£2 50

DOUBLE CENTURY

200 Years of Cricket in
.THE TIMES

Edited by
MARCUS WILLIAMS

WILLOW BOOKS
COLLINS
8 GRAFTON STREET LONDON WI
1985

Willow Books
William Collins Sons & Co Ltd
London · Glasgow · Sydney · Auckland
Toronto · Johannesburg

First published 1985
© Times Newspapers Ltd 1985
Introduction, notes and selection
© Marcus Williams 1985

British Library Cataloguing in Publication Data

Double Century: 200 years of cricket
in The Times
1. Cricket–History
I. Williams, Marcus
796.35′8′09   GV913

ISBN 0–00–218132–0

Designed by Humphrey Stone
Set in Times
by Ace Filmsetting Ltd, Frome, Somerset
Printed and bound in Great Britain by
Robert Hartnoll Ltd, Bodmin, Cornwall

CONTENTS

ACKNOWLEDGEMENTS

I cannot overstate my indebtedness to Gordon Phillips, a close and valued friend, who has a remarkable knowledge of the workings and history of *The Times*. His contribution towards this book has been prodigious – without him it *might* have been ready for the 205th anniversary – his resourcefulness at times of seemingly insurmountable crisis inspiring, and his service beyond the bounds of normal duty, such as highly competitive games of cricket with my small sons, utterly devoted.

Thanks are due to many others, notably: Tim Jollands, of Collins Willow, for his initial confidence and constant enthusiasm for the project, and a kindly editorial hand; to Humphrey Stone, who maintained a family link with *The Times* by designing the book and, particularly, its handsome jacket; to many colleagues at *The Times*, especially Michael Roffey, Picture Librarian, and his staff: Colin Wilson, Head Librarian, and his staff; Anne Piggott, Archivist and Records Manager, and her assistants; Norman Fox, Sports Editor and head of my department, and John Woodcock, Cricket Correspondent; to Stephen Green, Curator of M.C.C.; to another Stephen Green, Head of the British Newspaper Library, John Westmancoat, Information Officer, and other members of staff at Colindale; to Philip Spink, Librarian of The Advertising Association; to my wife, Wendy, for her patience, encouragement and practical assistance; and, of course, to all the writers, photographers and sub-editors whose work appears in *Double Century* and to Times Newspapers for readily giving permission to reproduce it.

The main works of reference consulted were: *The History of The Times* (vols. I–V); James D. Coldham's series of articles, *Some Early Cricket Reporters*, published in The Journal of the Cricket Society (vol. X no. 2–vol. XI no. 4); *Wisden Cricketers' Almanack*; and, not least, *The Times itself*.

INTRODUCTION

A daily newspaper is by strict definition ephemeral, but as recorder, commentator and interpreter of contemporary events it undoubtedly has a more enduring value. When a newspaper has managed to perform that function over a period of years – and has, moreover, come to be regarded as a national institution – it must contain a good deal that is worthy of study and preservation. When that institution, *The Times*, reaches its 200th birthday, it is also a cause for celebration – and how better to celebrate the occasion than to collect some of the best of its contents on a subject dear to an Englishman's heart throughout that period: cricket.

The story starts with the gentlemen of the White Conduit Club, the forerunner of M.C.C., and ends with a pair of England batsmen who had the presence of mind to mark *The Times*'s bicentenary year by becoming the first from their country to score double centuries in the same Test match innings. (To forestall inquiries the title of this book had already been settled before that happy coincidence.) The period embraces the whole panoply of cricketing giants: Beldham, Mynn, Pilch, Grace, Ranjitsinhji, Hobbs, Bradman, Sobers, Botham; but there is a fair slice of human life here too, from assault, divorce, fashion, libel, murder, the occult, politics, racial discrimination, riot and suicide to a cricketing dog, physically handicapped players and a pathetic paragraph about a Nottingham club forced to sell its pavilion to meet a rates demand of £36 but falling £11 short.

It is an awesome task to compress two centuries' writings, even on one topic, into a few hundred pages, not to mention the feelings of regret – and guilt – at not having the time to examine, while perusing miles of microfilm and sheaves of cuttings, what "The Thunderer" was saying about the French Revolution, or Waterloo, or World Wars, or the dozens of other cataclysmic events of the past 200 years. For the early decades, at least, selection was governed by the limited amount of cricket material that appeared in the paper, but this period will nevertheless be found rich in variety and entertainment.

The advent of an occasional feature article on cricket in 1875 broadened the field beyond the mainly factual and unvarnished reporting of matches, and the introduction, at the behest of the proprietor, Lord Northcliffe, in January 1914, of a light leading article (later known, and now fondly remembered by older readers, as the "fourth leader" and by older members of staff as "the funny") introduced a dimension of wit and humour which may surprise those who thought of *The Times* as dry and humourless. So felicitous, indeed, were the light leaders on cricket from the 1920s to the 1960s – notably those charming essays written by Bernard Darwin, Dudley Carew, Patrick Ryan and Peter Fleming (brother of the novelist, Ian) in the 1940s and 1950s – that although they are well represented in this book, there was a temptation to use all of them.

The light leaders apart, and because a newspaper's primary task is to provide information about current events, selection of the material has been dictated by its content and, occasionally, by the significance of its author: the quality of much of the writing is a considerable bonus and a tribute to the practitioners of the journalistic art. Although not every major cricketing event is covered, I trust that not many have been overlooked. In addition, room has been found for the minor: thus, while you will find the first big match at Lord's, the All England XI v. United England XI, the first Test matches played in Australia and England, Hobbs equalling Grace's record of first-class centuries, Holmes and Sutcliffe's first-wicket partnership of 555, Laker's 19 wickets in a single Test match, the unique tied Test match, the first World Cup final, and Bodyline (remember that *The Times* like almost all its British counterparts did not send its own man to cover the tour and seems, with hindsight, rather out of touch), you will also discover 19th century country-house cricket in Scotland, Grace playing table cricket, Hobbs visiting under-privileged children, a British author injured on the Hill at Sydney and, one to evoke memories in many cricket watchers, a lad consuming his sandwiches before the start of the lunch interval.

The publishers have been generous in allowing the book to stretch far beyond its original bounds, but even then limits have had to be imposed. The most convenient space-saving device, once I had recovered from heart-ache, was to condense all but a few of the scoreboards. However, the main individual performances (40 runs and four wickets upwards) have been included, together with the result of the match and, where relevant, the inter-mediate score for the day's play to which the report relates. In order to give period flavour the distinction between amateurs (with Mr., till 1921, and initials) and professionals (surname only), as indicated in *The Times* before being abolished at the end of 1962, has been retained. The initials themselves are those given by *The Times*, except where they were typographically or factually incorrect. Scoreboards from some of the early matches have been published in full for the sake of historical comparison and as a guiding principle thereafter, though there are exceptions, everything covered since its foundation in 1864 by *Wisden*, the most readily accessible cricketing reference work, has been abbreviated.

Profiles of leading players are presented either directly or through their obituaries (the latter not, as my wife avers, for reasons of morbidity but because there were few formal profiles of players of earlier days) and cricket also raises its head in leading articles – light and thunderous – law reports, arts and broadcast reviews, verse, the diary and personal columns, indeed just about everywhere in the paper at some time. Alas, much digging has failed to unearth the classic, though perhaps leg-pulling, advertisement in the personal column, from the period when it still appeared on the front page, which read: "Curate wanted for country parish, slow left-arm bowler preferred." Only one, very brief, letter – which was published in 1867 and is directly relevant to another item – has been included; cricketing letters to *The Times* were covered in *The Way to Lord's* (Collins Willow 1983; Fontana Paperbacks 1984).

To give an accurate picture of how *The Times* has covered cricket, in almost every case the text reproduced here is faithful to the original as published in the edition of the date indicated – this despite an urge to abbreviate or reorganize some of the pre-1914 match reports into more modern form (cf., for instance, the accounts of Cobden's match (June 1870) or Jessop's historic hundred against Australia (August 1902) with John Woodcock on the nail-biting finish to the Lord's Test match of June 1963). This adherence to the original may admit an occasional error of fact, but typographical blunders, it is hoped, have been remedied. In a few cases the text or headlines have been cut or amended in a minor way to suit the production of the book and all crossheadings have been omitted. There has been no attempt to impose a uniform textual style to cover two centuries; spellings and forms adopted by *The Times* at different stages of its history have thus been retained.

Cricket, as a rule, has had a healthy share of the space allocated in *The Times* to what used to be called Sporting Intelligence (only horse racing has had more), although until the 1980s sport was given but passing recognition by the editorial hierarchy. A most extreme example of this attitude was an extraordinary letter from the Editor, G. E. Buckle, to the Manager, C. F. Moberly Bell, in 1908 when he stated that it was "very clear that many of the sporting correspondents, and some of the best known ones, are people we should studiously keep clear of"; so it is not surprising that the first four volumes of the paper's official history, amounting to more than 3000 pages and published in the 1930s, ignored sport.

However, two of the chief proprietors in the 19th century, John Walter III and his son, Arthur Fraser Walter, were accomplished cricketers, both playing for Eton and the latter also winning his Blue at Oxford. Furthermore, A. F. Walter married into a cricketing – and light blue – family, his wife being a daughter of T. A. Anson, whom *Wisden* described as a "famous Cambridge wicketkeeper". By contrast with the Walters, Lord Northcliffe, who owned *The Times* from 1908 to 1922, had no love for cricket. In 1918 he wrote to the Editor:

> The article on baseball is quite good. There is just a touch of English hypocrisy in avoiding any reference to the fact that before the war cricket was dying, largely because of the canker of pro-

fessionalism and gate money. Baseball is an honest professional game, as is Association football. I do not imagine that the Victorian cricket will ever return. Cricket as described in "The Times" one hundred years ago – the quick, single-wicket game – must have been good sport, though nearly always played for large sums of money.

In 1919, the year of the abortive post-war experiment with two-day county matches, he fulminated:

I suppose we are right in giving so much space to cricket, though I am told by those who have been to see them that most of the county matches are very poorly attended, and chiefly by old men. I sent some Americans to see a cricket match the other day, and there was practically nobody there.

It is a relief to know that the proprietorial balance towards cricket was restored by Northcliffe's successor, the Hon. J. J. Astor, who played for Eton and Buckinghamshire. It was more than coincidence that during his presidency of M.C.C. *The Times* published its supplement, on 25 May 1937, to mark the club's sesquicentenary.

The Times has been fortunate in having some outstanding writers on the game, but, with a few exceptions, their identities were concealed until 1967 behind the mask of "Correspondent" – be it "Cricket", "Special" or simply "A" – or "Staff Reporter" or no signature at all. The names of members of staff were never disclosed on their reports for *The Times* until "Our Cricket Correspondent" was transmogrified into "John Woodcock, Our Cricket Correspondent" on 20 January 1967 (vid. introduction to chapter 4). However, the anonymity rule was less strict when well-known figures from outside the portals of Printing House Square contributed the so-called "turn-over" articles, which began on the right of the right-hand centre page and turned over on to the next page. Thus, Lord Harris's name appeared on an article about Amateurs and Professionals (1909), Sir Arthur Conan Doyle's on a tribute to the recently deceased W. G. Grace (1915) and that of the Australian Test player, J. W. Trumble, on a tribute to the "Demon" Spofforth (1928), while the Hon. G. W. Lyttelton had his name on a piece commemorating the hundredth Eton and Harrow match (1929) and Sir Donald Bradman on one in 1953 about the Australian touring party, with a protective "World Copyright" label.

Thanks to the Contributors' Marked Copies (bound or microfilmed volumes of *The Times* for almost every day since 1890 which indicate the source of each editorial item) it has been possible, almost certainly for the first time, to unmask the authors of many of the anonymous contributions. They are given belated recognition in the pages that follow, their names appearing between square brackets. In keeping with *The Times*'s persisting practice, leading articles and obituaries have been left unsigned.

Some familiar names who wrote for *The Times* sometimes went to great lengths – or were they having a joke at the paper's expense? – to conceal their identities. For instance, Pelham Warner, in his long series of Cricket Reminiscences published in *The Times* in 1919 and signed "From A Correspondent", used the first person "I" throughout but also referred in the third person to "Mr. Warner" and made so immodest at one point as to write: "In that match, 20 years ago, Mr. P. F. Warner played a faultless innings of 150". We also find Warner, before the First World War, reporting for *The Times* matches in which he was playing and sending a summary of the 1911–12 tour of Australia, from which illness prevented his taking an active part as the selected captain.

Similarly, Henry Leveson Gower sent dispatches from two tours of South Africa in which he was participating, in the latter as captain, and he continued to report matches for *The Times* after the First World War. G. J. V. Weigall, a great character of cricket in the early part of the century, is also to be found writing about matches in which he played and later about matches involving Kent, whom he served as coach. The constraints of *The Times*'s anonymity rule prevented these men from referring in print, and doubtless general conversation, to working for the paper, and the tradition died hard: even in 1980 members of A. C. M. Croome's family were unaware that he had been Cricket Correspondent of *The Times*, although they knew that he had, simultaneously, been Golf Correspondent of the *Morning Post*. Other Times . . .

MARCUS WILLIAMS
February 1985

I

THE FIRST HALF-CENTURY
1785 to 1834

In the year of The Times*'s birth (it was known as the* Daily Universal Register *for its first three years) organized cricket was already a schoolboy in short trousers, 'grand' matches for often large stakes being played between teams representing towns, counties or wealthy patrons. Hambledon was in decline as a cricketing power, but the White Conduit Club, based at Islington in north London, had come to prominence and its move across the city to Thomas Lord's new ground in Marylebone two years later helped to nurture the most famous cricket club in the world. It is not inappropriate, therefore, that the first item concerning cricket in the* Daily Universal Register *was addressed to the 'Lordling Cricketters (sic) who amuse themselves in White Conduit Fields'. The advice was tucked in the third column of page three of the four-page issue of Wednesday, 22 June 1785, between a report on the tobacco trade and, with modern echoes, news from Dumfries trumpeting the creation of several hundred new jobs.*

Coverage of cricket in these early years was patchy: thus, a dispatch from Canterbury in 1786 might tell readers merely that 'Saturday last the grand match of cricket, Kent against All England, was played at Windmill-Down, in Hampshire, which was decided in favour of the latter' and in 1804 MCC v All England might receive only two sentences; but in June 1787 reports on the first big match at Lord's, White Conduit v All England, amounted to a column, offering a useful sketch of the overall scene as well as tabulated scores, and towards the end of the period (25–27 July 1827) we have a splendidly graphic account of Sussex v England at Brighton with a great feeling of immediacy as The Times *correspondent rushes his report to the London mails for the next morning's edition. The speed of news gathering had made great advances since 1785, when the Catterick Bridge races of 29 and 30 March were not reported until 9 April! Pity the punter with his shirt depending on the results.*

Details of play were generally brief and factual, though there was an occasional critical comment: for example, a match between the elevens of Lord Winchelsea and Sir Horace Mann in 1787 was fiercely castigated as 'a hollow piece of business, when we consider that the players on both sides were allowed to be twenty-two of the best players in England'.

In addition to the serious matches we find delightful accounts of weird and wonderful goings-on: four men, average age 74¼, playing in Sussex (21 May 1788); one-armed 'veterans of the ocean' meeting their one-legged counterparts (10 and 12 August 1796); married women against maidens (20 June 1793); a match at Stanmore between gentry and commoners reminiscent of the encounter in L. P. Hartley's The Go-Between *(5 September 1828); and the most delicious morsel of the entire 200 years, a game on Harefield Common where a farmer named Trumper – truly a cricketing name with which to conjure – and his thoroughbred sheepdog defied odds of 5 to 1 to defeat two gentlemen of Middlesex (31 May 1827).*

22 *June* 1785. It is recommended to the Lordling Cricketters who amuse themselves in White Conduit Fields, to procure an Act of Parliament for inclosing their play ground, which will not only prevent their being incommoded, but protect themselves from a repetition of the severe rebuke which they justly merit, and received on Saturday evening from some spirited citizens whom they insulted and attempted *vi et armis* to drive from the foot path, pretending it was within their bounds.

2 *July* 1785. Thursday a great cricket match commenced in White Conduit Fields, between the gentlemen who usually play there, and the gentlemen of Kent, for one thousand guineas a side. It will be determined this day.

4 *July* 1785. Yesterday ended the grand cricket match in White-Conduit Field, which was won by the Gentlemen of the White-Conduit Club, by a majority of 306. The following is a state of each Gentleman's Innings:

White-Conduit Club	Innings. 1st 2d	Kent	Innings. 1st 2d
Ld. Winchelsea	11—16	Mr. Dyke	2—0
Sir P. Burrel	0—97	Mr. T. Taylor	0—0
Mr. Lenox	42—18	Mr. Smith	0—2
Mr. Peachey	19— 8	Mr. Edwards	2—0
Mr. Damper	6—17	Mr. Horsmer	22—1
Mr. Newman	15—56	Mr. Stanford	59—9
Mr. Wyatt	12—11	Mr. Thompson	4—0
Mr. G. Monson	4— 4	Mr. Amherst	7—9
Capt. Monson	29— 7	Mr. Whitehead	2—4
Mr. Tyson	3—17	Mr. Wilmot	7—5
Mr. East	20—17	Mr. Willard	0—2
By Runs	9— 7	By Runs	16—0
	170 285		121 28

4 *October* 1785. On Monday and Tuesday last was played on Langley Broom, a match at cricket between the county of Bucks and the county of Berks, with two of Farnham. Bets at starting were two to one in favour of Bucks; when Wells and Boult went in and were not parted till half past four o'clock the next day. The match was given up by Bucks, their opponents being 215 a head in the first innings.

2 *May* 1786; *Paris*, 16 *April*. On Monday last, a cricket match was played by some English Gentlemen, in the Champs Elyses. His Grace of Dorset was, as usual, the most distinguished for skill and activity. The French, however, cannot imitate us in such vigorous exertions of the body; so that we seldom see them enter the lists.

16 *May* 1786. The Noblemen and Gentlemen belonging to the Cricket Club in White Conduit Fields have made a match against the Kentish men, similar to that which afforded such excellent sport last year: and on Saturday a party of them had a practice with a few of the Kentish men in those fields, preparatory to the said match. Several ladies of quality were expected, but the uncommon high wind deterred them from attending, and it was with great difficulty that the tent was kept from being blown away. The Earls of Winchelsea and Caresford, young Lord Grosvenor, Sir Robert Farmer, &c. were present.

12 *January* 1787. A grand cricket-match was played on the day preceding Christmas-Eve at Mon Brilliant. But no particulars are mentioned, except that his Royal Highness the Duke of York attended, with a most splendid groupe of persons of fashion, and that the match was for a thousand guineas. In the evening there was a ball.

29 *May* 1787. A Grand Match will be played on Thursday, the 31st of May, 1787, in the new Cricket-ground, the New Road, Mary-le-bone, between nine gentlemen of the county of Essex, with two given men, against eight gentlemen of the county of Middlesex, with two gentlemen of Berkshire, and one of Kent, for One Hundred Guineas a side.

The wickets to be pitched at ten o'clock, and the match to be played out. No dogs will be admitted.

Grand Cricket Match

22 *June* 1787. A match for 1000 guineas a side was played on Wednesday at the New Cricket Ground, St. Mary-le-Bone.

The following is a List of the Players.

White Conduit Club.	*All England.*
Earl of Winchelsea	— Amherst, Esq.
Sir Peter Burrel	— Stanford, Esq.
— Hussey, Esq.	— Hofman, Esq.
— Dampier, Esq.	Mr. Bullen
— Drummond, Esq.	Mr. Aylward
Mr. Harris	Mr. Purchase
Mr. Clifford	Mr. Small, jun.
Mr. Taylor	Mr. Wills
Mr. King	Mr. Beldam
Mr. H. Walker	Mr. Small, senior
Mr. T. Walker	Mr. N. Mann

First day's Innings.

All England had the first Innings, and the Players went in the order undermentioned, and got the number of notches placed against their names.

All-England.

Mr. Aylward	93	Bullen	14
Beldam	17	Small, sen.	30
Hofman	43	Wells	8
Stanford	—		—
Amherst	20		239
Mann	11	Bye-balls	8
Small, jun.	3		—
Purchase	—	Total	247

White Conduit Club,

Only three Gentlemen went in owing to the day being far advanced;—as it was the agreement, that the wickets should be struck at eight o'clock.

Sir Peter Burrel	—	caught out the 3d bowl
Captain Dampier	20	and a by-ball, by which
— Hussey, Esq.	1	he got 3.
	—	
Total	24	

Umpires.	*Scorers.*
Lawrence and Hawkins.	Pratt and Nyland.

Upwards of 2000 persons were within the ground, who conducted themselves with the utmost decorum; the utility of the batten fence was evident, as it kept out all improper spectators.—The ground, though somewhat rough at present, will be laid out next year like a bowling-green.—A very good cold collation was spread under a covered recess, for the accommodation of the cricketers and subscribers.—Two tents were also prepared with refreshments for the spectators.

Yesterday the White Conduit Club renewed their innings, and got 113 notches.

Beldam and Small afterwards went in on the side of All England, and got 87 notches, without being bowled out, when the wickets were struck on account of the rain coming on. The game will be renewed this day, if the weather permits.

25 *June* 1787. Thursday being the 2d day—Mr. Dampier and Mr. Hussey resumed their play, not having been bowled out the preceding evening.

The numbers got in the whole by the *White Conduit Club*, taking a retrospect of the players and notches of yesterday, were as follow:—

Sir Peter Burrel	—	Lord Winchelsea	3
Captain Dampier	26	— Drummond Esq.	1
— Hussey, Esq.	21	Harris	5
J. Walker	11		—
King	19		104
H. Walker fell in running and out	—	Six bye-balls	9
Taylor	12		113
Clifford	6		—

This innings finished at half past three.

All England.

At a quarter past four, the *All England* Cricketters went in.

Small, Jun.	31
Beldam	52
	—
	83
Byes	4
	—
Total	87
	—

This number of notches were got by half past six in the evening,—when the rain prevented further play.

Friday, 3d day—*All England*

Small, jun. and Beldam, not being out the preceding evening,—went in again.

Small, jun.	11	Amherst	16
Beldam	11	Hofman	2
Purchase	3	Bullen	—
Aylward	15		—
Mann	5		107
Small, sen.	32	Bye-balls	3
Wells	12		Total 110
Stamford	—		—

White Conduit side then went in for their second innings in the following manner:

Thomas Walker	11	Drummond	1
Harry Walker	5	Harris	2
Taylor	20		—
King	2		83
Clifford	—	Bye-balls	2
Sir Peter Burrel	10		—
Mr. Hussey	10	Total	85
Mr. Dampier	13		—
Lord Winchelsea	9		

The match was finished a little before eight o'clock, when it was declared that *All England* were 246 a head.

Many persons of the first fashion were on the ground—the Duke of Bedford, Lord Derby, Lord Galloway, Mr. Fitzroy, Mr. Onslow, and many other gentlemen.

Beldam was by far the best player on the ground. Several capital betts were laid, but they were all great odds and in favour of *All England*.

12 *September* 1787. The cricket-match between the Hambledon Club and All England, began on Monday se'n-night on Windmill Down, near Hambledon, and was, after three days play, determined in favour of All England, by a majority of sixty-three notches.

10 *October* 1787. A few days ago, two Justices of the Peace sent their mandate to stop a game, which was playing for an evening's amusement, at cricket; but the messenger was desired to return with the players' humble service, and if they might depend upon justice being done them, they would be glad if the worthy Magistrate, for the sake of the peace, would do them the honour of coming to be umpires.

31 *October* 1787. Horse-racing is already on the wane in France, as it is in England. Cricket, on the recommendation of the Duke of Dorset, is taking its place, and making a far better use of the turf.

11 *February* 1788. Several *Dancing Masters* have lately arrived at CAM-
BRIDGE, for the purpose of teaching the *art of boxing—Cricket* and *trap ball*
have also become objects of study, and many of the *masters, fellowes*, and
graduates, have made considerable proficiency in these games, which they
pronounce to be truly *classic*, as having made a part of the ancient *Gym-
nastic* and *Olympic* exercises.

21 *May* 1788. On Tuesday last a cricket-match was played at Alfriston,
Sussex, by four men, whose ages added together amounted to 297 years.
The game was played with great spirit and activity, considering the age of the
gamesters, in the presence of a great number of spectators.

4 *September* 1788. On Tuesday morning at 11 o'clock died at Brightelmstone
his Grace the DUKE OF MANCHESTER. His death is supposed to have been
occasioned by a cold he contracted a few days ago, by lying upon the grass
after being heated by the play of a match at cricket. His Grace died with
great serenity and resignation. After his death, the DUCHESS returned to
London.

9 *September* 1788. We are sorry to be so well informed of the conduct of a
certain young gentleman near Brighton, and that it is so exceptionable as to
have been the means of several of the nobility not visiting that place this
season, as they usually have done. Descending to the office of a coachman
and driving his own carriage is not altogether compatible with high rank and
station, the more so when it is done in a public manner. The making of his
own lamplighter a partner at a game of cricket, is equally censurable. It
gives us much pain to make these remarks, but as we know this paper meets
the eye of the noble character we allude to, we hope the hint will be taken in
the same friendly manner it is meant.

Grand Match

11 *July* 1789. The Grand Match [at Lord's] between the GENTLEMEN of the
Mary-le-bonne Club and Essex, was yesterday decided, when the state of
the Game was as follows:

ESSEX first Innings   123
Second Ditto   —   152
Byes —   —   —   7
—282

MARY-LE-BONNE CLUB first Innings 106
Second Ditto 74
—180

Of course ESSEX were the winners by 102 notches.

12 *August* 1789. On Wednesday last a match of Cricket was played at Hackney, between the Gentlemen of the Club at that place, and the young Gentlemen of a school in the neighbourhood. The former, consisting of two grandfathers, four fathers, and such as had passed their prime, offered a challenge to an equal number of the latter, which was readily accepted. The juvenile appearance of the scholars, contrasted with the aged consequence of their opponents, afforded much mirth to the spectators. Victory at length declared itself in favour of the grown Gentlemen, who immediately shouldered their bats, and, with Mr. D—— at their head (who is lately returned from the attack of the Bastile, and who had formerly a command in the Hackney Association, and did great service upon an equal memorable occasion at Hoxton) playing on the violin, "See the conquering hero comes," proceeded to a tent erected for their accommodation, where they were received by some Ladies, who presented them with cockades, which was a representation of Hercules in the act of overcoming an infant, and depriving him of his rattle, with the motto, *"Veni, vidi, vici."* The Company afterwards partook of an entertainment, consisting of tea, lemonade, milk and water, and other refreshing delicacies, suited to their fatiguing situation, and the grandeur of the occasion. An oration of some length was afterwards made by their Treasurer, who gave a grand display of his rhetorical powers.

There is to be another trial of skill this day.

The Game of Cricket

PEACE and her arts we sing:– Her genial pow'r
Can give the breast to pant, the thought to tow'r,
Tho' guiltless, not inglorious souls inspires,
And boast less savage, not less noble fires.

Such is her sway, when CRICKET calls her train,
The sons of labour, to the accustom'd plain;
With all the hero's passion and desire,
They swell, they glow, they envy, and admire;
Despair and resolution reign by turns,
Suspense torments, and emulation burns. –
See! in due rank disposed, intent they stand,
In act to start – the eye, the foot, the hand,
Still active, eager, seem conjoined in one;
Tho' fixt, all moving – and while present, gone.
In ancient combat, from the Parthian steed
Not more unerring flew the barbed reed,
Than rolls the ball, – with vary'd vigour play'd,
Now levell'd, whizzing on the springing blade,

Now Toss'd, to rise more fatal from the ground,
Exact and faithful to the appointed bound.
Yet vain its speed, yet vain its certain aim,
The wary Batsman watches o'er the game;
Before his stroke the leathern circle flies,
Now wheels oblique – now mounting threat the skies –
Nor yet less vain the wary Batsman's blow,
If intercepted by the circling foe,
Too soon the nimble arm retorts the ball,
Or ready fingers catch it in its fall;
Thus various art with vary'd fortune drives,
And with each changing chance the sport revives. –
Emblem of many colour'd life – the State
By Cricket-rules discriminates the great:
The *Outward-side*, who place and profit want,
Watch to surprise, and labour to supplant;
While those who taste the sweets of present winnings,
Labour as heartily to keep their *Innings*.
On either side the whole great game is play'd,
Untry'd no shift is left, unfought no aid:
Skill vies with skill, and pow'r contends with pow'r,
And squint-ey'd Prejudice computes the *Score*.

In private life, like *single wicket play'rs*,
We get less *notches*, but we meet less cares. –
Full many a lusty effort, which at court
Would fix the doubtful issue of the sport,
Wide of its mark; or impotent to rise,
Ruins the rash, and disappoints the wise.
Yet all in public, and in private strive
To keep the ball of action still alive;
And, just to all, when each his ground has run,
Death *tips the wicket*, – and the game is done!

2 September 1790

This poem is attributed to James Love, c 1744, and differs in minor ways from the version in The Poetry of Cricket *(ed. Frewin, London 1964).*

4 September 1790. On Monday, August 30, began playing a Grand Match of Cricket, in LORD's Ground, Mary le Bonne, and finished on Thursday, Sept. 2d; four Gentlemen of the Mary le Bonne Club, with seven of Hants, against All England, for 1,000 Guineas.

ENGLAND			HANTS		
First Innings	——	177	First Innings	——	165
Second Innings	——	66	Second Innings	——	79
	Total	243		Total	244

Total for Hants Ten Wickets.

CRICKET was formerly an exertion of strength – it is now an application of skill. One of the *Walkers*, some time ago, continued his innings four hours, and got but nine notches.

23 *August* 1791. On Saturday last at the game of cricket at Ware, between Hertfordshire and Essex, the greatest shuffling took place that was ever known amongst Gentlemen. The County of Essex would not permit their last man to go in for the last run. Wy——, Esq. by gaining Ing—m, refused it! because it did not suit their INTEREST.

6 *September* 1791; *Nottingham, 3 September*. On Monday and Tuesday last was played in our Upper Meadow, a Grand Cricket Match for One Thousand Guineas, between the Gentlemen of the Mary-le-bone Club, and the Nottingham Club. A large space of ground was corded out for their reception, round which, divers standings were erected, and the days proving remarkable fine, contributed greatly to the accommodation of the company present. The spectators assembled were supposed to be upwards of ten thousand, such universal curiosity seemed to pervade with all ranks of people to be present at so noble and manly a pastime; and the extraordinary skilfulness displayed by the Mary-le-bone in all the various parts of the game was unequalled, and justly excited the astonishment of the beholders, by their superior agility.

MARY-LE-BONE

First Innings		Second Innings	
Ld. Winchelsea, c. Willows	12		
Lt. Col. Lenox, c. Chapman	6		
Hon. E. Bligh, b. ditto	3		
Ld W. Bentinck, b. Stephenson	1		
H. G. Monson, b. Chapman	10		
C. Anguish, Esq. not out	47	not out	
J. L. Kaye, Esq. stump out by Gilbert	18	not out	
Capt. Cumberland, b. Stephenson	13		
Capt. Markham, b. Chapman	3		
C. Louch, Esq. b. ditto	5		
— Towell, b. Stephenson	6		
Byes	1	Byes	1
	125	Total	126

NOTTINGHAM

First Innings			Second Innings	
W. Barker, b. C. Cumberland		0	b. Ld Winchelsea	12
W. Dexter, run out		0	b. Col. Lenox	3
W. Chapman, c. Col. Lenox		1	b. C. Cumberland	0
S. Hedderley, b. Winchelsea		19	c. Col. Lenox	1
E. Stephenson, b. Cumberland		4	c. H. E. Bligh	4
Jos. Gilbert, c. H. G. Monson		0	c. Louch, Esq.	0
S. Willows, b. Ld. Winchelsea		7	b. Col. Lenox	6
W. Warsop, not out		6	c. Capt. Markham	4
S. Muglestone, c. Ld. Winchelsea		2	c. Louch, Esq.	1
Hump. Hopkins, b. ditto		4	not out	18
James Stephenson, b. ditto		12	b. C. Cumberland	12
	Byes	8	Byes	1
		63		62
			Total	125

20 *June* 1793. A match of Cricket was played last week on Bury Common, in the county of Sussex, by *females*, the *married women* against the *maidens*; it was won by the married women, who had 80 notches more than the nymphs. So famous are the Bury women at this game, that they have challenged all England.

10 *August* 1796. Yesterday a curious cricket match was played at Montpelier Gardens, between 11 of the Greenwich Pensioners, wanting an arm each, against the same number of their fellow-sufferers with each a wooden leg. Not fewer than 5000 people were assembled on the occasion, who were highly entertained with the exertions of the old veterans of the ocean, who never acted against their most inveterate enemy with more energy, each party striving to quit the field victorious. The evening coming on, the contest could not be decided; but it was so much in favour of the Timber-toes, as never to be recovered by the dint of Arms.

After they had left the field, the nimble-fingered gentry endeavoured to draw a crowd together in order to follow their trade, and for a short time these fellows were never more dextrous; they had a long cord, and threw people down over it as they passed. A scuffle ensued, and several persons lost their watches and money. One or two of the crew were secured, and sent to Newington watch-house.

12 *August* 1796. On Wednesday morning the 11 men with one arm, and 11 men with but one leg, were brought by three Greenwich stages engaged for that purpose, to the new Cricket-ground, the back of the Montpelier Tea

Gardens, Walworth, when the match was played out, and the men with one leg beat the one arms by 103 runnings. After the match was finished, the eleven one-legged men ran a race of 100 yards distance for 20 guineas, and the three first had prizes.

11 *August* 1796. On Thursday last a Cricket match was played at Portsmouth, between eleven of that town against eleven of Southampton, for 100 guineas stake, and won by the former. Mr. COULSON, one of the latter party, unfortunately had his eye entirely struck out of the socket by the ball.

5 *August* 1802; *Brighton, 3 August*. The attractions of the day were, in the morning a Review of the Prince's Regiment by his ROYAL HIGHNESS; and the finish, or second match of Cricket, between the East and West Sussexers.

At the Review, which was at the Devil's Dyke, the PRINCE gave the word of command in person, and we need not add that this very fine corps of men went through the various evolutions with great precision and promptitude. His ROYAL HIGHNESS's manœuvres were rather too early for the attendance of many of the Fashionables of the place; nor was the Cricket Ground, until noon, paid more attention to. By that time, however, the fair Nymphs had dried their locks, newly wet by the moist embraces of old Neptune; the Man of Fashion had slumbered off the effects of last night's debauch, and exerted himself to draw on his *Dutch breeches* and high-polished boots. The curricle and sociable filled the circle of the Ground, and all the company who had nerve enough to bear the scorch of a noon-tide sun in the month of August were present.

The match was made between General LENNOX, on the part of the Men of West Sussex, and by Col. PORTER, for those of East Sussex, for five hundred guineas. The first match was played prior to the Races, and won by the East Sussex, as was the match of this day, it being gained by sixty-one notches. Amongst the Gentlemen-players were, General LENNOX, Colonel PORTER, Mr. UPTON, Mr. SMITH, Mr. MUSTERS, and Lord MILSINTOWN.

The PRINCE had a very small party to dine with him at the Pavillion; the company consisted of Sir H. FEATHERSTONE, Admiral PAYNE, Mr. DAY, Mr. NORTON, and Mr. TREVES.

Most of the Fashion go to Lewes to-morrow to be present at the Shew of Cattle, which is expected to be very gratifying to the amateurs in grazing.

Yesterday arrived here the Bishop of CHICHESTER.

Lord HARRINGTON is just arrived.

Fatal Instance of Over Exertion

22 *October* 1805. A match of cricket was played on Friday last, near Totter-idge, Herts, between two young men of the names of GREGG and CORDEROY, which was so well maintained, that forty-three and forty-five runs were made in the first innings. GREGG was caught out after making thirty-two runs in the second innings. CORDEROY went in, and made seven runs; he again hit the ball, and ran, but on arriving at the wicket he fell down and expired.

Cricket-match Extraordinary

5 *October* 1811. On Wednesday last a singular Cricket-match commenced at Ball's-pond, Newington. The players on each side were twenty-two women: eleven Hampshire against eleven Surrey. The match was made between two amateur Noblemen of the respective counties, for five hundred guineas aside. The performers in this singular contest were of all ages and sizes, from 14 years old to upwards of 40; and the different parties were distinguished by coloured ribbons: Royal purple for the Hampshire; orange and blue, Surrey. The weather being favourable on Wednesday, some very excellent play, and much skill was displayed; but the palm of that day was borne off by a Hampshire lass, who made 41 innings before she was thrown out. At the conclusion of the day, the first innings for Hampshire were 81, while those of the Surrey were only seven. Five to one on the Hampshire lasses: any odds offered, but no takers. Thursday the Surrey damsels kept the field with their second innings almost the whole of the day; but it rained so incessantly there was very little play. The game, it is expected, will not be concluded until Monday next; but the general opinion is, that Hampshire will gain the victory. Notwithstanding the unfavourable state of the weather, a great concourse of people attended to witness this singular contention; and although each party seemed to exert their utmost skill and activity against their adversaries, the utmost harmony and good humour prevailed amongst them.

7 *October* 1811. The cricket-match between the Hampshire and Surrey females, for 500 gs. a side, has terminated; the former won by 15 notches. Another match has been made.

Eton v. Harrow

31 *July* 1818. On Wednesday, after a long and severe struggle for the ascendant, the Etonians were beat by the boys of Harrow [at Lord's]. This well-contested match was won only by 15 runs. A short time ago the Etonians were beat by the Epsom club. They should contrive not to lose a characteristic which has been thought to distinguish them as much as making centos of Latin verse.

Great Cricket Match
and Dreadful Accident

2 *September* 1822. The great cricket match between 15 Sheffield and 11 Nottingham players, for which great preparations have latterly been making on the new ground at Darnal, near this place, commenced yesterday forenoon. The contest having excited a peculiar interest in and around the town, the concourse of spectators was proportionately great; never, perhaps, on any occasion, was witnessed an assemblage at once so numerous and respectable. Sheffield seemed almost to pour out the whole of its population, the roads being literally covered all the morning with crowds hastening to the scene of the expected enjoyment. Little was it then suspected, that before the expiration of the day the pleasure of it was to be dashed by one of the most afflicting accidents that we have had to record for some time back. The playing commenced; the weather, with the exception of one shower, was highly favourable, and all went on well till about four o'clock, when a large extent of scaffolding, which had been fitted up on the ground near the road side, for the accommodation of several thousands of spectators, having nine tier of seats, and being near 40 yards long, suddenly gave way, and precipitated its unfortunate tenants one over the other on the ground. Shrieks, screams, and groans rent the air on all sides; and the scene of confusion which ensued was indescribably affecting. Every hand was instantly engaged in extricating the sufferers; every possible accommodation offered, and every vehicle put in requisition to convey them away to their respective homes. It is with painful feelings that we have to add, that two persons were killed upon the spot, and between 40 and 50 more or less mained. We dare not vouch for our correctness, although we have endeavoured to gain the best information we were able; but amidst so much distressing confusion, the extent of the mischief cannot with accuracy be yet ascertained, and even the names of the parties we could not procure. Late last night 23 cases had been admitted to the Infirmary, four or five of which were pronounced very dangerous. – *Sheffield Advertiser, Aug. 27*

9 *September* 1822. In our relation of this sad calamity last week we mentioned that two persons were said to have lost their lives; we are glad to find that the statement was not founded in fact, and we have now the satisfaction to make a much more favourable report. Seventeen persons were admitted into the Infirmary (several of whom were able to return to their respective homes the next day); 6 were made out-patients, and returned home after being dressed, &c., making 23 in the whole – 19 males and 4 females. We are happy further to state, from undoubted authority, that the more serious cases are going on very favourably, and that all the other will most probably soon recover from the injuries received. On the day following the accident many were bold enough to mount the scaffolding again: and the consequence of such temerity was, what might have easily been predicted – another accident. Some wretch was base enough to raise a false alarm, and in the scuffle and hurry of escape, one man had his leg fractured. – *Sheffield Iris*

Fire in Lord's Cricket-ground

30 *June* 1825. About half-past one yesterday morning a fire broke out in a large building called the Pavilion, erected in the cricket-ground near the school of the orphans of the clergy, on the St. John's Wood Road. From the nature of the materials, which were chiefly of wood, although lately enlarged and beautified at a great expense, the fire in a very short time defied the power of the fire-engines and water, if there had been a sufficient supply of the latter, which happened not to be the case. In about an hour and a half after the commencement of the fire, the whole Pavilion was reduced to a heap of ruins, saving only the foundation, which is about three feet high of brick-work. So strong was the fire, that the wooden rails round the building were partly destroyed. There was a very valuable wine-cellar well stored in the Pavilion, belonging to the gentlemen of the various clubs who frequently play in the ground, which shared the same fate with the building. Happily no houses were near enough to the spot to be in the least danger, but some of the trees in the adjoining grounds were scorched. Yesterday a grand match of cricket was to have been played between the young gentlemen of Eton and Harrow Schools.

3 *August* 1826. On Tuesday last, the annual cricket-match of the Westminster scholars took place in the Play-field, Vincent-square, between 11 of the King's Scholars, and an equal number of young gentlemen belonging to the College, termed Town Boys, which was decided in two innings. The wickets were pitched at ten o'clock. Town Boys – First Innings, 21; second ditto, 55: total, 76. King's Scholars – First innings, 49. After the Town Boys had finished their second innings, the King's Scholars took their positions for 28 against

their opponents, and won the match cleverly with perfect ease, by eight wickets. During the contest an accident occurred by the ball striking one of the players, named Marsh, a violent blow on the left eye, which stunned him for the moment, but the young gentleman soon recovered from the shock, and manfully contended the match. An assemblage of ladies and gentlemen, the relatives and friends of the players, were on the ground during the contest, and we also noticed in the field Dr. Goodenough, the head master, Mr. Preston, and other gentlemen belonging to the College. Cooper and another, two principal officers of Queen-square, were in attendance, to prevent the intrusion of strangers, and preserve order.

Novel Game of Cricket

31 *May* 1827. A novel game of cricket was played, for a considerable sum, on Monday the 21st instant, on Harefield-common, near Rickmansworth, between two gentlemen of Middlesex, and Mr. Francis Trumper, farmer at Harefield, with the help of a thorough-bred sheep dog. In the first innings, the two gentlemen got three runs, and Mr. Trumper three for himself and two for his dog. In the second innings, the two gentlemen again got three runs, and Mr. Trumper then going in, and getting two runs, beat the two gentlemen, leaving two wickets standing. Before the game began, the odds were 5 to 1 against Mr. Trumper and his canine partner; but after the first innings, bets were so altered, that four to one were laid on Trumper and his dog. The match having been much talked of in the neighbourhood for two or three weeks, and the day proving very fine, there was a numerous attendance of spectators, who were much astonished at the dog's dexterity. The dog always stood near his master when he was going to bowl, and the moment the ball was hit he kept his eye upon it, and started off after it with speed; and, on his master running up to the wicket, the dog would carry the ball in his mouth and put it into his master's hand with such wonderful quickness, that the gentlemen found it very difficult to get a run even from a very long hit. The money lost and won on the occasion was considerable, as a great number of gentlemen came from Uxbridge and the neighbouring towns and villages to see so extraordinary a game.

Sussex v. All England

25 *July* 1827; *Brighton, 24 July*. The grand match of cricket, between the county of Sussex and all England, commenced here yesterday. The interest which it had excited is unprecedented, and it is doubtful whether, within the memory of man, so many persons were ever before assembled at a cricket-match. People have come, not only from all parts of Sussex, but from London,

and even distant parts of England; and the cricketting-ground, which is very spacious, and one of the finest in the kingdom, was literally thronged. The number of spectators present was variously estimated at from 3,000 to 6,000. All England took the first innings, and got only 27 runs: Mr. Budd, one of their best players, getting only 8, and Mr. Osbaldeston not one; indeed, he had not a single ball, having gone in last, and the tenth wicket going down almost immediately. Sussex then went in, and got 77 runs. At the end of their innings, it was past six o'clock, but all England again went in, and the first wicket being put down for 10 runs, all further playing was postponed till the next morning, it being then nearly half-past seven o'clock. Mr. Ward, the city member, plays on the side of all England, and Mr. Osbaldeston has also been brought forward to assist in retrieving their lost fame; but he is no longer what he was in former days. He has not played until now for some years; and having broken his thigh, has no longer the activity which he once possessed.

So great was the interest excited respecting this match, that Sir Hussey Vivian, who had fixed an inspection of the 7th Hussars, now lying here, for Monday and Tuesday, changed it to the two preceding days (Saturday and Sunday), for the purpose of enabling an officer of that regiment, Lieutenant Cheslyn, who is on the side of Sussex, to play in the match.

Two o'clock.

Five wickets of all in England are down; they have now fetched 65 runs, that is, 15 a head of Sussex. Two of the best players, Mr. Budd and Saunders, are now in, and seem to have just got into their play, the former having fetched 14, and the latter 18. There is, however, no chance of their beating Sussex. Three of their best men, Mr. Ward, Mr. Osbaldeston, and Marsden, have been in; Mr. Osbaldeston got only seven runs, and Mr. Ward only two or three. They can do nothing against the bowling of the Sussex men: I heard Mr. Osbaldeston say, they had no chance against it.

There is a good deal of betting. When Saunders went in, 5 to 1 was offered and taken, that Sussex would not win single innings. There is again this morning an immense concourse of spectators on the ground, although not quite so many as yesterday: and the town is almost in as much bustle as at the races. The match will in all probability be finished in the course of the day.

26 *July* 1827. The game of cricket took a most extraordinary and unexpected turn yesterday, after my letter was despatched. Saunders and Budd were then in, and kept up their wickets for a long time. At the conclusion of their innings, all England had got 169 runs, being 119 a-head of Sussex, who then went in; and at the close of the day's play, about half-past seven o'clock, three wickets had been put down for 11 runs only. In fact, fortune had completely changed, and the odds, which had, up to an advanced period even of their second innings, been greatly against England, now became as much in their favour.

Two o'clock.

J. Broadbridge, one of the best players of Sussex, has been put out this morning, without getting a single run. Seven wickets are now down, for only 53 runs, so that Sussex has still 67 to get, before they can win. Thwaites has just gone in: he is one of their best men, and so is Dale, who is in with him. If they can manage to keep their wickets and get a good many runs, the odds will change greatly. The only two men left are Lanaway and Lillywhite, neither of whom is a very good batsman, although the latter is a capital bowler.

Betting is now 5 to 1 on All England. Mr. Ward has just made a beautiful catch, by which Baker was put out; it was declared on the ground to be one of the finest things of the kind ever seen. The weather has been extremely favourable throughout the match.

It is said that another match will be made between Sussex and All England; and it is also reported, that a match of pigeon shooting is made for Mr. Osbaldeston to-morrow.   .

27 *July* 1827. The Cricket-match has at length terminated, after a most severe and well-contested struggle, in favour of all England, who have won, however, by 24 runs only. The anxiety which prevailed as the game approached to a close is past description; and it was increased by the fluctuations which almost to the last moment rendered victory doubtful. There has been a good deal of money lost and won by this match. Lieutenant Cheslyn, of the 7th Hussars, who played on the side of Sussex, had, it is said, lost 300*l* [£300]. The fielding of the men on both sides was remarkably fine, so much so, that upwards of 40 balls were at one time bowled without scoring a single run. The ground was most numerously attended, there being from 4,000 to 5,000 persons present each day.

5 *September* 1828. A match of cricket, which, from all the circumstances attending it, excited a vast degree of interest in the neighbourhood of Stanmore, Edgeware, and the adjacent county, for a considerable distance round, was played a few days ago at Bently Priory, the seat of the Marquis of Abercorn, and the residence of the present Secretary of State for Foreign Affairs, the Earl of Aberdeen, whose Countess is the mother of the young Marquis. The Marquis, who is much attached to every description of field sports, and is considered an excellent cricketer, formed a match to play himself, his brother Lord Claude Hamilton, Viscount Grimstone, the eldest son of the Earl of Verulam, the Honourable Mr. Bathurst, a son of Earl Bathurst, who were all there on a visit with the young Marquis, and all about his own age, together with six of his Lordship's servants, whom he selected, making in all ten players, against ten of the best players amongst all the tradespeople of Stanmore and Edgeware. These two ancient villages put forth, of course,

their best and picked men on the occasion; and the ten selected, at the head of whom was an Edgeware butcher, who is esteemed a crack player in those parts, went to meet their aristocratic opponents. A beautiful spot of ground, well adapted for the game, was selected by the Marquis in the Priory-park, and the whole of the grounds – and, indeed, of the mansion itself – were thrown open for the reception of the surrounding country, which poured in its population to witness this interesting contest, and every facility to view it was by orders from the young Marquis afforded to all comers, without distinction, rank, wealth, station, or dress. The wickets were set about 12 o'clock at noon, and the game commenced immediately after. At the beginning every thing seemed to run in favour of the lords, but in an early stage of the game, to the great regret of all present, the young Marquis, one of their best men, was bowled out. This unlucky event not only threw a considerable damp upon his Lordship's party, but gave a tremendous stimulus to the opposite side, and the butcher and his men for some time after carried on a slaughtering game, and seemed to have knocked on the head all chances of success to their opponents, when the young Lord Grimstone, apparently determined to snatch either victory or death from the butcher's grasp, went in and completed, in the most gallant style, 40 runs before he received a check, which brought the game to almost a hair's balance. Both parties now contended for victory with might and main, and carried on the game with varied success until the evening became too dusk to continue it any longer, and it being now announced to the young Marquis that the dinner party at the mansion had already been waiting a considerable time for his lordship's presence, both parties, to their mutual disappointment, were obliged to make it a drawn game, and they separated, all declaring that they never had a finer day's play in their lives, and the butcher vowed to his friends as he went homewards, that he was worked almost to a "marrow." Besides those already described as present to view this scene, there were the Countesses of Aberdeen, Verulam, and Bathurst, Lord Apsley, and several others of rank and fashion. From the commencement to the close, there were in every direction over the grounds, in tents and marquees, as well as in apartments laid out for the occasion in the mansion itself, a constant and abundant supply of cold meats, strong ale, bread and cheese, wines, jellies, negus, fruit, &c., for the use of all who felt disposed to partake of them; and there were upon the grounds upwards of 50 men-servants belonging to the Marquis and the three families of Aberdeen, Bathurst, and Verulam, in attendance all that day upon the visitors to the Priory. The Earl of Aberdeen was prevented from being present on the occasion by his Lordship being compelled on that day to visit His Majesty at Windsor, on important business. The young Marquis of Abercorn is a fine athletic young man, now in his 19th year. His Lordship has completed his studies at Harrow-school, and is shortly to be entered at College, together with his brother, Lord Claude, who is only about one year younger than the Marquis.

Eton v. Harrow

6 *August* 1833. On the morning of Friday, after winning the match with Winchester, the gentlemen of Eton entered the field at Lord's with 11 gentlemen of Harrow School, and a similar distinguished assemblage of spectators as honoured the contending parties with their presence on the previous day congregated on this occasion. We noticed upwards of 30 carriages, containing ladies, on the ground alongside the pavilion. The gentlemen of Eton went in first, and scored 86. Harrow then commenced batting, and 118 were obtained at the conclusion of the innings. The science displayed by both parties, but perhaps more particularly by Harrow, called forth the repeated and vehement acclamations of the spectators. The score at the termination of the game stood as follows:–

ETON		HARROW	
First innings............	86	First innings............	118
Second ditto............	57	Second ditto............	27
	143		145

2

THE SECOND HALF-CENTURY
1835 to 1884

The opening of this period sees more of the curious matches and the tantalizing coverage which, in August 1840, would say: 'CRICKET. – SUSSEX V. ALL ENGLAND. – *This match, which commenced on Monday, terminated on Tuesday in favour of All England by four wickets, after some of the finest play ever witnessed.' Ends! However, in 1842, one may assume under the influence of the new Editor, the formidable John T. Delane, regular reporting of MCC's and other major matches began. Space, however, was sometimes at a premium, witness the report of 14 June 1849 in this chapter and, on 9 July 1852:* 'THE COUNTY OF SURREY V. THE COUNTY OF KENT. *This interesting as well as great match was commenced at the "Oval" yesterday, when, as was anticipated from its character, it attracted a vast assemblage of spectators. The pressure of electioneering matters prevents us from entering into any detail of the play. The state of the score at the time of the discontinuance of the game for the day was as follows:–' (full scoreboards).*

It is probable that the main coverage at this time was in the hands of William Denison, the father of daily newspaper cricket reporting and a Parliamentary reporter too. Until his death in 1856, aged 55, he contributed as a freelance to many papers – hence an average night's sleep, he tells us, of less than four hours – and from 1843 to 1846 compiled his own cricket annual (vid. review 12 May 1845). Denison also found time to help to found Surrey County Cricket Club, for whom he played occasionally, and to be the first secretary. He is likely to have been responsible for some of the quite professional coverage appearing in The Times *at this period and for such a diatribe in July 1852 as:* 'Mr. Walker . . . will not take a sufficiency of practice to secure his "length," and so render his bowling that which in that case it would be, very dangerous, and very difficult to play. Would this gentleman but devote one-third of his time to bowling practice, he would arrive at the point we have pointed out. But his fancy is like that of most others of his standing – batting and slashing, not bowling practice.'

George Parr had already led the first English touring team overseas – to North America in 1859, when reports took almost a fortnight to reach the paper – and a cricketing prodigy named W. G. Grace had taken guard by the time Charles Box was appointed Cricket Reporter c 1867; in the following year he was entrusted with the selection of matches to be reported. Box, who published three cricket books under the pseudonym 'Bat', used to run a private school and was in his early sixties when engaged by The Times. *He is said to have kept aloof from his fellow journalists, preferring to sit alone in the grandstand. Box left* The Times *in 1880, the year of the Australians' second visit to England, and was succeeded as 'the regular cricket correspondent' by a much younger man, George Henry West, aged 29, who was related on his mother's side to a famous old cricketer, Squire Osbaldeston.*

The final entry for this second half-century, which had seen the first feature article on cricket in The Times *(The Cricket Season, written by one of the leader writers and book reviewers, A. I. Shand) published on 6 April 1875, marks the end of an era by recording the death of John Wisden. Although he once took all ten wickets in an innings* bowled *(vid. report 17 July 1850), he will forever be remembered as founder of the cricketers' almanack which bears his name. The book was edited by G. H. West for six years from 1880, beginning a link with* The Times *which is repeated a century later in the person of John Woodcock.*

17 *February* 1837. We have just had communicated to us another instance of His Majesty's liberality in promoting all establishments for the amusement and benefit of this town and county. It is generally known that a Sussex Cricket Club was at the close of last season established for the purpose of raising a fund, by subscription, to be expended in playing county matches; and His Majesty has been graciously pleased to transmit, through Sir Henry Wheatley, the sum of 20*l*. towards the undertaking, with a warm expression of His Majesty's desire to encourage the manly exercise of cricket, as a game which so peculiarly belongs to this country. – *Brighton Gazette.*

11 *October* 1838. A somewhat novel match of cricket was played on Wednesday between two female parties (married and single), in a field in the rear of a newly-erected public-house near Westend, kept by Mr. J. Vare. The fineness of the weather and the novelty of the scene drew together an immense concourse of spectators, who signified their delight by repeated rounds of applause. Vehicles of almost every description were also in attendance, from the dashing phaeton and pair down to the humble donky tandem; on the whole, there could not have been less than 3,000 persons present. The playing commenced in right earnest at 12 o'clock, the married ladies going in first, scoring 22 runs; the damsels then took the bat and scored 18. The dames then went in again and scored 27, making 49; the young ladies then went in and got 34, thus beating their opponents by three runs only. After the two first

innings, bets varying from 2 to 1 to 5 to 2 were freely offered on the married ladies and as freely taken. The fielding and batting of Miss Ann Cleaver, of Bitterne, and the Misses Caroline and Patience Lee, were particularly admired; indeed, they may be safely backed against any three boys under 18. The bowling of Mrs. Carter, on the married side, was also very good. The peculiar manner of the ladies in stopping and catching, or attempting to catch, the ball was highly amusing. When the game was over they all sat down to a comfortable tea provided by the landlady, and concluded the day's sport by a dance in the evening. It is proposed to play the return match this day week (Saturday) at the New Inn, Westend. – *Hampshire Advertiser*.

30 *July* 1840. A match of cricket was played at Ballinasloe on Wednesday, between the Teetotallers and the whiskey drinkers, which caused considerable amusement. The Temperance men mustered strong, and were backed by Lord Clancarthy and Admiral Trench. After a well contested game, the patrons of the mountain dew won the match by 35, and celebrated their victory in the evening by illuminating their houses, bonfires, &c., much to the discomfiture of the Mathewites, who fought a hard battle.

A Frenchman's Idea of Cricket

10 *February* 1841. We got up a tolerably good match behind the Hotel Royal, on the beach at Dieppe, for the amusement of the Duchess de Berri, in the year 1829. We mustered, with some difficulty, two elevens; the bowlers pitched their balls with scientific precision; the batters defended their wickets with great skill; short and long stops were on the alert; in fact, all the performers acquitted themselves most admirably. As soon as the first innings were over, one of the party who had been most active in the display of his athletic powers, approached the Duchess's carriage in the expectation of being complimented on his exertions; instead of which, one of the suite asked the gentleman, to his utter dismay and confusion, when this game of *creekay* was going to begin! – *The Sportsman in France*.

Extraordinary Match between the Greenwich and Chelsea Pensioners

19 *August* 1841. This novel match between the one-arm and one-leg pensioners came off on Monday and Tuesday, at Hall's Cricket-ground, Camberwell, by the permission of the Governors of the respective institutions, and excited much interest and mirth from the various falls which occurred during

the play. The charge of admittance to the ground was 6d., and on Monday there were full 2,000 present. It was obvious from the first that the Chelsea veterans, being much older, and at the same time mostly men who had lost a leg, would have no chance against the Greenwich tars. The result of the match thoroughly justified this conclusion, the Chelsea pensioners scoring only 19 runs, while the Greenwich tars got 176. The best of feeling and good fellowship pervaded both parties throughout, and it was not the least interesting part to witness the old boys dine together, reminding us in its truest sense of a "United Service Club." Mr. Hall, their worthy host, acted with the greatest liberality towards them. They had a good luncheon of bread, cheese, and porter before they commenced play, and for dinner quarters of lamb and roast and boiled beef in profusion. On their departure they each had a noggin to drink the Queen's health and 10s. in cash for their two days' exertions, besides their free passage to and fro. It is 16 years since a similar match took place between the two institutions, which was played in Montpelier-gardens, Blackheath, when the Greenwich heroes came off victorious.

Kent v. All England

14 *July* 1842. There never was perhaps in the annals of cricketing a greater triumph than the one achieved on Tuesday evening at Lord's, by the players of Kent in their match with eleven selected from the various counties of England, and in which they, after two days of unrivalled play, were proclaimed the victors by a majority of no less than 50 runs. The English cricketers are unquestionably the finest in the world, and the "Men of Kent" having now defeated, and without much difficulty, the *élite* of the gentlemen and professional players of this country, they are fairly entitled to the distinction of being styled the champions of the players of this fine game. For some time past this match has been the principal topic of conversation among the members of the metropolitan, suburban, and provincial cricket clubs, and consequently a speculative interest has been excited – indeed, bets to an immense amount have been pending on the result, and some idea may be formed of the anxiety with which that was regarded by those amateurs and players who were unavoidably absent and living in distant parts from the fact, that pigeon and horse expresses were despatched after each innings, communicating the state of the game. The weather being propitious on both Monday and Tuesday, the enclosure at Lord's presented a gay and animated appearance from the immense assemblage of spectators, more than four thousand of whom paid for admission. There were above 100 of the equipages of the nobility and other distinguished persons, including a number of the carriages of ladies of rank and fashion. The arrangements for the admission of the company and the convenience of the spectators were admirable, and reflected great credit on the taste and judgment of Mr. Dark, the sole pro-

prietor. It will be seen from the subjoined list that the players in this game were very nearly matched, the conditions being – Kent, five gentlemen and six players; and England, two gentlemen and nine players. They were as follows:– Kent – Gentlemen, Mr. N. Felix, Mr. W. D. C. Baker, Mr. C. G. Whitaker, Mr. W. Mynn, and Mr. A. Mynn. Players – Pilch, Wenman, Adams, Dorrington, Hillyer, and Cocker. England – Gentlemen: Mr. T. A. Anson, and Mr. C. G. Taylor. Players – Lillywhite, Redgate, Sewell, Good, Hawkins, Box, Guy, Fenner, and Barker. The wickets on Monday were pitched shortly after 11 o'clock, at which time the betting was very brisk, Kent for choice. There was a considerable variation in the odds during the game, particularly when any of the "crack" men got runs, or on their wickets being lowered. As the match was drawing to a conclusion the Kentish players were decidedly the favourites, 5 and 6 to 4 being freely laid on them, with but four takers. The players of Kent having won the toss, went in first, and made 120 runs. England scored 133. Kent in its second innings made 151, while England only scored 88. The play, altogether, was first-rate; that of Mr. A. Mynn was perfect; his bowling, which did great execution among the wickets of his adversaries, was universally admired, and his batting was also very fine. His brother, Mr. W. Mynn, Mr. Felix, Mr. Whittaker, and Pilch likewise displayed some pretty batting. Of the English players who particularly distinguished themselves may be named Hawkins, Box, Sewell, and Mr. Taylor. The latter gentleman, as a cricketer generally, is second to no one, and as a batsman has scarcely an equal. In the first innings of this match he injured his wrist, and in the second innings batted (and against the bowling of Mr. Mynn) with only one hand; yet he scored 19.

Gentlemen v. Players

29 *July* 1842. The annual match between 11 gentlemen and 11 players was commenced on Monday morning at Lord's, and terminated on Wednesday afternoon, when the former, contrary to general anticipation, came off victorious, winning the game easily and with no less than 95 runs to spare. This is indeed a triumph for the gentlemen when it is considered that their adversaries are the finest players in England. The success of the Kent 11 in their matches with Sussex and All England is in a great measure ascribed to the unparalleled scientific play, tact, and knowledge of the game displayed by Mr. Alfred Mynn; but certain it is that on this occasion the defeat of the professionals is solely attributable to the extraordinarily fine play that gentleman exhibited, particularly his bowling, by which in the first innings of the players he lowered the wickets of Fenner, Guy, and Rich, and caught Wenman and Hawkins, and in their second also bowled out Redgate, Box, Guy, Fenner, Wenman, and Hawkins, and caught Sewell. The gentlemen having won the toss, went in first; at which time, and also for some days previous, long odds

were freely laid against them, with but a poverty of takers, and in some instances bets of four to one on the professionals were booked, so sanguine were some of the members of the Marylebone club, and other amateurs, of their success. The confidence of these gentlemen, perhaps, arose from their acquaintance with the merits of the players, several being attached to the establishment at Lord's as bowlers with whom noblemen and gentlemen practise, and also the absence of Mr. C. G. Taylor, a most experienced cricketer, and one of the finest batsmen in the kingdom, who, doubtless, was prevented from appearing on the field on the side of the gentlemen in consequence of the accident he met with while playing in the late match of Kent v. All England at Lord's, by his left hand being injured by the ball. The Gentlemen in their first innings scored 76; their second innings amounted to 206; gross total, 284. The Players, in their second innings, cleared only 67. Hawkins, Redgate, and Lillywhite were put out without a single run, the two former by Mr. A. Mynn, and the latter run out. The game throughout was well contested, the play being of the first order. We have already spoken of that of Mr. A. Mynn, and it is best justice to his colleagues to say that they well supported him. Sir F. Bathurst, who bowled with Mr. Mynn, did great execution among the wickets of the Players, and the batting of Mr. Felix was universally admired. Mr. Mynn also batted uncommonly well, and of the 206 runs scored in their second innings, these gentlemen made 134 with their own bats. The Players seemed all abroad, and they could not resist the bowling of Mr. Mynn, who, possessing extraordinary muscular power, delivers the ball with a force quite irresistible, and with the most extraordinary precision. Fuller Pilch, who is esteemed one of the first batsmen of the country, was bowled out by Mr. Mynn without a single run, and in his second innings made only six; and Lillywhite, the best slow bowler of the day, was put out by one of Sir Frederick's peculiar balls, after scoring but 9 in his first, and 0 in his second, innings. Hillyer, Lillywhite, and Redgate, displayed some very excellent bowling, and Box, as wicket keeper, evinced his usual tact and adroitness. The fielding of both sides was capital. The ground each day was crowded with spectators, but at the Pavilion we missed several sporting noblemen and gentlemen, who usually attend the enclosure to witness the great matches, and who, it appeared, were at Goodwood. There was, however, a good sprinkling of fashionables, and among other distinguished patrons and supporters of the game present, we noticed the Marquis of Douro, Viscount Chelsea, Viscount Grimston, Lord M. Hill, Lord C. Russell, Lord W. Beresford, Lord H. Loftus, Lord F. Beauclerc, Lord Colberne, Hon. Colonel Lowther, Hon. S. Ponsonby, Hon. A. Savile, Hon. F. Savile, Hon. H. Agar, Hon. C. Agar, Hon. F. Craven, and an immense number of the Marylebone and other fashionable clubs who frequent this renowned sporting resort, and Mr. Robert Peel, the eldest son of the Premier.

The Marylebone Cricket Club

16 *May* 1843. At the anniversary dinner of this distinguished and celebrated club, which took place at the Clarendon Hotel a few days since, the Earl of Ducie, the president, in the chair, 35 new members were balloted for and elected, amongst whom were the Earl of Munster, the Hon. Henry Neville, Sir John Shelley, Colonel Fane, the Hon. Captain Vivian, Viscount Glamis, the Hon. Charles Neville, the Hon. Captain Lindsay, the Hon. C. B. Lyon, Captain Newton, &c. His late Royal Highness the Duke of Sussex was an honorary member, and his Royal Highness Prince Albert has been graciously pleased to become the patron of the club. Matches, appointed to come off during this season, have been arranged with the undermentioned clubs as follows:– St. John's Wood (to have come off yesterday), at Lord's; University of Cambridge, May 18, at Cambridge; Clapton Club, May 22, at Lord's; University of Oxford, May 25, at Oxford; Haileybury College, May 29, at Haileybury; County of Sussex, June 5, at Lord's; the Garrison of Chatham, June 8, at Chatham; University of Cambridge (return match), June 12, at Lord's; Northern Counties, June 19, at Lord's; Clapton Club (return match), June 22, at Clapton; Present Etonians, June 24, at Eton; Gentlemen of Hants, June 26, at Lord's; Rugby School, June 29, at Lord's; Present Harrovians, July 1, at Harrow; University of Oxford (return match), July 6, at Lord's; England, July 24, at Lord's; Garrison of Chatham (return match), July 27, at Lord's; Nottingham Trent-bridge Club, July 31, at Lord's; County of Sussex (return match), August 14, at Brighton; Northern Counties (return match), August 21, at Leicester; Nottingham Trent-bridge Club (return match), August 24, at Nottingham; and Gentlemen of Hants (return match), August 28, at Southampton. The following matches were also arranged at the anniversary dinner to come off at Lord's in the course of the season:– Two select elevens of England, May 29; Oxford versus Cambridge, June 15; Gents of England versus Gents of Kent, July 3; Kent versus England, July 10; Gentlemen versus Players, July 17; and the usual matches between Harrow, Winchester, and Eton, August 2, 3, 4, and 5. The two following return matches have also been arranged by the club to be played at Canterbury:– Kent versus England, August 7; and the Gents of England versus the Gents of Kent, August 10. A match will also be played in the county of Kent for the benefit of Wenman, on Thursday, the 17th of August. Altogether, the forthcoming season, with regard to the prospects of this distinguished and old-established club, is more promising than it has been during the last few years.

Marylebone Club
v. University of Cambridge

20 *May* 1844. The annual match between the Marylebone Club and the University of Cambridge was played at the latter place, on Thursday and Friday last in the presence of an immense assemblage of spectators. The former eleven won in one innings and 17 runs, whilst last year, the victory was gained by the University with 37 runs to spare. Upon the present occasion the score was, the University, 135 and 151, and the Marylebone, 303, whilst last year the University made 90 and 108, and their opponents, 50 and 111. The largeness of the Marylebone score last week was attributed to the bad bowling of the Cantabs, its characteristics being wildness and unsteadiness. Indeed, as with many bowlers of the present day, pace was aimed at in preference to the wicket, and it was quite a matter of chance as to whether the ball took its course towards the stumps. Hence the long hands of the Marylebone eleven. It is much hoped that by one of the amendments in the laws of cricket which have been proposed, and referred to a select committee of the Marylebone Club, with a view to the assimilation of the rule applicable to "wide" balls with that for "no" balls, that the "vice" of the throwing bowling, wildness and recklessness of delivery, without any attempt to direct the ball at the wicket, will be corrected, an end which will be accomplished in the event of the amendment being agreed to. A stronger proof that an alteration in the existing law is demanded could not have been brought forward than this match at Cambridge, for the Marylebone scored 44 for wides and byes alone. Of the 303 Captain Freer made 27, Mr. C. Whittaker 25, the Hon. F. Ponsonby 46, Mr. Garth 23, Mr. C. Morse 82, and Lillywhite 44, not out. On the part of the University, the runs were principally obtained by Mr. Dewing, who scored 4 and 32, Mr. F. Gruggen 13 and 9, Mr. E. Dowell 9 and 35, Mr. A. M. Hoare 22 and 3, Mr. H. Wroth 26 and 34, and Mr. J. Bowyer 12. The batting on each side was altogether as good as the bowling (especially by the University) was of an inferior description, for whilst Lillywhite did not tell so much as usual, Mr. Whittaker every now and then was almost as "far afield" as his antagonists. There were some brilliant hits by both parties, and the only astonishment was that, instead of 303, the Marylebone Club had not doubled that number. On Thursday week the latter club play the University of Oxford, when we hope to find that a different plan of bowling will be adopted, and that it will be characterized by a general endeavour to "bowl the wickets" and not by an attempt to deliver the ball with as much force as though the party were actuated by a desire that it should go into the adjoining county.

Gentlemen of England
v. Gentlemen of Kent

19 *June* 1844. The match between the gentlemen of England and the gentlemen of Kent was one of the most astonishing in the annals of cricket. It commenced on Monday at "Lord's" in the presence of one of the most distinguished assemblages we ever remember to have seen upon a similar occasion. The brilliancy of the scene, too, was very considerably enhanced by some extremely large marquees which have been erected for the fancy fair and promenade, which is to take place on Thursday for the benefit of the ship-wrecked mariners. The gentlemen of Kent went in first, and after some very fine play, scored in the first innings 116 runs, in their second 82, making a total of 198. Of these Mr. Felix made 22 and 18; Mr. A. Mynn, 32 and 0; Mr. Swann, 24 and 4; Mr. W. Wynn, 4 and 17; Mr. Fredericks, 8 and 0; Mr. E. Bayley, 1 and 19; Mr. C. Harenc, 9 and 2, &c. The gentlemen of England scored but 63 in their first hands, being thus 53 fewer than their opponents. At the commencement of the match the betting, of which there was a great deal throughout the contest, was 6 and 7 to 4 in favour of Kent; but as soon as the wicket of Mr. Felix had been lowered, the odds diminished to even. They, however, assumed their original position as soon as Kent had terminated their second hands; and when England had lost their first wicket in their second innings, the betting went up until as much as 7 to 1 were laid with some freedom. But the result of the game proved how little certainty of calculation there is in the play. They began their second innings with a majority of 135 runs staring them in the face. They went, nevertheless, to work with great spirit; but Mr. Craven and the Hon. R. Grimston were got down for two and three runs respectively. Mr. Haygarth was the first who made any stand against the terrific bowling of Mr. A. Mynn and the awkward balls of Mr. Fredericks. He obtained 19 in excellent style. Mr. C. Taylor hit away with his usual freedom, and in a very short space of time contributed 18 to the score. The match, however, was in reality won by the steady play of Mr. Gordon, and the resolute hitting of Mr. Kynaston, the former scoring, whilst he made 30 in his first, 32 (not out) in the second hands, and the latter 3 and 35 (not out). There were 17 byes and 12 wides. The new rule relative to "wide balls" was brought into operation only once during the match, and then 2 were run for a "wide" from Mr. Fredericks. This gentleman also gave one other wide, whilst Mr. Mynn bowled four singles, and Mr. Harenc five. England thus won by six wickets, greatly to the surprise of all the spectators. In future each run obtained for a "wide ball' is to be scored against the particular bowler by whom it is given, upon the scoring paper.

The Game of Cricket

14 *August* 1844. Baron Alderson, a few days since, addressed the following remarks to the grand jury of the county of Suffolk:– "In a neighbouring county which I passed through on the circuit this time, I had what I am afraid I shall not have here – a day of rest; and I went out into the country, and had the pleasure of seeing a match of cricket, in which a noble earl, the Lord-Lieutenant of his county, was playing with the tradesmen, the labourers, and all around him, and I believe he lost no respect from that course – they loved him better, but they did not respect him less. I believe that if they themselves associated more with the lower classes of society, the kingdom of England would be in a far safer, and society in a far sounder condition. I wish I could put it to the minds of all to think so, because I think it is true."

Enclosure of Kennington Oval

2 *May* 1845. This well-known place, which has for many years been used for the purposes of a nursery ground, is now being enclosed with high palings, in order to convert it into a cricket-ground, bowling-green, race-course, &c. This alteration will not be much liked by the inhabitants in the neighbourhood, as the grounds will be entirely hidden to pedestrians, instead of being open as before. – *Globe*.

Denison's Cricketers' Companion

12 *May* 1845. The object of this week is to present to the admirers and followers of the most noble and healthful of England's sports, cricket, a collection of all the best matches which were played in the past season at "Lord's," and in every part of the United Kingdom, together with other information of interest, and in some instances necessary, to the accomplished player as well as to the inexperienced learner. In the number before us the author appears to have carried out this intent with great success, for it contains the scores of nearly 200 matches, a minute review of the progress of the game in the summer of 1844, a list of the various noblemen by whom clubs are either supported or patronised, and the remarks of Mr. Baron Alderson upon the beneficial operation of such a proceeding; some strictures upon the "wild and reckless" system of bowling now so much in use, average tables in which are to be found about 120 names of batsmen, bowlers, and wicket-keepers, together with the laws of cricket. The book is published by Mr. Denison under the patronage of the Marylebone Club – a circumstance which would invest it with the character of an "authority." There is, too, an

additional reason why the *Cricketers' Companion* should be possessed by all who feel an interest in the game – it is the only annual collection of matches, and is published in a pocketable form.

Cricketing in Hyde Park

15 *September* 1846. On Friday evening the Foot Guards quartered at the powder magazine, Hyde Park, proceeded, according to custom, to play cricket on a piece of ground in the park adjoining the magazine, but they had scarcely pitched the wickets when they were ordered off by one of the constables, who would not allow them to play there. The soldiers remonstrated, and assured the constable that they were in the habit of playing there without any molestation. A crowd that had assembled, seeing that the constable was determined to prevent the soldiers having a game, commenced hooting and pelting him, when the soldiers, dreading that worse results might follow, very prudently withdrew, assuring the constable that they would lay the matter before their commanding officer. – *Globe.*

16 *September* 1846. We find on inquiry, that the paragraph we copied from the *Globe*, stating that the police had prevented the soldiers from playing cricket in Hyde-park on Friday last, is entirely destitute of foundation.

Lord Morpeth and Cricketing

19 *October* 1846. It may not be known to many, and we had the happiness of being one of the few who had become acquainted with the fact, that during the last three years – indeed ever since the noble viscount returned to his native shores – Lord Morpeth has been constant and unceasing in his efforts to cultivate cricket amongst all classes of society, but especially amongst those who are engaged in agricultural and manufacturing pursuits. It has not been an uncommon thing, in the progress of the period we have alluded to, to see his Lordship scoring throughout a match which has been played by the servants of his noble family against another club or a different parish; and his Lordship has been often heard to say that whenever the opportunity was afforded to him of furthering the practice or the interests of so national and healthful a sport he would not permit it to escape. It is gratifying, therefore, to find that one of his high and proud birth should carry into office the opinions and intentions which were expressed when holding the simple position of a private gentleman. Lord Morpeth, when merely the son of an earl, patronized, by his pocket and cheering presence and personal assistance, the first of England's pastimes. Lord Morpeth, now a Minister of the Crown, and consequently with increased power, has, in his official character, given

instructions, or permission, that nine acres of a park, which is even yet in the course of formation, the Victoria-park, situated somewhere below White-chapel, shall be reserved and prepared as a cricket ground for the inhabitants of the district. It is but fair to infer that the results which Lord Morpeth witnessed in Northumberland, from the constant commingling of classes in the practice of the game upon all who were engaged in the matches, or, indeed, in the pastime, has led to this step – one, too, which in the present rage for building, is the more acceptable, setting aside the peculiar circum-stances of this particular case, because even the small number of grounds which have been hitherto applied to the purpose of cricket are, we lament to hear, being considerably diminished. This proceeding of the noble lord comes with increased benefits and claims upon the sympathies of the public. It is a boon of vastly enhanced value, and in proportion is his Lordship entitled to the thanks of the world at large. We earnestly trust we may hear of further grants of land for the recreation of the people. A park is to be laid out in Battersea-fields; could not a portion be set aside for cricket? – *Sheffield Iris*

Married v. Single

14 *June* 1849. This match, after a contest of three days, was last evening brought to a termination at "Lord's" in the presence of a numerous assem-blage of spectators. The perusal of the score will prove this, – that the batting beat the bowling, or else we scarcely like to say so. On the present occasion the "fielding" in some respects on both sides was very faulty. At another time, when more space is afforded [*no more space was afforded*], we shall enter into a dissection of the play which has been exhibited as this contest has progressed, and offer some deductions which it is hoped may lead to an improvement in some points. The final score stood thus:–

MARRIED

Dean, b. Wisden	2	c. Nicholson, b. Wisden	..	19
Clark, run out ..	71	b. Wisden	..	0
Hillyer, l. b. w., b. Wisden	11	s. Nicholson, b. Wisden	..	32
Box, c. Kynaston, b. Chester ..	42	b. Martingell ..	..	37
N. Felix, Esq., c. Kynaston, b. Wisden	27	b. Martingell ..	..	0
A. Mynn, Esq., c. Wisden, b. Chester	2	c. Armitage b. Wisden	..	0
Earl Verulam, b. Wisden	2	b. Martingell ..	..	1
W. Pilch, c. Wisden, b. Armitage ..	4	b. Wisden	..	18
Daken, not out	26	Not out..	..	19
S. Whitehead, Esq., b. Wisden	0	b. Wisden	..	3
Lillywhite, c. Parr, b. Armitage	0	b. Wisden	..	0
		Byes, 16, wide, Chester, 1,		
Byes	16	Wisden 1 ..	..	18
	203			147

SINGLE

Hon. R. Grimston, b. Lilly-white	26	b. Hillyer	76
A. Haygarth, Esq., s. Box, b. Dean	24	s. Box, b. Hillyer	5
Guy, c. Hillyer, b. Lillywhite ..	0	b. Lillywhite	12
Pilch, c. Box, b. Dean	8	c. Mynn, b. Hillyer	5
Martingell, c. Mynn, b. Lilly-white	0	c. Whitehead, b. Lillywhite ..	1
Wisden, b. Lillywhite	0		
Armitage, c. Box, b. Dean ..	23		
Parr, b. Dean	61	b. Hillyer	3
Chester, b. Dean	3	not out	22
R. Kynaston, Esq., b. Lilly-white	1	not out	3
W. Nicholson, Esq., not out ..	23	c. Box, b. Dean	32
Byes, 6; no balls (Clark) 5 ..	11	Byes	12
	180		171

The single won by three wickets.

Gentlemen of Kent
v. Gentlemen of England

27 *August* 1849. This, the second grand match of the [Canterbury cricket] week, was played on Thursday and Friday. It was on these two days, as in preceding years, that the ground presented the most elegant and fashionable attendance. There was an immense ring of carriages, from which the fair occupants alighted, and either paraded along the upper portion of the ground, or took their seats in the canvassed pavilion, which, as heretofore, had been provided for their accommodation by the "Cricket Committee."

England having gained the toss, commenced their operations with the Hon. R. Grimston and Mr. Esrom, whose wickets were laid siege to by Mr. Harenc and Mr. Traill, whilst Mr. H. Andrews, of the Blackheath Clubs, was posted behind the wicket. With regard to the play of Mr. Grimston, bad luck attended him on the first day in the week, and having attached itself to him, then, it would appear that with all his anxiety and all his nerve, he was unable to release himself from its enthralment. Thus, in the present match, he was compelled to rest satisfied – no "satisfied" he was not – he was compelled to congratulate himself that his scores were not more insignificant than five in each hand. Mr. J. Lee took the place of Mr. Grimston; but had not been long at his post before he was caught by Mr. Felix, off a ball which was delivered by Mr. Dyer. Mr. Nicholson succeeded to this wicket, but just as he had scored half a dozen he received a peremptory notice to quit from Mr. Harenc. Mr. Hartopp came next, when without having previously been permitted to make the smallest contribution to the score, he placed his leg before the very goal which it was his duty to have secured by "other" means. It should be mentioned that this last named gentleman took the wicket which Mr. Esrom had been dismissed from by means of Mr. Bosworth having caught him from Mr. Harenc. His score was 13. There were now five wickets down, and only 37 were gained. Mr. Fellowes now made his appearance, but his efforts resulted in one only, when he was succeeded by Mr. Nash, who was soon afterwards joined by Mr. "Biffen" a "Norfolk" cognomen for an Etonian "Keate." By the gentleman from Hertfordshire and the late Etonian, a vigorous and effective stand was made against the onslaught attacks of the Kentish bowlers. Mr. Nash was the first to suffer himself to be overcome, but he had obtained as many as 16 prior to his being caught by Mr. Felix. His number contained three twos and a balance of singles. His vacancy was soon filled by Mr. Whitehead. The runs were once more made with some rapidity, whereupon Mr. Dyer was taken off and A. Mynn put on in his place in the following "over." After some little time had elapsed, Mr. Mynn found an uninterrupted path to the wicket of Mr. Whitehead, whose score amounted to eight only. Eighty runs had at this point of the game been registered with the loss of eight wickets. Mr. Mayne was the next, and quickly accomplished a one and a two, when he [Mr. "Biffen"] was bowled out by Mr. Harenc at a moment when his contributions had realized 18. 88 was now the number of England's score with the loss of nine wickets. Sir F. Bathurst was the last to come in, but he failed to offer any numerical aid to his side, seeing that he ran out without having scored. Thus the total of this innings was 89.

On the part of the Gentlemen of Kent Mr. Traill and Mr. Norton opened the proceedings. The bowlers were Sir F. Bathurst and Mr. Jonas Nash, an underhand slow bowler, the latter of whom soon disposed of Mr. Traill for 5 runs. Mr. Dyer thereupon joined Mr. Norton. This transplant from Blackheath, however, had only made two when he was caught by Mr. Esrom off Sir F. Bathurst. Then came Mr. Mynn, who was shortly beaten by one of Mr. Nash's slow balls, which he put back into that gentleman's hands. Kent had now lost three powerful wickets for 12 runs only. Mr. Felix then made not only his appearance but an effective stand with Mr. Norton against the bowling. A considerable addition was now made to the score, twos, threes, and fours multiplying to some extent, the batmen, one in particular, adopting the plan of "running in" [*running forward to meet the ball*] to make his hits – some people call this bad play – until Mr. Nash was taken off and Mr. Fellowes took the ball in hand. Both of the hitters, however, were so well "in" that the rapid pace of that gentleman was so far from effective that the runs were now and then obtained the more quickly, and therefore the slow bowler was fallen back upon. If Mr. Felix is required to make runs fast, put on the most rapid bowling you can procure, for his practice at the Catapulta has rendered him its master. Against slow bowling he will sometimes run up a goodly number, but, generally speaking, he is beaten by it. This result is easily accounted for: all his early practice was at fast bowling, and he has, since those days, looked at the slow pace as rubbish; yet he seldom plays against it without becoming one of its victims. In the course of time, and just when Kent had scored 59, Mr. Norton ran out, having as many as 20 runs attached to his name. He was followed by Mr. Harenc, who was soon caught by Mr. Fellowes, off Mr. Nash, without having scored. Mr. G. Burnett succeeded to the wicket, and achieved 13 runs, Mr. Felix still hitting away with great success and effect. Soon after Mr. Burnett had taken the bat, Sir F. Bathurst changed his end for bowling, and Mr. Fellowes took the ball from the other wicket. Still, Mr. Felix was not removable. By and by Mr. Burnett was bowled by Sir Frederick, but the Kent score had at that time increased to 120. Mr. Andrews came next. He was bowled by Mr. Fellowes without having made any addition to the score. Previously to this, Mr. Felix had "astronomised" a ball delivered by Sir F. Bathurst, which Mr. Nash caught, and this ended Mr. Felix's score. Mr. Bosworth came next and made two runs, whilst the other two wickets proved to be unproductive. The first day's play expired before the last of the Kent wickets went down, and therefore on Friday they were again at their posts. The result of the innings has been stated. England once more took the bat, and a reference to the score will show that had we space much opportunity was afforded for remarks and description. We can only point out that Mr. Whitehead scored 54 in a fine slashing style, that Mr. Nicholson obtained 20 by good steady play, that Mr. Fellowes "let out" to the tune of 20, and that Mr. Lee added 13 to the score in excellent style. The innings amounted to 145, by which Kent had to go in for 111 to tie and 112 to win. They could only make 95, and so they lost by 16 runs. The score stood thus:–

ENGLAND

Hon. R. Grimston, run out ..	5	c. Andrews, b. Harenc	..	5
Mr. C. Esrom, c. Bosworth, b. Harenc	13	c. Andrews, b. Traill ..	..	0
Mr. J. M. Lee, c. Felix, b. Dyer	3	b. Harenc	..	13
Mr. W. Nicholson, b. Harenc	6	s. Andrews, b. Traill ..	..	20
Mr. Hartopp, l.b.w., b. Harenc	0	c. Norton, b. Mynn ..	..	2
Mr. H. Fellowes, c. Norton, b. Harenc	1	run out	..	20
Mr. J. Nash, c. Felix, b. Harenc	16	s. Andrews, b. Harenc	..	5
Mr. Biffen, b. Harenc	18	c. Burnett, b. Harenc ..	..	1
Mr. S. Whitehead, b. Mynn ..	8	run out	..	54
Mr. H. B. Mayne, not out ..	3	b. Harenc	..	2
Sir F. Bathurst, run out ..	0	not out	..	7
Byes, 10; wide 6	16	Byes, 10; wide 6 ..	..	16
	89			145

KENT

Mr. J. Traill, b. Nash	5	b. Fellowes	..	6
Mr. H. Norton, run out ..	20	b. Nash	..	0
Mr. F. Dyer, c. Esrom, b. Bathurst	2	b. Fellowes	..	1
Mr. A. Mynn, c. and b. Nash	2	c. Esrom, b. Bathurst ..	..	3

Mr. N. Felix, c. Nash, b. Bathurst	70	c. Fellowes, b. Nash	5
Mr. C. Harenc, c. Fellowes, b. Nash	0	b. Fellowes	4
Mr. G. Burnett, b. Bathurst ..	13	b. Bathurst	4
Mr. H. Andrews, b. Fellowes	0	c. Lee, b. Nash..	35
Mr. F. Bosworth, b. Bathurst	2	b. Fellowes	0
Mr. G. Dickins, b. Bathurst ..	0	b. Bathurst	23
Mr. W. Baldock, not out ..	0	not out	0
Byes, 6; wide, 3	4	Byes, 10; wide, 4	14
	123		95

And so the Gentlemen of England won by 16 runs.

North v. South

17 *July* 1850. If any man on Monday morning had chosen to have advanced a passing remark to the effect that it was "possible," not to say "probable," that the "South" could be beaten in one innings by the "North," he would have been regarded either as a madman or a fool by certain persons. Nevertheless, such was the result of the present match. But the more extraordinary event was, that, notwithstanding that was the result, its end should have been accomplished in one day. The untutored will naturally ask how, with such a powerful eleven as was that which represented the "South," its representatives could be got out so quickly, and for so few runs. The reply is this, – in the first instance the "South" were totally unable in the first innings to play the slow bowling; for the little they had learnt in respect of that pace whilst Clarke was attached to the Marylebone club the members and players appear to have lost again; and then, in the second innings, young Wisden will be found to have taken vast liberties, for he dispersed 10 of the wickets. The score stood thus:–

SOUTH

1st Innings.		2d Innings.			
Dean, b. Wisden	3	b. Wisden	0
Mr. J. M. Lee, b. Clarke ..	5	b. Wisden	6
Caffyn, b. Clarke	9	b. Wisden	24
Box, b. Wisden	3	b. Wisden	1
Mr. N. Felix, st. Chatterton, b. Clarke	3	b. Wisden	0
Chester, b. Clarke	8	b. Wisden	17
Mr. R. Kynaston, b. Clarke ..	0	b. Wisden	0
Mr. A. Mynn, c. Burghley, b. Wisden	2	not out	17
John Lillywhite, not out ..	0	b. Wisden	0
Sherman, run out	0	b. Wisden	2
Sir F. Bathurst, b. Clarke ..	0	b. Wisden	4
Byes 2, leg byes 1	3	Byes 3, leg byes 1, no ball 1 ..	5
	36		76

NORTH

1st Innings.

Hunt, b. Sherman	..	..	..	7
Mr. R. B. Smythies, b. Sherman	..	..	4
Guy, b. Sherman	..	..	..	4
Parr, b. Bathurst	..	..	..	17
Mr. R. T. King, b. Sherman	..	..	13
Lord Burghley, run out	..	..	..	2
Chatterton, run out ..	..	..	..	0
Mr. R. F. Skelton, b. Sherman	..	..	0
Wisden, b. Mynn	..	..	..	22
Lord Guernsey, not out	..	..	..	27
Clarke, b. Sherman ..	..	..	..	13
Byes 14, leg byes 5, wide 3 ..	..	..	22

131

And so the South were vanquished in one innings by 19 runs.

Cricket under Difficulties

16 *August* 1850. At a return match between the young cricket club of Burneside and the junior members of the Kendal Club, one of the most remarkable features was the playing of Walker, a youth from Burneside, without hands, having been unfortunately deprived of those useful members by an accident at the paper mill. Maimed as he is, he can do anything in the game except bowl. He bats very tolerably, and certainly most extraordinarily for his means; catches a ball upon his chest, with the assistance of his arms; and throws up a ball with remarkable precision by means of his foot. – *Westmoreland Gazette.*

Cobden on Cricket

20 *September* 1850. Mr. Cobden has written the following reply to a request that he would become patron of a cricket club in the West Riding:– "Midhurst, Sussex, September 5, 1850. Sir, – I have no hesitation in allowing my name to be used as one of the patrons of the Wakefield Mechanics' Institution Cricket Club. It is a game with which I have been familiar from my childhood, it being universally played in this part of the kingdom. It is still a question, I believe, whether cricket had its origin in Sussex or Hampshire; but I remember that, upwards of 40 years ago, every village in these counties had its cricket-ground. Since that time it has spread throughout the north of England, and even into Scotland. It is a healthful, manly recreation; and, if the game be played under judicious rules, such as you have adopted, it is, in my opinion, the most innocent of all out-of-door amusements. Wishing your club good luck, – in other words, dry Tuesdays and Saturdays, I am, Sir, your obedient servant, RICHARD COBDEN."

Lane v. Barnes

Sittings in Middlesex, at Nisi Prius, before Mr. Baron PLATT
and Common Juries

15 *January* 1853. Mr. Serjeant Wilkins and Mr. C. Pollock conducted the case for the plaintiff, and Mr. E. James, with Mr. Needham, appeared for the defendant.

This was an action to recover compensation in damages for an injury sustained by the plaintiff in consequence of blows which had been inflicted upon him by the defendant.

It appeared that the plaintiff is a young man of about 19 years of age, and had been for many years the managing assistant to his father, who carries on the business of a house-decorator, painter, and paperhanger, in the Horse-ferry-road. The plaintiff was a member of a cricket club in connexion with the normal school at Westminster, and on the 19th of June, with other members, went to play a match against Dr. White's pupils, it being agreed that although those pupils belonged to the Westminster school, yet that the match should come off at Shepherd's-bush. The defendant, Christopher Barnes, who was the son of a surgeon, at Notting-hill, was one of the pupils selected to play. The Westminster boys took the first innings, and afterwards the normal school scholars "went in." In the course of their innings, however, a heavy shower came on, during which the parties took shelter in a shed belonging to the Wellington Tavern. The defendant and some of his companions also went into the tavern, where they had something to drink, and, subsequently, he and others appeared to be very much excited. When the rain subsided, the game, notwithstanding the wet state of the ground, was resumed. At this period the plaintiff, James Lane, and one of his brothers, were at the wickets. The defendant bowled a ball to the plaintiff's brother John. That ball hit John's leg, whereupon the defendant appealed to the umpire (his own brother) at his end, who gave it "out." The plaintiff said it was "not out," as the leg was not before the wicket. A dispute thereupon arose, and the lie was passed by the defendant to the plantiff, who as quickly, as he stated, returned the compliment. Further words of anger ensured, in the course of which the defendant struck the plaintiff on the nose. This action induced the latter to dare its repetition, when the defendant seized a bat from his brother, the umpire with which he attempted to strike the plaintiff, who, however, ran away, in the outset throwing his own bat away, fearing that he might lose his temper, and then do some serious mischief with it. The defendant followed him, and made many attempts to hit the plaintiff with the bat. He succeeded in the first instance in planting a blow on the back, which made the plaintiff stagger forward. The chase was continued for some further distance, and at length the plaintiff was brought down by a severe blow on the ankle. After this the persons upon the ground gathered round, and considerable irritation was manifested. Eventually a comparative reconciliation was arrived at, and the game was resumed, the plaintiff having a friend to run for him. The plaintiff, in his evidence, said that he was induced to go on with the game principally because the other side said they should take the ball.

Several questions as to the rules and customs of the game having arisen,

Mr. JAMES said they happened to have a considerable authority in cricket matters in court at that moment, and as they had in law certain reports of "leading cases," so he might say there were in cricket reports which he would call "Denison's Leading Matches" – a work which could be referred to to decide these questions. (Laughter.)

Having continued the game until about 8 o'clock, the plaintiff and his companions went home, but the former was so bad in his leg that he was obliged to be assisted. On the following day the leg presented such symptoms as induced the sending for the medical man of the family, and from that day (the 20th of June) until a fortnight since the plaintiff had been under the care of that gentleman, unable to do more than about three days' work during the whole of that period.

Dr. Burton Payne stated that he had been attending the plaintiff ever since the 20th of June, for an injury inflicted just below the point of the ankle. For the first two or three weeks it was a very simple matter comparatively, but from that time it presented a very serious aspect, as a violent inflammation of the ligamentary structure set in. Erysipelas had supervened twice or thrice, and among other severe medicines he had had to treat the patient with was that of mercury, to throw him into a state of salivation. The illness had been accompanied by great constitutional disturbance. It had been by his advice that the plaintiff had abstained from his ordinary avocations, because, having made two or three experiments on the subject, he had found that each had resulted in an increased amount of inflammation of the wound. His bill was something more than 17*l*.

Evidence was also given to show that even at one of his occupations, that of a decorative paperhanger, the plaintiff could earn from 2*l*. to 3*l*. a week.

At the conclusion of the plaintiff's case a consultation took place between the learned counsel on each side, which resulted in

Mr. JAMES intimating to the Court that his learned friend and himself had agreed to take a verdict for the plaintiff for 60*l*.

Verdict accordingly.

Death of Lillywhite

24 *August* 1854. The admirers of the manly game of cricket will be sorry to learn that this favourite son of the bat, the ball, and the wicket is no more. After a long and successful innings, cholera has at last "caught him out." He

died at his house at Islington on Tuesday of the prevailing epidemic. The deceased was much respected by the cricketing world, who gave him the title of "The Nonpareil." Lillywhite introduced round bowling.

Earl of Winterton's Eleven
v. Second Royal Surrey Militia

18 *August* 1855. This match will doubtless form one of Mr. Denison's "Curiosities of Cricket." Not only is it singular of itself that any "Eleven" should all be removed from the wickets without scoring even "one run," but the matter becomes the more extraordinary when Challen, one of the noble earl's bowlers, is a fast bowler, while there were several cool and dangerous bats opposed to him. It would naturally have been betted at very long odds that some one of the batsmen would have "fluked," if he could not have "played," a run, and that a "bye" or a "leg" or a "wide" would have come out as a common matter of course. But no not either one of these results came off, and so there will be found appended to this notice a score in which the "first innings" passed away without a run.

In the second hands of these military defaulters 106 were marked up. Thus stood the score:–

EARL WINTERTON'S CLUB

Earl Winterton, b. Dudley	5
Mr. W. Randall, b. Heyes	17
Heather, b. Heyes	9
Challen, c. Hartnell, b. Heyes	8
Challen, jun., c. Dudley, b. Heyes	15
Piggot, b. Heyes	0
Mr. J. Sadler, c. Ball, b. Hartnell	7
Viscount Turnour, b. Hartnell	7
Mr. T. Sadler, b. Hartnell	1
T. Taylor, b. Hartnell	7
Newman, not out	7
B., &c., 9	9
Total	**92**

SECOND ROYAL SURREY MILITIA

First Innings.		Second Innings.			
Pri. Dudley, b. Challen, jun.	o	c. J. Sadler ..	..	..	7
Pri. Plumbridge, b. Heather..	o	b. Randall ..	..	..	0
Lieut. Hartnell, b. Heather ..	o	run out ..	..	..	15
Capt. A. Marshall, b. Challen, jun.	o	b. Randall ..	..	..	23
Pri. Ayling, b. Challen, jun. ...	o	not out ..	..	..	9
Lieut. Pontifex, b. Heather ..	o	b. Challen ..	..	..	6

Cor. Heyes, b. Heather	..	0	c. Challen	..	..	..	10
Lieut. Ball, b. Heather	..	0	b. Heather	..	..	..	0
Major Ridley, not out	..	0	run out	..	..	..	0
Sergt. Ayling, run out	..	0	c. Sadler	..	..	..	1
Pri. Newbury, b. Heather	..	0	b. Heather	..	..	..	14
B., &c.	..	0	B., &c.	..	..	..	21
		0					106

The All England Eleven
v. The United All England Eleven

27 *July* 1858. This match was commenced yesterday at Lord's ground, and was for the exclusive benefit of George Parr. So well was he appreciated, that about 6,000 spectators attended the ground. The ground was especially honoured by the presence of the French Ambassador, the Duke of Malakhoff, who met with a most enthusiastic reception. The points of the game were explained to his Excellency, who seemed much to appreciate them, and he enrolled his name as a patron. About 12 o'clock "play" was called, the All England Eleven winning the toss and choosing to go in first. Diver and E. Stephenson took in their bats, and both preserved their wickets for some time by cautious play, Diver being the first to be dismissed, through giving a chance to Ellis after marking 13, by a four, a three, two twos, &c.; one wicket and 20 runs. H. Stephenson took the vacant wicket, and runs were made fast, but Ellis again took a chance, H. Stephenson retiring for 16, in which were three threes and a two; two wickets and 64 runs. G. Parr put in an appearance amid much applause, and some good batting was the consequence; E. Stephenson, however, succumbed to Bell after a well got 33, in which were a five, four fours, and three twos; three wickets and 87 runs. Caesar, in his innings of 24, made them quickly by three fours, a three, and two twos; four wickets and 114 runs. Tinley gave way to Caffyn after marking one; five wickets and 118 runs. Wadsworth then faced Parr, but after adding seven he was given out, leg before wicket; six wickets and 133 runs. Alfred Clarke was the next to appear, G. Parr being caught and bowled by Grundy for 28, comprising a four, a three, and two twos; seven wickets and 145 runs. Willsher joined Clarke and their hits were well judged, both making good scores; the latter, however, gave a chance to Wisden, 21 being his contribution, composed of a four, a three, and five twos; eight wickets and 173 runs. Jackson showed next, and he and Willsher made runs fast, both hitting hard; Martingell, however, like a cunning General, caught the latter from his own bowling after scoring 33; in his runs were a five, two fours, a three, and five twos; nine wickets and 233 runs. Gibson was the last man, and he and Jackson made a lengthened defence; Jackson, however, sent the ball into the hands of Wisden,

and retired with a score of 45, well got, by a five, two fours, three threes, and six twos. Gibson carried out his bat for five, and the innings terminated for 254 runs. On the part of the United Eleven Carpenter and Hearne scored respectively eleven and three (with three byes); total 17, when "time" was called.

28 *July* 1858. The merits of George Parr, as a first-rate cricketer, seemed to be duly appreciated by the cricketing public, for yesterday Lord's ground, on the occasion of his benefit, was thronged with spectators.

> ENGLAND 254 (J. Jackson 45)
> UNITED 87 (J. Jackson 6 for 40) and 70 (J. Jackson 6 for 28)
> Score after first day: England 254, United 17 for no wkt
> *England won by an innings and 97 runs*

Shocking Death of a Cricketer

14 *September* 1858. Within an hour after the close of the grand cricket match between the Eleven of England and Twenty of Rochdale, on Saturday evening, a shocking accident occurred on the railway, which produced a very painful sensation in Rochdale, and which terminated in the death of Mr. Thomas Hunt, the well-known cricketer. Gentlemen who reside in the neighbourhood of Oldham-road, Rochdale, have made it a very common practice, with a view to shorten the distance, to get upon the Lancashire and Yorkshire Railway at Milkstone, and to walk thence to the pavilion on the cricket ground, which abuts upon the line. Mr. Hunt, at the close of the game, was requested to stop in Rochdale, in order to attend a banquet at a quarter-past 7 o'clock, to be held at the Wellington Hotel. He refused, saying that it would cost him less to go home, and, after packing up his cricketing materials, he engaged a man named John Wild to carry them to the Rochdale station. Unfortunately, without any leave whatever, the example of walking on the line had increased very much during the match, and large numbers entered the cricket ground on Saturday that way. Mr. Hunt and the man Wild determined to walk upon it to the station. Wild went a short distance before Mr. Hunt, and the latter incautiously picked his road between the up rails; and, when he had gone a distance of about 200 yards and had nearly reached the houses at Milkstone, Wild heard the whistling of an engine, and turned round to look what it was. It was a train due at Rochdale station from Manchester at 6 50. He saw the danger in which Mr. Hunt was, but was too far off to render him the slightest assistance. He appeared to be in a complete state of bewilderment and unable to discover a place of safety. He turned round quickly, and in a moment was caught by the buffer of the engine, which threw him down on the rails. Both his legs and his left hand were across the rails, and in that position the train passed over him, cutting off both legs across

the calves, except a few shreds of skin and flesh, and smashing all the fingers of his left hand, over which the wheels seem to have gone in a slanting direction. Some of the passengers, attracted no doubt by the gay appearance of the cricket field, were looking out, and saw a man on the line and lustily called out. The driver did all that he could to stop his train, but was unable to do so until the accident had occurred. A number of people from the adjoining house jumped on the line to render assistance. The train went forward to the station to apprize the officials of the accident, and the people procured a labourer's truck close by, lifted the unfortunate man upon it, and conveyed him to the station, under the directions of Mr. Cross, the stationmaster. Mr. Hunt was then removed to the Fleece Inn, adjoining the station, Mr. Cross instantly telegraphed to Dr. Harrison, of Manchester, the company's surgeon, but he had left for Huddersfield. Mr. Ogden, surgeon, was then called in, and he sent for Mr. Bowers, and in a short time after Messrs. Sellars, Coventry, and Wood (assistants to Mr. Lawton) arrived, and rendered all the assistance they could to the unfortunate man. No hæmorrhage of any moment took place. The rough manner in which the limbs were mutilated caused the vessels to contract. Shortly before 9 o'clock Mr. Sellars announced that Mr. Hunt was dying. Mr. Cross had telegraphed for his wife, who was expected to meet him at the Manchester station. Dr. Molesworth, the vicar, was sent for to administer consolation to the dying man. The latter arrived just when the spark of life had fled, and Mr. Hunt's wife came by the train which leaves Manchester at 8.15 p.m., and was five minutes too late to see him alive. It has been reported that Mr. Hunt was intoxicated at the time, but this is not true; he had had a glass or two, and boasted, before leaving the ground, that he had spent very little during the match. He appears to have lost all self-possession, and the shock to his system by the accident produced almost immediate delirium, which continued till within a few minutes of his death, when he became sensible, but his voice was very feeble. He called for his friend James Clegg, who had never left him from the time the accident occurred. In person he was remarkably good-looking, being somewhat portly. He was much admired on the field during the match by the spectators. He was born at Chesterfield in the year 1819. By trade he was a coachmaker; but for the last 14 years he has been a professional cricketer, and a great portion of that time in the service of the Manchester Club, by whom he was much respected. He generally played with the United All-England Eleven, and in his time was considered the best single-wicket player in England. In the match at Rochdale Hunt was one of the professional players "given" to the Rochdale Club, and acted as its wicket keeper. He leaves behind four children – a daughter about 17 years of age by his first wife, and three children by his present wife, the eldest of whom is about nine years of age. – *Manchester Guardian*, of yesterday.

The Great Match at Montreal

6 *October* 1859. Our cricketing readers, no doubt, have been anxiously looking for news with regard to this exciting international match; they will be glad to hear, then, that the players of England had a pleasant voyage and were safely landed on the American shore. By advices from Montreal, dated Saturday, September 24 (per Electric and International Telegraph), we learn that the match commenced on that day, and that the Montreal 22 went to the wickets first, and by some very good batting made an innings of 85. All England commenced their innings, and when "time" was called they had scored seven runs for the loss of one wicket, which ended the day's play. The match was to be resumed on Monday the 26th of September, and when in possession of the full score we shall give it due publicity. The interest of the match created caused the assemblage of many thousands, numbers coming from all parts of Canada, and also from the United States.

11 *October* 1859. We have already given the result of the match between the English and Canadian players at Montreal; subjoined are the details furnished by the *New York Herald* of September 28:–

Montreal, 26 September. "The cricket match commenced on Saturday at noon, with the Canadians at the wickets. From the fast bowling they continued making runs, until Parr went on the 16th wicket and made sad havoc with his slows. The last wicket fell for 85 runs, leaving the Canadians rather nervous from their sad prospect of success.

"At 5 15 p.m. England sent Wisden and Grundy to the wickets, and after some pretty play Hardinge found his way to Grundy's stumps. Hayward was then sent in, and played steadily with Wisden till sundown, when the score stood seven for one wicket.

"On Monday at 11 30 a.m. they began to play, and at 3 o'clock the last wicket fell.

"The Canadians again faced the bowling, but when time had been called 17 wickets had fallen for 43 runs, Parr bowling splendidly, having taken six good wickets in half-an-hour. The nervousness of the first innings had taken strong hold, the slows finding their way faster to the wickets than the fast bowling. The game was stopped at twilight, the sun shining in the faces of the batsmen, with four wickets to fall on the side of the Canadians.

"The twenty-two are laughed at by their friends, who bet two to one on the twenty-two of the St. George's Club. The English eleven play splendidly, and it is a perfect picture to see them; but they will find their equals in the twenty-two at Hoboken. There were 6,000 people on the ground, and the military band played some fine selections. There were many ladies, military officers, and heads of departments witnesses to the match.

"The following is the score:–

TWENTY-TWO OF CANADA

First Innings.		Second Innings.		
Swain, b. Caffyn	4	c. Jackson, b. Caffyn	..	1
Surnam, c. Caffyn, b. Jackson	4	l.b.w., b. Caffyn..	..	7
Simmons, c. Jackson, b. Caffyn	2	run out ..	..	1
Bonner, b. Jackson	0	st. Lockyer, b. Jackson..	..	6
Fisher, l.b.w., b. Jackson	0	run out ..	..	3
Foudrinier, c. Cæsar, b. Jackson	6	b. Jackson	..	5
Hardinge, b. Caffyn	0	c. Lillywhite, b. Parr	..	0
Ravenhill, c. Jackson, b. Caffyn	2	b. Jackson	..	0
Earl, run out	4	c. Lillywhite, b. Jackson	..	6
Pickering, b. Caffyn	8	c. Lockyer, b. Jackson ..	..	0
King, b. Jackson	3	c. Stephenson, b. Jackson	..	3
Daley, b. Parr	19	run out ..	..	0
W. Smith, b. Jackson	8	hit wicket, b. Parr	..	2
Racon, run out	4	b. Parr ..	..	2
Morgan, c. Wisden, b. Stephenson	0	l.b.w., b. Parr	..	0
Swettenham, b. Parr	3	c. Lockyer, b. Parr	..	1
J. Smith, c. Stephenson, b. Parr	6	not out ..	..	0
Napier, st. Lockyer, b. Parr ..	0	c. Grundy, b. Parr	..	0
Ellis, c. and b. Parr	2	Leg byes, 4; wides, 2 ..	..	6
Prior, b. Jackson	3			
Tilston, hit wicket, b. Parr	0	Total	..	43
Kerr, not out	1			
Byes, 4; leg byes, 2 ..	6			
Total	85			

THE ENGLISH ELEVEN—First Innings

Grundy, b. Hardinge	2
Wisden, c. Hardinge, b. Fisher	7
Hayward, run out ..	17
Caffyn, b. Fisher	18
Parr, b. Fisher	24
Cæsar, b. Fisher	0
Diver, c. Pickering, b. Napier	3
Lillywhite, b. Napier	4
Lockyer, not out	19
Stephenson, b. Fisher	2
Jackson, b. J. Smith	10
B., 5; w., 6	11
Total	—117

"The nervousness and run-outs have defeated the Canadians, among whom are several British officers; but it was to be expected when they were pitted against such a magnificent body of cricketers.

Montreal, 27 September. "The play was resumed at 1 o'clock to-day, Ellis joining Smith, who was in last night. Smith was bowled by Parr for 17 runs, got by very pretty play. The remainder of the score stood as follows:–

Smith, b. Parr	..	..	..	..	..	17
Ellis, b. Parr	..	..	..	..	..	0
Kerr, c. Cæsar, b. Parr	..	..	..	..	..	2
Prior, c. Caffyn, b. Parr	..	..	..	..	..	1
Tilston, not out	..	..	..	..	..	0

"Making the total of the innings 63, leaving the eleven 39 [*32*] runs to get to win. They were obtained with the loss of two wickets, the score standing:–

Lockyer, b. J. Smith	..	..		..	..	10
Hayward, c. Bonner, b. J. Smith	..		..	..	17[*10*]
Caffyn, not out	..	..	..	..	..	4
Diver, not out	..	..	..	..	..	1
B., 2; w., 5	..	..	..	..	7—39[*32*]

Departure of the Eleven for Australia

21 *October* 1861. On Friday afternoon ten of the players selected to represent England in Australia mustered at the Surrey Tavern, Kennington-oval, and from there went to the station of the Great Northern Railway, King's-cross. They were accompanied by numerous friends, and upon the signal being given for the starting of the train a hearty parting cheer was given them, which was heartily responded to by them, all being in high spirits and sanguine of success. Mr. Mallam, the Australian agent of Messrs. Spiers and Pond, was with them, and several members of the Surrey Club and personal friends took places in the train, determined to accompany them to Liverpool. On arriving at Liverpool, they were joined by Iddison, the eleventh man, the twelfth (G. Wells) having started some few weeks back. On Saturday they went on board the Great Britain, and at parting the numerous friends and spectators gave them a ringing farewell cheer, and hearty wishes were expressed for a prosperous voyage out and a safe return home, crowned with the laurels of victory. Previous to leaving London the players called on Mr. J. Bartlett, of the Waterloo-road, who presented them with a handsome new bat each, of his own manufacture. The first match will be played in Melbourne, and is likely to take place on Boxing-day.

Death of an Old Cricketer

7 *November* 1861. It is our painful task this week to record the death of Mr. Alfred Mynn, which took place in London on Friday last, from a severe attack of diabetes. He was in his 55th year, and has left a wife and family to deplore his unexpected demise. The cricketers of England will read this announcement with feelings of the deepest sorrow, and more especially the few old veterans of Kent who now survive him; while all ranks and classes

will mingle their regrets with those who enjoyed his private friendship, or were his companions in many a hard-fought field. As a cricketer he was an honour to his country; as a man he was worthy of the greatest esteem. He was born at Twisden-lodge, in the parish of Goudhurst, Kent, on the 19th of January, 1807, being the fourth son of the late Mr. W. Mynn, who was the descendant of a highly respectable family, the two preceding generations of which were renowned for their gigantic stature and great proficiency in all atheletic games. These gifts Mr. A. Mynn inherited in a pre-eminent degree, standing 6 feet 1 inch, with an average playing weight of 18 stone. – *South-Eastern Gazette*.

Cricket in Australia

16 *January* 1862. Of the three absorbing topics of interest during the past month (says the *Melbourne Argus*) – politics, the sad news of the Victorian exploration party, and the anticipated visit of the All-England cricketers to these shores – the last has been on the increase as each succeeding week has lessened the period which must elapse before the arrival of the Great Britain. Already great preparations are being made for the reception of the Eleven. Subscriptions are being canvassed to fetch down the best players from the country districts, so as to organize a team worthy to cope with the Eleven. Practice has within the last week commenced on the Melbourne ground, by having 22 placed in the field – it being expected the Eleven will play against that number – but we fear that a great deal more practice will be required, as at present the fielding is inferior. Some little change of feeling was produced upon the arrival of the last mail, consequent upon the retirement from the Eleven of several players whose names were familiar as household words to most of our cricketers. At the same time, whatever effect such change may have upon the "books" of those who make the event one of money speculation, the one opinion exists – that our men will have plenty of work before them, even if they are beaten by a small majority. Every arrangement is to be made to fit our cricketing reserve for the thousands who will assemble on it from all quarters of the three colonies. It has recently been altered as to shape, and at the same time enlarged. Messrs. Spiers and Pond are erecting a grand stand, which will be 700 ft. long, and which will contain some thousands of spectators. They will also have other accommodation. The ground is in first-class order, and by the system of irrigation proposed the turf will be fresh and green even in the hottest weather in December or January.

Surrey v. All England

27 *August* 1862. This is not only one of the most extraordinary matches ever chronicled in the annals of cricket, but the most extraordinary. On Monday the match was commenced, at the close of the day's play England left off with 244 runs, with the loss of three wickets, Carpenter being not out with 61, and Hayward with 28. Yesterday, on the game being resumed, Carpenter and Hayward again occupied the wickets, the bowlers being Humphrey and Caffyn. Carpenter made up his runs to 94, comprising a five (drive), five fours, two threes, and six twos; four wickets and 338 runs. Carpenter was caught very cleverly by Stephenson off his own bowling. Anderson joined Hayward, and though a change of bowling was tried, Mr. Miller going on at Humphrey's end, the batting still prevailed. Lockyer left his post as wicketkeeper, and relieved Mr. Miller of the ball, Griffith taking Lockyer's place. No immediate effect took place, but, after two or three "overs," Lockyer succeeded in lowering Hayward's stumps, after a magnificent innings of 117, gained in a masterly manner. Among his hits were seven fours, five threes, and 12 twos. He was deservedly applauded, and both he and Carpenter received the "talent money" at the pavilion awarded by the Surrey Club. Five wickets, and 402 runs. The Hon. C. G. Lyttelton came next, and the batting still held the ascendancy. Mr. Lyttelton, however, was the first to part, Griffith cleverly catching him at the wicket off Mr. Miller, after marking 26, in which were two fours, a three, and three twos; six wickets and 445 runs. Iddison filled the vacancy, and it seemed as if the run-getting could not be stopped, though all that could bowl were made available. Griffith at the wicket, however, again showed his efficiency by catching Anderson, off Sewell, after a quickly got innings of 42, comprising two fours, a three, and six twos; seven wickets and 451 runs. Jackson followed, and in a short time gained 21, containing two fours, a three, and two twos; eight wickets, and 497 runs. Mr. V. E. Walker next appeared, and Iddison, who had been batting for some time remarkably well, at length succumbed to Mr. Miller. His score was 33, made up by three fours, six twos, and singles; nine wickets and 501 runs. Mr. V. E. Walker added a single, and was then bowled by Caffyn, Biddulph taking his bat out for two. The innings thus closed for 503 – the largest score ever recorded. England may be said to have occupied the wickets two days, for it was half-past 5 when the innings terminated. The fielding of Surrey was excellent, and no fault could be found with the bowling, beyond its not being equal to the splendid batting it had to contend against. The spectators seemed highly gratified at the cricket displayed, and testified it by their applause. Shortly before 6 o'clock Surrey commenced their innings by sending in Mortlock and T. Humphrey against the bowling of Mr. V. E. Walker and Willsher. Humphrey did not score; one wicket and 4 runs. Mr. Burbridge came next, and here we regret to state after a four had been scored

off Willsher from a "no ball," called by the umpire, John Lillywhite, and called so successively for four or five balls following, a "sensation" scene took place. Willsher threw the ball indignantly on the ground and left the field, followed soon after by the rest of the eleven, and all play was put an end to for the evening. For some time past it has been a moot point regarding "high bowling," and although the "cricket laws" define it, still it has been a growing fashion to get high, and with Willsher it is considered by some particularly so. But however this may be Willsher's high bowling has never before been interfered with, and, like that of others, perhaps, may have been permitted under sufferance. With this, however, we have nothing to do, it rests with the umpires to decide, and John Lillywhite being one of those functionaries, we think he was perfectly justified in calling "no ball' if in his judgment it was unfairly delivered. During the commotion the Surrey Club held a committee meeting in the pavilion, and it was urged that John Lilly-white had fulfilled his duties as umpire according to his honest conviction, and he stated that he should continue to do so, but as the Surrey Club were desirous that no interruption should take place in the match, he would resign. He did so, and another will be appointed. It was not altogether the "high bowling" that was objected to, but the umpire considered it a "throw." Willsher having apologized for his hasty manner in leaving the ground, the game will be resumed this morning.

> ENGLAND 503 (T. Hayward 117, J. Grundy 95, R. Carpenter 94, E. Willsher 54, G. Anderson 42)
> SURREY 102 (E. Willsher 6 for 49) and 154 for 6
> Score after second day: England 503, Surrey 15 for 1
> *Match drawn*

The law was eventually altered to permit what we now know as overarm bowling – vid. 11 June 1864.

6 *August* 1863. Dark, the cricketing purveyor, complains that in his trade he suffers from imitators. There are, he says, during the summer months, so many bats after Dark, with whom he has no connexion – *Punch*.

Paris Cricket Club

25 *May* 1864. The match played in Paris on Monday last between the P.C.C. and Sir Robert Clifton's Eleven, from Nottingham, was won by the latter with very great ease in one innings. The play of the conquerors was exceedingly admired by all the members of the P.C.C., as well as by the spectators, of whom a considerable number, French and English, were present. The committee of the P.C.C. have expressed their thanks to Sir Robert for the kind way that the Nottingham men played on the ground. No grumbling, but all

goodwill was the order of the day. The Paris Club did their best to make up for their play and the pitiful ground by giving a hearty reception to the men who had undertaken such a fatiguing journey. The Eleven went to Mr. Delton's to be photographed in their dress, which was very neat, the cap being blue, braided with gold, and Sir Robert's crest embroidered on the front. They have left Paris carrying with them all honour. The first day the Paris side made in both innings 51, and Sir Robert's side in one innings 175 – 92 of which were scored by G. Summers. The second day's play consisted of a scratch match, and the third day a return match was played, the Paris Eleven scoring 45 only, whereas the Nottingham men scored 171. The bowling was admirable, and the wicket-keeping was too sharp for the Paris men. With practice, and a professional bowler, the Paris Club will be able, it is to be hoped, to sustain better their honour in the next match, to be played shortly. The names of the 11 members of the P.C.C. were:– Sir H. Bromley, J. Arthur, E. A. Jones, T. Arthur, J. B. Mourilyan, F. Ludlam, W. Arthur, T. D. Arthur, T. Sprent, R. Hazelton, and the Hon. W. Vanneck. The 11 Nottingham were:– G. M. Royle, M. Fiddler, T. W. Burnham, G. Summers, F. Billyeald, T. Burrows, J. Dame, A. Fewkes, W. Wragg, T. Shrewsbury, and S. K. Kershawe.

"Law X"

11 *June* 1864. After the above match [Marylebone Club and Ground v. The University of Oxford], according to announcement, a very important meeting, of considerable interest to cricketers in general, was held in the Tennis-court adjoining Lord's Ground, to take into consideration the above law,

Lord DUDLEY presided, and having stated the object of the meeting,

Mr. C. MARSHAM rose, and read some correspondence from various clubs expressing their opinion on Law X. He then gave his own views on the subject, and concluded by moving that the law as it stood should be rescinded, and that the following be substituted:–

"The ball must be bowled; if thrown or jerked, the umpire must call 'No ball.'"

Mr. PERKINS briefly seconded the motion.

Mr. FITZGERALD (Hon. Sec. M.C.C.) said he was opposed to high bowling, and there ought to be restrictions upon it. He attributed all the large scores that were now made to high bowling, and thought that there were not so many good bowlers as there used to be, and that high bowling was much inferior to low. He opposed the motion.

Mr. R. T. P. BROUGHTON, after some preliminary remarks, moved an amendment, which was tantamount to the law remaining as it stood, which is as follows:–

"The ball must be bowled; if thrown or jerked, or if the bowler in the actual delivery of the ball, or in the action immediately preceding the delivery shall raise his hand or arm above his shoulder, the umpire shall call 'No ball.' "

Mr. R. KYNASTON seconded the amendment.

The Hon. F. PONSONBY said that this was not a new question. He could recollect that 30 years ago bowling was as high then as now, and although they tried to keep the arm down the umpires failed to enforce the law. Umpires were frequently abused for not doing their duty, and as there was a diversity of opinion among many persons as to the fairness or unfairness of a bowler, it was not to be supposed that the umpire could decide so as to give satisfaction to all. To allow high bowling, it was said by some, would be dangerous on rough ground; but care should be taken that grounds should not be rough. He strongly supported the motion.

The Hon. R. GRIMSTON made some very appropriate remarks in favour of the motion, and said it was true, as Mr. Ponsonby stated, they legislated for themselves (the M.C.C.), and he had no doubt the high position in which the club stood would be upheld by other clubs in carrying out the laws.

The Hon. F. CAVENDISH said he thought Mr. Marsham and Mr. Ponsonby had fully explained what was practicable, and it was no use trying to enforce what they could not carry out. He should give his support to the motion.

A MEMBER supported the amendment of Mr. Broughton, and thought that one more effort might be made to carry the laws into effect as they stood. (Cries of "Divide, divide!")

The CHAIRMAN rose and most ably commented upon the question, inclining much to the opinion of Mr. Broughton.

His LORDSHIP was about to put the amendment to the vote, when Mr. BROUGHTON withdrew it.

The CHAIRMAN then put the motion, which was carried by a majority of 27 to 20, amid much cheering.

Law XXIV., relative to "leg b. w.," was to have been discussed, but the motion was withdrawn.

Marylebone Club and Ground v. South Wales Club

22 *July* 1864. At Lord's Ground yesterday this match was commenced, the attendance being very scanty. South Wales went in first, and Mr. E. M. Grace made his first appearance since his arrival from Australia, but was not fortunate enough to score. Mr. W. G. Grace made a fine innings of 50, but the "leger" was taken by Captain R. Jones with 65, and the total of the whole was 211. Messrs. Teape, Hearne, and Nixon bowled.

SOUTH WALES 211 (Capt. R. Jones 65, Mr. W. G. Grace 50) and 79
M.C.C. AND GROUND 186 (T. Hearne 59, Mr. A. Infelix 47) and 28 for 1
Score after first day: South Wales 211, M.C.C. and Ground 47 for 1
Match drawn

This was W. G. Grace's first match at Lord's, aged 16 years and 3 days; he was dismissed for 2 in the second innings.

France v. Germany

16 *August* 1864. This event, which was a contest between two elevens of continental cricketers representing France and Germany respectively, came off at Homburg on Wednesday, the 10th inst. The honour of France was in the keeping of the Paris Cricket Club, while their antagonists were drawn from the English visitors at Homburg and the members of the Frankfurt Club. The game was played on a lovely spot in the grounds of the Kurhaus, and the scene was enlivened as well by a military band as by the presence of a large gathering of spectators of every nationality. The administration furnished the music and in every possible way exerted themselves to show hospitality and attention to their visitors, and both sides were loud in their appreciation of the liberality and courtesy which they had experienced. The visit of the Parisians terminated in a ball, given in their honour by the Homburg Club. The match was concluded in one day, and added another victory to the laurels of the Paris club. [*The Paris club won by an innings and 41 runs*]. On the Homburg side Messrs. Roberts and Conbro alone made respectable scores, while on the other side larger contributions were made, especially by Messrs. Gardiner and Mourilyan. The foreign spectators watched the proceedings with a marked attention, due probably rather to curiosity than to a critical admiration, for it was discovered to be the more generally received opinion that the game was to be played upon horses, which, up to the conclusion of the day's sport, had failed to arrive. One German gentleman, on observing the wickets scattered in all directions by a well-delivered ball, eagerly inquired, "And how many does that count?" We may, however, augur from the success of this contest that cricket at Homburg will henceforth be not merely an attraction, but a permanent institution of the place.

Cricket on the Continent

28 *August* 1865. A series of matches have just been concluded at Homburg. The first match took place on Tuesday, the 15th inst. between eleven gentlemen representing the Paris Club and an equal number composed of members of the Frankfort and Homburg Club. The match was concluded in one day, and the Paris Club proved victorious.

The great event of the week followed. Eleven Gentlemen of England v. Seventeen of the rest of Europe. The match was commenced on Wednesday the 16th, and that and the return match occupied three days.

The English Eleven was very strong all round, being composed of gentlemen whose reputation as first-rate players is well known, while the Seventeen comprised names celebrated in the cricketing world. England was victorious in both matches, and well sustained the cricketing reputation of the old country.

The smallness of the scores is mainly attributable to the state of the wickets, which was very difficult at first, but improved as the play proceeded. The grounds of the Kursaal were thronged each day with a brilliant assemblage, and the strains of the Austrian band enlivened the general enjoyment.

Surrey v. England

31 *July* 1866. This exciting match was commenced yesterday morning on the Surrey ground, Kennington-oval, and attracted about 4,000 spectators. The wickets were excellent, the turf being in fine order. England won the toss for choice of innings, and elected to go in first. Some rare run-getting ensued, the scores made being very large, against a variety of bowling, – Humphrey, Sewell, Jupp, Griffith (fast and slow), Mr. Miller, Mr. Noble, and Pooley (who had been wicket-keeping), all taking a turn, most of them three or four times. The batting completely "collared" the bowling, the wickets falling thus:– One for 9, two for 42, three for 90, four for 225, five for 242, six for 250, seven for 358, and eight for 421, Mr. W. G. Grace being (not out) with 187, and Mr. Round with 12. In most of the large scores hits for fives, fours, threes, and twos were frequent. The fielding of Surrey was very far from being up to the mark.

> ENGLAND 521 (Mr. W. G. Grace 224 not out, Payne 86, Mr. V. E. Walker 54, Mr. J. Round 42)
> SURREY 99 (Wootton 6 for 37, Willsher 4 for 32) and 126 (Wootton 4 for 40)
> Score after first day: England 444 for 8
> *England won by an innings and 296 runs*

The report omits to mention that W.G. had only recently passed his 18th birthday. He missed the final day of the match to run in, and win, a 440-yard hurdle race.

Harrow v. Eton

2 *July* 1867. The arrangements for this great annual public school match, which was fixed to come off at Lord's ground on the 12th and 13th of July, are likely to be interfered with owing to a lamentable accident which, it was

understood, had befallen one of the Harrow Eleven. The Harrow gentleman in question, it was stated on the cricket field upon good authority, while jumping over a hedge caught his leg against a sithe, cutting the limb most severely. The accident, it is said, will incapacitate him from playing.

To the Editor of The Times

Sir, – I beg most entirely to contradict the unfounded statement which appeared in your columns of the 2d inst., that Mr. Smith's accident will in any way interfere with the arrangements previously made for the Harrow and Eton match.

I remain, Sir, yours truly,
THE CAPTAIN OF THE HARROW ELEVEN.
Harrow, July 4.

Eleven of Lord Lyttelton's family v. Bromsgrove Grammar School

30 *August* 1867. A match, noticeable from the composition of the winning eleven, was played on Monday at Stagley-park, the seat of Lord Lyttelton, Lord-Lieutenant of Worcestershire. The match was between an eleven of the Bromsgrove Grammar-School and eleven of the Lyttelton family, composed of his lordship; his brothers, the Hon. and Rev. W. H. Lyttelton and the Hon. Spencer Lyttelton; and his lordship's eight sons – the Hon. C. G. Lyttelton, the Hon. A. V. Lyttelton, the Hon. N. G. Lyttelton, the Hon. S. G. Lyttelton, the Hon. A. T. Lyttelton, the Hon. R. H. Lyttelton, the Hon. E. Lyttelton, and the Hon. A. Lyttelton. The Bromsgrove eleven went to the wickets first, and put together a good score of 150, in the course of which Lord Lyttelton made a very difficult catch, holding the ball, though he fell and rolled over on the ground in the attempt. His lordship and the Hon. Charles Lyttelton commenced the batting for the "Honourables," but were soon parted, a straight ball taking Lord Lyttelton's wicket before any figures stood against his name in the scorer's book. The Hon. Charles Lyttelton was then joined by his brothers in succession, when some very good cricket was played, the last wicket falling with a total score of 191. The Bromsgrove eleven then went in again, but were less fortunate than in their first innings, scoring only 51, thus leaving the Lytteltons only 11 to make to win. These were made, without the loss of a wicket, by the Hon. N. G. Lyttelton and his brother Edward, and at the conclusion of the game the total scores stood thus:– Bromsgrove Grammar-School, first innings, 150; second innings, 51 – total, 201. Lord Lyttelton's eleven, first innings, 191; second innings, 12 – total, 203, with ten wickets to fall.

The youngest Lyttelton, Alfred, who went on to achieve fame as a cricketer and cabinet minister, was 10 years old at the time of this match. Edward, who was 12, rose to the headship of Eton, while Robert, aged 13, became a great student of the game and wrote regularly on it for The Times *– as, later, did his nephew, George (vid. introduction to chapter III).*

Eleven Aboriginal Black Australians v. Eleven Gentlemen of Surrey Club

26 *May* 1868. No truer test of the interest taken by the public in the performance of this team from the antipodes can be afforded than that of 7,000 persons congregated at the Oval yesterday, when the first match of a series projected to be played in the three kingdoms came off. Many and confused were the ideas generally entertained respecting these Aboriginals, both as regards their cricketing acquirements and their physical conformation. They represent the colonies of Victoria, Queenstown, South Australia, and New Zealand. Their hair and beards are long and wiry; their skins vary in shades of blackness, and most of them have broadly-expanded nostrils, but they are all of the true Australian type. Having been brought up in the bush to agricultural pursuits under European settlers, they are perfectly civilized, and are quite familiar with the English language. As most of their native names are polysyllabic, and not very euphonious, each has adopted a *sobriquet* under which he will doubtlessly be recognized in this country. Unfortunately, the best man of the party was absent through illness. In order that the lookers-on might be able to recognize each man, a sash differing in colour was affixed to his shirt. At 12 15 play commenced, and as the two leading Surrey batsmen approached the wickets the Blacks received them with vociferous cheering. Mullagh and Lawrence were the bowlers at starting. At 28 the first wicket (Mr. Noble's) fell, and at 42 Mr. Jupp was cleverly stumped by Bullocky. From the 10th to the 17th over only one run was effected. The bowling after this went off, and the score advanced with great rapidity. At the fall of the fifth wicket 124 runs were recorded in favour of Surrey. Mr. Baggallay was the chief scorer, and kept his wicket intact for three hours and a quarter. The innings closed at 5 15. Four bowlers were engaged. Lawrence bowled 49 overs (8 maidens); 90 runs were got off him; Mullagh, 52 overs (20 maidens), 100 runs; Bullocky, 5 overs (1 maiden), 14 runs; King Cole, 9 overs (2 maidens), 16 runs.

The Blacks commenced batting at 6 o'clock, and at 7 four of their wickets were down for 34 runs.

27 *May*. It will be remembered that with the close of Monday's play Surrey had completed an innings, and four Aboriginal wickets were down for 34

runs. Long before Tuesday's business commenced the Oval presented an unusual gathering of spectators. At 12 5 Mullagh and Twopenny, the "not outs," presented themselves at the wickets. Messrs. Frere and I. D. Walker resumed the bowling. In Mr. Frere's second over Twopenny was caught in the slips. Five wickets, 34. Lawrence then joined Mullagh, made a straight drive for three, and in the next over was caught mid off. Six wickets, 37. King Cole, in conjunction with Mullagh, brought up the score to 65, when Mullagh, who had defended himself with more skill than any of his party for upwards of an hour, was stumped off a slow. His hits were one five, two fours (chiefly drives), four twos, and singles. The remaining wickets fell quickly, as at 1 15 the innings closed for 83 runs. Being in a minority of 139 the Blacks had to "follow on." Lawrence and Bullocky appeared first. The bowling of Messrs. Miller and Boultbee was altogether different in its character to that brought to bear upon the Aboriginals in their first essay with the bat. 119 runs were obtained for the loss of six wickets. At 5 30 Mr. Frere went on at Mr. Boultbee's end, and after two overs had been bowled Mr. I. D. Walker relieved Mr. Miller. The change soon produced the contemplated effect. Mullagh, who had been in two hours, was bowled by a bailer from Mr. Frere, and the remaining wickets seemed quite bereft of real defenders. The innings closed at 6 30, when Surrey were declared winners by an innings and seven runs. It was apparent to every one on Monday that these Aboriginals had little or no chance against the cultivated team which Surrey had summoned to confront them with. Surrey's first innings proclaimed the second-rate character of the bowling. The blacks returned the ball quickly, but not with precision. Their batting, saving that of Mullagh, is sadly wanting in power, and in several instances it exhibited on the day in question a great deficiency in those defensive attributes which are requisite for a protracted stand against good bowling. In running between wickets their judgment is much at fault, both on account of slowness and hesitancy. Doubtless, some of these defects will be overcome by the practice with good players during their stay in this country. Score:–

SURREY CLUB—First innings

Mr. G. H. Jupp, st. Bullocky, b. Lawrence	..	.. 24
Mr. C. Noble, c. and b. Lawrence	..	.. 9
Mr. W. Baggallay, st. Bullocky, b. Lawrence	..	.. 68
Mr. I. D. Walker, c. King Cole, b. Mullagh	..	.. 1
Mr. G. Greenfield, c. Bullocky, b. Lawrence	..	.. 16
Mr. C. Calvert, b. Mullagh	..	.. 25
Mr. St. J. Boultbee, b. Lawrence	..	.. 37
Mr. R. Barton, not out	..	.. 16
Mr. M. Frere, b. Mullagh	..	.. 4
Mr. F. P. Miller, c. Redcap, b. Lawrence ..	..	.. 7
Mr. H. Hibberd, c. King Cole, b. Lawrence	..	.. 14
Bye, 1	..	.. 1
Total	..	.. —222

AUSTRALIANS

First Innings		Second Innings	
Bullocky, maroon, c. Walker, b. Frere	6	b. Miller	19
Tiger, pink, b. I. D. Walker	3	b. Boultbee	3
Mullagh, dark blue, st. Hibberd, b. Walker	33	b. Frere	73
Red Cap, black, b. Frere ..	1	run out	0
Lawrence, c. Calvert, b. Walker	9	b. Miller	22
King Cole, magenta, b. Walker ..	14	c. Walker, b. Miller ..	0
Dick-a-Dick, yellow, b. Frere	0	b. Boultbee	5
Twopenny, drab, c. Miller, b. Frere ..	1	b. Frere	0
Peter, green, b. Frere	0	b. Frere	4
Jim Crow, brown, b. Walker	10	not out	2
C. Dumas, light blue, not out	5	b. Walker	4
B., 5; w., 2	7	B., 4	0
Total	83	Total	132

Mar Lodge v. Abergeldie Castle

9 *September* 1868. On Wednesday last, the 2d of September, a very pleasant match was played on the ground in front of Abergeldie Castle, between eleven of the gentlemen and servants at Abergeldie and eleven gentlemen and servants from Mar Lodge. The weather was magnificent, and the play on both sides was as good as could be expected on a soft and spongy soil. Mar Lodge won the toss, and sent in Mr. Monck and Mr. Morton to the wickets, whence they were not dislodged till nearly 20 runs were scored. After their departure wickets fell somewhat rapidly, the only stand being made by Lord Macduff for 5 and Gruer for 11. The Abergeldie eleven then went in and were not got rid of till 86 were scored, of which Hook obtained 23 by some excellent play; Clark was next with 14, and after him came the Hon. Oliver Montagu, who woke up the field with some hits which reminded the Etonians present of "aquatic" doings in the lower shooting fields at Eton. The fielding of the Mar Lodge eleven was loose, and their bowling at first very much off the spot; later in the innings it improved very much. In the second innings of Mar Lodge Mr. Morton obtained 19 in good style, and Lord Macduff and Wright both played well for 8 and 7 respectively; but the other scores were small, and the innings closed for 57. This left Abergeldie 21 to get to win, which number they lost their four best wickets before getting. The bowling of Mr. Morton and Weston in this innings was very good, and the fielding of the Mar Lodge eleven showed much improvement. A capital catch by the Hon. Eustace Dawnay at point, and the Hon. H. Monck's long-stopping, both deserve notice. Nor in speaking of fielding ought we to omit to mention Cole, who kept wicket for Abergeldie in capital style. In the evening his Royal Highness the Prince of Wales gave a dinner party at the Castle, at which were present his Royal Highness the Prince of Wales, her Royal Highness the Princess of

Wales, Prince John of Glucksburg, Hon. Mrs. Hardinge, Hon. A. Denison, Captain Buckley, Viscount Macduff, Hon. H. Monck, Hon. E. Dawnay, Rev. A. H. A. Morton, Rev. C. F. Tarver, Mr. K. Sumner, Hon. George FitzClarence, &c.

Aboriginal Sports

14 *September* 1868. At an exhibition of native Australian sports by the aboriginal cricketers, at Bootle, near Liverpool, on Saturday, a boomerang, thrown by Mullagh, was carried by the wind among the audience. It struck a gentleman on the head, the brim of the hat saving the face from severe laceration. As it was, the boomerang cut through the hat and inflicted a severe wound across the brow. Surgical aid was at once procured, and the gentleman was able to return home.

Skating and Cricket in the Fens

15 *February* 1870, *Cambridge*. The Mere Fen, situate at Swavesey, about 11 miles distant from Cambridge, being flooded and frozen, has to-day [14 *February*] been crowded with spectators, a very large number of whom were members of the University, who travelled by special trains, which were run by the Great Eastern Railway Company. The accommodation for skaters can nowhere be exceeded, and several thousands of persons were present. The programme for the day included what is certainly a great novelty – viz., a cricket match on ice and a skating match for money prizes. In the cricket match, eleven members of the All England Eleven and of the University were pitted against 16 of the neighbourhood of Swavesey, with several members of the University. The wickets were pitched at 12 30, and R. Carpenter, the captain of the Englanders, &c., won the toss, and placed the 16 in first. Their innings lasted an hour and a half, in which time they managed to trundle together 125, of which number Mr. C. Baker made 77, which included one for 12 and another for 9. Mr. Graham, Trinity Hall, was not out, 24. J. Smith fielded wonderfully well, and it should be said that batsmen, bowlers, and fielders all wore skating pattens, and the ice was as smooth as glass. Shortly before 2 o'clock the eleven were put on their defence, and in about an hour had made 280 runs for the loss of eight wickets. Pryor made 37, starting with a 7. T. Hayward played some good all round cricket, and carried out his bat for 52, including five fours, four threes, and five twos. J. Smith retired when he had made 51, which included an eight, a six, five fours, &c. Mr. West (Magdalen College) scored 27 very merrily. After the cricket match a grand match was run off by 16 of the crack skaters of this part of the Fens, Mr. D. Long, the owner of the ground which was flooded, acting as starter and judge.

The course was about a mile round, and the deciding race was between E. Norman and G. Lack, both of Willingham. A good race for half the distance was rather easily won at last by Lack, who covered the distance in 2 min. 4 sec. The whole of the proceedings passed off without any casualties.

Dangers of Cricket

20 *June* 1870, *Nottingham*. George Summers, the Nottinghamshire cricketer, who was struck by a ball from Platts, in the match between Notts and Marylebone, on Wednesday, at Lord's Cricket Ground, died at his father's house at Nottingham this afternoon [19 *June*] from the injuries received, the blow having occasioned concussion of the brain. The deceased was only 35 years old.

Oxford v. Cambridge

29 *June* 1870. Viewed in all its bearings, the above match which was concluded last evening at Lord's, is perhaps the most remarkable since it was first played 33 years ago. To explain this a few brief remarks are necessary. Yesterday Cambridge commenced their second innings at 12 15, with 28 in arrear, and with a prevailing opinion that Oxford were the more effective eleven. First to appear at the wickets were Messrs. Dale and Tobin, as on the day previous. Messrs. Francis and Belcher followed Monday's programme in respect to bowling. From the 22d ball Mr. Tobin played on, when 6 runs only were scored. Mr. Money succeeded, made six singles, and played on also. Mr. Fryer lost his wicket from the first ball presented to him; Mr. Thornton joined Mr. Dale, and cut the second ball into the slips for four. Other runs of less note followed, till 40 were accredited to Cambridge. Mr. Thornton then tried the steeple hit, which Mr. Hadow surveyed with great calmness and judgment. On the retirement of Mr. Thornton came Mr. Scott, but his stay was unexpectedly brief. Five wickets were now down for 40 runs. With Mr. Yardley this dull aspect of affairs changed in an extraordinary manner. The leading bowlers were displaced by Messrs. Butler and Hill, but, as no beneficial effect to Oxford was manifest, Messrs. Hadow and Fortescue were brought forward. Then cross overs were had recourse to. Mr. Dale occupied his wicket for two hours and a half for 67 runs, and was at length most wonderfully fielded at long leg, very deep, by Mr. Ottaway. His chief hits were six fours (drives), two threes, and six twos. Mr. Mackinnon next joined Mr. Yardley, but soon deserted him. Nearly all the subsequent interest centred on Mr. Yardley, who got just 100 runs – a feat which has rarely, if ever, been accomplished in a match of this kind. The innings culminated in 206, thereby leaving Oxford 178 to tie. Seven bowlers were engaged, but the most successful were Mr. Francis, who in 43 overs (13 maiden) took seven

wickets for 104 [*102 elsewhere*] runs; Mr. Belcher, 29 overs (10 maiden) two wickets, 36 [*38 elsewhere*] runs; and Mr. Butler, two overs (one maiden), one wicket, eight runs. At 4 10 Messrs. Hadow and Fortescue commenced the final innings of the match, Mr. Cobden, as before, choosing the "gate wicket," and Mr. Bourne the pavilion. Mr. Hadow was caught mid on from the second ball of the third over before a run was scored. Mr. Ottaway, in conjunction with Mr. Fortescue, advanced the total to 72 before the second wicket (Mr. Fortescue's) fell. Mr. Pauncefote, not being very successful, left at 86, and Mr. Tylecote took his place. The bowling appeared now to be nearly used up, but by frequent changes and the judicious application of the means at hand for the ends desired, every chance was made the most of. In two hours and five minutes 100 runs were scored; this number was enlarged to 153, when the fourth wicket fell. Mr. Townshend came forward as the clock was striking 7, the time for drawing the stumps, but as the game was considered lost to Cambridge, it was suggested by some that it would be well to finish it. Mr. Ottaway was caught close to the ground after being at the wicket three hours. Mr. Townshend was caught next over in short slip for the smallest contribution possible, and Mr. Francis was given out l.-b.-w. in the succeeding over. There were now seven wickets down for 176. Mr. Butler came and was caught mid-off without scoring. Mr. Belcher had but one ball, which bowled his leg stump, and Mr. Stewart, the last man, who was only required to make three, failed most signally – bowled also from the first ball, and thus at 7 35 Cambridge were declared winners by two runs. Messrs. Cobden and Ward were the only successful bowlers out of the seven engaged. Mr. Cobden bowled 27 overs (10 maiden) and took four wickets, for 34 runs. Mr. Ward 33 overs (16 maiden), six wickets, 30 runs.

CAMBRIDGE 147 (Mr. A. T. Scott 45; Mr. C. K. Francis 5 for 59, Mr. T. H. Belcher 4 for 52) and 206 (Mr. W. Yardley 100, Mr. J. W. Dale 67; Mr. C. K. Francis 7 for 102)
OXFORD 175 (Mr. F. C. Cobden 4 for 41) and 176 (Mr. C. J. Ottaway 69, Mr. A. T. Fortescue 44; Mr. E. E. Ward 6 for 29, Mr. F. C. Cobden 4 for 35)
Cambridge won by 2 runs

This is the most famous encounter between the Universities, forever known as Cobden's match for his hat-trick which brought Cambridge victory.

English Cricketers in America

1 *October* 1872. The last experiment in itinerant cricket, the journey of the English Amateur Eleven to Canada, has, so far as telegrams inform us, been a brilliant success. The British Lion has consented to "walk round and show his muscle" to the Canadians, and he has done so to some purpose, making exceedingly short work, as might have been foretold, of the very weak teams which were all that the colony could bring into the field. The English expected

to win, and won; the Canadians probably expected to lose, and lost; so that both sides were well pleased, as they could reasonably be expected to be, though it would, perhaps, have been more pleasant to all if the colonists had shown more fight. How the Yankees will fare when opposed to the visitors we have yet to see, but we never had much doubt that they would share the fate of their fellow Americans, and even that little was removed when we heard that the Englishmen had won their United States' match at New York in a single innings by 108 runs, thus putting the Yankees much about on a cricketing level with the Canadians they had recently been beating in similar style at Toronto and elsewhere. It must be admitted that the British Lion has been well represented. Even if the best possible 11 of cricketers, amateurs and professionals, had been selected, three or four of the present team must have had places in it, and it would have been difficult to the last degree to get together a better set of amateurs under the circumstances, two of the originally selected 11 having fallen ill at the last moment. Of Mr. W. G. Grace there is no need to speak; his fame may be taken for granted here and in Canada; and there can be little doubt that a keen desire to see him at the wickets was the leading motive which impelled the "Old Dominion" folks to invite the Englishmen to cross the Atlantic and enter the lists with them. We are glad to find that he has not disappointed his hosts, as he has scored largely, though for some part at least of the time he was very unwell, and has maintained that singular superiority over all other batsmen, however good, that has always distinguished his play since his first appearance in London. But, beyond Mr. Grace, at least five others of the Eleven – Messrs. Ottaway, Hornby, A. Lubbock, Hadow, and Appleby – are up to Gentlemen and Players' form; nor are Mr. Harris, Mr. Rose, and Mr. Francis far below it; while the remaining members of the twelve, from whom the English Eleven are selected, are, Mr. E. Lubbock, well known and highly esteemed in Kent; Mr. R. A. Fitzgerald, of hard-hitting fame; and Mr. Pickering, whose name is new to us, and who probably fills up the place of one of the Messrs. Walker, of Southgate, who were unable to undertake the voyage. It is not a matter of wonder that such a side should put almost any number of colonial antagonists to the rout. The result of the play, so far as it has been reported at full length, is just what we might have expected. As far as the batting is concerned, Mr. Grace is, like Eclipse, "first, and the rest nowhere." He made 142 at Toronto on the 3d and 4th of this month, and other long scores elsewhere, while no one else has at present got more than 30 or so, though every one, or almost every one, has made a double figure. Mr. Appleby has bowled successfully, but the greatest results in that way have fallen to the luck of the insinuating persuaders of the wily Mr. Rose (that one rose without a thorn), who has played havoc with the colonial wickets, much as he did at Canterbury a season or so back. We are rather surprised to find that Mr. Grace did not come off with the ball, for he is bowiing much better this year than he has done for some years past. He has dropped his pace and improved his pitch by so doing, for the great height from which the ball is delivered makes it rise quickly and jump high, catching the best batsman every now and then in two minds as to how he ought to play it, and it is very fairly straight. However, the Canadians seemed to find it easy enough. As to fielding, the wicket-keeping of Mr. Ottaway seems to have attracted most notice. What sort of grounds the matches have been played on, and how far the colonial teams have represented the cricketing strength of the colony we do not at present know, but we think we may venture to believe that a very risky experiment, depending for its success not only on good luck and good management, but even more on good temper, has turned out well. There is, perhaps, no real use in these cricketing voyages; they only tell us what we knew before – that there is no such thing as making any handicap which shall bring together first-rate and third-rate cricketers unless the latter have bowlers given to them. Thirty-three indifferent players are hardly stronger than 22, for they only field poorly and get in each other's way. Still, the recollection of how the English force came, saw, and conquered is bound to stimulate the game in Canada, and teach the rising generation how fields were won, and so to do good service, in the long run, to the "cause of cricket over all the world," as a good old toast, drunk with enthusiasm after a cricket match at many a foreign station from Archangel to Singapore, has it. – *Land and Water*.

The Eton and Harrow Match

21 *July* 1873. The disturbance that occurred after the finish of the Eton and Harrow match has caused the committee of the Marylebone Cricket Club to issue the following manifesto: – "The committee regret that, notwithstanding all their efforts to prevent a scene of confusion at the termination of the Schools' Match, their efforts were frustrated by the unseemly conduct of some persons on the ground. Such scenes as those witnessed on Saturday would not occur if the partisans of both schools were to assist the authorities in checking the immoderate expression of feeling at the conclusion of the match. The committee appeal to the old and young members of the two schools to assist them in future in preventing a repetition of such disorder, which must inevitably end in a discontinuance of the match." – By order of the committee, R. A. FITZGERALD, Sec. M.C.C." We could venture to wish that the committee had been a little more explicit, and had said where the "scene of confusion" was, as it is just possible that they may refer to a crowd at the gate, which is said to have behaved itself ill. But we have little or no doubt that the crowd in front of the Pavilion is what is referred to, and we must admit that it is very properly found fault with. The noise and confusion were extreme, and lasted for a most unreasonably long time. If the police and those of the ground men who helped them had not been very peaceful and good-tempered the result of the scrimmage might have been really serious,

and as it was certain hats were broken and many toes trodden on, and it is said that one policeman was a good deal injured. But, though we object much to such horse-play, we cannot help thinking that too much has been said about it in some quarters. People who were not at Lord's, but who read the accounts of the match in Monday's papers, must have thought that there was something very like a free fight between Eton and Harrow going on, as soon as the match ended in favour of Harrow. Now, we who write were on the top of the Pavilion, just beyond the centre, during the whole of the row, and we can fairly say that we did not see one single blow struck in anger throughout. As far as we could understand the situation, the Eton boys, after Mr. Hadow and Mr. Shand on the Harrow side had been borne victoriously through the crowd, wanted to treat Mr. Buckland to the same sort of glorious but un-comfortable manifestation of sympathy. Probably Mr. Buckland either did not know this, or did not care for the honour, or was dressing and not presentable – anyhow, he did not respond, and the crowd surged up against the police in the vain hope of getting at him. This is the belief of those who could see best, being up above the crowd, *sua sine parte pericli*, not a dozen yards from the centre and kernel of the row, the middle entrance of the Pavilion. That there was really no violence worth mentioning may be proved sufficiently by the fact that more than one ex-Etonian near us had a brother or friend in the thick of the crowd, without feeling the faintest anxiety for his fate or even for the symmetry of his costume. "Just like a bully at the wall," said one of them at our elbow, using the technical name for their most crowded game at football, and he could not have hit the thing off better in one sentence. It was just like a rough game, such as football, and was, as far as the boys went, just as harmless. One rough fellow, not a boy, but a middle-aged man, tipped a policeman's hat off, but he did it from behind, and looked most innocently in the opposite direction when the policeman, who did not exactly like the liberty taken with his uniform, turned upon him. A few more of his stamp would have put the whole place in an uproar; but he was, most luckily, not seconded. And now that we have entered our protest against the somewhat exaggerated way in which this not very terrible disturbance has been treated, we must say that the committee are perfectly right in resolving to put down anything of the kind in future years. We must not expect too much of boys; but they really ought to learn to moderate their transports and confine themselves to the use of their voices. Even these might be advan-tageously toned down in some cases. "Well hit!" and "Well bowled!" are fair cries enough; but "Well fielded!" when an adversary misses a catch, and "Well asked!" when the umpire gives his decision in favour of the batsman, are, to put it mildly, errors in taste and judgment. We do not want boys to "take their pleasures sadly, after the manner of their country," for they will surely, like the rest of us, find plenty of sadness later on in life. But we venture to hope that they will henceforward have sufficient self-command to refuse to follow the bad example set to them by the "persons of unseemly conduct" referred to by the committee. Some of these worthy folks, hangers-on at the schools and other parasites and partisans of the most contemptible kind, are known to do what they can, year after year, to make and keep up a row, and they must have succeeded beyond their hopes on Saturday last. If one or two of them were taken in the act, and had a short but appropriate allowance of treadmill administered to them for their pains, society would be able to get on pretty well without them for a while, and they would learn a lesson that would be useful to them in future years. We commend this point to the attention of the M.C.C. committee for 1874. – *Land and Water*.

Australia

FROM OUR VICTORIA CORRESPONDENT

19 *February* 1874; *Melbourne, 2 January.* I need not describe anew our Christmas festivities, in which ice-pails are substituted for yule logs and fern leaves for holly. Plum-puddings and pantomimes appear simultaneously in London and Melbourne; but, having conceded so much to custom, we are free to find recreation more appropriate to our Midsummer holydays. The exceptional attraction of the year was the long-looked-for cricket match between 18 of Victoria and 11 of England, consisting of Messrs. W. G. Grace, G. F. Grace, Jupp, Humphrey, Greenwood, Oscroft, M'Intyre, Lillywhite, Gilbert, Southerton, and Bush. I give the names, that the value of our victory may be properly estimated when I write that the Victorians, who went first to the wickets, scored 266 against excellent fielding, and beat the 11 in one innings, with 21 runs to spare. Before the match the odds were 3 to 1 in favour of the Englishmen, and our unexpected success delighted all patriotic colonists, though many lamented the intolerable "blowing" which would follow it. There has not been much to complain of yet in this respect, and we are ready to admit that the 11 men were playing under disadvantages. It is said that they were not in good form – they had only 10 days' practice after a six weeks' voyage – and that the self-denial necessary for getting into condition at Christmas in an hotel among hospitable people was too much for human nature, and was certainly not practised by some of the professionals. Mr. Cooper, who made the top score of 84 for Victoria, had played in England with the Gentlemen against the Players in more than one match, and has not been many years in the colony. But, after setting off everything which detracts from the credit due to Victoria, there is an encouraging balance in favour of the Australian-born and Australian-made cricketers, who greatly distinguished themselves. Their bowling is said by our visitors to be equal to any in the old country, and as much might have been guessed from the score, which showed many of the champions clean bowled, including the redoubtable Mr. W. G. Grace. This is the third English eleven which has visited us, and each visit seems to have improved our play.

New South Wales

FROM OUR OWN CORRESPONDENT

9 *April* 1874; *Sydney,* 14 *February.* It is not to be expected that while turning over the files of the English papers and reading the records of a fortnight's fog in London we should not contrast our lot with yours and find ours to be much preferred. A climate which is fatal to cattle cannot be suitable for Christians. The passengers by the mail speak of their departure from the mother country as an escape from something terrible. We are ready to concede that there may be compensations in fog, and yet we prefer the immediate enjoyment of genial breezes and cloudless skies, in spite of the knowledge that the indulgence is apt to be attended with physical weakness. I have not yet had an opportunity of ascertaining what the All England Eleven (W. G. Grace's team, now here) think of the noble game under an Australian summer sun or during a hot wind. They have experienced both, and, having improved in play since they played and lost the first match against 18 New South Welshmen, we may suppose that the influences have not proved untoward. But to those who are not enthusiasts it seems impossible to find much pleasure in cricket while the thermometer stands at 90 degrees in the shade. Yet men were not only found to play it, but thousands of spectators surrounded the field from morn till eve. The first game, as I said, was won by the colonial 18, their runs being two in excess, with eight wickets to spare. This unexpected success led, of course, to a good deal of boasting and a cheapening of the British men. The play of the Graces in the single wicket match which was introduced to close the third day, however, served to modify this judgment. The next match between the All England Eleven and the colonial field was played at Bathurst, the numbers opposed being 22 and 11. The victory for the Englishmen was an easy one. Since then a more exciting game was played in Sydney, the All Englanders accepting a challenge from 15 picked men from Victoria and New South Wales. The former won by 218 runs. Several other matches are yet to be played.

Twelve of the Marylebone Club
v. Eighteen of America

4 *August* 1874. The appearance of the American cricketers in the Metropolis attracted a more than usually large company at Lord's yesterday. Only two hours and a half were devoted to cricket, as the main object of the visit was to exemplify the mode in which the Americans played their national game of base ball. Marylebone started batting on an excellent wicket at 12 25, with

Messrs. Courtenay and A. Lubbock. H. Wright, from the nursery end, and M'Bride were the bowlers. The fast underhand deliveries of the latter disposed of two wickets in seven overs for eight runs. Mr. Lucas then joined Mr. Lubbock, and brought up the score to 41, when the last-named was clean bowled. Just prior to luncheon Mr. Lucas was finely caught at point. Four hours elapsed before Messrs. Walker and Bird resumed the Marylebone batting. Doubtless the exertions of the Americans at base ball caused their fielding, which had hitherto been first-class, to decline, and consequently runs came quickly. At the close of the day M.C.C. had scored 88 for five wickets. [Because of rain the following day the match was not played out, M.C.C. scoring 105 and America replying with 107.]

Base Ball

Immediately after luncheon the two leading base ball clubs of America gave an exposition of their game. The play, however, was somewhat disappointing, compared with the previous tourneys at Liverpool and Manchester, as the Philadelphian Athletics threw many chances away by bad fielding, of which their opponents took most judicious advantage. The game, which commenced at 3 35, concluded at 5 45 in favour of the Bostons by 17 runs, as may be gathered from the following official score. The number of "outs" signifies the times the player was put out. Nine innings were played by each side :–

ATHLETICS			BOSTONS		
	Outs.	Runs.		Outs.	Runs.
M'Mullin (centre field)	3	1	G. Wright (short stop)	3	4
M'Geary (short stop)	3	1	Barnes (second base)	3	4
Anson (first base)	2	1	Spalding (pitcher)	1	4
M'Bride (pitcher)	3	1	M.Verg (catcher)	1	3
Fisler (right field)	3	1	Leonard (left field)	4	2
Batten (second base)	2	1	O'Rourke (first base)	4	2
Sutton (third base)	4	1	H. Wright (centre field)	4	1
Clapp (catcher)	4	0	Hall (right field)	4	1
Gedney (left field)	3	0	Schafer (third base)	3	3
Total	27	7	Total	27	24

NUMBER OF RUNS IN EACH INNINGS

Athletics .. 3 0 0 0 1 1 1 0 1 .. Total 7
Bostons .. 3 7 4 0 5 0 5 0 0 .. Total 24

Fisler hurt his hand in the second innings, and his place was taken by Murman.

The Cricket Season

[BY A. I. SHAND]

6 *April* 1875. Willow wood is cheap with us, bits of unenclosed land are happily still common enough, and English boys take as naturally to the bat as Scandinavians to their snow shoes. Englishmen, as a matter of course, carry their cricket about with them wherever they go, and lay themselves out to cherish it as a delicate exotic in the most uncongenial climates. Few of them, perhaps, are capable of such sustained exertions in the Tropics as Mr. Alfred Jingle in his famous match with Sir Thomas Blazes. Yet we believe the cricket ground to be an appurtenance of our barracks in the Blue Mountains of Jamaica, and sporting contemporaries publish reports of the game from the stations in the Mediterranean to those under the Southern Cross, where garrison "teams" come in conflict with the civilians who have exiled themselves from home in pursuit of fortune. The fact is that all Englishmen love the game – scarcely so much, perhaps, for itself as for its many associations. They have all learnt it more or less in boyhood, although the branch of education they followed so kindly may in many cases have been cut prematurely short when they had to betake themselves to the serious business of life. If, however, we may fairly be called a nation of cricketers, we owe it, as must be confessed, very much to the climate we are all so given to abuse. England is become the country of cricket, because it is the country of turf and flying showers and tempered sunshine. Even in England cricketers learn to appreciate these blessings after an unusual continuance of drought and sunglare. With a glass at "set fair" and a thermometer at 80 deg., the soil grows hard and cracks and bends, in spite of the most tender care and incessant rolling and watering. The sickly grass becomes more yellow as it dies at the roots, and as nature pines away the game grows positively dangerous. The swift balls glance off at the most unlikely angles, setting eye and agility alike at defiance and demoralizing the coolest master of the bat in spite of his panoply of defensive armour. An eccentric "shooter" takes a man in the region of the midriff with something like the effect of a spent cannon-shot, leaving him a reminiscence that may last for a lifetime. Then, although keen cricketers will pitch the stumps in any weather, just as hard riders will turn out in a deluge or boating men in a hurricane, yet sultry weather is in itself a serious take-off to enjoyment. As it happens, summers of the kind are the exception with us, and so we cricketers are seldom tried in that way; but foreigners, if we could fancy their taking to the game, would find it far more of a pain than a pleasure. Standing up to swift bowling on bare ground, baked hard as a brickfield, would be a severe trial even for the most chivalrous of Frenchmen, and if Spaniards and Italians were as energetic as they are indolent, the indispensable exertion would often be physically impossible.

When the French villager, in the fine season, has done with his hard day's work in the fields or the vineyards, he is suffering more or less consciously from the languor that comes of protracted heat. As for the Spaniard, he is still worse off, for he has generally to walk some miles from his toil to his village, and is pretty well exhausted by the time he reaches it. The summer life of our English villages presents, at any rate, from this point of view, a very different picture. The men and boys assemble on the village green when their work is over and the horses have gone home from the watering; wickets that show the signs of hard service are fetched out from the opposite publichouse, with the splintered bats that have been repeatedly sprung and spliced again. At least twenty-two of the loungers may be taken into the game, and though their style might seem wanting in scientific grace to skilled critics from "Lord's," yet, on the whole, they have the air of men who know thoroughly what they are after. It is true they have a dislike to standing on the defensive. But they cut and drive and sweep to long leg; they steal runs, or are stumped in trying to steal them, till the spectators get as thoroughly animated as themselves, and the village becomes a scene of hearty excitement, which is the best specific for hard-working men. They make the most of these long summer evenings, which are only to be enjoyed in perfection in a climate and latitude like our own. We have no idea of painting a rustic paradise. There is, sometimes, a little roughness in the play; there may be men who drink more than is prudent, and their language and the tone of their merriment may leave a good deal to desire. But they are far less likely to be hurting themselves or their families than if they had gone inside the publichouse and drawn their chairs round the table; they are unbending muscles and expanding chests that have been stooped over the hoe and the spade. Nor can cricket in the country be confined to a class, because you must have a certain number to make a pleasant game. Some of the younger employers of labour are pretty sure to stroll up to the green or the common when the Club is assembling to choose its sides; and even the sons of the squire may have arranged for an early dinner, and come out to dazzle their tenants and cottagers with the latest lights from the Playing Fields of the Universities. Nor need the Church withhold its countenance. If the Rector be wise, he will make a point of often taking his evening walk that way; and the lord of the manor ought to sub-scribe handsomely to send his parish team on its way rejoicing to play the annual match with some of the neighbours. It is that early training and blending of ranks that make possible these matches under difficulties at the Antipodes, and these early associations make the matches enjoyable in spite of the climate. When the wardroom officers of the gunboat on the Pacific Station pass the word forward for volunteers, they are pretty sure to make up a scratch eleven from the forecastle men who some time or other have taken keen pleasure in the game. The memory of the old times comes back to the players. The clearing among the mahogany trees recalls the village green, with its elms and horse-chestnuts, although the luxuriant glories of the tropical parasites may eclipse the clematis and dogroses of the English hedgerows. Kindly feeling is promoted as it used to be, discipline gains, and Her Majesty and the country are served the more efficiently that the officers and men can be brought together in a common enjoyment by common sympathies.

We have purposely dwelt upon cricket as it is played in the rough, because in its popular and less scientific aspects it is more beneficial, more picturesque, and more lively. But we know it would be rank blasphemy to slight the science of this game, and we hasten to disavow any such intention. Professional teaching is invaluable in bringing out the more delicate beauties; grace and power come generally by cultivation rather than instinct; and a man seldom does much credit, even to his local circle, unless he has seen good models to form his style upon. The professional elevens who stump the country do a useful work, and County Clubs would degenerate into hopelessly slovenly habits unless they were largely leavened by players who had been carefully taught and trained. But it must be owned that the great matches, where high gate money is taken and the ground kept carefully clear, prove not unfrequently to be the very reverse of exciting. We can imagine the intelligent foreigner or the uninstructed female intellect being sorely put to it to sympathize with the enthusiasm prevailing around them. Bowling brought to its modern perfection leaves few opportunities for telling display. It is all a man can do to keep his wickets. The field solemnly crosses and recrosses, like pieces shifted by machinery on a chess-board. The score mounts more deliberately than the men move. It is positively a relief when the bowling gets demoralized, or, in other words, when the play breaks down. When a long-reaching broad-shouldered batsman sees his way to taking liberties; when he can step out to slash and cut, "skying" the ball to unexpected points of the horizon, or fluttering by some tremendous drive the galaxy of beauty under the curtains of the pavilion, then only the decorous spectators forget they are connoisseurs, and begin to enjoy themselves in reality. Their human nature is having its way, and burst the restraints of artificial appreciation. "Lord's" and the "Oval" have their own attractions, like Piccadilly or Rotten Row; but for the type of a genuine English cricket match to show a stranger give us one like that immortalized by Dickens between the Dingley Dellers and the All Muggletonians, where a couple of neighbourhoods come together in easy rivalry and hearty good fellowship; where the game is played fairly well by men who make their practice a mere recreation, and where the players and their friends meet afterwards at dinner to close the pleasant day with cheerful conviviality.

Death of Box

13 *July* 1876. The third day's play in this match at Prince's [Middlesex v. Notts] was proceeded with at the appointed time. Mr. Ottaway, one of the not-outs for 44 runs, put on 62 before he surrendered to the varied attacks of

Notts. Next to him "extras" figured most prominently. The innings closed for 220 runs. It should be observed that Mr. Ottaway went in first and came out last. In his score were one five, four fours, seven threes, and nine twos. Shaw bowled 66 overs for 65 runs; Morley, 52 overs, 63 runs; Tye, 25 overs, 41 runs; and Oscroft, 16 overs, 26 runs. Notts now required 55 to win. Barnes and Selby were sent in to get them, but the latter was caught at mid-off from the fourth ball delivered. A. Shrewsbury then joined Barnes, and the score reached 10, when play was stopped by a sad event.

Box, the groundkeeper, had put up the plate on the telegraph signifying the first decade; he then went to his chair, fell backward, and expired three minutes afterwards. In consequence of this further play was abandoned. Deceased for many years held a foremost position as wicket-keeper, and has rarely been excelled.

County of Kent v. Marylebone Club

14 *August* 1876. In the long list of cricket marvels and curiosities few stand out, or are likely so to do, with greater prominence than those comprised in the last "Week at Canterbury." Three days of sunshine, with only an occasional passing cloud, were considered sufficient to play out the first match on the paper. But it proved otherwise; and with 1,132 runs recorded it was left unfinished. Towards this number Mr. Gilbert contributed 143, Mr. A. J. Webbe 117, Mr. W. G. Grace 100, and Lockwood 99. The second match was more remarkable than the first. Kent began the batting, and occupied the wickets the whole of Thursday. Nine wickets were lost in the meantime for 453 runs. To these 20 were added on Friday morning. Marylebone were singularly unlucky at the start, nor were they much befriended by fortune at any of the subsequent stages, being 329 runs in arrear at the fall of the tenth wicket. A "follow on" was inevitable, and 217 were obtained with four wickets down when play for the day ceased. No one attempted to forecast the result, and few, if any, dreamt that Mr. Grace would rub out the debt of arrears himself. But he did. This feat puts in to the shade that of Mr. Ward in 1820, whose score of 278 has till now been regarded as the most wonderful of its kind on record. The enormous total of 344 completed by Mr. Grace on Saturday occupied six hours and a quarter, thus giving an average of 57 runs per hour. He had to contend against all the Kent bowlers save one. Three of them went on three times and three twice. In one instance Mr. Yardley bowled from the right arm and then from the left. Never was a more striking exhibition of endurance against exhaustion manifested. To explain the progress it may be well to say that play began at 12 o'clock on Saturday, and in 90 minutes the overnight total of 217 advanced to 323, and ten minutes later the arrears were pulled off. At 4 35 Mr. Grace had scored just 300, and at

5 o'clock the figures 500 appeared on the telegraph, of which total Mr. Crutchley claimed no ordinary share. Mr. Turner, after resisting several changes of bowling, fell to the first ball delivered by Lord Harris. Six wickets 506. Now came the close of Mr. Grace's career – caught at mid off, and great was the joy thereat. His score of 344 contained 51 fours, eight threes, 20 twos, and 76 singles. There remained yet half an hour for play. This time was expended partly by Mr. Cottrell, caught at square leg for 10. Neither Captain Meares nor Mr. Goldney had a favourable opportunity for scoring, and when stumps were drawn 557 runs were announced for the loss of nine wickets; at the same time the match was declared drawn. Mr. Absolom delivered 39 overs for 105 runs; Hearne 35 for 91 runs; Mr. Foord-Kelcey 40 for 84 runs; Captain Fellowes, 28 for 63 runs; Lord Harris, 19 for 59 runs; Mr. Thomson, 20 for 52 runs; Mr. Shaw, 4 for 14 runs; Mr. Penn, 7 for 25 runs; Mr. Yardley, 8 for 27 runs, and Henty 2 for 7 runs. Umpires – Willsher and Hearne.

> KENT 473 (Lord Harris 154, Hearne 57 not out, Mr. W. Yardley 47; Mr. W. G. Grace 4 for 116)
> MARYLEBONE CLUB 114 (Capt. Fellowes 5 for 50) and 557 for 9 (Mr. W. G. Grace 344, Mr. P. C. Crutchley 84; Lord Harris 4 for 59)
> *Match drawn*

Grace's next two innings were 177 and 318 not out.

New Zealand

FROM OUR OWN CORRESPONDENT

2 *May* 1877; *Wellington, 8 March.* . . . The English cricketers have almost completed their New Zealand tour. They have played in all the chief centres of population, but with the exception of Canterbury, no New Zealand team has made a decent stand against them. However, their visit has been a source of much interest to the cricketing world within the Colony, which has had the opportunity of learning the extent of its deficiencies in handling the willow.

Victoria

FROM OUR OWN CORRESPONDENT

14 *May* 1877; *Melbourne, 22 March.* . . . You know the result of our great cricket match [*the first Test match*]. Australians will "blow," to use Mr. Trollope's word, about it for some time to come. It was played on the ground of the Melbourne Club, between Lillywhite's eleven and a combined eleven

of New South Wales and Victoria. We are told that it is the first match in which an English professional eleven has been beaten out of England. Each side was under a certain disadvantage. Pooley, the English wicket-keeper, had been left in New Zealand, and Allan, the best Victorian bowler, upon whose services the colonial eleven almost entirely depended in his department, suddenly retired, and a substitute had to be found at the last moment. The betting was altogether in favour of the Englishmen before the match began, but the splendid play of Bannerman, from New South Wales, soon altered the odds. He made 165 runs before he retired, not out, with his finger badly cut. The Englishmen declared that they had never seen a finer display of batting, not even by the great Grace. The other Australians brought up the score in the first innings to 245. The Englishmen then went in and made 196. The Australians followed and, with Bannerman disabled, made 104, leaving the Englishmen 154 to make to win, and a most interesting game was brought to a close with the fall of their last wicket for 108 runs, leaving our men the winners by 45 runs. This victory is certainly creditable to Australia. The scores were made against presumably the best English bowlers, among whom were Shaw, Emmett, Ullyett, and Southerton. The fielding of the team was excellent, and, although it is considered relatively weak in batsmen, Jupp, Charlwood, Greenwood, and Selby are said to be strong enough to give, at least, an average efficiency. As may be supposed, the game was watched with intense excitement by enthusiastic crowds, and those who could not get to the ground clustered round the newspaper offices to see the last despatches from the seat of war placarded on the door posts. It began and ended in good temper, and Lillywhite's pecuniary success must have consoled him for his defeat.

Marylebone Club and Ground
v. The Australians

28 *May* 1878. Over 4,000 persons visited Lord's ground yesterday to witness one of the most extraordinary spectacles that has occurred at this place for a long time past. The Australians were not thought very highly of in their recent contest with Notts, but they showed themselves in a very different light yesterday, for better fielding has rarely occurred. Marylebone were provided with a well-selected team, but with the exception of Mr. Hornby no one exhibited anything worthy the name of a defence. Mr. Ridley won the toss, and decided upon sending Messrs. W. G. Grace and Hornby to the wickets. Mr. Allan started bowling from the nursery end, followed by Mr. Boyle at the pavilion. Mr. Grace hit the former for four, but from the next ball he was caught at short leg. Mr. Booth's off stump was struck before he scored a run. Mr. Ridley then joined Mr. Hornby, and the score advanced to 25. At this stage Mr. Spofforth, a renowned bowler, very soon disposed of the latter.

In the next six overs seven of the Marylebone wickets fell for six runs. Mr. Allan bowled nine overs for 14 runs, and took one wicket; Mr. Boyle 14 overs, 14 runs, three wickets; Mr. Spofforth, five overs and three balls, four runs, six wickets. He took three wickets in three successive balls during his fourth over. C. Bannerman and Midwinter began the Australian batting at 1 30, and within two hours, including luncheon, the whole eleven were got out for 41 runs – only one double figure. The bowling was intrusted to Shaw and Morley. The first-named delivered 33 overs and two balls for 10 runs, and took five wickets; Morley the same number of overs, 31 runs, and also five wickets. Marylebone resumed batting with Messrs. Grace and Webbe; and great indeed was the disappointment caused by Mr. Grace's quick retirement, without a run. It signified little who went in, for Messrs. Spofforth and Boyle were determined upon their speedy dismissal. Four wickets fell for one run. Flowers and Wild held together long enough to bring the score up to 16. At 4 50 the innings closed for 19. The Australians required but 12 runs to win. This number cost them one wicket, so that the Colonials beat the greatest and most powerful club in the world by nine wickets. They were loudly cheered by the assembled multitude for the achievement. Umpires, Sherwin and Rylott.

M.C.C. 33 (Mr. F. R. Spofforth 6 for 4) and 19 (Mr. H. F. Boyle 6 for 3, Mr. F. R. Spofforth 4 for 16)
AUSTRALIANS 41 (Shaw 5 for 10, Morley 5 for 31) and 12 for 1
Australians won by 9 wickets

The Australian Cricketers

20 *September* 1878, *Leading Article*. Yesterday, it will be seen, the Australian Cricketers started on their homeward journey from Liverpool, visiting the United States in their way, and hoping, no doubt, to win fresh laurels there. The summer is over, the equinox is near, the days are shortening, the weather is breaking, and, warned by the signs of coming winter, our visitors from the Antipodes, like other birds of passage, have taken their flight. They may be congratulated on the complete success of their visit. If they have not been uniformly victorious, if they have succumbed now and again to the teams which the mother country could array against them, they have at any rate shown that the national game is as well understood and as diligently practised in Australia as it is at home, and that the mysteries of batting, bowling, and fielding are not the exclusive privilege of a small island in the northern hemisphere. This fact was at least partially disclosed some years ago, when an English professional eleven first made its way to Australia. But to the public of this country it was an event of striking significance that an eleven should come from Australia and should hold its own, always with credit and generally with triumph, against the best skill that could be pitted against it.

It seemed much more natural, as well as more soothing to the national pride, that a picked professional eleven should go to Australia in order to show the colonists what English cricket was like. The tables have now been turned. If the Australians had been generally overmatched in their adventurous enterprise, we should have admired and applauded their courage without being much surprised at their defeat. But they have given us no opportunity of indulging in this pleasing sense of compassionate superiority. They have shown us that, as far as cricket is concerned, Englishmen in Australia are as good as Englishmen at home. They have produced an eleven very hard to beat and quite impossible to despise. At times they have been rather easily defeated, as the best eleven must occasionally be even by inferior opponents; nor can there be much doubt that a picked eleven of the best English players, whether professionals or amateurs, would under ordinary circumstances be more than a match for them. Their opponents have not always been formidable, and some of the matches they have played have been very unequal contests. But the fact remains that they have met in fair field and have there beaten some of our best county elevens, and that out of thirty-seven matches they have won eighteen and only lost seven while twelve have been drawn, some of them manifestly and indisputably in their favour. With such a record to show it cannot be denied that they have more than held their own in an arduous campaign against some of the best opponents which this country could bring against them. Australia is not perhaps naturally so favourable a home for the game as England, but the success of the Australian cricketers is a proof that they have learnt to neutralize the disadvantages of climate by assiduous practice and skilful generalship.

It is the opportunity which the game affords for the display of the latter quality which gives cricket its real supremacy over all other games played with the ball. In tennis each player depends on his own skill and cunning, while in cricket each player, whatever his individual skill, is but a soldier in an army whose victory depends on the loyal co-operation of all. Each man bears his share in the struggle, but all yield allegiance to the trusted commander. To the recognition of this fact the success of the Australian cricketers has been very largely due. They have shown strong batting, varied and bewildering bowling, and skilful fielding, such as the best English cricketers could hardly surpass, but, in addition to all this, they have acquired the habit of working together, of seconding each other's play, and of combining the individual skill of each with the due subordination and co-operation of all. Thus, they have shown that not only can Australia produce individual cricketers who would do no discredit to the best English eleven, but that it can send forth an eleven capable of holding its own at all points against the strongest elevens of this country. To have made a good fight against us and yet to have been worsted would have been no discredit to Australia; it is more than creditable to have been victorious so often and to have defeated such redoubtable opponents. They have been hard to beat here; they should be invincible in America. Meanwhile, let us hope that our Australian visitors carry home with them the pleasant memory of a warm welcome as well as of a brilliant and well-earned success. We heartily wish them good speed on their homeward journey, and we are sure that we only express a universal sentiment when we say that their victories have been as satisfactory to their entertainers and rivals as they have been creditable to themselves.

Glocestershire County Cricket Club

14 *January* 1879. A special meeting of the Glocestershire [*sic*] County Cricket Club was held at Bristol on Friday evening. Mr. J. F. Norris, chairman of the committee, presided and there was a very large and influential attendance. The chief discussion occurred on rule 6, which, in the appointment of officers of the club left out the secretary, Dr. E. M. Grace, while another rule provided that the salaried secretary should be ineligible to vote. Major Versturme moved and Captain Warren seconded a resolution that the revised rule providing that the secretary, Dr. Grace, should not be an officer of the club should be adopted. Mr. W. G. Grace contended that the secretary should be considered an officer of the club, and said that in this and in giving the secretary the privilege of voting they could not do better than follow the example of the Marylebone Club. He proposed an amendment to that effect. The Rev. J. Dann seconded the amendment. The chairman said this matter arose from circumstances which, sooner or later, must have come before the whole body of subscribers. At a committee meeting held, he believed, on November 1, certain accounts were brought before the committee for their sanction as payment for certain playing members in a match at the Oval. It then appeared that the secretary, Dr. E. M. Grace, had sent to the Surrey Club Committee a claim of £102 10s. for those expenses, and the Surrey Committee had declined to pay it on the ground that it was exorbitant. The Glocestershire Committee had not seen the account before, and when submitted to them the majority of the committee also thought the amount excessive, though the majority of the sums, ordinary understood payments, they passed. The items of that account consisted of £4 10s. each (the ordinary out-of-pocket expenses) for the general body of the team; Mr. W. G. Grace, £15; Mr. G. F. Grace, £11; Mr. Gilbert, £8; Midwinter, £10; the umpire, £6; scorer, £5; and Dr. E. M. Grace, £20. After investigation they reduced the total amount to £80 10s., which the Surrey Club then paid. He and some of the committee who audited the accounts considered that they were not in a satisfactory state, and they were so made up that the committee had no control over the payments to playing members of the club. Dr. E. M. Grace, the secretary, complained of the charges made against him and repudiated them. While the chairman had audited the accounts he had endeavoured to adopt all the suggestions he had made, and had secured vouchers for all items, and

every item would be found revised. Though out of the £102 10s. charged for the match at the Oval Surrey only paid £80 10s. the committee thought proper to pay out of the club's fund the remainder, including his £20. Some gentlemen at the Surrey Club, when playing in the home match at Clifton College, were said to have stated that he had said the Glocestershire team were paid £10 each. He emphatically denied that he made any such statement. Immediately he heard of this false statement he wrote up for the names of the gentlemen who alleged that he had made such a statement, but he read a reply showing that he had not yet been able to get them. Two names of members of the Surrey Club who had made the remark were then mentioned. Mr. W. G. Grace's amendment was put and carried by 23 votes againt 17; and it was then carried as a substantive motion by 28 to 16. The old rule retaining the secretary as an officer therefore stands. Revised rule 10, for the appointment of a secretary at a salary, provided that he should be ineligible to vote. Mr. W. G. Grace moved as an amendment that this clause should be struck out, and the amendment was carried by 23 votes to 15. Other rules, including new ones providing that the accounts should be audited annually by a professional accountant, that only out-of-pocket expenses should be paid to those playing for the county, except where special arrangements are made by the committee, were carried, together with one providing for the appointment of a finance committee.

Presentation to Mr. W. G. Grace

23 *July* 1879. At Lord's yesterday a handsome clock and chimney ornaments, with £1,400 in money, were presented to this well-known cricketer. The presentation originated in Glocestershire, which is naturally proud of its pre-eminence as a cricketing county, due to the Grace family, and especially to Mr. W. G. Grace. Lord Fitzhardinge, who was chief speechmaker yesterday, alluded to the fact that the Prince of Wales was one of the donors. He said that the original idea was to purchase a practice for Mr. Grace, but he had talked the matter over with the Duke of Beaufort, and they thought that Mr. Grace was old enough and strong enough to choose a practice for himself. (Laughter.) He could only say on the part of the people of Glocestershire that they wished him as much success in his profession as he had gained in the cricket field. Mr. Grace expressed his gratitude in a brief reply, and Lord Charles Russell, as one of the oldest members of the Marylebone Club, added a few words. He was an old cricketer, and the greatest enjoyment he had had in the cricket-field for many years past was in seeing Mr. Grace play. He looked upon cricket as the sport of the people, from the prince to the peasant, and he was delighted to see that it was increasing in popularity year by year, and that in some respects also it was being better played. He had certainly seen better bowlers than Mr. Grace, but he could say, with a clear conscience,

that he had never seen a better field, and he had never seen any one approach him as a batter. More than agility was wanted in playing cricket. The game must be played with head and heart, and in that respect Mr. Grace was pre-eminent. Looking at Mr. Grace's playing, he was never able to tell whether that gentleman was playing a winning or a losing game. He had never seen the slightest lukewarmness or inertness in him in the field. His heart and soul were in the game. The Marylebone Cricket Club held its ground for the practice and promotion of good sound cricket, and it was for that reason they had such great delight in taking part in this testimonial to Mr. Grace, who was in every respect of the word a thorough cricketer. The clock bears the following inscription:– "Presented to W. G. Grace on July 22, 1879, on the occasion of the match Over Thirty v. Under Thirty, played in his honour at Lord's."

A Centenary Match

28 *June* 1880. A hundred years ago to-day a match was played at Sevenoaks between the Duke of Dorset's Eleven and a team selected by Sir Horace Mann, for a stake of £500. The Duke of Dorset, the third of the title, left an inclosure of land, part of his estate at Knole, Sevenoaks, to be "a cricket field for ever." The ground is well known as "The Vine," and has been the scene of many a well-fought battle. In order to commemorate this match, a game was arranged for Saturday last on the same ground by members of the Vine Club, the sides having been chosen by Earl Stanhope and Earl Amherst. The contestants seemed very evenly matched, as when an innings each had been finished there was only a difference of five runs between them. Earl Amherst's side went in a second time, and when stumps were drawn one wicket was down for 79.

England v. Australia

9 *September* 1880. No match has ever excited such general interest as that commenced at Kennington Oval on Monday between the Australians and England. Enormous crowds were present on the first and second days, and even yesterday the spectators were to be numbered by thousands. The fact of the match being played at all is a matter of general congratulation. After protracted negotiations, a team of English cricketers, under the captaincy of Lord Harris, entered the lists against the Colonials. The latter had experienced an almost triumphant career. Twice only have they had to bow to their opponents, although it must be admitted that in some of their contests they may be said to have had a charmed life, especially in that against Glocestershire. Unhappily, some questionable bowling at Scarborough disabled Mr. Spofforth, and although it was hoped that he would have sufficiently re-

covered in time to participate in the match against England, this was found impossible. This, of course, was a most serious loss to the Colonials, as the gentleman in question is thought by many persons to be the best bowler in existence. In spite of this drawback, the Australians were bold enough to meet eleven of our own players, who formed probably the strongest combination that has ever entered a cricket-field. All the elements of the game were represented to perfection. There were Drs. W. G. Grace and E. M. Grace, both well known for their hard hitting and good fielding; Mr. A. G. Steel, whose ability with the bat and ball has long been recognized; the Hon. A. Lyttelton, with a deserved reputation for wicket-keeping and batting; while Lord Harris, Mr. Penn, Mr. G. F. Grace, and Mr. Lucas are all players of marked ability. To this formidable host were added three of our best professionals. These were Barnes, known for his heavy scoring, and Shaw and Morley, the exponents of the two styles of bowling which are generally most effectual. A good piece of fortune attended England at the outset as they won the toss. A most perfect wicket was in favour of heavy scoring, and all the arts of which the Australians were masters were futile against the clever batting of many of the home team. Dr. W. G. Grace played an innings which will long be remembered. With the exception of a very hard chance in the long field when he had made considerably over 100, his batting quite equalled any previous performance. His brother, Dr. E. M. Grace, played carefully and well. Mr. Lucas, Lord Harris, and Mr. Steel batted brilliantly, and it was not until 420 were reached that the eleven were out. This was a most formidable number for the Australians to go in against. They played the game, however, pluckily and well. Misfortunes fell fast upon them in their opening venture. Their mainstay – Mr. Murdoch, the captain of the team – succumbed to a catch at mid-off which only a very clever fieldsman could have made. Bannerman batted in a clean style, and Mr. Boyle hit in grand form until he was obliged to retire for want of a companion. The visitors found themselves in a minority of 271; but although this was most disheartening, they played the game in their "follow on" with an ability and courage that called forth the most hearty acknowledgments of the spectators. Mr. Murdoch batted in a manner simply perfect, and, oddly enough, he beat Dr. W. G. Grace in the race for "top score" by a run and then remained unconquered. The second innings of Australia for 327 runs surprised every one, as a single-innings defeat seemed inevitable. Surprises are so general in cricket that many people were afraid that this characteristic of the game would be most unpleasantly exemplified. Three batsmen, whose efforts had produced 119 runs in the first venture, were dismissed for seven. Mr. Palmer kept dead on the wicket, and captured two excellent batsmen, the Hon. A. Lyttelton and Mr. G. F. Grace. Mr. Penn remained, and the Glocestershire captain had the pleasure of making the winning hit. Taken all round, the Australians were, without the slightest exaggeration, beaten at every point; but still they possess such merit as must command the admiration of all who witnessed their play. A tribute to their ability was made by Lord Harris in front of the pavilion after the match, and his wish that they would have a safe voyage home was heartily re-echoed by the spectators.

At 11 20 Messrs. Murdoch and Bonnor, the overnight not-outs, re-occupied the wickets, the former having made 79 in irreproachable style, and his companion 13. Morley and Mr. Steel continued the attack, and while the former escaped with very slight punishment in his first two overs, Mr. Murdoch cut and drove Mr. Steel for four each. The present year's Cambridge captain, however, had the satisfaction of completely defeating Mr. Bonnor. Thus seven wickets were down for 181 runs, and there seemed at this stage but little chance of an innings defeat being averted. Mr. Palmer filled the vacancy and commenced in promising style by driving a full pitch from Mr. Steel to the off side of the wicket for four. He was, however, destined to fall a victim to the Lancashire amateur, who, running from his position as bowler to mid-off, secured the ball which had been hit very high. With 84 runs still to make up, Mr. Bannerman joined Mr. Murdoch, and a most remarkable change was gradually worked. Both batted with exceeding steadiness. Mr. Alexander drove Mr. Steel to the long-on for four, but with this exception the runs were obtained by small items for some time. By ten minutes to 12 the completion of the second hundred was an accomplished fact. After this announcement had been made, Morley's bowling was remarkably difficult, as for five overs neither batsman could do anything against him. Mr. Steel's deliveries appeared exactly to the liking of Mr. Alexander, who in one over obtained two fours – a cut and off drive. This caused Mr. Steel's removal in favour of Dr. W. G. Grace at 217, which certainly checked the run-getting. A very fine leg hit for four from Morley had presently to be placed to the credit of Mr. Alexander, and a snick off Dr. Grace's bowling produced a similar number for the same batsman. This latter item increased the score to 230 by 25 minutes past 12, and immediately afterwards Mr. Murdoch, by a single, reached three figures. Mr. Alexander gained runs at a much faster rate than his companion. He cut Dr. Grace for three and played Morley hard to the leg boundary. The latter effort proved his last, as from the following ball he was neatly taken at slip. The retiring batsman's share of the runs secured during his stay amounted to more than two-thirds. Nine down for 239 runs. The interest was now extremely great, and every one concerned worked with determination, Morley bowling at his best and all the home team showing remarkable quickness in the field. The batsmen exhibited just as much anxiety to let no opportunity slip, and so matters progressed, the excitement growing with every addition, small or large, to the figures. A straight drive for four by Mr. Murdoch from Dr. W. G. Grace evoked much applause, and the next over from the Glocestershire captain, realizing five brought forth more cheering on the part of those present. At 2 50 Dr. W. G. Grace handed the ball back to Mr. Steel, whose first delivery was despatched by Mr. Moule to leg for four. A cut for three and an off drive for two, both by Mr. Murdoch, took the total to 263, when Shaw was tried in place of Morley. The slow bowler opened with three maidens, but in the meantime seven runs were obtained from Mr. Steel, four of them being for an off drive by Mr. Moule. Another run only was required to insure the Australians from what at the end of the second day's play seemed more than probable, and this at ten minutes past 1 was gained by Mr. Murdoch. Seemingly elated by their success, a more free style of play was adopted by both batsmen. The Australian captain drove Shaw to the off for four, and Mr. Moule obtained seven runs in a subsequent over of the same bowler. Morley, at 284, resumed in place of Mr. Steel, and the ten overs following the change yielded but five runs. A couple of rather fluky hits for four in one over from Morley preceded his displacement by Dr. W. Grace, off whom a cut for four by Mr. Murdoch advanced the total to 300 by 1 35. Mr. Lucas now assisted Dr. W. Grace in the attack, and for three overs not a run was scored off his bowling. Such a measure of success was not accorded Dr. W. Grace, for in the same number of overs 10 runs came, including a straight drive for four by Mr. Murdoch, who was playing as faultlessly as ever. Mr. F. Penn deposed Dr. W. Grace at 314, and seven runs in one over caused the Surrey amateur to be supplanted by Barnes. This change was resorted to at 324, and no advance was effected previous to the luncheon interval at 2 o'clock. Upon a continuance at 10 minutes to 3, Messrs. Moule and Murdoch had to meet the bowling of Mr. Steel and Barnes. The end of the venture soon arrived, Barnes at 5 minutes to 3 bowling Mr. Moule's off stump out of the ground. In this manner the innings closed for 327 runs. Mr. Murdoch, who came in when one wicket was down, made 153 (not out) of 319 runs scored while he was batting. His display was perfectly free from fault, and included a five, 18 fours, three threes, and 13 twos. Seven bowlers were engaged. Of these, Morley achieved the greatest share of success, but each of his three wickets cost 30 runs. Wanting 57 runs to win, England sent in Mr. G. F. Grace and the Hon. A. Lyttelton, opposed to whom were Messrs. Boyle and Palmer. The sixth ball disposed of Mr. Grace, whose place was taken by Mr. Lucas. The Hon. A. Lyttelton cut Mr. Palmer for four, but, with ten runs only registered, a fine catch at the wicket got rid of Mr. Lucas, the ball being well taken on the leg side. The association of Mr. Penn and the Hon. A. Lyttelton promised to amend matters, but at 22, after some not over-confident batting, the last named was clean bowled by Mr. Palmer. Barnes succeeded, and cut Mr. Palmer finely for four, but he was not destined to stay long. With 31 as the sum total, he played a ball to mid-on, where it was secured. Dr. E. M. Grace joined Mr. Penn, but, like his brother, Mr. G. F. Grace, was dismissed by the second ball he received. Half the wickets were now down for 26 [still required]. Dr. W. G. Grace went to the assistance of Mr. Penn, and steadily the runs required were obtained, the winning hit being made by the last-comer at about a quarter-past 4. Thus, amid the greatest excitement, a victory was declared for England by five wickets.

ENGLAND 420 (Dr. W. G. Grace 152, Mr. A. P. Lucas 55, Lord Harris 52, Mr. A. G. Steel 42) and 57 for 5
AUSTRALIA 149 (Morley 5 for 56) and 327 (Mr. W. L. Murdoch 153 not out, Mr. P. S. M'Donnell 43)
England won by 5 wickets

Mr. G. F. Grace

FROM OUR BRISTOL CORRESPONDENT

23 *September* 1880. The news of the death of Mr. G. F. Grace, the youngest of the famous cricketing family, 'the three Graces,' reached Bristol yesterday evening. So little was known of his illness that, in the face of the fact that he was announced, in conjunction with his elder brothers, to play in a match at Chepstow, the report was believed to be a hoax; but inquiry made at the residence of Dr. W. G. Grace proved that it was quite true. The young cricketer died about midday, at an hotel at Basingstoke, where he had been staying for the last eight or ten days. He was suffering from cold during the great Australian match, in which, it will be remembered, he did not make any show of his usual cricketing form; but on the following three days, the 9th, 10th, and 11th of the present month, he played with success in a match 'South of England *versus* Stroud,' running up a score of 44 in his last innings. On returning to his home at Downend, Glocestershire, where he lived with his mother, he complained of illness, but it was not sufficiently serious to interfere with his journey to Basingstoke, on his way to London. While there he was confined to his hotel by inflammation of the lungs, which became so severe as the week wore on that on Sunday or Monday he was visited by his elder brother, Dr. H. Grace, who, in the belief that he was much better, left him on Tuesday and returned home. A telegram received yesterday morning, however, was of so alarming a character that Dr. W. G. Grace started to Basingstoke at once. He went to Bradford-on-Avon, in Wilts, *en route* to get his brother, Dr. H. Grace, to accompany him, but at the Bradford station they received a telegram informing them that death had taken place. Mr. Fred. Grace was only 29 years of age, and throughout the successful career of the Glocestershire cricketers his manly and straightforward conduct and genial manners won him not only popularity, but the esteem of hosts of friends.

28 *September.* The remains of the late G. F. Grace, the famous Glocestershire cricketer, were buried in the family vault at the village church of Downend, Glocestershire, yesterday, in the presence of an assemblage numbering between 2,000 and 3,000 persons, many of whom had travelled long distances. So numerous were those who had expressed a wish to take part in the funeral,

that it took much of a public character. The Australian team sent a telegram of sympathy; many letters from all parts of the kingdom were received, and wreaths of flowers were sent by a number of friends who were unable to be present. The county team and members representing clubs at Cheltenham, Oxford, Bath, Chepstow, Bristol, Bedminster, Clifton, and other places attended, and walked in procession after the chief mourners.

Cricket at Odessa

5 *September* 1881. Our Correspondent writes from Odessa, Aug. 26:– "Last year the head-quarter staff in South Russia of the Indo-European Telegraph Company was transferred from Kertch to Odessa. The gentlemen composing it brought with them two institutions previously unknown here, an athletic club and a cricket club, and a day or two ago they had here their first public cricket match. I was unable to be present at it myself, but it is reported to have been a very successful and even brilliant affair. The ground looked gay with numerous tents, flags (especially Russian and British), festoons, and flowers. There was also a large and profusely-decorated marquée for the visitors, among whom were Prince Dondoukoff-Korsakoff, Governor-General of Odessa, M. Marazlee, the Mayor, a number of Russian officers and members of the civil and civic services, Her Britannic Majesty's Consul-General, the Consular representatives of other Powers, and a large attendance of ladies, both foreign and English. Play commenced at mid-day, and Prince Dondoukoff-Korsakoff and the other spectators evinced great pleasure and interest in the game. At 1 o'clock lunch was served, accompanied by an interchange of most friendly toasts and speeches. Soon afterwards some of the principal visitors left, but the match, played between representatives of the British colony at Odessa and representatives of that at Galatz, lasted until dusk, when the former were declared victors."

Cricket in 1882

20 *May* 1882, *Leading Article*. A large class of our countrymen probably blesses the present fine weather more as promoting cricket and other summer pastimes than for its beneficial effect upon the crops. Cricket this year came in with the blackthorn blossom, and seems to have reached its prime before most seasons are well begun. It is upon the tour of the Australians, whose visit is now one of the ordinary incidents of the season, that interest will be chiefly concentrated. It is said that the colonial team is stronger than ever – a rumour calculated to dismay those who bear in mind the drawn battle fought last autumn by Australians against the flower of our players. Their fielding is sure to be of the first quality. MR. SPOFFORTH and MR. PALMER

are formidable bowlers, although our batsmen have, through familiarity, lost the dread they once entertained of the former. As to the Australian batting, it is significant that in the course of the only two matches hitherto played MR. MASSIE has made an innings of 206, and MR. MURDOCH, the hero of the Oval match last season, one of 286, a score perhaps unprecedented in a first-rate match. Probably most of the counties will fare no better than Oxford and Sussex have fared at the hands of the Australians. It remains, however, to be seen with what success our visitors will encounter the crack representative teams of the M.C.C. and of All England.

Few will deny that these contests between English and Australian cricketers are a wholesome innovation upon the monotonous round of matches between county and county, between North and South, and gentlemen and players. The pitch of interest felt in county matches by all except the players is far from high. The "North v. South" contests evoke no enthusiasm. "Gentlemen v. Players," a match which was wont to excite the keenest partisanship, falls flat, partly because it is often repeated as many as three times during the season. The tendency, indeed, is to regard matches as mere opportunities for the display of individual skill. There are so many of them, each with its return match, and the same heroes change sides in and out with such perplexing rapidity, that we are apt to cease to follow the fortunes of a team, in order to admire those of the cricketing stars. The Australians, at all events, present the spectacle of a team which is nothing if not united, and which cannot be successfully met except by union. No match played against the Australians, whether by a county, a University, a club, or by a national team, can fail to be watched by all lovers of the game with an ardent interest. Crowds are sure to line, as they did last year, each green arena, and prevent the colonial eleven from repenting their visit to the old country. Cricket, indeed, was never so full of life and vigour as at present. The very tendency hinted at above is a symptom of redundant energy and public interest. We are all so fond of watching the game that the natural classifications of players by the place they live in will not suffice. More matches the public must have, even if genuine local spirit suffers thereby. The Australians, therefore, step in at an opportune epoch in the history of the game. When a nation is tired out with internecine feuds, a common enemy exerts a rallying influence. The recent visits of the Australians may in the same way inspire our too highly organized system of matches with fresh life. Their success – for we need not hesitate to predict for them a success at all events equal to last year's – will set English cricketers wondering where the secret of it lies. It is not enough to say that the Australians have a cricket season of nine or ten months in the year. In our four or five months our best players manage to squeeze in as many playing days, or more, than the Australians can afford in the course of their long summer. With us cricket matches, first-rate and even second-rate, are played all day and every day in the six. On the other hand, Saturday is the only day on which much cricket goes on in the colonies. It is a truth which may not be very palatable to those who assert the natural supremacy of Englishmen in the game, that cricket here is made more of a business than in Australia, where men wear cricket proficiency lightly, as a flower.

It is our national habit, and no bad one either, to play with all our might; nor would it be seemly to utter a word in disparagement of the pomp and ceremonial, significant of earnestness, with which cricket or any other sport is surrounded. Proceeding upon the principle that to do a thing well you must be always doing it, our best players, to witness whose skill the public are willing to pay, divide themselves into two classes, between whom a hard and fast line is drawn. But there is this affinity between the "gentleman" and the "player," that both make a business of the game, in the sense that for a certain time during the year both do nothing else. The amateur is, of course, an enthusiastic cricketer. So, as a rule, is the professional, although we have heard more than one declare that if he could help it he would never more touch bat or ball. But one is often tempted to wonder whether the gentlemen who play steadily from May to September for their county, for the M.C.C., for "North" or "South," for the "gentlemen," for England, and for number-less other teams and clubs, have any other taste or occupation in life. That they have sufficient leisure thus to spend their time is matter for envy to men who have to work during at least some portion of the week. That they are willing thus to exhibit their wonderful prowess is reason why we should be grateful. But the singleness of their tastes in the way of amusement is rather calculated to surprise. Do not some of them long to see the world – that is, parts of it other than those to which a cricket-pitch is to be found – during the choicest season of the year? Or have they no other social impulses, such as, for instance, towards the society or their families or friends by the sea-side or in the Highlands? It is almost treason thus to tempt our amateur cricketers from their allegiance; but these questions proceed from pure curiosity. It may be conjectured, however, that some among them who, miscalculating the duration of their enthusiasm, engage themselves to play throughout the season are heartily weary before their last match is played. Our gentlemen players, therefore, make a business of pleasure. The professional, on the other hand, takes a pleasure in his business, and, as businesses go, we can imagine none more pleasant. He is generally a capital fellow, whose only failing is to spend improvidently what he earns easily. It is no small tempta-tion to a mere youth, emerging suddenly from local celebrity, to find himself overloaded with admiration and paid on a handsome scale. That his head is seldom turned with praise, and that his success does not very often sink him in dissipation, speaks well for the general manliness and healthy character of the class. The cricket professional is more deserving than most of those who minister to human pleasure. It is only lamentable to think that the goal of his aspiration is, too frequently, to be the proprietor of a publichouse.

England v. Australia

30 *August* 1882. Our Colonial visitors have added another match to their long roll of victories obtained during the present season, and this, too, the most coveted of them all. Few of the 20,000 spectators on Kennington Oval yesterday were prepared for such a result, even within less than an hour of its accomplishment. In spite of the fact that the rain, which had been falling at intervals during the early morning, had increased to a heavy downpour by 10 o'clock, there was at this hour almost a complete belt of spectators round the field of play, who, protected by umbrellas, macintoshes, &c. maintained their positions throughout all discomfortures. Before 11 there was a break in the clouds, and the rain ceased. It was fortunate for the Australians that they had to go in first, as the wicket played far easier than it otherwise would have done. They did not obtain so many runs, however, as was expected of them. Mr. Massie hit vigorously, and his performance was very praiseworthy, in spite of his escape at the hands of usually so reliable a fieldsman as Mr. Lucas. Mr. Murdoch batted in his usual finished style, and Mr. Bannerman hit with great care. Beyond these none of the team did much. Mr. Hornby seemed to know the bowling which would most baffle the batsmen, and varied it accordingly, while he altered the disposition of the field with great judgment. Peate's bowling was again excellent. The small total of 85 which England had set them to win caused the match to be regarded by most people as a foregone conclusion for them, and this confidence was increased when the third wicket fell for 51. Thus there remained seven batsmen to be dismissed and only 34 runs to get. The Australians, however, although defeat stared them in the face, played with that thoroughness which we pointed out yesterday as being one of their most admirable characteristics. Two more wickets speedily fell. Yet, with five to go down and only 19 to get, it seemed almost impossible even in the game noted for its surprises that the home team should not be able to get them. Every ball was watched with the keenest interest; but batsman after batsman succumbed with a rapidity that soon caused great anxiety on the part of the on-lookers, and at length, after victory appeared to be almost within their grasp, the English Eleven found themselves beaten by seven runs. Mr. Spofforth sustained the reputation which secured for him the title of the "demon" bowler, as in the double innings he claimed 14 wickets for 90 runs. It is needless to say that the excitement was intense, and that the winners were warmly congratulated on their success. True, they had the best of the wicket, which played very treacherously during the English innings. Still the gallant manner in which they played an uphill game when there seemed no hope of success will cause their victory to be a subject of lasting admiration.

With 38 runs on the wrong side of their account, the Australians started batting again at 12 10. Messrs. Bannerman and Massie were their representatives. Barlow bowled the opening over from the Pavilion end. Mr.

Bannerman cut the first and last balls for two each. Ulyett conducted the attack from the other end. His second delivery Mr. Massie drove to the off. Read saved the ball from reaching the boundary; but a possible, though difficult, opportunity of running Mr. Massie out, was missed, owing to the ball being returned, in the opinion of many, to the wrong end. This player then secured seven runs in two overs of Barlow's by a cut and a square-leg hit. Each batsman having made a single, a very fine hit round to long leg by Mr. Massie for four caused 20 to be registered as the result of a quarter of an hour's play. This feat he speedily supplemented with a square-leg hit to the boundary, and at 25 Peate superseded Ulyett, and Mr. Studd displaced Barlow. Some very lively batting was now shown by Mr. Massie. The first ball of Mr. Studd's he hit finely to the on for four, and then drove Peate on either side of the wicket for like amounts, which caused the arrears to be rubbed out at 20 minutes to 1. Having secured another four from Mr. Studd by driving him to the boundary, that gentleman gave way to Barnes. The first ball sent down Mr. Massie raised to long-on, but Mr. Lucas failed to hold it. Mr. Bannerman made a cut for two, which brought the total up to 50 at ten minutes to 1. Mr. Massie continued his free hitting, and having obtained six runs by on and off drives from Peate, Mr. Steel was tried in lieu of the Yorkshireman. For a few overs these variations did not seem to disconcert the batsmen. Mr. Massie, however, having sent a ball of Mr. Steel's to deep square leg for four, was clean bowled by the next, the leg stump being knocked out of the ground. One for 66, as many as 55 having been obtained by the retiring batsman, whose chief hits were nine fours, two threes, and three twos. Those who expected to see some of Mr. Bonnor's tall hitting must have been sorely disappointed. Ulyett resumed again in place of Mr. Steel, and the change proved most happy, as the fourth ball struck Mr. Bonnor's middle stump right out of the ground. Mr. Murdoch came in, but did not long have the society of Mr. Bannerman, who before another run had been obtained was easily caught at mid-off. Mr. Horan remained while nine were obtained, but then played a ball tamely into the hands of Dr. Grace at point, while from the next ball Mr. Giffen, who supplied the vacancy, was served in the same manner. Half the wickets for 79 runs. Messrs. Murdoch and Blackham were associated, the most notable hit for a little time being one to leg for four by the latter. The total having reached 99, rain fell somewhat heavily, and an adjournment for luncheon was made a quarter of an hour earlier than usual. The interval over, Peate and Barlow proceeded with the attack against Messrs. Blackham and Murdoch. Ill-fortune attended the colonists at the outset. From the last ball of the opening over from Peate Mr. Blackham was well taken at wcket. Six for 99. Mr. Jones supplied the vacancy. A square-leg hit for a single by the Australian captain caused the three figures to be signalled at ten minutes to 3. Mr. Jones made six by cuts for two and four in an over of Barlow's. During the next nine overs Mr. Murdoch monopolized the little run-getting that was shown. Seven were gained by him, all by on drives, the most important being one for three off Barlow. With the score at 113, Mr. Murdoch hit a ball to leg, which was fielded by Mr. Lyttelton, who threw it at the wicket; the object was missed, and the ball went to Dr. Grace, who as Mr. Jones was out of his ground, put the wicket down, the batsman being adjudged run out. Mr. Spofforth's stay was brief and valueless – clean bowled. Eight for 117. Mr. Murdoch next had the companionship of Mr. Garrett, and at 25 minutes past 3 120 runs were registered. After this the innings speedily terminated, both the remaining wickets being taken in an over of Mr. Steel's. Mr. Murdoch was run out in attempting a third run, while Mr. Boyle was bowled, leg stump. Total, 122; time, 3 20.

With the apparently easy task of getting 85 to win, England started on their second venture at a quarter to 4. Dr. Grace and Mr. Hornby were placed in opposition to Mr. Spofforth (gasometer end), and Mr. Garrett. The opening over was a maiden, but a single by each batsman resulted from the second and the third overs. This moderate rate of run-getting was relieved by Mr. Hornby driving a ball of Mr. Spofforth's to the on for four, while in the same over he made a lucky "snick" to leg for two. Two overs subsequently, however, his off stump was struck, while Barlow, who followed, had his wicket upset by the first ball he received. One and two for 15. Dr. Grace and Ulyett were partnered, and for a time all went well. At ten minutes past 4 an off-drive for two caused 20 to be signalled. Dr. Grace then made seven in an over of Mr. Spofforth's by two on-drives. A change was consequently deemed desirable and this bowler crossed over, while Mr. Boyle went on at the gasometer end. This alteration in the attack did not bear fruit for a considerable time. Besides minor hits, Dr. Grace and Ulyett were each accredited with one to deep square leg for four. The "50" was attained at 4 35. One only had been added to this number when Ulyett was splendidly caught at wicket. Three down. Mr. Lucas came in, but without having much opportunity to score, he was separated from Dr. Grace, who was easily caught at mid-off. Four for 53. The Hon. A. Lyttelton came in, and started by scoring a single and three in an over of Mr. Spofforth's. Two maidens followed, and then the new arrival obtained two somewhat luckily and supplemented this by a very clean leg-hit to the boundary. Now followed a great display of patience on the part of the batsmen. Twelve overs were sent down without result and a single only was obtained in 17. The 18th proved fatal to Mr. Lyttelton, whose wicket fell to an excellent ball of Mr. Spofforth's, which struck the top of the middle stump. Half the wickets for 66. There were still, therefore, five to fall, and only 19 to get for victory. Mr. Steel joined Mr. Lucas, and the latter elicited considerable applause by a late cut from Mr. Boyle, which yielded four runs. This, however, was soon followed by misfortunes. The first ball of Mr. Spofforth's next over Mr. Steel returned to him, while Read, who succeeded, had his mid and off stumps struck by the third. Six and seven for 70. Only five runs were added, three of them byes, when Mr. Lucas played the ball on. Eight for 75. Mr. Studd and Barnes joined partnership, when only ten runs were required – a task which such batsmen as these would have been expected to accomplish without difficulty. The professional, however, was speedily caught at point. Nine for 75. Peate, the last man, sent the first ball he received to square leg for a couple. This hopeful start was not followed up, and in the same over he was clean bowled. Total, 77. The Australians thus won by seven runs.

> AUSTRALIA 63 (Barlow 5 for 19, Peate 4 for 31) and 122 (Mr. H. H. Massie 55; Peate 4 for 40)
> ENGLAND 101 (Mr. F. R. Spofforth 7 for 46) and 77 (Mr. F. R. Spofforth 7 for 44)
> *Australia won by 7 runs*

This match gave rise to the 'Ashes' obituary notice in the Sporting Times *the following Saturday.*

8 *April* 1884. We regret to learn that Mr. John Wisden (the once celebrated cricketer) died at his house, Cranbourn-street, Leicester-square, on Saturday last.

3
THE THIRD HALF-CENTURY
1885 to 1934

The start of this chapter sees MCC celebrating their centenary in an era still dominated by W. G. Grace. The regular interchange of tours between England and Australia is well under way and destined to extend to South Africa, West Indies, New Zealand and India by the close of the period. By then Don Bradman is the outstanding figure, but the link between Australia and the Mother Country had been under threat of severance because of Bodyline – although viewed through the leading articles emanating from Printing House Square in 1933 it seems the fuss arose from the rantings of a few sensationalists.

Major matches were given full coverage in The Times *during this half-century and the early part of the Edwardian era brought several articles in a lighter vein from E. B. Osborn, boxing correspondent, classical scholar and devotee of cricket, which give a foretaste of the fourth leaders. It is a mark of the expansive times – and the absence of photographs – that a piece, say, on The Crowd at Cricket might extend to 2500 words (though even this was outdone by a summary of the 1888 Australian tour that ran to more than 4000).*

George H. West, Cricket Correspondent at the start of the period, died in 1896, after several years of illness. He was 45. News of his death seems to have taken a while to reach the contributions department at The Times, *who for several days afterwards were still ascribing the sporting coverage to him. Another apparent anachronism persisted years later in that area: as late as the 1930s C. F. Pardon was being credited for parts of the cricket news – although he had been dead since 1890. The explanation is that the name of the founder was being used rather than that of the organization he founded, the Cricket Reporting Agency (also known as Pardon's, though I believe nowhere else as C. F. Pardon's).*

Ernest Ward, who earned the sobriquet 'Sporting' to distinguish him from other Wards on the staff, took over coverage of important matches from West without, it seems, being given the title of Cricket Correspondent. From 1902 until the First World War R. H. Lyttelton, member of a famous cricketing brotherhood and for five decades a vehement advocate of reform of the lbw law, assumed as 'Our Special Correspondent' responsibility for many of the leading games, although Ward, until he joined the Morning Post, *and Philip*

Trevor, later of The Daily Telegraph, *did some of the Tests. It should be remembered that in those days, for* The Times, *Oxford v Cambridge, Gentlemen v Players (the Lord's match) and Eton v Harrow were of equal importance to Test matches – to the extent that in 1921 virtually a page was devoted to a preview of Eton v Harrow with four-inch deep pictures of all the participants. (A sign of changed standards was thundered home 60 years later when, for one season,* The Times's *coverage of the match came several days, and several irate telephone calls, later and comprised only brief scores.) Much of the Eton v Harrow coverage between the Wars was in the hands of Robert Lyttelton's nephew, George, who was praised by Bernard Darwin, the famous Golf Correspondent of* The Times, *for producing the 'best prose of the time'.*

When Test cricket resumed in England after the First World War A. C. M. Croome, a former schoolmaster and Oxford cricket and athletics Blue, covered the matches as 'Special Correspondent', although when the third Test clashed with the university match, F. B. 'Freddie' Wilson went to Headingley and Croome to Lord's. Wilson, a former Harrow and Cambridge cricket captain and rackets and real tennis Blue, was proud to boast that he had reported some 20 different sports for The Times. *The title of Cricket Correspondent at this time was held by Sydney H. Pardon, magisterial editor of* Wisden *for 35 years and another all-round journalist who wrote on racing and the arts, as well as cricket, for* The Times. *His cricket writing for the paper appears to have been confined to feature articles or previews of important fixtures, but his successor, Croome, continued to report matches – not to mention his duties as Golf Correspondent of the* Morning Post! *– when he became Cricket Correspondent after Pardon's death in 1925.*

Croome, whose life had been saved by W. G. Grace in 1887 after he had seriously injured his throat on the spiked railings of the Old Trafford pavilion trying to save a boundary hit, died in 1930 and was succeeded by R. B. 'Beau' Vincent. A long-standing member of the sports department, Vincent had been a 'Special Correspondent' on cricket since 1927 and seems to have been the first Times *Cricket Correspondent to be a salaried, rather than retained, member of staff.*

The Centenary at Lord's

14 *June* 1887. Rarely has a club attained such longevity and then found itself in the zenith of its fame as that which the Marylebone Club are celebrating this week at Lord's. Its formation in 1787 arose, it would seem, through an almost chance meeting of the Earl of Winchelsea and the Hon. Colonel Lennox. These gentlemen induced Thomas Lord – a cricketer himself of no small repute – to open a ground at St. Mary-le-bone on the site where Dorset-square now stands. Subsequently Lord's removed to the North Bank, and thence to the ground in the St. John's-wood-road, where its headquarters now exist. The first recorded match on Lord's original ground was on May

31, 1787, in which T. Lord himself played. It was followed within just a week of a century ago by a match between England and the White Conduit Club (with six men given) at Lord's. This practice of a side having players allowed them was far more general then and for many years subsequently than at present. Indeed, during the latter end of the last century matches usually depended on the individual prowess of a player, and sometimes the contests were made for heavy sums. These were either risked by the players themselves or else provided by some wealthy patron – much in the same manner as we now have professional oarsmen, runners, walkers, and others, supported by some admirer. We find in 1794 on Lord's Ground a match being played between Eight Gentlemen of the Marylebone Club (and four men given) against Eleven Gentlemen of London for 500 guineas a side. In this Thomas Lord took part, and in the double innings obtained 12 wickets. Even 50 years before this it is stated that in 1735 a great match was played at Moulsey Hurst, in Surrey, between his Royal Highness the Prince of Wales and the Earl of Middlesex, eldest son of the Duke of Dorset, for £1,000 a side; eight of the London Club and three out of Middlesex played for the Prince and the Kentish men for the Earl. One glimpse of the altered state of the metropolis is caught from the fact of Marylebone playing London, thus implying that Mary-le-bone, as it was then spelt, was distinctly an outlying district. The playing for heavy stakes naturally led to much betting and certain quarrels. This was particularly the case in single-wicket matches, which were then and until quite recent years very popular. Thus we find "the lion of Kent, the bold and manly Alfred Mynn," so noted for his personal achievements. Gradually, however, the ability of the individual merged into the reputation of the club, which, when once firmly established, caused single-wicket matches to be of rarer occurrence. Even then for a time betting existed; but it gradually ceased. Though, at its outset the records of the Marylebone Club are so bare as to leave its earliest doings almost in a cloud, it is certain that, once well established, it has always held the indisputable position it now so deservedly occupies. It must be remembered that the laws which governed the game a hundred years ago were in a very crude state. If for nothing else, the early attention to and careful revision of these laws by the Marylebone Club would alone entitle them to the respect of all lovers of the game. It could have been by no means so easy a task as cricketers may be prone to imagine that the laws were gradually formulated into their present shape. Not only has cricket such a charm for the players themselves, but throughout the summer it affords healthy recreation to hundreds of thousands, and is watched with a keenness, a subdued feeling of enjoyment, and withal an enthusiasm quite free from the artificial excitement and feverishness engendered by betting. Thus the inherent vitality of cricket is proved beyond question. To enumerate the long roll of exploits with which the name of the Marylebone Club is associated would be to give the history of cricket since it has become indisputably the national game. It is gratifying also to reflect that the freehold of the ground on which they play is now their absolute property – obtained after many vicissitudes. It is now without doubt the ambition of all cricketers, whether amateur or professional, to appear in a match at Lord's, and in the chronicles of the scores the appearance of a player at Lord's seems to be made almost the starting-point of his career. We are, perhaps, apt to think that players of the past were much superior to those of the present. Yet it is probable that two teams never entered the field so skilful at all points as those celebrating the centenary at Lord's. In glancing at the names of the players engaged in the match, it is curious to note that neither in the Marylebone nor in the England team is there a representative of a county which in bygone days has produced so many good cricketers. Sussex at one time could put a team into the field able to vie with any in England. In fact, it is not too much to say that the name of Lillywhite was a household word in connexion with the game. On more than one occasion Sussex has met England single-handed and defeated them. Yet at the present time it does not, in the opinion of those intrusted with the selection of the teams, possess a single player, able to take part in this centenary match. Nor can the elevens chosen, with any show of reason, be found fault with. In the two teams, Gloucestershire furnishes Dr. W. G. Grace (the greatest cricketer of his and, in the opinion of most people, any other day); Lancashire sends Mr. A. N. Hornby, Pilling, Barlow, and Briggs; Nottinghamshire, Barnes, Gunn, Flowers, Shrewsbury, and Sherwin; Yorkshire, the Hon. M. B. Hawke, Bates, Hall, Rawlin, and Ulyett; Surrey, Mr. W. W. Read, Lohmann, and Maurice Read; Middlesex, Messrs. A. J. Webbe, J. G. Walker, and A. E. Stoddart; and Kent, G. G. Hearne.

The weather yesterday was charming, and if it is true that it can never be too hot for cricket the votaries of the game had nothing left to wish for. Long before the hour set for a beginning many took up their positions. The whole of the covered seats were crowded, as were also those along the tennis side of the ground. Members also fully availed themselves of their opportunities. The seats in front of the pavilion and members' enclosure were well filled and the roof itself was crammed.

Within a few minutes of 12 o'clock the appearance of England in the field showed that Marylebone had won the toss. Mr. Hornby and Dr. Grace opened the innings, and Lohmann delivered the first over from the pavilion end. After a single by Mr. Hornby Briggs bowled from the nursery end. In the fourth over Lohmann, fielding at slip, injured his hand and retired for a few minutes. Meanwhile Bates bowled in his place. The fielding and bowling were very close. Mr. Hornby at last drove Briggs finely to the off for four, and soon afterwards he repeated the stroke. At 19, however, Mr. Hornby returned the ball. Barnes joined Dr. Grace, but with only four added the latter was beaten by a ball from Lohmann. Two for 23. Mr. Webbe's stay was brief and unproductive, as without alteration in the figures he was out to a brilliant catch by Briggs, who secured the ball high up with his left hand, running from cover-point. Three for 23. Gunn joined Barnes. Runs were still obtained with great difficulty, until at 36 Barnes was clean bowled. George Hearne and Gunn improved matters. An off drive for two by the Kent man brought 50 on the telegraph board after an hour and a quarter's play. Two runs later, however, Hearne was bowled, and half the wickets were down. Mr. Walker started promisingly, making a fine cut for two, but was then dismissed by a clever catch at slip. Six for 55. The Hon. M. B. Hawke was next on the order. He made a hard off drive for four from Lohmann, and in the following over from that bowler his companion secured four by a similar hit. Although the bowling was twice changed, the total was 85 for six wickets at luncheon. Lohmann and Briggs conducted the bowling after the interval. Mr. Hawke was at length clean bowled. Forty runs had been added since the fall of the sixth wicket. With seven batsmen out for 95 Flowers aided Gunn. The 100 was reached at 3 o'clock. Gunn completed his 50 at 3.20. Flowers was bowled at 125, and Gunn had Rawlin for a partner. The former soon had the misfortune to play on. He had been in two hours and 10 minutes, and his 61 were obtained in splendid style; his chief contributions were three fours, three threes, and 12 twos. Sherwin, the last man, and Rawlin hit freely, and put on 39. Bates now clean bowled Sherwin, and the innings was over at a quarter past 4. Pilling had kept wicket to quite his old style, and the total reached 140 before the first extra was recorded.

Shrewsbury and Mr. Stoddart began the England batting at 4 35. Barnes and Rawlin were the bowlers. Now came one of the best displays of batting that has been seen at headquarters for some time. The bowling underwent almost every conceivable change, while the field was frequently varied. With the exception of a hard return chance by Mr. Stoddart (the ball also glancing to mid-off), the batting was perfect, and they played out time, runs having been obtained at the rate of 80 an hour. The company on the ground numbered about 8,000, among whom were Prince Christian, Lord Charles Russell, Lord and Lady Londesborough, Lord Winterton, Lord Sondes, Lord Erskine, Lord Bessborough, Lord Bingham, Lord Anson, &c.

M.C.C. AND GROUND 175 (Gunn 61; Lohmann 6 for 62) and 222 (Barnes 53, Dr. W. G. Grace 45, Flowers 43; Bates 5 for 46, Briggs 4 for 77)
ENGLAND 514 (Shrewsbury 152, Mr. A. E. Stoddart 151, Mr. W. W. Read 74, Ulyett 46; Barnes 6 for 126)
Score after first day: M.C.C. 175; England 196 for 0
England won by an innings and 117 runs

Cricket Reporting

5 *September* 1887, *Leading Article.* Cricket reporters are upon their trial. Their offence is that they have introduced a classification of counties into major and minor, or first-class and second-class. They also talk learnedly of

championships and premierships, against the peace of mind of old-fashioned cricketers, and against the statute in that behalf by the M.C.C. provided, according to which every county is as good as another county. And the public prosecutor is of great reputation. "F.G.," [Frederick Gale] whose rejoinder to the defence of the reporters we publish this morning, is easily recognizable, through the thin disguise of initials, as a NESTOR of the cricket-field. "The theory of these self-constituted authorities," he argues, "is that any one of their own ear-marked first-class counties – provided that they play not less than eight matches among each other without defeat – shall take precedence and be champion over any other which suffers a defeat." He illustrates the vicious operation of this rule by the performances of Notts and Surrey last year. Notts played 14 county matches – won seven, drew seven, and were not defeated once. Surrey played 16 county matches – won 12, lost three, and drew one. Besides this, Surrey twice defeated the Australians. Yet, upon the system of reckoning which "F.G." denounces, Notts was the champion county of 1886. Thus a county has every motive for playing as few county matches as possible, and spinning out as many as it can for a draw, "instead of taking an honest licking like a "good cricketer and sportsman."

We deplore as much as "F.G." the formation of a close aristocracy among the cricketing counties. But is he not blaming cricket reporters for what is not their fault? These poor people are pitched upon as somebody to hang, because they are nearest to hand. They are treated by "F.G." as a sort of "ring" which pretends to confer sham degrees of merit. While professing entire gratitude towards the Press for its services to cricket, he reminds its unfortunate representatives that they are only flies on the chariot-wheel. But it was not reporters who created the gulf which separates, let us say, Surrey from Suffolk. If cricket chroniclers ignored the wide difference between two such counties, they would be shutting their eyes to plain facts. It is very well that the M.C.C., in the democratic spirit which becomes cricketers, should regard all counties as equal; nor should we like to see this nominal equality disturbed. But to say that all counties are equal is no more true in point of fact than to say that all men are equal. "F.G." must blame mightier forces for requiring that this disparity should be recognized. Cricket reporters "but echo back the public voice." The classification of counties, and the minute comparison of the performances of those counties which are placed in the front rank, are the natural result of the extraordinary interest which is felt now-a-days in cricket, and, indeed, in all forms of athletics. Always popular, cricket has become vastly more popularized during the last twenty years. This impetus to the game has made competition keener, and has produced something of a mania for canvassing "results" of county cricket during each season. It is not a movement which can be arrested by refusing to notice it. Nothing will satisfy enthusiasts but measuring the prowess of the various counties. "F.G." complains in effect that they use a tape measure. But it seems to us that, although the method is rough and ready, the correctness of the result, so far as a division into first and second class counties goes, is beyond challenge. Who can name a single county, out of the twenty or so which possess elevens, regarding which there is any doubt in which category it ought to be placed at the present time? Nor is it credible, with all deference to "F.G.," that any county's pecuniary prospects can suffer through being ranked in the right division. If it is only second-rate, larger "gates" will not be drawn by describing it as first-rate. People know a great deal too much about the merits of county elevens to be deceived by adjectives. As to "F.G.'s" criticism upon the rule itself, that it favours "stonewall tactics," there would be much truth in what he says if the rule were applied in a hard and fast manner. It may have been applied too rigidly in the matter of Notts and Surrey last year, although that is a matter of opinion. But everybody, cricket reporters included, now recognizes that it is only a rough and ready rule of thumb. It only creates a presumption which may be rebutted by other circumstances. For instance, the analysis we publish this morning shows that Middlesex, during this season, out of 10 matches lost only two and won four. Yet public opinion, to which reporters have deferred, unites in ranking Middlesex below both Lancashire and Notts, the former of which counties has lost three and won ten matches out of 14, while the latter, with the same number of engagements, has been defeated in three contests and victorious in eight. And the best answer to "F.G." is that no one has yet invented a better test of merit, capable of being put in the form of a definition.

It would be more healthy if there were more love for cricket itself and less excitement about "results." Cricket, as "F.G." is never tired of preaching, is only a game, the intrinsic beauties of which deserve admiration far more than a long roll of successes. In an ideal state of things score-sheets would be torn up after the match was over. Away with tabulated returns and averages and all the rest of the paraphernalia, and let us enjoy our cricket match in a quiet, contemplative atmosphere, without the fear of the end of the season before our eyes, applauding to the echo the smart fielding of cover-point or the stopping of a deadly shooter, but treating with cold silence the unscientific hit out of the ground for six! Fain would we journey back to the rare days of which "F.G." delights to tell, and dwell in oblivion of that irrepressible arithmetical calculation which takes place at the beginning of September. But the emulative spirit of our countrymen will not have it so. The modern cricket-lover is too often a mere statistician. He has at his fingers' ends records, and batting and bowling averages, and county championship returns; and yet he sometimes has a hazy idea of what is meant by "playing with a straight bat." For these people "F.G." is right in entertaining scorn. But even among genuine cricketers the intense spirit of competition which is the chief feature of modern cricket precipitates itself in a worship of success. To attempt to stem the tide of invidious comparison would be idle. The best thing under the circumstances is to insure that, if restless spirits insist upon knowing the truth, it shall be the whole truth. In any case "F.G." is needlessly apprehensive of the advent of the betting-ring in cricket. Surely the moderns, who have long ago banished the matches for money, which "F.G." remembers so well, have given no ground for anticipating so doleful a relapse.

A Theatrical Cricket Match

17 *July* 1888. On the Recreation Ground at Paddington yesterday afternoon a return game between ladies and gentlemen of the theatrical profession was decided before a numerous company of onlookers. On the first occasion the gentlemen, although batting with broomsticks, gained a somewhat easy win, so that in the present match they were further handicapped. In addition to the broomsticks they had to bat and field left-handed, the penalty for picking up the ball with the right hand being an allowance of three runs to their opponents. An amusing incident occurred by a lady who was batting having the politeness to field the ball herself, but the penalty was not enforced, and she was allowed to continue her innings. The ladies, most of whom played under assumed names, scored 60 to the gentlemen's 23, and thus won by 37 runs.

Germany

27 *May* 1890; *Berlin*, 26 May. . . . An international cricket match was concluded to-day between the eleven of the English Berlin Cricket Club and that of the "Bold Club" of Copenhagen. The game, which was played on the Tempelhofer-field, excited considerable interest among the Berlin public. It ended in favour of the Danish club. Herr von Gossler, Minister of Public Instruction, and other distinguished persons were present, and followed the play with evident interest. The score for the Berlin club was – first innings, 46; second innings, 45; for the Copenhagen Club, first innings, 70; second, 99. The best score on the English side, 16 runs, was made by Mr. A. W. Thomson, while on the Danish side, Mr. Smart, the only Englishman in the eleven, headed the list with 31 runs.

Middlesex v. Somerset

23 *August* 1890. Tie matches are of such rare occurrence that the remarkable contest which ended at Taunton yesterday between Middlesex and Somerset will long be remembered. There was only the difference of a single on the first innings, and Middlesex, after appearing likely to win easily, were got out for 126. It is curious that Middlesex should have been concerned in two other

notable tie matches – viz., in 1868 and in 1876 on the Oval, against Surrey in each case. In 1883, on Kennington Oval, Gentlemen v. Players also resulted in a tie. There are, doubtless, many cases in cricket of less importance. Fine weather was experienced at Taunton on what proved to be the last day of the "Week," while the attendance was bigger than in any previous year. On Thursday evening Somerset had begun their second innings and had lost one wicket for four runs. Four batsmen were out for 20, but Messrs. Hewett, Roe, and R. Palairet played so well that the innings lasted until just before luncheon and realized 127, the number that Middlesex had to make for victory. The visitors lost two wickets for 28 – Messrs. Stoddart and Jardine. Rawlin, however, stayed while his captain batted vigorously, and the third wicket did not fall until 73. Subsequently 114 runs were recorded for five wickets, so that, as only 13 were wanted to win, there was every probability of the easy success of Middlesex. But Mr. Webbe, who had batted with great brilliancy, was given out caught at wicket, and then matters went badly with the metropolitan side. Mr. Henery was finely caught at mid-on, Mr. Ford was bowled, and Burton returned the ball. Nine for 125. Mr. Dauglish came in when two runs were required. These he attempted to make by one hit; in going for the second he lost his wicket, and, amidst great excitement, the result was a tie. Mr. A. J. Webbe, the Middlesex captain, scored 100 runs in two innings against good bowlers and on an indifferent pitch. He was unfortunate in being unable to gain the victory, but Somerset played very well, and their achievement against their formidable opponents will not readily be forgotten.

SOMERSET 107 (Mr. J. B. Challen 49; Hearne 8 for 55) and 127
MIDDLESEX 108 (Mr. A. J. Webbe 43; Tyler 5 for 64) and 126 (Mr. A. J. Webbe 57; Mr. S. M. J. Woods 5 for 61)
Match tied

Somerset were at this time a second-class county. They achieved first-class status as a result of their fine form in 1890.

George Parr

24 *June* 1891. George Parr, one of the greatest of English cricketers, died yesterday at Radcliffe-on-Trent. His name is almost a household word wherever the game is played. Parr made his mark early, and following his first appearance at Lord's in 1845, he took a prominent part in cricket for a quarter of a century. He succeeded Fuller Pilch as the leading batsman of the day, a position that he easily held for about ten years; and then in turn he gave way to such men as Hayward, Carpenter, and E. M. Grace. Parr was associated all his life with Nottinghamshire, which he captained for several seasons. Apart from this, he was manager of the famous All England

Eleven, and when this combination lost his influence it survived only a few years. Parr was a tremendous leg hitter. He lived in a day when bowlers were given to bowling on the leg side. Twenty years have elapsed since he dropped out of the ranks of important cricket. His very best season was in 1857, and one of his most notable feats was the 130 for Notts v. Surrey in 1859. Parr was born in May, 1826, and was thus in his 66th year.

Mr. Frederick Gale on Cricket

4 *July* 1891. Last night, at the Westminster Town-hall, Mr. Frederick Gale delivered a lecture "On Cricket," including his personal reminiscences of the game and of its votaries. In the absence of the Hon. Alfred Lyttelton, who is on circuit, the chair was taken by the Rev. Charlton Lane. On the platform were sketches of the old Bat and Ball inn at Hambledon, of the picture representing cricket as it was played in 1743, and of the different kinds of bats in use since the middle of the 18th century. Mr. Gale began with a brief review of the history of cricket, pointing out that the germ of the game was to be found among the Greeks and the Romans. One of its earliest followers in this country was Oliver Cromwell. For some time after the accession of George I, it was under a cloud; the Government were nervous in those Jacobite times about large crowds coming together, and the *Gentleman's Magazine* subsequently took up the cudgels against it. Of the hostility it encountered some indications might be found in "Waverley" and "Red Gauntlet." It might be described as a mongrel, since it came from rounders, club ball, hockey, tip-cat, and other ancient sports. As though to illustrate one point in the national character, its laws had been pretty much the same for 120 years, and the wicket the same since 1817. The lecturer then gave a description of a village cricket match 60 years ago, of old Lord's in or about 1841, and of the changes he had witnessed in the art and science of bowling. Incidentally he mentioned that Mr. Richmond, R.A., now in his 83d year, had been present at now fewer than 78 matches between the Gentlemen and the Players. Cricket grounds were now much better than they used to be; in fact, he thought that they had been rendered too easy, too much like a billiard table. The large difference made in the conditions by the institution of boundary hits was also dwelt upon. A vote of thanks to the lecturer – who, it is understood, intends to pass the rest of his life in Canada – was moved by the chairman, seconded by Mr. Harvey Fellowes (the once famous bowler), and very warmly carried.

England v. Australia

7 January 1892, *Leading Article*. After a series of victories over minor opponents the English cricketers in Australia have succumbed to a representative Australian eleven. For five days has this struggle of heroes gone on; for Australians have no prejudice against starting a match upon a Friday and ending it in the middle of the following week. Fortune first wooed the eleven commanded by DR. W. G. GRACE. They went in against 240, and topped that very formidable score by 24 runs. In the second innings the Australians made 236 – four runs less than in their first. The situation of our English champions – with 213 to get to win and a rather worn-out wicket to get them on – was trying to any cricketer with nerves. Where, indeed, is the cricketer who is proof against panic – the panic which sets in when a big score must be made, and the early batsmen fall short of what was hoped from them? At any rate, the English eleven, in spite of the fairly good example set by DR. GRACE, ABEL, and MR. STODDART, failed by 54 runs to reach the Australian score. Thus the great match is over, to be followed in the fulness of time, no doubt, by others, in which the temporarily dejected mother-country may hope to wipe out her defeat. In the first flush of mortification some may whisper that LORD SHEFFIELD's team does not represent the full strength of English cricket. Perish the unworthy excuse! LORD SHEFFIELD's eleven is very nearly, if not quite, the best that we could put in the field. It lacks, indeed, SHREWSBURY and GUNN; but it comprises DR. GRACE, who, upon the fast grounds of Australia, has quite regained his old freedom of play, ABEL, who ranks third in the list of batting averages for the past season, BEAN, who stands fourth, MR. STODDART, MAURICE READ, MR. M'GREGOR, and the five best bowlers that the mother-country possesses – LOHMANN, SHARPE, PEEL, ATTEWELL, and BRIGGS. On the other hand, the Australians may complain that we have robbed them of MR. FERRIS – not to speak of MR. MURDOCH and MR. SPOFFORTH. Our eleven represents English cricket as fully and fairly as any Australian team which has visited us of late years represented Australian cricket. Naturally the visiting eleven is always at a slight disadvantage; and perhaps it is as well that it should be so. Those at or near to the scene of one of these international struggles necessarily take a keener and closer interest in the result than a people thousands of leagues away. It would have been a grievous blow to the Australians to have been defeated upon their own soil; we Englishmen have suffered severely in spirit upon those rare occasions when our colonial kinsmen have beaten us upon our own dunghill. But it is impossible to feel so absolutely depressed when we have not presided at our own obsequies; when these are conducted in the Antipodes, and when bare particulars, stripped of circumstance and incident, are flashed over here by ocean cable. We can console ourselves in any case by reflecting that there is no finality about these contests. Neither side is utterly crushed. An indefinite vista of matches, belonging potentially as much to the vanquished as to the victors of to-day, stretches across the tracts of the future. Perhaps the popularity of this competition in national sport between the different parts of the Empire is worthy of the serious attention of statesmen. MR. J. ASTLEY COOPER'S proposal for the periodical holding of a grand Imperial athletic festival may not be as ambitious as an all-embracing scheme of Imperial Federation. But it is superior in one important respect, that, instead of imposing irksome burdens and fetters, it would foster a taste which the Anglo-Saxon race in all corners of the world cultivates with enthusiasm. MR. ASTLEY COOPER proposes rowing, running, and cricket contests. There is something fascinating in the idea of such a Pan-Britannic gathering, recalling the Pan-Athenian festivals of old. Its value might be only sentimental; but those who scan the field of politics, even colonial politics, see that sentiment is still a great power in the world.

The Lady Cricketers

16 *March* 1892. At the Lord Mayor's Court yesterday, the case of "Rowney v. Wood" came before the Assistant Judge (Mr. Roxburgh). It was a claim by Miss Agnes Rowney, one of the lady cricketers, to enforce payment of £11 from the defendant, who had taken over the lady cricketers as a financial speculation. At the trial of the action the plaintiff said that the lady cricketers went on tour of the provinces, and when the venture came to a standstill for want of funds the defendant stepped in and became virtually the proprietor, undertaking to pay the salaries of the girls. This the defendant denied, but the jury found against him, and the plaintiff now endeavoured to enforce payment. The defendant said that he was an agent and undertook all sorts of business, but he was doing none just now. He had an office in George-yard, Lombard-street, for which he paid 7s. 6d. per week rent. He lived at Kew in a house rented at £100 a year, but his wife paid that rent. The house was now being given up because he could not really afford to pay for the journey to and from the City. He had no means to pay the plaintiff: the case was really decided against him on perjured evidence. An order was made for 8s. per month.

The English Team in India

26 *December* 1892; *Bombay,* 24 *Dec.* Lord Hawke's team to-day sustained their first defeat since the commencement of their Indian tour. At the close of play yesterday the visitors had lost six wickets for a total of 51 in their second innings, and thus required 152 to win. Mr. C. Wright and Mr. Hill,

the not-outs for 14 and 17 respectively, to-day continued the innings, but the former was dismissed almost immediately without adding to his score. Mr. Foljambe then joined Mr. Hill, and runs came somewhat more freely for a time. The latter, however, was unable to improve matters to any extent, and was doing his utmost to avert defeat, but succumbed after adding 23. Mr. Maclean, the last man, contributed eight, and the innings closed for 93, thus leaving the home team victorious by 109 runs. The fielding of the Parsees was most smart, and frequently evoked loud applause from the spectators.

Cricket in Roumania

19 *June* 1893; *Bucharest*, 18 *June*. The Crown Prince and Princess of Roumania were to-day present at the first cricket match played here between elevens of Bucharest and Braila. Their Royal Highnesses were enthusiastically received. The Braila eleven won the game by 17 runs.

Cricket at Spitzbergen

17 *September* 1894. The following communication, forwarded to us by Lord Sheffield, will doubtless prove of interest to cricketers:–
    "The Earl of Sheffield and Alfred Shaw played cricket in August last at Spitzbergen, in lat. 77 20, at midnight. This is the highest northern latitude in which cricket is recorded to have been played."

Middlesex v. Gloucestershire

31 *May* 1895. At Lord's yesterday, the scene of so many of Dr. Grace's great cricket triumphs, the most wonderful player of our time achieved another feat marked by all his old excellence. From noon until nearly half-past 6 he was at the wicket, and then, being a little wearied by his hard work under a hot sun, in a declining light he was beaten by a ball from Dr. Thornton, which kept low and which he played outside. It must be something of a record even for Dr. Grace to make over a thousand runs in the first month of the season. By his 169 yesterday his aggregate for the ten innings played by him in a little over three weeks reaches 1,016. The champion seems to have taken a fresh lease of his cricket life. He seemed determined to make a big effort yesterday to get the thousand runs, and this and the fine bowling and fielding caused an unwonted steadiness in his play. Before luncheon he batted beautifully; but afterwards he was a little slow in getting back his game – in fact, for a few overs he played Mr. Nepean's slows very badly, and once or twice put the ball up dangerously towards the fieldsmen. Still, the

exercise of more care and his anxiety to reach the four figures did not make his cricket less attractive. There was all the old power in the drive and the cut, while few balls to leg escaped unpunished. Dr. Grace has played many a quicker innings; but the bowling and fielding were very good, and Hearne and Rawlin were especially difficult to score from. He made some bad strokes and narrowly escaped being run out midway through his innings. He was batting altogether for a little over five hours, and was ninth out at 362. An idea of his rate of scoring will be gathered from the fact that he made 50 out of 108 in an hour and a half; his 100 were scored out of 198 in three hours, and his last 69 occupied two hours and a half. He hit 21 fours, five threes, and 11 twos. At the different landmarks, so to speak, of the innings the crowd of 7,000 who had come up to Lord's were very enthusiastic, and when at last it was over the champion had a wonderful reception, the members in the pavilion rising to applaud him.

The early players of Gloucestershire all helped their captain. Mr. Kitcat stayed while 83 were added, and Mr. Dearlove, a Bristol cricketer of promise, contributed 23 towards the 73 put on for the fourth wicket. But unquestionably the brightest period of the day was the hour between 4 45 and 5 45, when Captain Luard hit brilliantly and made 64 out of 105 by nine fours, two threes, six twos, and singles. He was eventually caught at slip, being sixth to leave at 347. The last four wickets went for 19 runs. Some good catches marked the Middlesex fielding; but the most wonderful piece of fielding was when Mr. Webbe, running in from extra mid-off, caught Mr. Dearlove wide and low down with his left hand. Gloucestershire's innings took up the whole of the day. The home side are very strong; but the visitors are without Murch, whose bowling may be sadly missed to-day.

GLOUCESTERSHIRE 366 (Dr. W. G. Grace 169, Capt. A. H. Luard 64; Dr. G. Thornton 4 for 52) and 46 for 5 (Dr. G. Thornton 5 for 20)
MIDDLESEX 200 (Mr. G. F. Vernon 62; Mr. G. L. Jessop 5 for 88, Painter 4 for 42) and 208 (Rawlin 83, Mr. R. S. Lucas 70; Painter 8 for 67)
Gloucestershire won by 5 wickets

Grace's achievement – 1000 runs in May – was indeed a record, since equalled by Hammond (1927) and Hallows (1928). Four others have scored 1000 before June.

The W. G. Grace Testimonial

17 *June* 1895, *Leading Article.* The proposed testimonial to MR. W. G. GRACE has been taken up by the Marylebone Cricket Club, and may fairly be said to have assumed a national character. After communications between the Gloucestershire County Club and the central body at Lord's, the latter has appointed a committee, and, as we have already stated, has issued an appeal which, as it has good reason to hope, will meet with a cordial

response from those who take an interest in our national game, not only within these islands but throughout the British Empire. The opportunity indeed is unique. Not only has there never been a cricketer who, as batsman, bowler, field, and captain, is comparable to MR. W. G. GRACE, but while other great cricketers commonly disappear after ten years, or fifteen at the most, he has filled the foremost place for more than thirty years, and during the present season, at forty-seven years of age, has proved himself a more formidable batsman than ever. It is very natural that this should have touched the imagination of England, and that a characteristic expression should be given to what is a universal feeling. We are a testimonial-giving nation. As LORD BEACONSFIELD once said, we are an emotional people and we are at the same time a practical people; we admire, and we like to reward those who have aroused our admiration, and to reward them in a way that both we and they are likely to appreciate. Our spirited contemporary, the *Daily Telegraph*, was the first to apply this truth to the case of the champion cricketer, and we are glad to learn that the success of its "shilling testimonial" has already been great. Many thousands of shillings, many hundreds of multiples of shillings, have poured into its coffers, whence we presume they will be transferred to the common purse that is being formed by the M.C.C. The other local funds all over the country will go there too, whether the Gloucestershire fund, or those from other county clubs, or those which we assume are coming into existence in every town and village which possesses a cricket club and reads a sporting paper. London admirers of MR. GRACE had better send their contributions, large or small, direct to the secretary of the Marylebone Club, or to the account of the fund at SIR SAMUEL SCOTT's bank in Cavendish-square.

It is needless to say much of MR. W. G. GRACE and his achievements. His praise is in all the cricket clubs. For a month past his rejuvenescence has been the theme of all the dinner tables, the railway carriages, the public-houses, and above all, the public schools. Wherever English folk congregate, they have exchanged notes of admiration about the hero of a thousand fights and of a hundred centuries. He began making big scores at the age of fifteen, and went on doing so till over forty, when there came an apparent check, and when it seemed that the muscles were becoming too stiff for first-class cricket, and that the veteran would soon have to cease from active warfare. The present season has shown the public that they must not judge too hastily about the limitations of the powers of first-rate men; for during May, aided no doubt by the wonderful weather which made cricket a joy for batsmen and a purgatory for bowlers, he not only beat all other people's records, but his own. To score a thousand runs in a single month in first-class matches is an unheard-of performance, and, as though to make us believe that he could easily repeat it, on the very day of the publication of the Marylebone appeal MR. GRACE, in playing for that club against Kent, appropriately scored a hundred and twenty-five. It is scarcely surprising that performances of this kind, while they indicate that in certain respects the standard of the game itself has advanced, should also have contributed to increase its popularity. The thirty-two years of MR. GRACE's career have seen many changes, and notable among them is the immense growth in public favour of all amusements, and of cricket in particular. Those of us who are old enough to remember the days, we do not say of ALFRED MYNN, but of JACKSON, PARR, and LOCKYER, cannot fail to be struck, whenever they visit the Oval, with the difference between the scene presented now and the scene as they remember it. In those days, on a very great occasion, five thousand people might have been present; to see an ordinary match certainly not more than a few hundreds; but now the rising banks of seats are thronged, not with a fashionable crowd of the leisured classes who come to chat, to see their friends, and to show their toilettes, but with serious-looking men, whose whole minds through the long summer afternoons are set upon the critical watching of the game. Nor is this the case in London alone. All the first-class counties, and others which live in hopes of entering that charmed circle, have their almost faultless ground, their eager public, and their array of matches; and we need not say that the Universities and the great schools are more than ever nurseries of the game. If we were concerned to trace everything to its causes, we should place first among the reasons for this remarkable development of the love of cricket the general liberalizing of the standards of life which this last generation has seen, and, as a necessary adjunct to this, that development of the means of communication which lies at the bottom of so many of the changes that have come over the world during the past half-century. Fifty or even thirty years ago the British middle class, speaking generally, was still half consciously ruled by a survival of the old Puritan idea that amusements as such were morally wrong. Of course, it would not have admitted the charge if stated in that bald manner; it would have explained that amusements were not all wrong, but only that many of them were dangerous – the theatre and the racecourse in the first degree and others in a minor measure. Whether there was any justification for this half-instinctive fear of the seductions of this life we will not now discuss; it is enough to remark that in the case of the vast majority of English people it exists no longer. The most virtuous folk only draw the line at the racecourse. They go to the theatre whenever they can spare the money and the time. Church and Dissent alike encourage working lads to join cricket clubs and any other organizations that can give them health and pleasure. In a word, the old sharp antithesis between the good and the agreeable has faded away, and people have come to wonder how it could have existed so long. With regard to the popular love of national games, and especially cricket, this withdrawal of the veto, if one may so express it, has been followed by the growth of a positive passion, thanks to the publicity given by the sporting Press. The supply of news has created its own demand; the demand has in its turn stimulated the supply. All the school boys in England read the cricket news, and have at their fingers' ends the performances of GRACE and STODDART, of RICHARDSON and GUNN; and if the London clerk is often slack in his employer's service he is pretty sure to be a master of the last information about bowling averages and about the chances of the county championship. Summers like those of the jubilee year and of 1893 and such as that through which, to the ruin of our fields and gardens, we are now passing have their natural effect in the same direction; few can resist the charms of watching a cricket-match, with its almost certain episodes of great scores, on days like these.

All this makes it perfectly natural that, when England happens to possess a cricketer alike unrivalled for his performances and for his staying power, the country should wish to do him honour. Many would have been glad to see his name in the Birthday list, since Lord's is at least as national as the Lyceum and since a PRIME MINISTER who twice wins the Derby might be supposed to have a fellow-feeling for the man who has made the other national sport illustrious. Failing this recognition, that which was contained in the letter of the PRINCE of WALES was not without importance, and this action of the Marylebone and Gloucestershire Clubs and of our enterprising contemporary may be regarded as a kind of popular response. It is the practical English variety of the honour which many nations have conferred, not only upon their warriors, but upon such of their sons as have distinguished themselves in the contests of peace. The Greeks used to crown their Olympic victor – we can at least make ours comfortable. Even the champion cannot go on making centuries for ever; even his quick eyes, pliant hands, and iron muscles must before long feel the power of the insidious years. We trust that the present movement will have the effect of making a provision which, when the inevitable day of his retirement arrives, will cause him not to regret that he sacrificed, during the years of his prime, his profession to the national game, and was content to be, instead of a busy country doctor, the greatest cricketer in the world.

I Zingari v. Gentlemen of England

[BY G. H. WEST]

21 *June* 1895. The Zingari in a fitting manner celebrated their jubilee at Lord's yesterday when their side against the Gentlemen of England was one of the most brilliant that could well be got together. Mr. A. G. Steel snatched a few hours to visit once more the scene of his triumphs alike for Marlborough, Cambridge, Marylebone, and England, and he found himself in the midst of the flower of English amateur cricket. As for the Gentlemen, Dr. W. G. Grace, in consequence of county matches, was unable to command a strong bowling team. The very best conditions prevailed, and the condition of the pitch at

Lord's showed that the old ground could still furnish the best of batsmen's wickets. It was satisfactory to find that the public, in the rush for county cricket, have not wholly deserted the game when played without the feverish excitement engendered by the championship. The pavilion and members' enclosure were crowded as they have not been before this season, and the general cricket community was represented by a company some 5,000 strong.

The Zingari have rightly preserved the amateur traditions of their organization for 50 years. It is interesting to quote the following minute from their records having reference to the origin of the now famous club: – "In July, 1845, F. Ponsonby, S. Ponsonby, J. L. Baldwin, and R. P. Long . . . found themselves at supper at the Blenheim Hotel. They then and there formed a club, christened the same, framed rules, and the following day informed W. Bolland that he was perpetual president, and 20 of their friends that they were members of I Zingari." "Fred" Ponsonby (the late Lord Bessborough) was the central figure of the famous cricketing party, of which the majority are now no longer living. Tom Taylor ("the liberal legal adviser" of the club) and Robert Grimston (the hon. treasurer) were among the original members. Mr. J. L. Baldwin, the first vice-president, and Sir Spencer Ponsonby-Fane, also an original member, were both at Lord's yesterday; and the former received the hearty congratulations of his many friends in the pavilion. Sir Spencer Ponsonby-Fane, who is honorary treasurer to the M.C.C., is one of the most familiar figures at Lord's.

There was no lack of excellence in the cricket. When the Zingari went in first, it was thought, in view of the weakness of the bowling, that the last might not be seen of them by 7 o'clock. The way in which Mr. Hewett and Mr. Jackson started supported this view; but Dr. Grace's lobs effected the first separation, and then Mr. Fry and Mr. Burnup did nearly all the rest of the execution, and by half-past 4 the formidable Zingari were out for 289. The Gentlemen were lucky to dismiss them for this total; but it is one of the curiosities of cricket that a wonderful batting team will sometimes give way before moderate bowling. The secret, of course, often lies in the inclination of the batsmen to hit out at almost everything. Mr. Fry was especially successful with the ball. The batting honours were well distributed among the side. The longest partnerships were 75 by Mr. Hewett and Mr. Jackson, 56 by Mr. Stoddart and Mr. Mordaunt, 42 by Sir T. C. O'Brien and Captain Wynyard, and 59 by Captain Wynyard and Mr. Steel. These stands were respectively for the first, third, fifth, and seventh wickets, and all were the result of fine batting. Mr. Hewett hit ten fours in his 51 out of 75 in 70 minutes, and Captain Wynyard, whose driving was clean and of great force, made nine fours, four threes, and two twos. Mr. A. G. Steel's 38 was a well-finished innings, but a trifle cautious. The Gentlemen were batting from 5 o'clock to 7. Dr. Grace played excellently until he was quite beaten by a ball from Mr. Steel. Mr. Massie made his 26 in a quarter of an hour, and the other best things were the catches by Mr. Mordaunt in the long field and by Mr. Vernon at cover-point.

I ZINGARI 289 (Capt. E. G. Wynyard 56, Mr. H. T. Hewett 51; Mr. C. B.
Fry 5 for 75) and 293 (Mr. A. E. Stoddart 92, Capt. E. G. Wynyard 51; Mr.
C. B. Fry 5 for 102)
GENTLEMEN OF ENGLAND 411 (Mr. W. G. Grace jun 79, Mr. V. T. Hill
73, Mr. C. J. Burnup 66 not out, Mr. C. B. Fry 43) and 172 for 0 (Dr. W. G.
Grace 101 not out, Mr. A. Sellers 70 not out)
Score after first day: I Zingari 289, Gentlemen of England 148 for 5
Gentlemen of England won by 10 wickets

Somerset v. Lancashire

17 *July* 1895. Dr. W. G. Grace's record for a first-class match of 344 for
M.C.C. v. Kent, at Canterbury, in 1876, after standing for 19 years, has at
last been beaten, and to Mr. A. C. MacLaren, the old Harrovian, belongs the
honour. Mr. MacLaren yesterday, at Taunton, after batting all Monday and
well into Tuesday, made 424, so that he exceeds Dr. Grace's figures by 80.
Another record is also made by Lancashire, inasmuch as 801 is the biggest
innings ever made in county cricket; and it has only twice been exceeded in
first-class matches, the instances being the 843 by the Australians against
Oxford and Cambridge Past and Present, at Portsmouth, in 1893, and by the
Non-Smokers' 803 against the Smokers in 1887 on the East Melbourne
Ground in Australia. Yesterday, at Taunton, Lancashire, who on Monday
made 555 for the loss of three wickets, completed their innings for 801, after
eight hours' actual batting. Mr. MacLaren was seventh to leave at 792, when
a catch in the long-field disposed of him. He played splendidly from the time
he went in, and his success, following on his fine feats in the colonies with
Mr. Stoddart's team, will be universally esteemed. The highest individual
score ever made in any match was the 485 by Mr. A. E. Stoddart for Hampstead v. Stoics in 1886. In the present match Mr. MacLaren was batting
seven hours and three-quarters, and his best hits were one six, 62 fours, 11
threes and 37 twos. After Mr. MacLaren had gone the Lancashire innings
was rapidly finished. Somerset fared badly, and there was little in their two-
and-a-half hours' batting in the first innings and when they followed on
against 658 the score was left [at 58 for 1].

LANCASHIRE 801 (Mr. A. C. MacLaren 424, Paul 177, Ward 64, Mr. C. H.
Benton 43, Sugg 41; Mr. L. C. H. Palairet 4 for 133)
SOMERSET 143 (Briggs 4 for 59, Mold 4 for 75) and 206 (Mr. S. M. J.
Woods 55, Mr. G. Fowler 46, Tyler 41 not out; Mold 5 for 76, Briggs 5 for
78)
Score after second day: Lancashire 801; Somerset 143 and 58 for 1
Lancashire won by an innings and 452 runs

Robert Abel's Benefit

12 *August* 1895. The "gate" of the Surrey and Yorkshire match, which begins to-day at the Oval, will be devoted to the benefit fund of the Surrey professional batsman, Robert Abel. Abel entered the Surrey ranks at the beginning of the eighties, when the county's cricket was at a low ebb, and his great skill as a batsman has enabled him to keep his place to a time when the county is in its most prosperous years. While the rapidity of Surrey's rise to the foremost position has been mainly due to the development of wonderful bowling skill, beginning with Mr. Roller and Mr. Horner, and going on with Lohmann, Beaumont, Bowley, Lockwood, and the latest, and greatest perhaps, Richardson, the batting has also contributed its fair share, and for this Abel has worked with consistent excellence.

Warwickshire v. Yorkshire

9 *May* 1896. The fast wickets which are prevalent on most important grounds was yesterday productive of a gigantic score at Birmingham. Yorkshire beat all previous records for the highest score in an innings by obtaining 887. The previous best in first-class cricket was achieved by the Australian cricketers in their last tour on July 31, August 1, 2, and 3, 1893, at Portsmouth, when they ran up a total of 843 against Oxford and Cambridge Universities Past and Present. The highest score in any match was made by the Orleans Club, when their total was 920 against Rickling Green, in August, 1882. On the present occasion not only was the record for highest score beaten, but the individual achievements of the team are unprecedented, as four of them – Lord Hawke, Mr. F. S. Jackson, Wainwright, and Peel – all made three figures. There are many instances of three "centuries" in one innings, but on no previous occasion has there been four. Thursday night's position of 452 for seven wickets left no one prepared for the extraordinary feats of yesterday. But Lord Hawke and Peel (the not-outs with three and 37) carried the score to 740 before their partnership was severed. The full stand amounted to 292, this number being secured in three hours and three-quarters. Lord Hawke then played on. In his splendid innings of 166, in which hard driving was the characteristic, he made only one mistake, and that was a chance to mid-off with his figures at 151. The vigour of his play may be gleaned from the fact that he was credited with 21 fours, seven threes, and 13 twos. Peel, for a long while afterwards, found in Hirst such a useful partner that there seemed a probability of even a fifth individual 100. Profiting by an escape at 27 Hirst hit out freely, and had made 85 out of 136, put on in an hour and three-quarters, before Santall got him caught; his chief hits were 15 fours. Hunter's stay proved brief, and the innings closed for 887. Peel, who had gone in late on

Thursday afternoon when five wickets were down for 339, carried out his bat; in his 210, which had occupied rather less than seven hours, were 16 fours, 14 threes, and 17 twos, while he had one five (four from an overthrow). He was badly missed at slip with his score at 17, and there was a shade of a chance to mid-off when he had made 119. This is the best batting performance he has ever done for his county. The falls of the wickets in the innings are interesting. They were:–

1	2	3	4	5	6	7	8	9	10
63	124	141	211	339	405	448	740	876	and 887

The nearest approach to four hundreds in an innings was by Essex against Somerset last season at Taunton, when in a total of 692 Carpenter scored 153, Mr. C. M'Gahey 147, Mr. A. P. Lucas 135, and Russell 99. Ten bowlers were tried yesterday, and, as may naturally be concluded, the fielding became a little slack at times.

YORKSHIRE 887 (Peel 210 not out, Lord Hawke 166, Wainwright 126, Mr. F. S. Jackson 117, Hirst 85, Moorhouse 72; Pallett 4 for 184)
WARWICKSHIRE 203 (W. G. Quaife 92 not out; Hirst 8 for 59) and 48 for 0
Score after second day: Yorkshire 887
Match drawn

Oxford v. Cambridge

[BY G. H. WEST]

4 *July* 1896. If the honourable traditions of cricket are to be preserved there must be no more tactics such as those which were employed in the afternoon of yesterday, of all places at Lord's, and in such a match as Oxford v. Cambridge. Is it cricket to tamper with the natural course of a match? A great majority of the members on the pavilion, which was crowded, apart from the outside public, gave unmistakable signs of their opinion. And these were not favourable to the Cambridge procedure. Naturally Mr. Frank Mitchell, the Cambridge captain, wanted to adopt the course most likely to succeed; but his instructions to his bowler to send down no-balls in order to make up the Oxford score to such a number as would prevent the follow-on were far removed from the region of sportsmanlike conduct, and were hardly within the spirit of the game as generally understood.

The ninth wicket fell at 188, and Oxford were then within a dozen runs of saving the follow-on. Mitchell quickly grasped the situation, and, with his bowlers and field fatigued by nearly four hours' hard work, he saw that it was the interest of Cambridge to prevent their opponents from going in then a second time. So, no doubt under instructions, Shine, when Lewis came in, twice went over the crease and bowled two no-balls, both of which went to the boundary, and then from the next ball four byes were scored. When the crowd realized the tactics of Cambridge there went up a great shout of "Cricket!" "Play the game!" "Shame!" and other cries. The end of the innings came in the same over, Shine bowling Cunliffe. So Oxford had saved the follow-on. Many members in the pavilion joined very strongly in the demonstration of dissent at the action of the Cambridge men, and there was a round of groans for them instead of the usual cheers. There should not, of course, be any sentiment in the pastime; but keenness can be shown without breaking the bounds of honourable play. With the pitch showing signs of breaking, and with his men fatigued, the Cambridge captain strove to get the best of the wicket, and he allowed his keenness to override one of the first principles of the game. No doubt he will find the support of a great many people who think only of the means to secure success. But it is not cricket in its highest form. Mr. F. S. Jackson, in 1893, when the old rule of 80 was in force, adopted the same policy; but in that instance it was a case of diamond cut diamond, for the Oxford men were attempting to lose their wickets when Mr. C. M. Wells settled the question by bowling some wides in the neighbourhood of square-leg. This incident really brought the alteration in the law of follow-on. Such scenes as these of yesterday are not good for the village and small clubs who look to Lord's for their principles.

Mr. Mitchell's policy has so far attained success that Cambridge are in a very strong position. Already they are 271 runs ahead and have two wickets to fall, and after last night's rain Oxford will have to achieve no ordinary feat in the fourth innings to win, for the pitch is sure to be slow, and if there is any sun may be reduced to that condition known in cricket language as "sticky." Yesterday was a day full of exciting incidents. The breakdown of some of the famous Oxford batsmen – it is strange how cricketers of great repute fail in this match – the attempt of Mr. Leveson-Gower and Mr. G. O. Smith to save the side, the vigorous batting of Mr. Hartley, and the catch that got out the first-named were things that held the spectator until late in the afternoon. Then there was the furious bowling of Mr. Jessop, who seemed bent on maiming some one; his own wicket-keeper and Mr. Leveson-Gower were very badly knocked about, especially the latter, who was "doubled up" in one case, in another had a bad blow on the hand, and was hit in sundry places. This short stuff that Mr. Jessop was bowling was very dangerous, and he should have endeavoured to keep a better length. Mr. Leveson-Gower, however, is a model captain and cricketer; and, although so lame towards the close of his innings that he could not get forward quickly enough, he stuck to his batting for an hour and a half. Mr. Smith's 37 was a very fine piece of cricket. As if offended by the conduct by which Cambridge got the third innings of the match fortune seemed to veer quite round after this. Mr. Cunliffe's fine pitch and considerable break were too much for many of the Light Blues, four of whom he bowled out, while Mr. Hartley's slows were always a good length and were always difficult to play. But when Cambridge were going to pieces there came a brilliant innings by Mr. Norman Druce, whose beautiful style and power in the drive seemed to win back some of the friendliness of the company, who, after the "no-balls" incident, had received the Cambridge men and their performances in reproving silence. This batting of Mr. Druce turned the game once more for Cambridge, and Oxford's prospect of winning rapidly dissolved when the rain came at the finish. The fielding of the Dark Blues was as brilliant as ever, and whatever happens the match 1896 will often be remembered for this characteristic of the Oxford eleven. Young Mr. Grace had the misfortune to completely fail in batting, and Dr. W. G. Grace and Mrs. Grace, who were among the spectators on the grand stand, were quite grieved at the ill success of their son. Dr. Grace himself has never got a "pair" in his long career in important cricket.

There was a much larger attendance at Lord's yesterday than on the opening day. The figures ran from 17,000 to 18,000, and with the weather until late in the day bright the scene during the promenade was very brilliant. The auxiliary ground, generally known as the Nursery, presented a remarkable spectacle during the luncheon interval: for it was here that nearly all the picnic parties were mustered . . .

CAMBRIDGE 319 (Mr. C. J. Burnup 80, Mr. C. E. M. Wilson 80, Mr. E. H. Bray 49; Mr. J. C. Hartley 8 for 161) and 212 (Mr. N. F. Druce 72, Mr. E. H. Bray 41; Mr. F. H. E. Cunliffe 4 for 93)
OXFORD 202 (Mr. J. C. Hartley 43) and 330 for 6 (Mr. G. O. Smith 132, Mr. C. C. Pilkington 44, Mr. H. D. G. Leveson-Gower 41)
Score after second day: Cambridge 319 and 154 for 8; Oxford 202
Oxford won by 4 wickets

Reform of the follow-on law was demanded immediately but not effected until 1900. The margin for a three-day match was increased from 120 runs to 150 and, more importantly, enforcement of the follow-on became optional.

England v. Australia

Second Test

[BY G. H. WEST]

20 *July* 1896. At the end of the second day of the great test match at Old Trafford the English eleven appeared to be in a hopeless position; but on the third afternoon they almost had the game in their hands, and were beaten by only three wickets. It was a great victory for the Australians, and every one will be ready to congratulate them. Englishmen, with their rich resources of cricket, can well afford to be generous to their colonial friends in the matter of congratulation; for in matches, recognized as representative, the English

eleven have a great preponderance of victories [11 to 3]. K. S. Ranjitsinhji's batting and the bold attempt subsequently made by England to pull the match out of the fire made Saturday the greatest day of the match and the five or six thousand people who went up to the Manchester ground intead of seeing the expected easy win for Australia had a splendidly keen fight over which to grow enthusiastic. And the end might have been closer had a catch not been dropped when there were yet nine runs to win. The man who did most to rescue England from ignominious defeat was K. S. Ranjitsinhji, who in his not-out innings of 154 played in the course of a stern uphill fight, exceeded all the many other brilliant feats in his comparatively brief career as a cricketer. Some cricketers were, on principle, against the inclusion of Ranjitsinhji in the English side. The Marylebone Club committee thoroughly weighed the matter, and, while recognizing the wonderful ability of that cricketer, thought it scarcely right to play him for England against Australia. And Mr. Perkins, on behalf of the M.C.C., sent a letter to K. S. Ranjitsinhji explaining the reason why the M.C.C. did not choose him. But the Lancashire committee did not follow the M.C.C. precedent, and their policy proved immensely successful. Ranjitsinhji is playing cricket this season in a way that recalls to many Grace's great years in the seventies. The easy precision of his batting is wonderful, and he has developed that short-arm stroke on the leg side to a degree never before attained by any one. Brown, of Yorkshire, practises it at times; but with nothing like the consistency or success of Ranjitsinhji. In an innings of over three hours the Indian Prince scarcely made an ill-timed hit, and he contributed 154 to a total of 305, while in the double innings he was credited with 216. These figures fully demonstrate how ill England would have fared without him. He and Mr. Stoddart and Lilley were in fact the only English batsmen who can be said to have played up to their form. But on Saturday nothing could be said against the manner in which the Englishmen by their fielding and bowling strove to win the game. The fourth innings even with only 125 to score is a trying ordeal when there is so much at stake. And on Saturday the Australians, who had so far been playing a winning game, almost suddenly became involved in a hard fight for victory. How well Richardson and the others bowled, and how excellent was the fielding may be gathered from a simple statement of fact – at the end of two and three-quarter hours the Australians found themselves with seven men out for 100 runs and 25 more wanted. Fortune then fluttered back to the visitors, whom she never forsook for any lengthened spell in this match; and a dropped catch and a few small hits followed and the match was over. Richardson's pace and pitch were worthy of the great Surrey bowler, and were sustained for the three hours and 10 minutes which it took the Australians to make their 125. Throughout the match he did nearly all the hard work with the ball. The Lancashire executive should have made a much greater effort to have another good bowler in the side, and the fact that Lohmann, Mold, and Pougher were all too unwell for cricket does not wholly exonerate them from blame. It was the Australians' third victory over England since the institution of this particular match in England, played for the first time in 1880. The third and last of the test matches will be decided at Kennington Oval on August 10 and following days. It may be pointed out that the English score of 305 is the highest so far made against this season's Australian team as K. S. Ranjitsinhji's 154 is the first three-figure innings played against them.

The morning was dull, and rain threatened, when at 11 35 England renewed their second innings, in which four wickets were down for 109. So that 72 were still necessary to save the innings defeat. Ranjitsinhji, not out 41, and Brown started steadily to the bowling of Giffen and Jones. Brown soon began to score freely; but in his attempts to force the game he did not show much of that fine, clean batting for which he has grown famous, and, having made 19 out of 23 added for the partnership, he was easily caught in the slips. Five for 132 was the record when MacLaren joined Ranjitsinhji, who by careful batting ran to his 50 after a stay altogether of an hour and a half. Having got thoroughly set, Ranjitsinhji began to force the game in great style. He was very severe on Giffen, four of whose overs yielded 26 runs. But just when there was a prospect of a long stand MacLaren hit too quickly at a ball from Trumble and gave an easy catch on the off-side. With only four men left England were still two runs behind, so that their prospect was very bad. However, a change was at hand. Lilley, finding Ranjitsinhji doing so well, contented himself with steadiness. Ranjitsinhji when nearing his 100 went straight along, and he hit the bowling all over the field. He ran to his 100 in two hours and ten minutes, his last 50 having been obtained in 40 minutes. Lilley had a single increased to five by an overthrow; but soon afterwards, with Giffen back again, he hit a ball hard to short leg, where Trott brought off a wonderful catch; he knocked the ball up and caught it at the second attempt. Fifty-three had been obtained during the partnership. Ranjitsinhji went on forcing the game, and had some assistance from Briggs and Hearne; but the side were all out by a quarter to 2 for 305. Ranjitsinhji had a great reception on his way back to the pavilion. In his brilliant innings of 154, not out, he gave no chance whatever; he was batting rather more than three hours; and he hit 23 fours, five threes, and nine twos.

On their previous form the Australians, it was thought, would easily make the 125 necessary to win. But the fourth innings is nearly always a very difficult one to play. Iredale and Darling started to Richardson and Briggs. Neither batsman seemed very confident; but Darling got some lucky strokes away through the slips. Indeed, the runs were only scraped together. Hearne, who came on for Briggs, had a beautiful pitch, and could not be hit, and Richardson was bowling in great form. A ball from the Surrey man struck Iredale, whom he directly afterwards bowled. The first wicket fell at 20, and six runs later Giffen was beautifully caught in the slips by Ranjitsinhji, while at 28 a fine catch at wicket on the leg side by Lilley standing back got out Trott. England, with a prospect of winning, bowled and fielded with great brilliancy. The Australians played with care, and the score went to 45, when Darling also fell to the wicket-keeper. Gregory and Donnan stayed together some time; but the bowling was too good to be hit. Eleven overs by Hearne were actually sent down for four runs. The 50 had gone up in an hour and 20 minutes. Briggs came on again for Hearne, and at 79 he got Gregory caught at short leg for 33, a very fine score under the conditions of the cricket. With five men left, the Australians wanted 46 runs. Donnan was out at 95, and at 100 Hill was caught by the wicket-keeper. Only three wickets remained and 25 runs were wanted. Trumble and Kelly very slowly secured these; but when 12 of them had been made Lilley missed Kelly standing back at the wicket off Richardson. It was an irreparable blunder. So by 6 o'clock the Australians had won the match by three wickets.

AUSTRALIA 412 (Mr. F. A. Iredale 108, Mr. G. Giffen 80, Mr. G. H. S. Trott 53; Richardson 7 for 168) and 125 for 7 (Richardson 6 for 76)
ENGLAND 231 (Lilley 65 not out, K. S. Ranjitsinhji 62) and 305 (K. S. Ranjitsinhji 154 not out, Mr. A. E. Stoddart 41)
Australia won by 3 wickets

Killed in a Cricket Field

1 *August* 1896. At Potter's-bar, on Thursday afternoon, teams representing the Enfield police and the villagers were about to play their annual match, and three of the Potter's-bar men – Robert Finch, Alfred Bennett, and John Willmot – went into the field to have a litle preliminary single-wicket practice, Finch taking the bat, Bennett bowling, and Willmot fielding. Finch "skied" the second ball sent down, and his two companions ran to bring off a catch, but in their eagerness they came into violent collision, and Willmot's head struck Bennett under the chin. The force of the impact was such that both men came to the ground and neither was able to get up. Artificial respiration was tried, and various other remedies were applied, with the result that Willmot came round. Bennett, however, did not revive, and Dr. Fowler, who was hurriedly summoned, found that his neck had been broken by the shock of the collision and that he must have been instantly killed. The unfortunate man, who was a gardener, was 32 years of age, and leaves a widow and one child.

An Early Indian Writer on Cricket

[BY A. LANG]

24 *August* 1897. K. S. Ranjitsinhji is not the only nor the earliest Oriental sage who has made cricket the theme of his meditations. Mohummud

Abdullah Khan was first in the field with his "Cricket Guide" (Lucknow, 1891). The example before us is marked "First Edition." "I mean," says our Eastern author, "to entertain my readers with these few pages, that will decidedly be of great use and benefit to them." Mohummud is entirely successful in his project of entertaining us. He inculcates a cautious style of play from the beginning. "Even those who are very good and noble, say next door to angels, turn so rash and inconsiderate at certain moments." This is very well said; many a wicket falls, from inconsiderate rashness, and a desire to hit out of the ground. We have known Mr. Jessop himself to fail in caution. Temper, we learn, must be kept. It does not do "to seem in field as if treading on a volcano and even look daggers at their dearest friends and darlings." Thus, if the wicket-keeper is one's darling, one must not frown when he fails to take a catch.

The young Indian cricketer is a soaring human boy, who "aspires every breath of National Congress." But politics must here be excluded. The stumps, if properly pitched, "evidently prevent the ball from passing through," and, adds our author with Oriental subtlety, "give every possible sensation to the least touch or stroke felt by any consequence of the game." Here the delicate distinction between animate and inanimate nature appears to lose itself in a higher unity. As the poet makes Brahma say –

> I am the batsman, and the bat,
> I am the bowler, and the ball,
> The umpire, the pavilion cat,
> The pitch, the roller, stumps, and all.

So regarded, the stumps may be spoken of as feeling "every possible sensation." With a mild wisdom our author now warns the young reader never, on any account, to umpire when two elevens of his friends are engaged. But where "an out-station team" is playing, your side, at any rate, will stand up for your decisions. Avoid "ordering a batsman out, unless you are appealed to by the opposite party." "Each and every one of the umpires must avoid using insulting terms, or playing on bets, with any one of the fielders, or persons in general, in his capacity of being an umpire." As a man, he may do as he pleases; as an umpire, not so. To be objected to, and dismissed, is "very disgraceful and a cause of shame to the players, as well as to the umpire himself." There appear to be three creases at each wicket, the bowling crease, the return crease, and the popping crease. This is unusual. "Follow on" is also difficult. A scores 100, B only 20. "Under these circumstances A may not intentionally take the bat, but," says our mentor mystically, "nurse the idea of giving a dam and over defeat to B by allowing him to play the second innings as well, in order to make up and realize his score to the best of his exertions and endeavours." The technical term, "to nurse the idea of a dam and over defeat" seems peculiar to Oriental cricket, but probably contains no profane significance. "Two trial balls are only allowed in every match to each party." This, also, is an innovation, which, long ago, would have been very useful to Mr. G. B. Studd, when Mr. Evans's first ball nearly sent his bails into the nursery. "Behave like gentlemen when the game is over; avoid clapping and laughing in the faces of the persons you have defeated." This is excellent advice. Next observe the Oriental care for documentary evidence. "If you have any book to be signed by the captain of the opposite side, confessing his defeat by so many runs, please do it like men." The precaution is not usually taken in this country. As to no-ball, the umpire must call it "when not absolutely satisfied with the bowler's style of aiming the stumps," which, apparently are used as missiles. "It is no-ball when the bowler finding the striker out of his ground aims at the wickets to have him 'run out,'" and the case ends in any run or so, then the run is to be taken down as "no-ball." The "case" is obscure and the circumstance rarely occurs. But the batsman is out if the bowler hits the wicket with a throw, for you can be run out of a no-ball. Byes, we learn, only occur off no-balls and wides. What follows trenches on metaphysics.

"After the striker has made six runs, and you call 'Lost,' then there are only six runs in his favour; but if the striker has scored only two or three runs, and you say 'Lost ball,' surely he will receive $2+6$, or $3+6$, as the case may be." But who would call "Lost ball" in the circumstances? Not easier is this:– "If one of the strikers is made 'run out,' then the remaining one must not leave his wicket, unless next player comes in, and even then both the parties must agree to the proposal of the striker leaving his position in order to complete his innings." This rule is calculated to puzzle the M.C.C. The number of balls in an over "differ in different climates. In some parts of England they count only four balls to an over, while at others they take six," in accordance, obviously, with climatic variations in various parts of our island. But, in India, they "avoid extremes," and bowl five balls to the over. This sagacity deserves our imitation. "Devout lovers of the duty of umpiring call 'last but one,' at the fourth ball, a very common practice, although by mistake prevailing." The next aphorism is delightful. "During one and the same over the bowler is allowed to change his ends as often as he may desire, but he cannot possibly bowl two overs in succession." Thus Jack Hearne bowls his first ball from the pavilion, the next from the nursery end, the third from the pavilion, and so on, the whole field changing with each ball. The batsman's first duty is to collect his senses. "You are not going to face a cannon ball, but, on the other hand, you are going to examine your own ability and capacity as a striker." If applauded, "raise your nightcap a little;" they always play in nightcaps. "You must hit when needed, and block when possible." "Block some dangerous balls as they may come across your bat." You are l.-b.-w. "if the ball would, in the umpire's opinion, have hit the wicket;" a good rule for bowlers. As to wicket-keeper, "I would like this man to be of a grave mind and humble demeanour," though why he should be humble does not appear. Wicket-keeper faces long-stop "with the stumps under his arms." Point must be "of slender form," like Dr. W. G. Grace.

"He must take special care to protect his own person when fast bowling is raging through the field." "The fielders must never sting the player with tants, if they turn him out, for this often results in something disagreeable to human mind." Our author concludes thus, "Now, fare you well, my young readers. I am going to take leave of you, in order to finish this interesting petty work of mine on cricket game." Our mentor adds his date on the back of the cover; it is 1891. Probably he could, by 1897, make some changes in a work truly original, and, to cricketers, instructive.

The author of this article is, in all probability, Andrew Lang, journalist, man of letters and writer on cricket. Assuming the identification to be correct, "the poet" from whom he quotes is himself ("Brahma", after Emerson)!

The Marylebone Cricket Club

[BY ERNEST WARD]

1 *March* 1898. The secretaryship of the M.C.C. possesses an importance that extends far beyond the limits of the 4,000 membership of the club, and since the impending resignation of Mr. Henry Perkins became known late last autumn the extensive constituency of cricket has developed a keen interest in the chances of the many aspirants to the honour. The question was definitely settled yesterday at the Queen's-hall, Langham-place, where there gathered perhaps the most representative company of cricketers ever assembled. The floor of the large hall was crowded to overflowing, and the gallery had to be resorted to by many of the members. The full strength of the meeting was variously estimated at between 1,200 and 1,500. It may be at once stated that the first of the committee's recommendations, the text of which is given below, was carried unanimously:–

"That Mr. F. E. Lacey be elected secretary. The committee have gone carefully into all the applications, over 50 in number, for the post, and have come to the unanimous conclusion that Mr. Lacey is the most suitable candidate."

The executive of the club had been put to extreme trouble by a candidate whose claims had been passed over continuing to oppose the choice of the committee, and, in addition to a strong whip to the members generally, an appeal, signed, amongst others, by Lord James of Hereford, Lord Justice A. L. Smith, Sir R. T. Reid, the Hon. Alfred Lyttelton, and Sir Edward Grey, appeared in *The Times* of Friday last urging the support of the committee. This action was taken in order to avoid the consequences of a snatch vote, but at the last moment the opponent of the committee withdrew his candidature. Had this been done earlier great inconvenience would have been saved to many members who had come from all parts of the country to support the committee.

Mr. F. E. Lacey, the new secretary of the Marylebone Club, was a distinguished hard wicket batsman in his day at Cambridge, and there are many good judges who think that he should have been given his "blue" long before his last year. Since he came down Mr. Lacey has played for Hampshire, but only intermittently . . .

The proposal that a pension of £400 a year should be granted to Mr. Henry Perkins, the retiring secretary, was put by the president, who made appreciative reference to the 22 years' service Mr. Perkins had given to the Marylebone Club. In the course of his speech he stated that when Mr. Perkins became secretary the membership was under 2,000, and now it stood at considerably over 4,000.

The motion was unanimously agreed to, and Mr. Perkins was elected an honorary life member of the club.

The New Pavilion at the Oval

[BY ERNEST WARD]

30 *March* 1898. There has been a transformation at the Oval from the old irregular pavilion to the new palatial structure since Surrey towards the end of last August, playing perhaps their best cricket of the season, beat Lancashire, in spite of which result the subsequent course of events gave to Lancashire the championship. The old pavilion and the old tavern with all their cricket traditions have been swept away, and there now stands in their place a handsome red-brick pile of buildings which commands the admiration of all those who pass along the Harleyford-road to Vauxhall and the West-end. Perhaps the disappearance most regretted by old stagers is that of the old players' room, with its rickety staircase, long ago turned over to the cricket reporters for use as a luncheon room, the walls of which could have unfolded many a tale of the great deeds on the Oval in the sixties and seventies. Of course, the pavilion tablet recording how Surrey in one year long ago won the whole of its matches, including one against the champions of those times – Cambridgeshire – has been preserved, and will duly ornament the walls of the new big room. But apart from this everything has disappeared. And now the members of the Surrey Club have a palace wherein to dine and to watch and talk cricket. The Surrey executive have adopted thoroughness as their watchword; and the cost of the change, instead of being rather more than £20,000, is likely to be considerably above £30,000. Their action under the new conditions of the 30 years' lease from the Duchy of Cornwall at an increased rental from £99 to £750 was to a large extent compulsory. The new red-brick building, with Bath stone facings, has a frontage of 300ft. It much surpasses in its imposing nature its model – the Lancashire pavilion at Old Trafford, Manchester – and also the handsome red-brick and terra-cotta work at Lord's. Nothing has been allowed to interfere with the symmetry of the building;

and perhaps the Press, who hitherto enjoyed on the Oval their best view of the game in the kingdom, will be the first to raise an outcry about their position. But even if their view is less excellent than it was their convenience has been well studied in the way of comfort and in the important matter for evening papers of getting the work to the telegraphic department. Both inside and out the buildings are in a very forward state; but the contractors – Messrs. Foster and Dicksee, of Rugby – are greatly indebted to the openness of the winter for the advanced state of the works, for it is hoped that the place will be finished early in May. The first match (Surrey v. Derbyshire) is not until May 19. For the new tavern some 28ft. of the space in front of the old building has been absorbed in order to provide a better way between the pavilion and the hotel then that which by its narrowness was a source of constant danger in the old days of a big match owing to its getting continually congested by visitors wishing to get from the west to the east side of the ground. This alteration still leaves a good approach to the Oval gates by the curve which has been made. The best places for following the game have been given, and quite rightly, to the gentlemen engaged in the cricket; their dressing and sitting rooms command an exact end-on view of the cricket pitch, while the professionals have almost an equally good position. The Surrey committee are to be commended for striking out a fresh line in their thought for the players' comfort. The old professional box tacked on to the pavilion at Lord's is always an eyesore to many of the Marylebone Club members. On the ground-floor of the pavilion the secretary has a room commanding the whole of the ground, and immediately above him is the committee's place. The public have not been forgotten, and a spacious luncheon-hall has been constructed at the back of the hotel for their convenience. The only thing essential now is good cricket; and if this is not forthcoming this season it will be no fault of Apted, the ground man, whose keen interest in his work in looking after the turf has brought the Oval to better condition than it usually is at this season of the year. There is a fine growth of grass and not a weed is to be seen. In fact, only the last few days' severe weather has postponed the application of the mowing machine.

Gentlemen v. Players

[BY ERNEST WARD]

19 *July* 1898. Three years ago the whole cricket world was talking of the wonderful rejuvenescence of Dr. W. G. Grace, who had then completed his 100 "centuries" and every one rushed in to contribute to something like a national testimonial to the greatest cricketer of all time. The three summers which have passed since then have dealt kindly with Dr. Grace. The champion, as he is familiarly called, is still the cricketer of the day, and it was his

50th birthday and his 34th appearance in Gentlemen v. Players at Lord's that the thousands went to the M.C.C. ground yesterday to celebrate. Only the other day "W.G." almost beat Essex off his own bat and by his skill with the ball; and his form generally has been very good. Every one familiar with cricket must have Dr. Grace's great achievements at his fingers' end; how he played in Gentlemen v. Players at the age of 16, how he almost broke the hearts of the big fast bowlers in the seventies, how he has thrice achieved the feat of getting two 100's in the same match, and how he has more than once taken all ten wickets in one innings. It may almost be said that in Dr. W. G. Grace's career for the last quarter of a century or more is to be found the history of the game. And yet on his 50th birthday, not out of compliment, but simply he was indispensable, he was playing for the 34th year in succession in the Gentlemen's team at Lord's. In order to appropriately celebrate the jubilee of Dr. Grace the M.C.C. committee decided to defer their big test match until his birthday, and so loyally were the Marylebone Club supported by the counties that no other first-class fixture in any part of England was arranged for the first three days of this week. Everything was favourable for the match; the weather was worthy of July, and the wicket hard and true, and the elevens, if open to some criticism in the selection, were full of fine talent. It was therefore not surprising to find the crowd run to 20,000, for the public paying for admission alone was officially returned at 17,423. This record was, of course, exclusive of members – and the pavilion was very crowded – and others with the privilege of admission to Lord's. There is nothing of the social picnic element about a Gentlemen v. Players crowd at Lord's; everybody is earnest in attention to the game, and yesterday the huge company was enthusiastic in its reception of the great cricketer, though somewhat disappointed that the luck of the toss prevented them from seeing him at the wicket.

The cricket day was absorbed by the batting of the Players, who had not completed their innings at half-past 6, when, with a wicket to fall, they were 328 runs on. That the Players had to fight hard for their score was beyond doubt; but, though Dr. Grace made the most of his bowling, which was backed up by much excellence in the field, he could well have done with either Mr. Cunliffe, the Oxford captain, or Mr. Bull, of Essex, one of whom should surely have been given a place. But Mr. Kortright's great pace, the slows of Mr. Townsend, and the variable length and pace of Mr. Woods were quite enough for a majority of the Players. Gunn was really the stumbling block against the Gentlemen's triumph in bowling; and in his first half-hour he played neither Mr. Kortright nor Mr. Townsend very well, but when once set the great Nottinghamshire batsman was superb to watch. His lovely style, the fine wrist and forearm power which he got into the drive and the cut, and the delicacy of his placing on the leg side were worthy of the master that he is in batting. Then for those who liked it there was the more robust work of Storer, and later on came a dashing innings by William Brockwell, of Surrey. The keenness of the fielding kept the runs down as much as anything, and Mr. A. C. MacLaren deserves especial commendation; he had most to do, and he did his work exquisitely. Gunn's 139, it ought to be pointed out, is the highest individual score ever made in the Lord's match for Players v. Gentlemen . . .

PLAYERS 335 (Gunn 139, Storer 59, Brockwell 47; Mr. C. L. Townsend 4 for 58) and 263 (Storer 73, Gunn 56, Tunnicliffe 44; Mr. J. R. Mason 4 for 47)
GENTLEMEN 303 (Mr. A. C. MacLaren 50, Mr. F. S. Jackson 48, Dr. W. G. Grace 43; J. T. Hearne 5 for 87, Lockwood 4 for 82) and 158 (Mr. C. J. Kortright 46; J. T. Hearne 6 for 65)
Score after first day: Players 328 for 9
Players won by 137 runs

Lord Hawke and the Test Matches

19 *July* 1898. The meeting of county representatives to discuss the points raised by Lord Hawke in connexion with future matches between England and Australia in this country was duly held in the pavilion at Lord's ground yesterday afternoon. The Hon. Alfred Lyttelton, M.P. (president of the Marylebone Club) was in the chair, and the others present were Dr. W. G. Grace (Gloucestershire), Mr. John Shuter (Surrey), Lord Hawke (Yorkshire), Mr. S. H. Swire (Lancashire), Mr. W. Wright (Notts), Mr. A. J. Webbe (Middlesex), Mr. F. Marchant (Kent), Mr. C. E. Green (Essex), Mr. H. T. Hewett (Somerset), Mr. H. F. de Paravicini (Sussex), Mr. C. E. de Trafford (Leicestershire), Mr. Walter Boden (Derbyshire), Mr. W. Ansell (Warwickshire), and Dr. Russel Bencraft (Hampshire). The meeting was strictly private, but the following official statement was issued:– The first resolution – unanimously carried – was that the M.C.C. should appoint a board to govern future test matches between England and Australia at home. It was afterwards agreed:– "That such board be comprised of the president of the M.C.C., five of its club committee, and one representative from six of the first-class counties selected by the M.C.C. to send a representative. The president of the M.C.C. to have a casting vote." It will be seen that yesterday's proceedings were for the most part formal in character, all details as to financial and other arrangements in connexion with the test matches next year being left to the newly-established body. Lord Hawke, however, clearly carried his point in getting the test matches placed under the control of a specially constituted board.

Record Score

24 *June* 1899. The extraordinary score of 501 not out was made at Clifton College, yesterday, by a boy named A. E. G. [*sic*] Collins. He was playing in a house match for Clarke's-house v. North Town, and as the innings is not yet complete – nine men being out for 650 – he will have a chance to-day of still further increasing his score. Collins is only 14 years of age [*not until August*], and has so far been six hours at the wickets. He is the first batsman in the world to make five hundred runs in a single innings.

28 *June* 1899. A. E. G. Collins, the young schoolboy of Clifton College, who has been taking part in a house match, continued on various afternoons, got to the end of his innings yesterday by the dismissal of the last member of the side. He carried his bat through the innings of 833 for 628. He was at the wicket seven hours, and hit one six, four fives, 31 fours, 33 threes, and 146 twos. The previous best score was Mr. A. E. Stoddart's 485 for the Hampstead Club against the Stoics in August, 1886.

The Australians v. Sussex

31 *July* 1899. That most true of all grounds – the Hove, Brighton – remained kind to batsmen for the third day, when Trumper, one of the most skilful members of the Australian Eleven, established a record by scoring 300 runs not out. This is the highest individual innings ever played for or against the Australians in England, and, curiously enough, it was at Brighton that the previous best was recorded, when Mr. W. L. Murdoch made 286 against Sussex in 1882 which is generally acknowledged to be the year when the Australians had the most brilliant side ever sent to this country. It was the year that England lost on the Oval by seven runs. Trumper, although one of the last to be selected for this year's team, is one of the most accomplished of their batsmen. He comes down very straight on the ball, and perhaps, amongst a variety of strokes, his best is that by which he gets away a ball pitched on his middle and leg stumps. It is something of a Ranjitsinhji stroke, but it generally gets the ball well away in front of square leg. Trumper went in at 3 o'clock on Friday, first wicket down at 62, and he was not out with 300 to his credit when, at 4 o'clock, the Australians closed their innings at 624 for four wickets. He gave no chance until he was in his third hundred, when Marlow might have caught him at mid-off. Thirty-six fours, six threes, and 29 twos, were his chief hits. Sussex, going in a second time, began badly, but when Fry, Brann, and Ranjitsinhji had gone for 41 runs there was a stand by Killick and Collins that saved the match. The game was eventually drawn.

SUSSEX 414 (Mr. C. B. Fry 181, Killick 106; Mr. C. McLeod 5 for 91,
Mr. H. Trumble 4 for 75) and 143 (Killick 57)
AUSTRALIANS 624 for 4 dec (Mr. V. Trumper 300 not out, Mr. J. Worrall
128, Mr. S. E. Gregory 73, Mr. J. Darling 56 not out)
Match drawn

West Indians v. London County

12 *June* 1900. The West Indian cricketers, consisting of white colonists and
coloured players, opened their tour in this country yesterday at the Crystal
Palace. They were kept in the field the whole day, and at the close had not
dismissed all their opponents. Barton and Woods are both good bowlers, with
an excellent knowledge of pitch, spin, and pace; and the fact that they had
to make their *début* on a perfectly true pitch and against a splendid batting
side was a piece of ill-fortune. The visitors fielded well, and the catches of Mr.
Constantine and Mr. Cox in the long field were beautifully judged. It must
have been a little disheartening to the visitors that Dr. Grace and Mr. J.
Gilman made 136 for the first wicket. Dr. Grace played beautiful cricket for
his runs; on such a hard wicket he may not have come forward quite so much
as he did in his more youthful days, but his game was perfect. Mr. J. R.
Mason, the Kent captain, however, played the great innings of the day by
making 126 in a couple of hours. His off-driving was superb, and any leg ball
was easily dealt with. He hit 20 fours, and was eighth out at 381. There was
other good batting by Mr. Lawton, Mr. Murdoch, and Mr. Parkes.

14 *June*. The West Indians were beaten yesterday by an innings and 198 runs.
In less than a couple of hours Dr. Grace and Mr. Mason got the side out a
second time. The wicket helped the bowlers. The West Indians did their best
within a week of their arrival in this country, and no doubt they will play
much better cricket as they get used to English weather and the condition
of the grounds.

At luncheon yesterday in the Crystal Palace pavilion Dr. Grace took the
opportunity of publicly welcoming the West Indian team. Mr. A. Warner
thanked the Englishmen for their reception, and said that they had come to
learn cricket and he felt sure that whatever were their match results the trip
would be beneficial to West Indian cricket. Mr. W. L. Murdoch pointed out
in a very good speech that the same spirit of humility existed among the
Australians when they first visited England in 1878. He was sure that the
West Indians would as years went on develop their talent as Australia
had done.

LONDON COUNTY 538 (Mr. J. R. Mason 126, Mr. H. R. Parkes 106 not out, Dr. W. G. Grace 71, Mr. J. Gilman 63, Mr. E. H. S. Berridge 50, Mr. A. E. Lawton 46)

WEST INDIANS 237 (Mr. P. A. Goodman 74, Mr. P. J. Cox 53; Mr. J. R. Mason 5 for 50) and 103 (Mr. J. R. Mason 5 for 43, Dr. W. G. Grace 5 for 52)

Score after first day: London County 432 for 8

London County won by an innings and 198 runs

Oxford v. Cambridge

[BY ERNEST WARD]

6 *July* 1900. The University match was begun yesterday at Lord's under conditions in every degree favourable. The wicket was perhaps a little slow in the morning, but the ball came along at a nice easy pace, and after the luncheon interval the pitch steadily improved for batting. Cricket, like other sports, has suffered in its interest this season by the effects of the war, but yesterday the attendance in the later hours of the match must have exceeded 10,000. The weather was generally bright; but the promenade lacked some of its usual brilliancy.

With regard to the cricket, we are able to give only a few general observations. The Marylebone Club executive have recently shown much hostility to the Press at Lord's; and yesterday the cricket reporters were exiled from the grand stand to a position in the north-east corner of the ground, from which it was impossible to secure an accurate idea of the play. Our representative's application to the secretary of the club for a place where the game could be followed was met with a curt refusal.

The Oxford eleven were seen (by the more fortunate) to splendid advantage, for they not only made the highest score recorded in the annals of the University match, but Mr. R. E. Foster had the distinction of establishing an individual record. His 171 beat Mr. K. J. Key's 143, made in the Key and Rashleigh year of 1886. Yesterday was a great day for Oxford, for, following the superlative batting skill of Mr. Pilkington and Mr. Foster, the worn-out Cambridge bowling was severely treated by Mr. Martyn. The Cambridge men fielded excellently, but the fortune of war was unkind to them. The Oxford men were quick to appreciate their position. To begin with, they for a while did badly, and the catching of Mr. Champain at mid-off and of Mr. Knox in the slips made two wickets down for 22. Thereafter everything was for Oxford. Mr. H. C. Pilkington, who possesses a thoroughly Etonian style, never played better cricket; his cutting and off-driving must have pleased the most exacting followers of the R. A. H. Mitchell school. He and Mr. Foster made 168 for the second wicket, and Mr. Pilkington's hits included 13 fours. Mr. Foster was fourth out at 281 to a catch in the long field: he made 171 out of 259 in three hours, and hit 24 fours. He played a fine forward game, and his stroke in front of cover-point was tremendously strong.

7 July. The protests of the Press failed to make any impression on the august Marylebone Committee, and the reporters at Lord's yesterday were again left to gain the best impression they could of the play. It was impossible to get an accurate idea of the cricket from the new Press stand. The action of the Marylebone Cricket Club needs explanation, seeing how much benefit the club has derived from the Press.

With only small opportunity of following the play, we again confine our-selves to a few general remarks on the game. The Oxford innings was yester-day quickly over. Mr. Martyn was vigorous to the end, and his 94, made in less than three-quarters of an hour, included 16 fours. Cambridge were batting from just after midday until the drawing of stumps at half-past six. Mr. Moon hit hard and well; but the cricket of Mr. Wilson and Mr. Taylor was that most admired. Both played very soundly, and later in the Cambridge innings there was splendid work by Mr. Day and Mr. Dowson. These players prevented any danger of the follow-on. Mr. Day hit hard, and Mr. Dowson gave a fine illustration of forward and back play on a hard pitch. The follow-on was easily saved, and in the present position of the game a draw seems inevitable. The Oxford fielding was fairly good, but the bowling apparently lacked sting. It was a brilliant day for the game, and there was an attendance of over 10,000 people.

OXFORD 503 (Mr. R. E. Foster 171, Mr. H. Martyn 94, Mr. H. C. Pilkington 87, Mr. B. J. T. Bosanquet 42; Mr. A. H. C. Fargus 4 for 153, Mr. E. M. Dowson 4 for 163) and 219 for 6 dec (Mr. H. C. Pilkington 45, Mr. R. E. Foster 42)
CAMBRIDGE 392 (Mr. T. L. Taylor, Mr. E. M. Dowson 65, Mr. L. J. Moon 58, Mr. S. H. Day 55, Mr. E. R. Wilson 45) and 186 for 2 (Mr. L. J. Moon 60, Mr. J. Stanning 60)
Score after first day: Oxford 480 for 8
Score after second day: Oxford 503, Cambridge 358 for 8
Match drawn

10 July. The following statement has been issued by the M.C.C. Committee with a request for publication:–

Complaints having been made by the Press as to the accommodation pro-vided for their representatives in the grand stand, and the number of such representatives having now reached upwards of 40, the committee of the M.C.C. provided the present stand with seats to accommodate that number.

A portion of the building has during the 'Varsity match been occupied and warmly approved by old cricketers of high standing. No other stand to accommodate so large a number of representatives of the Press is in the existing conditions possible. Further consideration to the matter, however, will be given by the committee with the object of giving the Press, if possible, even better accommodation in the future.

For the Gentlemen v. Players match on 16–18 July the Press returned to the grand stand and in 1901 a new Press box was built.

Mr. Richard Daft

19 *July* 1900. All cricketers will learn with regret of the death yesterday morning at his home, Radcliffe-on-Trent, of the famous Notts cricketer Richard Daft. Born on November 2, 1835, he was in his 65th year. His career in public matches which began in 1858, came to an end in 1881, but ten years later he reappeared for Notts in one match, playing against Surrey at the Oval on the August Bank Holiday. He began and finished as an amateur, but from 1859 to 1880 inclusive he played as a professional. In his young days he divided honours as a batsman with the late Tom Hayward and Robert Carpenter, and at the beginning of the '70's he had no superior except Dr. W. G. Grace. In his own opinion the best innings he ever played was 118 for North against South at Lord's in 1862 in James Grundy's benefit match, but this was only one of many fine displays that he gave. It was probably no better than his 111 not out against George Freeman's bowling at Manchester for the All England against the United All England eleven in 1867. The biggest score he ever made in first-class cricket was 161 for Notts against Yorkshire at Trent Bridge in 1873. Daft was always a master of style in batting, standing up to his full height, and was equally good to look at whether he scored fast or slowly. Like Carpenter, he was a back player, but the methods of the two men were in strong contrast, Carpenter playing so much lower. Whether or not Daft at his best was as fine a bat as his successors in the Notts eleven Shrewsbury and William Gunn is quite a matter of opinion, but in making comparisons it must always be borne in mind that the wickets in Daft's day were by no means so true and easy as they are now and that as a natural consequence scores all round were much smaller.

England v. Australia
Fourth Test Match

[BY ERNEST WARD]

28 *July* 1902. Australia won an extraordinary match at Old Trafford, Manchester, on Saturday, by three runs. The result was the more surprising as at one period the Englishmen seemed to have the match in hand. But the Australians played a fine uphill game, and their bowlers were supreme. Mr.

Trumble's length and Mr. Saunders's pitch and break were wonderful. England had the game in their hands before luncheon, and the 100 went up with only five men out. But then the side collapsed. The wicket certainly helped the bowlers, but it looked as if the Englishmen should have won quite easily. Mr. Darling seemed to upset the whole English side by the placing of his field. He got his men close in, even for such forcing players as Mr. Jackson and Mr. MacLaren, and his bowlers kept up too good a length to be hit. The Englishmen seemed to become afraid. Instead of going forward and hitting the bowlers off their pitch, they played back cautiously at everything. Mr. Trumble and Mr. Saunders were remarkable in their break and length, and the Englishmen, having once dropped their game, could not recover it. The occasion was too much for them, and it was quite pitiful to see such a splendid side going to pieces in the way they did. In fact, England failed as they did at the Oval 20 years ago in the game of 1882. They made a splendid start, and, after getting the game quite in their hands, lost it. The Australians have now won the rubber of the test matches, but no doubt the Oval match in August will attract great attention. The executive of the Lancashire County Club are to be congratulated on the excellent arrangements they made for the comfort of the 20,000 spectators of the match on Saturday.

After the heavy night's rain the umpires, Moss and Mycroft, considered the pitch unplayable for an hour after the arranged time. The game was renewed at mid-day, when Mr. Trumble and Mr. Kelly, the not-outs, went on with the batting. The wicket was very soft, and a foothold was difficult to get. Rhodes sent down a maiden to Mr. Kelly, and then from the last ball of Tate's first over at the other end Mr. Trumble was leg-before, a decision of Moss's that met with much apparent dissatisfaction from the batsman. Nine wickets were down for 85. Mr. Saunders joined Mr. Kelly, and after four maidens had been sent down Mr. Kelly got a single, and then Rhodes got Mr. Saunders caught in the long-field by Tyldesley, a beautifully judged catch. Rhodes had immediately before appealed for a return catch, but Moss, umpiring at short-leg, gave the batsman in. The balance of the innings had lasted 20 minutes for the odd single. Lockwood's bowling figures were unaltered from those given in *The Times* of Saturday, but Tate finished with a good analysis, making amends to some extent for missing Mr. Darling on Friday.

England wanted 124 to win, and went in at 20 minutes to 1. Mr. MacLaren and Mr. Palairet started with great care. The English captain soon seemed at home and got rid of some very difficult bowling. Mr. Noble and Mr. Trumble bowled superbly, and the score was still only 12 at the end of half an hour. Mr. Noble once quite beat Mr. Palairet, the ball coming along at a great pace and just missing the off stump. In the next over from Mr. Trumble, Mr. Palairet made a bad stroke to short-leg (Mr. Gregory just missed it) and Mr. MacLaren, after being appealed for leg-before, drove Mr. Trumble almost to the boundary, but the ball was well fielded by Mr. Duff just in front of the screen. After this there was no particular incident in the cricket for a few overs. The score was up to 24 at the end of half an hour, when Mr. Darling changed his bowling and put on Mr. Saunders at Mr. Noble's end. There were some clever short runs. The wicket was helping the bowlers tremendously and Mr. Trumble and Mr. Saunders were keeping a fine length and getting much work on the ball. Mr. Palairet was nearly caught at short-leg by Mr. Gregory, who made a great effort to get to the ball with his right hand and fell in making the attempt. Mr. MacLaren and Mr. Palairet showed courage and resourcefulness, and, although constantly beaten, they struggled on to 36, as the result of 50 minutes' batting before luncheon. With the weather threatening England still wanted 88 to win.

After luncheon Mr. Trumble started the bowling from the lower end, and from the fifth ball of the over Mr. MacLaren made a drive to the boundary. At 44 Mr. Palairet was bowled by a break-back from Mr. Saunders. Tyldesley came next, and then Mr. Trumble, who was getting a lot of work on the ball, nearly got Mr. MacLaren caught at short-leg by Mr. Gregory. Tyldesley made a beautiful cut for four from Mr. Saunders, and got a clever single on the leg side. The 50 was reached in just over an hour, by means of a clever stroke by Tyldesley to leg. Mr. MacLaren made a grand drive for four from Mr. Saunders, and was then twice beaten without the ball hitting the wicket. Mr. Trumble overpitched one to Tyldesley that was promptly hit for four. But with the field well placed on the leg side there were some narrow escapes. Tyldesley was caught at short-slip at 68, getting forward to a short one. There was a great cheer for K. S. Ranjitsinhji, but almost directly Mr. Mac-Laren, who had been batting for more than 75 minutes, was out to a well-judged catch at long-on. Three for 72. Abel was next in and the score was speedily taken to 76, when a sharp shower drove the cricketers to the pavilion for a quarter of an hour. England had now only 48 to get with seven wickets left, and the wicket was scarcely affected by the rain. Mr. Trumble and Mr. Saunders were the bowlers. Abel got a couple of pretty strokes on the leg side for two each, and then getting to the other end he got two nice hits from Mr. Trumble, who, with a beautifully placed field, tried to get him at long-on. Abel hit hard, and the ball each time cleared Mr. Duff. K. S. Ranjitsinhji was not at home, and shortly afterwards was leg-before to Mr. Trumble at 92. Mr. F. S. Jackson had a splendid reception. At 97 Abel hit across at a break-back from Mr. Trumble and was bowled. Five for 97. The pitch was now obviously helping the bowlers and the fielding was strong. The 100 had gone up, but the ball was very difficult to get away. Mr. Saunders sent down a couple of maidens and then came a lucky three through the slips to Braund. The score reached 107, and then Mr. Jackson hit too quickly at a full pitch and gave mid-off an easy catch. Lilley came in next, England wanting 27 to win. Braund got a fluky three in the slips that fell just short of Mr. Armstrong. At 109 Braund was beautifully stumped. Rain then began to fall. Mr. MacLaren had been saving Lockwood for emergencies; and the famous old Surrey player was very much cheered when he went in. Mr. Trumble, after an ineffectual appeal for leg-before, bowled him completely, leg stump, with the third ball, and eight wickets were down for 109. Rhodes came next, and hit a short one from Mr. Saunders over the ropes. Lilley was missed being run out through a bad return by Mr. Hill, but in the same over the latter secured him by a grand catch at deep square-leg. Nine for 116. A heavy shower drove the players to the pavilion, and there was no more play for three-quarters of an hour. Tate, the last man, hit the first ball he had from Mr. Saunders for four, but in the same over his off stump was bowled down, and amid great excitement Australia won the game by three runs.

> AUSTRALIA 299 (Mr. V. Trumper 104, Mr. C. Hill 65, Mr. R. A. Duff 54, Mr. J. Darling 51; Lockwood 6 for 48, Rhodes 4 for 104) and 86 (Lockwood 5 for 28)
> ENGLAND 262 (Hon. F. S. Jackson 128, Braund 65; Mr. H. Trumble 4 for 75) and 120 (Mr. H. Trumble 6 for 53, Mr. J. V. Saunders 4 for 52)
> *Australia won by 3 runs*

England v. Australia

Fifth Test Match

FROM OUR SPECIAL CORRESPONDENT [R. H. LYTTELTON]

14 *August* 1902. Whatever may be said about the unsatisfactory weather that cricketers have experienced this season, the year has produced two struggles that can never have been surpassed for excitement. England has lost the rubber, but her defeat at Manchester and her victory at the Oval will never be forgotten, and both were much to her credit.

Every batsman on his way to the wicket yesterday felt that on his success or failure depended the fate of the match. In other words, the match was always in a critical position, and every run had to be fought for. The bowling of Mr. Trumble could not have been better. Every variety of pitch and break back seemed to be at his command, and he never sent down a ball of bad length. In this he was a very different bowler from Mr. Saunders, who bowls a very difficult ball, but many very bad ones – of such bad length that a child would score from them. Mr. Trumble bowled from the pavilion end from half-past 11 in the morning until 4 in the afternoon. He was never taken off, nor was his bowling once collared in an innings of 263.

At the end of the second day's play Australia were 255 runs ahead with two wickets in hand. No rain had fallen in the night, but it was generally thought that the wicket would be slow and easy. There was, however, a heavy dew, and the wicket up to luncheon time was very difficult and never became easy all day. Only seven runs were added to the Australians' score. Indeed, the Australians may be said to have lost the match chiefly by their failure in batting on the second day when the wicket was not difficult. As at Manchester, they collapsed in a way that was unworthy of a strong batting side. Lockwood's five wickets cost only 45 runs – a very good performance.

At 11 35 England began the last innings on a wicket that appeared made to suit the Australian attack, and the first three wickets fell for ten runs. The chances were quite four to one on Australia at this stage, and six to one when the fifth wicket fell at 48. The batsmen did not play well, but there was every excuse on such a wicket and against such bowling. But Mr. Jackson was still in, and wonderfully free was his play. To him is due, to a very large extent, England's victory. On five occasions in the last five test matches has Mr. Jackson had to go in at a critical moment for his side, and only once did he fail. There is no batsman in the world whose nerve is so surely to be relied on. When he was joined by Mr. Jessop the great stand that paved the way for victory was made. Up to lunch time the wicket was so difficult that nobody could have felt surprised if either batsman had got out; but they stayed in and brought the score to 87, though Mr. Jessop appeared to give a chance of stumping, and was missed by Mr. Trumper off a difficult chance in the long field. Runs came far faster after luncheon, Mr. Jessop putting in some of his finest work, while Mr. Jackson was content to take things steadily. Too much use was made of Mr. Saunders, who was now bowling a very bad length and was freely punished by Mr. Jessop. Three full pitches and one long hop were bowled consecutively, and 17 runs were scored from one over. Mr. Jackson was then caught and bowled by Mr. Trumble for 49, after an hour and 40 minutes' first-rate batting. The match appeared to be lost when he left. Hirst came in next and he, Mr. Jessop, and Mr. Jackson were the three heroes of this famous innings. It must, however, be confessed that Hirst looked very like being l.-b.-w. to Mr. Trumble almost immediately after he went in. Mr. Jessop continued his hitting, and sent Mr. Trumble twice in an over into the pavilion. Mr. Armstrong relieved Mr. Saunders, and was vigorously hit by Hirst. But Mr. Jessop must have longed for Mr. Saunders again. He could not hit Mr. Armstrong's leg balls with a little break on in his usual style, and the new bowler got him caught at short leg. Seven wickets were now down for 187, and 76 runs were still wanted. Mr. Jessop has accomplished several very wonderful performances in his life, but has frequently, both here and in Australia, failed against the colonial bowling. But as long as cricket history lasts will this great performance be remembered. He ran risks, as every man must who makes more than a run a minute, but he only gave two chances, and one of them was very difficult. He completely demoralized Mr. Saunders. His wonderful success must have been a great cause of rejoicing to those who, in spite of so many failures, have urged his claim to represent England; and all these failures will be forgotten long before this great feat of fierce hitting against first-rate bowling and fielding and on a difficult wicket. Out of 139 runs scored while he was in 104 came from his bat. On several occasions during this innings the prospects of England looked well, but, as so often happens, at a critical moment a wicket fell. Mr. Jackson, Mr. Jessop,

Lockwood, and Lilley all got out just when the chances might have veered round in England's favour. Seventy-four runs were wanting when Lockwood went in, 49 when Lilley succeeded him, and 15 when Rhodes, the last man, came out of the pavilion. All these men played with nerve, but Hirst was the real hero. Nothing seemed to put him out. Indeed, he played with more confidence than in the first innings, and his hits were hard and along the ground. Lockwood stayed while 27 runs were scored, but his share was only two. Lilley got 16 out of 34 by good batting, but was dismissed by a good catch by Mr. Darling at mid-off. Rhodes then came in, and it is not likely that he will ever again have to face a more trying ordeal. Nobody could have risen to the occasion better. Hirst went on the even tenor of his way, and Rhodes stopped the straight balls and judiciously left alone the rising off balls from both Mr. Trumble and Mr. Noble. And thus the runs were slowly hit off, Rhodes making the winning hit amid a scene of excitement that can never be forgotten. Mr. Darling is so experienced a captain that it may seem presumptuous to wonder why he was so unwilling to make use of Mr. Noble's bowling, but he undoubtedly was wise to keep on Mr. Trumble all the time. In the whole match Mr. Trumble bowled 65 overs for 12 wickets at a cost of 14 runs each – a splendid performance.

When all the conditions under which these last two test matches were played are considered, it must be conceded that it was a wonderfully fine feat of England's to lose the first match by only three runs and to win the second by one wicket. Several good judges yesterday said that for England to get 200 runs on the wicket would be a very fine performance, and they got 263. The Australians threw no chances away, and their fielding and throwing were magnificent, Mr. Hopkins especially doing grand work. But Englishmen may justly claim for their side superiority in batting on a bowlers' wicket, though, with the exception of Mr. Jackson, no batsman shows the skill of Shrewsbury and other great batsmen of former years. Until this season the Colonials have not had much practice on bowlers' wickets, but the blot on their escutcheon is their collapse in batting on the second day both at Manchester and at the Oval. In both cases the Englishmen had the same wicket to play on; perhaps it was a trifle more difficult, but their batting was better. It may be that the fall of Mr. Trumper on both these occasions demoralized the side; and this need not be a matter for surprise, for such things are common, and Mr. Trumper is the greatest bat in the world.

In this last match Australia had the advantage of occupying the wickets the whole of the first day, the only period when run-getting and batting were easy. Notwithstanding this fact, the English side, who never once in the match had anything but a difficult wicket to bat on, won the match; and this more than redeemed their reputation. The Australians, however, have won the rubber, and hearty congratulations must be given to them. They may have had the best of the luck, but this is part of the game, and every true sportsman will give them the credit of being the better side.

AUSTRALIA 324 (Mr. H. Trumble 64 not out, Mr. M. A. Noble 52, Mr. V. Trumper 42, Mr. A. Hopkins 40; Hirst 5 for 77) and 121 (Lockwood 5 for 45)
ENGLAND 183 (Hirst 43; Mr. H. Trumble 8 for 65) and 263 for 9 (Mr. G. L. Jessop 104, Hirst 58 not out, Hon. F. S. Jackson 49; Mr. V. Saunders 4 for 105, Mr. H. Trumble 4 for 108)
England won by 1 wicket

Arthur Shrewsbury

20 *May* 1903. Arthur Shrewsbury, the famous Notts batsman, committed suicide at Gedling, near Nottingham, last night by shooting himself. His indifferent health had occasioned anxiety for some time. He had been under treatment locally for a return of an old internal complaint and had become very despondent, although he had the assurance of his medical adviser that there was no organic disease. Upon the advice of friends he went to London about a month ago, and stayed for a brief period at a nursing home, returning then to the residence of his sister at Gedling. He committed suicide with a five-chambered revolver. One bullet penetrated the left side of the chest, and, this not being effective, he turned the weapon to his right temple, death from the latter bullet proving almost instantaneous. He was fully dressed at the time, having been out an hour or so previously.

Shrewsbury was born on April 11, 1856, and made his first appearance at Lord's for the Colts of England against the M.C.C. and Ground in 1873. Even as a lad of 17 he had given proof of exceptional ability, and no doubt was entertained in Nottingham that he would develop into a county player. For the Colts at Lord's he did nothing out of the common, scoring four and not out 16, but the way in which he got his runs and his finished style of play made a strong impression. A few weeks before, for the Colts of Notts against the County Eleven at Trent Bridge, he had headed the scoring with an innings of 35. By reason of ill-health he did little or nothing in 1874, but the following year found him a regular member of the Notts eleven, and in 1876 he made his first hundred in a big match, scoring 118 for Notts against Yorkshire at Trent Bridge. In May, 1877, he made 119 for the Players of the North against the Gentlemen of the South at the Oval, this being his first hundred on a London ground; and his position among the leading batsmen of his time was then assured. Still, though everybody recognized his ability, he did not in these early days obtain anything like the number of runs he has made during the last 20 years. Over and over again he showed fine cricket, but it could not be said that he was a great scorer. The turning-point of his career came when, in the winter of 1881-82, he paid his first visit to Australia with the team selected and managed by himself, Alfred Shaw, and James Lillywhite. He was in bad health when he left England, being, indeed, too unwell to journey from Nottingham with the rest of the team; but the sea voyage and the Australian climate set him up, and from that time forward his career was one of almost unbroken success. In this first Australian trip he did very well, coming out second to the late George Ulyett in the batting averages in eleven aside matches; and when he came back to England he was a different man, being much stronger and more robust than he had ever been before. In 1882, for Notts against Surrey, in the August Bank Holiday match at the Oval, he played an innings of 207, and from that day he was by general consent the first professional batsman in England. Going on from success to success, he reached his highest point in 1887 – a summer of brilliant weather – when he played eight innings of over 100 in first-class matches, and had for the whole season the extraordinary average of 78. In the previous year, 1886, however, he played an innings which he himself always considered the best of his life – 164 for England against Australia, at Lord's. That innings, played against the bowling of Palmer, Spofforth, Garrett, Evans, and Giffen, on a wicket that during the first afternoon varied in pace from hour to hour, was indeed a masterpiece of batting. After the season of 1887 he paid his fourth visit to Australia, and did great things, scoring 232 against Victoria, at Melbourne, and 206 against All Australia, at Sydney. Remaining in the Colonies to look after a football team, he was absent from English cricket in 1888; but he was back again the following year, and played regularly till the end of 1893. In this last season he had another great triumph for England against Australia, at Lord's, scoring 106 and 81. In 1894 he played no first-class cricket; but he reappeared for Notts in 1895, and continued to assist his county regularly up to the end of last summer. Last year he headed the Notts batting with an average of 52 and an aggregate of 1,153 runs, and for the first time in his career made two separate hundreds in one match, scoring 101 and not out 127 against Gloucestershire, at Trent-bridge.

The characteristics of Shrewsbury's batting were too well known to need any detailed description. Wonderfully strong back play in a style peculiarly his own and perfect timing accounted mainly for his extraordinary success. No one ever had a more accurate judgment of the length of bowling, the certainty with which he scored on the on side from anything like a short-pitched ball being astonishing. When at his best – that is, between 1888 and 1893 – he had certainly no equal either in England or Australia on a wicket rendered treacherous by rain. It must be said against him that he had much to do with popularizing the leg play which has been so much indulged in during the last 20 years, and he was always a batsman to save rather than to win a match; but apart from this his batting left no room for fault-finding.

Table Cricket

11 *November* 1903. Yesterday, at Wisden's showrooms, Dr. W. G. Grace and Mr. A. Weintrand gave an exhibition of a greatly improved form of the game of table cricket. The game has been invented by Mr. Weintrand, with additions and rules by Dr. Grace, and is suitable either to the house or the garden. The wickets, which are, of course, of a very small size, are placed on a table, and a popping crease is marked out. The bowler delivers a ball, rather larger than the ordinary racket ball, from an instrument provided with a strong spring which he holds in his hand. This instrument has been cleverly devised, and the bowler, with practice, can alter the pace of the ball and get on a considerable amount of break either from the off or the leg. The batsman may play either with one or both hands; for a defensive game the latter method is the easier, but greater force can be put behind the ball when only one hand is used. Fieldsmen are placed in convenient positions, and the batsman can be out in almost all the nine ways known in cricket. The scoring can be varied at will, and, if the game is played out of doors, the batsman can run his runs in the ordinary way. The game combines amusement with a good deal of real skill. With beginners the batsman certainly has an advantage, but when the method of delivering the ball has been thoroughly learnt the bowler, if anything, holds the upper hand.

The First Test Match

18 *December* 1903, *Leading Article*. The English eleven in Australia have followed up their early successes by winning the first of the test matches by the substantial margin of five wickets. The match will be a memorable one in cricket history, not only for the fact that several "records" have been broken, but also as a very complete and splendid example of a cricket drama on a great scale. The number of runs scored and the time occupied in getting them are both "records" for such matches, and so, too, is MR. R. E. FOSTER's magnificent innings of 287, which is higher by 76 runs than MR. MURDOCH's 211 at the Oval in 1884. But more remarkable than the mere numerical eclipse of previous achievements is the general character of this week-long contest – its sustained and stubborn vigour, so the game was fought out hour by hour and day by day, without favour of fortune, under perfectly equal conditions, fairly and squarely to the end. Our victory, it will be readily admitted, was chiefly due to the quite exceptional effort of MR. FOSTER; and it was contested, after the first three days, by an uphill fight of a kind for which the Australians are famous, and of which they have never given a finer example than this. There is only one thing to be regretted in the proceedings,

and that is an unfortunate outburst of temper on the part of the Sydney "larrikins" over a decision by an umpire, in which even some of the members of the club seem to have joined. Such exhibitions have occurred before in Sydney, and are not unknown even in England, where, however, they usually proceed only from the baser partisans in county games. The English captain, MR. WARNER, took up a firm line in the matter, and we must trust to the determination of the captains, and of the respectable spectators, to see that there is no repetition of such a scene.

The composition of the English eleven, which was got together by the Marylebone authorities, was criticized with great severity in certain quarters before it left these shores. There were some who resented the selection of MR. WARNER as captain in preference to MR. A. C. MACLAREN, and the consequent refusal of the latter to join the party; there were others who considered that the absence of MESSRS. MACLAREN, JACKSON, and FRY, not to mention MR. JESSOP, would be fatal to the chances of the team. The good judges deplored the absence of those famous cricketers, in spite of all the efforts which have been made to secure their adhesion; but they considered that out of the material before them the M.C.C. had made the best possible selection both of captain and of men. The team is indeed a very powerful combination; it is strong right through in batting, for RHODES, the last man to bat at Sydney, made his thousand runs this year. It does not take the field without six bowlers, including the redoubtable Yorkshiremen, RHODES and HIRST, now the two finest English bowlers, with the exception of LOCKWOOD at his best. Above all, the men are, each and all of them, the right sort of cricketers for the task – keen, good-tempered, active, and loyal, and, with hardly an exception, on the right side of their cricket prime. Are we, then, to hope that MR. WARNER's men will win the rubber and recover for the cricketers of this country the supremacy which they have temporarily lost? We must not be too sure. We must remember that both the last elevens which visited Australia from this island won the first test match at Sydney, and that neither of them scored another win in the whole set. We must remember that, although Australia just now seems very weak in bowling, it is stated that her finest bowler, MR. TRUMBLE, who did not play in the match at Sydney, has promised to appear in all the other four. Let it be added that Australia possesses in two of her youngest players, MESSRS. HILL and TRUMPER, two batsmen who are without superiors anywhere in the world; and in all her representatives men of nerve, grit, and determination not second to our own. When all is said, and when it is remembered that up till now the present English team have carried all before them, we do not believe that we have ever had a fairer chance.

England won the series by three matches to two.

Tom Emmett

1 *July* 1904. The famous TOM EMMETT, whose death at the age of 63 was reported yesterday, was probably the most popular professional cricketer who ever appeared. He had a long career, and for years was one of Yorkshire's greatest all-round cricketers, while on three occasions he visited Australia, and he was a constant performer in Gentlemen v. Players matches. He was a cricketer of whom it may be said that there was nothing certain in him except his uncertainty. Originally famous as a bowler, he frequently bowled wides but frequently also an unplayable ball even on the best of wickets. With an odd, angular sort of delivery, he was in his early days very fast, and on the old-fashioned Lord's wickets very dangerous. He bowled all lengths and directions, and was therefore somewhat expensive; but, first with George Freeman and subsequently with Allan Hill, he was a most effective bowler for his county, and, indeed, for any side. As a batsman he had some of the same characteristics that he had as a bowler in his complete disregard of the conventional. Originally mainly a hitter, he became later on quite a steady player; but nobody could prophesy what he would do. A half-volley that nine batsmen out of ten would hit to the ropes Emmett would play gently back to the bowler, while a good-length ball he would jump out at and hit for four. No cricketer was keener or more cheerful, no day was too long for him or too hot. He would bowl one end and field anywhere, and was as popular as a jovial Yorkshireman naturally would be who always was cheerful, always worked his hardest, and always played the game. After his retirement from first-class cricket Emmett was for some years coach at Rugby School.

English Games in France

FROM A FRENCH CORRESPONDENT

2 *May* 1905. It is not a herculean task to describe the development of games in France, for though athletics have made a remarkable stride during the last few years they are still far from having made their way among the people, while the upper classes of society, which are snobbish to the backbone, confine their attention to the fashionable sports which expense forbids to any but themselves . . .

The obstacles to be faced by hockey lead on to the consideration of cricket. The "national game" is only played in France by about half-a-dozen clubs, composed almost exclusively of Englishmen who have been unable to abandon their beloved game. About 1896 the Albion Cricket Club was founded under the presidency of Mr. Willan. Unwilling to be left behind, the Standard Athletic Club also formed a team, and the two clubs played friendly matches till 1897, in which year the first championship was founded. Only three teams competed to begin with, and the Albion, which was composed of the best units, won the championship three times running. In 1900 the Standard succeeded in wresting from them the coveted title, but had to relinquish it in the following year to the Albion, which held it till 1902. In 1903 the Compiègne Cricket Club, thanks to Thorpe, a good bowler and a good bat, won the championship in a field of five competitors. Finally, in 1904, the Standard, which had succeeded in getting together a first-rate team, beat the Stade Français, the Albion Cricket Club and the Compiègne Cricket Club. Our cricket elevens are far from having any value. A batsman who makes two figures is considered good; when he reaches 50 he excels. As for three figures, such things are unknown, for the record (made by Atrill four years ago) is 96. But it must be stated in defence of our batsmen that the pitches they play on are anything but favourable. Some of them are covered with stones. The heavy expenses necessary to making a proper pitch are beyond the means of our clubs, and they cannot count on the spectators to increase their funds, for the simple reason that there are none. The public in France takes no interest in cricket, of which it does not understand the subtleties, and it sees no fun in "hitting a ball with a stick." The Frenchman gets impatient at waiting his turn to go in, and would like to be either batting or bowling the whole time. In a word, cricket is not sympathetic to the French temperament. There are scarcely a dozen Frenchmen who play the game, and most of them play it abominably.

Alfred Shaw

17 *January* 1907. Alfred Shaw, the well known cricketer, died last night, at Gedling, Nottingham. He was born in 1842 at Burton Joyce, a village near Nottingham. In those days it was safe to assume that most men born near Nottingham were cricketers, and Shaw was no exception to the rule. His first appearance for his county was in 1864, and he at once foreshadowed his future excellence, for the first time he bowled in a county match he got six Kent wickets for 31 runs. He was a leading member of the famous Nottingham eleven for 24 seasons, and it was a common opinion that he was shelved too soon. In support of this it must be mentioned that after giving up all first-class cricket for seven years he played for two seasons for Sussex, and showed much of his old bowling skill, and this at the age of 52 and 53. Shaw became a member of the ground staff at Lord's in 1864, and remained there for 16 seasons, and after the superannuation of Grundy and Wootton was the leading bowler of the club. Few cricketers have ever lived who had so long, so successful, or so varied a career. For 24 years he played for what on the whole was the leading county, for 16 years he was at Lord's, for two years he played for Sussex; in 28 matches he played for the Players against the Gentlemen;

five visits he made to Australia, in three of which he was an active player; twice he went to America; and, finally, he acted as umpire for ten years.

The length of his career proved that he was a slow bowler, for no fast bowler could have stood the strain of so much cricket. He bowled slow with a very short run, and his arm was about on a level with his shoulder, and it would be impossible to see an action that took less exertion. For the first seven years Shaw was a medium pace bowler, but after that he was a real slow bowler, and it was as a slow bowler that he made all his great feats. In 1874, for the M.C.C. against the North of England, Shaw got all ten wickets in the first innings for 73 runs; and in 1875 he dismissed seven M.C.C. batsmen for seven runs, all clean bowled except one, and five of them were W. G. Grace, I. D. Walker, Lord Harris, C. F. Buller, and A. W. Ridley. Shaw was not a bowler who was likely to suffer on account of having no adequate support. For the first six or seven seasons he was in the famous Notts elevens that had as bowlers Grundy, Wootton, Tinsley, McIntyre, and J. C. Shaw, and as these went off Morley, Attewell, Flowers, and Barnes came on the scene. It was in conjunction with Morley that Shaw performed many of his best feats, and a better combination it would be impossible to find.

If Shaw had not been a grand bowler he would have been a very good batsman, and he was generally good at a pinch; but he always thought that it was impossible to be good at both, so he did not take batting seriously; but he was a sure catch at short slip. As a bowler Shaw was quite unlike the bowlers of the present day, who bowl with very high action, with all paces, every variety of length, good, bad, and indifferent, and go in for leg-breaks. Such bowling is a result of too good wickets. Shaw never bowled a bad ball, and, though he varied his length, he never bowled a real long hop or an overpitched ball; and he was almost the last of the great bowlers whose whole principle of bowling was accuracy. If he had a fault it might possibly be said that he was apt to bowl too much for maidens, but it must be remembered that in Shaw's early days if the bowler had accuracy he was bound to be successful. Assistance from the wicket was much more in evidence in those days, and if to this was added accuracy of length and direction and some break from the off, nothing more was wanted. On the whole, considering the length of his cricketing career and of his so frequently bowling against W. G. Grace in the height of his fame, Shaw may be considered the leading slow bowler of cricket history, the career of Peate, a possible rival in the way of accuracy, having been so short.

Middlesex v. Somerset

[BY PHILIP TREVOR]

23 *May* 1907. Albert Trott, for whose benefit the match between Middlesex and Somerset was played, accomplished a wonderful bowling performance

at Lord's yesterday morning, one indeed which has never been equalled according to the authentic records of first-class cricket. Trott twice did the "hat trick" in the course of a single innings. On the first occasion he got four men out with successive balls, and he only missed the wicket by about an inch with the fifth ball. The details of his bowling are sufficiently interesting to merit exact rehearsal. Left with the task of getting 264 runs in order to win the match Somerset began batting with Mr. Palairet and Braund, and there was nothing in the early play to suggest the collapse which followed. Braund played sound cricket, and Mr. Palairet made a number of excellent scoring strokes in his best style. The score was taken easily enough to 56, and then Mr. Palairet was caught at cover-point. Mr. Beldam and Mignon had been then replaced as bowlers by Trott and Tarrant. Mr. Johnson came in, made a few hits, and was then finely caught by Trott off Tarrant's bowling, the second wicket falling with the total at 74. Lewis succeeded him, and this was the beginning of the end. He was leg-before-wicket to Trott after making a single. Then Mr. Poyntz came in, only to be deceived in the flight and bowled first ball by Trott. Mr. Woods suffered a similar fate next ball, apparently trying to make a chop stroke. With the defeat of Mr. Woods Trott accomplished the "hat trick," but his success did not end there. Robson was the next man to face him, and his fate was the fate of his predecessors. He was, too, clean bowled, and he was, therefore, Trott's fourth successive victim. It was only by an accident that Mr. F. M. Lee did not become his fifth. He hit at the ball bowled to him and missed it. For the moment it seemed from the pavilion that that ball had hit the wicket as well. Mr. MacGregor, the wicket-keeper, evidently thought that that was so, for he did not take it, and four byes were the result. It was a wonderful over, and one is scarcely likely to see one like it bowled again in a first-class match. Mr. Lee made seven runs before being caught at short slip by Trott off Tarrant's bowling. Then Mr. Mordaunt, who had made four runs, faced Trott. He made a poor stroke to mid-off, and was easily caught by Mignon. Mr. Wickham succeeded him, and was bowled first ball. Bailey, the last man in, had to take the one ball of the over which remained to be bowled. He hit it up into the air, and Mignon made another easy catch. Thus Trott did the hat trick for the second time in the course of half an hour. Neither the excellence of his bowling nor the failure of the Somerset batting is to be explained away, but it is only fair to state that the light was very bad at the time. But that defective light was even the primary cause of Trott's success was not the case. Two or three of his victims he deceived in the flight of the ball, and the uncomfortable necessity of batting under unpleasantly dramatic conditions no doubt was responsible for the rather poor efforts which some others of his victims made.

Still the fact remains that his was a great achievement, and it will long be remembered by those who saw it. It is rather exceptional for a professional cricketer to do himself especial justice in his benefit match, and, although Trott had made 30 odd runs in one innings, his comparative failure in this game had up till yesterday morning been generally regretted. He made the most ample amends by the way in which he brought the match to an end. In one respect his success on the field had a touch of irony in it. The game was all over by lunch time. Had it lasted well into the afternoon, as at one time seemed probable, there would certainly have been a large attendance of the public, and Trott would have been the financial gainer thereby.

It was a very disappointing finish of the match for Somerset. Braund carried his bat right through the innings, and Mr. Palairet's batting has already been mentioned; but the display of the other men on the good wicket was inexplicably weak. With 50 runs scored no wicket had fallen, yet the total when the tenth wicket fell was less than a hundred. Few, indeed, were prepared for the victory of Middlesex by so many as 166 runs. Yesterday, in *The Times*, some insistence was laid on how much depended on the first and best of the Somerset batsmen, even presuming that the wicket remained good. Somerset, in spite of the return to the eleven of Mr. Palairet, are unusually badly off for first-class batsmen; and even in this match it must not be forgotten that the respectable total made by them in the first innings was largely due to mistakes in catching made by the Middlesex men. The cry is usually for bowlers nowadays. Somerset are not by any means lacking in bowling talent. They at any rate compare favourably in this respect with, at least, a bare majority of the counties which are officially first class. But they need two or three men capable of getting runs when a wicket is favourable to the getting of runs.

MIDDLESEX 286 (Tarrant 52, Mr. P. F. Warner 46, Mr. E. S. Litteljohn 44; Lewis 4 for 88) and 213 (Mr. E. S. Litteljohn 52)
SOMERSET 236 (Braund 59, Mr. P. R. Johnson 57; Tarrant 6 for 47) and 97 (Trott 7 for 20)
Middlesex won by 166 runs

Village Cricket

FROM A CORRESPONDENT [J. E. VINCENT]

12 *September* 1907. In the Celtic fringes stretches of grass which even approach the level are rare, and cricket clubs are therefore few and far between. Hence, perhaps, the Scotch, the Irish, and the Welsh, able-bodied races all three and capable of producing football-players of exceptional merit, can seldom boast that they have brought forward even a second-class cricketer. How can they hope to do so? Sons of these races who are at school in England play cricket, no doubt, in term time, but when they have sung "Jam repetit domum Daulias advena" (at least a month too early as a matter of natural history) their cricket season is over in nine cases out of ten. They go home to shoot, to fish, to play lawn tennis, to swim, to sail, to row; but

not to play cricket; and many a one of them, his knowledge of English village life gained from "Tom Brown's Schooldays" and from study of the ancient records of cricket or, if he have some delicacy in literary taste, from Miss Mitford's "Our Village," envies the life of his school-fellows in the summer holidays as he imagines it to be. He pictures to himself every rural village possessed of a spacious village green, where squire's sons, parson's sons, farmer's sons, village lads, the blacksmith, the carpenter, and the wheelwright play on terms of equality, while the elders look on with critical eyes, and, now and again, an unknown spectator may be one of the great men of the county club on the look-out for a promising colt. There may be some foundation for this idea in village cricket in the first-class counties; but it is a fond delusion so far as some other counties are concerned. Writing in the heart of Berkshire I have jotted down the names of 15 adjacent villages as they came to mind. One has a magnificent village green; one or two have strips of roadside grass on which small boys may just contrive to play a game of cricket; the rest have nothing in the way of a cricket ground except where, usually with a good deal of outside help, they are able to pay for the ground.

Still, since cricket is the national game, it might be imagined that, except in the matter of ways and means, there would not be the slightest difficulty in starting a flourishing cricket club in an English village. Such was the expectation with which last year I took a part, more leading than it was ever intended to be, in starting a cricket club for a village where boys and young men were many, but there were no facilities for cricket. Money having been obtained in adequate amount without much difficulty, and a pitch – really a good one in the midst of a spacious and level pasture – with an infinity of trouble, and a captain having been discovered who really played a very sound game. But matters began to go amiss almost at once. At our first meeting – villages are fond of meetings although nobody ever says anything when the meetings are assembled – we elected a captain and a committee, with power to add to their number, and fixed the annual subscription at one shilling. A committee sat to consider the question of purchasing the "tackle," as we call bats and balls and the like, for several hours, and an animated debate was carried on, the debaters, for the most part, not having the remotest idea what ought to be paid for them. Eventually the captain and I were deputed to make up our own list, and the "tackle" was ordered at our discretion. Before it came a steam-roller weighing 15 tons improved the pitch vastly in the course of an afternoon, but when the "tackle" came trouble began at once. Some half-grown boys, who had paid their subscriptions, took it out on a wet evening and were immediately dispossessed by louts who had not paid. Hearing this the next morning, I went down that evening to act policeman and found the louts, or most of them, quite willing to pay if they could find a trustworthy recipient of their shillings. Such a one was found in the village carpenter, and a practice game began at once. But the village idea of practice was that batting was not bad fun, though none of them could bat at all; that bowling was better sport – and most of them could bowl rather well; but that fielding was the last thing to be thought of. Very small boys might long-stop in pads, bowlers sometimes wore them, but nobody ever batted in them, and nobody would field. The other players, both sides alike – for sides were always picked – and a few footworn spectators, lay on the ground and smoked about the spot where short slip would stand in the ordinary course of things. Remonstrance and example were both wasted on them (as they always are wasted in our village), and the only way of shifting that loafing knot was to go in oneself determined to tap long-hops to the off smartly back-handed, as if one were a left-handed man hitting to leg. This stroke did not often come off; but the backward sweep of the bat produced a moral effect.

The next trouble was that, although every member of the club worked with his hands, none of them would help in mowing or rolling the pitch. These duties thus fell to the captain and, occasionally, to me, being undertaken in my case with the hope of putting them to shame; but the hope was always disappointed. What they were paid to do they would do; and the majority of them certainly felt that they ought to be paid for playing in practice games. In fact, they played only to oblige "the quality," making it very plain all the time that their hearts were set on the football season. Yet at the same time they were exacting, complaining bitterly if their captain did not put in an appearance every evening to coach them, although not one of them ever paid the smallest attention to his instructions. They complained also that he was clean in his habits and dress, and, as each individual member at the club felt himself entitled to be in the village eleven in every match, whereas the captain usually chose those who played a little less ill than the rest, and these happened also to be cleaner than the rest, discontent was rampant. Once, during my absence from home, they deposed the captain; but a letter to the effect that I should have neither difficulty nor scruple in drying up the stream of subscriptions at its source, and disastrous defeat in the one match played without him, restored the *status quo ante*; and I have never known, in a small way, a more sportsmanlike action than that of the captain in returning to the service of those who had flouted him.

The village was always full of the desire for victory. Indeed the excitement with which the issues of our little matches were awaited was a joyful thing to me. Occasionally, since we are not far from Oxford, a good-natured college club, not naturally given to cricket, is kind enough to send over as weak an eleven as it can find. Even so the village cannot win, and how low the standard of cricket is may be judged from the fact that more than once, between half-past 2 and half-past 6 on a Saturday, there has been time for each side to have a second innings and for both sides to have tea. By the gentlemen, however, they do not mind being beaten; but inter-village matches are played in a very earnest spirit. Scornful are the comments when Slogdon-in-the-Marsh imports players from the neighbouring town, but, somehow or other, we won the majority of our village matches last year. Then came the football season, in which, on the whole, we did very well. The captain – a new one for football, chosen, it is believed, because he was profuse of beer – usually played in his funeral trousers, and smoking a cigarette, in the responsible position of centre forward; and the flaring shirts of the players, purchased out of the club funds, were often worn over ordinary clothes. The football season ended. The ground, with more difficulty than before, was secured for another year. Membership declined, and those who consented to join for cricket made it plain that they did so as a favour to me and to my like and in the hope of football to come. Yet we have lived through our cricket season; have won our share of matches, in spite of the rain and of the fact that the farmer took a crop of hay off most of the ground as well as taking a large rent; and, on the whole, the enterprise is probably worth carrying on even in the face of discouragement. What has been gained? Well, the young fellows do not always sit idly at the corners when work is over, spend a little less time at the public-houses, greet one with a half-smile instead of a surly stare in the village street, and have developed some spirit of local patriotism. The gain cannot be called great, but at least it is a beginning. It is an uphill task, however, failing a curate with a good leg break. Anglican as I am, I must confess that the most useful man in the club, at all events socially, occupies a Nonconformist pulpit on Sundays.

Cricket in the Parks

FROM A CORRESPONDENT [E. B. OSBORN]

7 *August* 1908. Nothing could be more interesting to the true lover of cricket than a stroll through one of the parks and open spaces of London on a fine Saturday afternoon in the height of summer. If these patches of green on the map be the "lungs of the metropolis," then one might say that the hundreds of white fleeting figures seen there are the leucocytes of the body municipal. For all the pathetic crudeness of their efforts, these youthful players are actually striving to prevent the physical decay of a nation, far too large a proportion of which is now compelled to live and die in huge prison-cities.

In these green playing-fields of London a greater battle than Waterloo – the battle for the renewal of the nation's wasted physical force and will-power – is being fought sturdily, steadily, and, let us hope, victoriously. It is true that good batting or bowling, or even decent fielding is not often seen in the parks. Clearly nine in ten of the players have not been taught the rudiments of the game, and have not tried to think out its theory for themselves. Here and there curious instances of physical mimicry may be observed. Since Mr. Jessop is still the chief popular favourite, it is always easy to find some small, square-set batsman who has adopted his crouching attitude and hits at everything without anything like the success of his model. It is human nature to imitate the mannerisms of the great, and human nature abounds in London's free cricket-fields. I had hoped that the appearance of his Highness the Jam Sahib at Lord's would have led to a revival of the so-called "Ranji play" among the boys who play in the parks on Saturday afternoon. But a careful survey of nearly all the games going on in Regent's Park on a recent Saturday did not reveal the presence of a single professed imitator of that incomparable artist. The "Ranji" of the parks, it should be pointed out, asserts his right to the title by clubbing straight balls to the leg side and then flourishing his bat with a turn of the wrist. Much more often than not the ball is not touched; whether it hits the wicket or not, the flourish is faithfully executed. However, it would appear that Mr. Bosanquet's achievements and those of the best South African bowlers have not escaped the notice of London's free cricketers. "Let Joe try his wrong 'uns" was the advice given to the captain of an eleven (defined as "medium 16") in my hearing. Joe went on two overs later – a captain must be deliberate in acting on unsolicited advice – but the only resemblance of his deliveries to those of Mr. Bosanquet consisted in the fact that wides were not infrequent. But, as a rule, only the old-established favourites are flattered by imitation. Miniature Abels, with the secretive look of a groom and a fondness for leaving balls wide of the off-stump to the long-stop, may still be seen. The Cockney legend that Abel, really a very straightforward batsman, got most of his runs by a kind of cunning coping still survives in the parks. Only careful coaching could eliminate this and other fallacies and persuade the London working boy that he must first achieve orthodoxy before imitating the heterodox methods of the great players with a personal style whose names are pavilion words on the lips of men.

There is a limited amount of space for cricket in Regent's Park and the other pleasances which are Royal demesnes. In such a place as Kew Gardens cricket is out of the question, of course, but I cannot help thinking that more accommodation for so humane a pastime could be, and ought to be provided in the Royal parks. In some of the small open spaces controlled by the borough councils – e.g., in Paddington Recreation Ground, the drainage system of which compares so favourably with that of Lord's on the hill above – there is accommodation for the game; but the total amount under this heading is not very large. As a matter of fact, the London County Council does much more for the cricketer of very small means or no means at all than all the other public bodies in the metropolis and its suburbs. The total number of reserved match grounds provided this season by the London County Council is 442, accommodating nearly 10,000 players every Saturday afternoon between May 1 and September 30. The total number of matches recorded last season was 29,010. In addition a very large number of players are provided for on unreserved ground, where on any fine warm half-holiday the air is thronged with flying balls, and the lack of serious accidents is really amazing. It often happens on these congested areas that short-leg on one fielding side is back-to-back with point in the next game, and a hard hit travels through four or five matches in being. I have a pleasant recollection of seeing an Oxford captain, who was helping a team of East-end boys, make a brilliant catch at cover on the unreserved ground at Peckham-rye. Unfortunately the ball he caught had been driven out of somebody else's game, and the catch was no compensation for his failure to trouble the scorer. As a rule the reserved pitches are well kept, though generally rather slow or "morose," to use the epithet of a slow bowler in the sixth standard, and the out-field is often rough. But it is quite possible to play decent cricket on these pitches.

Colleges and public school missions are now numerous in London, and those in charge of them do all in their power to encourage cricket and the other *ludi humaniores* which are wholesome exercise for mind and body and a salutary discipline for youths who would otherwise spend all their leisure in the sorry-go-round of London street life. I know several good cricketers who devote an hour or two of their spare time every week to the pleasant and profitable task of coaching the young cricketers of the East-end and of South London, that vast and monotonous wilderness of mean streets – streets coloured blue (which denotes respectability within a week of starvation) in Mr. Charles Booth's wonderful map of London, a veritable spectrum analysis of the financial standing of its million families. No investment of one's leisure returns higher interest. The boy of the London streets is amazingly quick – rather more so than the average public school boy – in taking the hints of a competent coach and soon learns to field well and bat in decent form, though the fact that he cannot get regular practice prevents him from attaining real excellence as a rule. He is by no means effuse in his thanks, but he will never forget the kindness of those who teach him how to play cricket and to make a sensible use of his riotous activities.

Unquestionably cricket is the best antidote to Hooliganism; experience has proved the truth of this assertion not only in the case of London, but also in that of Melbourne where the "larrykin" (who may be succinctly defined as a meat-fed Hooligan) invariably deserts his "push" or band the moment he takes to cricket in downright earnest. As Mr. Arthur Morrison has assured, the typical Hooligan is a keen, high-strung creature, whose nervous energy and lust for adventure have been diverted into an improper channel. Persuade him to play cricket – boxing is Mr. Morrison's prescription, but other equally competent social physicians prefer cricket – and fast bowling on a London County Council pitch, which is invariably fiery after a week's sunshine, will provide him with all the excitement he requires on Saturday afternoon. And, as has been hinted already, he will always remember his coach. I still cherish a bundle of letters from the boys of an East-end club – they were very human boys – several of which were received, long years after I had resigned my office of coach, at queer little post-offices in the wilds of the Canadian North-West. Some such all-sufficient reward will be given to every other cricketer who thus invests a portion of his leisure.

Hambledon Redivivus

FROM A CORRESPONDENT [E. V. LUCAS]

4 *September* 1908. The announcement is made that on September 10, 11, and 12 a cricket match will be played on Broadhalfpenny Down between the Hambledon Club and an eleven of All England.

At the close of the cricket season we have come to expect a few fixtures that are *hors concours*, merely friendly and sporting, when the strain of the championship struggle and average hunting is lightened; but not for a long time has there been so interesting and provocative an announcement as the above. For it fires the imagination, as indeed it was meant to; one sees visions of wind-swept turf, of quaint and dignified players in knee-breeches and ribboned hats, and a gathering of Hampshire farmers looking on and baying "Tich and turn." The bat is curved like a banana and there are only two stumps. The bowlers bowl underhand, bringing the ball to the eye before delivering it. The scorers sit on an isolated bench cutting the runs on a stick. That or some such scene do the words Broadhalfpenny Down conjure up in the mind of any one who knows his Nyren.

The forthcoming Hambledon match, on the old ground of the club famous in the latter half of the 18th century, will, however, not be a dramatization of Nyren or an archaeological reconstitution. It will be modern and serious. Not according to the old laws (which is perhaps a wise decision and one that will certainly be welcomed by the umpires), but the new; nor in the old costume (which also, we can believe, must be a relief to the players themselves); but two very excellent early customs will be revived; all hits will be run out, and the ground, save for an enclosure for carriages, will be free. Cricket matches undoubtedly should be free; certainly any match should be that attempted to reproduce the glorious past.

Nor will the contest be fought out on the virgin turf of the Down. It was all very well for David Harris and Lumpy Stevens to walk over the ground in the early hours of the match days in that distant era and carefully pitch the wickets to embrace such hillocks as favoured their peculiar methods. But such refinements have passed from the game, and passed for ever, before a Socialism that prescribes a level sward to all alike. For this match, therefore (and let it be hoped, for many similar matches to come), a pitch has been made by Hopkins, the Hampshire ground-man at Southampton, who has worked on the new turf at intervals all the year.

One other change in the game. It is unlikely that the following three Laws of Cricket, as revised by the M.C.C. in 1830, and printed in Nyren's book, will be operative:–

BETS.
If the runs of one player be laid against those of another, the bets depend upon the first innings, unless otherwise specified.

If the bets be made upon both innings and one party beat the other in one innings, the runs in the first innings shall determine the bet.

But if the other party go in a second time, then the bet must be determined by the number on the score.

We cannot be too grateful to think that cricket has ceased to attract the betting-man, although there are few signs that he did the early game much harm.

Any step that can bring sentiment again into first-class cricket is to be welcomed; for a hard utilitarianism and commercialism have far too long controlled it; and the new conditions of the game as a spectacle, demanding for its success as a spectacle a sufficiency of "stars," have made it necessary that the principal participants in the first-class game to-day should be prepared to give so much time to it as practically to be debarred from any other occupation – thus converting what began as an occasional pastime, and was meant to be an occasional pastime, marked by geniality and rapture, into a more of less mechanical trade. Its glorious uncertainty must and will always save cricket and cricketers from the worst depths of professional mechanism; but the fact remains that a three-day match to-day can be a scene of little joy and little enthusiasm.

It is for this, as well as other reasons, that we are pleased to hear of the preparations that have been made for the revival of the Hambledon Club and the repetition of a Hambledon and All England match. It is well also that cricketers should be reminded now and then of the antiquity of their game, and in these days of pageants and the celebration of England's past the early years of cricket are as worthy of reproduction as scenes in the lives of Henry VIII and Elizabeth. In a sense, the match next week will be a pageant. It will have also an historical value in the circumstance that during one of the intervals of the game will be unveiled the granite obelisk that has been erected immediately in front of the old Bat and Ball Inn (once kept, it is on record, by John Nyren's father, the famous "general" of the Hambledon Club in its best days) to commemorate the sanctity of the spot. The obelisk bears this inscription :–

> This stone marks the site of the ground of the
> Hambledon Cricket Club. Circ. 1750–1787.

It will be unveiled ceremoniously, the deed being performed by a suitable hand, possibly that of Dr. W. G. Grace; possibly by a younger, smaller, but, in another walk of life, more illustrious personage.

The particular match which the promoters have in mind for celebration is that played exactly one hundred and thirty years ago, on the same ground – Broadhalfpenny Down – between the Hambledon Club and All England. That also began on September 10 (in 1777), and England won by 54 runs, making 146 and 187 against Hambledon's 117 and 162.

The names of the All England XI, of which Mr. Jessop is to be the captain (or "general") next week, have yet to come; but the Hambledon Club will be represented by eight members of the Hampshire Eleven, two ordinary members of the Hambledon cricket team, and Mr. C. B. Fry, who has been the principal mover in the project, if not the "onlie begetter" of it. He has found the most willing supporters in the Rev. W. G. G. Thompson, of Binsted, Mr. E. Whalley-Tooker, the Hambledon captain, Mr. J. A. Best, the late Hambledon secretary, the Rev. H. Floud, the present Hambledon secretary, Mr. E. M. Sprot, the Hampshire captain, Mr. A. J. Hill, Major Butler (who possesses a screen on which are pasted the Hambledon scores from 1750 to the year of the old club's extinction), and Mr. Hyde Salmon Whalley-Tooker, whose punch bowls and dinner plate, as used by the original Hambledon men, will be on view in one of the tents during the match.

The London and South-Western Railway Company will make it easy for the match to be reached, the best station for Hambledon being Droxford. It is also accessible by the light railway from Cosham.

Hambledon beat the England team by five wickets.

Australia v. England

Second Test Match

8 *January* 1908; *Melbourne, 7 January.* There was a truly sensational finish to the Test match here to-day, the Englishmen winning by one wicket after their position had seemed quite hopeless. They wanted 73 to win when their eighth wicket fell, and 39 runs were still required when Fielder, the last man, joined Barnes. Amid ever-increasing excitement, these two batsmen finished off the game, Barnes making the last hit with the score at a tie. By general consent it was a magnificent close to a splendid match. Barnes and Fielder had a great reception as they returned to the pavilion. They were patted on the back by enthusiastic spectators, and the cheering was loud and prolonged.

Mr. Justice Cussen, the president of the Melbourne Club, in congratulating the winners, said that a more exciting match had never been played on the Melbourne ground. Both on leaving the ground and on arriving at their hotel the Englishmen were tremendously cheered. There was a good deal of dull cricket during the six days, but the finish made ample amends for everything. Despite the length of time over which the game extended, public interest never declined, and the prospect of a keen struggle attracted a large crowd to-day. The wicket remained good to the end.

The weather was muggy at the start of play. Set to make 282, the Englishmen had scored 159 yesterday for the loss of four wickets, so that they had 123 to get with six wickets in hand. Braund and Hardstaff, not out, with 17 each, continued the innings, Noble and Cotter bowling at them. Only three runs had been added when Hardstaff, in trying to hook the first ball bowled by Cotter, skied it and was caught deep on the leg-side. Five wickets for 162. Rhodes came in, and with his score at 2 gave a difficult chance off Cotter to

McAlister at slip. From the next ball Cotter appealed confidently for leg-before-wicket against Braund, and was much disappointed when the umpire gave his decision in the batsman's favour. With the wind behind him, Cotter was bowling at a great pace and Noble was making the ball swerve. Before very long, however, Noble thought changes of bowling desirable. He gave way to Saunders at 184 and put Armstrong on in place of Cotter at 196. The second change at once met with success, Armstrong's fifth ball bowling Braund. Six for 196. Braund was at the wickets nearly an hour and three-quarters for his 30. Though so slow and cautious, he played in excellent style. Among his hits were two fours. Crawford joined Rhodes, the cricket being now keen to a degree. In playing Armstrong, Crawford was repeatedly "stuck up." Two runs having been added, Rhodes was run out, Armstrong fielding the ball very smartly at third man and returning it at lightning speed. Seven wickets for 198. Barnes followed, and 200 went up when the innings had lasted just over four hours and 40 minutes. Crawford made a magnificent hit for six on the on-side from Armstrong, but from the next ball, amid a roar of disappointment, he was badly missed at mid-on by Saunders. At this point he had scored nine. He did not profit by his luck, as after getting another run he was caught at third man.

The match now looked all over, eight wickets being down for 209. Humphries became Barnes's partner, and at 216 Cotter and Noble took up the bowling again. Armstrong had taken two wickets for 30 runs. At lunch time the total was 221, Barnes and Humphries having made seven each. When the game was resumed, Cotter and Saunders shared the bowling. By cautious play the score was increased to 231, when Armstrong bowled once more in place of Cotter. The batsmen were watchful and defensive in their methods, and the crowd followed every ball with the closest attention. Humphries was cheered on getting a ball from Armstrong away on the leg-side. The total reached 243, and then Humphries was out leg-before-wicket. He looked very much disappointed as he walked back.

With 39 runs wanted, Fielder joined Barnes. Though the Australians seemed to have the match in their hands, excitement ran high. Gradually the score rose, both batsmen playing with confidence. At 254 Noble relieved Saunders, and then at 261 Cotter displaced Armstrong, who crossed over to Noble's end. The tension was now extreme, the spectators counting the runs required. At 275, or only seven to win, Noble put on Macartney for Cotter. The ladies shrieked as each run was obtained, and men stamped their feet. The batsmen were very smart and eager in running between the wickets. At last Fielder made the game a tie, playing Armstrong to mid-on. Saunders returned the ball, and Carter, the wicket-keeper, fell over. Then, amid intense excitement, Barnes, with a single in the direction of point, won the match.

The *Argus* describes the match as "the game of a life time," and praises the plucky way in which the last three English batsmen rose to a great occasion.

The aggregate attendance was 91,388, and the total receipts were £4,070. This is nearly a record.

> AUSTRALIA 266 (Mr. M. A. Noble 61, Mr. V. Trumper 49; Mr. J. N. Crawford 5 for 79) and 397 (Mr. W. W. Armstrong 77, Mr. M. A. Noble 64, Mr. V. Trumper 63, Mr. C. G. Macartney 54, Mr. H. Carter 53; Barnes 5 for 72)
> ENGLAND 382 (Mr. K. L. Hutchings 126, Hobbs 83, Braund 49; Mr. A. Cotter 5 for 142) and 282 for 9 (Mr. F. L. Fane 50)
> *England won by 1 wicket*

Amateurs and Professionals

BY LORD HARRIS

22 *January* 1909. It is with considerable hesitation that I respond to the invitation to write something about the troublesome question of "Amateurs and Professionals" in the more popular pastimes. The cobbler must stick to his last, and I naturally take "Cricket" as my guide.

Why is it then that in two of the most popular pastimes – football and athletics – so much ire can be roused over the question of amateur and professional, while in a third – cricket – it is viewed with a calm indifference? Last year the world of Association football was rent in twain over it; and humble and harmless individuals who, for the sport of the thing, had patronized the Football Association were ostracized by that body because they thought they might with equal justice patronize the game as displayed by the Amateur Football Association. Now the Rugby football world is apparently convulsed by somewhat similar causes. Why is it that we do not allow the subject to trouble us in the cricket world? Have we reached Nirvana? I think not; there seem to be plenty of enthusiasm and activity still; or are we still struggling through stages of development long anterior to that reached by other pastimes? Surely not, for in cricket we have had an acknowledged and welcomed professionalism for two hundred years. May we not rather assume that we have passed through the scathing fires, and may we not without arrogance suggest that what may seem indifference is in truth the wisdom of experience, and possibly worth studying, and that from our store of experiences may be gleaned some facts that may help other pastimes to treat the problem with less rancour?

Deep in the records of the committee of the M.C.C. will be found a sapient definition something to this effect:– "That cricketer is not an amateur who makes a profit out of playing the game." That has a fine legislative ring about it, but unfortunately it fails in an important particular – it omits to define what is "profit"; and what that may be no man, despite Dr. Johnson and W. and R. Chambers, and auditors galore, can say for certain. However, it was a very innocent and innocuous effort at definition, and has been relegated to its appropriate place on the pavement of good intentions. It is at least 20 years since that axiom was laid down, and it may be 2,000 years before any cricketer will attempt to utilize it. And why? Because we do not see any urgent necessity for keeping up a marked distinction between amateurs and professionals – marked distinction, that is to say, resting on remuneration, for a much clearer line of distinction exists, namely, the daily avocation, the profession of the man; that is perfectly well known, and there is no need to seek for a more accurate definition.

The real distinction is not whether A receives £5 or £2 for playing in a match, not whether B receives £200 and his expenses, or £50 and his expenses for representing England in a tour; but does he make his livelihood out of playing the game, is it his daily occupation in its season, does he engage himself day in and day out to play it from May 1 to August 31? If he does, then he is a professional, and he knows he is a professional; and he recognizes as convenient, and bows to those social regulations which distinguish the amateur and professional at cricket; and what are these? Well, little more than this, that the rule of the ground should be observed; and that the guests should accept the arrangements made by their hosts. For instance, the arrangements as regards dressing rooms and sitting rooms are not identical on all grounds, but whatever they be they are accepted without demur.

On some grounds therefore the amateurs approach the wicket from a different gate in the pavilion from that used by the professionals; on others both use the same. It is simply, as already said, a case of courteously accepting the rule of the ground on which you play. The dress of both classes is identical as supplied by county clubs, and the only way nowadays that one can distinguish an amateur in the field is that many of them prefer to play bare-headed. From old practice the prefix "Mr." or the affix "Esq." is still used; but no one lays any particular store by them; and if the English professionals – say, in an England v. Australia match – asked that initials only should be used it would probably initiate a universal change without any one's feelings being the least hurt. Therefore after two centuries of comradeship on the field amateurs and professionals have agreed that in the republic of cricket there is no need to encourage disputations on the definition of an amateur. What the professional is is quite clear, as clear as day; but he, knowing that the amateur regards him as his comrade, does not trouble his head what words should be used to describe clearly what is the difference between them as cricketers, because the difference is not irksome or undignified to him. In the republic of cricket the prizes go to the best, and the best can demand – perhaps successfully – the best terms. Well, that is the reward of efficiency, and "ca' canny" is not likely to upset that natural rule at cricket.

At this moment there appears to be a dispute between some of the best Australian cricketers and the Australian Board of Control as to what proportion of the "gate" shall be given to the members of the next team of Australian cricketers. It is a purely local question, and though a share may largely exceed the highest income earned by any English professional the question of amateur and professional will not be raised thereby. Our visitors will accept such arrangements for their entertainment as the English clubs make for them without question, just as our English teams accept those made for them on their colonial tours, whatever the social *status* of this or that individual may be.

We have, in my opinion, reached that very conviable stage where "Manners make the man," not money, whether that be taken in the form of "wage" or of "expenses." We have all for years past, of both classes, been trying to raise the *status* of the professional cricketer, and successfully; and the higher he has risen the closer have become the bonds of comradeship between him and the "amateur," and the rude and abusive professional will now be avoided by those of his own profession as markedly as by amateurs. The game in its highest forms is controlled by clubs of which the professionals are valued *employés*; they do not as a general rule seek membership, and therefore they do not infringe on purely amateur cricket; but, if an amateur club does play against one which includes professionals among its players the *status* of the former is in no way affected.

The above is the position as regards amateurs and professionals in cricket, in my opinion. I can imagine this description will considerably startle some cricketers; but I think after strict examination they will admit its correctness, and I hope they will be able to feel thankful that we have arrived at such a stage. If so, we may justifiably recommend it for the consideration of the supporters of other pastimes in case there are elements in it adaptable with advantage to them. As to that I do not venture to advance an opinion. I stick to my last.

Tea Intervals

FROM A CORRESPONDENT [E. B. OSBORN]

3 *June* 1909. There is no denying that the tea interval, which was unknown to our cricket-playing forefathers, is a bad quarter of an hour for the spectators of modern first-class cricket. Even those critics who believe that whatever is is best are disposed to agree with the veterans who regard this new fashion as a symptom of "slackness" on the part of the present generation of cricketers. No constant incumbent of the hard and abbreviated benches at Lord's or the Oval can help noticing that the crowd, individually and sometimes collectively, resents the loss of time involved, and is injured in its temperament, if not in its temper. Unfavourable criticisms are heard here and there, and when undue advantage is taken of the privilege of tea and talk in the pavilion – as at Lord's recently, when nine wickets were down in the Australian innings and the players began to leave the field, which would have led to a cricketless half-hour broken only by the speedy fall of a bowler's wicket – the resentment

of the spectators is apt to be expressed in unseemly terms. On the occasion in question the cry of "loafers" was taken up all round the field. Afterwards, when the players returned, there was hearty applause; and the visible hesitation of Mr. Warner and others to take full advantage of the law, unwritten and written (which would have given them 15 minutes for tea and the customary ten minutes between one innings and another), was privately praised in a very handsome manner. It would have been hard lines on the many industrious persons who, having applied the provisions of the Daylight Bill to their own proceedings, or having toiled at high pressure since 9 o'clock, had been able to get up to Lord's from their offices in order to see the Australians batting or fielding, if nearly half an hour of play had been cut out. I sat next to one of these sporting spectators from "the city," and he thought that the tea interval should be abolished, a pail of water and ice and oatmeal being carried round the field of play at 4 30 p.m. for the benefit of cricketers who did not appreciate the advantages of cherishing a "righteous thirst" (Nyren would have admired the phrase) until the dinner hour.

The arguments for and against the tea interval are not at all concerned with the opinions and predilections of the average spectator. We must not allow cricket to become subject to crowd-law. The true issue is – do cricketers really require a tea interval? Really this is a particular instance of the general question – is afternoon tea a necessity for the modern Englishman? It cannot have escaped the attention of the most casual student of social institutions in this country that all sorts and conditions of workers now take a cup of tea or coffee in the course of the afternoon, and that it is taken as a stimulus to mental exertion when the mind begins to suffer from the pressure of continuous work. Tea and a little talk certainly refresh the mind even if, as some doctors say, the former makes for nervousness. Lecky's theory that the introduction of hot drinks, tea, coffee, and cocoa, was a great civilizing influence may be practically applied in this case. The social amenities of the tea table, even if ladies cannot be present, are at least as important as the stimulus to further exertion supplied by the actual tea-drinking. To come to the particular case of the cricketer's tea interval, it must be remembered – the fact is often forgotten by those who do not play – that cricket is a mental as well as a physical diversion, a social as well as an athletic pursuit. On either score, then, it would appear that the cricketer is as much entitled to afternoon tea and the social amenities which accompany it as the mere spectator who, if he went home or remained at his office instead of hastening to Lord's in order to cultivate "cricket's manly toil" by proxy, would in all probability indulge in the mild and mellow delights of the tea-table. All he does, if he avoids resorting to a place where refreshments can be obtained, is to do his tea-drinking, like his cricket-playing, by proxy. In country house and village cricket matches the tea interval is almost always taken to give the players an opportunity of meeting and talking with visitors who have driven over to watch the game and for other good reasons. For all one knows to the contrary, marriages may be made in this little social heaven of the tea interval.

Why should county cricketers, merely because their play entertains large numbers of strangers, be deprived of the same privileges which are often – as will be seen by any spectator who sees what becomes of the fielders during the 15 minutes' recess – turned to good account, humanly speaking? A flower-cup of Hippocrene, not a pot of tea, is what their souls commonly desire. In the case of the Australian players, who are our guests, the abolition of the tea interval would be not only inhospitable, but also inhuman. In the Colonies tea is often taken at all three meals, and the drinking thereof is a habit not to be eradicated. In Australia, as in Canada, urns of hot tea, a cooling drink in sub-tropical summers, are carried out in the afternoon to toilers in the field. It would be inconvenient to follow this example on a public cricket ground. The ball might be hit into the tea-urn, thus giving rise to legal difficulties and worrying the umpires – men, by the way, to whom the mental relaxation afforded by the tea interval is invaluable. It is a well-established fact that Australian teams often have a bad quarter of an hour, catches being missed or batsmen dismissed far below par value, halfway through the afternoon's play. Presumably this is the result of wanting tea when tea is not quite ready; and it would not be humane, indeed it would be inhuman, to attempt to deprive them of a customary solace, especially when they have already paid a penalty for desiring it. Let our guests boil the "billy," metaphorically speaking, at 4 30 p.m. punctually, and concerning the tea interval let so much have been said.

Fast Bowling

FROM A CORRESPONDENT [E. B. OSBORN]

30 *June* 1909. Some authorities, candid critics of latter-day cricket, are of opinion that good fast bowlers – men who have control of the ball as well as pace through the air and from the pitch – are not nearly so numerous to-day as they were a generation ago. They would have us believe that the art of bowling fast, like the ability to throw the cricket-ball one hundred yards or more, is slowly dying out because – here comes in the note of pessimism! – the number of players with the required physique, the long elastic muscles of a Spofforth or a Richardson, is gradually diminishing. At the risk of being condemned as *laudator temporis acti*, the writer is disposed to give a qualified assent to these conclusions. There is certainly a scarcity of fast bowling properly so-called both in England and in Australia at the present time. Not a few of those who are called "fast" bowlers in this country and play regularly for their counties would have been thought little more than medium-paced twenty years ago. The fact that Mr. Cotter is their only fast bowler of any ability would seem to argue that the present generation of Australian

cricketers are even worse off than we are for fast bowling. And yet the combination of height, strength, stamina, and agility which makes the physique – the "piratical physique," as it has been called – of the fast bowler is not uncommon among Australians, many of whom can throw as well as any of the ancient champions.

When that mighty cricketer Mr. Spofforth first visited England he was terrifically fast not only through the air but also from the pitch – much more often than not the ball came straight through – and the power of changing his pace without any perceptible alteration of action added greatly to the deadliness of his deliveries on all kinds of wickets. Afterwards he changed his methods somewhat, his average ball being fast medium with a pronounced break back; but a large percentage of his victims fell to his very fast ball – in the writer's judgment the fastest delivery that has been seen on a cricket-ground since 1878. It was certainly faster than the terrific throw with which Crossland would end his overs. On the whole Mr. Spofforth was the fastest of modern fast bowlers – any comparison with Mynn and the other antique bowlers is impossible, our cricketing forefathers having been a non-scientific race and unable to record their observations – and it is highly probable that he was the cleverest. Next in merit comes Richardson, who was certainly superior to any of the fast bowlers of to-day. Both Mr. Spofforth and Richardson bowled to hit the stumps, wisely ignoring the dubious advantages of the "off theory" which wastes time and gives the batsman confidence. The former's chief object was to get wickets, not to keep the runs down – and at the height of his game he would take a wicket in an average of 17 balls. In a word, he was never thinking of his bowling average, and that is the hall-mark of the grand style of bowling in every age.

Fast bowling, like hitting, should be the business of amateurs rather than of professionals. It cannot have escaped the notice of the observant that the professional bowls fast not because he finds such activity exhilirating, but because it is a profitable pursuit, a sure passport into county cricket. And there can be no denying that nine in ten of the professional fast bowlers who show promise of great things in early years are ruined by overwork. Warren, of Derbyshire, is a case in point. A few years ago he seemed good enough to play for England, and competent judges believed that he would train on into a second Richardson. To-day, as a result of the constant strain and overwork of county cricket, he is in the ruck of ordinary fast bowlers, and is not likely to be picked again to play in England v. Australia. The touch of *diablerie* has vanished from his deliveries, and his pace appears to have slackened. Similar examples of a failure to improve or even to maintain the fast bowler's first fine careless rapture could easily be multiplied.

Less obvious, but real enough and by no means occluded from the eyes of the observant, are the evil effects of the billiard-table wicket. In the old days, before turf was fed with marl, the fast bowler who kept a good length could always hope for success. On the impeccable wickets of recent years a good length ball may be forced into the long field by means of strokes which would have been too speculative on the old sporting pitches (on which, in his boyhood, the writer picked daisies!); and the modern fast bowler, in his anxiety to keep down the runs rather than to break through the batsman's defence, customarily pitches somewhat short of a good length.

Fortunately, England still possesses a few fast bowlers of merit. Both Fielder and Buckenham keep a good length, and find it more profitable to do so than to try to bounce the timid batsman out. On his day – generally a hot day, when the muscles are most elastic and the bowler, like the sprinter, gets more pace out of himself – the former is little, if at all, inferior to Richardson in his prime. His fault is that he takes rather too long a run, which is a waste of energy. (Why are not young fast bowlers taught to take a run of the right length as long jumpers are taught? Too little attention is paid to such details in training young cricketers.) Too long a run, as the case of Mr. Knox proved, if proof were necessary, is an inevitable cause of breakdowns. But of all our orthodox fast bowlers the best is Mr. Brearley. His run is no longer than necessary, he has an easy flowing action, and his slight swerve from leg and occasional breakback add to the difficulty of his length bowling. It is never safe to attempt forcing his good length balls into the long field. If he were more skilful in masking a change of pace and had Mr. Spofforth's instinct for the weak points of batsmen, he would be the greatest bowler of his age. As it is, he is a bright exemplar of the τό καλὸν of his art in an unprincipled and barbarous generation. His position in the bowling averages does not really give a true idea of his value to a side. His wickets cost 13·28 runs apiece. But he gets a wicket in fewer balls than any other bowler. This is a point which should be taken into consideration in the statistical survey of the comparative merits of bowlers. It was on the score of balls per wicket that Lohmann's superiority to his compeers was manifest. He, like Brearley, bowled to get wickets, not to collect maiden overs. The following list of what may be called the averages of attack of a number of bowlers of the season (based on the figures of June 21) is worth studying:–

	BALLS PER WICKET.
W. Brearley	25·65
J. H. B. Lockhart	26.12
Thompson	32.49
F. Laver	33·17
Blythe	33·36
Leach	33·8
H. A. Gilbert	34·38
Dennett	35·09
Wass	35·7
Jayes	37·
Rhodes	43·02
Hirst	46·94

Imperial Cricket

27 *July* 1909. Mr. F. E. Lacey, the secretary of the M.C.C., yesterday issued the memoranda of the minutes of the [first] Imperial Cricket Conference, together with the rules for Test Matches and a table showing the practical working of the scheme.

RULES FOR TEST MATCHES

1. Test Matches are those played between representative elevens of England, and of Australia, and of South Africa, also between elevens of Australia and South Africa.

2. A cricketer who has played in a Test Match for a country cannot play for any other country without the consent of each of the contracting parties.

3. Qualification by Birth. – A cricketer, unless debarred by Rule 2, is always eligible to play for the country of his birth.

4. Qualification by Residence. – A cricketer, unless debarred by Rule 2, may elect to play for any country in which he is residing and has resided for not less than four years immediately preceding, and thereafter shall always be eligible to play for that country.

SUGGESTED PROGRAMME OF INTERNATIONAL GAMES

Main Principles. – 1. No team from any country shall pay visits in two successive seasons.

2. Each such team shall pay a visit to and receive a visit from each other country in every cycle of four years.

TABLE SHOWING PRACTICAL WORKING OF THE SCHEME

Cycle 1909-13.				Cycle 1913-17.
Year.		Months.	Countries meeting.	Next round
1909	..	May to August ..	Australia in England ..	1913
1909-10	..	November to March ..	England in South Africa ..	1913-14
1910	..	May to August ..	—	1914
1910-11	..	January to March ..	South Africa in Australia ..	1914-15
1911	..	May to August ..	South Africa in England ..	1915
1911-12	..	November to March ..	England in Australia ..	1915-16
1912	..	May to August ..	Triangular contest	1916
1912-13	..	March to April ..	Australia in South Africa ..	1916-17

In view of the triangular contest in 1912, South Africa defers its visit in 1911 until 1912, and Australia's visit in 1913 is advanced one year to 1912.

SCHEME FOR THE CONTEST.

1. England, Australia, and South Africa shall play each six Test Matches in England, each playing the other three matches against the other.

2. Each country shall take one-half of the gross gate taken at the Test Matches in which it takes part; the net proceeds of stand money to be pooled

for the benefit of the ground on which the match is played and the counties.

3. Each visiting team shall, in addition to Test Matches, play, if possible, at least one match with each first-class county and with the M.C.C.

4. The Board of Control shall fix the dates of the Test Matches before July 31, 1911, to enable the county secretaries to make their programmes without undue inconvenience.

5. (a) For the purpose of providing for the complimentary and other stand tickets each contesting party shall receive 100 free stand tickets, and shall have the option of purchasing 500 additional stand tickets for each Test Match at the current rates, and that no other provision shall be made in this respect. Such option to be exercised at least 14 days before the match for which the tickets are required.

(b) For the convenience of accurately ascertaining the amount of gate money to be divided the sale of stand tickets shall in no case include the entrance fee to the ground.

6. That not more than three days be allotted to each match.

7. (a) The price of admission to all Test Matches be 1s.

(b) The price of admission to all matches other than Test Matches shall be arrived at by arrangement between Australia, South Africa, and the local authorities on whose ground such matches are played.

UMPIRES

The umpires in Test Matches shall be selected by a committee equally representative of each country.

Canterbury Week

FROM OUR SPECIAL CORRESPONDENT [GUY CAMPBELL]

3 *August* 1909; *Canterbury*, 2 *August*. Last night and this morning, in response to much anxious tapping, the glass remained quite steady, and in any ordinary year the weather prospects, at all events to to-day, would be fairly promising. But the summer which we are still patiently enduring laughs at barometers and precedents, and, though it was not raining when the Middlesex match started, we shall be very lucky if we get an uninterrupted day's cricket. Still we must be grateful for small mercies, and it was something to be thankful for that the only shower before lunch did not last very long, though it was heavy enough to delay play for some time and to bring out the famous Kent "Tompaulins."

Concerning these there has been a certain amount of controversy. But, when they are seen in use, it is not easy to understand why they should be objected to. They consist of a sheet of canvas 12ft. long, raised about 3ft. off the ground by a ridge-pole in the centre, and closely pegged down at the sides. The air passes freely through them from end to end, and as they only extend 2ft. in front of the popping-crease they actually cover a smaller part of the wicket itself than is often the case when sacks of sawdust are used, and they certainly make it possible for the bowlers to secure a foothold when in ordinary circumstances it would be all that they could do to stand. Also they have the additional merit that they can be put down and taken up in about a tenth of the time that it takes to lay down and sweep up the conventional sawdust. In all probability Kent's lead in this matter, which is due to the ingenious brain of Mr. Tom Pawley, will next year be followed by all the counties.

One other innovation seen to-day on the St. Lawrence ground is not altogether so satisfactory from an æsthetic point of view, though it will add greatly to the comfort of a fair number of the spectators. This consists in the addition of a red-tiled two-storeyed annexe to the pavilion, in the position which has hitherto been sacred to I Zingari tent. There was some talk of cutting down the great elm at the left side of the pavilion, but we have been spared this act of vandalism, and the annexe has been built beyond the tree. It is not in itself very beautiful and one does not want to see the St. Lawrence ground converted into a sort of Lord's, with an unsightly mound-stand taking up a quarter of the circle of the ground. However, so far no great harm has been done, though it is rather a shock to see I Z. banished to a tiny tent on the other side of the ground.

The order of the tents is practically the same as it was last year. Next to the bowling-screen opposite to the pavilion comes the hospitable abode of the Band of Brothers, and after them the names of the various hosts are Lord Harris and Mr. J. Howard, Mr. Marsham, the East Kent Club, Colonel Hardy, Lord Guilford, I Zingari, Mr. Wheler, Captain Hatfeild, Mr. Elmer Speed, 21st Lancers, The Buffs, Mr. Samuelson, Mr. Prescott-Westcar, The Old Stagers, Mr. P. B. Neame, the Mayor of Canterbury, and the Canterbury and Conservative Clubs. Besides the tents there was to-day a good show of carriages. The various stands were very well filled, and all round the rest of the ground the Bank Holiday crowd sat and stood nine or ten deep, and were rewarded for their faith in Canterbury Week weather by seeing a dashing display of batting by Mr. Hutchings and Humphreys, so that, though the rain began again at 2, they were generally speaking in a wonderfully amiable and contented frame of mind. The streets of the town are as usual gay with strings of flags and pennants, which flap and flutter cheerfully in the fresh breeze; and if only the breeze keeps away the rain, as it promises to do, the Canterbury Week of 1909 will be as brilliant and as cheerful as any of its long list of forerunners. There is even a possibility that the grey clouds may roll away before the end of the week, and show us the almost forgotten blue skies which we still believe exist behind them. That is not a prophecy. It is a pious hope, which is set down here to be contradicted or confirmed to-morrow.

But, however manfully one may struggle to be cheerful, there is no getting away from the facts that rain is damp and haymaking in August is depressing work, especially when there is no sun to make it by. And hay, and not hops, seems to be the staple industry of Kent at the present moment. All the way down from London the fields are either still uncut or are covered with sodden swathes. And yet the farmers have the pluck to come to Canterbury to cheer the cricketers on to victory. Their hay crop may be nearly ruined and their hops wofully short, but as long as they can see Kent bravely struggling to win the championship, and Messrs. Day and Dillon and Hutchings, and Woolley, and the rest, turning the best length balls of the enemy into hops that are long they are proud and happy men. After lunch cricket went on till tea-time, and the Kent eleven have so far done very well. But then once more the rains descended and play had to stop, and from 5 o'clock onwards a dreary procession of disappointed spectators wended its way down to the town and its drooping and bedraggled flags.

And then, to crown all, the irony of fate had ordained that the play to-night was to be *Peter's Mother*, surely the most depressing and gloomy comedy that ever was written. A dying man receiving the death sentence from his doctor, an impending operation, the Boer war, Boer prejudices, and the monumental male selfishness of Peter and his father – is it possible to think of a more dismal collection of subjects? And yet the playing of *Peter's Mother* not only ended but redeemed the day. It was almost as exhilarating, because of the way it was acted, as Mr. Hutchings's batting.

The "Importation" of Cricketers

[BY R. H. LYTTELTON]

6 *September* 1909. The season is now practically over, and the weather has been uncertain all through. Many matches have lately been drawn, but one match, between Middlesex and Gloucestershire, was finished in one day, an unusual occurrence in these times and notable in this case as showing what a great cricketer can do. Tarrant went in first for Middlesex and carried his bat through the innings for 55 runs; he also bowled all through both innings of Gloucestershire and took 13 wickets for 67 runs. It may be said that Tarrant is a better bat on bowlers' wickets than any of his fellow-countrymen at the present moment. This performance of his recalls an even better performance of Braund's some years ago against Yorkshire, a very much stronger side than Gloucestershire. Australia has lost a very great cricketer owing to Tarrant's having left his native country.

The unfounded rumour that Mr. Bardsley was going to qualify for an English county has brought out a protest from Mr. C. E. Green against the whole system of the importation of colonial players. There can be no doubt that he is right in his contention. Middlesex have been the worst offenders, and their position of late years has been very largely due to Trott and Tarrant.

It is to be hoped that cases like these and that of Marshal, the Surrey player, will not be repeated. If an amateur like Mr. Smith, of Northamptonshire, chooses to come and reside in England and qualify for a county it is a different matter, provided that he plays as and is a *bone fide* amateur, although even this is not altogether to be encouraged; but when a professional does so it is only a flagrant instance of commercialism in cricket, and the present dispute in the football world shows what a deplorable state of things may prevail in this respect. If a colonial cricketer was born here, and chooses to come back after many years' residence in a colony – as was the case with Mr. C. Bannerman in 1878, who was born in Kent, and Mr. Carter, of this year's Australian eleven, who is a Yorkshireman – nobody would object to his playing for his native county, for place of birth is rightly held to be paramount in these matters; but it ought to stop there.

A Review of the Tour

FROM A CORRESPONDENT [H. D. G. LEVESON GOWER]

28 *February* 1910; *Port Elizabeth*, 7 *February*. By winning the second Test Match at Durban the South Africans have placed themselves in a very strong position, and their prospects of winning the rubber are particularly bright.

Cricket is proverbially an extraordinary game, and it is continually providing extraordinary surprises; but after what has happened it is scarcely conceivable that the visitors can carry off the three remaining fixtures. Immense importance was attached to the Durban match by both sides. By many it was regarded as the great test; the South Africans, it was said, were practically certain of winning the Test Matches played at Johannesburg and almost certain to be defeated in the two matches to be played at Cape Town. Therefore, the issue must depend on the Natal game. We have never supported this argument. We do not think there is any greater certainty that the South Africans will win the next Test Match at Johannesburg than that the Englishmen will gain victories in the two to be played at Cape Town. The first two Test Matches – the first one especially – were productive of close games; there is no reason to suppose that the three remaining fixtures will not be fought out without equally close results.

It is a little difficult to know what to make of either of the Test Match teams. Both have been the subject of criticism, and both have in certain respects more than realized expectations, and in other respects have fallen a long way short of expectations. When the M.C.C. team was selected, although there were some who found fault with its composition, on the whole it met with the approval of the many. It could not be claimed for the side that it was absolutely representative of the best English cricket, but it was generally conceded that it was a powerful combination, and one of very great possibilities. Certainly in one department of the game – in bowling – it was exceptionally strong; and in reviewing the bowling that took place in England last season it is not very easy to see how it could have been materially strengthened, unless Barnes, one of the finest bowlers at the present time, had been included. There is the fast bowler in Buckenham, the left-handed bowler in Blythe, the medium pace bowler in Thompson, and the unorthodox bowler in Mr. Simpson-Hayward [lobs], with such excellent changes as Rhodes, Woolley, and Hobbs – six recognized first-class bowlers, a formidable attack.

Has the bowling, then, come up to expectations? In a sense it may be contended that it has, but not to that extent which was claimed for it. Except in the Transvaal match no opposition side has really made any sensational total. At the same time, individually the bowlers have been rather a disappointment. Blythe, it is true, has not played in either of the Test Matches; but when opposed to the Transvaal team he gave the batsmen very little trouble, and except against the Western Province and in the return match against Natal at Pietermaritzburg his bowling has fallen far below his usual high standard – in fact, on his showing, he is at the present time inferior to both Rhodes and Woolley. In these circumstances it would seem that Mr. Leveson-Gower was justified in omitting him from the side in the Test Matches. It is to be hoped that before the next great game at Johannesburg Blythe will have regained his form, for a bowler of his class might make all the difference between the success and failure of his side. Buckenham has not been consistent enough, and Thompson has not been as difficult as his past performances on matting wickets in other countries led one to believe would be the case. Rhodes has proved a most useful change, and has rendered much service on many occasions in keeping down runs. Mr. Simpson-Hayward has been a great success. With the exception of Mr. White, Mr.Snooke, Mr. Faulkner, and Mr. Nourse, none of the opposing batsmen in the Test matches played the lobs with confidence. Mr. Sinclair, Mr. Schwarz, and Mr. Zulch have been mastered by him on almost every occasion they have met him, and the value of this kind of attack has been thoroughly demonstrated.

But it is not in bowling that the weakness of the visiting team has been apparent; it is, as was feared when the side left England, in the batting. On paper the English Eleven has many good batsmen, but in actual practice it has too often happened that the side are dependent upon two men. Again and again have Hobbs and Rhodes given the M.C.C. a great lead. Again and again those who have come after have proved unequal to the task of pushing home the advantage. On their reputation in England Mr. Fane, Denton, and Woolley should all be capable of making many runs in the best company; but they have failed most often when most has been expected from and required of them. There is no one on present form in the same class as Hobbs in the eleven. Rhodes is a good way behind him, but with the possible exception of Thompson, who has done admirably in the Test matches, he holds second place very far in front of the remainder.

But if the Englishmen are largely dependent upon two batsmen for runs, it can with equal force be urged that the South Africans are dangerously dependent upon two bowlers for wickets. Up to the present in the Test matches Mr. Faulkner and Mr. Vogler have had to carry practically the whole of the attack upon their shoulders. This is the more surprising, because the South Africans' great strength was once thought to be in the variety of their attack. Mr. Sinclair, Mr. White, Mr. Snooke, Mr. Schwarz, Mr. Stricker, and Mr. Nourse are all bowlers, but none of them seem capable of taking wickets. They are now being used as understudies to Mr. Faulkner and Mr. Vogler, but the two latter only are expected to secure wickets. Up to the present they have done everything that has been required of them; but what would happen if either of them was incapacitated one cannot imagine.

Leveson Gower (unhyphenated) was captain of the touring side, which ultimately lost the series 3-2. South Africa's decisive victory came in the fourth Test at Cape Town, when F. L. Fane deputized – as he did also in the final match – for Leveson Gower.

Eton v. Harrow

[BY R. H. LYTTELTON]

11 *July* 1910. This season of 1910 is about half over, and has already been made famous for close finishes; but nothing has quite equalled the great match between Eton and Harrow, which ended on Saturday in the most dramatic victory for Eton that could be conceived. Until about 25 minutes before the end it never looked possible that Eton could win; but really great boy-bowling and fielding, and perhaps a visitation of nerves – most natural in the circumstances – that came over the Harrow boys brought about an Eton victory by nine runs. So hopeless was Eton's position at the end of their second innings that many Etonians had left the ground; but there were quite enough at the finish to make the scene when all was over a memorable one, and most pardonable pandemonium reigned for fully half an hour.

The weather on Saturday was cold and sunless until a few minutes after five, when the sun struggled out. The wicket, however, never varied all through the match; it was slow, although not very difficult, because the ball came too slowly off the pitch; but it frequently got up, and bowlers could get a lot of break on. When play began Eton had lost five of their best wickets and required 93 runs to save the follow-on. Of this number they got 27, none of them showing any sign of ability to play the Harrow "googly" bowler Alexander [*later Field-Marshal, Earl Alexander of Tunis*], who got three wickets for seven runs. The other bowlers bowled steadily, while the fielding could not have been surpassed, a catch by Turnbull at short-leg being worthy of especial notice. There is no need to say much about Eton's start in the second innings. They followed on 165 runs behind and had lost four wickets for 47 at luncheon, nobody except Birchenough showing any form against Alexander, who again seemed difficult to play.

So far in the match Eton had not in batting made any show at all. Two batsmen had made 43 runs, or about half the runs that came from the bat; and nobody would have been surprised if the whole side had collapsed for about 100 runs. Things looked even worse when, shortly after luncheon, Steel was caught; for five wickets were down for 65, and 100 more runs were wanted to avert defeat by an innings. The turning point of the match arrived when Wigan joined Fowler. There was not much of a stand, but Eton supporters were thankful for small mercies; and when Wigan was bowled for 16 the sixth wicket had added 40 runs, and, moreover, Fowler had got set. Boswell joined his captain and played an admirable innings of 32; and both he and Fowler did much for their side, not only by scoring fast and hitting the bowling, but by causing a deterioration in the fielding, for several catches, not all easy ones, were dropped. The ground fielding and throwing were so good that perhaps too much was expected; and it may be that the extreme keenness caused the dropping of catches as fieldsmen are apt to shut their hands just a little too quick when on the full stretch. Boswell played as good an innings as any in the match, showing both nerve and skill, and his stand with Fowler added 57 to the score.

At this stage Eton sympathizers were looking a trifle less gloomy – at all events some batting form had been shown; but the position was nearly as hopeless as ever, for one run was still wanted to save the innings defeat and seven wickets were down. Worse remained, for Fowler was caught at 166 and Stock was out leg before wicket at 169, so that with one wicket to fall Eton were four runs ahead. Fowler is probably a useful and dangerous rather than a good bat, but his nerve and pluck were splendid on Saturday, and, without running any risks, he fairly pulled the game round and made possible what was to follow. After the fall of the ninth wicket there was a most exhilarating half-hour's cricket while Manners and Lister-Kaye, especially Manners, hit the bowling all over the field. There were no half-measures about Manners's play. He did not hit recklessly at straight or off balls of at all a decent length; he waited instead for the well-pitched-up ball, with which he made no mistake; and when Lister-Kaye was caught Eton, although in a desperate plight, had at any rate retrieved the position to a certain extent, for in the circumstances 219 was a very good score.

The rest of the match was simply astounding. The Harrow Eleven – seven of whom had played in the match the year before, and were therefore more or less experienced – had not once been beaten this season, and were confronted with the apparently simple task of making 55 runs; moreover, all through the match up to this point they had been fairly on top of their opponents. The most sanguine Old Etonian would have compounded for a five-wicket defeat; and, as already stated, many had left the ground. Two hours remained for cricket, so there was no playing against the clock, and the wicket was not more difficult than it had been at any time during the match. Jameson and Wilson opened the batting, as in the first innings. Fowler began the bowling from the Pavilion end, and with his first ball, which was a good one, clean bowled Wilson. Hopley then came in and quickly made two 4's; and the fact that a dozen more of such hits would have won the match for Harrow confirmed the impression that the match was as good as over. Lister-Kaye bowled three overs at the Nursery end, being then replaced by Steel, and no further change was made. After Hopley had scored his two boundary hits Fowler set his teeth and almost before one had taken in the position Hopley and Turnbull were respectively bowled and caught, and three wickets were down for eight runs, all scored by Hopley. Turnbull looked as if he had gone in with instructions to knock Fowler off his length; and whether this was so or not he skied the ball to the deep field, where Boswell judged it well and made an easy catch. The powerful figure of Earle was then seen at the wicket, and for a few minutes his hitting looked like pulling the match off for Harrow. He scored the next 13 runs and looked most dangerous, but then was caught at short-slip. From the Pavilion the catch looked a doubtful one, but the umpire gave him out. Four wickets were now down for 21 runs, and things were getting exciting; but as far as the result was concerned the general opinion was expressed by an experienced cricketer, not connected with either school, who remarked that it was a pity that 90 runs had not been wanted instead of 55, for then there would have been the possibility of an exciting finish.

Jameson was defending with skill, but so far had not made a run. Then wickets began to fall so quickly that it was really difficult fully to comprehend how things stood. Monckton, Hillyard, Blount, and Straker were all out, three of them victims to Fowler and one of them to Steel. The ball with which Steel dismissed Blount was a short one, but it hung a little, and the batsman played too quick; Hillyard was caught at mid-on off a hit that might have been harder, but the catch was a good one, as the fieldsman was very close in. Eight wickets were down for 27 runs, when Jameson scored two runs. He had actually gone in first and had seen eight wickets fall in 40 minutes before he himself had scored a single run. Not many minute. before he had been badly cut over, and at 32 he was clean bowled by Fowler. Graham was then in and was joined by Alexander, Harrow wanting 23 runs to win. Alexander raised hopes by the way he shaped, for he seemed full of confidence, and the pair added 13 runs. Eton's fielding could not have been surpassed, as every man did his work, and there was only one "extra." Fowler was bowling with great precision, and it speaks well for the nerve of the two Harrovians that they put on 13 runs. The end came a minute or so before 6 o'clock. Alexander played inside a ball from Steel for the break. The ball went straight on, he was well caught at short-slip, and Eton had won by nine runs.

A more exciting match can hardly ever have been played. The electric rapidity with which the fortunes of the game changed in the last hour was truly remarkable. When all was over, of course, many were heard to say that had Harrow gone for a hit they must have won the match. Three of them to all appearances did go in to hit, but the result was that Hopley was clean bowled for 8, Turnbull caught for o, and Earle caught for 13. Fowler's bowling in the very beginning of the last innings, when he got the wickets of Wilson, Hopley, Turnbull, and Earle for 21 runs, was at once the direct and indirect cause of the defeat of Harrow. Directly he got these four out and indirectly he affected the nerves of the others that came after. Those who have watched cricket for years can recall too many cases of nerves affecting a whole eleven to be surprised or to blame Harrow for this. The picked English team in 1882 could be equally blamed for nerves. They, too, had a paltry score to make on a soft wicket to win; they lost the match by 7 runs, and they also after the match were told that they ought to have gone in more for hitting. Furthermore, they were men and the Harrow Eleven were boys; and to boys the bowling of Fowler was probably more formidable than Spofforth's was to England. Harrow played the game well until Fowler's skill with the ball proved too much for them. In the management of the Harrow bowling there was rather too much changing. Five bowlers could not have been wanted for an innings of 67 runs, and too little use was made of Alexander. Supporters of Eton felt more comfortable when he was not bowling.

The Eton Eleven have every reason to be proud of themselves. After fighting with all the worst of it for nearly the whole match, they rose to the occasion after the fall of the fifth wicket in the second innings. There were three of them especially that did splendid work. Boswell in his innings of 32 played splendidly against the Harrow bowling and fielding at the height of their success, and Manners hit in a way that cannot be praised too highly for its courage and dash. But in the whole history of public school cricket nothing better can have been seen than Fowler's play on the second day. As captain he managed the match well, as a batsman he played an excellent innings of 64 when the game appeared to be hopelessly lost, and, finally, by a really fine piece of bowling, he pulled the match out of the fire. It was a splendid performance and a glorious wind up to a great match, that reflects great credit on both sides.

HARROW 232 (Mr. J. M. Hillyard 62, Mr. T. B. Wilson 53; Mr. A. I. Steel 4 for 69, Mr. R. St. L. Fowler 4 for 90) and 45 (Mr. R. St. L. Fowler 8 for 23)
ETON 67 and 219 (Mr. R. St. L. Fowler 64, Hon. J. N. Manners 40 not out)
Eton won by 9 runs

Musical Cricket

FROM A CORRESPONDENT [E. B. OSBORN]

30 *August* 1910. In those pellucid intervals when they are not calculating averages and percentages to several places of decimals or chronicling So-and-so's 99th wicket or 999th run, certain publicists (let us choose the name that dignifies rather than the name that degrades the business of writing round about cricket) wax magniloquent on the subject of the rights and wrongs of the crowd at a cricket match. Two years ago it was the question of the tea interval which disturbed the minds of these friends of the people and dislocated their grammar. Last year they discussed the subject of suspensions of play while the ground was recovering from a drenching (last season it was a case of "the rain it raineth every day," and the weather has been even more exasperating this year) and assured us that such breaks in the entertainment provided for those who had paid down their money at the turnstiles could no longer be tolerated.

These agitations, sad to say, were not without effect. Tea intervals were dropped on several county grounds, where the authorities, for mercenary reasons, think more of satisfying the sixpenny spectators than of the comfort of cricketers, who after all are not members of music-hall troupes, and have a right to indulge in tea-and-talk when the whole civilized world is doing the same. And this season, as a result of last year's agitation by the friends of the professional spectator, weird engines have been provided to protect the pitch from the effects of rainfall, though nothing has been done – for nothing can be done – to prevent the drenched outfield from being scarred and cut up by the men who are scouting out and cannot keep their footing.

It is now proposed to "enliven" county cricket matches for the benefit of spectators by means of bands, and the experiment has actually been tried at Lord's – Lord's of all places in Cricketdom. There can be no objection, of course, to instrumental music during the luncheon interval when those who do not care to leave the ground, preferring sandwiches and cricket gossip to a formal meal, often find that time trickles away slowly, spasmodically, reluctantly – like the contents of a full bottle. Nor, if the musicians chose to stay and watch the match, would any rational person refuse them the opportunity of performing suitable pieces (such as "Home, Sweet Home," "Pack, Clouds, away," &c.) while play is suspended owing to a sudden downpour or the darkening of the heavens by a suspended fog. As long as it is not a case of interfering with the physical and mental comfort of the actual players, everything possible should be done for the greatest possible happiness of the greatest possible number. But it is nothing less than an outrage against the spirit and traditions of cricket to allow a band to perform while play is going on. At athletic sports music is not out of place; but as regards cricket, the good old rule "Don't mix your arts" comes into full play. Cricket is a complete art in itself – epic, or dramatic, or lyric, as the man and the moment may determine – and the intrusion of the finest and most finely-rendered music is felt by the cricketer who puts brains into his batting, or bowling, or fielding and respects his art, himself, and his fellow-artists as an intolerable impertinence. Moreover, the spectator who really knows the game and is able and willing to concentrate his mind on what is happening on the "perilous pitch" does not want to be bothered with a band; when deeply moved by the consideration of some crisis, some dramatic turning-point in the history of the *funera nefunera* of a well-contested match, he will describe the most charming music as a noise and a nuisance – adding the appropriate adjectives which, winged words as they are, would be as inappropriate in print as swallows in a cage.

Some cricketers, no doubt, would merely grumble to themselves if a band were allowed to interfere with the business of their game, in which every stroke or stratagem is an "intellectual thing," like a tear or a laugh. But others will speak out in the emphatic language of the wisdom of intolerance (a kind of wisdom unwisely despised in this complaisant age) if the Lord's experiment is made a precedent. Mr. C. I. Thornton, going in to take his innings at Scarborough, once ordered a band to stop playing, and the order was obeyed. He was dismissed without scoring – no doubt there remained something of his *saeva indignatio* at an artistic outrage while he was at the wicket for the first fateful few balls – and his successor, sad to say, went in without rebuking the musicians. There must be other instances of the same timely outspoken common sense in the annals of first-class cricket. To descend from great things to small, the writer himself when going in to try to stop a rot in a village match annexed in passing a concertina which, in the hands of a small boy, had vexed the souls of many that afternoon. The small boy said, among other things, "Don't excite your silly gizzard" (curious phrase!) and was then taken home by his governess, but the concertina was given into the charge of the home team's umpire. It is perhaps only fair to tell another short story, which shows that in certain circumstances the attendance of a band might make for the betterment of the game. Playing against a lunatic asylum, the writer skied the ball to deep square-leg, and the catch was judged to a nicety and held by the fielder, a gentleman with delusions alleged to be having a lucid interval. Excited by the applause (in which the writer forgot to join) he ran rapidly round the field and was not caught by the attendants, who appeared from nowhere, until ten minutes had been wasted. One of the doctors subsequently said that, though quite harmless, he was very susceptible to the charms of music. Had there been a band in attendance the incident might never have occurred; for example, he might have missed the catch.

Let us then consent to the presence of bands at matches played on the grounds of lunatic asylums, but refuse to invite them to Lord's and other places where cricket is the sport of persons with a whole mind in a wholesome body. All batsmen will agree with this declaration of policy, which has the politic merit of making a concession to the enemy. Bowlers may not be quite so eager to withstand the innovation. They are in the habit of turning all perturbations of the natural order of things (differences of pace in the pitch, cross-winds that help their swerve, &c.) to their own advantage and the confusion of the batsman, their natural enemy; and some of them may regard the music that distracts his attention as an addition to the number of their incidental allies. But they all have to wield the willow, and the majority are anxious to be regarded as batsmen and moved up in the order of going in – a boon for which they will cheerfully resign some portion of their skill in bowling. Let us then appeal to them as batsmen, deceiving them for their own good, to strengthen the forces of opposition.

If their music could be made incidental (in the theatrical sense), the band might be tolerated on county grounds. For each characteristic stroke or bowling stratagem we might have a *leit-motiv*; a late cut or a googly would elicit from the band a characteristic musical phrase. A cricket symphony, composed by an English variant of Richard Strauss, might be permitted. It would begin, of course, by introducing the motive of the mowing machine, the sound of which, heard in the early morning of a mid-summer's day, is so delightful to the ears of cricketers. The time is not yet come for such delicate inventions; until it does bands must not be admitted to the nation's chief playing grounds because a few spectators wish to have their ears tickled. Admit a band for that unreasonable reason, and before we know where we are there will be (as Mr. Punch has suggested) side-shows, electric theatres, and small *cafés chantants*, and switchbacks, and flip-flaps, and aunt sallies, and all the rest, doing a brisk business round the field of play. This very thing has happened in the case of American baseball, a fine game till the professional spectator spoilt it and vulgarized its surroundings. Unless the spectator be cockered up, we are told, county cricket will become bankrupt! The sooner, the better – for then county elevens will be chiefly composed of authentic amateurs, which is just what ought to be. Besides, if a band be allowed to settle at Lord's there will be no limit to its depredations. It will get into the *dedans* when a great tennis match is on. Horrible thought!

Golfing Cricketers

[BY BERNARD DARWIN]

13 *September* 1910. Although Mr. de Montmorency is now a better golfer than he is a cricketer, it would not be inaccurate to class him among the golfing cricketers; indeed, he is the best of that numerous clan. One would not

apply the term to such players as Mr. Balfour-Melville or Mr. Herman de Zoete, because these two began to wield both a bat and a club in early youth. Mr. de Montmorency, on the other hand, was already a good cricketer and had left his public school for a year or two before he began to play golf at all; and to have done that will presumably constitute a man a golfing cricketer, until such time as that expression ceases to have any meaning, through all little boys' beginning golf in the nursery.

There are nowadays a large and distinguished body of golfing cricketers, and it is rather interesting to watch how their early upbringing affects their golfing methods. Mr. Croome, who is one of the very best of them, has absorbed golf so thoroughly into his system that he has not only a graceful but a genuinely golfing style; it is only when he is off his game that a tendency to pull himself up on both toes at once at the top of the swing gives a faint clue to his origin. One very great cricketer, Mr. Alfred Lyttelton, always gives one the idea that he did not begin to play golf in a sufficiently arrogant frame of mind. In the humble desire to learn he cultivated a swing of exaggerated length with a rather elaborate turning movement of the wrists. Good player though he is, it may be permissible to wonder whether he would not have been better still if he had merely stood up to the golf ball by the light of Nature and slashed it to the boundary with the contempt it deserved.

Among many other cricketers, Mr. George Brann drives a very long ball in a peculiar style. The club begins to go back in a perfectly orthodox fashion; then, when it has travelled some little way, it suddenly changes its course and describes a most formidable flourish over Mr. Brann's head. It resembles the flourish of Massy, but is far more pronounced, and there is a large proportion of hit in the stroke to a small one of swing; still, there are very few longer drivers, nor are Mr. Brann's golfing merits by any means confined to his long game. Dr. W. G. Grace began golf at a rather more advanced age than these other cricketers before-mentioned, and his swing is therefore more curtailed. Needless to say, however, there is much to admire about it. The body is kept very still and the ball is hit wonderfully crisply and cleanly; better than either is the action of the wrists, which so acute and experienced a critic as Braid has declared to be an absolute model for all golfers.

The Yorkshire Captainship

FROM A CORRESPONDENT [E. B. OSBORN]

27 *September* 1910. The final retirement of Lord Hawke from the captainship of the Yorkshire County Eleven will be sincerely regretted by cricketers throughout the country, who have regarded him for a whole generation as one of the institutions of the game. It is true his appearances in that capacity have been infrequent during the last two seasons – this year the whole burden

of leadership has fallen on his lieutenant, Mr. E. J. Radcliffe. Even now, after 28 years' service as captain, and despite the inevitable falling-off in his run-earning and run-saving powers, his unquestioned genius for getting the most and best out of his men would make him well worth his place in the eleven.

As a batsman Lord Hawke has always done his share of the work. Since he came into the Yorkshire eleven in 1881 he has scored 23,473 runs (including ten centuries) for the county in 692 completed innings, which gives him an average of 29·4, quite enough from a captain who never, or hardly ever, lost runs by missing catches at a crisis. In point of fact this statistical computation is really no criterion of the value of his batting. Going in rather late as a rule he has been the sticking partner, so to speak, in scores of unexpected stands; and on many occasions it was due to him that the game was pulled round after a series of disastrous failures on the part of Yorkshire's leading batsmen. In Lancashire, the keen and critical rival of his county, his sturdy defence and vigorous driving were always admired and regarded as an important factor in the annual battles of the Roses; and the Old Trafford spectators would sigh when a catch went to him, well knowing that he had the safest pair of hands in his eleven. "Yon chap's a (adjective) sand-bank" said one of the spectators in moleskins when he took a difficult chance and characteristically refrained from chucking the ball up. "All ah can say," said a comrade, "is, if he is a lord, we could 'appen do wi' more like 'im."

But it was as captain that he was indispensable to his side. As every captain must be who is in charge of an eleven chiefly composed of professionals, he was a strong disciplinarian, who could be stern on occasion. Before he became captain, the Yorkshire team, though surprisingly rich in individual ability, was an undisciplined horde. A professional captain may sometimes get the best out of his fellow-professionals on the field – it is not often so – but invariably his authority terminates with the close of the day's play. Lord Hawke soon gave his men to understand that there was no room in the Yorkshire Eleven for a player who thought he could do as he liked off the field, provided he obeyed orders while the game was going on. In a very short time he had his men in hand; and for many a long year it was never necessary for him to assert his authority overtly, everybody knowing the firm will that lay behind the dignified geniality of a leader who was also a comrade. A significant trait of the captain whose authority is firmly based on the respect and confidence of his men is his ability to seek and take advice from the long-experienced professional without any loss of prestige. Lord Hawke was always able to do this; he would consult Tunnicliffe or another, whenever that course seemed advisable, and was never afraid of letting the other players, to say nothing of the crowd, see that he did not consider his own judgment infallible at all times. Off the field he was the Yorkshire professional's best friend. He proved himself of opinion that you can dress and talk and lunch with any man who is good enough to play cricket with. People from the north of England, a not unduly democratic region, are always a little annoyed when they come south and find that amateurs and professionals do not associate off the field. Still it would be unjust to dismiss the southern fashion as mere snobbishness. Off the field Lord Hawke has always regarded himself as a trustee of the Yorkshire professional's future welfare. The latter has not to shift for himself during the winter, thus incurring a loss of *moral* that must diminish his value to his team – and to himself. In the matter of talent money Lord Hawke's sympathetic knowledge of his men has been usefully expressed. Probably the custom of a money reward for a score of 50 has been more often a cause of wasted time and opportunities than the professional batsman's wish to cultivate his average. The plan of giving marks for conspicuous services in the field – for a score in proportion to its usefulness, for fine bowling at a crisis, for a good catch at the critical moment – and dividing up a fund of prize-money at the end of the season is obviously a long step in the direction of applied common sense. No wonder that the Yorkshire professionals have a deep affection for their old captain, and that cricketers throughout the country sympathize with them in their loss.

Sussex v. Nottinghamshire

Extraordinary hitting by Alletson

22 *May* 1911. Probably nothing has been accomplished either at Brighton or on any other enclosure more remarkable than the hitting seen in this match on Saturday. Alletson gave a most extraordinary exhibition of rapid and fierce scoring. He has always been known as a batsman with strong punishing powers, but on Saturday, going in when his side were apparently in a most hopeless position – Nottinghamshire with seven wickets down in their second innings being only nine runs on – he accomplished the extraordinary feat of scoring 189 runs out of 227 in 90 minutes.

He scored 47 runs in 50 minutes before luncheon, but this was just the beginning. Afterwards, when he had Riley, the last man, as his partner, the latter played the part of the quiet onlooker. Alletson took the game into his own hands and treated Killick and Leach as though they were a pair of schoolboys. He began by scoring nine runs off each bowler in the first two overs, and then hit Killick for 22 in one over. Thirteen came from Leach's second over, and he reached his 100 in 75 minutes, having made his second 50 in 20 minutes.

He now proceeded to hit Killick for 11 in the following over and Leach for 17 in the succeeding one, and then came the crowning point – 34 runs in one over from Killick, and that bowler sent down two no-balls, so that the hitter had eight balls to deal with. He scored from seven of them, hitting three 6's and four 4's. He had thus since lunch made 115 runs out of 120 from seven consecutive overs, and R. Relf was then put on for Leach, and was hit for 15 in his second over; and then Cox, after being twice sent to leg for four, got Alletson extremely well caught by Smith standing with his back to the grand stand.

Some idea of the remarkable character of the closing stages of this wonderful innings was that Alletson scored his last 89 runs in 15 minutes, and with two or three exceptions all his runs came from tremendous drives. Twice he sent the ball over the grand stand, once into the pavilion seats, and on five other occasions he cleared the ring either to the on or off. His score was made up by eight 6's, 23 4's, four 3's, ten 2's, and 17 singles. He made 142 out of 152 in 40 minutes after lunch, the latter figures being the amount of the stand for the last wicket.

Sussex were left with 237 runs to get to win in three hours and a quarter, and were nearly beaten, though R. Relf and Vine gave their side a brilliant start. When they left wickets fell quickly and Sussex played to avert defeat. Killick and Leach stayed together for an hour, and the match ended in a draw, Sussex with only two wickets to fall being 24 runs short of the number required to win. The defects of the new scoring system were seen in that Sussex by their lead on the first innings gained three points and Notts one.

NOTTINGHAMSHIRE 238 (G. Gunn 90, Mr. A. O. Jones 57; Killick 5 for 14) and 412 (Alletson 189, Iremonger 83, G. Gunn 66)
SUSSEX 414 (Killick 81, Vine 77, Leach 52, R. Relf 42) and 213 for 8 (R. Relf 71, Vine 54; Riley 4 for 82)
Match drawn

Mr. E. M. Grace

22 *May* 1911. We regret to record that Mr. E. M. Grace, the well-known cricketer, and brother of Dr. W. G. Grace, died on Saturday at Thornbury, Gloucestershire.

Edward Mills Grace was born in November, 1841, and was thus in his 70th year. He had been Coroner for West Gloucestershire since 1875 and Registrar of Births, Deaths, and Marriages for his native district. He was four times married, was a bold and thrusting rider to hounds, and, finally, as a cricketer was for nearly 40 years Secretary of the Gloucestershire Cricket Club, and played first-class cricket for 35 years.

It is doubtful whether any cricketer that ever lived could have been more enthusiastically fond of the game or have had a more varied experience. It is true that he went to Australia only once and had not been to other parts of the world, like many of our modern cricketers; but he took part in every kind of match in this country that cricket can produce. An International match against the Australians, Gentlemen v. Players, North v. South, matches against odds, the most trivial village match – they were all alike to E. M. Grace; one and all he played with the utmost keenness and with wonderful success. When he began first-class play in 1860 batsmen played on orthodox lines. They kept the right foot firm, and never were known to leave a ball alone or to pull or hit across the wicket. But orthodoxy in cricket was never in E. M. Grace's way at all; and he was probably the first great cricketer who systematically pulled off balls to the leg side. This was not solely because he wanted to hit where no fieldsman was standing, but because he was a far stronger player on the leg side than he was on the off. But his chief characteristic as a batsman was his wonderful eye. In cricket, as in other games, it is generally the case that the orthodox player is able to play a good game for a much longer time than the unorthodox. Hand and eye fail as a man gets older, but if the style is there the runs will come, though at a slower rate. E. M. Grace had no style, strictly speaking, and no orthodoxy; but his eye was marvellous. Although after 1870 his first-class play was confined mainly to county matches, much fewer in number than they are now, he was selected in 1880 to represent England in the great International match of that year; and then for the first and last time in cricket history did three brothers appear in an International match. E. M. Grace went in first with his more famous brother and played a characteristic innings of 36; and in the same year he scored 65 and 41 against the Australians, with F. R. Spofforth on the side, which was not the case in the International match. It has always been said that these two innings astonished Mr. Spofforth, who never dreamed that anybody could be found who could pull his best length balls so daringly.

As a bowler E. M. Grace was successful without being really good; but there were many bowlers in the '60's who, simple enough on a perfect wicket, were good enough to get wickets on unprepared and bumpy pitches, and E. M. Grace was one of these. He bowled both round-arm medium pace and lobs, but his lobs were not of a high class, though they played havoc in the numerous country matches of which he was so fond. Fifty years ago cricketers used to "specialize" and field in one place; and E. M. Grace as a point was as famous as R. T. King in the '40's, or as Tinley, Carpenter, and F. W. Wright of his own day. He used to stand far closer to the batsman than is the case now, and when Dr. W. G. Grace was bowling he was a perfect terror to "tail" batsmen. Nobody was quicker in his movements or more daring, and he used to take the ball almost off the bat, a method of fielding most terrifying to the nerves of inferior batsmen.

It is difficult to select his greatest performances, as there is such a large period of time to choose from. E. M. Grace was one of the three (W. G. Grace was another, and the late V. E. Walker was the third) who scored a century and took 10 wickets in one innings in the same match. E. M. Grace's match was at Canterbury, where he was playing as a substitute for M.C.C. against Kent, a purely amateur match of the best class, in 1862. He went in first and carried his bat through the innings for 192 and proceeded to take all 10 wickets in Kent's second innings. In 1863 he played a fine innings of 73, playing for Twenty-two of the Lansdown Club at Bath against the bowling of Tinley, Jackson, Tarrant, Willsher, and Hayward, a very strong lot; and in the same year an innings of 52 against Thirteen of Kent at Lord's made a great sensation at the time. In 1882 he played an innings of 122 against Lancashire; this was one of his best innings, for he gave no chance, and Nash, Crossland, Barlow, and Watson were four very good bowlers. But he played in few first-class matches in which he did not make his mark, and his boundless enthusiasm and unfailing high spirits were invaluable assets to his side.

In purely country cricket E. M. Grace must have surely scored more runs and taken more wickets than anybody who ever lived. Many of these matches were played on small grounds, and the presence of a man who for many years would have been selected for the best English Eleven in an ordinary village match must have been a lesson to his opponents. E. M. Grace scored innings of one, two, or three centuries as long ago as the early '60's; what he would have scored in these days, when wickets are so easy, may be imagined. In 1863 he made more than 3,000 runs, and he still played in his own village as late as 1909. Altogether between the years 1851 and 1899 he scored 72,482 runs and took 10,006 wickets.

The M.C.C. Team in Australia

An appreciation

FROM A CORRESPONDENT [P. F. WARNER]

5 *April* 1912. "England batted better, fielded better, and bowled better than we did, and we have no excuses to make; we were fairly and squarely beaten." These were the words in which Mr. Hill, the captain of the Australian Eleven, congratulated the English cricketers on winning the rubber, and his generous opinion has found an echo throughout Australia.

There can be little doubt that the potent factor in England's triumph has been the magnificent bowling of Mr. F. R. Foster and Barnes. In each of the last three Test Matches they gave their side a great start, and there has never been such consistently fine bowling on perfect wickets. Barnes is probably not so fast as he was six or seven years ago, but he has lost nothing in accuracy or spin, and he possesses the faculty of making the ball go from leg after pitching. It is not exactly what you might call a leg break, and it is much more than a mere "go with the arm"; it is, in fact, something between the two. This is the ball which has worried the Australian batsmen so greatly, and much of their trouble comes from the difficulty of detecting whether this ball or the one that will break from the off is on the way. Barnes bowls well to his field, and, while his length is immaculate, he varies the flight of the ball, especially when bowling his leg break, extremely well. He is, on all wickets, the finest bowler in the world to-day – that at all events is the opinion of Australia.

From the pavilion Mr. F. R. Foster appears to be medium in pace, but when the ball strikes the ground the velocity seems to be trebled, and if the batsman and the wicket-keeper should miss the ball it will reach the boundary almost as quickly as anything that Mr. E. Jones, Mr. Kortright, or Mr. Brearley ever bowled. And what a lovely, natural, and absolutely unforced action Mr. Foster possesses. Two or three steps, a graceful skip, a short run, and he delivers the ball. Never in first class cricket has a bowler been seen who has hit the batsmen so frequently on the legs as Mr. Foster has done this tour. His bowling makes such haste off the pitch that even such accomplished players as Mr. Trumper and Mr. Armstrong have apparently, on occasions, not had time to get into position to play their stroke. In his first few overs Mr. Foster has made the ball swerve into the batsman, but even after the newness has worn off the ball he has been able to keep almost all of his fieldsmen on the leg-side. To justify such a disposition of the field a bowler needs to be wonderfully accurate, and his accuracy is one of Mr. Foster's greatest merits. Moreover, he makes the batsman play at four balls out of five, for he pitches the ball on the leg stump, or just off it, and his "leg theory" is no confession of weakness as "leg theory" bowling so often is. It has a very positive value, and on the majority of English wickets, on which the ball rises considerably higher than on Australian pitches, the batsmen may expect some very nasty knocks. Apart from his superb bowling, Mr. Foster has batted excellently in a free and charming style, and he is undoubtedly the finest all-round cricketer England has discovered for many a long day.

Mr. Douglas's bowling has also been a contributing factor in England's success. In the first Test Match at Sydney he bowled very well, taking four wickets for 50 runs in Australia's second innings, and in the third Test Match he rendered good service by bowling steadily and taking two wickets for 71 runs in the long Australian second innings. But in the second innings of the fourth Test Match he bowled in a form only slightly inferior to anything Mr. Foster and Barnes had shown. His bowling on that occasion was a revelation, for not only did he take wickets, including those of Mr. Hill, Mr. Armstrong, and Mr. Minnett, all clean bowled, for 46 runs, but he bowled with such life and fire that no one would have been surprised had he obtained an even better analysis. He will return with a greatly increased reputation, and he is certainly a much improved bowler, for not only is he accurate in length, but he makes great pace off the ground. Mr. Douglas has done so splendidly since that there is no harm now in saying that he did not captain the side at all well in the first Test Match. It was generally agreed at the time that he made a great tactical error in not beginning the bowling with Barnes and Mr. Foster, nor did he have a "grip" of the team on the field. The experience, however, gained then was of great value, and he deserves to be warmly congratulated on the success of his subsequent efforts. He improved match by match as a leader and never spared himself.

Apart from Mr. Foster, Barnes, and Mr. Douglas, England's bowling has been only moderate. J. W. Hearne, who was regarded in England as a bowler who might on his day turn the fortunes of a match in half an hour, has been a complete failure, for the reason that he has never struck a length, full pitches, long hops, and half-volleys being plentiful. It is probable, however, that his loss of form is only temporary. Whenever he has bowled a good length ball it has always wanted playing, though on these perfect wickets the amount of break he can impart to the ball is not great. Hitch sustained an injury early in the tour which kept him out of the team for nearly a month, and he was just beginning to bowl in something like his true form when just before the fourth Test Match he again broke down. It has, therefore, been scarcely possible to form an opinion as to his true merits. Woolley has taken an odd wicket here and there, but Australian pitches give no encouragement to a slow left-handed bowler.

The magnificent bowling of Mr. Foster and Barnes, who are regarded here as the finest pair of bowlers England has ever sent to Australia, has received adequate backing in the fine batting of Hobbs and Rhodes, and, in a lesser degree, of Gunn, J. W. Hearne, and Mr. Foster himself. Hobbs has been in wonderful form, and Rhodes bats better and better match after match. His second innings against New South Wales was a magnificent display of free, confident batting, with very hard hiting on the off side. Gunn is a better and more reliable batsman in Australia than in England, and J. W. Hearne has more than fulfilled Mr. Warner's expectations as a batsman, if he has been useless as a bowler. He it was who taught the team in the first Test Match the correct way to play Dr. Hordern's googlies, and there is every reason to hope that he will develop into one of the greatest batsmen of his time. He ought indeed to be a second Hayward. Mr. Foster bats in an easy and natural style, and he has been very consistent. Woolley's 56 in the fourth Test Match at Melbourne was a beautiful innings, but he has over and over again been dismissed just when he seemed set. Mead has been disappointing, for he tumbles over his bat and is not good at slow bowling. Nor has he timed the ball well. The fielding has been good; there was no long field to compare with Mr. Ransford or Mr. Bardsley, but the catching has been sound and reliable, and Smith is a really great wicket-keeper.

Warner, the appointed captain of the side, was taken seriously ill after the opening match and did not play again on the tour.

Australia v. South Africa

Easy victory of Australia

[BY E. B. NOEL]

29 *May* 1912. Australia beat South Africa at Manchester yesterday by an innings and 88 runs.

The South Africans finished their first innings at about half-past 4 for a total of 265. They were thus 183 runs behind, and they followed on, but in their second innings, on a good wicket and against bowling which was not deadly, they collapsed utterly, and by half-past 6 the whole side were out, and the match had been lost and won. No one dreamed for a moment when they went in a second time that the game would be finished that night, but Mr. Faulkner's dismissal in the second over was the prelude to a series of disasters.

A "record" was set up by Mr. Matthews. There have been "hat tricks" in Test Matches before – Bates, J. T. Hearne, and Mr. Trumble have accomplished the feat – but no one until yesterday had done so twice in a Test Match in one day. Mr. Matthews in the first innings took the last three wickets – Mr. Beaumont's, Mr. Pegler's, and Mr. Ward's. In the second innings, when five wickets were down, he bowled Mr. Taylor and caught and bowled Mr. Schwarz and Mr. Ward. Mr. Ward was thus the unfortunate victim of the third ball on each occasion.

The South African first innings was interesting, as cricket always is when batsmen have to fight hard for runs against good bowling. A bad start was made and four wickets were down for 54 runs. A great batting feat by Mr. Faulkner at one moment looked likely to be crowned with the success of saving the follow-on – he and Mr. Beaumont were together, the score was 265 for seven wickets, and only 30 more runs were wanted – but then Mr. Matthews, bowling from the Stretford end, accomplished his first "hat trick"; Mr. Beaumont was bowled and Mr. Pegler and Mr. Ward were out leg-before-wicket to very similar balls. The wicket was again easy, but there was more life in it than on Monday, and the ball travelled much quicker in the outfield.

Mr. Faulkner's batting was the one bright feature of the innings; much depended on him, and he rose to the occasion. His task was to stay there and bat to score, not quickly but steadily, and for over four hours he played the soundest of cricket, hitting the ball to the boundary when an opportunity presented itself, which was not very often. He was once badly missed, at mid-on by Mr. Whitty, when he had made 36, and he made two bad strokes towards third man, but apart from these there was no mistake in his innings. Mr. White's batting deserves the greatest praise. He came in at a critical time, and although he was obviously in pain and could hardly use his right hand (which was split yesterday) at all, he stayed in for a long time while nearly 100 were put on. For a batsman with such beautiful strokes and forcing power as he it must have been in a sense most galling to have to stay in and do nothing but keep the ball out of his wicket. He could not, of course, put any power into his strokes, but his innings was a fine display of physical and moral pluck.

Mr. Whitty's bowling in the first South African innings stood out as conspicuously as Mr. Faulkner's batting. For a long spell after luncheon from the Stretford end, with the wind blowing crosswise, he bowled really well;

he made the ball swing and come off the pitch with much fire; he bowled practically no bad balls, and it took all the skill of even Mr. Faulkner to play his bowling, while some of the others were all at sea. He bowled 34 overs in the innings and only 55 runs were hit off his bowling, a record which speaks for itself. . .

The Australians had bowled well and the field had been cunningly placed, but, except Mr. Faulkner, who alone saved the side from bad disaster, and Mr. White who was so severely handicapped, the batting on the whole was poor. Mr. Emery, who shared most of the attack with Mr. Whitty, is a most interesting bowler, for his methods are so enterprising. He bowls all sorts of balls (long-hops and full-pitches are quite common), but he was never heavily punished off the full-pitch. Probably it drops at the last minute quickly and unexpectedly; at all events, time after time the batsman missed the ball. Mr. Gregory, Mr. Matthews, and Mr. Macartney on the off-side were beautifully quick in the field, as was Mr. Minnett in "the country."

The Australians sent the South Africans in again at about a quarter to 5. By half-past all hopes of a fight were over and an hour later the match was finished. It was decided that Mr. Faulkner should bat first; probably it was thought that after a rest he would be all right again, for he had looked tired towards the end of the first innings, although he had rightly spared himself by not running quickly between the wickets. Whether the policy of putting him in first was right or not, a great disaster befell the side at once, for in Mr. Kelleway's first over from the City end Mr. Faulkner was clean bowled by a good ball and the best batsman of the side was gone. Mr. Nourse, who came in next, has for the most part this year played stolid on-side cricket; yesterday for some reason he discarded this method and went all out for his off-side shots. He made one or two lovely hits, but was caught from a bad stroke – he did not get his left leg across at all – at third man. Mr. Snooke was dismissed at the same total, 22, and at 43 Mr. Hartigan was bowled by a really fine ball from Mr. Whitty. Four men were now out. Mr. White came in and for a short time he and Mr. Taylor withstood the attack, but both were out in quick succession with the total at 70, Mr. White caught at the wicket off Mr. Kelleway's bowling and Mr. Taylor clean bowled by Mr. Matthews. Mr. Schwarz came next, but was caught and bowled off the first ball he received. Mr. Ward met with precisely the same fate, and then with his next ball Mr. Matthews in his first Test Match in England set up a "record" which will probably stand for many a day, that of a double "hat trick." Four wickets had fallen for 70 runs, and now eight men were out and not a run had been added. Mr. Beaumont made two 4's and then Mr. Mitchell was bowled. Mr. Pegler came in, 17 more runs were scored by hard hitting, and then Mr. Beaumont was bowled, and the match was over.

On a good wicket South Africa had been dismissed in well under two hours for a total of 95 runs. It was a collapse of the worst description, due, moreover, to really bad batting, but such things, after all, are the life and soul of cricket.

The Australians have played very well in this match, which will add to their reputation as a side. Mr. Matthews, of course, will look back on it with especial gratification. He bowls right-handed, medium pace, and makes the ball turn either way, chiefly from leg, and come quickly off the pitch.

The South Africans' form was too bad to be true, and it is to be hoped that this may only be the darkest hour before the dawn and that they will show their real ability later.

> AUSTRALIA 448 (Mr. W. Bardsley 121, Mr. C. Kelleway 144, Mr. T. J. Matthews 49 not out; Mr. S. J. Pegler 6 for 105)
> SOUTH AFRICA 265 (Mr. G. A. Faulkner 122 not out; Mr. W. J. Whitty 5 for 55) and 95 (Mr. C. Kelleway 5 for 33)
> *Australia won by an innings and 88 runs*

The Failure of "Googly" Bowling

3 *June* 1912. It is rather remarkable to note the comparative inefficiency of "googly" bowling – to judge it solely by results – in the more important matches which have been played this season. For instance, in the first Test Trial match at the Oval Clark took one wicket for 68 runs; Mr. Carr in the second Test Trial match at Lord's, none for 91; Mr. Schwarz, Mr. Faulkner, and Mr. White in the Test Match at Manchester, four wickets between them for 226.

In cricket mere figures are often very misleading – neither at Lord's nor at Manchester did the lifeless wickets help the "googly" bowlers at all – but it does seem that practice in playing the "googly" has robbed it of some of its terrors. It is said that Dr. Grace, after watching some "googly" bowling a few years ago, observed, "I am glad they didn't bowl like that when I was playing." If this is so he paid this form of bowling the highest possible compliment but no doubt in his prime he would have lost no time in discovering how to master it. For to some of the best of modern batsmen – Hobbs and Rhodes, for instance, and some of the left-handed players, such as Mr. Bardsley – it has apparently no real terrors.

The theory that a "googly" bowler will have a very short life at his best seems to be confirmed. Mr. Schwarz and Mr. Faulkner are not, it must be admitted, the bowlers they were. This is not argued from their non-success at Manchester, for on that wicket it was most difficult to make the ball come quickly off the pitch, a quality which is one of the great essentials of this bowling. But this year they have never bowled, as Mr. R. E. Foster once wrote in "Wisden," so that "it is like playing Briggs through the air and Richardson off the pitch." How much greater an effort is required to bowl the "googly" than other forms of bowling only those who have acquired the art can say, and they are at present few in this country out of thousands who have made the attempt; indeed, the spectacle of bowlers and non-bowlers alike attempting between the fall of the wickets to bowl down "googlies," generally without a suspicion of "google' in them, is now a commonplace in all cricket. But if the effort required is much greater, and if such a bowler can only last a few seasons, it is obvious that a professional cricketer who is a bowler only and must look to the future will think twice about acquiring a style of bowling which might reap for him a harvest of wickets for three or four years and then leave him "on the shelf," so far as bowling is concerned. But it must be remembered that all "googly" bowlers in modern first-class cricket, from Mr. Bosanquet onwards, have acquired the style when they have been grown men. In South Africa it is said that every small boy now bowls the "googly": and if this bowling is developed in the earlier stages of a cricketing life before the muscles become set, it may be that the effort will not be in proportion nearly so great.

Death of Tom Richardson

4 *July* 1912. A Reuter telegram from Chambéry, of yesterday's date, says:– "The body of a man, described as John Richardson, 45, of Richmond-green, Surrey, who has been staying at Aix-les-Bains with his family, was found to-day at a spot above the Bout du Monde cascade near here. Death appears to have been due to cerebral congestion."

The "John" Richardson in the above telegram is presumably a telegraphic mistake for "Tom" Richardson, the once famous bowler, whose residence is at Richmond-green, and who, it was known, was seriously ill at Aix-les-Bains.

Tom Richardson had for some years past dropped out of first-class cricket, but he will be remembered as the greatest fast bowler of his day. Born in 1870, he came out for Surrey in the season of 1892, and had marked success in matches against the counties, which were not then reckoned first class. In the following year he went into the front rank, and for five seasons he remained at his very best. Indeed, no fast bowler in modern days was ever so consistently successful as he was from 1892 to 1897 inclusive. Considering the excellence of the grounds on which he had to bowl his achievements were remarkable. In first-class matches he took 174 wickets in 1893, 196 in 1894, 290 in 1895, 246 in 1896, and 273 in 1897.

He was never the same after his second visit to Australia in the winter of 1897-8. There was a marked falling-off in his form in 1898, and, increasing greatly in weight, he gradually lost his old pace and spin. He still took a good many wickets – as many as 159 fell to him in 1901 – but he was no longer the bowler he had been in his prime. He took 115 wickets for Surrey in 1903, bowling very well in that wet summer, but a year later he dropped out of the eleven, only taking part in four matches. No county in our time has had two such fast bowlers as Richardson and Lockwood at their best. The late George

Freeman is often spoken of as the greatest of fast bowlers, but the wickets on which he played were for the most part inferior to those on which Richardson won his fame.

The Triangular Tournament

23 *August* 1912. The Triangular Tournament ends in a victory for England. The result is:–

	Played.	Won.	Lost.	Drawn.
England	6	4	0	2
Australia	6	2	1	3
South Africa	6	0	5	1

There can be little doubt that England were the best side of the three, that the Australians were better than many people expected them to be at the beginning of the year, and that South Africa were unlucky.

The English side may not be so strong in batting as some of its predecessors, although it would be hard to find a better first pair than Hobbs and Rhodes; and down to Nos. 6 or 7 they were strong. In bowling there was in Barnes one great bowler, who can bowl well on almost any kind of wicket and who must be placed in the class of the great bowlers of the world. His value has been incalculable. Whether on fast wickets England might have been short of bowling is impossible to say. In this apology for a summer the Test Matches have suffered as much as any others. On sticky wickets the bowling has been sufficient for all requirements, and as an all-round cricketer no one has done more than Woolley, who has made runs and taken wickets consistently. Mr. Fry may not have been an ideal captain in certain respects – great captains are not born every day – but if he has had shortcomings, no one has worked more wholeheartedly and with greater keenness for the side. His efforts have been crowned with success, and he is to be heartily congratulated.

The Australians had a most consistent and sound batsman in Mr. Bardsley, a fine batsman in Mr. Macartney, a most attractive player in Mr. Jennings, and the dogged and patient defence of Mr. Kelleway. But the body and tail of the side were not dependable. They had no great bowler, although they have a number who bowl well at times, and a good deal of it looks puzzling "stuff."

To judge the Triangular Tournament by the measure of public support it has received, it has not been a success, and probably in this generation it will not be repeated. But it has at least been an interesting experiment. The one really disheartening thing has been the weather.

A Suggestion to Prohibit
Left-handed Batting

12 *May* 1913. A keen critic of the game, after having read Mr. R. E. Foster's contention that the leg-before-wicket rule might be altered so as to apply to the off-break only, at once remarked, "What is to happen in the case of the left-handed batsmen?" Another critic observed, "There ought to be no left-handed batsmen," and it is possible that there is a good deal in the theory which he proceeded to elaborate. In effect it was as follows:–

The left-handed batsman is a nuisance to all but his own side, to whom he is most valuable. Bowlers do not as a rule bowl so well against him; there is great trouble and waste of time in changing the field during the overs, and it is difficult to arrange it scientifically for both right-handed and left-handed batsmen without the necessity of comparatively long journeys for some of the fieldsmen. Now it is probable – indeed, almost certain – that a boy at the beginning of his cricket career, even if he be naturally left-handed, can be taught to bat just as well right-handed, in the same way that many boys who are naturally right-handed have been taught or have taught themselves to bowl left-handed. Thus if left-handed batting had never been allowed at cricket, there would have been no hardship.

Of course it would be absurd to suggest that those who have grown accustomed to bat left-handed could change in riper years. But there is much to be said for the suggestion of a rule that, say, after the year 1925 no one should come into cricket as a left-handed batsman. The result would be that all boys would from now onwards be taught to bat right-handed; the left-handed batsmen now playing would automatically disappear in the process of time, and left-handed batting would cease to exist. This critic admitted that left-handed batting was a distinctive art and that in a sense the game would be poorer without it, but he held that the advantage of doing away with the trouble of changing the field, &c., would more than compensate for the loss. The idea may be rather revolutionary, but it is certainly not unworthy of consideration.

The Late Mr. Alfred Lyttelton

9 *July* 1913. There was a most impressive scene at Lord's, where the University match was being played. On the stroke of 12 o'clock, the hour of the memorial service at Westminster, the umpires took off their hats. The 13 cricketers in the field did the same and stood reverently at attention. Then every one in the pavilion, which was filled in all three tiers, rose, as did the spectators in all parts of the ground, and all remained standing for some

minutes in unbroken silence. It was a most striking tribute of the general affection felt by the cricket-loving public for the man and the athlete who had gained so many of his gallant triumphs on the greatest of cricket grounds.

County Cricket on Trial

FROM A CORRESPONDENT [F. B. WILSON]

4 *May* 1914. The cricket season proper opened quietly on Saturday, and the very fact that several counties are changing their usual programme and starting games on Wednesdays and Saturdays, instead of Mondays and Thursdays, proves that the public are, at last, to be recognized rather than the players. Whether the experiment makes for the good of the game is a moot point; and whether it will "draw" the apparently reluctant public is another.

Cricket as a game can never die while we have our public schools and our universities. It will be the national game for many years, because the men who have played it and supported it will wish their sons to do the same. To play in the Eton and Harrow match will always give a boy, when he becomes a man, a claim to honour, and the Eton and Winchester match is on nearly the same plane. A cricket Blue will stand only second to a rowing Blue so long as the universities exist.

This season sees county cricket trembling in the balance, for without popular support it must die. Undoubtedly, Association football has hurt county cricket. People will come from Newcastle or Liverpool, Birmingham or Manchester, Glasgow, and even Dublin, to see the Final Tie for the Association Cup, in spite of the heavy expense and the loss of time, for they know that they will see the whole match from start to finish. People in these mercantile days want a big return for their money. One hour and a half's football, with a definite result, gives the spectator a table topic for the ensuing three months; a whole day at cricket, interesting though it may be, very seldom decides a match, and it is the decision that draws the money. The man who goes to a big boxing match knows that there will be a decision given or a definite finish; whether he agrees or disagrees with the decision he has seen all that there was to see, and therefore can improverish his store of adjectives in explaining the why and wherefore to unwilling auditors who did not see the particular contest.

Cricket is voted dull nowadays because there are not the overwhelming personalities on every county side that spectators have become accustomed to in great matches. There is no W. G. Grace playing at the present moment; there has been and will be only one W. G. Grace. But, wonderful player and personality, he could only play for one side at a time! Sometimes one hears it said, "Why are there no other men that play like Jessop?" "I am glad there are none," said Mr. Trumble, after the famous Test Match in 1902. In modern days the Jam Sahib of Nawanagar always drew a crowd; so did Mr. Trumper whenever he played in England. Earlier, Mr. C. I. Thornton and Mr. G. J. Bonnor were always supposed to be "hitting against each other," and it used to be said that the bowler who dismissed either of them for a small score was more likely to be hissed than applauded for his achievement.

Unfortunately, at the present moment there does not seem to be the same "county spirit" as there used to be. Perhaps it is owing to the fact that people have to work more strenuously than they had to 20 years ago. They are still keen to know how the cricket of the day is going, but they do not turn up in numbers, and numbers mean gate-money, and gate-money means every-thing to a county, stoutly though the authorities may deny it.

First-class cricket is no spectacular game now; nor can it ever be again, for with the perfect wickets has come in a disposition on the part of the batsman to wait till runs are given him, rather than to go and gather them for himself. In the time of our fathers it was dangerous to hit at a straight half-volley, because it might shoot dead – a real "daisy-cutter." Anything wide of the wicket was "vermin" and to be shot at as such.

But in those days they did not know the in-swerve or the swerve from leg. As wickets have become more perfect, as batting has grown more methodical, so has bowling become more teasingly accurate and more varied. Frankly, first-class cricket of the present day is the dullest of all games unless the spectator really understands the game and takes an intelligent interest in it; but, given that, it is still the finest game in the world on a jolly day. The placing of the field for certain batsmen, the traps that tempt by apparent mistakes, the use of the wind for one player, the substitution of a "googly" bowler for another – such things can be noted and enjoyed by the man who knows and loves the game.

It was said many years ago that the visits of the Australians were "not likely to help county cricket because the big matches were likely to sap the loyalty of 'the county.'" Of the Triangular Test Matches it was said that "they were likely to furnish a surfeit of unhealthy excitement, which would defeat the purpose of wholesome cricket among those who have its best interests at heart." No doubt both remarks, if somewhat grandiose, have more than a little application. County cricket must be the object of the young player who has done well at his university; by county cricket alone can he improve, and hope to graduate first into the class of a "Gentlemen v. Players" player, and, later, a member of an England team. But, however good a player, he has to be made by his surroundings, and his surroundings are very largely made up by his audience.

Probably the spectators in county cricket do not know what a great power they wield. They are much more important than the critics in the pavilion, even to a young player; to an old player, who knows, they are "the members of Parliament." It means a lot to a captain of a side to know that the men in the sixpenny seats are still loyal to the county. If he makes no runs he is sorry for their sakes, but glad and proud to think that they are more sorry for his. It is a great comfort to take back to the pavilion with o against your name.

Death of Mr. A. G. Steel

Cricketer and King's Counsel

16 *June* 1914. The death occurred yesterday, of heart failure, at 12, Cleveland-gardens, Hyde Park of Mr. A. G. Steel, K.C., Recorder of Oldham and the well-known cricketer.

Allan Gibson Steel was born in 1858, being the son of Joseph Steel, of Liverpool, and Kirkwood, Lockerbie, and was educated at Marlborough and Trinity Hall, Cambridge. He was a barrister by profession, was called to the Bar by the Inner Temple in 1883, and was Recorder of Oldham from 1904 to the time of his death. He took silk in 1901. By 1897 he had a very large practice and appeared in almost every Admiralty case of any importance in the Liverpool Courts. When Mr. (now Mr. Justice) Horridge left Liverpool in that year Mr. Steel became the leader of the local Bar. He was greatly loved on the Northern Circuit, and in Liverpool he had innumerable friends who were attracted to him and held by the charm of his personality.

As a cricketer, Mr. A. G. Steel was one of the greatest in the history of the game. He was one of the few – the late Mr. William Yardley, the late Mr. R. E. Foster, and Mr. F. S. Jackson are others that may be mentioned – whose genius for the game enabled them to play great innings when short of practice. He was the first great bowler who possessed the art of concealing from the batsman the way the ball was going to break, and yet he was far more accurate in length and direction than most bowlers even in these days. Mr. Steel was four years in the Marlborough Eleven, captain in 1876 and 1877, and his side in these two years were victorious over Rugby mainly owing to his batting and bowling. On going to Cambridge he stepped at once into the ranks of the greatest cricketers of England. He was a Freshman in the celebrated Cambridge Eleven of 1878, captained by Mr. Edward Lyttelton, which won every match, eight in number, including one against the Australians. He was at the top of the Cambridge averages both in batting and bowling and created a "record" by heading the bowling averages for the year against all the bowlers of England – in that year Shaw, Morley, and Emmett were in their prime. This certainly never has been done since by any other under-graduate, and Mr. Steel did it as a Freshman. It was a totally new style of bowling, and the late Mr. Alfred Lyttelton, who kept wicket to him all the season, said he never felt certain that he could judge which way Mr. Steel's bowling was going to turn. In the four years that Mr. A. G. Steel played against Oxford he scored 184 runs with an average of 30 and took 38 wickets at a cost of 9 runs a wicket.

Mr. Steel played 11 times for the Gentlemen against the Players at Lord's and did great things both with bat and ball, but in his case, as in so many others, bowling went off or became better understood, while batting improved.

His first Test Match against Australia was played at the Oval in 1880, and altogether he played in 13 representative Test Matches against Australia, four of which were played in Australia, when he was a member of the Hon. Ivo Bligh's team, 1882-3. Mr. Steel scored 135 not out at Sydney, but probably the great innings of his life was played at Lord's against Australia in 1884, when he scored 148 against the bowling of Spofforth, Palmer, Midwinter, Giffen, and Boyle.

Mr. Steel was not exactly a stylish batsman to look at, as he was short in height and did not stand quite upright, but he was quick on his feet, and he used constantly to jump out of his ground to Spofforth's slow ball. He had a good cut and though not a hard hitter he could hit all round the wicket and was a fast scorer. His bowling was slow and overhand. For Lancashire he did great service, though he did not play regularly. To take his career as a whole he must be placed in that small band of grand all-round cricketers who, with Dr. W. G. Grace as the greatest, made the cricket of England glorious during the eighties.

Mr. Steel was the joint author with Mr. R. H. Lyttelton of the Badminton book on cricket, and his chapter on Bowling was a great contribution on the subject.

Tunbridge Wells Week

Social events of the cricket festival

[BY H. PERRY ROBINSON]

15 *July* 1914. Tunbridge Wells has not been too fortunate in the last few years in the weather for its cricket week. The ideal weather of the first two days of this year's festival, therefore, has been all the more welcome. The town, attractive at any time, is gay with bunting. Each evening, in spite of the special programme of entertainments, the streets are crowded, particularly the Pantiles, the orderly row of lime trees of which are illuminated with red, white, and blue electric lights. The attendance at the cricket yesterday was very large, and popular as the victory of the home team was, it is a pity from the purely social standpoint that their success should have been gained so easily as to leave to-day blank.

There are not many grounds anywhere which present so beautiful a sight as does the Nevill ground on the occasion of a great match. The site, ringed round with foliage as it is and with the wide view over a rolling tree-covered landscape, is peculiarly fine. Beyond the grand stand, the pavilion, and the members' enclosure, runs the line of private tents with their bright flags fluttering, and all the rest of the circuit of the ground yesterday was banked with spectators, behind whom an almost continuous file of motor-cars and carriages was drawn up.

The new pavilion, built to replace that which was burned down early in the year, is an ornate and by no means unpicturesque building of red brick and red tiles with white woodwork. It was only just completed in time to be ready for the cricket week, but now, with the borders in front of it filled with rambler roses, sweet Williams, and other flowers there is little to tell how new it is. Unhappily the new structure can never contain the precious relics which were destroyed with the old.

The bandstand and the enclosure presented a gay scene yesterday with the ladies' frocks and many coloured sunshades; a scene that appeared all the more animated when the band was playing. The psychology of band playing at a cricket match is a much vexed question. Many batsmen find it hard to keep up a patient defensive game to the music of a two-step. Yesterday after-noon the band came to the end of an exhilarating march, and in the dead silence which succeeded, Russell, after playing a most careful innings of 42, stood still while a ball from Blythe broke into his wicket. Probably the ball came in a great deal, but to the spectators it seemed as if the batsman's immobility was part of the silence which followed the cessation of the music. Who knows but that if the band had played a few bars more Russell would have smacked that ball to the boundary?

Each evening the band, which is that of the East Kent Mounted Rifles, gives a concert on the Pantiles. In addition, the Strolling Players, with Mr. Gilbert Ferme, are giving a series of concerts in the Great Hall. Last night and on Monday there was a performance of *The Duke of Killiecrankie* at the Opera House by amateurs, the company consisting of Mrs. C. F. Clapham, Miss Evelyn Barnes, Miss L. Tewson, Mr. Neville Stone, Mr. R. L. Sevenoaks, Mr. T. H. Sleddall, Mr. F. D. Barnes, and the Rev. H. H. Hockey. On Friday evening the subscription dance will be given in the Pump Rooms, under the patronage of Mrs. Cheale, Mrs. Emson, Mrs. Lees, Mrs. F. B. Manser, Mrs. Newgass, Mrs. Silcock, Mrs. Shepherd, and Mrs. Snelgrove. In addition to the foregoing events there is a great deal of private entertaining being done, and prizes are awarded for the best illuminations and decorations of business premises. Only a continuance of the fine weather is needed for a most successful and enjoyable week.

One may take it for granted that it is only the love of cricket in the Kentish people which makes possible the success of the various "weeks" at Ton-bridge, Tunbridge Wells, Maidstone, Canterbury, and Dover. And what is also certain is that the "weeks" contribute enormously to maintain and spread the popularity of the game. There is no budding cricketer at school at Tun-bridge Wells who does not dream of some day playing for his county on the Nevill Ground before such an assemblage as gathered there yesterday.

Death of A. E. Trott

Famous cricketer found shot

31 *July* 1914. The death is announced of Albert Edward Trott, the well-known Australian and Middlesex cricketer. He was found dead in bed yesterday by his landlady at his residence in Denbigh-road, Harlesden. Trott had a wound in the temple and a Browning pistol was found beside him. The police and a doctor were summoned, but death was practically instantaneous.

For some considerable time Trott had been an in-patient at St. Mary's Hospital and only left that institution recently. He was 42 years old, and had lived for nearly 3½ years at Harlesden.

Trott was a very great cricketer and a man who, in spite of faults, was quick to win affection. The modern professional is very different – and in many ways superior – to his predecessor, but in older days there were many more of the class that may be called "characters," and Trott was essentially one of these.

The feat, probably, that his name will always be remembered by is that of being the first, and at present the only man who has ever hit a ball over the present pavilion at Lord's. Possibly there may have been bigger hits on the ground. Long did Trott persevere in his ambition to make this feat, and at last he achieved it. He used the most enormously heavy bat in his efforts – it is rumoured that it was over 3lb. – and his batting powers suffered probably in his many attempts. Trott was essentially an all-round cricketer, a very great, and in some ways unique, bowler, a good hard-hitting batsman, and a glorious field, particularly in the slips.

A younger brother of Harry Trott, the famous Australian captain, he had made his mark in Australian cricket before he came to England and was engaged as a member of the M.C.C. staff, and qualified for Middlesex, for whom he did great service in the late '90's and the early years of the century. His great years were 1899 and 1900, when he achieved the feat of getting over 200 wickets and making 1,000 runs, which so few cricketers have accomplished. For a number of seasons afterwards he was one of the mainstays of the Middlesex side, but his batting deteriorated and then, after a time, his bowling. He was comparatively quite young when he retired from first-class cricket and should have had many more years of cricket in him. He was, of course, a member of the Middlesex team that won the Championship in 1903.

Another "record" that stands to his name is that of doing the "hat trick" twice in a single innings (in one instance taking four wickets in four balls). This was accomplished in his benefit match against Somerset at Lord's in 1907.

His claim to greatness as a cricketer will rest chiefly on his bowling. He was essentially one of all paces and all kinds of balls, and was never afraid to try experiments, even at the cost of runs, to get a man out. His fast "surprise" yorker was as good a ball probably as any bowler of normally medium pace could spring upon the batsman. There was no apparent change of run or action, and then down it would come as fast as anything the fastest bowlers could do. For all batsmen Trott at his best had terrors, and the best admitted that he was most interesting to play, because one never knew what was coming next.

In minor matches for the M.C.C. he was especially deadly. It is rumoured that one victim, who happened to play against him in two matches running, was clean bowled four times first ball. In his great years he was as good a bowler as there was in England. As he was an Australian he had no opportunity of Test Match cricket in his English cricket days. As a batsman he was at his best a great deal more than a mere hard hitter, though he loved "having a go." In the last year or two he had been a first-class umpire and had proved himself a most capable one.

Mr. R. H. Spooner Wounded

25 *October* 1914. News has been received in Liverpool that Mr. R. H. Spooner, the cricketer, has been wounded. Mr. Spooner is a lieutenant in the Lincolnshire Regiment. His brother, Captain Spooner, was mentioned in dispatches.

The Press Bureau confirm with regret that Mr. Spooner has been wounded and add that no further details are available.

Suicide of Mr. A. E. Stoddart

A great cricketer

6 *April* 1915. We regret to announce that Mr. Andrew Ernest Stoddart committed suicide by shooting himself with a revolver on Saturday night at his residence in St. John's Wood.

Stoddart's name will always live as one of the really great players of cricket and Rugby football – the only man who has ever captained England both in a Test Match and a "Rugger" International. Born at South Shields in 1863, he was in his prime as a cricketer in a great heyday of cricket popularity – the late 'eighties and early 'nineties. Middlesex, the Gentlemen, and England – he did great work for all. It was as a batsman that he was most famous, and a beautiful bat he was, scoring fast in the old-fashioned attacking style, with all the shots, drive, cut and glance, and yet with quite a sound defence. He could hit balls of all paces and all lengths, and he dearly loved a duel with a fast bowler.

Among his most famous innings were 215 not out, against Lancashire at Manchester in 1891, and 151 for England against the M.C.C. at Lord's in

1887, when he and Arthur Shrewsbury raised the total to 266 for the first wicket. In 1886, for Hampstead against the Stoics, he played an innings of 485 – at the time the highest individual score on record. He was a great favourite of the Lord's crowd in the palmy days of Middlesex cricket, when his friend Mr. A. J. Webbe was captain of the side, and truly did Mr. Norman Gale write of him:– 'When Stoddart makes her hum up at Lord's.'

In Australia his name was a household word, and his happiest recollections were of his Australian trips. He paid four visits to Australia – in 1887, 1891, 1894, and 1897 – on the two last occasions taking out his own team. He was a fine field, and a well-known professional once said to him:– "Mr. Stoddart, if you had been a professional you would have been a great bowler." But he was a much better bowler than many people imagined. In 1898 – his last full season in county cricket – his batting average was 52.

Brilliant as he was at cricket, he was equally so as a three-quarter; his play at Blackheath, when he was captain of "the Club" for some years, and for England was a household word. Between 1886 and 1893 he played in 10 Rugby internationals, and would certainly have played in more but for the fact that in two of the intermediate seasons England, owing to a dispute with the other unions, had no international matches. He was fast, full of resource, and a splendid kick. It was a memorable drop kick he made against a gale of wind that, giving Middlesex victory over Yorkshire by a goal to four tries, led to the rules of the game being altered. At that time a goal counted more than any number of tries.

Stoddart never believed in coaching; he said if a game was in one it would come out. He had never paid much attention to coaches himself, and he was a great example of a born player of games. One of the kindest of friends and most sympathetic, he was always encouraging to and thoughtful for the young player, and his loss will be widely mourned.

At the inquest held at Marylebone yesterday Mrs. Ethel Stoddart said that last year her husband had to give up his secretaryship of Queen's Club on account of bad health and nervous breakdown, and had done nothing since. He was a temperate man but lately had been depressed, and said that life was not worth living. Last year he was treated for an attack of influenza and a sea voyage was arranged for him, but it did not take place. Lately he had been very moody. He was in financial difficulties and lost all his money through the war, and that had preyed on his mind and worried him.

Late on Saturday night he took a pistol out of his pocket, laid it on the table, and said he was tired of it all and was going to finish it. The witness advised him to wait until they could consult their friends the next day. She picked the pistol up and they had a slight struggle for it, but she gave it back to him after having found it was unloaded, and took from him a full box of cartridges. He then put the pistol into his pocket and later went to bed. Before midnight she went to his room and saw him in bed. There was blood on his cheek. She called for help and then found that he was dead. There was no smoke in the room, and no report had been heard. Lately he had been forgetful and irritable, and even when she had rustled a paper he had asked her not to do so, saying it would drive him mad. It was afterwards discovered that he had another box of cartridges in his possession.

Isabel Dalton, a friend, also said Mr. Stoddart was moody and restless. He was happy at home, but had had a good deal of money trouble. The witness was called by Mrs. Stoddart on Saturday night, and saw him in bed with a revolver in his right hand. She had heard no report, and was certain that his mind was affected by his troubles.

Dr. Lindsey Saunders, of Maida-vale, said he was called late on Saturday night. Stoddart had a bullet wound in the brain on the right side, and the bullet was found embedded in the skull on the opposite side of the head. The heart was enlarged, as was usual in the case of athletes, and the lungs showed commencing pneumonia, which would increase despondency owing to its depressing effect. Death was due to the bullet wound, which, in the opinion of the witness, was self-inflicted.

The jury returned a verdict of "Suicide while of unsound mind."

The Greatest of Cricketers

An appreciation of Dr. Grace

BY SIR ARTHUR CONAN DOYLE

27 *October* 1915. The world will be the poorer to many of us for the passing of the greatest of cricketers. To those who knew him he was more than a great cricketer. He had many of the characteristics of a great man. There was a masterful personality and a large direct simplicity and frankness which, combined with his huge frame, swarthy features, bushy beard, and somewhat lumbering carriage, made an impression which could never be forgotten.

In spite of his giant West-of-England build, there was, as it seemed to me, something of the gipsy in his colouring, his vitality, and his quick, dark eyes with their wary expression. The bright yellow and red cap which he loved to wear added to this Zingari effect. His elder brother, the Coroner, small, wizened, dark, and wiry, had even more of this gipsy appearance. I speak, of course, only of the effect produced, for I have no reason to think that such blood was in his veins, though, following Borrow, I am ready to believe that there is no better in Europe. There was a fine, open-air breeziness of manner about the man which made his company a delight and added a zest to the game. He was, of course, a highly educated surgeon, but he had rather the fashion of talk which one would associate with a jovial farmer. His voice was high-pitched, considering the huge chest from which it came, and it preserved something of the Western burr.

His style and methods were peculiar to himself. In his youth, when he was tall, slim, and agile, he must have been as ideal in his form as in his results. But as this generation knew him he had run to great size and a certain awkwardness of build. As he came towards the wicket, walking heavily with shoulders rounded, his great girth outlined by his coloured sash, one would have imagined that his day was past. He seemed slow, stiff, and heavy at first. When he had made 50 in his quiet methodical fashion he was somewhat younger and fresher. At the end of a century he had not turned a hair, and was watching the ball with as clear an eye as in the first over. It was his advice to play every ball as if it were the first – and he lived up to it. Everything that he did was firm, definite, and well within his strength.

I have had the privilege of fielding at point more than once while he made his hundred, and have in my mind a clear impression of his methods. He stood very clear of his wicket, bending his huge shoulders and presenting a very broad face of the bat towards the bowler. Then, as he saw the latter advance, he would slowly raise himself to his height, and draw back the blade of his bat, while his left toe would go upwards until only the heel of that foot remained upon the ground. He gauged the pitch of the ball in an instant, and if it were doubtful played back rather than forward. Often he smothered a really dangerous length ball by a curious half-cock stroke to which he was partial. He took no risks, and in playing forward trailed the bottom of his bat along the grass as it advanced so as to guard against the shooter – a relic, no doubt, of his early days in the sixties, when shooters were seen more often than on modern grounds.

The great strength of his batting was upon the off side. I should not suppose that there was ever a batsman who was so good at controlling that most uncontrollable of all balls, the good-length ball outside the off stump. He would not disregard it, as is the modern habit. Stepping across the wicket while bending his great shoulders, he watched it closely as it rose, and patted it with an easy tap through the slips. In vain, with a fast bumpy bowler pounding them down, did three quivering fieldsmen crouch in the slips, their hands outstretched and eager for the coming catch. Never with the edge of the bat but always with the true centre would he turn the ball groundwards, so that it flashed down and then fizzed off between the grasping hands, flying with its own momentum to the boundary. With incredible accuracy he would place it according to the fields, curving it off squarely if third man were not in his place or tapping it almost straight down upon the ground if short slip were standing wide of the wicket.

In no shot was he so supremely excellent, and like all great things it seemed simplicity itself as he did it. Only when one saw other great batsmen fail did one realize how accurate was the timing and the wrist-work of the old man. When he was well on towards his 60th year I have seen him standing up to Lockwood when man after man was helpless at the other wicket, tapping those terrific expresses away through the slips with the easy sureness with which one would bounce a tennis ball with a racket. The fastest bowler in England [*usually said to be Ernest Jones, the Australian*] sent one like a cannon-shot through his beard with only a comic shake of the head and a good-humoured growl in reply.

Of his bowling I have very clear recollections. He was an innovator among bowlers, for he really invented the leg-theory a generation before it was re-discovered and practised by Vine, Armstrong, and others. Grace's traps at leg were proverbial in the seventies. His manner was peculiar. He would lumber up to the wicket, and toss up the ball in a take-it-or-leave-it style, as if he cared little whether it pitched between the wickets or in the next parish. As a matter of fact this careless attitude covered a very remarkable accuracy. His command of length was absolute, and he had just enough leg spin to beat the bat if you played forward to the pitch of the ball. He was full of guile, and the bad ball which was worth four to you was sent, as likely as not, to unsettle you and lead you on.

Those who knew him will never look at the classic sward of Lord's without an occasional vision of the great cricketer. He was, and will remain, the very impersonation of cricket, redolent of fresh air, of good humour, of conflict without malice, of chivalrous strife, of keenness for victory by fair means, and utter detestation of all that was foul. Few men have done more for the generation in which he lived, and his influence was none the less because it was a spontaneous and utterly unconscious one.

The Funeral.

The funeral of Dr. Grace took place yesterday at Elmers End Cemetery, Beckenham. The mourners included Mrs. W. G. Grace, Captain C. B. Grace, R.E. (son), Mrs. Dann (sister), and Mr. C. L. Townsend (Gloucester Cricket Club), and others present were:–

Lord Hawke and Mr. John Shuter (M.C.C.), Lord Harris, the Jam Sahib of Nawana-gar, Captain P. F. Warner, Mr. F. G. J. Ford, and Mr. G. MacGregor (Middlesex), Captain H. D. G. Leveson-Gower (Surrey), Mr. H. W. Bainbridge (Warwickshire), Mr. J. R. Mason, Mr. C. J. Burnup, Mr. R. N. R. Blaker, and Mr. W. M. Bradley (Kent), Mr. C. E. Green, Mr. A. P. Lucas, and Mr. O. R. Borradaile (Essex), Lieutenant A. C. MacLaren (Lancashire), Mr. J. A. Bush and Mr. R. E. Bush (Gloucestershire), Mr. Frank Townsend and Mr. R. Fenton Miles (members of the Gloucestershire Eleven in 1871), Sir George Riddell, Mr. C. I. Thornton, Mr. P. J. de Paravicini, Mr. E. H. D. Sewell, Mr. H. J. Hill, Sir A. Priestley, M.P., Captain G. J. V. Weigall, Mr. R. J. Cooper-Murray (Sydney, N.S.W.), Mr. C. Wreford-Brown, Mr. A. T. Kemble, Mr. S. A. P. Kitcat, Mr. G. Brann, and Mr. Alec Hearne.

Sir Home Gordon writes:– "Messrs. Constable have invited me to write a lengthy memorial biography of Dr. W. G. Grace. Lord Hawke, President of the M.C.C., has consented to write the introduction. May I appeal through your columns to all who possess documents, anecdotes, and reminiscences kindly to forward them as soon as possible to 2, Cheyne-walk, S.W.? Everything will be carefully returned in a few weeks."

Cricket Reminiscences

Great Hitters

FROM A CORRESPONDENT [P. F. WARNER]

3, 7 *June* 1919. Opinions differ as to who is the greatest hitter the world has ever seen. Mr. C. I. Thornton, the Australians Mr. G. J. Bonnor and Mr. J. J. Lyons, Mr. W. H. Game, and Mr. G. L. Jessop all have their admirers, but the biggest measured hit is credited to Mr., afterwards the Rev., W. Fellows, who, in 1856, at practice on the Christ Church ground at Oxford, drove a ball 175 yards from hit to pitch, Charles Rogers, the groundman, being the bowler. This was an immense hit, especially when one remembers that in those days bats had not the wood they have to-day, but it was carefully measured by E. Martin, of the Kent XI, from 1845 to 1851, and there is no reason to doubt its authenticity.

In spite of this hit of Mr. Fellows's, most cricketers, however, will, I fancy, award the palm for big hitting to Mr. Thornton, who, in an Eton and Harrow match, drove a ball over the pavilion at Lord's into the Secretary's garden. This was in 1868, when the pavilion was much smaller than the present one, but it was none the less a mighty blow. A year or two later he scored 20 runs off a four ball over of Mr. David Buchanan's, and once, in practice at Brighton, he hit a ball out of the Hove ground and down the Western-road. But perhaps Mr. Thornton's most wonderful performance was for the Gentlemen of England v I Zingari, at Scarborough, when he scored 107 runs in 29 strokes, hitting no fewer than seven sixes. One hit almost disappeared in the "central blue," and went over a block of high houses, and dropped in Trafalgar-square. Another huge hit of his was off Tom Emmett, also at Scarborough, which Tom declared had gone into the sea! On the Oval, early in the 70's, he hit a ball of James Southerton's so far that it caused Pooley, the Surrey wicketkeeper, to exclaim, "So 'elp me God, Jimmy, I believe its gone on to Brixton Church!" After this hit Southerton used to lie awake at night wondering what would happen to him if Mr. Thornton drove the ball straight back at him.

Southerton, like Mr. David Buchanan, did not play first-class cricket until he was well on in life, for he was 40 when he appeared in the Surrey XI in 1867, but between that year and 1879 he took 1,002 wickets.

Mr. G. J. Bonnor was a magnificent specimen of a man, and a tremendous hitter, but on looking through "Wisden" one finds that he had many failures and inconsistencies, and in general ability he was greatly surpassed by his fellow Australian, Mr. J. J. Lyons, who used to go in first with Mr. Alec Bannerman, who, by way of contrast, once took seven hours to score 91 runs in a Test Match at Sydney in 1892, thereby emulating the feat of Scotton at the Oval in 1884.

The catch and bowl with which George Ulyett dismissed Mr. Bonnor in the Test Match at Lord's in 1884 is still talked of, and Mr. Lyons once hit a ball so hard that it broke some of the pickets that fence in the Adelaide ground. Mr. Game I never saw play, but from Mr. Jessop's bat I have seen many wonderful hits. Mr. Jessop was never so long a driver as Mr. Thornton or Mr. Bonnor, but he was by far the best bat of all the hitters, his consistency in scoring being little short of marvellous, especially when one remembers that he took his life in both hands and went for the bowling at once.

It has been said of Mr. Jessop that he reduced rustic cricket to a science, and certainly there has never been any cricketer quite like him. He crouched in his position at the wicket with one hand at the bottom of the bat handle and the other at the top, and, to the purist, he defined every canon and rule of the game. But then he was a genius, who knows no rules, and a terror to all bowlers on all sorts of wickets. Mr. Jessop could cut as well as anyone, and as he was also an expert at the "hook" stroke it was no use bowling short to him. Mr. Kotze did so in the England v. South Africa match at Lord's in 1907 with disastrous results to his analysis. A very great professional bowler had a theory that the best way to get Mr. Jessop out was to bowl him a straight ball, just over a half volley in length, and not quite a "yorker," on his first coming in to bat, as he was, he alleged, apt to hit over, and across such a ball; and I have seen this bowler defeat Mr. Jessop in this manner, and, contrariwise, I have seen the same bowler pulverised by him.

When the West Indians played Gloucestershire at Bristol in 1900 Mr. Jessop scored a "century," hitting six fours in one over, when all the black members of the team sat down on the ground and shrieked with laughter at their own discomfiture. Mr. Jessop did not come off in Australia, where the wickets were too fast for him, and where the ball keeps rather low, but his 104 at the Oval in August, 1902, for England is one of the great innings in the history of the game. Ill-health caused Mr. Jessop's retirement, but that stocky active figure crouching at the wicket, but ever on its toes, ready to spring out to meet the bowling, will not fade from the memory of the many thousands to whom he has afforded such unalloyed pleasure. Of his perfection as a cover or extra cover I hope to write later.

Another mighty hitter was Albert Trott. The pages of "Wisden" are strewn with the tragic deaths of many a professional cricketer, and poor Trott's end was very sad. To him falls the honour of making even a bigger drive than Mr. Fellows's, for playing for M.C.C. v. The Australians at Lord's on July 31, 1899, he drove a ball of Mr. Noble's clean over the top of the pavilion, the ball pitching in the garden of Philip Need, the well-known, and much liked, dressing room attendant at Lord's.

I was sitting in the front seats of the pavilion when the hit was made, and I remember how Trott found the range with a couple of sighting shots, one pitching just short of the pavilion rails, and the other on the seats. In fact, he seemed to be making a "bracket," as the gunners say, and then came this historic hit. It was not possible to measure the distance accurately because the pavilion and tennis courts and Need's house intervened, and no one knew the exact spot where the ball fell.

In May of the same season Trott had made almost as big a hit off Tate, the Sussex bowler, the ball hitting the cornice on the right hand top side of the pavilion on which "M.C.C." is scored, the ball bouncing back into the top balcony. Trott used to play with a bat which, if it did not weigh as much as Mr. William Ward's, must have turned the scale, at the very least, at 3lb., and I fear this hit off Mr. Noble's bowling spoilt his batting, for ever afterwards he went about trying to "carry" pavilions.

But the best innings Trott ever played was 164 for Middlesex v. Yorkshire at Lord's, in 1899. On that occasion, after a very quiet beginning, he hit with terrific power, one drive off Wainwright's bowling striking the pavilion rails with such force that the ball came back almost to mid on, where the Hon. F. S. Jackson picked it up and handed it to the bowler. Trott gave one chance late in his innings deep on the on side, and the explanation of the fieldsman for not catching him was amusing, for, said he, "at first I didn't see her up against that — blackboard (the big scoring board), and then when I sees her up there and a-coming to me, I says oh — it, and I leaves it!" In that match, 20 years ago, Mr. P. F. Warner played a faultless innings of 150, and only a few days ago he scored another "century" on his favourite ground.

The Game and the Spectator

28 *June* 1919. Do the cricketing public appreciate fine bowling as they did in the seventies and eighties? Judging by the attitude of the spectators in the years just before the war, and in the match at Lord's this week between the Gentlemen of England and the Australians, when some exceptionally fine bowling by Mr. Falcon and Mr. Douglas evoked not one single hand-clap or cheer, except from their own colleagues, they do not.

The spectators applaud any batsman who makes a good score, be the bowling good, bad, or indifferent, but a successful piece of bowling on a good wicket is put down to the weakness of the batting, and little or no credit is given to the bowler. Possibly all that has been written about "brightening" cricket may have something to do with this attitude, but it shows an appalling ignorance on the part of those who watch cricket, and one almost blushes when one remembers that the pavilion at Lord's, the headquarters of cricket, received in stony silence and with utter indifference the remarkable effort by Mr. Falcon and Mr. Douglas.

In a certain Gentlemen v. Players match before the war one of the amateur batsmen was greeted with ironical cheering because on first coming in after his side had made a bad start he played two maiden overs from the redoubtable Barnes, who was bowling superbly on a wicket on which the ball was inclined to "pop." We live in a quicker age, and though a democratic form of Government is, no doubt, the most suitable for the time we live in, I should be very sorry indeed to see the government of cricket in the hands of the democracy, for they would probably order out any batsman who was guilty of playing a maiden over, and the guillotine would descend on the neck of the man who did not score 50 runs an hour, irrespective of whether the wicket was true or false, and whether the bowling was the best or the worst in England. Lord's is, of course, rather a "cold" place, and the criticism there is of a somewhat frigid and unemotional character, and one is glad to be able to record that in a recent match at the Oval, between Surrey and Hampshire, the fine bowling of Kennedy and the exceptional fielding of the Hampshire eleven evoked such enthusiasm that the pavilion and ground "rose at" the players and gave them a wonderful reception.

But take it all in all the public do not understand, or do not appreciate, fine bowling. Now this was not always so, as a glance at Wisden's Cricketers' Almanack of past years will show. Opening "The Cricketers' Bible," as Wisden has been called, for the year 1876 one reads tremendous praise for Alfred Shaw's bowling in the match between the M.C.C. and Nottinghamshire, which was played at Lord's on June 14 and 15, 1875.

The M.C.C. had a capital side, including "W.G.," Mr. I. D. Walker, Mr. W. H. Hadow, Mr. A. W. Ridley, Mr. C. F. Buller, Mr. A. J. Webbe, and Lord Harris. And Nottinghamshire, with Alfred and J. C. Shaw, Morley, Martin McIntyre, Oscroft, Richard Daft, and Arthur Shrewsbury, were at full strength. The comments on the game are decidedly interesting:

"Mr. W. Grace was one hour at wickets scoring his ten runs, and one hour and ten minutes making his 35; he was thoroughly put on his defence by Alfred Shaw, and one of the few batting treats of the match was the defence of Mr. W. Grace against the rare bowling of Alfred Shaw; over after over was played in truly great form, shooters being got down upon with marvellous sharpness, but those enjoyable struggles between bat and ball ended in victories to Shaw, who clean bowled the crack in both innings. . . . Mr. I. D. Walker was one hour scoring his 13 runs, and Mr. Hadow was precisely 38 minutes at wickets for his first innings of one run." Mr. A. J. Webbe, "the colt from Oxford," made a pair of spectacles, being run out in his second innings after "being called by Mr. Grace for a desperately sharp run."

Alfred Shaw's full analysis for the match was:–

	O.	M.	R.	W.
First Innings ..	54	35	39	2
Second Innings ..	41.2	36	7	7

"Such marvellous bowling as this to such high-class batsmen has no equal in the history of the game. It brought out the full defensive powers of Mr. W. Grace, Mr. Walker, Mr. Hadow, Mr. Ridley, and Mr. Buller, none of these great hitters being able to get the ball away for runs, and during their stay at the wickets the attack from Alfred Shaw and their defence was indeed splendid cricket that will long be remembered with admiration."

The M.C.C. scored 153 and 98 to their opponents' 114 and 75, winning the match by 62 runs. "W.G." bowled 83 overs, 38 maidens, for 86 runs and nine wickets, Mr. Ridley taking ten wickets for 46 runs with his lobs. This was the year in which Mr. Ridley, the Oxford captain, put himself on at the crisis of the University match, and bowling Mr. W. S. Patterson and Mr. A. F. Smith won the match for his side by six runs. Mr. Ridley's generalship was highly praised, but I wonder what would have been said if a couple of fours had been hit off him! Cricket is very like war. If the leader brings off a good stroke he is a Marlborough, a Napoleon, or a Foch; if he fails stones are thrown at him!

But to return to Wisden. In the Gentlemen v. Players match at Lord's in 1879, Mr. A. P. Lucas, at the end of the first day's play, was 15 not out, in scoring which runs he had occupied one hour and 23 minutes. That 15 not out of Mr. Lucas's was indeed a splendid sample of defence, worth journeying many miles to witness; indeed the compiler of this book knows one who left a sick couch to witness this match, and who says that Mr. Lucas's 15 not out that day amply repaid him for the pain and discomfort he suffered from the ungenial weather. The wicket was sticky and the bowling of Alfred Shaw, Morley, Barlow, and Barnes very fine indeed, but I fancy some modern spectator could he have been present on that occasion would have inquired of Mr. Lucas why he didn't hit 'em.

Again, in the Gentlemen v. Players match at Lord's in 1880, Alfred Shaw began by delivering 14 successive maiden overs at the start of the Gentlemen's second innings to "W.G." and Mr. A. P. Lucas, and in 55 minutes only 17 runs were scored. But there are several other instances to prove that the scoring in days gone by was not faster than it is to-day, and that a keen duel between batsmen and bowlers was keenly appreciated. How seldom in these days does one hear a succession of maiden overs applauded, the great majority of the public appearing to think that slow scoring of necessity implies indifferent batting.

Cricket is not like baseball, and any attempts to "brighten" it or to put a "hustle" on it would spoil it. It is, as Mr. E. V. Lucas put it in a delightful article in Punch on December 4 of last year, "an intricate, vigilant, and leisurely warfare, and the fact that every moment of it is equally fraught with possibilities and openings for glorious uncertainty makes it peculiarly the delight of intelligent observers, none of whom finds dullness in the spectacle of a batsman, no matter how stubborn, defending his wicket successfully against 11 opponents. First-class cricket calls for such very special gifts of temperament and skill that only the fittest survive; and all their actions are worth study."

A World XI

22 *July* 1919. The Martians have challenged us at cricket, and I have been deputed to select a World XI to play against them.

I am somewhat appalled at the difficulties of my task, but as I have already had the temerity to choose both an English and an Australian side, I will take my courage in both hands and go boldly for this the last and biggest fence of all. I will, as usual, select the bowlers first. We shall want five, on modern wickets four bowlers are not enough, and we will ask the Martians to play the match at Lord's, a fitting arena for so unique a contest. The captain of the Martians, like the great von Moltke, of whom it was said that he could be silent in seven languages, does not talk much, but he is a very astute leader, as becomes his race, and we cannot afford to leave anything to chance in the composition of our team.

We have three countries from which to choose our side – England, Australia, and South Africa. America is the home of baseball, but there is one corner of that vast Continent where cricket flourishes, or used to flourish, Philadelphia, and the home of Mr. J. B. King, a remarkably fine fast bowler. Mr. King was one of the first of the "inswingers," and with his high action and good length he was an awkward customer on any wicket. Had he been an Englishman or a Briton from beyond the seas in Australia or South Africa, his reputation would be even higher; as it is, he is recognized by all good judges of the game as a bowler of high distinction. Still, he was not, for all his ability, a Lockwood or a Richardson, and I shall therefore retain Lockwood as the fast bowler.

Barnes, of course, has a place. On all wickets he is a master, and Australian cricketers have over and over again remarked to me that "Barnes is the best bowler England has ever sent to Australia." The Australians are not only sound, but generous judges, and I remember Mr. Warwick Armstrong's reply when I asked him whether there was anything wrong with the wicket when Barnes accomplished his wonderful performance at Melbourne on New Year's Day, 1912:– "No, just fine bowling." I never saw "The Demon" in the heyday of his fame, but from what I have heard and read of his bowling he cannot be left out of a World's XI, especially as the match is to be played at Lord's, and not at Sydney, Melbourne, or Adelaide. Mr. Spofforth was no batsman, and I fancy he was not a particularly good field, but his bowling was of superlative quality and he shall be my third bowler.

My fourth bowler will be Mr. Noble. Many would, no doubt, select Mr. C. T. B. Turner, "the Terror," but these Martians are a fine side, and Mr. Noble was a better batsman and a better field than Mr. Turner, and, of course, a very fine bowler. It is, however, with reluctance that one leaves out Mr. Turner, who threw all his energy into every ball he bowled and who was a rare fighter. The choice of the fifth bowler causes me anxious consideration. Shall I use "W.G.," whom I shall play as a batsman, as a bowler, or shall I give South Africa a representative, and call on Mr. G. A. Faulkner, on his day a most difficult googlie bowler, who on a sticky wicket in the Test Match at Leeds in 1907 actually took six wickets for 17 runs? Mr. Faulkner was also a great batsman – he made no fewer than 1,651 runs with an average of

61·14 in the eleven-a-side matches during the tour of Mr. P. W. Sherwell's team in Australia in 1910-11 – his scores in the Test Matches being 62, 43, 204, 8, 56, 115, 20, 80, 52, 92, and a fine fieldsman in the slips.

Then such names as Mr. A. G. Steel, Mr. George Giffen, Mr. Macartney, Mr. Armstrong, Mr. Jackson, Lohmann, Woolley, and Hirst instantly occur to one, though I did not give Hirst a place in my England XI, probably an error on my part as he was for years our champion all-round cricketer, and is still a good man at a crisis, as he showed in Gentlemen v. Players at Lord's last week. If I play Lohmann I weaken the batting somewhat; and I will, therefore, pass over this wonderful cricketer, and, taking into consideration the fact that he is a left-handed batsman, a beautiful field anywhere, and a slow left-handed bowler – which, so far, the team lacks – who is invariably successful on sticky wickets, I will select Woolley. Mr. Blackham shall be the wicket-keeper, though Mr. Sherwell and Mr. E. A. Halliwell, of South Africa, Mr. MacGregor, and Lilley have strong claims. The remaining places I will award to "W.G.," K. S. Ranjitsinhji, Hobbs, Mr. Trumper, and Mr. C. Hill, and the side in the order of going in would be:–

> Dr. W. G. Grace.
> Mr. V. Trumper.
> K. S. Ranjitsinhji.
> Hobbs.
> Mr. C. Hill.
> Mr. M. A. Noble (captain).
> Woolley.
> Lockwood.
> Mr. J. McC. Blackham.
> Barnes.
> Mr. F. R. Spofforth.

If the wicket is really sticky I shall play Mr. Faulkner, vice Lockwood, as this will give us another batsman, and a googlie bowler. Mr. Faulkner shall, therefore, be 12th man but I shall have a very careful look at the pitch before discarding Lockwood, as if he could get a proper foothold he could bowl on any wicket. This side has seven superlatively good batsmen – eight if Mr. Faulkner plays – plenty of bowling, and several slip and country fielders, Hobbs at cover, and "the prince of wicket keepers" behind the stumps. Mr. Noble shall be captain, and he will be a match for the silent and clever Martian leader. Some moderns would prefer Lilley to Mr. Blackham, because of his greater run-getting power, and I expect the selection of Woolley to be criticized; but Mr. Blackham, by general consent, had no superior, and the fact that Woolley is a left-handed batsman weighs with me. Two such left-handers as Mr. Hill and Woolley, with Mr. Noble sandwiched between them, might well turn out an awkward problem for the Martian bowlers, and further I do not like taking the field without a slow left-handed bowler. Moreover, should the wicket at Lord's be wet, Woolley is as likely as anyone on the side, excepting Mr. Trumper and Hobbs, to make runs.

In his letter to *The Times* of July 18, Mr. C. K. Langley, to whom I am exceedingly grateful for his flattering references to these reminiscences, wonders why Mr. F. R. Foster was not included in either the first or second England teams. Mr. Foster was undoubtedly a beautiful cricketer, but it is hard to see who could have been left out of the first XI for him, and in the second XI I preferred George Hirst, who possesses a wonderful, all-round record over a long period of years. Tyledesley, too, a batsman with no superior in modern times, especially on a sticky wicket – his innings of 62 out of a total of 103 runs, eight of which were extras, on a veritable glue-pot at Melbourne on January 5, 1904, is, perhaps, the classic innings on a wicket of this kind – and a great long fielder, I could find no place for in the first XI, and there are several other famous men who are left out of not only the first XI, but the second XI, as well, but then the difficulties of selection are almost insuperable.

1 *August, Sydney.* Mr. Frank Iredale, the best known writer on cricket in Australia, considers the following World XI better than that chosen by the correspondent who has been writing his Reminiscences in *The Times*:– Mr. G. H. S. Trott or Mr. M. A. Noble (captain), Dr. W. G. Grace, Mr. Victor Trumper, K. S. Ranjitsinhji, the Hon. F. S. Jackson, Mr. C. Hill, Peel, Richardson, Lohmann, Mr. F. R. Spofforth, and Mr. J. McC. Blackham.

A Fieldsmen's XI

16 *August* 1919. It has often been said that perfect fielding would make even the weakest bowling comparatively strong, and, though I am not prepared to go so far as that, there is no doubt that an eleven which was composed of men who were one and all experts in the field would seldom have a very big score made against them, be their bowling ever so "delicate."

The finest and most zealous fielders occasionally make mistakes, it being but human to err, but the great fieldsman will save literally hundreds of runs in the course of a season, and his energy and zeal will act as an inspiration to his comrades and will imbue his side with a great enthusiasm. There is no finer sight in cricket than an eleven fielding for all it is worth. Selecting imaginary teams to play against Australia, for example, is a fascinating, if difficult, task, and we will suppose that the Australians have asked England to put into the field against them, at Lord's or the Oval, an eleven selected from men who are actually taking part in first-class cricket to-day, the qualification for inclusion being that each member of the side must be an A1 fieldsman.

Let us begin with the wicket-keeper, and for this post I will select Mr. G. E. C. Wood, of the Cambridge eleven. He is young, and on his form in the University match he is without a superior at the moment. Brown, of Hampshire, and Hendren, of Middlesex, shall be my next choices, and you cannot put either of them out of place in the field. I do not remember seeing Brown field in the slips, but I feel sure that if required he would fill that position as satisfactorily as he does every other, for his activity and eyesight are extraordinary, he can throw, and his hands are of the size that swallow a cricket ball. Hendren, I am inclined to think, is the best all-round fieldsman we have. He is a great slip, a beautiful off-side fieldsman, a daring short leg who does not object to standing right under the bat, and a long fielder who is not only a dead sure catch, but a sprinter who cuts off the fours. Hitch, of Surrey, is another who can field anywhere, and Hobbs shall be our cover-point, Woolley will be one of the slips, and Mead, of Hampshire, the other. Mead is not a good outfield; he can neither run fast nor throw hard, but he is an extraordinarily fine slip, and in this position I have seen him bring off some really great catches.

So far we have Mr. Wood, Brown, Hendren, Hitch, Hobbs, Woolley, and Mead. We want four more, and these shall be Barratt, of Nottinghamshire, an extremely fine mid-off, not, perhaps, so good as Brown, but very good indeed; Humphreys, of Kent, who has made a speciality of fielding at mid-on, and is the best fielder in this position in England; Walden, of Northampton-shire, reputed the finest field in the Midlands and North of England, a superb cover or extra cover, and almost equally good in the long field; and, finally, Mr. H. C. McDonell, of Hampshire, a wonderful field to his own slow bowling, no hit being too hard for him to catch or to stop, and efficient anywhere near the wicket. It is on record that Mr. McDonell caught a bats-man at third man off his own bowling. The match was Old Wykehamists v. Bradfield College, and a skied mis-hit went in the direction of third man. Mr. McDonell had followed up the ball on the off-side, and, perhaps not alto-gether trusting third man, he took the catch himself. Our side is now com-pleted, and the order of going in would be:–

1. Hobbs (Surrey).
2. Humphreys (Kent).
3. Mead (Hampshire).
4. Woolley (Kent).
5. Hendren (Middlesex).
6. Brown (Hampshire).
7. Mr. G. E. C. Wood (Cambridge University).
8. Mr. H. C. McDonell (Hampshire).
9. Hitch (Surrey).
10. Walden (Northamptonshire).
11. Barratt (Nottinghamshire).

The men who compose this eleven have been selected purely for their qualifications as fieldsmen, but the first five are also tip-top batsmen, and the remainder are dangerous hitters. Moreover, Mead, Woolley, and Brown are left-handed, an added source of strength to the team and a distinct annoyance to their opponents. The bowling is not by any means strong; Hitch, Woolley, and Barratt are the only recognized bowlers, but Mr. McDonell is a distinctly useful slow bowler, especially with so fine a lot of fieldsmen to assist him, and Humphreys is by no means to be despised as a left-hander. It would be interesting to see whether a great many runs would be made against such a side. My own opinion is that on a hard, true wicket they would obtain a good deal of exercise; but this is exactly what the spectators would like, for they would have plenty of opportunities to admire and to realize what a large number of runs can be saved in a long innings by really fine fielding.

Certain natural qualifications are necessary to enable any cricketer to become a great fieldsman, but "keep your mind on the game and expect every ball to come to you" is an excellent maxim for every cricketer. Practice, too, can do a great deal to improve one's fielding, and is most interesting and amusing, especially off the "cradle," from which slip catches fly in all directions. Capital practice for long field, cover, and mid-off catching may be had by getting someone to hit the ball to you at various distances and paces, but it is a great mistake to hit long field catches too high. One seldom or never gets abnormally high catches in matches, and they only tend to bruise the hands.

Do not practise fielding on very cold days. The only result will be bruised hands, missed catches, and consequent loss of confidence. Many catches are missed because on our modern grounds, with their huge stands and pavilions, it is often difficult to follow the ball. Lord's is notorious in this respect and one has often seen a long fieldsman at the nursery end run the wrong way, it being hard indeed to see the ball until it rises above the pavilion. Many catches, too, are missed through sheer nervousness. Here practice does much good. As the "Jubilee Book of Cricket" says:– "Nervousness often disappears as experience grows. A steeple high catch in the country begins to lose its terrors when one has caught a dozen such the evening before at fielding practice."

This series of 26 "Cricket Reminiscences" was republished in book form the following year.

"A Leisurely Warfare"

5 *August* 1919, *Leading Article*. The average Englishman is a leisurely being who will not be hurried, a fact which may explain why our national game is cricket, for "cricket," wrote MR. E. V. LUCAS once in a delightful article, "is an intricate, vigilant, and leisurely warfare." There was never a better definition of our game, which is played wherever Englishmen are gathered together. It is played in mean dark streets where the wicket is a lamp-post, the pitch a pavement, and the players in their happy imaginations Trumpers and Blythes. It is played on all our village greens and commons; it is played at all our schools, great and small, at our universities, and at our country

houses. It is played in all our Dominions and in all foreign countries where there are Englishmen. It was played on all the battlefields of the Great War. It is not understood of the people of other countries, but we who understand it love it, because it is "a leisurely warfare" fraught always with amazing possibilities. No cricket is more pleasant than country house cricket, and the Canterbury Week which began yesterday is the best of the year. Its revival is a sign that all is well with our great game. The "Old Stagers," who appeared first in 1842, are acting again, and the old stagers of cricket are discussing the games of the past on the famous ground. There are house parties at all the great houses in the neighbourhood. Originally the property of Kent alone, the week is now the property of all who love the game. The thoughts of the spectators, and of thousands who are there only in thought, will not forget the figures of many men who "played cricket" to the last, and especially those two great Kent players, COLIN BLYTHE and KENNETH HUTCHINGS, worthy successors of the immortal ALFRED MYNN – BLYTHE, physically frail but mentally a giant, who could bowl out a whole side on a perfect pitch, and HUTCHINGS, an Apollo whose fielding and batting were the delight of all.

Death of William Caffyn

An Old-time Cricketer

30 *August* 1919. William Caffyn, who died at Reigate on Thursday night, belonged to a time so long gone by that only the oldest *habitués* of the Oval and Lord's – grey-haired and stricken with years – can have seen him at his best.

Caffyn was in his 92nd year, and his real career in English cricket ended when, after the tour of George Parr's team in Australia in the winter of 1863-64, he accepted a position as coach, and stayed behind in the Colonies. Returning to England in 1872, he played that year and in the following season in a few matches for Surrey, but it was far too late to begin again where he had left off. His day was over, and he soon dropped out of public notice. At his zenith he was Surrey's best all-round player – the star of an eleven that had the glory of beating, more than once, the full strength of England. Of that famous band there is still one survivor, Mr. E. Dowson, who was at the Oval a week or two ago, bearing quite lightly the burden of 81 years.

Caffyn did as much as anyone in the fifties to make Kennington Oval a popular resort. He and Tom Lockyer, the never-to-be-forgotten wicket-keeper, were special favourites of the enthusiasts who came to be known as the Surrey crowd. A column could be written about the matches in which F. P. Miller's eleven took part. A tablet in the pavilion at the Oval sets forth the details of a season in which not a single game was lost. The matches were few, but the beaten opponents included England and the North. Expert opinion differed in comparing Mr. Miller's side with the eleven that in later years, with Mr. John Shuter as captain, won back for Surrey the first place among the counties. Curiously enough Mr. Frederick Burbidge, who shared in the far-off triumphs, gave his preference to the modern side, but Mr. V. E. Walker as long as he lived retained a robust faith in the old combination. It was for England against Surrey at the Oval in 1859 that Mr. Walker took all 10 wickets in one innings with his lobs and made a score of 108 runs.

At this distance of time it would be futile to compare Caffyn with modern cricketers, but on one point there can be no doubt. As a batsman he loved a good pitch, and as he could, on occasions, get his century 60 years ago, he would have found himself very much at home on the carefully-prepared pitches of these days. On the rough wickets at Lord's he fell far below Hayward and Carpenter.

Caffyn won quite as many matches for Surrey by his bowling as by his batting. Learning the game years before the law was altered, he bowled medium pace with a purely round-arm delivery. The change that removed all restriction as to the height of the arm was made in 1864, just when he had settled in Australia. Whether he had any special virtue of spin or peculiarity of flight, let those decide who played against him. He may have had no particular merit beyond great accuracy of length, but the fact remains that he took a lot of wickets.

Retirement of John Tyldesley

6 *March* 1920. In a letter to the Lancashire County Cricket Club J. T. Tyldesley, the famous batsman, has announced his intention to retire from first-class cricket. He said that he only played last year at the request of the new captain, Mr. Kenyon, and that he was not fit enough to stand the strain of another season. He expressed his gratitude for the courtesy and appreciation he had always received.

Few professional cricketers have been more popular than Tyldesley, and not one has deserved popularity more. He has had a wonderful career, and among the batsmen of his generation he will rank in cricket history with the very best. Success came to him at the outset and he never looked back. In retiring now he leaves off while still first class.

Tyldesley was 46 in November, but there was little sign of age in his batting last summer. Indeed, in many matches he played with all the brilliancy of his best seasons. He was very doubtful as to the wisdom of returning to the field after a break of four years, but the desire to help his county through the first season of peace overcame his reluctance. Some physical trouble had to be fought against. His eye and wrist were as unfailing as ever, but his legs – he suffered severely at one time from varicose veins – were not what they had been. No doubt he found the long hours of the two-day match fatiguing. There is no need just now to go into details of Tyldesley's career, but one may recall the fact that on three occasions he made a hundred for England against Australia – 138 at Birmingham in 1902 and 100 at Leeds and 112 not out at the Oval in 1905. His hundreds for Lancashire can be counted by the dozen.

No batsman in our day has surpassed him on the off side. From the time he came out for Lancashire in 1895 his cutting was a marvel of skill. So far from being only a fine weather batsman, he could get runs in all conditions. It has been said that during his second visit to Australia – with Mr. Warner's team in the winter of 1903-4 – he played the innings of his life on an almost impossible wicket at Melbourne, getting 62 when no one else could look at the bowling.

Mr. Warner's Triumph

1 *September* 1920, *Leading Article*. Yesterday was a great day for cricketers, and seldom can lovers of the game have had such good and sincere cause for rejoicing as they had last night over the result of the Middlesex and Surrey match. The victory of Middlesex, which was thoroughly well deserved, and was due as much to sound strategy as to skilful play, decides the County Championship in a way which cannot fail to give satisfaction; for the alternative, had Middlesex failed to get Surrey out in time, would have caused much disappointment. Lancashire, in spite of their want of success against their more formidable competitors, stood every chance, thanks to the method of scoring the Championship points and the caprice which governs the allocation of matches, of coming out first on the list; and, if public opinion had grown restive the Committee of the M.C.C. might have been put into the awkward position of having to consider whether they ought not, by virtue of a power possessed by them, to override the reading of the points and decide the Championship on other grounds. But most happily for the game, at the close of its first season after the return to three-day matches, all the gloomy clouds of possibility have been swept away in the last hour, and the sunset sky is clear. The Championship may not in itself be the be-all and end-all of good cricket, and not every one who desires to see the game flourish may attach an equal importance to its results; but some such trial for supremacy, some such climax, is almost inevitable; and, as long as the present system is in force it is important that the winner should be indisputably the best eleven.

Middlesex can amply justify the position which it has just won. The county has been admirably led, and has had in MR. WARNER a captain who combines all the virtues which a county captain should possess. That he should lead his side to victory, and to a victory which brings so satisfactory a sequel in its train, on his last appearance in first-class cricket, is eminently befitting. Fortune is often fickle in cricket, but it smiled on the Middlesex captain yesterday. The close of his long and honourable period of devoted service to the best interests of the game could not have been staged in more appropriate circumstances. Yesterday's match was such as all cricketers, who are, because they play the game, all good men, desire to see and to bring about. That things do not always go so ideally in the cricket field is not a valid reason for good men to be grumbling; and true cricketers do not, in fact, dwell upon the more disappointing side of the national game. Every now and then they receive their full recompense, and the moment is well worth living for. Such a moment awaited them at Lord's last night, and "all time's story remembers." MR. WARNER will not forget it, and no captain left the field for the last time with cheers better deserved.

The Test Matches

2 *March* 1921, *Leading Article*. The five Test Matches are over, and Australia has set up a record for this class of cricket by winning them all. Yet, when the English team left these shores it was the general opinion not only that they were practically the best all-round combination that the country could produce, but that they were, in spite of their pronounced weakness in batting after the first five or six men, a really fine side. The conclusion is obvious. Either their ability had been over-rated, or, making all due allowance for their not doing themselves justice or enjoying the best of the luck, their conquerors were an exceptionally good Australian eleven. On the whole, we are inclined to believe that this last inference represents the true state of the case. None of the English bowling seemed to have the sting required for Australian wickets, and for some reason too many catches were dropped by players who at home were known to have particularly sure hands. But these failures can hardly account for the obvious superiority of their opponents. In the five matches, Australia scored nearly 600 more runs than England for twenty-seven fewer wickets, and their average score per wicket was forty-six to England's twenty-seven. Till they are seen over here this summer it is not possible to compare them with previous elevens from the Dominion, but it certainly looks, from this distance, as if they deserve to be ranked high in the list. MR. DOUGLAS claims that the men under his command were a happy family, so that a last possible explanation of their failure – a fatal and inevitable source of weakness, when it exists – is ruled out, and MR. ARMSTRONG and his team deserve on all grounds the heartiest congratulations from the motherland of cricket on their fine achievement. A word must be said, however, on the reports of "barracking" and occasional heated criticisms of decisions given by the umpires which have from time to time been cabled across. Both are entirely foreign to the true spirit of the game, which,

though it is, after all, only a game, has unwritten laws which cannot be broken with impunity, more especially in international contests. We have no doubt that when the English side comes home, it will be found that the reports with regard to the attitude of some of them towards the umpires have been exaggerated. With regard to the stories of "barracking," it appears that it has been partly due – especially in the last match of the series – to the annoyance felt by some of the spectators at the tone of certain journalistic messages sent home by members of the English side [*Rockley Wilson and Percy Fender*]. People in this country are hardly in a position to judge of the contents of such messages. But, whatever may have been the practice up till now, recent events have clearly proved that the system which tolerates them is undesirable and harmful. In Test Matches, at all events, cricketers should be cricketers and not amateur journalists and descriptive reporters and critics of the games in which they engage. We sincerely hope that this is the view which will be taken by the M.C.C., and that in future no one will be chosen to represent England except on the understanding that when he becomes a Test Match player he lays aside his pen.

Eton v. Winchester

Great Innings by J. L. Guise

[BY S. F. OXLEY]

27 *June* 1921. Eton beat Winchester at Agar's Plough on Saturday by seven wickets. Winchester made a great effort in their second innings, but were unable to make up for the failure in the first.

The feature of the Winchester second innings was the magnificent batting of J. L. Guise, who went in first, and was the last man out. He hit up 278 out of a total score of 381, and was, unfortunately, run out in an effort to get the bowling. His display was one of the finest ever witnessed on the Eton Playing Fields. Some say he gave a difficult chance before he had scored, but this is disputed. He certainly hit the ball hard and cleanly, and it was noticeable that he very rarely missed a leg ball. His scoring strokes included over 40 to the boundary. Overnight he had made 87, and at the luncheon interval on Saturday he had raised his score to 243. The total was then 345 for nine. Afterwards, he made 35, at which point Barber threw his wicket down smartly from some distance out – half-way to the boundary on the leg side.

Guise received a great ovation on returning to the pavilion, his score of 278 generally being regarded as a "record" for the series of matches between the two schools. His innings occupied over four hours. With the exception of B. Pinney and A. R. V. Barker, none of the other Winchester batsmen reached double figures, their batting, in fact, being rather feeble.

G. O. Allen again was the best bowler on the Eton side, and by taking four wickets for 74 runs brought his analysis for the match to nine for 94. He kept a good length, and bowled no fewer than 27 overs in the second innings. The other Eton bowlers were very moderate, but, taking into account the great heat and the long time they were out in the field, the Eton team fielded very well.

Eton were left to score 184 runs in order to win, and quickly lost G. K. Cox, who was run out badly before he had scored [*this detail is omitted from Wisden's account*]. R. Aird and the Hon. D. F. Brand then put on 71 runs before the latter was bowled by J. L. Guise for 12. Brand had played very carefully, Aird doing most of the scoring. P. E. Lawrie joined Aird, and both played brilliant cricket. Aird, although feeling far from well, played most attractive cricket, his strokes to leg being particularly brilliant. He gave a chance when he had made about 50, but he has seldom batted better, and he is undoubtedly the prettiest bat in the Eton eleven. His hits included 18 fours. Aird, who was still not out at the finish, was helped by Lawrie to make victory quite certain. Lawrie also hit very powerfully, and only two runs were required to win the match when he was out to a catch at cover-point. T. C. Barber joined Aird, and shortly afterwards made the winning hit, the game being over just before 5.30.

The Winchester bowling and fielding were excellent. Raikes probably was the best bowler in the two teams, and he captained his side splendidly. Macmillan again fielded magnificently at cover-point. The game was a most interesting one to watch. The wicket wore very well, and much credit was due to Austin, the groundsman, for its condition.

> WINCHESTER 57 (G. O. Allen 5 for 20) and 381 (J. L. Guise 278; G. O. Allen 4 for 74)
> ETON 255 (P. E. Lawrie 92, G. K. Cox 64; T. B. Raikes 7 for 92) and 184 for 3 (R. Aird 112 not out, P. E. Lawrie 42)
> *Eton won by 7 wickets*

The Test Matches

BY S.H.P. [SYDNEY H. PARDON]

20 *August* 1921. Despite the defence put forward for him by Mr. C. B. Fry, I think that Mr. Armstrong was much to blame in reducing the last stage of the Test Match at the Oval to a mere exhibition – in fact a farce. He might surely have shown a little consideration for the thousands of people who had paid their money to see serious cricket. It would have been so easy to avoid all risk of friction or unpleasantness. If, when he found his fast bowlers unable to get a wicket, he had gone on himself and kept the runs down for an hour, not a word would have been said. Assuming that he took the course he did as a protest against our custom of restricting Test Matches to three days,

the moment of so doing was ill-chosen. The Australians beat us at Nottingham in two days, at Lord's in considerably less than two days and a half, and at Leeds with nearly an hour and three-quarters to spare on the third day. This year, at any rate, the matter of time has not been a burning question. More than that, the match at the Oval would, if the rubber had depended on it, have been played out to a finish.

I have been told that when England went in to bat on the Tuesday, with a little more than three hours left for play, the Australians thought that they had just an off-chance of winning the match. The extreme energy with which Mr. Gregory and Mr. Macdonald bowled the first few overs suggested some hope of snatching a victory. The two fast bowlers have done such startling things this season – they got Middlesex out in double quick time at Lord's for 90 – that they might easily have given us a scare. Happily Russell and Brown faced the onslaught so coolly and, apart from one ridiculously short run, played with such discretion that a draw very soon became inevitable. Then Mr. Armstrong changed the bowling, and serious interest was at an end. Without grudging Russell his success, I cannot help feeling sorry he made a hundred. A Test Match hundred obtained under such unreal conditions does not deserve the place that must be given to it in the records.

In the light of his score of 182 not out – the highest score ever made for England against Australia in this country – it is sad to think that Mead should have played in only two of the five Test Matches. Slight injuries – a bad finger and a blow on the head – caused the Selection Committee to leave him out at Lord's and Leeds, but I believe that he was very anxious to play on both occasions and felt keenly disappointed. He was not among the players picked for the first match, at Nottingham. His great innings at the Oval may be regarded as the chief consolation of our disastrous season. He was batting for five hours and, against ground fielding less perfect than that of the Australians, he would have made considerably over 200. With all his good qualities, he is strictly utilitarian as a batsman. One admires his fine all-round hitting and his impregnable defence, but he plays so low that his style affords no joy to the eye. Woolley, when set and hitting, is as good to look at as the most attractive right-handed batsmen.

The fact that 30 men appeared for England in the five Test Matches is sufficient in itself to prove how heavily we have been handicapped. We have never had a real England eleven, merely a succession of scratch teams. Vastly different was the state of things in 1912 – the year of the Triangular Tournament. Then, we only called upon 17 players, eight of whom took part in all six matches. The changes from match to match were so trifling that the strength of the combination was not in the least affected. Best of all, we had, with Barnes and Mr. F. R. Foster playing, the solid foundation in every game of highest class bowling. It so happened that Mr. Foster was only deadly in our first match in the tournament, but the South African and Australian batsmen always faced him with a certain degree of apprehension. They knew that at any time he might be irresistible. Barnes was our match-winning force, taking 39 wickets to Mr. Foster's 13.

This year we have had no bowler good enough to make the Australian batsmen fearful of the morrow. Parkin would have been more formidable if he had not gone to Australia and been on the losing side in the Test Matches there. Still, he has been by a long way our best bowler, and I cannot think that the most judicious use was made of him. He ought always, in my humble judgment, to have been put on first and given his choice of ends. The measure of our weakness in bowling could be gauged by the extent to which we depended on Colonel Douglas. He is, of course, an excellent bowler – zealous and untiring – but in an England eleven of pre-war strength, he would have been no more than second change.

Our fielding in the Test Matches – deplorable at Lord's – was made to look worse than it was by the extraordinary brilliancy of that of the Australians; but in this matter, as in bowling, there were difficulties that could not be overcome. In order to get the solid batting that served us so well at Manchester and the Oval, some sacrifice was inevitable. We were obliged to play men who can only field near the wicket. When one recalled Hobbs and Mr. Jessop, our coverpoint fielding at the Oval was a sorry sight. That brilliant fielding is not an Australian monopoly was proved to demonstration in the University match.

Presentation to George Hirst

11 *October* 1921. Lord Hawke, at Leeds, yesterday, paid a great tribute to George Hirst, when making a presentation to the well-known cricketer.

He referred especially to the good sportsmanship shown by Hirst whether the day went against or favoured his side. "You never condemned, you always cheered," he said. "You were the best county cricketer of our time, and it was a great honour to you to captain the Players against the Gentlemen in your 50th year."

Hirst, returning thanks, said that his jump from a village lad to a county cricketer was big, but his retirement was a greater change. "I want to retire," he continued, "before becoming a nuisance. Cricket goes in cycles. Australia, within a few years, will meet the same treatment as England suffered this year."

The presentation took the form of £700 of War Stock and a cheque for £39.

The Canterbury Week

FROM OUR SPECIAL CORRESPONDENT [G. J. V. WEIGALL]

7 *August* 1922; *Canterbury, 5 August.* The first match of the week was set apart for Woolley's benefit.

His great career as a cricketer is too well known by the cricket-loving public to go into detail. It is enough to say that he has made 20,000 runs and has taken nearly 1,500 wickets in first-class cricket. He started playing for Kent in 1906, and ever since then he has been a tower of strength to his side in all departments of the game. The writer, who first saw him on the Tonbridge ground, which is within a 100 yards of Woolley's home, some 20 years ago, predicted that he would be an England player some day. To-day he is the finest all-round cricketer in the country, and probably in the world.

His style, certainly, is ideal both to watch and to try to copy. Whatever he does when batting is most graceful. He is the modern-day Palairet. The grace and ease of his attack and defence is unsurpassed, and unlike many present-day players, he is never guilty of making an unorthodox stroke, and his timing of the ball when driving is the perfection of what timing should be. In all that he does while he is batting there is a simplicity of method which is the essence of correctness and which gives the onlooker ample time to recognize the stamp of a really great batsman. Although popularly supposed to be almost a hitter Woolley's defence and back play are actually his strongest weapons, so correct are his methods.

Regrettable Scene at Trent Bridge

Player Ordered off the Field

1 1 *September* 1922. Play in the match between Nottinghamshire and Hampshire, at Trent Bridge, yesterday, was marred by an extraordinary incident, which ended in Newman, one of the visitors' bowlers, being ordered off the field by his captain.

Newman was at some pains to re-arrange his field before trying the experiment of bowling round the wicket, and a section of the crowd subjected him to some barracking, which was renewed when he again hesitated before beginning his next over. The sequel was that Major Tennyson took him off and ordered him to the pavilion, Newman, in his anger, kicking the wicket down as he retired. In a conversation afterwards Major Tennyson said that Newman's offence was using objectionable language.

Cf. 19 *June* 1973.

Old Bats

2 *October* 1922, *Leading Article.* With the end of the cricket season comes a putting up of weapons and, when the player's critical eye compels his reluctant decision, a great pensioning off of old friends. The ball which, on an August day, when the sun gave a dry surface to a sodden pitch, won a match and secured a reputation, is thrown to the puppies, who treat it, not as a prince among balls, but as a round thing like any other round thing which is good to gnaw; and the bat, which flashed so splendidly in the hour of its July triumph, is seen to have survived its usefulness, and is given over to the attic's unending shadows. Not all bats are thus finally abandoned. To some a reprieve is granted for another season, and they are anointed with oil and covered with winter baize. Others, whose remarkable achievements have earned for them a taste of immortality, are inscribed with dates and figures and hidden in a secret place. A few – and these the aristocrats of the game – are attached to pavilion walls, there to encourage with an illustrious history bored cricketers of future generations when they have grown tired of the club photographs and are wishing the rain would stop. Who shall say what score or what occasion justifies this gentle vanity of preservation? None but the harshest materialist would find fault with the whim that keeps for a little while the bat with which its owner scored a century for his country or his university. And if a hundred may redeem it, the sentimentalist will argue, why not ninety-nine? There can be no answer, for no rigid limitation can ever be put upon men's pardonable desire to keep beside them a few relics, however useless before the world, by which old age may proudly remember its youth. Yet, those who hesitate between keeping and throwing away may care to be reminded, by the letter from the secretary of the London Playing Fields Society, which we published recently, that a third course lies open to them. London children, for whom new bats gleam only in shop windows and in the hands of others, are in need of old bats and of sporting material of every sort. It is an appeal which should rescue many a well-tried warrior from the dull obscurity of an attic. In the children's hands he is yet a King, though his Ministers are changed; among the apples and the cobwebs he is a useless and, as all good cricketers must believe, an unhappy exile.

Mr. J. W. H. T. Douglas as Prosecutor

Attempt to Obtain Money by Fraud

2 *September* 1924. At the Stratford Police Court yesterday, HOLMAN ARTHUR MENDAY, 39, described as an accountant, of no fixed abode, was charged, on remand, with attempting to obtain £2 by false pretences from Mr.

John William Henry Tyler Douglas, the Essex cricketer. The prisoner, whose name was originally given as Kerry, was now further charged with obtaining £2 by fraud from Captain T. Jameson, of Walton-place, Chelsea.

Evidence was given last week that while Mr. Douglas was at the Army Sports Ground at Leyton on Saturday, August 23, he received a telephone message from a man who gave the name of Hill. Douglas had played with a man named Hill, and when the man at the telephone said one of his motor-lorries had broken down in the neighbourhood, and asked if Mr. Douglas would advance one of his men £2 to pay for the repairs, the prosecutor said he would. Later, his suspicions were aroused, and the prisoner was arrested. At the police station he admitted that he had telephoned to Mr. Douglas, and that his tale was untrue.

Detective Rogers said that the prisoner had made a statement in which he said he had, since leaving a situation in Buckingham Palace-road, met a man who induced him to join in frauds of this kind. They had, with the help of a young woman, got 30s. from a Mr. Thomas. He called on Sir William Plender, but got nothing; but after that they got £2 from a Colonel White, £2 from Captain T. Jameson, and £2 from Lord Swaythling.

After evidence on the second charge. Detective Rogers stated that the accused came from a very good family, but in 1911 he was convicted for stealing a dividend warrant. He afterwards joined the Army and got commission rank. After leaving the Army in 1920 he was employed by the Metropolitan Water Board for six months. His downfall was due to drink and gambling. He had also confessed that he had got £1 by fraud from Mr. Lacey, of the M.C.C., at Lord's Cricket Ground.

The prisoner made no defence to the two charges, and was sentenced to three months' imprisonment with hard labour on each charge, the sentences to be concurrent.

Colonel Jackson's Harrow Days

6 *March* 1925. COLONEL F. S. JACKSON, distributing the prizes at the Harrow Boys' Secondary School on Wednesday, said he had found it a great deal easier to distribute prizes than to win them at Harrow School. His clearest memories of school life at Harrow were those of the playing fields, where he spent happy times before the taint of politics got hold of him. In those days he never dreamed he would find himself a Governor of Harrow School, but he took the appointment as a compliment to one who, though not an academic success, was privileged to help his school on the playing fields. In the same house as himself at Harrow were the present Prime Minister, Mr. Baldwin, Lord Peel, and Mr. Amery, whom they always found at the top of the form, and Mr. Churchill, the Chancellor of the Exchequer, whom he was asked to look after as a little boy. When he was at Harrow his master

endorsed his report: "Jackson thinks too much of his cricket." Later, when Harrow beat Eton at Lord's and he took 11 wickets, his master wrote to his father: "Jackson still thinks too much of his cricket, but I am very glad he does."

Records

23 *July* 1925, *Leading Article*. England is waiting for news in an expectant hush. At any moment, nay, at the very moment these words are being written, HOBBS may be hitting the four to leg, from a full-pitch sent him by some kindly bowler, which shall make the number of his hundreds equal to that of W. G.'s. And a little later he will make yet another, and W. G.'s record will be a record, in inverted commas, no longer. This has been an iconoclastic summer. MR. WILLIAM WARD's "longest hands" at Lord's of 278, after standing for a hundred and five years, has been beaten by HOLMES, and MR. ENTHOVEN has equalled the achievement of the immortal YARDLEY [*a century in the University match*]. Indeed, since he made his two hundreds in successive years, the record-mongers say that he has surpassed it. It was not long since that the incredible NURMI beat GEORGE's mile, and, of the records upon which we have been brought up, only BROOKS's jump of 1876 still survives. That may go too if MR. VAN GEYSEL gets a fine day instead of a wintry wind for the University Sports. Everything seems to be crumbling around us.

Yet there ought in all this to be no cause for lamentation. It is absurd to talk of W. G.'s record being "in danger." He is secure for ever on his lonely height, incomparably great. Nor should anything be able to touch YARDLEY, to whom MR. COBDEN has borne the finest testimony that any cricketer could desire. "I have often known him," he wrote, "back his runs against W. G. GRACE's when they were playing on the same side, and win his bet." In the case of MR. WARD there is no sting, because we think of him as mythological rather than real. JOHN NYREN dedicated his book to him, so that he seems to belong to the "thymy pastures" of Hambledon, where sported the elder gods. Still it is difficult not to "murmur a little sadly." The printed table of statistics abides when those who saw and played against and can appraise great men have passed away. That fact cannot be altered, not even by the most unimpeachable arguments to the effect that conditions change and that it is impossible to compare one generation with another. It is an argument to which we ourselves have not perhaps paid enough attention when advanced by our elders, and so it may be only right that we should be punished, as we shall be, in our turn. Only it seems a pity that some records cannot be treated as was TOM CRIBB, who, having held the championship unchallenged for nearly ten years, was expected to fight no more and was dubbed champion for the rest of his life.

This regret of ours has in any case something illogical about it, for, however strongly we may feel it, let us but be on a cricket ground with HOBBS's score in the eighties and we shall hold our breath as hopefully as any man in Surrey and crow as lustily when the three figures break at last on the telegraph board. This is no doubt partly due to the psychology of the crowd of which we are a fraction, for the crowd always wants to bring home a winner and to believe that it has helped him to win. But there is also the feeling – and a right and proper one – that it would be churlish to deny his meed to a fine player. So let us cheer HOBBS with all sincerity. All we ask is that no effusive statistician shall rub it into us too hard. After all, as the wise MR. MITFORD said, "All is vanity but cricket," and some day some one may even beat HOBBS.

An Early View of Cricket

5 *August* 1925, *Leading Article*. There is scarcely a custom or an institution now thriving among us which has not had to fight for its life. Everything, small and great, from Summer Time to the aseptic method of surgery, has been fiercely opposed and ridiculed in the period of its innovation. Even pastimes, of which the harmlessness is now so obvious that it is difficult to understand how men ever thought them harmful, have been attacked by reasonable people with the most solemn rhetoric.

So it has always been. Even golfers can remember a time of glorious martyrdom when golf was supposed to lead to drink, the desertion of wives and the angry chastisement of children. But hitherto cricket has generally been considered exempt. There it is – a quiet, peaceful, decorous game, perfectly fitted to exercise the sons of gentlemen. Have we not, indeed, been told again – particularly by those who feel that lawn tennis is effeminate and that the study of wild flowers and birds by small boys is only an excuse for loafing – that cricket is the foundation of Imperial and manly virtue, and is the source of "that spirit of unselfish team-work which has undoubtedly made England what it is"? It is not easy to believe that it was ever regarded as a coarse and dangerous pastime which men of breeding ought at all costs to avoid. Yet we have the indignant evidence of DR. WILLICH to prove that cricket was not always an honourable game. DR. WILLICH compiled a Domestic Encyclopædia in the year 1802 – about the time, it is to be presumed, when the Battle of Waterloo was being so successfully fought in the neighbourhood of Windsor. "Cricket," he explains, is "an exercise or game performed with bats and a ball. This sport was formerly confined solely to the labouring class of people, but is now becoming daily more fashionable among those whose rank and fortune entitle their countrymen to expect a very different conduct." So much for the writer's aristocratic frown, but this is not all. DR. WILLICH, like others after him, had the best and gravest reasons to fortify him in his prejudice. "Although," this moderate man continues – "although we have on all occasions enjoined proper muscular exercise, yet we strongly reprobate that of cricket, which is in all respects too violent, and, from the positions into which players must necessarily throw themselves, cannot fail to be productive of frequent injury to the body. Indeed, we have witnessed several melancholy accidents which lately happened in our neighbourhood; and dislocations of the hip joint in particular are by no means uncommon from the awkward posture occasioned by employing both arms at the same time in striking a distant object." It might be supposed that "our neighbourhood" was exceptionally unfortunate in having erratic bowlers and batsmen who could not resist a tempting wide. But DR. WILLICH is not to be so easily discounted. His medical fears are less important than his unerring social instinct. "We trust," says he, "the time is not very remote when this game, like pugilism, will be utterly exploded by all who possess a correct taste and have any regard for their constitutions as well as for their respective situation in life."

Hobbs 101

The Champion's Record Equalled

[BY E. H. D. SEWELL]

18 *August* 1925. There was a thoroughly interesting day's cricket at Taunton yesterday, when a huge crowd assembled in the hope and expectation of seeing Hobbs score his 126th hundred and so equal Dr. W. G. Grace's record of centuries. Hobbs had made 91 not out on Saturday and at 11.37 yesterday morning he duly accomplished this feat after play had been in progress for 12 minutes. Surrey's first innings ended at 2.35 for 359 and, making light of their deficit of 192, Somerset made 256 for three wickets by the close of play, Mr. MacBryan playing a magnificent innings.

The best cricket of the day and the match came in the afternoon, when Mr. MacBryan, playing England cricket, and Young were making 184 for Somerset's first wicket in their second innings. The late start was due to the fact that the authorities wished to give as many spectators as possible a chance of witnessing Hobbs's feat, if it was to be done.

At 11 o'clock the queue at the gate was nearly half-a-mile long. In obtaining the necessary nine runs Hobbs had 17 balls bowled to him in the course of five overs. With three singles, a 4 off a no-ball, and two more singles he reached his hundred. The crowd gave him a very warm reception and the Somerset players crowded round to congratulate him. After Mr. Fender had taken him out a drink, the exact nature of which was not disclosed, the game proceeded, Hobbs playing the next six balls from Mr. Robertson-Glasgow without scoring. Three overs later he was very well caught on the leg-side by Mr. Hill.

It is as well to give the complete details of this historic innings. Hobbs batted for two hours and 50 minutes and scored off 59 of the 192 balls bowled to him, hitting eight 4's, two 3's, 12 2's, and 39 singles. He gave only one catch, when he had made 14, but narrowly escaped being run out at 87, when Mr. Knight sacrificed his wicket for him, and again at 90. By scoring this hundred Hobbs equals the late W. G. Grace's total of centuries, but has now to make 19 more to equal Dr. Grace's total of hundreds in first-class cricket in this country. He also equalled the 13 centuries in a season scored by Mr. C. B. Fry, Tom Hayward, and Hendren. He received a great ovation on retiring to the pavilion to cope with a deluge of telegrams.

After the tension of Hobbs's hundred, the dismissal of Mr. Jardine, who might have been caught in the slips twice in one over off Mr. Robertson-Glasgow when he had made 32 and 34 respectively, came as a slight relief. Mr. Fender, hitting at everything, skied a ball towards square leg. Mr. Hill started for the impossible catch, doffing his hat in the first few yards. Having run ten yards he flung away one glove and a little farther on he flung away the second one, thus blazing his trail with articles of attire. He was, however, unable to grab the ball as it fell. In the meanwhile Mr. Fender and Mr. Jardine were ambling up and down the wicket; at last Mr. Hill got to the ball, and returned it to mid-on; the batsmen attempted a fourth run, but Mr. Ingle's return to the bowler being accurate. Mr. Jardine was run out. Mr. Fender made several glorious strokes during his stay of 50 minutes, his straight and off driving being magnificent. He was mainly responsible for the third hundred being scored in 40 minutes.

Peach was striking frequently and well when he turned a ball on to his wicket at 322, and Mr. Fender, in the following over, was well stumped at 325. At the luncheon interval the score was 331 for eight wickets. The Surrey innings ended soon after the interval. Somerset's out-cricket was splendid, the ground fielding and throwing-in both being good, and the bowlers were very wise to keep the ball so straight for Hobbs.

It is noteworthy in concluding this description of a day's cricket that will become historic that it was against Somerset at Bristol in May, 1895, that Dr. Grace scored his hundredth century. He made 288 out of 474, and the Somerset wicket-keeper, the Rev. A. P. Wickham, said that during Dr. Grace's innings he had only four balls to take. In this respect there is parity between Dr. Grace's 288 and Hobb's 101, for it is probable that Mr. Hill did not have more than 12 balls to handle behind Hobbs.

SOMERSET 167 (Young 58; J. H. Lockton 4 for 36) and 374 (J. C. W. MacBryan 109, Young 71, Hunt 59; P. G. H. Fender 5 for 120)
SURREY 359 (Hobbs 101, P. G. H. Fender 59, D. R. Jardine 47) and 183 for 0 (Hobbs 101 not out, Sandham 74 not out)
Score after second day: Somerset 167 and 256 for 3; Surrey 359
Surrey won by 10 wickets

Mr. Baldwin on Test Matches

Australian Eleven entertained

21 *April* 1926. The members of the Australian cricket team were the guests of the London District of the Institute of Journalists, yesterday, at a luncheon at the Criterion Restaurant, Piccadilly. Mr. Alan Pitt Robbins, chairman of the district, presided, and the company numbered over 350.

The following message was read by the Chairman from the Prince of Wales:–

I am desired by the Prince of Wales to ask you to convey to the members of the Australian cricket team his Royal Highness's best wishes for a pleasant stay in this country. His Royal Highness is looking forward to meeting the members of the team during the summer. – SIR LIONEL HALSEY.

Lord Forster, formerly Governor-General of Australia, had accepted an invitation to be present, but he telegraphed expressing great regret that a mishap to his motor-car prevented him reaching London in time for the luncheon. "Please say," his message stated, "how sorry I am, and offer my warmest greetings to my Australian friends."

The CHAIRMAN also said that a message of regret at not being able to be present had been received from Mr. J. H. Thomas, M.P. He was taking a hand in the negotiations concerning the coal dispute.

Mr. BALDWIN, who was cheered on rising, proposed the toast of "Our Australian Guests." He said – There is an unfortunate difference between Mr. Robbins and myself. He said he had no speech to make, but some messages to deliver. I have no message, but I have to make a speech. (Laughter.) One of the messages he delivered reminded me of a circumstance which I am quite sure is unfamiliar even to Mr. Warner and Sir James Barrie. That is, that the Prince of Wales once captained an England Eleven and was beaten; but that was 200 years ago. (Laughter.)

I find it difficult to express to the Australian team what their visit means to old men like myself who, though no great performers, have followed with the keenest interest from the days of early childhood the performances of the giants of cricket right across the world. To us the mere word "Australia" smacks of romance and we think of our childhood and those great names upon which we were brought up, and we seem to see once more the demon bowler at work – the great Spofforth – who is still living among us in London. (Cheers.) And we have here my old friend Sir Kynaston Studd, who tells me that his body is still scarred with bruises received from that giant arm. (Laughter.) We all think of the names of those, some of whom are with us, but some, alas! have passed over – those great bowlers, Charlie Turner, Hugh Trumble, and Ernest Jones. We seem to see once more Victor Trumper and Clem Hill, who has reminded us of his presence lately in a way most likely to attract the attention of the British public. (Laughter.) There was George Giffen, and, perhaps, above all, those two romantic figures, one of whom I am rejoiced to hear from Mr. Smith is still living – the great Blackham, who taught every cricketer in the world how to stand up to fast bowling without a long-stop. And there was one, no longer with us, who gained the admiration of everyone – Bonnor, whose throw-in from the country was a thing no man that ever saw it can forget. I tell the present team that if such giants as those I have named are with them to-day – I gather that there are – then indeed we shall have to look out for our laurels.

But this game of cricket, the nursery of which are the villages of England, has cast its seeds across the ocean, and nowhere has a mightier tree grown from that seed than in Australia. There is nothing that has been imported from this country that has flourished there like cricket. The only remarkable thing to my mind is that the other great English export from this country which though it has flourished so much in Australia yet has been kept out of the team. I know not by what means, is rabbits. (Laughter.) In these few words of mine wishing to welcome the Australians I want to say a word of cheer to Mr. Warner. (Hear, hear.) I want to ask him not to allow his nerves to be unduly rattled by the Press barrage under which our opponents are advancing to fight us. (Laughter.) I can assure him I have passed through those barrages unscathed. (Laughter.) I can assure him that the quality of the ammunition which will be employed can be no better than is manufactured by the directors of the fire. In those circumstances I hope he will keep up his spirits and his courage.

And to the Australians I would say we offer them here to-day the warmest welcome. (Cheers.) We hope the weather will be good. We hope the games will be played out. There are two matches in this country which perhaps occupy a peculiar position for those who are directly interested in them – the Oxford and Cambridge and the Eton and Harrow. It was on the morning of the Oxford and Cambridge match that my younger son – as I had been at Cambridge – said to me, "Don't let us have any of that nonsense to-day about letting the best side win." (Laughter.) No true sportsman in those two matches ever feels that. (Laughter.) But in every match the Australians are going to play I say from my heart let us have the finest cricket and let the best side win. (Cheers.) I ask you to rise and drink the health of the team, and I couple with the toast the names of Mr. Collins, who is no stranger to this country, and Mr. Smith, the manager of the team. (Cheers.)

The toast was enthusiastically received. . .

SIR JAMES BARRIE was loudly cheered on rising to propose the toast "Cricket." He said :– How much sweeter those sounds would be to me if I had got them for lifting Mr. Mailey over the ropes. (Laughter.) If I were to say one-tenth of what I could say about cricket, especially about my own prowess at it, there would be no more play to-day. (Laughter.) Once more I buckle on my pads, I stride to the wicket. I take a look round to see how Mr.

Collins has set his field – and, oh horrible! I see Mr. Gregory waiting in the slips. (Laughter.) What can he be waiting for? I get one consolation from Mr. Gregory's name – he is obviously a MacGregor. I have no doubt that he inherited his bowling from his ancestor, Rob Roy MacGregor, who, as the books tell us, used to hurl rocks at the stumps of the Sassenach. (Laughter.) Mr. Gregory is now joined in the slips by Mr. Hendry and Mr. Mailey. Three to one! (Laughter.) I don't know what they think they look like, with their arms stretched out imploringly, but to me they look as if they were proposing simultaneously to the same lady. (Laughter.) Even though one of them wins her, what can he do with her? I hope they will remember this in the first Test Match, and that it will put them off their game. (Laughter.)

The first Test Match! Fancy speaking that awful mouthful in words of one syllable. All the awful words this year are to be in one syllable. The three T's – Test, Toss, Tail. (Laughter.) The first Test Match is about to begin. We are all at Trent Bridge. The English captain wins the toss (loud laughter) – and puts the Australians in. I think he must have something up his sleeve. I don't quite catch sight of his face, but I saw him having a secret conversation with Mr. Warner's old Harlequin cap, and I believe they are up to something. (Laughter.) Maurice Tate takes the ball. You know his way. He then puts his hand behind his back; an awful silence spreads over the universe. The Prime Minister, in the House of Commons, in the middle of his speech is bereft of words. (Laughter.) It has been said, probably by Mr. Gregory, that drowning men clutch at straws. On a balcony in the pavilion nine members of the Australian team pick up straws and clutch at them. (Laughter.) Mr. Noble pauses in the middle of drawing up the complete Australian averages of the tour. Mr. Hill in Australia is suspended between Heaven and the inkpot. (Laughter.) Maurice Tate takes a little walk which is to be followed by a little run.

My lords and gentlemen, pray silence while Maurice Tate delivers his first ball. There is now nothing to be heard except Mr. Gregory letting fall his straw. Tate comes rushing forward and sends down, not the ball, but the seam. (Laughter.) What does that mighty roar from the onlookers mean? Have the Australians already made four, or does it mean, in journalistic phrase, "The next man in is Macartney"? Much good that will do us. (Laughter.) Then there is Ponsford, who, I am told, has only been out twice in the last five years. (Laughter.)

I suppose I am the only man in the room who knows what is to be the constitution of the English XI. Mr. Warner and his committee don't know – at least I haven't told them. (Laughter.) On such occasion as this it may seem cruel to damp Mr. Collins, but I suppose the truth is best, and I am afraid I must tell him that this year there is no hope for his gallant but unfortunate company. (Laughter.) Our team is mostly new, and is at present hidden away in cellars. Our fast bowler – I mention this in confidence – is W. K. Thunder, who has never been known to smile except when he hears Mr. Gregory referred to as a *fast* bowler. (Laughter.) Of our batsmen, I shall merely indicate their quality by saying that Hobbs is to be 12th man. (Laughter.) Of course, things *may* go wrong. There is the glorious uncertainty of cricket. Even the Prime Minister – in the only game in which I saw him play – in the first innings he made one, but in the second innings he – was not so successful. (Laughter.) But even though Australia should win – this time – I have a rod in reserve for Mr. Collins. (Laughter.) In that case I shall myself choose the Scottish XI. (Laughter.) My first choice is MacGregor, with him Macdonald, Macaulay, and Macartney. (Laughter.) Two other names as Scotch as peat are Hendry and Andrews. A. W. Carr is my captain, M. D. Lyon my wicket-keeper, and there are still Douglas, Nigel Haig, MacBryan, and Armstrong. With this Scottish XI I challenge the Australians. The game not to be played on turf or matting, but, as always, on our native heather. (Laughter.)

In conclusion – for I was out long ago (caught Gregory) – in conclusion, as Mr. Grimmett said when he went on to bowl in the last Test Match – let us pay our opponents this compliment, we are sure that if we had not thought of cricket first, they would have done it, and whether we win or lose, O friendly enemy, you cannot deprive us of our proudest sporting boast, that it was we who invented both cricket and the Australians. (Laughter.) And let us not forget, especially at this time, that the great glory of cricket does not lie in Test Matches, nor county championships, nor Sheffield Shields, but rather on village greens, the cradle of cricket. (Cheers.) The Tests are but the fevers of the game. As the years roll on they become of small account, something else soon takes their place, the very word may be forgotten; but long, long afterwards, I think, your far-off progeny will still of summer afternoons hear the crack of the bat and the local champion calling for his ale on the same old bumpy wickets. It has been said of the unseen army of the dead, on their everlasting march, that when they are passing a rural cricket ground the Englishman falls out of the ranks for a moment to look over the gate and smile. The Englishman, yes, and the Australian. How terrible if those two had to rejoin their comrades feeling that we were no longer playing the game! I think that is about the last blunder we shall make. I ask you to drink to the glorious toast of cricket, coupled with the name of one of the greatest of all cricketers and one of the greatest of cricket captains. Mr. Warner. (Cheers.)...

Crockett to Stand at Lord's

31 *July* 1926. R. Crockett, the famous Australian umpire, has for the first time in his life come "home," and will remain in England until the close of the cricket season. He was invited to officiate at Lord's when the M.C.C. played the Australians there. But the boat on which he was a passenger was delayed by an outbreak of fire, and he did not arrive in time to accept the invitation. Unless, however, some unforeseen accident should occur he will be seen in

action, and repose, at Lord's on August 11 and 12, when the Australians play a game with a team of public school boys. Crockett's assistance will add distinction to what must in any event be a unique occasion in the lives of 15 young cricketers. The Olympian umpires, such as were C. K. Pullin and Robert Thoms, do more than avoid errors of observation or judgment in deciding questions of fact; they encourage the players to blend two occasionally antagonistic virtues – generosity and keenness. The applause which will greet Crockett when he comes out of the Pavilion at Lord's will indicate that his name is known and honoured in England as well as in his own country.

On Chosen and Choosers

24 *June* 1926, *Leading Article*. Londoners (if the weather is kind) are to have their first Test Match this week, and the thoughts of a considerable part of the population are concentrated on the chances of a seat at Lord's. Yet it is doubtful whether the actual play arouses greater interest than, and it is certain that it does not arouse such strong feelings as, does the preliminary business of choosing an English eleven. A few months ago the omission from the Australian side of a famous cricketer produced "nothing less than a natural conwulsion" on the other side of the world, and at this moment there are many worthy persons in this country honestly trying to understand how the Selection Committee could have been so stupid as to differ from them. There are some things that we know we cannot do – we do not, for instance, think that we could jump six feet high or drive an aeroplane; we may have some doubt as to whether we could command an Army Corps; but, whatever the game, we all believe that we could choose the best possible side. It is a proof of our touching faith in the newspapers that we sometimes think we could do so without having seen the candidates, merely by the daily reading of their achievements over the breakfast table. We may indeed call ourselves in a deprecatory tone "the man in the street," or preface our criticisms by the remark "Of course, I suppose they must know best"; but this is the merest pretence and we are fully convinced that *we* know best. Many critics, moreover, are not content to pity the ignorance of the official Selectors, but impute to them motives of complicated baseness. It cannot be that Dumkins and Podder have been preferred to Luffey and Struggles on the simple and transparently absurd ground that they are the better players. If they had habitually played for big, overbearing Muggleton instead of poor little Dingly Dell there would have been a very different story to tell. The name of Podder is, as all the world knows, "associated with property," and Podder's selection is suspect accordingly. Otherwise reasonable people become the most parochial of patriots. The always smouldering feeling of distrust between North and South flares up on a sudden. The fact that there are two Loamshire men in the team and none from Stonyshire, although Stonyshire is ahead in the

County Championship to the clear extent of a decimal point, is capable of only one explanation.

There are other critics, of a pleasanter and more childlike turn of mind, who feel not bitterly but sadly about the omission of their favourites. They have an affection for particular players which they could hardly explain on any logical grounds. They are romantic creatures to whose imagination the unknown makes an irresistible appeal. They do not think much of Surrey, a suburban sort of county in which perhaps they live themselves; but Yorkshire, grim, black, and mysterious, must be the home of heroes. If LUKE GREENWOOD and EPHRAIM LOCKWOOD were still in the land of the living, they would have to be chosen for the beauty and romance of their names. Why cannot England again have a wicket-keeper who was splendidly christened Mordecai? Thus from various sources a stream of disapproval always pours down on the devoted heads of the Selectors, nor can it ever be entirely stemmed, even by a series of victories of the chosen players. It is the delightful part of this form of criticism that we can never be proved in the wrong. If A with his medium-paced bowling of impeccable length has slain his thousands, that erratic genius B with his googlies might have slain his tens of thousands. If there were no victories, then, of course, we can say to the Selectors with Mrs. Nickleby, "I don't make it a reproach to you, my love; but still I will say that if you had consulted your own mother —." In fact, it is a game of heads we win and tails they lose, and the utmost they can hope for is not to be shot on the ground that they are doing their best.

England v. Australia

Fifth Test Match

FROM OUR CRICKET CORRESPONDENT [A. C. M. CROOME]

19 *August* 1926. England, 280 and 436; Australia, 302 and 125. We have won! And after all the lean years we were more than half-pleased. We began to cheer when the Australians' innings was little more than half over, and at the finish we charged, ten thousand of us, across the ground, and massed ourselves in front of the pavilion, where we shouted for the 11 men who had won the game, and for the Chairman of the Committee which selected them. We shouted even more loudly for Mr. Collins and the members of his team. We wanted them to know that we appreciated the high standard of keenness and honourable conduct which they have set up and maintained in this and all their other matches.

This final Test match has been an extraordinarily interesting game. There were grounds for fearing that England had missed a golden opportunity by omitting to make at least 400 on the first day, after Mr. Chapman had won the toss on a perfect Oval wicket. But the Australians declined the offered chance.

In fact their later batsmen had to extricate the side from a nasty hole. Still it seemed likely that we should have to pay for Saturday's comparative failure in batting. The thunderstorm of Monday night, followed by hot sunshine on the following morning, produced a wicket on which 200 was a remarkably good score against first-rate bowling. Hobbs and Sutcliffe made more than that number between them and raised the aggregate of their combined scores in the last ten Test matches against Australia to something like 2,300. Every moment that has passed since they were parted has emphasized the magnitude of their performance. England's last nine wickets fell at rather frequent intervals and when the Australians went in to make 415, they were put out for 125.

The explanation is simple. We had Rhodes on our side. Larwood, Tate, Geary, and Mr. Stevens all bowled well. Larwood, in particular, rendered valuable service by getting rid of Mr. Woodfull and Mr. Macartney. But these bowlers might possibly have been worn down. From the moment that Rhodes went on the match was over. Rhodes has learnt no new tricks since he used to bowl one end for nearly half the time that England were in the field, and his length is not so regular as it was. Yesterday he sent down a full toss and two long hops to leg, balls which he could not bowl in his palmiest days. The unbowlable ball has had some very distinguished victims in this match. Hobbs, Mr. Macartney, Mr. Bardsley, and Mr. Andrews have all given away their wickets to it. The specimens released by Rhodes were all properly hit for four. Otherwise they found themselves playing forward when they would fain have played back, and he used the spin which his fingers impart to the ball to make it break back sharply, leaving those who will to swerve. On a biting pitch the best batsmen in the world cannot take root against a flighty left-hander who places a man at silly mid-off, another not quite square with the wicket at the point of the bat, and pitches the ball well up on the leg stump, making it break back to hit the top of the off, unless it is stopped by the bat; for there is no second line of defence to this form of attack. Only the two left-handed strikers, Mr. Bardsley and Mr. Gregory, were even moderately comfortable when facing Rhodes. And he took Mr. Bardsley's wicket. In this he was fortunate, for the fatal ball must be included in the category of the unbowlable.

The Australians have been beaten and even in the moment of defeat they are generously glad of it. They think that the result will do much good to the game of cricket "at home." It will, if English batsmen have learnt the lesson of wise conservatism which Australian example can teach. I do not myself think that the rain which interrupted play between 1.15 and 3 o'clock made the Australians' task more impossible than it already was. At no time yesterday was the pitch so difficult as it had been on Tuesday morning, when Hobbs and Sutcliffe were – Hobbs and Sutcliffe. Rhodes needed no rain; the faster bowlers might even have preferred that none should fall. What is not matter of opinion is that Mr. Collins may have chanced giving away as many as 20 runs by consenting to resume play so promptly after the shower ceased. But he and his men have come many thousands of miles to play cricket, and have fulfilled their purpose.

The concluding stages of the game were watched by the Prime Minister and an important section of his Cabinet. Some, at least, of them must have been late for their afternoon appointment.

A few spots of rain fell just before noon, but the weather seemed set fair when Rhodes and Geary took guard against Mr. Mailey and Mr. Gregory, the latter bowling for the first time from the pavilion end with no screen behind his arm. Mr. Gregory soon had Geary caught at the wicket and Rhodes played him a trifle diffidently, though he drove an over-pitched ball in great style to the pavilion, and once and again condescended to cut the short one. Tate hit very hard and with discrimination, but Rhodes was out leg-before to Mr. Grimmett, who superseded Mr. Gregory. The fatal ball kept low. Larwood stayed a while and watched Tate make four extremely ponderous hits to the on boundary. He himself brought off a glorious drive for 4 through Mr. Andrews and then was bowled by a googly. Strudwick stayed for nearly two hours while the rain fell and then was caught at silly mid-off.

Mr. Collins sent in Mr. Ponsford with Mr. Woodfull this time, and the bowlers were Larwood and Tate. The heavy roller had been used for the full time allowed, but Larwood at once made the ball fly and might have had Mr. Ponsford out if Geary had not been too far forward at third slip. Geary was moved to the left, and in Larwood's next over caught Mr. Woodfull, whose stroke was not one of his best. Mr. Macartney came in, the man for whom only himself can determine the limits of the possible. He took a couple of minutes to look at the bowling, and then set himself to spoil it. He off-drove Tate, forced a fast rising ball from Larwood off his chest to the leg boundary, and cut him splendidly, though he only got a single for the last stroke of the three. But to the intense relief of every Englishman present, from Mr. Chapman and the Prime Minister downwards, he shortly afterwards cut an almost similar ball to Geary at third slip. Mr. Chapman had a special reason to be elated, for a moment before he had strengthened the field behind the wicket on the off side for Larwood's bowling. Rhodes was called up to stand in the gully and Geary placed precisely where the decisive chance went. The dismissal of Mr. Macartney was of such vital moment that it has caused me to anticipate the order of events. Rhodes had previously been put on in place of Tate, and without another run scored he had Mr. Ponsford caught at backward point. A ball of perfect length broke back the breadth of the wicket and reared up sharply. No first-rate batsman's back stroke can be certain to keep that ball down, though the village blacksmith might mow it to square-leg for 6. Larwood actively and intelligently dived forward from backward point and got a hand under it as it fell. Mr. Collins and Mr. Bardsley were now partnered, but not for long. Mr. Collins got something like Mr. Ponsford's ball, and snicked it to short slip.

Mr. Andrews batted as freely as if the pitch were fast and true. He made some delicious strokes off Rhodes on the off-side, most of which were stopped with apparent ease by Hobbs, and he hit a couple of his loose balls very hard to the on boundary. Since the match was practically won I could with equanimity have watched Mr. Andrews play a long innings in the manner of his opening. But it was not to be. He hooked a short ball from Larwood quite well, but not with the driving part of his bat, and Tate at short leg took a nice catch with his right hand. Mr. Gregory made some powerful strokes before hitting rather recklessly at Tate and getting himself caught at mid-off. Mr. Bardsley dealt with Rhodes better than anybody else, but his efforts at the off balls of the faster bowlers were not convincing. Ultimately Rhodes got his wicket with a long hop which Mr. Bardsley skied to short leg.

As in the first innings Mr. Oldfield and Mr. Grimmett played first-class cricket. Rhodes could deceive neither with his flight and gave way to Mr. Stevens, who bowled for this turn medium pace. His first over was expensive, but in his second he made Mr. Oldfield play a yorker on to his stumps. Mr. Mailey made one slashing cover-drive off Geary, but was clean bowled by him and, catching Strudwick napping, was able to pocket the ball.

Each of our bowlers got at least one wicket. The fielding was exuberantly keen and Strudwick kept wicket splendidly on a pitch which constrained Mr. Oldfield to let 19 byes. It was pleasant to see Mr. Chapman captain his side so ably – and alone he did it. No doubt he had discussed strategy and tactics in the pavilion with his staff officers, but on the field he relied on his own judgment. The demeanour of his colleagues indicated clearly their absolute approval of his direction.

ENGLAND 280 (Sutcliffe 76, A. P. F. Chapman 49; A. A. Mailey 6 for 138) and 436 (Sutcliffe 161, Hobbs 100)
AUSTRALIA 302 (J. M. Gregory 73, H. L. Collins 61) and 125 (Rhodes 4 for 44)
England won by 289 runs

Lord Darnley

A Brilliant Cricket Career

11 *April* 1927. Lord Darnley, better known to cricketers as the Hon. Ivo Bligh, whose death is announced on another page, had a short and brilliant cricket career, but most unfortunately, just as he was on the point of securing the highest honours, he had a breakdown in health, and after this he went back, and three years later had to abandon the game.

Lord Darnley first played for Eton in W. F. Forbes's celebrated eleven in 1876, and made 73 runs against Winchester and 12 against Harrow. He was not so successful in 1877, but he was awarded his "Blue" in his first year at

Trinity, Cambridge, in, perhaps, the best side Cambridge ever turned out, in 1878. He played four years for Cambridge, and was the exact contemporary of A. G. Steel, H. Whitfield, and P. H. Morton. In 1879 his best innings was 113 not out against Surrey, and he was with Alfred Lyttelton at the head of the averages. In 1880 he made 70 and 57 not out against Yorkshire, 90 against the Gentlemen, and 59 and 13 against Oxford. It was after this season that his health gave way, and he was never the same batsman again, but for Kent in 1880 he scored 105 against Surrey, 69 not out against England at Canterbury, and 73 against the Gentlemen, also at Canterbury; and his position was then so high that it was a nice question whether he would be selected to represent England against Australia in the only Test Match played at the Oval, but G. F. Grace was finally chosen.

In 1881 his health prevented him from playing more than three matches for Cambridge, though he was captain, and he did nothing of note that year, and dropped altogether out of cricket in England in 1882. He was, however, captain of an English eleven in Australia in 1882 and 1883, but though the side won the rubber of the Test Match and altogether had a successful tour, Lord Darnley could do little because of his health, and in five 11-a-side matches only scored 64 runs with an average of eight. After the season in Australia Lord Darnley's appearances were intermittent and for the most part ineffectual, and his health made him give up active participation in the game altogether after 1883. But he retained his great interest in it and was President of the M.C.C. in 1900. He was also President of the Kent County Club in 1892 and 1902.

Lord Darnley was very tall and of slender build, but he made full use of his height and had very strong wrists, was as fine a cutter as any of his contemporaries, and was a good hitter all round the wicket. He had one fault, and that was that his defence was marred by a crooked bat, but he had so good an eye that he was not so much handicapped as might have been expected.

If his health had been good Lord Darnley would have been one of our best tennis players. He had an enormous reach and his strength of wrist gave him command of a heavy stroke, but just as he was promising to reach the highest place among amateurs – second, in fact, only to Alfred Lyttelton – he had to drop the game. He played for Cambridge against Oxford in 1879 and 1880, and won both double matches and the singles in 1880. He was also a good and very hard-hitting rackets player, and won the singles against Oxford in 1879.

Lord Darnley was born in March, 1859, the son of the sixth earl, and succeeded his brother in 1900. He was elected a representative peer for Ireland in 1905, and was Deputy Lieutenant and County Alderman for Kent. He married in 1884 Florence Rose, daughter of the late John Stephen Morphy, and leaves one daughter and two sons, the elder of whom, Lord Clifton, of Rathmore, succeeds to the earldom. Lady Darnley was appointed D.B.E. in 1919.

A notable event in the art sales of 1925 was the sale at Christie's in May of that year of Lord Darnley's collection of pictures by old masters, English and foreign, 91 lots, which produced the unexpected total of £70,758 9s. Seventeen pictures reached four figures, including Hoppner's portraits of Lady Elizabeth Bligh (10,200 guineas) and of the fourth Earl of Darnley (3,100 guineas); Sir Joshua Reynolds's "The Calling of Samuel" (6,700 guineas); Gainsborough's portrait of Mrs. W. Monck (4,800 guineas); and Sir Antonio Mor's Portrait of a Lady (4,200 guineas).

Proceeds of Benefit Match

Seymour v. Reed

(BEFORE THE LORD CHANCELLOR, LORD DUNEDIN, LORD ATKINSON, LORD PHILLIMORE, AND LORD CARSON.)

HOUSE OF LORDS

25 *May* 1927. The HOUSE, by a majority, allowed this appeal from an order of the Court of Appeal (42 *The Times* L.R., 414) reversing by a majority an order of Mr. Justice Rowlatt (42 *The Times* L.R., 377) affirming a decision of the Commissioners for the General Purposes of the Income Tax Acts for Lower South Aylesford, Kent.

The appellant was a well-known cricketer in the employment of the Kent County Cricket Club, and the question for determination was whether he was assessable under Schedule E, rule 1, in respect of a sum of £939 odd, being the net proceeds derived from a benefit match played at Canterbury in 1920 under the direction of the club for the benefit of the appellant.

The club's regulations for the staff contained a provision as to benefits and tours. That provision (so far as material) was as follows:–

(1) The Committee reserve to themselves an absolute and unfettered discretion as regards benefit matches, the collection of subscriptions in connexion with such matches, and dealing with the net proceeds of such matches in any way they may think desirable in the interest of the beneficiare.

If a professional cricketer was granted a benefit, it was granted on the express understanding that he should allow the proceeds to be invested in the names of the trustees of the club during the pleasure of the committee. The income derived from the invested proceeds was paid to the beneficiaire. The invested sum was always handed over to the professional cricketer when his career as a cricketer was over, or when he found an investment, such as a share in a business or a farm, of which the trustees approved.

The net proceeds derived from the benefit match, together with certain other sums obtained by public subscriptions, were invested by the club in the purchase of certain investments at a total price of £1,492 odd. The dividends on those investments, from 1921 to 1923, less income-tax, were received by the club and paid over to the appellant. Certificates of deduction of income-tax from the dividends were furnished to the appellant by the secretary of the club and the appellant preferred claims for repayment of income-tax for the relevant years, on the footing that the dividends formed part of his income.

In 1923 the investments were realized and the proceeds, amounting, with the addition of certain other moneys, to £1,914 odd, were paid by the club to the appellant and applied by him, with the approval of the trustees of the club, to the purchase of a farm.

In 1923 the appellant was assessed, under Schedule E, in the sum of £939 odd for the year 1920-1921 in respect of the net proceeds derived from the benefit match.

On appeal, the Commissioners discharged the assessment, and their decision was affirmed by Mr. Justice Rowlatt, on the ground that the money in question was a personal gift and not such remuneration as would constitute income for the purposes of income-tax.

The Court of Appeal by a majority (the Master of the Rolls and Lord Justice Warrington, Lord Justice Sargant dissenting) reversed the decisions of Mr. Justice Rowlatt and the Commissioners.

Sir John Simon, K.C., and Mr. W. T. Monckton appeared for the appellant: and the Attorney-General (Sir Douglas Hogg, K.C.), the Solicitor-General (Sir Thomas Inskip, K.C.), and Mr. R. P. Hills for the respondent.

JUDGMENT

The LORD CHANCELLOR, after stating the facts, said that the question was whether the sum of £939 16s. fell within the description contained in Rule 1 of Schedule E of "salaries, fees, wages, perquisites, or profits whatsoever therefrom" (i.e., from an office for employment of profit) for the year of assessment so as to be liable to income-tax under that Schedule.

Those words, and the corresponding expressions contained in the earlier statutes (which were not materially different), had been the subject of judicial interpretation in cases which had been cited to their Lordships. It must now, he thought, be taken as settled that they included all payments made to the holder of an office or employment as such, that was to say, by way of remuneration for his services, even though such payments might be voluntary, but that they did not include a mere gift or present (such as a testimonial) which was made to him on personal grounds and not by way of payment for his services. The question to be answered was, as Mr. Justice Rowlatt put it: Was it in the end a personal gift or was it remuneration? If the latter, it was subject to the tax; if the former, it was not.

Applying that test, he did not doubt that in the present case the net proceeds of the benefit match should be regarded as a personal gift and not as income from the appellant's employment. The terms of his employment did not entitle him to a benefit, though they provided that if a benefit were granted the committee of the club should have a voice in the application of the proceeds.

A benefit was not usually given early in a cricketer's career, but rather towards its close, to provide an endowment for him on retirement, and, except in a very special case, it was not granted more than once. Its purpose was not to encourage the cricketer to further exertions, but to express the gratitude of his employers and of the cricket-loving public for what he had already done and their appreciation of his personal qualities. It was usually associated, as in this case, with a public subscription and, just as those subscriptions, which were the spontaneous gift of members of the public were plainly not income or taxable as such, so the gate-moneys taken at the benefit match, which might be regarded as the contribution of the club to the subscription list, were, he thought, in the same category. If the benefit had taken place after Seymour's retirement, no one would have sought to tax the proceeds as income. The circumstance that it was given before, but in contemplation of retirement, did not alter its quality. The whole sum – gate-money and subscriptions alike – was a testimonial and not a perquisite. In the end, when all the facts had been considered, it was not remuneration for services, but a personal gift.

He was of opinion that the appeal should succeed and that the order of Mr. Justice Rowlatt should be restored, with costs here and below, and he moved their Lordships accordingly.

LORD DUNEDIN gave judgment to the same effect.

THE DISSENTING JUDGMENT

LORD ATKINSON differed. He said that he could not find anything in the case suggesting that the club, or its committee, had any motive, object, or aim in giving the benefit of the match to Seymour, their officer, other than to reward him for the efficient discharge of the duties of his post. He thought that when no reason was shown for the gift to an official such as Seymour of the large and substantial prize through the medium of the benefit match, it must in reason be assumed that it was given to him for the efficient and satisfactory discharge of the duties he was employed to discharge and, if so, that the reward came to him from his employment. He was, therefore, of opinion that the judgment of the Court of Appeal was right and should be affirmed.

LORD PHILLIMORE and LORD CARSON gave judgment agreeing with the Lord Chancellor.

Solicitors. – Messrs. Halsey, Lightly and Hemsley.; the Solicitor of Inland Revenue.

This judgment established the principle that cricketers' benefits should be tax free, but cf. November 1954.

On Being a Good Hater

8 *July* 1927, *Leading Article*. It is a satisfactory spiritual outlet to indulge once a year in a good, clean, thorough-going hate, and for such indulgence there is no better opportunity than the Eton and Harrow Match. Hatred; which we have to bottle up because we are ashamed of it, is a miserable and degrading thing, but on this occasion such of us as have the right to do it can give free rein to our feelings; the only thing that ought to make us ashamed is the knowledge that we used to hate, that we should like to hate, and that through some creeping palsy of the emotions we have lost the power of hating. This annual orgy is all the more reviving to the spirits because we come to it with appetites fresh and unjaded; for three hundred and sixty-three days in the year we are the best of friends with our hereditary foes, and then for two days we really let ourselves go; as long as these two days last we say with Mme. Defarge, "Tell the wind and fire where to stop, but don't tell me." And yet there is about our sentiments a certain quality that was lacking in the hatred of that "frightfully grand woman." It is not without a certain chivalrous courtesy. We may lunch on the coach of an enemy both with safety and with pleasure. We may even praise, perhaps with some artificiality of phrase, a fine piece of play by some one on the other side; but there are clearly understood limits to our self-restraint. We may be eating the enemy's ice; but if in the middle of it one of his wickets falls there is no law of chivalry to forbid us yelling ourselves hoarse. Were the positions reversed he would do the same by us. Everything is open and above board. "I wish him no ill," said a lady watching a golf match, "but I wish he was in a bunker." On this occasion we wish the enemy eleven no ill whatever except that they were one and all in the deepest bunker that was ever dug.

It cannot be denied that this hatred is rather a prostrating indulgence. The agony of some particularly crucial moment is of course dreadful while it lasts, but that which in the long run is hardest to bear is the shouting of the other side. There always seems something so raucous and underbred about it. "Mitchell was clean bowled for 26," wrote SIR NEVILLE LYTTELTON of the match in 1861, "playing carelessly at a short shooter, and I have seldom heard such a yell of triumph as greeted his downfall." Doubtless that yell was a severe test of Etonian tempers, and even now, sixty-six years afterwards, it is difficult to read of it without a momentary glint of fierceness in the eye. Mere applause when the enemy is making runs can be borne; it is the fall of one of our own wickets that tests the Christian that is in us. The supreme comfort is that there is no nonsense about wishing the other side to win. It happens at the present moment that Eton has had a long run of successes, but for an Etonian to say to a Harrovian that he hoped Harrow would win ought to be a lie, and would certainly be an impertinence. We need not even pretend to be glad that the other side has won, however glorious the circumstances. That tepid virtue of impartiality may be left to those of other schools. If there be any who hold this an "unsportsmanlike" view, let them search their own consciences. Do they not begin to say "May the best man win" when they have lost their stomach for the fight and are tolerably sure that their own side is going to be beaten?

Death of George Giffen

A Great All-round Cricketer

FROM OUR CORRESPONDENT

30 *November* 1927; *Adelaide,* 29 *November.* George Giffen, the famous cricketer, who had been seriously ill for 18 months, died in a private hospital this morning at the age of 68. Giffen's undying enthusiasm for the game was shown by his coaching, every summer, until illness prevented him, the teams of boys who began to play in the Adelaide Park Lands punctually at 6 a.m., and he always remained with them for over two hours. Giffen also took the boys' international and inter-State matches, and made running comments on the play, which was so illuminating that a regular circle was formed, which became one of the most popular features of big cricket days.

In 1923 a "benefit" game was played at Adelaide on behalf of Giffen at the suggestion of Joe Darling, an old College friend, who is now a farmer in Tasmania and a member of the Legislative Council, and a substantial sum was realized. Giffen was a letter sorter in the General Post Office for over 43 years and retired early in 1925 on allowance and pension, which, combined with his cricket "benefit," made him independent. Clem Hill pays Giffen the tribute of describing him as Australia's greatest all-round cricketer. Giffen was born in Adelaide on March 27, 1859.

As a batsman Giffen possessed a wonderfully fine defence. He stooped a little but had a great variety of strokes with great freedom in his use of the bat, and was exceptionally strong in driving. He bowled right-hand, rather below medium-pace, with considerable spin and well-concealed change of flight and pace. He used to send down with much effect a slow ball, very high-tossed, which, seeming to be coming well up to the batsman, pitched short, and resulted in many a "caught and bowled." It was expected that Giffen would have charge of the Australian team which toured England in 1886, but his merits as a leader were not commensurate with his merits as a player.

Giffen first visited England in 1882 as a member of the team which beat England at the Oval by seven runs, and so vindicated Colonial cricket. As the side included Spofforth, Boyle, Garrett, and Palmer – four of the finest bowlers of the time – Giffen was overshadowed, and while they averaged 150 wickets at a cost of less than 13 runs each, he had to be content with taking 32 wickets for 22 runs each. Still, he had a brilliant success against the

Gentlemen of England at the Oval, where he took 11 wickets for less than 10 runs each – eight in the first innings for 49 runs – and contributed largely to a memorable triumph. Nor had his batting powers at that period fully de·veloped, but his record of 873 runs with an average of 18 was a vastly bigger thing than it would be regarded on the easy wickets of to-day. He showed a marked advance in 1884, and, two years later, headed both batting and bowl-ing averages, scoring 1,454 runs, for an average of 25, and taking 162 wickets for 16 runs each. Giffen declined invitations to join the Australian teams of 1888 and 1890, but was a member of the side captained by Blackham in 1893, and also of that led by Harry Trott in 1896. In these years, however, though he came out with a fair record for the whole of each tour, he accomp-lished little in the representative games. Giffen, indeed, in England scarcely reproduced his Australian form, which was of so high a class that he used to be referred to as the "W. G. Grace of Australia."

Among Giffen's best performances in Australia were his 203 at Adelaide in 1887 for South Australia against G. F. Vernon's team; 237, and 12 wickets for 192, for South Australia v. Victoria at Melbourne in 1891, and in the following season an innings of 271 and 16 wickets for 166 runs for South Australia against Victoria at Adelaide; he made 45 (out of a total of 166) and 205 for South Australia v. New South Wales at Adelaide in 1893. Most remarkable of all, perhaps, was his all-round performance in scoring 161 out of a total of 586, and 41 in a total of 166 for Australia v. Stoddart's team at Sydney, in December, 1894, as in that match he also took eight wickets, and yet was on the losing side. The bowling of Peel and Briggs on a ruined pitch won the match for England by 10 runs. In the winter of 1883, at Sydney, for the fourth Australian team against the Rest of Australia, Giffen took all 10 wickets in an innings for 66 runs. Two years later, at Adelaide, for South Australia against Victoria, he scored 20 and 82, and took 17 wickets.

Giffen's highest score in England was 180 v. Gloucestershire, at Bristol, in 1893. He had his greatest success as a bowler in England during the season of 1886, when 16 Derbyshire wickets fell to him for 101 runs, and in five consecutive innings he dismissed 40 batsmen at a cost of 222 runs. He did the "hat trick" three times – for South Australia, against G. F. Vernon's team, at Aldelaide, in 1888; against Lancashire, at Manchester, in 1884; and against an England eleven, at Wembley Park, in 1896.

Altogether in first-class matches, Giffen scored 12,501 runs, at an average of 29, and took 1,109 wickets, at a cost of 21 runs each. In matches between Australia and England he made 1,238 runs, and took 103 wickets.

Cricket

Our countrymen of England who winter here at ease
And send abroad their cricketers to fight across the seas –

They long to win the rubber, but inwardly they know
  The game's the game: howe'er the luck may go.

They know the English skipper may cry "a head! a head!"
And t'other like a kangaroo may toss a tail instead.
But cricketers can smile away the force of Fortune's blow,
  For a man's a man: howe'er the luck may go.

To field upon a field of brick, to bowl beneath the blaze,
To bat and bat and bat and bat for days and days and days,
And then to lose – there's something wrong – but no! but no! but no!
  The game's the game: howe'er the luck may go.

All men alive are cricketers, and stand to face the odds,
And some will trust in cunning tricks and some in heathen gods:
But you, my son, were born and bred where what I say is so –
  The game's the game: howe'er the luck may go.

HENRY NEWBOLT.
2 *February* 1928

Lord's, 1928

Lord's – Lord's on Wednesday evening!
  Cambridge fieldsmen crowding round,
Oxford's hardly a chance of saving it –
  Hardly a chance, but still you found
    Elderly cricketers gnawing their sticks,
    Blameless Bishops, forgetful of Jix,
    Publicly praying at half-past six,
And prayers and curses arise from the Mound
  On that head of carrots (or possibly gold)
With a watchful eye on each ball that's bowled –
  And a deadly silence around the ground.

Lord's – Lord's on Friday evening!
  Two men out and an hour to play –
Lose another, and that's the end of it,
  Why not call it a harrowing day?
    Harrow's lips are at last on the cup,
    Harrow's tail unmistakably up,
    And Eton? Eton can only pray
For a captain's heart in a captain's breast,
And some decent batting among the rest,
And sit and shiver and hope for the best –
  If those two fellows can only stay!

Stay they did – can we ever forget it? –
Till those who had bidden us all despair
Lit their pipes with a new assurance,
   Toyed instead with the word "declare":
      Harrow's glorious hours begin,
      Harrow batsmen hurrying in,
      One and all with the will to win,
   Cheers and counter-cheers rend the air!
      Harrow's down with her colours flying,
      Great in doing and great in dying,
   Eton's home with a head to spare!

C. A. A.
16 *July* 1928

The initials are those of Dr. Cyril Argentine Alington, headmaster of Eton and formerly of Shrewsbury, where he once employed Neville Cardus as his secretary. The Times *paid Dr. Alington 3 guineas for this contribution: Sir Henry Newbolt received 2 guineas.*

The World's Best Bowler

F. R. Spofforth

BY J. W. TRUMBLE

26 *July* 1928. For some time past I have been hoping that some other Australian cricketer who had, before my time, been on tour with Spofforth when he was at his best, and who had also seen the prominent bowlers of more recent times, would publicly uphold his right to be considered the world's greatest bowler. This title has recently been claimed for Barnes. As the challenge has not otherwise been taken up I feel impelled to suggest reasons why Spofforth should be rated second to none.

I played with him and against him in Australia and toured England with him in 1886, and, as I happened to be an all-round player and slip fieldsman, my opportunities of studying his bowling were exceptional. Spofforth struck me as being a very remarkable man possessed of rare mental ability and of other assisting personal qualities which enabled him to bring to a successful conclusion almost anything he took in hand. He started as a fast bowler and then studied medium-pace and slow bowling, his objective being a completely disguised combination of the three paces; and those who saw him bowling at his best will remember to what perfection he attained in this direction. His action on delivery was exactly the same for all of the three paces, and it was in his magnificent concealment of change in the pace of his bowling that he stood out from all other bowlers of all time.

Spofforth had a different grip of the ball for each pace of the three paces he bowled, and it must have necessitated for him very strenuous practice to secure accuracy with the grip he had for his very slow ball. But he could do many remarkable things with his hands, even to throwing a new-laid egg a distance of 50 yards or so on turf and causing it to fall without breaking. Nobody ever fooled good batsmen with the slow ball so completely as did Spofforth. I remember an exciting match between England and Australia, at Sydney in 1885, which Spofforth won by the successful use of this very ball. Flowers and Maurice Read were well set. Spofforth had bowled Read a fast one outside the off stump, which was left alone. The slow ball then came along in action, delivery, and flight apparently a reproduction of its prececessor. Read played forward to it and completed his stroke before the ball had arrived. He then tried to pull his bat back to cover his wicket, but was too late to prevent the ball getting through to the stumps. I look upon this as the cleverest ball I ever saw bowled, and I am sure Maurice Read will well remember it. We won by six runs, and just before the dissolution of this partnership the match looked any odds on England.

Spofforth was an off-break bowler. He was very accurate in direction and pitch in all paces, and could vary his pitch and direction to a very fine point. As a rule he had only one slip standing fairly well up. When he intended to send down his very fast ball he usually signalled this to the wicket-keeper and slip when on his way back from the wicket to start his run. Even on wickets which would help him a lot Spofforth would not put on more break than was necessary to attain his purpose, and even then the break ball would be mixed up with balls coming straight on. Consequently Spofforth's bowling was always dangerous for leg-before-wicket decisions. His most effective break ball was of medium pace beautifully pitched about on the off stump, requiring forward play, and which, if it beat the bat, would about get the leg stump. I saw him at Oxford in 1886 when he took in the first innings eight wickets for nine runs, of which seven were bowled with the type of ball that I have described, and to which all the batsmen played in the same way. In our 1886 tour we had a strong bowling side, including Spofforth, Palmer, Giffen, Garrett, and others, but before very long Spofforth impressed me as being in a class by himself. That apparently was W. G. Grace's view, for he said that, however well set he might be and however good the wicket, he never felt sure "Spoff" would not bowl him out next ball.

Spofforth, like Grace, was a great master in strategy and resour⸗ fulness. He quickly sized up a batsman, and soon realized his strong and his weak points and rather preferred to tackle a batsman on his pet strokes than otherwise. He was never more dangerous than when luring a batsman on to indulge in his favourite strokes. Many instances might be given of his successes in this direction. As a sample of his resourcefulness when in a tight corner, I may instance his strategy on the occasion of an important match in this country. Two of the opposing batsmen were set and scoring freely. Spofforth, after trying hard without success to effect a separation, then proceeded ostentatiously to alter the positions of his field, packing several of them behind the wicket and down the gully as is done for very fast bowling. He then started his run to the wicket at top speed, but instead of the expected very fast ball the batsman got a slow one which took him completely by surprise, as in expectation of a fast delivery he had his stroke partly made when the ball left the bowler's hand. The result was a soft return catch which Spofforth safely took. In a State match at Sydney, Bonnor, after previously threatening to do so, attempted to hit Spofforth out of the ground. He let go at what was apparently the right ball, but, instead of hitting it out of the ground, sent it up to a tremendous height over mid-on's head. The catch was missed, but Bonnor took no further risks.

Probably Spofforth's greatest performance was his 14 wickets for 90 runs in that historic Test Match at the Oval in 1882 which Australia won by seven runs. It may be remembered that England on going in a second time had to get only 85 runs in order to win. With three wickets down the score stood at 51, and the batsmen undisposed of to make the remaining 34 runs were Grace, Lucas, Lyttelton, Studd, Steel, Read (M.), Barnes (W.), and Peate. When Grace was out two runs later the Australians felt that they had a chance. It was then that Spofforth was seen at his best. The scene has often been described: Spofforth, all out, tearing along like the "Demon" he looked; Boyle, the most daring of fieldsmen, close up in front at mid-on; Blackham in keen expectancy behind the stumps, with the field crowding in and keyed up. What an ordeal, almost terrifying in character for the later batsmen to face as wickets kept falling! Then we come to the closing scene, with Peate (about the worst bat of his time) lashing out at Boyle with fatal results and declaring subsequently in justification of his action that he could not trust Mr. Studd. In this innings Spofforth took seven wickets for 44.

As a student in the art of bowling Spofforth stood out from all other bowlers and would, in my opinion, have been able to cope with the difficulties of present-day concrete-conditioned wickets better than any other bowler and be still the best of them all.

In conclusion, let me confess that being accustomed in my profession to citing authorities I deemed it to be of some value to obtain a backing for my opinion as to Spofforth's superiority over all other bowlers, and I accordingly had a conference before recently leaving Australia with Garrett, Blackham, and my brother, Hugh Trumble, and I am able to say that they are in complete accord with me. I was particularly desirous of securing my brother's opinion, for, besides knowing Spofforth's bowling, he had experience in the field of all the other great bowlers who might be taken into account. As regards placing a bowler next to Spofforth we were in a difficulty, for, in our view, three or four of them come close together. We are inclined to give preference to Barnes for second place. Finally, if I may digress, let me add that we hold that in batting Grace stands first, with Trumper next to him.

Cricket on New Year's Day
More History Made at Hambledon

[BY DUDLEY CAREW]

2 *January* 1929. On Broadhalfpenny Down, Hambledon, where cricket may be said to have had its illustrious beginnings, a 12-a-side cricket match was played yesterday, New Year's Day, between the Invalids, a club captained by J. C. Squire, and the Hampshire Eskimos, captained by E. Whalley-Tooker.

Such a game – the outcome of a mild resentment that football should invade the cricket months of May and August – could have been treated in many ways. The most obvious and the most deplorable would have been the farcical – 22 men playing a travesty of the game that would have been an insult to the legendary shades that dwell by "The Bat and Ball." Dickens cricket can be overdone, and the teams yesterday managed admirably to preserve a proper Pickwickian spirit without showing that lamentable Pickwickian interest in the attributes of cricket, rather than in the cricket itself, that must always shock those who take their cricket with proper seriousness, however good Dickensians they may be. Still, Mr. Jingle would have been sufficiently at home on Broadhalfpenny yesterday. The multitude of photographers and cinema operators might have confused him, but he would have loved the band, which played a march especially composed for the occasion by Peter Warlock, the general heartiness, the ale at – for cricketers – the most famous of all taverns, and he would have looked forward to luncheon at "The George," with the thumping of beer-mugs and the singing of appropriate songs.

It had been arranged to play the game, whatever the weather, unless the ground lay either deep under water or wrapped in Stygian fog, but, as it happened, the day was far more pleasant than anyone has the right to expect in January. It was certainly cold, cold enough to make it extremely probable that the word "caught" would be suspiciously conspicuous by its absence on the scorecard, but it was dry and, for the most part, sunny. Those who got up in the middle of the night and made their several ways to what surely must be one of the most inaccessible spots in England were rewarded in many happily different ways. They had, in the first place, the pleasure – amusement would, perhaps, be an unkind word – of watchimg men who had not handled a bat for four months batting on a matting wicket which was equally ready to help the ball jump to an intimidating, in January a positively dangerous, height, and to make it shoot in a way that reminded one of another age. In the second, they had what one is tempted to call the unique experience of seeing hounds meet on a ground on which a cricket match was actually in progress. Strung out across the pitch, outlined against a sky of delicate blue, the horses and the hounds made up a picture that carried one back on the instant to the eighteenth century. The line of motor-cars seceded, the cinema operators disappeared, and time quickly slipped back 50 years, and, to complete the illusion that the day had been carefully picked and stolen from history, hounds found in the country below the down and streamed over the fields, as clearly etched in the frosty sunshine as on an old print.

And last, but far from least, there was a desperately exciting finish which tempted even the most timid from the shelter of the motor-cars and set them cheering as vigorously as though they were at Melbourne watching Larwood take the last Australian wicket and keeping the Ashes in England.

J. C. Squire won the toss for the Invalids, and those versed in the intricacies of mid-winter cricket immediately prophesied that the score of 80 would win – a prophecy that was very pleasantly borne out by events. From the curious way the ball behaved in the outfield – everywhere, that is, except on the actual matting – it was obvious that running between the wickets would call for either considerable judgment or a high degree of low cunning, and the Invalids were deficient enough in both these qualities for three of their number – including one who had travelled 600 miles and survived a motor accident – to meet with that melancholy fate, "run out." For all that, however, the Invalids put together the highly respectable score of 89. A. D. Peters made 20, and made them as though he was playing in mid-July after making three consecutive 50's, B. W. O'Donnell hit the first 4 of the match and collected 16, while, in an age of records, H. P. Marshall must be mentioned for being the first Harlequin captain to hit 6 off a lob bowler on Broadhalfpenny Down on New Year's Day.

Going in against a total of 89, the Hampshire Eskimos, who should have revelled in the conditions, made a disastrous start, losing three wickets for nine runs to the accurate bowling of R. H. Lowe, who bowled with any amount of energy up the hill and into the wind. The match looked over, but H. Clark, whose catch at cover-point off a hard drive of Marshall's must have struck the Invalids as ominous, proceeded to use a cross-bat to bowling that was inclined to be short with immense vigour and effectiveness. The score rose by leaps and bounds, and the hearts of the spectators – Eskimos to a man – with it, but a brilliant piece of stumping on the part of W. T. Monckton got rid of F. E. Macey, Clark's most valuable partner, and, when he had brought victory within the grasp of his side, Clark was himself bowled by O'Donnell. He played a splendid fighting innings, and the chance he gave produced one of the best bits of cricket in the match. The ball went high to Squire, fielding deep at square-leg. Squire judged it and got under it perfectly, but a catch that would have been made in June was turned by frozen fingers into a January miss. However, with 75 runs on the board and only seven wickets down, the odds were on the Eskimos, but some really good bowling by Peters and O'Donnell brought to an end a match which, in its own unpretentious way, has made, and deserved to make, cricket history.

INVALIDS 89 (E. Andrews 4 for 33)
HAMPSHIRE ESKIMOS 78 (H. Clark 42; B. W. O'Donnell 4 for 11)
Invalids won by 11 runs

Eton v. Harrow

The Hundredth Match

BY THE HON. G. W. LYTTELTON

12 *July* 1929. "According to the generally accepted record" should perhaps be added in Wisden's tactful words, for no Harrovian admits the validity of the 1805 match, averring that it was nothing but a holiday "scratch" game arranged by Byron for Harrow and Kaye for Eton. J. A. Lloyd, who captained Harrow, said later that Byron played very badly and should not have been in the eleven at all. What Byron thought of Lloyd is not known, but as he himself made 7 and 2 (11 and 7 according to his own account) and Lloyd a "pair of spectacles," his repartee was ready winged. The only authority for the score is a half-sheet of notepaper anonymously sent to the Hon. R. Grimston, whence it found its way into "Scores and Biographies." There it rests, a bone of contention till the end of time.

About the match in 1857, with which Harrovians contemptuously compare the 1805 match, there is no obscurity. Dr. Goodford forbade any Etonians who were not leaving to take part in it; and the M.C.C. deputed Mr. Hervey-Bathurst and Mr. Ponsonby to select two sides. As these included several players who had left, the omission of the match from the regular series appears reasonable, and Harrovians must console themselves with the fact that one Shakspear says Harrow won in 1804, and that in the matches between 1805 and 1818, of which the records were lost in the fire of 1825, oral tradition gives them at least one victory and is silent as to any defeat. In any case, even when all the chosen players turned up, which was by no means always, those early matches were very haphazard affairs. There were, of course, no boundaries, and a fieldsman pursuing a ball hit into a hostile patch of the crowd would have to play a frenzied game of hide-and-seek before recovering it, while the score mounted merrily. In 1827 the score itself was wrongly added, and the result had to be adjudged by the committee. In 1858 it was decided beforehand that rain should be ignored, and Eton played an innings among pools of water.

But quite soon partisanship seems to have reached that pitch where the joy of victory is only just worth the agony of suspense. The story of Lord D—, who in 1840 hired a cab to drive him two miles away from the intolerable strain of a close finish, returned to find his side victorious, and then drove cheering from his cab all down Regent-street and Portland-place, will be sneered at by none of those who, *mutatis mutandis*, followed his example during "Fowler's match," though Bob Grimston hoping to change Harrow's luck by changing his trousers may be allowed to remain unique.

In some ways feelings ran higher than in these more decorous days. The not wholly genial act of "barracking" in all its branches was familiar to our fathers and grandfathers. The staccato yelps which accompanied a bowler's run, the crude comments on peculiarities of appearance or gait, the exposure of imagined crimes of the "Who biled the salt bait fer soup" order – all these have passed to the Antipodes for ever. But it is still the shouting which makes this match different from all others. Once the game is fairly started the uproar begins, and continues with crescendo effects as soon as a finish is dimly sighted. You may spend Friday in tolerable equability, even though your side be in the toils. But by Saturday afternoon philosophy has gone, and it is not cheerfulness that has broken in, but an exquisitely uncomfortable blend of hope and terror of "what has been and may be again" – those incredible collapses, those miraculous recoveries, made possible and almost natural by the electric atmosphere.

Nor does a run of success diminish one iota of the excitement. Eton had the best of matters until the middle of the century, but through the fifties and sixties Harrow won 11 times to Eton's once, six times in one innings. The reasons for this manifest superiority are various. Harrow certainly had the pick of the players, for against five Etonians who played in Gentlemen v. Players Harrow can put 11. The grounds may have had something to do with it, the spongy turf of Upper Club being, until it was relaid in 1860, a poor training-ground for the shooters of Lord's. The coaching probably had more. For 50 years, according to the noble inscription in the Old Harrovian Club, Robert Grimston and Frederic Ponsonby taught "skill in cricket" to Harrovians. Eton had no instruction of such quality until G. R. Dupuis, and still more R. A. H. Mitchell, lifted Eton cricket out of the Slough of Despond in which it had sunk in 1859. Then, although there has always been disparity of numbers (in 1843 Harrow won with an eleven chosen from 87 boys against the 600 of Eton), it is certain that, before the classic magnificence of "Mike's" batsmanship had set a new standard, unattainable but none the less compelling, most Etonians were "wetbobs." The great Alfred Lubbock was taken straight into the eleven from the Boats, and his brother Montague, who faced the terrific bowling of R. Lang without pads or gloves and made top score, was actually second Captain of the Boats at the time.

In the last 60 years neither side can plead unequal conditions, whatever dark suspicions the more implacable partisans may throw upon the age of some unusually hirsute or muscular antagonist. The earliest photographs make the players look hardly younger than Test Match teams of to-day, and some of them must have been men of conspicuous brawn. What of the Eton bowler Kirwan, who clean bowled 13 men in 1834, and is simply called "the fastest of all bowlers"; and the great trio, Marcon, Yonge, and Fellows, of whom Marcon is said to have broken a man's leg at Oxford and Fellows made the ball hum in its flight? What of Emilius Bayley, whose 152 in 1841, though thrice surpassed since, still rises like an Everest among schoolboy feats of the past? The mists of legend hang tantalizingly about these names, for in their day cricket reporting was undiscriminating and jejune, and had nothing to say even in 1860 of A. W. T. Daniel's 116 and Mitchell's 70 out of 98, which all the reminiscences declare to have been of matchless excellence.

But somehow in 1860 we seem to be on modern ground, possibly because that year saw the first of the drawn matches which have since occurred so much too frequently. In 1864, after Harrow had resumed her tale of victories, came another innings on which reminiscences are uniformly dithyrambic – C. F. Buller's 61, played before a picturesque assemblage of 1,600 carriages and 300 horsemen. It was in this match that boundaries first came into use, counting 3 (4 in 1870 and afterwards). It also introduced A. N. Hornby to Lord's, a very Puck of the cricket field, weighing under 6 stone and 5ft. 3in. in height. Then the great names and events come thick and fast – W. B. Money's lobs, and Thornton's annihilation of them, and Ottaway's impenetrable defence, and a great vintage of University and Gentlemen cricketers (Eton's 1868 side, though it lost at Lord's through over-confidence, contributed no fewer than five men to the Gentlemen's eleven), and several matches dominated by one great player such as A. W. Ridley with his century and the lobs that beat Cambridge by six runs, and A. J. Webbe, whose repute gave Etonians nightmares and who nearly beat them off his own bat, and the brilliant all-rounder W. F. Forbes.

The spectacle of one player standing head and shoulders above the rest was commoner in the last century than it is now. Whether purposely or not, the coaching, judging by the scores, used to produce elevens consisting of one or two class batsmen and a tail. Another explanation is that the Lord's wickets of old demanded a touch of genius for a long innings, and grudged any success beyond a few swipes and snicks to the rash and the unsound.

The seventies were on the whole an Eton decade with her dynasties of Lytteltons and Studds, but after 1877 came another long period when Harrow seemed to play in general rather the sturdier cricket. Between 1876 and 1903 Eton won three matches and lost 12. In the matter of great names there is not much to choose, apart from F. S. Jackson and A. C. MacLaren, who must have been monarchs of any glen. There was a fine finish in 1878, when Eton failed by 20 to get over 200 in the fourth innings – a feat which has only been achieved once in this match, in 1914 – and a magnificent tussle in 1885, when a triple race between Eton, Harrow and Time ended in a victory for Harrow by three wickets in the last over but one. It was clearly the nerve of E. M. Butler that pulled Harrow through, but the foundations had been laid by a gigantic stand of 235 for the second wicket in the first innings by E. Crawley and A. K. Watson.

The fifth year of the last four decades has always provided something startling. In 1895 Harrow had the narrowest of shaves, the last two men surviving the necessary eight balls; and in 1905 Eton had a still narrower one, for P. A. Methuen and N. C. Tufnell stayed for 33 stricken minutes and one ball actually hit the wicket, but the bail did not fall, nor did Eton. There was no match in 1915, but in 1925 Eton again scraped home unbeaten after five wickets had fallen with a purgatorial two hours still to go. Then there was the 1900 match in which, at 3 o'clock on Saturday, Eton were 100 ahead with only two men out, and Harrow so acquiescent in the approaching draw that K. M. Carlisle threw up a deliberate full-pitch for A. A. Tod to complete an admirable 100. But it bowled him instead, and in the next over Carlisle had found the patch which gave three balls out of four a sharp off-break that Schofield Haigh would not have disowned, and Eton tumbled out. Later on E. G. Whately found it too, and put Harrow through the ordeal by fire before they emerged faint but victorious by one wicket.

The tide turned Etonwards in 1903, and has never since ebbed, save in 1907, when M. C. Bird made history with two sparkling and chanceless centuries, and in 1908, when G. E. V. Crutchley's 74 on a wet wicket was achieved with a mastery and grace not seen in schoolboy cricket since MacLaren's 76 in 1890. Eton's many victories, well and toughly as they have been won in a spirit of resolute confidence, the imparting of which was the special faculty of C. M. Wells, pale of course before "Fowler's match" in some ways perhaps the most unforgettable finish that any living spectator has had the chance of seeing. Dramatically it was a less well-balanced match then the Old Trafford Test Match of 1902, where from the beginning, every hour had its thrill; for the cricket for a day and a half moved heavily under a leaden sky with Eton pitifully overmatched. But the finish was a sort of Cobden's over prolonged through an innings, an almost appalling revelation of the ease and suddenness with which Fortune can reverse her wheel when within an inch of its full circle, and of the unpredictable stress which a great cricketer can bring to bear upon opportunity.

The revelation bit deep into Harrovian consciousness, for it was many a year before Harrow elevens shook off their grievous memories and ceased to see behind Victory's most affable beckonings the nightmare visage of 1910. That they have done so now is clear to anyone who remembers last year's match, when both sides were deaf to all else but the clear summons to adventure that is surely cricket's authentic voice. Even Etonians have been heard to say that they would have welcomed a Harrow win after so grand a struggle, and to complain that the edge of the ancient rivalry has been somewhat blunted by Eton's monotonous success. Such quixotry may be laudable; it may even be sensible; but it is safe to say it will not survive the first Harrow yell to-day, or even perhaps the first sight of those austere square-cut caps.

Eton and Harrow

Some of the Dresses

13 *July* 1929. The centenary match between Eton and Harrow was begun yesterday at Lord's in perfect cricket weather, and before one of the largest crowds which have in recent years attended the match.

The favourite material for the women's gowns was flowered chiffon in all colourings on light and dark backgrounds. These were made with long uneven skirts and floating scarves and many had little coats to match. There were also many lace frocks in pale shades. There were many more large hats than small, and they were trimmed with a big posy on one side or with floating ends of velvet or ribbon. It was essentially a day for sunshades and these were to be seen in every variety of gay and brilliant design.

Princess Arthur of Connaught, who was accompanied by Prince Arthur, wore a gown of heavy beige crêpe de Chine, patterned with green and red flowers, and a green hat. The Duchess of Northumberland wore a gown of raspberry-pink and black printed chiffon with a large pink hat, bordered with black. She was accompanied by the Duke of Northumberland, Earl Percy, and Lord Hugh Percy, and her two young daughters, the Ladies Elizabeth and Diana Percy, who wore simple frocks of hyacinth pink and straw hats.

Mrs. Stanley Baldwin, in a fawn georgette and lace dress with a feather-trimmed hat to match and carrying a pale yellow parasol, was among the early arrivals, as was also the Duchess of Roxburghe, in a black and white figured chiffon dress with a close-fitting hat. Lady Violet Astor was in a black chiffon dress patterned with small pink and blue flowers, and a small hat to match, and Marchioness Curzon of Kedleston, in white, was accompanied by her daughter, Mrs. Edward Rice.

Viscountess Craigavon was accompanied by the Hon. James Craig and her daughter, the Hon. Aileen Craig, who wore a brown figured chiffon dress. Miss Ulrica Thynne wore a yellow chiffon frock with an uneven hemline and a big black hat. Others to be seen were Mr. B. Thynne, Colonel Hardy, Mrs. Hugh Lubbock, Mr. Mark Lubbock, the Countess of Hardwicke, who wore pink and blue chiffon with a black hat, Major Guy Gold and Miss Anne Gold, and Lady Meyrick in yellow and beige chiffon. Lord North was with Lady North, who wore green flowered chiffon with a black hat, and Viscountess Folkestone, who was accompanied by Viscount Folkestone, was in chiffon patterned with large pink roses and a brown hat.

There were also to be seen Lord Harris, Mr. Le Marchant, Mr. Austen Leigh, Lieutenant-General Sir William and Lady Pitcairn-Campbell, who wore almond-green, Colonel W. M. Gordon, V.C., Lady du Cros, and Lady Cullen of Ashbourne. Viscountess Coke, who wore a dress of flowered chiffon with a grey background, was accompanied by the Hon. Sylvia Coke, in brown crêpe de Chine, patterned with yellow and orange spots. Mrs. Mills wore black and red with a large black hat. Mrs. William Ogden was in a green and yellow chiffon dress, and Lady Chesham wore black. Lady Angela Scott wore white and Lady Alice Scott was in hydrangea blue and beige lace with a green hat, and Mrs. Neville Chamberlain was in cool green.

Among those who entertained luncheon parties in their boxes or coaches were:—

Viscount and Viscountess Bearsted, among whose party were General and Mrs. Hamilton, Miss Jean Hamilton, Mr. D. Parker, and their son, the Hon. Peter Samuel. Lady Bearsted wore a black and yellow figured chiffon dress with a black straw hat and a black parasol. Major Colin and Lady Margaret MacRae, the latter in pinky-beige chiffon with a brown hat, were on their coach with Miss Barbara MacRae, who wore a beige and blue flowered georgette dress with a blue picture hat to match. Lady (John) Noble was on a coach with her two daughters, Miss Noble and Miss Rosemary Noble; Lady Noble wore a beige lace dress with a large red straw hat, and she carried a blue parasol. Lord and Lady Gainford entertained the Hon. Mrs. Beaumont, who wore a white georgette dress with a pale green hat.

The Earl and Countess of Bessborough, who were accompaied by Viscount Duncannon and Lady Moyra Ponsonby, entertained at luncheon the Hon. Geoffrey Brand, Lady Gweneth Cavendish, the Duchess of Roxburghe, the Marquess of Bowmont, Lady Irene Congreve, Mrs. Montague Elliott, Miss Elliott, Major-General Sir John Ponsonby, Captain and Mrs. Neville Flower, Miss Anne Flower, and Mr. Arthur Ponsonby.

The Duke and Duchess of Devonshire entertained a party in a box, as did Lord and Lady Leconfield, and among others who had boxes were Field-Marshal Viscount Plumer and Viscountess Plumer, who wore black and white, with a black hat trimmed with aigrettes; Brigadier-General the Earl of Lucan, Mr. Anthony de Rothschild, Mrs. Bulteel, who was dressed in black; the Marchioness of Crewe, the Countess of Wilton, Mrs. Lionel de Rothschild, Colonel Geoffrey Glyn, Lady Penrhyn, Lord Dundas, the Marquess of Londonderry, Mrs. Euan Wallace, and Mr. and Mrs. Gerard Leigh. Lord and Lady Hastings were in the Marquess of Abergavenny's box.

Among others who had coaches and carriages were Lord Wraxall, Brigadier-General Sir Norman Orr-Ewing, the Hon. Henry Dewar, Mr. P. H. G. Gold, whose party included Sir Archibald and Lady Gold. Mr. and Mrs. Peter Gold, Mr. Ulric Blyth and Mr. Ormond Blyth, the Hon. Claud Lambton, Sir Cosmo Bonsor, Mr. C. H. Goschen, Sir Edward Goschen, Sir Thomas Brocklebank, Sir Guy Campbell, Lord Cornwallis, Earl Fitzwilliam, and Mr. W. W. Grantham.

Others to be seen during the day were:—

The Earl of Rosebery, the Duchess of Devonshire, the Hon. Sir Harry Stonor, Lady Trenchard, Sir Godfrey Baring, Lord Wodehouse, Lord Hailsham, Archbishop Lord Davidson, Lord Armstrong, Lord and Lady Cromwell, the Earl of Chesterfield, General and Mrs. Hamilton Skene, General Melliss, Mrs. Humphrey Wyndham, Mr. and Mrs. Cator, Mrs. Hamilton Cotton, Mrs. Blair Oliphant, Colonel and Mrs. A. F. Maclaughlin, Captain Glover and Miss Bower, Mrs. Coryton, Captain W. S. Ronaldson, Mrs. Cory Yeo, Mrs. Bertram Hall, Mrs. Frank Blundell, Mrs. le Rossignol, Miss Heron Watson, Miss Hawkshaw and Miss Ruth Hawkshaw, Mr. Haskett, Mrs. A. Walter, Miss Broughton, Mrs. H. Waller, Mrs. Joseph Pike, Major Peel, the Earl of Shaftesbury, Lord Howard de Walden, the Duke of Buccleuch, Lieutenant-Colonel W. G. Lucas, and Lieutenant-Colonel G. Booker.

Lord's

7 September 1929, *Leading Article.* The last important game of the season has been played at Lord's, and to many it will seem that the year has ended. One sigh of satisfaction there will soon be heaved by the groundsman who has suffered agonies of anxiety in a desperate struggle against the effects of frost and drought. But his individual relief fades into nothingness before the regrets of the faithful myriads whose eyes and hearts have turned these many months, morning and evening, to the sacred city of their game. Of that city the Pavilion is the temple. Valhalla is perhaps the better word. For there the heroes are, lining the walls in honourable portraiture, or the seats in un-questionable flesh and blood. Cheek by jowl they sit, from the elders, who could, and generally do, tell the youngsters a thing or two about hitting the ball, to the youngsters themselves, atoning for their deficiency of years by a calm confidence that no one can tell them a great deal about anything. Theirs is a sanctuary undesecrated by the foot of woman, one of the last asylums of the merely male in an epicene world. Proud sons are there, intro-duced by fathers, and even prouder fathers introduced by sons, but the proudest and fondest mother, wife, or daughter knocks at the door in vain. Men tolerate no such rival near this throne, where they sit, aloof like gods watching the strife of mortals, dispassionately bestowing praise and blame. Behind them, in the tranquil depths, sheltered from the tumult and the shouting lies

> "that council hall
> Where sit the best and stateliest,"

giving law to cricket, and wielding, without other than moral sanction, a world-wide sway.

But what can they know of Lord's who only the Pavilion know? Spatially and numerically, the centre of gravity lies outside the Pavilion rails. There dwell the nameless thousands, young and old, male and, increasingly, female, for whom the humble shilling habitually opens the gateway to the Elysian field. They are no sybarites. Not for them the fat hamper on the coach-top, the collation in the private box, or even the luncheon room. Dispatch-case or brown-paper parcel meets all the needs of the old campaigner. It is no shame to eat in the full glare of the public eye at Lord's. The most highly respectable people in the most highly respectable seats, even "friends of members," unblushingly devour the homely sandwich and banana as a preliminary to the stroll across the turf to inspect the pitch with a knowing eye. As befits the citizens of a world centre, the Lord's crowd is catholic in its sympathies. Its units are, first and foremost, lovers of the game, not of a side. They will applaud a brilliant stroke, or shake their heads over a doubtful decision, impartially for friend or foe. Rare instances of a different deportment do but serve to throw into relief the massive good conduct of the main attendance. The regular Lord's man unhesitatingly traces to "visitors" any outburst of partisanship or impatience. For these devoted thousands the glory of life now suffers temporary eclipse. With them into the darkness go middle-aged enthusiasts, of sedentary occupation, who make a practice of setting aside a week or so of their holiday with the firm intention of spending every possible moment of it at Lord's. With them go, too, the veterans, to whom membership of the M.C.C. is the most effective insurance against the tedium of age, and who may be heard, pathetic inversions of schoolboys towards the end of term, mournfully counting to one another the days of Lord's that the year still holds for them, only six days more, three days, the very last day. For these, and for countless others, London without Lord's could hardly be considered London. MR. LORD builded better than he knew. It will not be thought a disproportionate reward that his name should belong at once to the household and to the world, and should be immortal.

Mr. C. I. Thornton

16 *December* 1929. Mr. A. B. Potter writes:– May I venture to suggest a slight correction of a detail in your obituary notice of C. I. Thornton? For his last two years at Eton he was called "Bunjam," which was subsequently shortened to "Bun." The story was that he was fielding long leg in a School cricket match in Upper Club, and, feeling hungry, he called out to Joby, who was standing near with his little cart of ices, cakes, and buns: "Joby, give me a bunjam." This delicacy consisted of a bun split open with jam inserted between the two halves. Thornton did not hesitate to eat this on the field! I never heard him called Buns, and I first saw that nickname in print about 25 years ago.

He was a genial good fellow. I knew him intimately, as I was his fag for two years, and a kinder, more considerate fagmaster never lived. His chief characteristic was self-confidence. On the Friday morning of the Eton and

Harrow match, 1868, the year he was captain, as he was leaving my tutor's house, he called back to me: "Potter minor, I will bet you sixpence that I win the toss, win the match, and make the biggest score," which showed that he was not troubled with nerves. He did win the toss and make the biggest score, but he lost the match, owing to his two best bats, Ottaway and Tritton, doing so badly.

Mrs. W. G. Grace

25 *March* 1930. Mrs. Grace, widow of Dr. W. G. Grace, the famous cricketer, died at her home at Hawkhurst, Kent, on Sunday, at the age of 76.

Mrs. Grace was formerly Miss Agnes Nicholls Day, daughter of Dr. Grace's first cousin. They were married at the close of the cricket season of 1873, when Dr. Grace was 25. He had then been playing in first-class cricket for eight years, and within a few days of the wedding he took a team out to Australia. The team included his brother, G. F. Grace, his cousin, W. R. Gilbert, Jupp, and Lillywhite. Mrs. Grace accompanied the party, and the tour became known as his "honeymoon tour." Like Mrs. Martha Grace, "W.G.'s" mother, Mrs. Grace always took a keen interest in cricket. On one occasion she attended the Oxford and Cambridge match when her eldest son, the late W. G. Grace, junior, played for Cambridge, and opened the innings for his university. He had the misfortune to register two "ducks," and as he returned to the pavilion the second time, with all eyes turned towards him, his mother and his sister sat with tears slowly falling down their cheeks.

The funeral will be at Elmers End, Beckenham, at 2.45 to-day.

A Last Innings

The Brigadier's Exit

FROM A CORRESPONDENT [BRIGADIER-GENERAL HUGH HEADLAM]

29 *April* 1930. There comes a time when a man begins to realize that his cricket days are over. The thing first began to dawn on me when I noticed that the captain of the side, whenever he started to set his fielders, invariably began by saying, "General, will you go point?" So I decided to chuck it; but I would go down with colours flying; I would get up a side, I would captain it, I would play a captain's innings, and then I would retire "to make room for younger men." Accordingly I decided to challenge one of the battalions of the brigade to a match. It gratefully accepted the honour. What else could it do? And when the great day came I had collected a very useful side, including several of the star turns of the garrison. It was a bright, sunny day; rather

warm perhaps; but this is to be expected at the beginning of the hot weather in India.

I made an initial error of a kind a captain should never make: I lost the toss. The battalion batted first. It made 101 runs, about 18 of which were the result of my non-bending. I also missed catching the best batsman before he had scored; he then proceeded to make 37. I thought it a difficult catch, and there were sympathetic remarks of "hard luck" from two or three soldiers who were included in my side; but from a chance remark from a subaltern which I happened to overhear later on, my opinion as to the difficulty of the catch was not shared by some of my side.

We started well. Fifty was up on the board before a wicket had fallen. With the abnegation of the great man, I had put myself in last, and it now looked as if I should not get an innings at all. But a new bowler was put on, one of the last draft just out from home, who was reported to be useful. He clean bowled two of my best bats in his first over and three more in his next. Five for 53. Then we pulled ourselves together and the score laboriously mounted up. But wickets continued to fall. We reached 100, but the ninth wicket fell next ball. Two runs to get to win and one wicket to fall, and I was that wicket. I confess my heart bumped; but here was the chance I had asked for – the Captain's innings.

As I strode out into the bright light which beats upon a batsman in India my courage returned. At any rate, I felt, I looked the part. I was wearing a dazzlingly white polo helmet; I remembered that at the time of purchase I resented paying £3 for this hat; now I felt that it was worth it. My shirt was a wonderful creation cut short above elbows and made of some patent stuff full of small holes. My trousers were a dreaminess of creaminess and creases. My socks were — (but no one could see them so that was all right). My boots were simply "It." I had borrowed pads and gloves, but not before I had noted they were of the best make; the gloves were covered with a sort of Chevaux-de-frise of black indiarubber and had the right military touch. My borrowed bat had some sticking plaster in the correct place and the autograph of a famous cricketer and about umpteen crosses on its face; these, for some reason, suddenly reminded me of the marks put at the end of most of the soldiers' letters which I had to censor in France years ago.

I reached the wicket. The umpire obligingly told me my bat was covering middle and leg. Taking the lump of chalk from behind the wicket, I drew a beautiful straight line along the coconut matting from the bat to the wicket. At any rate my hand was steady. I had a look round at the position of the fielders. I noticed with satisfaction that there was no one on the boundary between short-leg and mid-on; that is my favourite place for a drive in the air, which I confess, however, has many times caused my downfall. One run to tie, two to win. I faced the bowler. I felt my stance was all that it should be, and I did not forget to raise my left toe from the ground. The bowler was the successful last-drafter; but what matter? A two is an easy thing to get. The last-drafter took a longish run and then flung the ball at me. Long before the ball left his hand I had quite decided that whatever sort of ball it was, it was to go to my favourite place on the boundary.

The ball hit the bat. At such moments thoughts come like a flash; my flash was a hope that somebody in the crowd of spectators had one of those long-distance high-velocity cameras which photograph cricketers in action; this great shot of mine, I felt, was one which should be recorded. Then an extra-ordinary thing happened. The ball was not taking its proper course to the boundary; it was going slowly, but beautifully straight, direct to mid-on. Unless anything unforeseen happened to it, it would hit him full in the stomach. Alas! Something did happen to it. The fielder, no doubt as self-protection, put his hands in the course of the ball. The ball stayed in his hands. I was out. The match was lost.

Speechless, I walked back to the tent accompanied by the batsman from the other end. We were received with respectful cheers; at least I think they were cheers. I sat down and took off my armour. The soldier audience was moving away behind the tent. I heard a man say, "'Bout time Brigadier give oop cricket." He has done so.

Australians at Worcester

Bradman's Big Score

[BY R. B. VINCENT]

2 *May* 1930. The Australians have wasted no time in demonstrating their immense scoring power, and D. Bradman in particular took his first oppor-tunity to justify all the kind things that have been written about him. That they scored 492 for eight wickets against Worcestershire before their innings was declared closed at Worcester yesterday is not in itself a great feat, when the poverty of the bowling is considered, and the fact that two batsmen between them made 369 of the runs suggests other failures.

This is just where the score card is completely misleading. Bradman and Woodfull certainly were the great men of the day, but it was obvious that there were others who, had the occasion demanded, could have made big scores. One man after another, they all bore the stamp of true Test Match class until a'Beckett showed a tendency to lift his head and to hit the ball in the air, a thing undreamed of until he came in. If they possess, as a team, any one particular virtue in their batting, it is without doubt their amazing quickness of footwork, and in this respect Bradman is perhaps even more remarkable than the others. Bradman does not lift up his bat straight, but over and over again he makes the stroke in the end absurdly simple by the speed of his footwork, and never once did he make the slightest suggestion of hitting the ball in the air until, having made 236, he skied a full pitch to be caught at square-leg. It was a beautiful innings made all the more delightful by the fact that the Worcestershire bowlers, who had bowled so badly on Wednesday evening, did yesterday keep pegging away, maintaining at least a decent standard of accuracy.

Until he had made 200 Bradman took no undue liberties, but he found time composedly to play almost every stroke which the most greedy spectator could ask to see. His drives, whether straight or square, were equally certain. His late cutting was perfect, always with the full blade of the bat coming down on to the ball, and his forcing strokes off his right leg were beautifully timed, but the most welcome of all his strokes was his true, honest on-drive.

Woodfull, by contrast, was not so exciting, nor was he any more unlikely to get out, but he is a more pleasurable batsman than when he was here last. The short back lift and exaggerated follow-through are still there, but he has opened up new avenues of scoring, and his duties as captain seem to have cheered him up. McCabe is nearly as polished a batsman as Jackson, and Richardson, whose fielding in any position had been the brightest feature of the play on Wednesday, although he was not timing the ball yesterday, is clearly a most dangerous batsman for any side to allow to become set. Essentially an aggressive player, he has a very strong forearm, and will leave his mark on many a white palisade before the tour is over. Consider also that neither Kippax nor Ponsford, both names spelling thousands of runs, was playing, and the probability of yesterday's big score being repeated fairly frequently is clear.

The game was continued yesterday on as perfect a May day as the imagination of a poet could think of, and again a big crowd, which increased when the shops closed at midday, came to see what could never be anything more than an exhibition of good cricket by one team and long suffering by the other. The Australians had scored 199 for the loss of Jackson's wicket. Bradman being not out 75 and Woodfull 95. Bradman, who is always a busy batsman, at once looked for runs, but quite rightly his captain was the first to score a century on the tour. Bradman soon followed suit, having then been in for just under two hours, and nothing very startling happened until Woodfull, having scored 121, suddenly disclosed the fact that he had an edge to his bat. It was nothing like a chance, but the ball went behind the wicket instead of in front of it. He had made only 12 more runs when, lying back to hook a ball from Brook, he looked up a shade too soon, and Brook had the great honour for a young man playing for the first time for his county, of bowling the so-called unbowlable. Bradman, in the meantime, was taking runs as he chose, not only guiding Root through his leg trap, but on-driving him past mid-on. Only 18 runs had been added for the third wicket when McCabe produced the first really lofted stroke of the innings and was well caught by Root, running back at mid-on.

Richardson started uncertainly, but he was beginning to see the ball when Bradman drove a ball from Wright hard back at the stumps at the other end, and to which the bowler just got a finger with Richardson out of his ground. Fairfax did not put his left leg across to the third ball he received and was caught at second slip, and so five wickets were down for 366. a'Beckett was a little disappointing after what had been seen before, but he stayed in until the luncheon interval, when the total was 380, Bradman then being 173 not out. After the interval Bradman went on his cheerful way and a'Beckett, although he threatened to give someone a catch, did not actually do so until Gilbert accepted a not very easy chance at mid-on. Oldfield did not last long, but soon afterwards Bradman reached his 200, the result of 250 minutes' batting. He then became even more aggressive, and Root's policemen were moved back to a safer beat. When he had scored 215 Bradman gave his first chance, hitting the ball back hard at Brook, who could not quite hold on to it. Eventually, having done all that was asked of him, his great innings, which included 28 4's, came to an end with his first miss-hit, and shortly afterwards the innings was declared closed.

Worcestershire went in to bat again at 10 minutes to 4, 361 runs behind. This time Fairfax, with Wall, instead of a'Beckett, opened the bowling, but it was not long before Hornibrook was put on at Wall's end. With the score at 25, Jewell trod on his wicket, and one run later Nichol was caught in the slips by Hornibrook, who made a lot of ground to anticipate the catch. Luckily the wickets did not fall too quickly, for the day was much too beautiful for anything but a full day's cricket; but at 40 Wright was run out in trying to get a second run from a leg-bye, and at 75 Gibbons was bowled by the best ball that Hornibrook had bowled in either innings, a ball which did turn from leg, and quickly at that. Grimmett was not quite the master of the situation that he was in the first innings, Walters and Fox inclining to take liberties with him, and the close of play came without another wicket falling.

WORCESTERSHIRE 131 (A. Fairfax 4 for 36, C. V. Grimmett 4 for 38) and 196 (Root 48, C. F. Walters 44; C. V. Grimmett 5 for 46)
AUSTRALIANS 492 for 8 dec (D. G. Bradman 236, W. M. Woodfull 133; Brook 4 for 148)
Score after second day: Worcestershire 131 and 103 for 4; Australians 492 for 8 dec
Australians won by an innings and 165 runs

The Jam Sahib's Gift to Sussex

14 *May* 1930. The Sussex County Cricket Club have received the following cable from their President, the Jam Sahib of Nawanagar:–

"Hope visit you June. Have instructed bankers to remit you £1,000 as my contribution to the club's funds as President. Please request committee to accept same on behalf of club. Convey congratulations to Duleepsinhji (his nephew) for his fine score, and hope that he will secure his team many more and that he will uphold honour of English cricket and Indian name. – Maharajah."

Prince of Wales' Theatre
"Badger's Green"

BY R. C. SHERRIFF

Doctor Wetherby	.. ..	HORACE HODGES
Major Forrester	.. ..	LOUIS GOODRICH
Mr. Twigg ..	.. ..	SEBASTIAN SMITH
Mr. Butler ..	.. ..	FELIX AYLMER
Mr. Rogers ..	.. ..	FREDERICK BURTWELL
Dickie Wetherby	.. ..	ROBERT DOUGLAS
Mrs. Wetherby	.. ..	MARGARET SCUDAMORE
Mrs. Forrester	.. ..	HILDA SIMS
Mr. Butler's Secretary	..	MAISIE DARRELL
Mary	..	KATHLEEN HARRISON

13 *June* 1930. Mr. Sheriff promises in the opening act of his new play to write a first-rate comedy of village life. *Badger's Green* is hardly that. The promise peters out in a lot of pleasant farcical fun and a gallant attempt to compress into one short scene all the gentle humours and ironies and excitements of cricket. There are seven runs to win and three wickets to fall. Batsmen knowing that the supreme crisis of their lives has arrived go out of the marquee with the desperate light of battle in their eyes, and come back to explain how the sun contrived to blind them just as the ball left the bowler's hand. At last there is only one man left to go in, and four more runs are needed. Who should the last man be but the building speculator who has come down to vandalize the village? If his evil designs are not to fall through he must leave at once to catch the train at Guildford; will he prefer the chance of scoring the winning hit to the chance of large profits? Of course he will, for, like all Mr. Sheriff's characters, he is an essentially decent fellow.

The scene is less familiar on the stage than in fiction, perhaps because the audience can only see the game in the mirror of a few anxious faces, and so misses much of the excitement. Something less uproarious and more amusing is suggested when we first meet the rival autocrats of Badger's Green in Dr. Wetherby's sunny library. Imagine Mr. Horace Hodges as a vain and fussy little gentleman, who, remembering all that he has done for the village, resents the pushfulness and the easily gained popularity of a comparatively youthful major represented by Mr. Louis Goodrich. Imagine the trouble these too obstinate men give the meek and mild little clerk, so delightfully sketched by Mr. Sebastian Smith. They are both as touchy about their record of public service in the village as any statesmen who have found a larger arena. Who is to bear responsibility for the black and yellow striped marquee which has made the cricket field look like a circus, who for the decline of the archery club, who for the shortage of batting gloves in the last match but one? Their quarrels touch parochial life at so many points that we are all persuaded that Mr. Sheriff has taken as his model for Badger's Green the village we ourselves know best. The coming of the vandal and the impression made upon the three old gentlemen by the smoothly seductive tongue which Mr. Felix Aylmer wags so pleasantly are also in the hey of comedy, but the rest of the play ought perhaps to be called a wild "lark." Last night both actors and audience seemed to enjoy themselves – with the possible exception of Miss Maisie Darrell, who was given a quite unintelligible part to play.

Cf. 27 June 1938.

In Nottingham – Now

13 *June* 1930, *Leading Article*. Half a century ago, when the Australians (without F. R. SPOFFORTH) played their first Test Match on English turf and were beaten by five wickets, England was captained by LORD HARRIS, who had under him the three GRACES, A. G. STEEL, A. P. LUCAS, ALFRED LYTTELTON, FRANK PENN, BARNES, SHAW, and MORLEY. On the Fourth of June this summer, fifty years on, LORD HARRIS turned out once more for his annual match at Eton on Upper Club. Since that first match at the Oval – specially memorable for W. G. GRACE's big score of 152 in the first innings and W. L. MURDOCH's 153 not out in the second, and even more, to those who saw it, for the wonderful catch in the long field by which G. F. GRACE dismissed the mighty Australian hitter, G. J. BONNOR – there have been many cricket changes, none of which, says LORD HARRIS, has impressed him so much as the far greater importance now attached to the game than in the days of those early giants. Of that particular change the most obvious signs are the increase in the number of Test Matches (there was only one in 1880) and in the number of days given up to them regardless of the rival claims of county cricket, the multiplication of stands for the seething crowds of spectators, and the telegraphing and telephoning and broadcasting and printing of avalanches of written words, describing and analysing the play and the feats and failures of the players. For the next few days (weather permitting) masses of people throughout Great Britain and Australia will be eagerly waiting for the latest results and details of the friendly strife at Nottingham, all because twenty-two young and middle-aged men are playing at bat and ball. In Nottingham itself a huge score-board, erected in the market square, will, it is said, enable those for whom there is no room on the ground to follow every stroke of the game, and the telephone service to Australia is to be specially opened for four hours on Saturday afternoon and perhaps for all day. Intelligent foreigners, born in less favoured climes, may be forgiven

if they shrug their shoulders and hold up their hands in amazement at the spectacle of a whole nation, not to say an Empire, gone, as it must seem to them, cricket mad. But the natives of these islands, secure in the knowledge that cricket is the game of games and not without some knowledge of its finer points, will pay no heed to the polite superiority of well-meaning cynics, so long as they themselves may follow, vicariously or in person, the exciting chances and changing fortunes of the match.

Bradman 309 Not Out

All Records Broken

FROM OUR SPECIAL CORRESPONDENT [R. B. VINCENT]

12 *July* 1930; *Leeds* 11 *July*. The Australians early to-day had reason to fear that the luck of the Leeds ground, notoriously antipathetic to England, had at last turned against them, for it was announced that Ponsford, in addition to Fairfax, would be compelled by illness to stand down from the team. They obtained, however, some measure of comfort by obtaining the first use of a pitch which although it played yesterday even easier than that at Lord's had done on the first day, is so covered with bare patches that it is impossible to believe that it can last four days. The use they made of their advantage of winning the toss was to score 458 runs for the loss of only three wickets, and so must surely at least have placed themselves clear of any danger of being beaten.

But whatever may happen during the next three days this has been Bradman's match, for by scoring 309 not out he has made the highest individual score which has ever been made in a Test Match, so, at long last, beating the 287 made by R. E. Foster at Sydney during the tour of 1903-1904. That he would achieve this feat before the end of this tour was expected by all who have seen him play. He came near to it at Lord's, and in every game of importance he has shown a sureness of scoring power to which there has seemed no limit. How high he ranks among the greatest batsmen the world has ever known is not yet established, but at the moment, and at his age, his promise has been exceeded by none. It is idle to compare him with his great predecessors, Victor Trumper, who was no doubt more graceful, or C. Macartney, who was more impertinently shattering, but for sheer and continual efficiency his performances are truly astounding. To-day he pulverized the English bowling not with the abandon of Macartney, who, like Bradman, also scored 100 runs before luncheon on the same ground, but by a display of batsmanship which in ease of scoring combined with absolute security could not be surpassed. To mention the strokes from which he scored most of his runs is to go through the whole range of strokes known to a modern batsman. Once or twice he demonstrated an idea which is not generally understood, but at no time did he take anything approaching a risk, and he cannot have hit the ball in the air more than three times during the day. It was in fact an innings so glorious that it well might be classed as incomparable, and how the Yorkshiremen loved it.

On a pitch of such easy pace and against a batsman of such superb technique, supported as he was by Woodfull and Kippax, no bowler of the present generation could have been expected to do wonders, but it must be admitted that on the whole the English bowling was colourless and undistinguished. Apart from a poor over by Tyldesley during his first spell and some full pitches later in the day from Leyland, no complaint can be made of the accuracy of the bowling, but there was a complete absence of sting in it, and only Hammond at one time gave the impression that it was worth keeping a bowler on for another over because of the threat of a wicket falling. Larwood came off the pitch no faster than was comfortable to the batsmen and scarcely ever made the ball come back. Tate only once or twice could get the ball past the bat, and Geary could do little more than keep the runs down by an astute placing of his field. Altogether Duckworth must have had the quietest day behind the stumps that he has had for a very long time. The splendid fielding of many members of the team was spoiled by the inability of one or two to get down to the ball, but Chapman had an easier task in spreading his men out than he had had in the first two matches, and he made things easier for himself by declining to allow Hammond and Hobbs to remain anchored in their habitual positions.

Larwood started the bowling with a fairly strong wind blowing from the direction of mid-on, and he had K. S. Duleepsinhji, Hammond, and Geary respectively at first, second, and third slip. Sutcliffe was at deep fine-leg and Leyland at third man. For Tate Duleepsinhji was dropped back to third man and Leyland trotted across to deep square-leg. Off the fifth ball of Tate's first over the unlucky Jackson was caught at forward short leg, but the crowd had then to wait from 20 minutes to 12 until five minutes past 3 before the next wicket fell, by which time the score had been taken from two to 194, and still with the imperturbable Bradman grinding out the runs. Woodfull played just such an innings as is expected of a workmanlike No. 1 batsman. His own rate of scoring may have been slow, but the real value of his batting lay in the fact that he made things seem so simple for his illustrious partner. Woodfull early in his innings certainly did edge one ball from Larwood through the slips, but otherwise never offered the bowler the least glimmer of hope.

Bradman, without in any sense forcing the pace or taking any liberties, at once took runs whenever they were offered. He scored 11 runs in one over from Larwood, which included a beautiful stroke past cover-point in which he lay right back to place the ball through the opening and a stroke off his legs to the on boundary. Geary came on at Tate's end at 30, and during a fairly long spell he did contrive to keep Bradman reasonably quiet, and Tate, going on at the other end, was granted his one solitary excuse for scratching the back of his head when he barely missed Woodfull's off bail. Tyldesley was tried in place of Geary at 48, but even his three out-fieldsmen could not prevent full pitches from being hit for 4, and Geary had to be brought on again at the other end to steady the game. Bradman greeted him with the first really impudent stroke he had so far played, an amazing hook only just wide of mid-on from a ball outside the off stump. This he followed with a square cut, also for 4, and at 1 o'clock the English bowlers bore every appearance of hoping that a batsman would get out, rather than of suspecting that they would get him out. Hammond was given a trial, but he did not bowl so well then as he did in the afternoon, and Bradman reached his 100 out of 128 runs scored from the bat when he had been in for only 85 minutes, and that without ever suggesting that he was in a hurry. At the luncheon interval the total was 136, of which Woodfull's share, though only 29, had been of the greatest value.

Both Bradman and Woodfull hit Geary, who started the bowling after the interval, square for 4 and so Hobbs was moved back from cover-point to the boundary, a defensive move which was indicative of what was to follow. Bradman played one superb late cut off Larwood, but in the same over he played the first bad stroke of his innings and was lucky to see the ball sail in the air safe out of reach of second and third slip.

Hammond, having relieved Larwood, produced a spell of sustained attacking bowling at the end of which he had the satisfaction of getting a ball through more quickly than Woodfull expected and so at last a wicket fell when the spectators had become prepared to see the same pair together for the rest of the day. The arrival of Kippax, however, was not much encouragement to the bowlers. He was twice late in one over from Larwood, but, that little trouble once over, he settled down to play with the ease which Bradman had been showing. Things looked rather desperate for England before the tea interval, when Tyldesley and Leyland, neither of whom showed the least sign of taking a wicket, were kept on for half an hour, but by this time Bradman had eased down a little, reserving, perhaps, his energy for his great achievement later in the day.

Bradman scored his 200 out of 268 on the board, but two minutes later he should have been caught off a skier by Tate at mid-on, but Tate was curiously slow in starting to make the catch. Kippax also had an escape when he had scored 24, but this was a very hard chance, high up to Leyland at mid-off, and England had no manner of consolation until a wicket fell in the only way one was likely to fall – a glorious catch by Chapman at backward point dismissing Kippax, who is as good a No. 4 as his captain is a No. 1. Just before this Bradman had made his record-breaking stroke, and no ground in the world, not even his own Sydney, could have offered him such sincere and prolonged congratulations as did the crowd at Leeds.

AUSTRALIA 566 (D. G. Bradman 334, A. F. Kippax 77, W. M. Woodfull 50; Tate 5 for 124)
ENGLAND 391 (Hammond 113, A. P. F. Chapman 45, Leyland 44; C. V. Grimmett 5 for 135) and 95 for 3
Score after first day: Australia 458 for 3
Match drawn

England v. Bradman

12 *July* 1930, *Leading Article*. On August 27 D. G. BRADMAN will reach the ripe age of 22. The number of runs he will have made by that time is mercifully still unknown. His first two scores on English turf were 236 and 185 not out; and early in the season, with 252 and 191 against the bowlers of Surrey and Hampshire, he joined the select band of English batsmen – only four in all – who have made 1,000 runs off their own bat before May was over. After that he was fairly quiet till he came to the Test Matches, in which he has scored 131 in the second innings at Nottingham, 254 in the first innings at Lord's, and now, in his first and still unfinished innings at Leeds, 309 out of 458. His total for the season is exactly 2,000. In the three Test Matches alone he has already made more runs than any Australian batsman has made before in a completed rubber, and has easily outdone all previous Test Match records with the bat. He does not merely break records; he smashes them. In the first innings at Lord's, and again yesterday at Leeds, the play resolved itself in each case into a duel between England's bowlers and fielders on the one side and one young Australian on the other; and no one has any doubt as to who had the best of it. Apart from all questions of style and grace, the object of the batsman in the game of cricket is to make runs. Without as a rule troubling, like ordinary mortals, to play himself in, DON BRADMAN sets about the bowling directly he gets to the wicket, and goes on making them all the time. The most ardent advocate of brighter cricket could ask no more of him, except, perhaps, that he should occasionally – say rather oftener than once in a hundred or so – put a ball in the air. At his present rate of scoring it may take him a year or two before, like the holder of the one record that is still left for him to beat, he has a century of centuries to his credit. But that is for the future. For the moment it is enough that at Leeds, to quote our Special Correspondent, he "pulverized" the English bowling by a display of batsmanship which, for ease of scoring, combined with absolute security, was beyond all criticism.

Team Spirit in the Empire

Jam Sahib of Nawanagar on Cricket

11 *September* 1930. The Jam Sahib of Nawanagar, who responded to the toast of "Cricket" at the dinner given by Sir Kynaston Studd to the Australian Cricket Team at Merchant Taylors' Hall, spoke of the influence of cricket and of the team spirit on Imperial relationships. In the course of his speech he said:–

The British Empire stands for team work. It stands for cooperation; for the co-ordination of separate individual effort to a common purpose. And that common purpose is the realization, on the part of each constituent of the Empire, of its greatest and its best stature, both moral, mental, and physical. Just as the great game which we are now honouring is pre-eminently a cooperative enterprise, in which the individual effort is subordinated to the fortunes of the team, so the British Empire stands for something greater than the fortunes of its individual entities. The countries which together compose the British Empire constitute the greatest cricket team which the world has ever seen. Just as the members of a cricket team differ from each other in stature, in personal characteristics, in ability of one kind or the other, so the various components of the British Empire differ widely among themselves. But, in the one case and in the other, it is not with a series of individual units which we are concerned, but with a great team working for common good by bringing out the best from each component member.

These post-War years are admittedly difficult. There are adjustments to be made in our Imperial team. Some of our players seem dissatisfied with their place in the team; there are some whispers, although of the most irresponsible kind, of resignation. It is occasions such as this, far more than the stress of a crisis, which test both the skill in the captain and the loyalty of the team. Every cricketer knows how easy it is on certain occasions to allow himself to become discontented, if he starts brooding over his own individual case. . . . Yet it is precisely this kind of temptation which cricket teaches us to avoid at all costs. How often have I wished that all the political leaders in all the countries of the Empire were cricketers! For if they had undergone the training and the discipline of the great game, I am sure they would find it easier than they appear to do at present to think first and last of the team. I am not a politician myself . . . but I cannot help thinking that all of us in this great British Empire need more of the spirit which cricket inculcates; we need more team work, more patience, and more unselfishness; we need more of the true spirit of cricket.

For cricket is more than a game; it is really a manner of living. It is certainly among the most powerful of the links which keep our Empire together. So long as we can maintain in that Empire the spirit of sportsmanship which cricket inculcates, so long shall we be ready, as a team, to meet and defeat any adversity which the future may hold for us. If the bowling is difficult, let us present a straight bat with courage and with determination. In the crisis of the Great War Britain captained the Imperial team to a great victory; I am perfectly certain that in the more difficult times of peace that same captaincy will be characterized by wisdom, patience, and generous good will.

The Princes of India, to whose order I have the honour to belong, have been very old members of Great Britain's team; and both on easy and on difficult wickets they have tried their best to play with a straight bat for the Empire. In times of peace, as in times of war, you will always find us ready. We are united with you and to you in the bond of devoted loyalty to the King-Emperor. Throughout the period of adjustment of relations between Great Britain and India, upon which we are now entering, I am certain that the Indian Princes will do their best to play a part worthy of their best traditions. Like good cricketers, they endeavour to keep up their wickets even under the most difficult circumstances. You can rely upon us in the future, as you have relied upon us in the past, to play the game, and to give every support in our power to the harmony and to the success of the Imperial team. (Cheers.)

The Oberon Disaster

Mr. J. W. H. T. Douglas's Death

FROM OUR CORRESPONDENT

22 *December* 1930; *Copenhagen* 21 *December*. The Finnish steamers Arcturus and Oberon (as announced in the later editions of *The Times* on Saturday) came into collision in the Kattegat, east of Läsö, on Friday night in a dense fog. The Arcturus, a powerful vessel, stove in the starboard side of the Oberon from midships to stern. In half a minute the Oberon had a list of 80deg., and three minutes later she had gone down. Of the 60 members of her crew 36 were saved, but of her 22 passengers only four. The following English passengers were among those lost:–

Mr. J. W. H. T. DOUGLAS, the cricketer.
Mr. J. H. DOUGLAS (his father).
Mr. ERIC VICKERS, of West Hartlepool, who was engaged in the timber trade.
Mr. WILLIAM MILSOM, Mrs. BERTHA MILSOM, and their daughter (Mr. Milsom, formerly of Cleckheaton, Yorkshire, was engaged in the textile industry in Finland).
Mrs. MARY MARTIN.
Mrs. WILLIAMS, wife of the Copenhagen representative of the Dunlop Rubber Company, and her child.
The remainder of the passengers lost were Finnish. . .

Some of the passengers and crew seem to have been unable to get on deck at all on account of the steamer's heavy list; others who jumped too late into the sea were drawn down with the ship. There was no time to lower the boats and only one was let loose when the steamer sank. Four of the crew who were struggling in the water managed to get in this. Captain Erik Hjelt was on the bridge with his wife and daughter and jumped into the sea with the girl in his arms. He was saved by the boats of the Arcturus, but the child died from her immersion in the cold water. His wife jumped to the other side of the steamer and was lost. Mr. J. W. H. T. Douglas vainly tried to help his father, but both were drowned. Mr. Vickers, having reached the Arcturus, saw Mrs. Martin and her child struggling in the water and again jumped in in order to help her, but all three were drowned. . . .

Mr. J. W. H. T. Douglas, who was head of the firm of Messrs. John H. Douglas and Co., timber merchants, had been in Finland about six weeks on a business journey. His father, who was formerly head of the firm but had lately retired, made the journey in his company as a holiday and to meet again friends he had made in Finland during his many business visits there in past years.

"Sammy" Woods

9 *May* 1931. Old Brightonian [E. J. Oakley] writes:–

I should like to add a short postscript to "Joseph's" charming tribute to the late "Sammy" Woods. I have been waiting expectantly for some pen abler than mine to write such a tribute on behalf of his old school, Brighton College, where I had the privilege of fagging for him in the mid-eighties.

The college cricket XI in those far-off days, including as it did, in addition to "Sammy," George Cotterill, the late "Billy" Wilson, H. D. L. Woods (Sammy's younger brother), N. C. Cooper, L. H. Gay, and C. H. Waymouth, must surely have been one of the strongest XIs ever turned out by any public school.

To see "Sammy" come out of the pavilion with his cheerful grin and stop a "rot" by his favourite method of "tip and run," with an occasional hit of a loose ball clean out of the ground was a sight for the gods.

As a bowler he was, of course, in those school days, in a class quite by himself, and I have a keen recollection of the school wicketkeeper standing back half a pitch length behind the wicket, and on more than one occasion fielding a flying stump while the ball reached the boundary! I think I am correct in saying that the late Gregor McGregor was practically the only amateur wicketkeeper who could stand up to the wicket and take "Sammy's" bowling with either hand, when at his fastest.

Though no scholar, "Sammy" was popular with every one, masters and boys alike, and to the boys he was a hero, and although his exuberant spirits and superabundant vitality led him into many a scrape, he never made an enemy. May the turf he loved lie lightly on him.

Hendren's Benefit

23 *May* 1931. The match between Middlesex and Sussex, which will be begun at Lord's to-day, is reserved for the benefit of E. ("Patsy") Hendren. Hendren, who was 42 in February, first played for Middlesex in 1909; his first 100 for the county was made in 1911 – against Sussex. Hendren has played in Test Matches and M.C.C. matches in many countries, and has been for many years one of the most reliable, and often versatile, British batsmen. He has had to play every game as a batsman in his time, from scoring at the rate of two runs a minute to simply attempting to save the game by playing five balls in an over and stealing a run off the sixth to steal the bowling.

There is not a place in the field – except wicket-keeper – in which Hendren is not of Test Match class: his catching at short slip and at short leg has for years been very brilliant. Hendren is still fast in the outfield, holds all his catches, and throws beautifully without wasting any time. Hendren has deserved his place in every Test Match or M.C.C. tour for which he has been selected, though had he been a lesser player his unfailing good spirits, his jolly wit, and an ability to play the clown without hurting anyone's feelings would have told greatly in his favour as a good companion. It is to be hoped that the weather holds good and that the match holds such exciting hours of play as it did last year. In the corresponding match of 1930 H. J. Enthoven made two separate hundreds for Middlesex and K. S. Duleepsinhji two separate hundreds for Sussex. The Sussex team are always a "draw" at Lord's, and many people will go there, apart from Hendren's deserved benefit, to see K. S. Duleepsinhji as captain. Middlesex are playing six amateurs. N. Haig, whose injured right hand is quite sound, at least so far as batting is concerned, will captain Middlesex, and the other amateurs are I. A. R. Peebles, R. W. V. Robins, G. O. Allen – all of whom played against Australia last year – Enthoven and G. C. Newman, who has captained the side this year while Haig has been laid up.

"Rain Stopped Play"

11 *June* 1931, *Leading Article*. The British language has many melancholy phrases, but to the man for whom the summer exists solely that cricket may be played the curt three words "rain stopped play"are more poignant and depressing than any phrase MR. A. E. HOUSMAN could devise in the most prolonged pondering on the "iniquity on high." The scores on the back pages of evening papers inform the enthusiast who will hear of no county other than Blankshire that Blankshire has made the creditable score of 130 runs for one wicket at lunch; but his mind, running on ahead in eager anticipation, wonders what happened in that half-hour afterwards. It is sometimes a fatal

period. Did not a great authority on the game once write that lunch was a most valuable change bowler? At any rate the stop-press column will either confirm his fears or banish them; and then, instead of the intoxicating "185 for 1" or the calamitous "153 for 4," there is the unadorned announcement that rain has stopped play. It is as though a man in the middle of an exhilarating monologue on a subject very near to his heart suddenly discovered that the people to whom he was speaking were all asleep. His mind had been inspired, ready to answer an objection or strengthen an argument, and then, after all, the mental activity was wasted – his words and his enthusiasm had all been vanity.

The man who was actually watching Blankshire at the moment when the umpires, after exchanging that peculiarly significant look which umpires, alone of men, possess, took off the bails and proceeded with the players to the pavilion, is even worse off than he who reads of the disaster in the stop-press column. In an age when miracles are at a discount it remains miraculously true that, when the groundsmen trundle out their curious and cumbersome machines for protecting the wicket, a ground which, a moment before, had been teeming with humanity becomes forlornly empty. As the last flanneled figure disappears into the pavilion, he draws after him all the vitality which an hour before had made the ground a place of energy and enthusiasm; and not only does the spirit go, but the flesh vanishes also. There were 5,000 people, and suddenly there are at most 500, and not even, to invent a collective noun, an exaggeration of refreshment bars can explain this sudden depopulation. No, they are gone, and there is nothing but an expanse of green, nothing but rows and rows of empty seats mournfully aware that their hour of service is over. Will they ever again be used by the race of man? When the rain comes down at a cricket match, it not only stops play for the moment but conveys the malignant, irresistible suggestion that never, in no matter how remote an age, will cricket ever be played again. If MR. CHESTERTON really spent some of the most purple hours of his life in a waiting-room at Clapham Junction, he has times ahead of him even more imperially coloured if he will go to a cricket ground on which rain has just stopped play.

England's New Captain

FROM OUR CRICKET CORRESPONDENT [R. B. VINCENT]

11 *June* 1931. Mr. D. R. Jardine has been invited by the selection committee appointed by the Board of Control for Test Matches at home to captain England in their one and only game against New Zealand this year. He has accepted the offer, and so for the moment we know that a reliable cricketer will be in the side at Lord's on June 27.

Test Matches mean a great deal when we read of what D. Bradman did to our bowlers last season, when we saw, and realized, how much more C. V.

Grimmett meant to that Australian team, but little did the spectators at Lord's, Leeds, or the Oval know how much we missed when D. R. Jardine was not in our side. Had he played for England last year the run of the games might have been very different. As a Test Match batsman, his ability is indisputable, but for the moment, with so many others claiming the honour of captaining England, his claim has yet to be proved. Those who have chosen to attract popular opinion are at once dismissed, but there are others, who have played the game long, and always as it should be played, who have been passed over.

The Selection Committee, not failing to understand that the time has come to pick a team as young as Australia sent over here last year, had to find a captain to be worthy of playing in that side. Whether our young amateurs can afford the time to go here and there is not their business, but it remains for that committee, not forgetting the lesson they should have learned when the South Africans were here in 1929, to build up an entirely new side. Australia, by discarding many of their old choices and by winning the rubber last year, gained, on the turnover, four years. Mr. Jardine can be relied upon – provided he is given the material – to show what the young men can do here.

Mr. C. T. Studd

28 *July* 1931. The Rev. Robert Hindle writes:–

With reference to Mr. C. T. Studd's part in the Test Match of 1882, the story that was set on foot after that memorable match was lost is that Mr. Studd begged Mr. A. N. Hornby not to send him in. It was said that Mr. Studd sat with three sweaters on and shook with nervousness. As a result, Mr. Hornby kept him back, with the result that all the wickets were down before Mr. Studd received a ball, and the match was lost by seven runs. The following is Mr. Studd's story, given in the course of a letter I received from him in 1926:–

"I see from a newspaper that now they declare that I asked Hornby not to let me go in. Of course that is without the shadow of a foundation in fact. The only truth of the whole matter as stated is that the weather was cold and that we sat in the committee room with the windows closed because of the cold. Except that such strange things happen in cricket none dreamed we should be beaten. There were less than 80 runs required to win when we began our innings. When we had made over 50 for two wickets everything was over bar the shouting, as they say. Runs had come freely enough. Then came a time when the best English batsmen played over after over and never made a run. If I remember right something like 18 or 20 overs were bowled without a run, maiden after maiden. Then these got out. Hornby, on his own account, began to alter the order of going in. I believe he did ask me if I minded, and I said 'No.' Then things began to change, and the procession began. Hornby told me he was holding me in reserve. So I went in eighth man and saw two wickets fall, but I never received a ball. Now here are facts. Nobody dreamed, half an hour before the finish, that we could be beaten. Fifty odd out of 70 odd had been made, and eight men still to go in. What reason could there be for my nerves being bad as stated by Hornby? Again, if Hornby believed me to be nervous, he should have put me in first. That is what is usually done."

The foregoing was written to me as a familiar friend, and in self-defence after I had suggested that he was strung up as was the case in 1882. It was very unlike "C. T." to take the trouble to defend himself or to sound his own praises in any way.

Cf. 30 *August* 1882. *Studd's figures are faulty.*

The Late F. S. Ashley-Cooper

4 *February* 1932. A correspondent [R. C. Robertson-Glasgow] writes:–

Mr. Ashley-Cooper was the "Grammarian" of cricket. A life-long invalid, and for that reason unhappily almost a recluse – though a very present friend to many by correspondence and the medium of print – he proposed to himself, without thought of gain, but from a deep love of cricket, a task whose immensity might well have deterred the leisured enthusiast enjoying full health, and he more than achieved it. His monumental compilations of statistics, involving exhaustive research, a daily application to detail, and an encyclopaedic cataloguing, need not here be more than remarked. But I should like briefly to recall my first and, I think, only meeting with him. Having indulged in some rather puerile levities on a part of the history of cricket in a manner that could not have been wholly congenial to his sincere love of the annals of the game, I unwittingly made mild banter of some fabulous works of one "Historicus," unwittingly, for that was one of Ashley-Cooper's pen-names. We met shortly afterwards at a cricket dinner, and my apology was received with a courteous kindness that I cannot forget. He told me then that he never appeared on public occasions, and that he was bound to pay heavily for this one deviation from his rule. Many writers on the game owe him a debt: and even the foolish clown, however much he may "gag," is lost without his libretto. Surely Browning's lines, with a small change, are applicable to so unswerving a devotee:–

> Patience a moment!
> Grant I have mastered cricket's close-fill'd text,
> Still, there's the comment.
> Let me know all! Prate not of most or least,
> Painful or easy!

Lord Harris

26 *March* 1932, *Leading Article*. Wherever cricket is played, but especially in Kent, Australia, Bombay, and by members of the M.C.C. all over the world, the news of the death of LORD HARRIS will be received with a pang of keen regret. For nearly half of his long life he was a prominent figure on the cricket field at home and overseas, and from 1906, when he played in his last match for Kent, he held a unique position as perhaps the best known and most influential of the Elder Statesmen of the game. It was characteristic of his love of cricket and of his old school that till within a few years of the end of his life, long indeed after he had retired from first-class cricket, he made a regular practice of turning out to play for the Eton Ramblers in the Upper Club match at Eton on the Fourth of June. Captain of the Eton Eleven sixty-two years ago, and at different stages of his career, of Kent (from 1875 to 1889), and of England, he was President of the M.C.C. in 1895, and played innumerable matches for Oxford, the Gentlemen of England, I Zingari, and the Band of Brothers, besides doing invaluable work in the cause of cricket in India during the five years when he was Governor of Bombay. He was by no means merely a cricketer, for he rendered good service to his country in Ministerial appointments at home, and in various military and civil capacities here and overseas. But while cricket lasts he will be remembered for what he did for the game in his own county, and therefore far beyond its borders. In a letter written on his eightieth birthday and printed in this journal only a year ago he advised the rising generation to get all the cricket they can. "You do well," he said, "to love it, for it is more free from anything sordid, anything dishonourable, than any game in the world. To play it keenly, honourably, generously, self-sacrificingly is a moral lesson in itself, and the class-room is GOD's air and sunshine." No man in England had a better title to give that parting message than the fine cricketer and Old Stager who has now gone to his rest.

29 *March* 1932. A correspondent [C. L. R. James] writes:–

The late Lord Harris will be regretted in many places, not least in the West Indies, where he was born. He always had a warm spot in his heart for the land of his birth. He visited the West Indies periodically and, when in the seventies, met a negro septuagenarian who had been his playmate in childhood. Of late years he was a staunch supporter of West Indian cricket. He saw some of the games played by the M.C.C. team of 1926 and, his birthday happening to coincide with the Second Test in Trinidad, members of the M.C.C. playing in the match paid the veteran Test cricketer a charming compliment. He was asked to put on the pads and the Hon. F. S. G. Calthorpe, Hammond, Kilner, and Holmes, of the M.C.C., and H. B. G. Austin and George Challenor, of the West Indies, bowled at him. Even on the uncertain matting wicket and encumbered by coat and waistcoat, Lord Harris showed good form, playing forward with the left foot to the ball in the old style. There was no trace of the modern habit of getting unnecessarily in front of the wicket – which he condemned in the famous article on Modern Batting written for Wisden's Almanack over 20 years ago. During his short stay in 1926 he of his own accord visited the offices of the *Sporting Chronicle* (the leading sporting newspaper in the West Indies), and in an interview lasting nearly two hours discussed with the editor matters of importance affecting West Indian cricket.

Mr. J. R. F. Turner writes:– In 1924-25 I made strong appeals to the late Lord Harris to encourage, promote, and foster the boys' cricket movement and not in vain. He wrote me for many details *re* the Oxford Boys' Cricket Scheme, with special reference to the aspect of finance. I was able to give him every information. His final letter to me in 1925 was as follows:– "You need be under no apprehension. We have now got the matter well in hand as far as approaching the local education authorities in London, and I dare say if we can come to terms with them the M.C.C. will be disposed to make a public appeal." They did come to terms, and an appeal was broadcast, and ever since the boys' cricket movement has not only gathered strength in the Motherland, but also overseas in South Africa, Australia, New Zealand, Canada, and even British Guiana. A few years ago I attended the annual general meeting of the Club Cricket Conference at Fyvie Hall. Some 700 delegates were present, and Lord Harris was in the chair. I shall never forget his impassioned rhetoric in appealing to all those present to do their level best to bring cricket succour to the elementary school boys. It may be rightly claimed for him that, in his wisdom and vision on behalf of the rising generation, he contributed largely to the sterling success achieved.

A First-wicket Record
Fine Performance by Sutcliffe and Holmes

[BY DUDLEY CAREW]

17 *June* 1932. At Leyton, at exactly 1 o'clock yesterday, Sutcliffe, by hooking a short ball of Eastman's to the boundary, broke, in partnership with Holmes, the record first-wicket stand of 554 runs set up by two other Yorkshiremen, Brown and Tunnicliffe, in 1898. Sutcliffe promptly got out to the next ball, but the excitement was not yet over, for, as soon as A. B. Sellers had declared the innings closed and the players had reached the pavilion, the figures 555 on the score board, which meant that the record had been broken, were changed into 554, which meant it had only been equalled, and it was not until half an hour later that the new record passed into cricket history.

It would have been the cruellest ill-fortune had a mistake of one run on the score-board robbed the batsmen of the full fruits of their triumphs, for their respective innings were so consistently and unfailingly sound that the strokes which sent the ball to any direction other than that which they intended could be counted on the fingers of two hands. The pitch was, of course, perfect – the record could hardly have been broken had it not been – but the secret of Holmes and Sutcliffe's success lay not in the pitch nor in the short-comings of the Essex bowling but in their endurance, their unfailing patience, and their vast technical resources.

Sutcliffe's 313 was his highest individual score, and it enabled him to reach his 1,000 runs for the season, but Holmes has six times exceeded the 224 he made yesterday and on Wednesday. When Essex went in, Verity, who took five wickets for eight runs, and Bowes consolidated the work Holmes and Sutcliffe had begun and got the home side out for 78 runs. Following on, Essex lost five wickets for 92 runs, and so finished up the day needing 385 runs to save the innings defeat with five wickets in hand.

The weather was fine and sunny and a large crowd was present when Holmes and Sutcliffe went in to bat again yesterday morning. Nichols and A. G. Daer opened the bowling for Essex, but the batsmen began as they had left off, and soon after Holmes had driven Daer beautifully past mid-off to the boundary Sutcliffe beat the 456 made by E. R. Mayne and W. H. Ponsford in Australia with a square-cut for 4 off Nichols. After an hour's play the score had been raised to 500, and it was becoming more and more obvious that only time stood between the batsmen and the world's record. What happened at 1 o'clock has already been described, and, when everything was finally reduced to statistics, it appeared that Sutcliffe gave no chance and hit one 6, one 5, and 33 4's, and that Holmes, who might have been caught at the wicket when he had made three, hit 19 4's.

Essex lost L. G. Crawley before luncheon, and afterwards they collapsed completely on a pitch which was almost as good as it had ever been. Bowes, however, bowled with any amount of life and brought the ball back quickly, and with the total at 19 he got rid of Pope and Cutmore, who played outside a ball that came back, in the same over. O'Connor made 20 and then became Bowes' fourth victim, and when Verity bowled Nichols with a full-pitch and caught and bowled C. J. Bray by the time the total had reached 60 a real recovery was out of the question. Indeed, Verity bowled so well that the innings was all over by 4 o'clock for a total of 78, and Essex followed on 477 runs behind. Crawley, in his second innings, made some fierce drives, one of which led to Leyland's retirement from the field, but he, O'Connor, on whom the Essex batting is not a little dependent, Pope, and Cutmore were all out before the score had passed 50. Eastman and Nichols, however, prevented the Essex second innings from being a replica of the first, and they had almost doubled the total when Eastman hit a ball straight into Barber's hands at long-on.

YORKSHIRE 555 for 1 dec (Sutcliffe 313, Holmes 224 not out)
ESSEX 78 (Verity 5 for 8, Bowes 4 for 38) and 164 (Nichols 59 not out; Verity 5 for 45, Bowes 5 for 47)
Score after second day: Yorkshire 551 for 1 dec; Essex 78 and 92 for 5
Yorkshire won by an innings and 313 runs

Verity's Remarkable Record
Ten Wickets for Ten Runs

[BY DUDLEY CAREW]

13 *July* 1932. The match between Yorkshire and Nottinghamshire at Leeds, although it had sufficient excitement in itself, will be remembered always for the bowling of Verity. At luncheon yesterday Nottinghamshire, who led by 71 runs on the first innings, had scored 38 runs for no wicket, but they were all out for 67 runs, and Verity had not only done the hat trick, but had come out with the extraordinary analysis of:–

O.	M.	R.	W.
19.4	16	10	10

Bowlers have taken 10 wickets in one innings many times before, but never at such a fantastically small cost as Verity took his yesterday. The result of the match, thanks to Verity's astonishing achievement, was an easy win for Yorkshire by 10 wickets, with nearly an hour to spare.

Yorkshire declared at their overnight total of 163 runs for nine wickets and so seemed to put the future conduct of the match in Nottinghamshire's hands – they might choose to force the pace and declare in time to give themselves a reasonable chance of getting Yorkshire out, or they might concentrate on making sure of the first-innings points. Defeat at the time seemed out of the question.

The rain on the previous evening held up play until 12.30, and the hour's cricket before luncheon, during which Keeton and Shipston scored 38 runs together, suggested that the first-innings points were Nottinghamshire's objective. Keeton started off by hooking two short balls in Bowes's first over for a 4 and a 3, but this violence was not kept up, and later on Verity bowled seven maiden overs in succession. Both Keeton and Shipston had scored 18 runs at the interval, and the manner of their batting afterwards suggested that Nottinghamshire were definitely reconciled to their gain of five points.

With the total at 44, however, Verity, who before luncheon had only one slip and now had two, got Keeton caught by Macaulay, his original first slip. This reinforcement of the slips argued a certain increase in the difficulties of the pitch, and the batting of Walker at the beginning of his innings against both Verity and Macaulay, who was bowling round the wicket to two slips and two short-legs, confirmed the impression that the ball was turning more quickly. At 47 Shipston touched a ball of Verity's with the edge of his bat, and was caught at the wicket, and A. W. Carr was out before he had scored in almost exactly the same way he had been in the first innings, only this time Barber took the catch in front of the sight-screen instead of at long-off.

The pitch was now definitely difficult, and at 63 Verity took his fourth wicket when Walker played a perfectly correct stroke, found the spin too much for him, and was well caught low down with his right hand by Macaulay at first slip. Harris, playing in much the same way, was caught at second slip off the next ball, and Verity then proceeded to perform the hat-trick by getting G. V. Gunn l.-b.-w. with a good-length ball which came straight through. One run later, at 64, A. Staples provided Verity with his seventh successive wicket, and Larwood, hitting out, was beautifully caught by Sutcliffe running back from extra cover-point.

Verity now had the chance of doing the hat trick twice in one innings. As a matter of fact Lilley scored three very lucky runs off the ball that might have given it to him, but Verity's bowling had changed the match right round, and Nottinghamshire, and not Yorkshire, were now in danger of defeat. Although Verity missed doing the hat trick twice he got rid of Voce and S. Staples with two successive balls in the same over as Lilley scored his three runs, but, unluckily for him, Nottinghamshire had no twelfth man to bat for them. Since luncheon Verity's analysis read:–

O.	M.	R.	W.
12.4	9	10	10

Certainly the pitch became increasingly difficult, but, while Verity could not have accomplished his astounding success without its aid, it was only an accessory after the fact to his flight and length, which continually made the batsmen play the strokes they did not wish to after the ball had pitched. The turf and his finger spin did the rest.

Nottinghamshire lost 10 wickets for 29 runs after luncheon, and Yorkshire were left with 139 runs to win and with nearly $2\frac{3}{4}$ hours to spare. Holmes and Sutcliffe started off by scoring 50 runs in 40mins. The pitch was by no means perfect, but they hit the loose ball hard, and at tea time 81 runs were on the board, of which Holmes had scored 43 and Sutcliffe 30. After tea the batsmen made light of the bowling again, and the runs were obtained in 100 minutes without loss, Holmes having nine 4's in a delightful 77. He also completed his 1,000 runs during his innings. This was the seventy-second time that the Yorkshire opening pair have put on 100 runs for the first wicket.

NOTTINGHAMSHIRE 234 (Larwood 48, Lilley 46 not out; Leyland 4 for 14) and 67 (Verity 10 for 10)
YORKSHIRE 163 for 9 dec (Holmes 65; Larwood 5 for 73) and 139 for 0 (Holmes 77 not out, Sutcliffe 54 not out)
Yorkshire won by 10 wickets

Death of Mr. F. C. Cobden

13 *December* 1932. Mr. Frank Carroll Cobden, whose death has occurred at Capel Curig, North Wales, was the hero of perhaps the most sensational piece of bowling in the history of cricket.

In the Oxford and Cambridge match of 1870 Oxford, set 179 runs to win, had made 175 for the loss of seven batsmen and thus, with three wickets to fall, wanted only four runs for victory when Cobden began the over which will be for ever memorable. The first ball was hit by F. H. Hill for a single, the stroke being one which would certainly have sent the ball to the boundary had it not been brilliantly fielded by mid-wicket – as to whether this was mid-off or mid-on even those taking part in the match differ. S. E. Butler was caught off the second ball, T. H. Belcher bowled by the third, and W. A. Stewart by the fourth, with the result that Cambridge snatched an extraordinary victory by two runs.

Born at Lembley, Nottinghamshire, on October 14, 1849, Mr. Cobden was in the Harrow XI in 1866, and in the match against Eton, which Harrow won by an innings and 136 runs, he took five wickets for 37 and three for 10, or eight wickets in all for 47 runs. He left school early, and going up to Trinity College, Cambridge, he was given his Blue in 1870 and in the two following years, taking on the occasion of his great triumph eight wickets for 76 runs. He was an excellent fast round-arm bowler, and very straight, spoken of 60 years ago as "one of the best who has appeared in any eleven" and described as being a better bowler at school than at any time afterwards. He stood nearly 6ft. high, and weighed 12st. He generally fielded at mid-on, and was a free and powerful hitter.

Mr. Cobden had three sons and a daughter, and he is survived by his second wife.

Cricket and Chewing Gum

20 *December* 1932, *Leading Article*. The Victorian Women's Cricket Association, an Australian rather than a nineteenth-century body, have a problem before them much more far-reaching than the problems before the Australian Board of Control. The Board of Control have to decide how far members of the Australian Eleven may carry on journalism, and whether men who are, upon occasion, allowed someone else to run for them may also, if they plead a stiff forefinger, have someone else to write for them. These questions turn on the health of the players and journalism, which is proverbially a life of late hours and dissipation, is frowned upon as being bad for young cricketers. To the argument of the would-be journalists that the best doctor is a good income, and that the profits of their pens will make them leap about the field

in an ecstasy of solvency, bringing off impossible catches in order to have plenty of copy for their articles, the Board have no particular answer at the moment. What is plain is that among Australian men cricketers a simple criterion of health is what has to be applied.

No responsible man, whatever his views on this matter, is suggesting that unfairness will creep into the match. Any member of the Australian Eleven who uses his journalistic appointment to attribute high scores to himself and ducks to his opponents or rivals will find that he will only be able to establish his own version in a limited area and for a short time. It is far otherwise, however, with the women cricketers and the Victorian Women's Cricket Association. They are vexed with a question of health and fitness which also goes to the very root of cricketing ethics. At a recent match between two women's elevens at Melbourne the complaint was lodged that one of the teams had used chewing gum to fix the bails to the wicket, so that the slow bowler, the bowler of lobs or sneaks, had little chance of getting a wicket, even if she hit the stumps. No one wants to prevent women cricketers from chewing gum. Indeed lovers of the game, who know what formidable enemies to cricket and champions of lawn tennis the Americans are, must welcome a practice so calculated to win friends for cricket in the important New World. Fielding is often monotonous and uneventful and the very time for chewing, and batswomen who sit in the pavilion waiting to go in cannot very well be forbidden to chew then or expected to leave off in the middle. On the other hand it is plain wrong that the gum should be allowed to play any part in the game itself. The instance under investigation is but one example of the excessive changes it can make in the game, merely by being affixed to the bails. The changes are even more striking when the gum is attached to the ball itself, as it is only too easy for googly bowlers to do, and the need for the adhesive roller over the pitch is going to complicate the already difficult problems which captains have to think about.

It is the custom in Australian Test Matches for the spectators to throw about a good deal of orange peel. But this is at present chiefly aimed at over-eager spectators in the front. At the most it complicates matters for the out-field. But the moment it is believed that a bowler is bowling gum theory ardent partisans will appear with their catapults to project on to the pitch their own external contributions to the state of the wicket. If it is the experience of women cricketers that the bails are knocked off too frequently, it will be far better that they should learn from the humble but not impoverished owners of cokernut shies how to make bails lie deep in the stumps, so that when the wicket is hit they may but tremble and settle down again. But there must be no isolated and individual readjustments such as seem to have occurred. It is one thing for a batswoman to be allowed to smooth out the pitch with her bat to prevent bowlers from gaining unexpected advantage from a special worn patch. It is something quite different to allow them themselves to doctor the pitch or the wicket. Women cricketers are more fully

It is recommended to the Lordling Cricketters who amuſe themſelves in White Conduit Fields, to procure an Act of Parliament for incloſing their play ground, which will not only prevent their being incommoded, but protect themſelves from a repetition of the ſevere rebuke which they juſtly merit, and received on Saturday evening from ſome ſpirited citizens whom they inſulted and attempted *vi et armis* to drive from the foot path, pretending it was within their bounds.

INSET The first reference to cricket in *The Times*, 22 June 1785.
ABOVE Lobs, top hats and curved bats for the match between the Regency CC of Brighton and Hambledon on a packed Brunswick Lawns, Hove, August 1946.
BELOW The cradle of cricket: the players of Hambledon CC and Downing College, Cambridge, pose in front of the famous Bat and Ball Inn at Broadhalfpenny Down, Hambledon, June 1931.

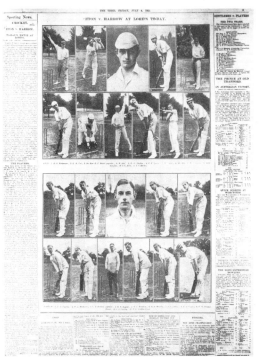

ABOVE LEFT The best part of a page was devoted in *The Times* to the preview of Eton v. Harrow in 1921.
BELOW The lunchtime promenade of spectators at Eton v. Harrow 1928 filled a large part of the revered Lord's turf.
ABOVE RIGHT The founder of Lord's (Thomas Lord) featured on the front page of *The Times* M.C.C. Number, 25 May 1937.

ABOVE No new thing under the sun: spectators rush on to the field at the end of the final Test match at The Oval in 1930 to applaud Australia's victory. Note, however, that they are making for the pavilion, not the players.
BELOW The mighty Bradman on his way to a third successive double century beneath the cathedral at Worcester in 1938. His partner is Badcock, who, on his first appearance in England, shared in a fourth-wicket partnership of 277.

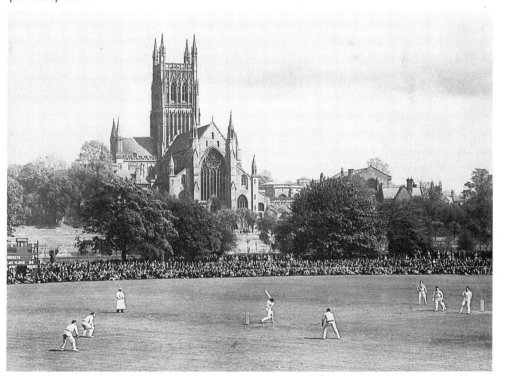

ABOVE LEFT A.C.M. Croome, Cricket Correspondent of *The Times* 1925-30.
ABOVE RIGHT John Woodcock, Cricket Correspondent of *The Times* since April 1954 and, since the 1981 edition, Editor of *Wisden* as well. This photograph was taken by Denis Compton at Port of Spain, Trinidad, in 1968.
BELOW R.B. (Beau) Vincent, Cricket Correspondent of *The Times* 1930-51, bids farewell to his Sports Editor, Oliver Beaumont, at Tilbury, September 1950 en route for Australia. Alas, illness forced Vincent to come home without covering a match.

ABOVE Bernard Darwin *(left)* and A.P. (Patrick) Ryan, authors of many of the wittiest 'fourth leaders' on cricket. Darwin is best known for his outstanding writing on golf.

BELOW LEFT "What did I do to deserve this, skipper?" Ian Botham appears to be asking Mike Brearley at Edgbaston, July 1981.

BELOW RIGHT P.G.H. Fender at 90, a grand old man of cricket pictured at his home in August 1982. Like Brearley, Fender contributed to a special cricket number of *The Times*.

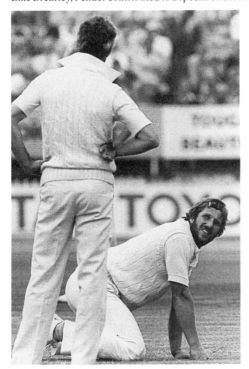

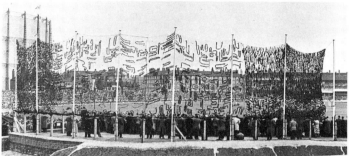

W. M. Lawry, c. Knott, b. Brown 0

I. R. Redpath, c. Cowdrey, b. Brown 4

R. M. Cowper, c. Graveney, b. Snow 8

K. D. Walters, c. Knight, b. Brown 26

A. P. Sheahan, c. Knott, b. Knight 6

I. M. Chappell, l.b.w. b. Knight 7
G. D. McKenzie, b. Brown 5

J. W. Gleeson, c. Cowdrey, b. Brown 14

B. N. Jarman retired hurt 0

N. J. N. Hawke, c. Cowdrey, b. Knight 2
A. N. Connolly, not out 0
Extras 6
Total 78

ABOVE Because a photographic agency had exclusive rights at Test match grounds *The Times*'s picture editor, Ulric Van den Bogaerde (father of Dirk Bogarde), designed a special long-range camera, seen here in use on a rooftop overlooking The Oval in 1951. Five years later camouflage nets obstructed the view and forced *The Times*'s cameramen to another vantage point.
BELOW A change of policy by the cricket authorities admitted newspaper photographers in 1972. This was the first picture of a Test match at Lord's taken *inside* the ground by a *Times* photographer (published on the front page, 23 June 1972) and shows Dennis Lillee winning an lbw appeal against John Edrich. The fielders are (from left): Rodney Marsh, Ian Chappell, Keith Stackpole, Greg Chappell and David Colley.
RIGHT How the front page of 25 June 1968 told the story of Australia's collapse to 78 all out against England at Lord's.

Soviet Union to defer repayment of Polish debt

Moscow, August 16 — The Kremlin has announced measures to ease Poland's financial crisis after a summit meeting between Soviet and Polish leaders, but has withheld judgment on the political course taken by Warsaw.

Rallies and marches planned for tomorrow, to protest against the detention of political prisoners in Poland were called off tonight, thus averting what could have been a major confrontation with the authorities.

The organizers of the rallies, in five towns, which were to have been followed by a march on Warsaw unless three anti-Communist dissidents were released from detention, announced that all protests were suspended for the time being.

The march had been condemned by Solidarity, the independent union movement, and the Roman Catholic Church. The Government had promised to stop it with all available means.

The Solidarity branch in Plock, west of Warsaw, which was to have been one of the assembly points for the march, said about 500 extra police with armoured vehicles had been brought into the town.

A full communiqué on the summit talks on Pravda today showed Moscow has pledged to postpone repayment of about £4,300m (now worth about £2,300m) in credits until the mid 1980s, and raise supplies of raw materials and consumer goods to Poland.

Western diplomats said the nists "to implement successfully the decisions of the party congress aimed at strengthening the Polish United Workers' Party as a Marxist-Leninist party and consolidating the position of socialism in society".

Diplomats said that amounted to Soviet approval for only a part of the congress decisions and did not suggest Moscow shared Mr Kania's view that it had plotted a course out of the country's difficulties.

It also indicated the Kremlin was still dissatisfied with the Polish party's pledge to continue policies of liberalization and reform, an important part of the programme put forward at the congress.

The communiqué's description of the climate at the talks also indicated that the two sides remained seriously divided on basic policy questions.

It said the meeting was held in an atmosphere of "fraternal friendship and comradely mutual understanding". Usually Soviet bloc leaders are said to have reached "full unity of views" at such meetings. Diplomats said the wording used for the Crimean talks was at least as cool as the official description of the last Polish-Soviet summit in March.

After that meeting, which was termed "cordial", Moscow released a statement saying Mr Brezhnev had called on Mr Kania to change the course of events in Poland following months of political liberaliza tion.

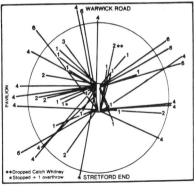

∗∗ Dropped Catch Whitney
∙ Stopped + 1 overthrow

WARWICK ROAD · PAVILION · STRETFORD END

Was Botham's innings the greatest ever?

By John Woodcock, Cricket Correspondent

Ian Botham's innings was, of its kind, perhaps the greatest ever played and the chart details its progress. It began just before half past two in the fifth Test match at Old Trafford on Saturday afternoon, when England, in their second innings, were 104 for five after starting the day at 70 for one. With a relentless display of tight fielding and accurate bowling, Australia had recovered from an apparently hopeless position to one from which they could well win.

In 34 overs, Boycott, Gower, Gatting and Brearley had fallen to Alderman and Lillee, while a mere 34 runs were being

England cricketers than to see a hard won advantage against Australia being gradually whittled away. Contrasting with England's abject surrender was Australia's uncontrollable joy.

The cheers which greeted Botham were of desperate encouragement, the position scarcely less fraught than at Headingley where he made his historic 149 not out. His 118 on Saturday was an even finer innings. It was more calculated for one thing, and less chancy.

At Headingley, he played a wonderful, unforgettable slog, but it was also a lucky one. On Saturday, with a full sense of responsibility, he played

end and Whitney at the other. When Alderman did take the new ball, immediately it was due, Botham had made 28 from 53 balls. At the other end, Tavaré was taking good care of himself, not scoring much but relieving Botham of the anxiety of seeing a partner in distress. Of the 149 they added together, Tavaré's share was 28.

Botham had been in for 65 minutes when the new ball was taken. At 150 for five, one or two of the England side were to be seen watching the cricket again. Tavaré, wrapped in his cocoon, had completed the slowest half century ever

was caught at the wicket, he had made another 90 runs in 49 balls. Off Alderman's first over with the new ball he took seven; off Lillee's, 19. In the remaining nine overs in which he received a ball he made six and 10 off Alderman, five, six and 13 off Lillee, eight and seven off Bright and one and eight off Whitney. I refuse to believe that a cricket ball has ever been hit with greater power or rarer splendour.

Where England's earlier batsmen, apart from Tavaré, had found survival impossible, Botham made the boundaries seem far too short and the wicket far too good. When

The fastest hundred in Test cricket, in terms of balls received, was by the West Indian, Roy Frederick, at Perth in 1975; it took him 71 balls. In 1902, the mighty Jessop scored 102 against Australia at the Oval in 75 balls; at the Oval in 1948, on the Saturday, with the new the balance, Botham's hundred took 86 balls (one fewer than at Headingley), though he was out from five to 118 in 20 balls.

It was an innings that could have been played in the best place only by a man of astonishing power. Botham's attack on the new ball was a mixture of crude strength and classical orthodoxy.

ABOVE A memorable innings — and front page — 17 August 1981.

BELOW Advertisements for *Times* cricket from 1926 *(John Wisden's Cricketers' Almanack)* and the 1970s.

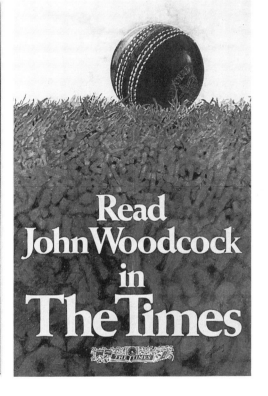

ABOVE Typical English cricket scene — 1: spectators shelter during a snow shower at The Parks, Oxford, May 1967.
BELOW Typical English cricket scene — 2: play on the village green at Wombourne, Staffordshire. This photograph was included in a *Times* exhibition at the Guildhall Art Gallery, London, in 1956.

equipped than are men for this doctoring. The shine on the new ball can be taken off by the same cosmetics which keep the shine off the nose, and much can be done with powder to mitigate slipperiness. Bowlers would find it useful to dye particular important spots on the pitch, rolling their heads on it while waiting for the next batswoman. All these tendencies must be voluntarily checked, or the Victorian Women's Association will have to forbid the presence of handbags and the use of cosmetics altogether. And then what chance will poor old cricket have of increasing its present quite slight popularity among the more influential half of the human race?

Australia Wins

4 *January* 1933, *Leading Article*. After a hard-fought and exciting game, in which day by day first one side and then the other seemed to have the upper hand, Australia won the second Test Match decisively by 111 runs. In the last day's play England's eleven batsmen failed to make 100 runs between them. It has been a bowlers' match throughout. In the four innings there was only one total of over 200, and the aggregate score of 727 gives the tiny average of 18 runs per wicket. Not since the Trent Bridge match of 1921, when the aggregate was 521 and the average 17 for each wicket that fell, has Test Match scoring been anything like so low. In every one of the twenty-five matches played since that date one side or the other, and sometimes each of them, has scored in one or both innings totals of over 300, rising to Australia's 729 for six wickets at Lord's in 1930. The respective aggregates in the last two Melbourne matches in the season of 1928-29 were 1,497 and 1,554, and the averages per wicket 40 and 44; so that it is difficult to avoid the conclusion that the moderate total in this year's match was due rather to the players than to the Melbourne wicket. In other words the bowling on both sides was uniformly good, and some of the batting dismally weak.

Still, apart from the disappointing failures of some of the best batsmen of both countries, there is comfort in the reflection that a check to the mammoth scores which the public now seem to look upon as their birthright might be all for the good of the game. Nor would there be any damage to the harmony of the present series, and to Test Match cricket in general, if it were to be freed from the atmosphere of artificial excitement by which in these days it is increasingly surrounded. Before this last match began and while it was was in progress so much has been said and written in both countries about the fairness or unfairness of this or that line of tactics, so many outsiders have wasted their time and energy in telling the two captains what they ought and ought not to have done and left undone, that, but for the unruffled common sense with which both have steered their course, the chorus of conflicting advice and criticism might well have put a severe strain on the nerves and judgment both of themselves and of their teams. The less of such talk there is in future the better for all concerned. Each side has now won a match; the lists are set for the remaining three; it is high time to cut the cackle and get on with the game.

"Body-Line Bowling"

19 *January* 1933, *Leading Article.* In due time, no doubt, the M.C.C. will send a considered and courteous reply to the cable of protest against what has begun to be called "body-line bowling" which they received yesterday from the Australian Board of Control. Meanwhile an attempt to give some idea of how the matter strikes the average Englishman may not be amiss. First of all there is nothing new in the kind of bowling to which exception is now taken. Really fast bowlers are as rare as truly great statesmen. But they do every now and then spring up, both here and in the Dominion, and have been known before now to hit the batsman as well as the wicket. English players who some years ago suffered many a shrewd knock from the bowling of MCDONALD and GREGORY – not to speak of JONES in still earlier days – have the right to recall their own experiences to those who are now criticizing the tactics of LARWOOD and his Captain. Australians know as well as our men that the game of cricket is not played with a soft ball, and that a fast ball which hits a batsman on the body is bound to hurt. They also know that, so long as a "shock" bowler is not deliberately bumping down short-pitched balls or purposely aiming at the batsman, his bowling is perfectly fair. It is inconceivable that a cricketer of JARDINE's standing, chosen by the M.C.C. to captain an English side, would ever dream of allowing or ordering the bowlers under his command to practise any system of attack that, in the time-honoured English phrase, is not cricket. To do the Australians justice the grievance at the back of their complaint is probably neither the pace nor the direction of LARWOOD's deliveries. What they apparently do object to is the array of leg-fielders – corresponding to the closely packed posse in the slips and the gully when the bowler exploits the off-theory – on whom the English captain relies to increase the effectiveness of his fast bowlers. But in that policy there is nothing dishonourable or unsportsman-like or foreign to the spirit of the game. After all, the object of every fielding side is to get their opponents out for as low a score as possible. If with that aim in view JARDINE has made more use of the "leg-theory" than other Captains before him the development is largely due to the fashion of the two-eyed stance and the modern batsman's habit of covering the stumps with his legs, thereby preventing the bowler from getting a clear view of the wicket, and incidentally making it more likely that he himself will be hit.

In the opinion of the Australian Board of Control bowling of this type has become a menace to the best interests of the game, is causing intensely bitter feelings between players, and unless stopped at once is likely to upset the friendly relations between Australia and England. Their protest, which is at once a warning and an appeal, is the direct outcome of the Adelaide Test Match. Apart from the skilful bowling that in the first innings sent back to the pavilion seven such batsmen as SUTCLIFFE, JARDINE, HAMMOND, AMES, FINGLETON, MCCABE, and BRADMAN for an average of fewer than five runs apiece, the game was remarkable for the dogged pluck with which the batsmen of the two teams that followed them retrieved for the time being the fortunes of their side. Those first two innings were a constant succession of ups and downs, brimful of excitement, as English and Australian players in turn, fighting with their backs to the wall, upset all the calculations of the prophets. Under normal conditions these fluctuating changes and chances would have been enough in themselves to win for the Adelaide match a niche of its own in the annals of Test Match cricket. Unfortunately it will be remembered rather as a game in which good-humoured barracking degenerated as the play went on into angry booing on the part of the spectators, irritated by the failure of their idols, and to acrimonious comments in the pavilion and elsewhere on the particular style of bowling which was one of its causes. On the other hand let it be remembered that the crowds on the mounds, in spite of their disappointments, showed that they could cheer as well as barrack their English visitors, and that OLDFIELD and other Australian batsmen who were hurt by our fast bowlers were the first to own that the bowlers were not to blame.

Any breach in the mutual good will and friendliness between the players of the two countries which have survived the ordeal of many a desperate encounter over a period of more than half a century would be a cricketing disaster of the first magnitude, and the M.C.C. may be trusted to do everything in their power to prevent the dismal forebodings of the Board of Control from coming true. It is difficult to conceive the possibility of their placing a ban on any particular type of bowling or to see by what authority they could instruct the captains of Test teams or any other eleven how to place or not to place their men in the field; but no doubt the common sense of the two great governing bodies of the game will be able between them to hit upon some means of coming to a satisfactory agreement. In all probability the present delicate and difficult position would never have arisen but for the irresponsible chatter of elderly critics in the pavilion and in the Press, and the craving in some quarters for sensational news-stories which has magnified words or incidents natural enough in the heat of a hard-fought battle.

The M.C.C. Reply

24 *January* 1933, *Leading Article.* The reply to the protest of the Australian Board of Control against what is called "body-line" bowling was unanimously settled yesterday by a special and largely attended meeting of the full

committee of the M.C.C. held at Lord's, under the chairmanship of LORD LEWISHAM. The effect of the resolution adopted by the committee and subsequently cabled to Australia is that the ruling authority of the game has no hesitation in standing by the captain of the English side and the bowler or bowlers to whose methods objection has been taken. Furthermore, if the Board should consider it desirable to cancel the remainder of the programme of the present tour, the M.C.C. would give their consent, though with great reluctance. In the circumstances their action in supporting the captain, the team, and its managers, in whom, as they say, they have complete confidence, was inevitable. By the terms of the protest the bowlers in question, and therefore their captain, were accused of unsportsmanlike conduct. That charge, which is not and cannot be proven, the M.C.C. committee could not possibly accept. To do so would be to admit that the tactics of which the Board of Control complains are an infringement of the laws of the game, an accusation which the Board itself, in spite of the strong language used in its protest, has never ventured to make. There was nothing unfair or unsportmanlike or contrary to the spirit of the game in the tactics of the English captain and his men.

Besides their offer to call off the remaining matches, if that is the desire of the Board of Control, the M.C.C. intimate that if the Board wish to propose a new law or rule it shall receive their careful consideration. That clearly, and not the abandonment of the rest of the present tour, is the regular and constitutional line of procedure. By their promise to consider a proposal for a change in the laws, and by expressing their hope that the situation is not now so serious as seemed to be indicated by the Board's cable of protest, the M.C.C. are holding out an olive branch which, in the best interests of the game in both countries and throughout the cricketing world, it is earnestly to be hoped that the Board may see their way to accept. Nothing could be more disastrous than a breach, even if only temporary, in the cordial relations which have for so long existed between Australian and English cricketers. The protest was cabled in the heat of a contest in which, in the opinion of those who sent it, some of the English bowling was causing intensely bitter feelings. But the dignified spirit in which it has been received and answered by the M.C.C. committee is the strongest proof how deeply they and the whole of this country (and, it may be said with confidence, the Australians themselves) would regret any change in the friendly relations between the cricketers of the two countries.

Leg-theory and Body-bowling

A Word for the Bowler

FROM OUR CRICKET CORRESPONDENT [R. B. VINCENT]

1 *February* 1933. The text of the reply of the Australian Board of Control to the message sent to them on January 23 by M.C.C. was announced yesterday, and will be found in full on page 10. For the moment the important fact is that the remainder of the programme is not to be cancelled and the English captain is free to employ whatever bowling tactics he considers suitable in the two remaining Test matches. If, however, there is any recrudescence of the disorderly behaviour which marred the third Test Match at Adelaide it is possible that M.C.C., without further discussion, may issue orders for the abandonment of the tour.

So long as tactics of the English bowlers remained the despair of the Australian batsmen and the butt of Australian criticism the matter could be regarded as little more than as a passing incident in Test Match history. But when once a formal protest had been made to M.C.C. the situation became serious. The M.C.C. Committee quite naturally refused to believe that their captain could have been guilty of any action which could be considered "unsportsmanlike" – an unfortunate word that for the Board of Control to have used – and since then every one interested in the welfare of the game has been trying to probe the rights and wrongs of the case.

An analysis of the whole matter has not been helped by a confusion between three quite different types of bowling – "bumping" bowling, "leg-theory" bowling, and this new specimen called "body-line" bowling. The fact that fast bowlers have always been liable and tempted to bang down a short ball has nothing to do with this present discussion, and the retort that McDonald and Gregory when bowling to a normally placed field occasionally hit our batsmen is not properly a comment on "leg-theory" as such. Nor can "leg-theory" bowling, as it has been accepted in the past, be considered a sufficient cause for complaint.

There have been at least three types of "leg-theory" bowling to which batsmen have become accustomed. First there is the left-handed bowler, such as F. R. Foster or Voce, who makes the ball go away with his arm and must of necessity rely upon a carefully placed field on the leg-side, and who straightens up the ball to hit the stumps. Foster was able to exploit this to the full by bowling round the wicket, but Voce cannot bring the ball back sufficiently and therefore bowls over the wicket; hence, no doubt, the accusation against him of "body-line" bowling. When he bowls round the wicket the ball travels diagonally from a point outside the return crease to fine long leg, which even if it is a "straight" line certainly is not a "body" line. Secondly, there is the medium-paced right-handed "in-swinger," a type of bowling employed most thoroughly by Root, against whom there has never been a charge of unfairness. Thirdly, there is the case of the normal medium-paced right-hander who either because the state of the pitch or the habits of a particular batsman affords an opportunity changes from bowling over the wicket to round the wicket and brings his men on to the leg-side. Macaulay, who is one of the most intelligent and accurate of our bowlers at the present time, frequently does this successfully, and no one could regard this as anything but good bowling.

None of these three types of bowlers has been regarded as unfair, even if a persistence of such bowling is liable to make the watching of cricket a dull affair in that it must mean the loss of many of the most beautiful strokes in cricket. I have in recent years been exasperated with continually having to make a note that a batsman was caught at "forward short leg," "backward short leg," or "fine leg," but that does not mean that the bowling has not been both good and effective. Over and above that there has been employed a purely negative form of "leg-theory," in which the ball is pitched consistently outside the leg-stump to waste time. It has been bowled by Australians, and deserves no comment. But now suddenly a definitely fast bowler has taken it into his head to bowl to a field placed on the leg-side, and at once "leg-theory" has become "body-line," not because Larwood is doing anything different from what has been accepted as normal in the past, but because he is doing it fast.

In the opinion of Australians the "leg-theory" has ceased to be clever or amusing and has become dangerous. If this type of bowling, now called "body-line," is to be deemed unfair or contrary to the spirit of the game, then it can only be controlled by limiting the pace of the bowler, or else by destroying the whole theory of bowling to a leg-side field, which has been evolved by previous bowlers of a lesser pace. And surely, when everything is being done to readjust the balance between batsman and bowler, it would be utterly reactionary merely to tell bowlers that they must go back 50 years and start all over again in an effort to find a way of curtailing a batsman's fun?

For Old Cricketers

The batsman stands to hide his wicket,
   The bowler at his body aims:
Tho' these perfect the "art" of Cricket,
   Do they improve the best of games?

– The game we played with zest, and, after,
   Homeward thro' meadows scented warm,
Rehearsed, re-played, with generous laughter,
   Victor and vanquished – arm-in-arm.

Q. [SIR ARTHUR QUILLER-COUCH]

Death of Mr. A. Jackson

A Great Loss to Cricket

16 *February* 1933. The death of Mr. A. Jackson at Brisbane yesterday at the age of 23 is an inestimable loss to the world of cricket in general and to Australian cricket in particular. Such high hopes had been placed in this young man that he had already been spoken of as a second Victor Trumper, and there were many in his own country who firmly believed that he was a greater batsman than Bradman! Be that as it may, it was sufficient that he was "Archie Jackson," a cricketer whose graceful style and charming personality had already endeared him to cricketers in England, who saw in him the spirit of all that is best in modern Australia.

After his triumphs in his own country Jackson had a disappointing season in England in 1930, but no one could fail to perceive the elegance and genius of a cricketer which only ill-health could prevent from fulfilment. He had clearly modelled himself on Alan Kippax, with all that great batsman's unaffected mannerisms, even to the shirt-sleeve rolled low on the forearm with the safety pin to keep it immaculately in place, and, like his master, he was a deflector rather than a striker of the ball, more suited perhaps to the fast wickets of Australia.

In England Jackson never gained sufficient confidence to play to the pitch of the turning ball, but on occasions when it came more quickly on to the bat he played some beautiful innings, and in the last and decisive Test Match at the Oval, when both courage and skill were demanded, his innings of 73 had a determining effect on the run of the game.

Jackson first attracted attention when he was at school at Balmain, Sydney. Joining the Balmain club he did not long remain in the lower grade, and in 1926-27, when only 17 years old, he had his first experience of State cricket with New South Wales. Jackson scored prolifically from the start, and his first season of Sheffield Shield cricket yielded him 464 runs with an average of 58. The next summer he accomplished a feat performed by no other player of his age – that of scoring two 100's in a match – putting together innings of 131 and 122 against South Australia. When the M.C.C. team, under the captaincy of A. P. F. Chapman, toured Australia in 1928–29 Jackson, by scoring 164, saved his country from collapse in the fourth Test Match which England won by 12 runs, and for his State he played innings of 162 and 90 at Adelaide. Jackson's 182 in the Test Trial match – regarded as his most beautiful innings – made certain of his inclusion in the 1930 Australian team which toured England. He was a reliable fieldsman in the deep, and had a splendid return. Jackson was a native of Scotland, having been taken to Australia when he was only six months old.

England Regain the Ashes

Some Reflections

FROM OUR CRICKET CORRESPONDENT [R. B. VINCENT]

17 *February* 1933. England, when they won the Fourth Test Match at Brisbane yesterday, regained the Ashes, which they had lost at the Oval in 1930. On that August afternoon there was a feeling that Australia, with a successful team which included many young men, had asserted a superiority which it would take some seasons to shake.

At the beginning of last summer there was still but little indication of the great things to come, but gradually as the team took shape so hope increased. Early in the tour it was evident that England had the making of an excellent side; the Australians, from one cause and another, were faced with difficulties, until at last England's triumph was definitely expected.

That so remarkable a reversal of form should have occurred is due almost entirely to two men, D. R. Jardine and Larwood. The English captain no doubt had in each match a team of reliable and efficient players, each of whom played his part nobly, but in the conditions which prevail in Australia a particular solidity of purpose is demanded, and this virtue Jardine possesses to the fullest degree. His appreciation of the situation was admirable, and, once he had made up his mind, events followed almost at his dictation. Unreasonable complaints were made from time to time of the dilatoriness of the English batting, but Jardine stuck to his point, hammered away, and now to him full and ungrudging credit must be given for a splendid victory.

Larwood, for his part, transformed the spirit of Test Matches, which had become to be considered a batsman's rightful amusement, into being a bowler's affair. He set the tune and controlled the play, for it was he, splendidly supported as he was by G. O. Allen, Voce, Verity, and Hammond, who was the particularly disturbing influence to the Australian batsmen. His record of 28 wickets for 502 runs in these four matches in no measure explains the influence which he brought to bear on the results. As an example of fortitude and stamina alone his performance has been remarkable, for it seems that whenever he was called upon for yet one more desperate effort, even in the most sweltering heat, he responded to the utmost. Comparisons, especially among fast bowlers of different generations, are futile, but he must assuredly be granted a place among the greatest and most willing of his kind.

Jardine's greatest difficulty has been in establishing a satisfactory order of batting, for he was not provided with a suitable partner to Sutcliffe. He sacrificed himself by going in first in this last game, but his proper place is at No. 5, where his remarkable power of concentration means everything to a side which shows signs of instability. Sutcliffe has again done splendidly, this time in circumstances which were not controlled by the batting side, but

England has a great deal to owe to the courage of batsmen lower in the batting order.

This game at Brisbane will always be thought of as "Paynter's match." It was only a game of cricket, but even those least interested in it must have felt that something noble had been achieved at the other end of the world when this sick little Lancastrian came from hospital to the heat and anxiety of a Test Match to save his side from the imminent threat of defeat. Certainly had it not been for his brave effort, and the imperturbable Verity, not even Larwood could have prevented England from having yet to fight out the issue at Sydney next week.

And if England have their heroes, so too have Australia, for no two men could have tackled the situation more gallantly than W. M. Woodfull and W. J. O'Reilly. The Australian batsmen as a whole seem to have lacked utterly a proper reply to Larwood's bowling, but throughout Woodfull did everything that a captain can do by personal example to pull his side through, and O'Reilly, with very little support, continually kept the English score within reasonable limits. T. Wall also has banged the ball down without sparing himself, and it is not extravagant to assert that the perseverance of the Australian bowlers, limited as it may have been in quality, has been one of the most resplendent features of these four Test Matches.

AUSTRALIA 340 (V. Y. Richardson 83, D. G. Bradman 76, W. M. Woodfull 67; Larwood 4 for 101) and 175
ENGLAND 356 (Sutcliffe 86, Paynter 83, D. R. Jardine 46; W. J. O'Reilly 4 for 120) and 162 for 4 (Leyland 86)
England won by 6 wickets

The King's Message

The King has sent the following telegram to Lord Lewisham, the president of the M.C.C.:–

As patron of the M.C.C. I wish you to convey to the team in Australia my warm congratulations on their victory. I have followed with the closest interest the ups and downs of the last match.

GEORGE R.I.

In addition D. R. Jardine received the following messages:–

THE M.C.C.:– "Splendid! We congratulate you all very warmly and thank you all very much."

THE PRIME MINISTER:– "Heartiest congratulations to you and all your team. We looked forward to hearing of hard-fought games with our old rivals on the cricket field and a win for us this time. Well done! – J. Ramsay MacDonald."

MR. J. H. THOMAS:– "Bravo! The Ashes are won; but they are secondary to the great fighting spirit and good sportsmanship shown by both sides. – J. H. Thomas."

THE LANCASHIRE COUNTY CRICKET CLUB:– "Lancashire's heartiest congratulations to you and team on winning rubber. Splendid performance. – Colwyn, president, committee, and members."

THE YORKSHIRE COUNTY CRICKET CLUB:– "Yorkshire's cricketers congratulate you and your team most heartily on your well-deserved victory."

NOTTINGHAMSHIRE COUNTY CRICKET CLUB:– "Warmest congratulations on recovery of the Ashes. Glad our Nottingham men have done their share."

A telegram was also received by D. R. Jardine from Mr. A. J. Lyons, the Prime Minister of Australia, congratulating England on a notable victory. The M.C.C. received a message of congratulation from the Australian Board of Control and have sent a reply.

The Maharajah of Nawanagar

4 *April* 1933. Mr. F. W. Bain writes:–

Here is a true story of "Ranji" which might interest your readers, few of whom in England will have heard of it. I was an inconsiderable member of a team that was playing against Kathiawar when Ranji was at the height of his fame. I have rarely seen so enormous a crowd, come from all parts of India to Poona to see their champion play. Ranji was caught third ball in the slips by Deas of the K.O.Y.L.I. In the second innings he was caught again third ball very smartly by Bond of the Gunners. As he went off Ranji said to me with a smile, "It's the only time in my life I ever made a pair of spectacles." The dismay of the spectators may be imagined. But we managed to put him in a third time – and then he made 70, so to say, in the twinkling of an eye.

England v. West Indies
Century by Jardine

FROM OUR CRICKET CORRESPONDENT [R. B. VINCENT]

26 *July* 1933. The second Test Match between England and the West Indies was left drawn at Old Trafford yesterday. There was just one moment when, with Headley out, Clark bowling quite fast, and Hammond supporting Langridge in the manner of the best short slip in the world, the possibility of a finish was suggested. England, however, were without Macaulay, who cannot put a boot on to his foot, and it was just Macaulay they wanted, for the ball was turning after luncheon, and Macaulay's leg-trap would have been more threatening than Clark bowling to the chance of a deep long-leg holding a catch.

There was quite a lot of talk in Manchester about body-line bowling, but really it mattered very little, for unless a bowler is as accurate as Larwood no batsman such as Jardine, playing right on to the top of the ball, or Constantine, hitting it fiercely off his eyebrows, is likely to be much troubled. Clark in fact bowled at one time to three slips, there is not much body-line in his bowling, and when Martindale and Constantine flung the ball at Jardine and Robins in the morning there was only one fieldsman creeping really close under the bat on the leg side. Jardine and Robins, when play was continued in the morning, could not possibly have been expected to attempt any grandiose gesture, for the match was then already almost stone dead. Jardine played first Martindale and then Constantine as easily as possible and also Valentine, who, when his turn came, was as quick off the pitch as any of the accredited thunderers. Robins, whatever the situation, can be relied upon to make a match of it. This season he has been stumped an almost incredible amount of times, and yesterday he tried his best for over after over again to provide the wicketkeeper with a chance. Later, when the West Indies were in a rather uncomfortable position, Constantine behaved in precisely the same way.

Runs came along. Jardine made his 100, the first that he has ever effected in a Test Match, and that is a truly remarkable statistic, and Robins made his 50. Suddenly the whole face of the game changed, not because England made more runs, but because they lost more wickets. Robins was stumped, as he had promised so often to be, and Jardine was caught at backward point so close to the ground that he may be excused if he wondered whether he was out. It had been a magnificent innings, during which, on Monday afternoon, he had been barracked at the one and only time when England had the least possible chance of losing a grip of the game. Verity never had a ball to play at all, for Clark was the last of three batsmen who tumbled out with the score unaltered.

The West Indies therefore gained a lead of one run on the first innings, but it was not long before that one run meant very little, for Barrow hit a ball of fair length from Clark on the splice and was caught at short-leg. Roach, who attacked Clark and Wyatt, bowling as an opening bowler in place of Macaulay, batted almost as well as he had done that day at the Oval when he scored a hundred and more runs before luncheon. Headley again had to stop any possibility of nonsense, and if there is any better or later cutter than he I would like to see him. England's captain saw that the pitch was taking spin: he had Langridge on at one end, Verity at the other, and in between times a small measure of Robins, who from the manner in which the ball curled off the bat was obviously making it do all manner of tricks.

Roach was the first to go, leg-before to a ball so far pitched up that it might be called a yorker. Headley then followed, caught and bowled by a ball which Langridge must have held back, and when Grant stretched continuously down the pitch, but more often than not stopped the ball with his bat, the match again seemed closed down. Hammond made two lovely catches at second slip. They move him when the ball is doing anything from first to second slip, and, placed there, he advances nearer and nearer to the batsman. The fielding of Hammond in that particular position was the best thing seen in the match. There was then just an outside chance, with five wickets down for 118 runs at 4 o'clock, but Constantine pranced down the wicket, a most imposing notice was paraded round the ground to say that the cricketers were to be allowed to catch an early train, and so another Test Match came to an end.

> WEST INDIES 375 (G. A. Headley 169 not out, I. Barrow 105; Clark 4 for 99) and 225 (C. A. Roach 64, L. N. Constantine 64; Langridge 7 for 56)
> ENGLAND 374 (D. R. Jardine 127, R. W. V. Robins 55, Ames 47, C. F. Walters 46; E. A. Martindale 5 for 73)
> *Match drawn*

Two Bank Holidays

Hobbs Then and Now

FROM A CORRESPONDENT [ALAN PITT ROBBINS]

8 *August* 1933. One passed through the turnstiles of the Oval yesterday morning with curiously mixed feelings. A perfect August day, a typical Surrey crowd, and the possibility of a century by Hobbs – what more could one ask for? But all the time there was the memory of another August Bank Holiday, another crowd of 15,000 spectators, and another notable innings by the Surrey hero. That was the last county cricket that many of the spectators saw for five years. By midnight on the following day England was at war and in a few days the Oval was in the position of the military authorities.

Nineteen years have passed since that day, and yet in many respects the scene at the Oval seemed scarcely to have changed. There have been minor modifications of the view from the roof of the Pavilion. The gas-holders are in the foreground as of old, but on the skyline Big Ben is in its steel splints and the roofs of the new buildings at Millbank have made for a brighter London. In the Pavilion there are the same portraits and other reminders of the great figures of the past, but there is now a War Memorial to those members of the Surrey Club who made the supreme sacrifice. Around the ground the spectators do not seem to have changed at all, and even in the two contending teams there are some who took part in the match which began on August Bank Holiday, 1914.

In 1914 Hobbs accompanied Tom Hayward to the crease to open the Surrey innings; with Sandham as the junior partner he performed the same duty yesterday. Mr. Fender and Mr. Carr are still in their respective teams after 19 years and in 1933 as in 1914 the familiar names of Gunn and Hardstaff appear in the Nottingham eleven, but the players belong to a different generation. But there comparison ends. Of the giants who helped Surrey to win the championship in 1914, Strudwick now wields the scorer's pencil; Hitch has donned the umpire's white coat; E. C. Kirk, like Whysall, of Nottingham, lives only in the hearts of those who love cricket whether it is played on the county ground or the village green.

It was a glorious day's cricket on August Bank Holiday in 1914. The match began on the Monday, not on Saturday, as at present, and Hobbs obliged the crowd by making his highest score of the season, 226, in four hours and 20 minutes. "Wisden" records that in his innings he used almost every stroke in the batsman's collection. Yesterday he was more sedate, but there was the same artistry, the same ability to make good bowling look commonplace when Surrey were in a tight corner; and yesterday he once more obliged with a century, the 196th of his illustrious career, making 133 before being caught. In 1914 Surrey scored 472 for five before the close of play, but afterwards rain robbed them of any chance of victory.

At the same time a mile or two away Sir Edward Grey was telling the House of Commons of the course of events which had apparently made war inevitable. On the following day war was declared and many of those who had spent the Bank Holiday at the Oval were flocking to the Colours. Surrey played a few more matches, including two at Lord's, while the Oval was in military occupation, but the outcry against the continuation of county cricket was so great that at the end of August the committee unanimously cancelled the remaining fixtures. But to many hundreds of cricket lovers who spent the Bank Holiday at the Oval the flawless innings of Hobbs and the whole setting of the game provided a fragrant memory during the weary winter months of military training which followed.

The Heritage of Cricket

Mr. Jardine's Tribute to the Game

17 *August* 1933. Mr. D. R. Jardine was the principal guest at Foyle's Literary Luncheon, held at Grosvenor House yesterday. Sir John Squire presided over a large gathering.

In welcoming Mr. Jardine SIR JOHN SQUIRE said that they had heard all about him recently. He was the "Monster from the Antipodes," "Douglas the Killer, who tells his men to go out and shoot the balls straight at their heads and don't care twopence about cricket." He fully bore out his reputation as the cave man. (Laughter.)

MR. JARDINE said that cricket was the peculiar heritage of this country. In the world as it might be in the future it seemed that there was going to be perhaps more leisure for a lot of people than was the case hitherto. He did not know whether that was because of the march of science or the displacement of human beings by machinery. Ever since the earliest Greek civilization the test of culture had been the ability to make good use of one's leisure.

It was important that the way in which the future world might spend some of its leisure should be written about, and that some of the romance of any sport, if it had romance, should be brought out. So many of the people who wrote about cricket to-day could write exceedingly well about the green grass and the conversation in the crowd. What was needed was some genius who could draw an accurate picture of Australian barrackers in full cry, who could bring out the best that was in a game which made its appeal in literature, which had a future, he hoped, and had a past.

The game of cricket had a great history, and it was one of the few of our sports left which had not to date been speeded up. He said that with due deference to the pace of the English bowling. He had, however, been told that cricket did not produce the thrills of dog racing or dirt-track racing. The only worthy definition of cricket he knew was that given by a New Zealander, as follows: "That beautiful, beautiful game that is battle and service and sport and art."

Mr. H. D. G. LEVESON-GOWER proposed "Literature and Cricket," and said the one could not be separated from the other.

Mr. ALEC WAUGH, responding, said that the literature in relation to cricket was small in comparison with the literature that had been inspired by other branches of sport. But, small though it was, it was lovingly cherished by its admirers. The literature of cricket had for the most part, in fact almost entirely, not been contributed by professional writers. Speaking as a writer of fiction, he would say that the great difficult in regard to writing about cricket was the absence of what was called an obviously romantic interest. He did not know if any young woman had ever been proposed to on a cricket-ground, but he could imagine that many girls had broken off their engagements because they had been dragged round to watch cricket matches. The real literature about cricket was written by cricketers; that was, by people who had been moved to write on a subject that they really understood.

Over

11 *October* 1933, *Leading Article*. The dispute over cricket between England and Australia must be held to have stirred public feeling more widely than any of those inter-Imperial controversies that come before the Judicial Committee of the Privy Council. If the questions raised in the sphere of law are probably more complex, that which has perplexed the lovers of sport has certainly been more delicate and more embarrassing to social relations. To LORD HAILSHAM and his colleagues, therefore, the thanks of all English cricketers are due in generous measure for their patient and tactful diplo-

macy, which, having evoked a worthy response at the other end of the cable-line, has now ended a situation that none could contemplate without distatste. For, however confident of the rightness of his cause, no man can rid himself of the uneasy feeling that there is always something ridiculous, and generally something discreditable, in quarrelling about a game. The quarrel is now over, and, it is to be hoped, will be quickly forgotten.

The terms of settlement are such as to leave no sore feeling on either side. There is not complete agreement upon the question of "body-line" bowling – a term that, since it does not occur in the final Australian message, we may hope is now used for the last time. But it is legitimate to say that on the points that matter the agreement is complete, and that those which still divide opinion have ceased to matter. The Australian Board of Control maintain, as they have maintained throughout, that such bowling as amounts to a direct attack upon the batsman is against the spirit of the game. The M.C.C. agree, as they have agreed throughout. Leg-theory bowling of the long-established type is agreed to be perfectly legitimate. These principles govern the proceedings of both English and Australian bowlers in the future. Whether the particular form of attack adopted by MR. JARDINE's bowlers in Australia falls under the first category or the second is a question of fact, relating only to the past. The disputants can safely retain their own opinions, while refraining, according to the spirit of the new agreement, from obtruding those opinions violently upon one another. There remains the question of tactics for next summer's matches. In this matter the M.C.C. rightly make no formal pledge which would either limit the freedom of the captain of 1934 or imply a censure on the captain of 1933. But they will not resent an intelligent reading between the lines. It is clear then that MR. JARDINE, who is once again leading a team on their behalf, retains their full confidence. On the other hand, the particular kind of fast leg bowling that has been the source of controversy is likely to be dropped. It will not be dropped because it is illegal; it will not even be dropped because it is against the spirit of the game. It will be dropped because it interferes with our Australian friends' enjoyment of cricket – and consequently with our own. That is a final reason, which goes deeper than any question of law or custom.

For the same reason it is gratifying to note that the Board of Control intends to make a corresponding concession to English preference. The free Australian spectator of cricket has been accustomed to claim a wide liberty of criticism, which knows few limits upon either its choice of language or the vocal intensity of its expression. Without wishing to deny the lawful rights of Australians, English cricketers have shown some dislike of the manner of their exercise; and the Board of Control have accordingly promised that they shall be controlled. No doubt Australians, in complying with the Board's desire, will laugh a little at English sensitiveness to barracking. They will perhaps be the readier to forgive us if we allow ourselves a smile at their denunciations of LARWOOD's bowling. It will do no harm if the two parties, in a friendly way, laugh at one another. It is the first step towards laughing at themselves. That desirable consummation may be looked for long before next year's Australian team have completed their very welcome tour.

The Foundling Site

Batting Demonstration by Hobbs

10 *April* 1934. Since the London elementary schools will re-open to-day, the holiday play centre on the Foundling Site "broke up" yesterday. For some hundreds of children on their Bloomsbury playground this last day of the Easter holidays was made memorable by the visit of Jack Hobbs.

Mr. Hobbs, in whites and pads, walked to the matting wicket which had been pitched for him, and for a time he demonstrated how to drive and cut, and glance to leg with an imaginary ball. Then certain boys were deputed to bowl to him, and the spectators watched him for half an hour, hitting beautifully and as hard as he might with safety in a small space.

The pavilion – a row of chairs parallel with the pitch – was occupied by officers and members of the Foundling Site Appeal Council and the friends and sympathizers to whom they were at home during the afternoon. The company included Lord Crewe, the president; Mr. Stuart Bevan, M.P., the chairman; Mrs. G. M. Trevelyan, honorary secretary; Mr. J. H. Leal, honorary treasurer; Professor G. M. Trevelyan, O.M.; Lord Hampden; Lord Rennell; Miss Dorothy Ward; and Mrs. Hobbs. The boys crowded close to the temporary fence which marked off the pitch.

Mr. Hobbs brought with him in his car 10 new cricket bats, a gift for the play centre. The bats will be awarded in the coming season to the boys whose performances on the Foundling Site are judged the best.

England Win in an Innings

Verity's Great Bowling

FROM OUR CRICKET CORRESPONDENT [R. B. VINCENT]

26 *June* 1934. England beat Australia in the second Test Match at Lord's yesterday by an innings and 38 runs, a remarkable result at 6 o'clock on the third day of the match, even if rain had fallen heavily during the week-end. The King, who watched the play in the morning, went on to the field at half-past 12, when the two teams were presented to him.

Obviously England had the luck of the game which came from winning the toss, but at no time yesterday did Australia have to bat on a wicket appreciably more difficult than that on which England was striving to save the game in the fourth innings at Trent Bridge. So far as these games have gone each side has had its opportunity, well and truly taken. No two opinions will agree on the exact state of the pitch at Lord's yesterday. It was inclined to pop in the morning; after an hour's play it became easier; and in the afternoon, playing appreciably faster, it took spin much more to the bowler's fancy. Certainly it was never anything approaching to a sticky wicket, and Verity, the great and undisputed hero of the match, had all the time to make the Australian batsmen believe that it was just a little more unkind than in fact it really was.

Helped as he was by a queer lack of confidence among the Australians, to whom the very sight of sawdust may suggest unknown horrors, Verity's achievement must be written down as one of the greatest in the whole story of Test Match cricket. In the first innings he took seven wickets for 61 runs in 36 overs, and in the second innings eight wickets for 43 runs in 22 overs. Only one bowler before has taken 15 wickets in a match between England and Australia, W. Rhodes at Melbourne in the tour of 1903-1904.

For the greater part of the day yesterday he bowled from the Pavilion end with three slips to the right-handed batsmen and three short-legs to Darling and Bromley, and during all this time one saw only one ball which was pitched not of the length he meant. Continually he made the batsman play to the ball, whether going with his arm, or coming back to offer a catch to Hammond at third slip and Hendren at silly mid-off. It was indeed a great bowling performance, a left-handed bowler taking just the slight chance that was offered him.

It may sound unkind to the Australians, and perhaps a trifle ungenerous to Verity, but, if the truth must be told, the batting was a little feeble. Woodfull in the second innings, by putting the whole of his body between the pitch of the ball and the stumps, did his noble utmost to keep one end intact, and Chipperfield played two gallant innings, but the Australians themselves would be the first to try to forget some of the meagre strokes that were offered. No one who saw it can ever forget the crude manner in which the great Bradman gave his wicket away when so much depended upon him. For all that, bad strokes or not, it was a great victory for England, and now all is again to be played for.

The match was continued in the morning, only after the players had taken up their position with the score at 192 for two wickets, and had ambled back to the Pavilion before a ball had been bowled because of bad light. Ten minutes and out they came again, with Bowes bowling from the Nursery end and Verity at the other. Bowes, it should be said, bowled well and ill in turns; when he was good he looked likely to take a wicket, more than once being able to bring the ball back up the hill. He had periods all through the match, however, when he became slower than medium and shorter than ordinary. Verity can always make the ball stand up, and it was therefore not surprising to see him pack the slips, with Hammond moved first from short to second, and then second to third slip. The first wicket fell when Brown, who had played so well on Saturday evening, waved his bat at a ball well outside the off-stump from Bowes, and was caught at the wicket, three wickets then being down for 203 runs.

Thoughts of a follow-on at once flew round the ground, and I must at once plead guilty having said during the Test Match at Nottingham that in a four-day match a side 200 runs behind could be sent in again. This law of cricket applies only to matches in Australia. We knew at this moment that it was only 150 runs, and we were encouraged to believe that even so England could do it when Darling, attempting a hook, was caught at backward short-leg, the score then being only 204 and 87 runs more wanted to save the follow-on. One run later McCabe was caught at second slip off Verity, the nastiest ball that Verity bowled all day, quick off the pitch and spinning away from leg to the off-stump.

When bowling to Bromley Verity looked for catches close in on the leg-side, but Bromley took four runs between the fieldsmen, and Geary, who seemed handicapped by a bad leg, came on in place of Bowes. With the score at 218 Bromley was out as Verity had intended he should be, caught at short-leg off a ball which jumped up a little. Oldfield, in the beginning of his innings, was lucky in playing the ball somehow and somewhere just clear of Verity's cluster of slips, and when he played out to the ball one could not help feeling that the deeper fieldsmen were just a few yards too deep, several strokes landing the ball first bounce into their hands. With a definite bite in the pitch R. E. S. Wyatt tried Leyland at the Nursery end, but his length was irregular, three full-pitches in two overs being unhelpful to the occasion. Just at this moment, when Oldfield by driving Leyland to the sight screen insisted on a deep fieldsman, there was an impression that England was a bowler short. Hammond, who next to Verity was the best of England's bowlers, had a spell from the Pavilion end and Verity was tried at the other.

Chipperfield had some awkward moments from Verity, but he was the most likely to hold out, once hitting Hammond straight to the boundary. Another spell of Geary meant little, and 40 runs had been added for the wicket before Oldfield, playing forward, was well caught, high up, at second slip. The threat of a follow-on was once more upon the Australians, and it was only delayed by Grimmett's streaking two 4's through the slips off Bowes before he was bowled. At the luncheon interval Australia, with only two wickets to fall, still wanted 18 more runs.

O'Reilly afterwards did his utmost to allow Chipperfield to make the runs, but at 284 he let loose at a well-pitched-up ball, missed it, and was bowled. Wall, without a run added, was leg-before-wicket, and so Australia followed on 156 runs behind.

The second innings was begun at a quarter to 3, Wyatt starting his bowling with Bowes, from the Nursery end, and K. Farnes, who was not very comfortable on an injured foot. England's captain knew when he sent Australia in again that he had only half a bowling side, but he no doubt felt that if wickets were to fall it were better that they were Australian wickets, and his trust in Verity was profound. Only 10 runs had been scored when Brown was caught on the leg side trying to hook Bowes, who, as in the first innings, had started well.

Woodfull's anxiety was shown when McCabe came in to bat next in place of Bradman, and it was not long before Wyatt showed the full force of his attack by putting Verity on at the Pavilion end with Hammond at the other to relieve a patently tiring Bowes. McCabe twice in one over from Verity was lucky to escape being caught in the slips, and Woodfull once put the edge of his bat at the last moment to a ball from Hammond which might have hit his middle stump, but which went for four runs.

Verity, even when bowling to McCabe, was now well on top, and the turn of the game came when McCabe drove a ball hard at Hendren at silly mid-off. The catch was held, and the bottom was knocked out of Australia's batting. Bradman, rather in the manner of the Bradman of 1930, played some workmanlike strokes until, with the score at 57, he suddenly perpetrated the worst stroke he has ever made in his life. He slashed, crooked bat, against the break to Verity, and, skying the ball, was caught by the wicket-keeper. Darling was all but bowled by the first ball he received from Verity, who by now was merely waiting for wickets, and at 94 the Australians suffered their final blow when Woodfull, playing back to a leg-break, was caught at extra slip. He had not made many impressive strokes, but so long as he was there Australia was alive.

Darling at 94 was bowled by Hammond, who most certainly had deserved a wicket, and one run later Verity took a good catch off his own bowling, high and to the right, to get rid of Bromley. Then the cheering broke out full-hearted, and the wickets fell accordingly. Oldfield, who might have been a nuisance, was leg-before-wicket; Grimmett, who also can be tiresome, was caught at third slip from the first ball he had; and Chipperfield, who had had a nasty blow from Hammond, was caught at first slip.

Verity was bowling to batsmen whom he knew he could get out, and the end came when Hendren, rolling on his back, caught Wall close in under his bat.

ENGLAND 440 (Ames 120, Leyland 109, C. F. Walters 82; T. W. Wall 4 for 108)
AUSTRALIA 284 (W. A. Brown 105; Verity 7 for 61) and 118 (W. M. Woodfull 43; Verity 8 for 43)
England won by an innings and 38 runs

Sevenoaks Vine Festival

The Game as it Was

FROM OUR SPECIAL CORRESPONDENT [DUDLEY CAREW]

23 *July* 1934. Looking back on the match and disregarding the motor-cars and the crowds dressed in clothes of 1934, the match that was played at Sevenoaks on Saturday was marvellous in its fidelity to the game and to the year 1734, when Sevenoaks Vine became a cricket club. The whole scene was an old print come miraculously to life, and those among us who have talked and written sentimentally of the charm of white figures moving on green grass suddenly realized what a lot we have lost since coloured small clothes and individual wigs gave way to flannel trousers and the formal cap.

So far as one by no means word perfect in the rules of the time could tell, the anachronisms were few and unimportant. Lord Sackville's XI. started off by bowling an over of "grubs" – then surely the orthodox, the only, ball – but afterwards both sides bowled their lobs to a length, and surely what we now know as a length was a distinctly later innovation. Then, too, there was the throwing. On coming to think of it, there seems no reason why the first man who ever threw a stone should not have thrown it much as Bradman throws in from the deep to-day, but, for all that, there was something not quite in harmony with the leisurely spirit of the times in the vigorous sprinting and throwing in full-pitch to the wicket-keeper indulged in by the members of both sides. It was undoubtedly cricket, but was it 1734?

However that may be, from first to last the match, and, indeed, the whole week was an unqualified success. The town all through the bi-centenary celebrations has been gay with flags, and half an hour before the match began the ground was a blaze of colour, with the scarlet uniforms of the band and the clothes of the Ladies of Quality showing up prominently. What a beautiful period for dress it was for women, every movement was formed and persuaded into grace and dignity. Just before 2.30 the Sackville coach arrived on the ground and was driven round to the cheers of a crowd which must have numbered neary 5,000. Major-General the Lord Sackville and Captain the Viscount Gage, who captained the Gentlemen of Kent and the Gentlemen of Sussex respectively, just as their ancestors captained them 200 years ago, then tossed and Lord Sackville (a non-playing captain) lost.

The wickets were pitched, the creases cut (1734 was innocent of white-wash), the scorers armed with tallies squatted on three-legged stools in what would now be the gully at one end and mid-on at the other; the umpires took up positions which must have made it extremely difficult to give any decision whatsoever, and the two strikers, C. L. Norman and Major R. P. Birchenough, strode out with their bats over their shoulders. All was as it should be and the match was duly begun. It was soon apparent that, curious as the bats were in shape, they had plenty of drive in them and that the placing of the field was a matter of extreme difficulty. A truly cunning bowler might, it is true, have bowled fast grubs outside the leg-stump and packed his leg-side field much as – but that is another, and less edifying, story. When Sir Waldron Smithers came in he quickly showed that he was going to have nothing to do with that stroke which is the natural birthright of small girls playing to indulgent brothers on tennis lawns. He proceeded to drive the ball hard and often and he looked like getting even more than his 33 when he was out to a brilliant caught-and-bowled. Eight Sussex wickets were down for 89, but the tail players seemed to have picked up a few hints from the failure of their predecessors and the final score was 123.

Kent, in the persons of G. D. Durtnall, who, incidentally, has had a successful week with the bat, and T. A. Grose, looked to have a more expert knowledge of the particular technique acquired, but, for all that, Birch-enough bowled both Grose and H. J. Taylor while the score was in its infancy, and Durtnall himself was caught and bowled after he had scored 21. S. G. Smith, however, pulled and drove ferociously, and, although he was out before tea, he had scored 45 out of the 88 runs on the board. The parade at tea suggested the Canterbury Week with a sprinkling of Old Stagers who had just been playing in a Congreve comedy.

Afterwards H. M. Sayers and T. W. Morgan went on batting steadily, and soon after 5 o'clock they gave Kent the victory by six wickets. The game did not end there, however, and nearly 200 runs were scored before the final ceremony of singing "Auld Lang Syne" brought a historic match and a historic bi-centenary to an end.

CAPTAIN THE VISCOUNT GAGE'S XI 123
MAJOR-GENERAL MCLEOD SACKVILLE'S XI 124 for 4 (S. G. Smith 45)
Sackville's XI won by 6 wickets

4
THE FOURTH HALF-CENTURY
1935 to 1985

In the wake of Bodyline the first half of this final era was comparatively tranquil, although by the late 1950s the game in England was in financial distress after the flush of post-war enthusiasm. By contrast, the last 20 years or so have been beset by revolution* and controversy, which have often dragged cricket off the sports pages on to the main news pages; the ending of the amateur-professional distinction; one-day and Sunday county and international cricket; the severing of links with South Africa and banning of English Test players; intimidatory bowling; the Packer invasion; and internecine rivalries in Yorkshire which have riven in twain the most famous cricketing county. To quote from a Letter to the Editor published in 1968: "We used to turn from the depressing political news to the cricket page for relief; now the cricket page is depressing and as political as any other." At least the chapter ends on an uplifting note, with, for the first time, two England batsmen scoring double hundreds in the same Test innings. In the context of this book their "Double Century" double could not have been better timed.

"Beau" Vincent continued as Cricket Correspondent during the early years, which are typified by the gaiety of the fourth leaders. Neville Cardus told a nice story involving Vincent, which gives some more flavour of those pre-war days; it concerns the England v. Australia match at Lord's in 1938, "the beginning of the typewriter efficiency epoch in cricket reporting". Vincent, sitting next to Cardus in the press box, searched his pockets (where he was also alleged to keep his dentures) in vain and asked his neighbour: "Got a pencil?" Cardus produced the stub of one and gave it to him. Cardus then conducted his own search, turned to his colleague and said: "Forgot to bring any copy paper. Got some?" Vincent tore several sheets from his pad and handed them over. Next morning the typewriters had produced numerous small paragraphs, but Vincent and Cardus had a column and a half each.

---

*A revolution in *The Times* – apart, of course, from the regular appearance of news on the front page from 3 May 1966 – was the abolition in July of the same year of a unique feature, a full cricket scoreboard throughout a match. Its replacement, to make more space, by a summary of previously completed innings and the full details only for an innings in progress on the immediate day's play, drew letters of protest, though not as many as the Sports Editor feared.

During MCC's tour of Australia in 1946–47 The Times *shared Cardus's Test match reports with* The Manchester Guardian; *for the next visit, in 1950–51,* The Times *decided to send its own man for the first time. Alas, Vincent, uncomfortable at travelling outside London to cover a Test match, broke down completely when he reached Australia and retired soon afterwards from his post. Raymond Robertson-Glasgow, known affectionately as "Crusoe" after an opponent had returned to the dressing room to tell the next man in that he was out "first ball from a chap named Robinson Crusoe", stood in as Special Correspondent for that tour and the following summer Geoffrey Green, already achieving distinction as* The Times's *Association Football Correspondent (not to mention a stint as Lawn Tennis Correspondent), doubled as Cricket Correspondent. When Green became Sports Editor, briefly, in 1954, a new Cricket Correspondent was recruited in John Woodcock, whose journalistic career had begun in 1950 as E. W. Swanton's assistant and film cameraman in Australia [vid. report 22 August 1951] and had continued with Test match coverage for* The Manchester Guardian. *Woodcock was appointed on 26 April 1954, at 27 the youngest of all* The Times *Cricket Correspondents, and to this day remains in office, his tenure already, by 10 years, greater than that of any of his predecessors. Widely respected in the cricket world and now the doyen of the press box, he has since 1981 followed in the footsteps of George H. West and Sydney H. Pardon by combining his post on* The Times *with the editorship of Wisden.*

Woodcock – the Sage of Longparish (his Hampshire home) he has been dubbed by a fellow Times *cricket writer, Alan Gibson – holds a particular distinction in the history of the paper: apart from contributing perhaps four million words to its columns he was the first specialist staff correspondent to be named above one of his articles. He had been sent at short notice to South Africa to cover a Test series against Australia and was to work for both* The Times *and its new bedfellow,* The Sunday Times. *The editor of the Sunday paper sought permission to use Woodcock's byline with his first dispatch for them, to be published on 22 January 1967.* The Times, *having kept the identity of its Cricket Correspondent secret – in its own columns at least – for so long, but having taken the momentous decision to name all Correspondents from 23 January, felt that it could not be "scooped". So, when Woodcock previewed the third Test match on 20 January, his mask of anonymity was duly removed. Named or innominate he has been, and remains, compulsive breakfast-time reading for myriad readers of* The Times.

New Player's Great Achievement

20 *May* 1935. A hitherto completely unknown cricketer, 20 years of age and making his first appearance in a first-class match, stole all the honours at Frome on Saturday. Somerset, after having six men out for 107 runs, finished with a total of 337 and followed up their advantage so well that they dis-

missed five Essex batsmen for 87 runs. Harold Gimblett, the young player in question had the unique distinction of scoring a century on his first appearance in a county match, which has been done only once before for Somerset, by B. L. Bisgood at Worcester in 1907.

Not only did Gimblett, who is an all-rounder from Watchet, in Somerset, score a 100, but he did it in the remarkable time of 63 minutes, and so is in the running for the Lawrence trophy awarded for the fastest 100. Against the well-varied and accurate Essex attack Somerset found themselves engaged in an uphill struggle, but Gimblett completely altered the aspect of the game. Showing what was, in the circumstances, amazing skill and resource, he made 50 in 28 minutes, reached three figures in 63 minutes, and altogether hit up 123 in 80 minutes. Gimblett did not give the slightest chance and hit three 6's and 17 4's. Judged upon this performance, Gimblett is a born cricketer and, as he bowls fast medium extremely well and is a smart fieldsman, it seems as if Somerset have made a real discovery. Andrews followed Gimblett's example and trounced the Essex bowlers. His 71, including three 6's and five 4's, in 50 minutes was a brilliant effort.

When Essex, with two hours left for play, went in to bat Wellard, keeping a fine length, caused a collapse. Only Rist, who plays football for Charlton Athletic, faced him with any confidence. He stayed for rather more than an hour and a half and his 41 included six 4's. Wellard, who got plenty of pace from the pitch, claimed five wickets for 36 runs and was helped by two fine slip catches by J. W. Lee.

SOMERSET 337 (Gimblett 123, Andrews 71, Lee, F. S. 41; Nichols 6 for 87)
ESSEX 141 (Rist 41; Wellard 5 for 66, Lee, J. W. 4 for 26) and 147 (Lee, J. W. 5 for 67)
Score after first day: Somerset 337, Essex 87 for 5
Somerset won by an innings and 49 runs

Lord's and Leather-Jackets

11 *July* 1935, *Leading Article*. In the second Test Match South Africa won the toss and the game. In the University Match Cambridge won the toss and the game. The conclusion is too obvious to be disputed. To win the toss at Lord's this summer is to win the game. The reason is not so easy to see as the fact. Creeping, materialistic minds will seek for physical causes; and some will hasten to an explanation which has been a blessed refuge to every side beaten at Lord's this summer. It is all the fault of the leather-jackets. Whereon other minds of the same order will reply that to talk of the larva of the daddy-longlegs or any other sort of long legs is a silly point; and that the dusting of Oxford's jacket had nothing to do with the leather-jackets, which had done the pitch little harm. While both sides are flatly contradicting each other, higher minds will tell them that, like the disputants in the old nursery poem

about the chameleon, they both are right and both are wrong. The toss and the leather-jackets won the match for Cambridge; but not by the dull, matter-of-fact method of making the bowling difficult. No! there are such things as *imponderabilia* – causes hidden from the materialist, but perceptible by the psychologist. Oxford men – even Brasenose men and cricketers – are notoriously sensitive, imaginative, psychic. The idea means more to them than the fact, the spirit than the matter. Legions of leather-jackets, a pitch of soft mud irregularly set with pointed flints, could not have put the very feeblest of the Oxford batsmen off his game, but that the dread of something underground puzzled the will. The idea of leather-jackets, the awful spectre of leather-jackets, the mental picture of their foul and hidden orgies, the ineluctable fate of having to bat twice after Cambridge on a wicket beneath which leather-jackets might still be teeming after their creepy-crawly kind – that was the doom that turned the Oxford hearts to ice, the Oxford knees to water, the Oxford bats to walking-sticks for graceful use between pavilion and wicket and back again.

Imagination, it is rumoured, is not hotly cultivated at Cambridge; but there is no knowing what PROFESSOR SIR ARTHUR QUILLER-COUCH may not have been up to, nor what effect the science of SIR JAMES JEANS and of PROFESSOR SIR ARTHUR EDDINGTON may not insidiously have worked upon the strict Cambridge ethos. And, unless the terror that now haunts the wicket at Lord's can be exorcised before next season, the University match may be reduced to the wearing of clean flannels and blues, and tossing up, and luncheon, and nothing more. The fear of the leather-jackets may not be real; but, like the young person of Deal, sensitive players hate the fear that they fancy they feel; and, as the complaint is one of suggestion, so must the remedy be. When leather-jackets, having ruined a lot of golf greens, were under discussion in this journal in 1932, it was recorded that leather-jackets were a favourite food of starlings. Lord's has leather-jackets; Trafalgar Square has starlings. If the leather-jackets will not go to Trafalgar Square (which is unlikely), the starlings must be taken to Lord's. They might be taken by aeroplane, as the winter-bound swallows were once taken South from Austria. Small boys might be forbidden to ask for autographs until they could prove that they had brought one or more starlings to Lord's. Some grandiose political scheme might include the organization of the unemployed into corps of beaters, to drive starlings up Regent Street and Portland Place (with the B.B.C. making records of the starlings' chatter and of the appropriate speech of a leading politician) into the Regent's Park, and so to Lord's; and flocks of starlings, collected overnight in cages, might be released each morning at the beginning of play. The thought of the presence of the avenging hosts would set at rest the imaginative terrors of sensitive cricketers; and the starling might be to Lord's what the goose was to the Capitol.

A Chat with Ranji

The Great Cricketer Remembers

BY J. B. BOOTH

26 *August* 1935. Test matches, whatever may be their virtues or their vices, have, besides a trick of making history, the effect of rousing Laudator Temporis Acti from his slumbers; and in present-day conditions the gentleman is too often more than a little peevish.

When he comes in with his old music, the note is sadly apt to be harsh. Perhaps it was always so, and from now and then having right on his side he has grown to consider himself infallible, and to hug himself joyfully at the thought that he has outlived the best of everything. In such a case, an occasional antidote has its merits. There is nothing new in this; 20 odd years ago the cricketing Laudator was much the same as he is to-day, and was all the better for the occasional antidote expertly administered.

Thoughts such as these sent me to an old diary, in which were scrawled notes of a talk with Prince Ranjitsinhji in 1912, when, one evening during the Scarborough festival, he chatted freely of the sportsmen of the past, and of changes in the cricket world. It was a cold, wet summer, and, fresh from India, the Jam Sahib shivered and dug his hands deep in his trouser pockets. Those same hands had not, however, lost their cunning, and more than once brought off the lightning catch that made their owner famous in the field. Age had told a little; the Prince was slower between wickets, but the great batsman was still there, and the panther-like spring at any fielding chance seemed as lithe as of old. Some of the Pavilionites, whose own chests had "slipped," professed to regret that the Jam was "putting it on," but most of the girth was amassed in the dressing-room. Feeling the cold intensely, each day he bought something fresh at the hosier's – an extra vest, another cholera belt, a woollen waistcoat – and had the cold lasted he certainly would not have been able to pass out of the dressing-room door.

Shrewd, modest, good-humoured, the Jam had strong views on the game he loved, and in that old diary I find some hastily written notes of his views and opinions as he expressed them one evening that week to a few friends. He didn't believe in "Test temperament"; in fact, jeered at it. "There's no such thing," he said contemptuously, "except amongst Pavilion cricketers." Then someone asked the obvious question. "Charles Fry is the best bat in the world at the moment," he declared roundly, "because he's the soundest. He can play on any wicket. That's the test. Some fellows are better on slow wickets, some on fast; they're all the same to Fry."

Then came the other obvious question. "On the whole, I'd call W. G. the greatest cricketer of all time. Not that he was a greater bat than half a dozen, at least, but because he was a pioneer. W. G. was the first of the great all-rounders. Look at the history of the game, from the old top-hat days, the days of Mynn, Carpenter, Pilch, and the rest. One, you read, was a back player; another depended on a forward game; another was a stonewaller; another a hitter. Each had a speciality he relied on. Grace could do anything, and, in spite of his weight, was a magnificent field, to say nothing of his bowling. If it hadn't been for the old man there would have been no Steel, Ulyett, Lohmann, Barnes, Hirst, Jackson and the others."

"How would you compare W. G. with Trumper?" someone asked.

"You can't compare the incomparable. Each at his best was incomparable. Trumper too, was a pioneer. Twenty years ago at Eton he'd never have got his colours, simply because his strokes were unorthodox. All reformers start as heretics. Look at what they had to say about Jessop."

As to the greatest bowler, he would not commit himself. In make and action, I remember, he seemed to think Tom Richardson the ideal fast bowling machine. "In spite of his pace, the naturalness and ease of his action took so little out of him that he could – and did – bowl unchanged for hours, with no diminution in pace, length and sting." The modern fast bowler – "modern" being the year 1912 – with a tendency to lose length and become exhausted after a dozen overs, the Jam Sahib seemed to regard a trifle contemptuously, as a sort of hothouse plant.

Taking things as a whole, the Prince roundly asserted that the general average of cricket had vastly improved in his own time. "When I began," he said, "there were only about a hundred really first-class players in the game. Now there are at least four times as many."

The Jam Sahib had one surprise for most of his little audience. "Of course, W. G. didn't have modern wickets to bat on," observed someone. "Grounds have improved enormously." And to our vast astonishment Ranji would not have it for a moment. "Don't you believe it!" he retorted. "Forty years ago there were some wickets every bit as good as the best we have to-day. W. G. told me that himself. Lord's, the Oval, the St. Lawrence ground at Canterbury and about half a dozen others were as good then as now."

Out of the recent past come these haphazard reflections of one who was, perhaps, the greatest batting reformer in the history of the game, the player of whom Andrew Lang wrote: "I cannot write an account of Ranji's batting, because I am not a really great poet."

A Few Words from Dr. Grace

Obiter Dicta of 1884

BY M. H. SPIELMANN

2 *September* 1935. While the memory of great cricketers of the past is being revived the record of a conversation which I had in 1884 with Dr. W. G. Grace may be welcome.

That was the year in which he was held to have surpassed his achievements for a long while before, and in which his performances against the Australian team in particular were so brilliant as completely to dispel the previous year's growing impression that "the Doctor was growing old and stale."

During the rather absurd match, as we thought it, of "Smokers v. Non-Smokers" (September 16, 1884) I was his guest in the pavilion at Lord's. Grace was a non-smoker, but he scoffed at the idea that anything was to be proved by the result of the match. "The rules of health for a cricketer," he said, "are merely the ordinary common-sense ones; moderation in all things, and above all plenty of rest. Tobacco moderately used certainly does no harm." At that moment Gunn, "far out in the country," made the catch which dismissed Stanley Christopherson. "It's the most wonderful catch I've ever seen in my life," commented Grace – and he was once more the elated and enthusiastic schoolboy who at the age of 18 had played for England v. Surrey and had carried his bat for 224.

"Are you as good now, do you consider, as you were then?" I asked. "My defence is as good," he replied, "but I can't punish the bowling as I used to do. Besides, as you get older you lose your activity and can't field so well. I shall play only for the county next season; and I shall take only three weeks' holiday. Cricket interferes with my practice; patients don't like an assistant, however good he is. I have a good practice which increases every winter when I am at home, and decreases every summer when I am in the cricket field. And it makes me wonder if I shall ever get to Harley Street." Cricket was in his blood, thanks to both his parents, as he explained: "My father was a very keen cricketer, and my mother, as you know, had a passion for the game and took great pride in her youngsters' play."

With a wonderful memory he began to detail some of his past performances and I put in a remark about his self-confidence. "Self-confidence?" he questioned. "I have never gone in to bat without my knees knocking together from nervousness throughout the first over!" (What an encouragement and consolation for the rest of us poor humble outsiders.)

"Spofforth says that you are far and away the best cricketer in England; and after you A. G. Steel. Do you agree?" "So I read," he replied, smiling. "A. G. is a grand all-round cricketer, and I would rather have him on my side than any other cricketer I know. You will always find," he went on, "plenty of good cricketers cropping up from time to time, and some years will bring more than others. . . . You will find that all counties have a run of success and then of bad luck. Look at Lancashire, which was at the top of the tree and is now worse than Gloucestershire. But we've got Painter, a new man." (Poor Painter. The Doctor could be very hectoring in the heat of the game, and as the professional let it be known "It's Painter here" and "Painter there" until he "sometimes wondered if he loved his Chief as much as he thought he really did." But as to his veneration he never had the slightest doubt.)

Grace maintained that the rules of cricket were good and sufficient, but needed to be made plainer for the umpires, who evidently did not always understand them! In support of this view he cited the case which at the time was being widely discussed. The middle stump had been bowled so as nearly to fall out of the ground, but owing to the outside stumps pinching the bails failed to fall. "If the stumps and bails had been properly made and pitched," said W. G., "the thing could not occur. But as it happened the umpire had to give his verdict, and tying himself to the word and not to the spirit of the rule he gave it not out. I should certainly have given it out."

For a moment he was silent. "Smokers v. Non-Smokers," he muttered and shrugged his shoulders. "What next, I wonder? What does it matter? – it's always cricket." "Remember," he added as a farewell, "the first essential in a good innings is to get safely through the first over. By then you ought to have played yourself in; it's the first over that settles you. Remember my knees: but that's between ourselves."

'Willow the King'

30 *April* 1936. To anyone who loves cricket with that strange, mystical love which makes a man regard the winter months as though they were so many traitors to a glorious and lovely cause, the closing days of April bring the indescribable thrill of the knowledge that summer and cricket are coming into their own again. Last night there was broadcast *Willow the King*, "a cricket miscellany with actors from the village green, the county ground, and even from Elysian Fields." The broadcast was written and arranged by Mr. Herbert Farjeon, and in verse, song, and prose does its best – and a very good best it is – to put into words the atmosphere of the game wherever it is played, whether in back gardens, in villages among club cricketers, or on the solemn, protected pitch of a Test Match.

The broadcast begins with the welcome note of the cuckoo and the sound of a roller, and then goes on to explore all those delightful avenues which lead into the heart of cricket. There is the pavilion gossip – "Do you remember C. S. T. Dash, good fast bowler?" and the erudite reply: "That wasn't C. S. T., that was C. S. D." – there are the stumbling exchanges of courtesies after the battle of the village green has been lost and won, and there is an impassioned appeal for the revision of the law that the juvenile player in the garden shall be out should he hit the ball over the wall. How, it was rightly demanded, can a small boy indulge his natural instincts and hit a full pitch on the leg-side for six and glory when the penalty is the surrender of his bat to the bowler? And why does not the M.C.C. get up a fund to pay all glaziers' bills incurred in the playing of good, spirited, and honest cricket? There follows a reading of Mr. Neville Cardus's record of that never-to-be-for- gotten Test Match at Old Trafford in 1902, when the unfortunate Tate at square-leg dropped Darling at a critical moment and was himself bowled when England needed only four runs for victory. This broadcast miscellany was a fitting prelude to the start of the first-class season this week.

Cheap Wickets at Lord's

FROM OUR CRICKET CORRESPONDENT [R. B. VINCENT]

29 *June* 1936. The bowling of Amar Singh, the batting of Leyland, and the wicketkeeping of both Duckworth and D. D. Hindlekar between them prevented the play during the first day of the Test Match at Lord's on Saturday from being anything but amiably futile. All-India, who were told to bat first on a wicket which might have been difficult if the sun had shone more strongly after Friday's rain, started well enough, but after the first wicket had fallen there was no reason or sense in their batting, and when England went in to answer a score of 147 with a total of 132 for seven wickets there was little to suggest that we were watching a game glorified by the name of Test Match.

The crowd thoroughly appreciated the quick fall of wickets, sickened as they have been on previous occasions by a glut of runs, but they must have known that they were wickets rather shabbily taken. G. O. Allen, captaining England for the first time, had a look on his face which declared that if he won the toss he would send All-India in to bat, the dropping of the unlucky Gover was a further indication of the purpose of the selectors, and even those who insist that W. G. Grace preferred emphatically to bat first whenever he had the chance had to admit that Allen was right.

It must be borne in mind, however, that this is not a single-innings match and that the value of Gover on the second day might be more valuable than that of Langridge on Saturday. The wicket actually was never difficult, and the strongest telescope in the world could not have discovered any exaggerated turn of the ball once it had touched ground. The telescope was not much wanted except when Amar Singh and Mohamed Nissar were bowling, for a more riotous display of full pitches and long hops can never before have been seen in a Test Match. Poor in quality the cricket may have been, but exciting also it was, for one never had an idea that swells such as these could get themselves out in such an amazing manner. . . .

> INDIA 147 (G. O. Allen 5 for 35) and 93 (G. O. Allen 5 for 43, Verity 4 for 17)
> ENGLAND 134 (Leyland 60; Amar Singh 6 for 35) and 108 for 1 (Gimblett 67 not out)
> Score after first day: India 147; England 132 for 7.
> *England won by 9 wickets*

Queen Willow

9 *September* 1936, *Leading Article*. There is "sweet English music" in the words men have used to praise the cricket-bat, the pliant, springy, glossy, sweet-sounding blade. With no inkling of its real nature they have honoured it as King Willow. With what now seems masculine cocksureness the poet sang:–

> "Willow the King is a monarch grand,
> Three in a row his courtiers stand."

For a century there has been no suspicion that King Willow could be a fraud, or that sex might enter into the matter. But presumption must now yield to truth and the world know that the true willow is a "she," that she is the bat's mother and no other. King Willow has been caught out; his offspring are suspect; they are not chips of the old block. For the experts say that the male willow is too often a hybrid and degenerate, who will wilt and warp in the battle with the ball. Now and then a male will pass the test of true willowhood; then he is a king among bats, a he-bat. But the traditions of cricket, it seems, have descended on the distaff side. Tardy honours must be paid to many scarred and bandaged and anointed "shes," Amazons of the game, who have stood up to fast balls, lashed at low ones, and stared the googly undaunted in the face. No longer, then, is "it" or "he" the bat's pronoun. No ill-advised personification this, as FOWLER might call it. "She" is the one and only word for a thing that has been found to be feminine.

Habit of course dies hard in a summer game, and the revelation has come late in the season, too late to affect the players and the counties whose exploits our Cricket Correspondent sums up this morning. But in Australia there will be cricket and a whole summer for controversy. Would it be too much to ask of a Test team that they should establish "Queen Willow" in the language before they reach Australia? Otherwise it must be left to the first match-winner who pats his bat lovingly and calls "her" a beauty. Or to the first batsman who comes runless from the wicket cursing the fickleness of feminine nature. After all, "she" will be no intruder; every cricketer with a fancy felt long ago that the manliness of cricket had been exaggerated. The ball, it is true, fierce, red, and glossy, is a masculine thing. But the soft soothing whites and greens of cricket have always shown a feminine touch.

Now that we know the truth about the willow, questions will be asked about the ash, the pine, and the yew. Have the oar and the cue, the racquet and the golf club a similar secret of sex? They too are often blamed for fickleness of form, and, what is more, women have used them as effectively as men. No one can say that of the cricket bat, which is sullen and timid in a woman's hand. The batmakers assert with some scorn that the racquet and the club have felt the cold hand of steel, that even though they might be female in origin they are no longer pure wood. For such hybrids, as for the late King Willow, the only word is "it." But the case of the cricket willow is beyond argument. Could there be a clearer claim on the well-known chivalry of cricketers than the cause of one who has served them gracefully, manfully, and anonymously? Let the Gentlemen of England close the season with a toast and the cry: "King Willow is dead. Long live the Queen!"

"Little" Cricket
The Stonyhurst Game

FROM A CORRESPONDENT [REV. HERBERT THORNTON]

12 *September* 1936. There cannot be more than a score or two of people now living who have taken part in a game of "Stonyhurst cricket" as it flourished under primitive conditions at the college rather more than 60 years ago. If I am not mistaken it went out of favour in 1873, and though spasmodic attempts to revive it occurred from time to time, it was never reinstated in its original glory, and for quite half a century has been extinct. But before all memory of it perishes it may be worth while to call attention to the way in which the peculiar features of that game seem to throw light upon the earlier stages of cricket proper. In many respects they show points of agreement with eighteenth-century records, and in particular with the pictures of that date, including those in Sir Jeremiah Colman's collection, which was not long since exhibited in the Tate Gallery.

At Stonyhurst the new form of cricket with the Marylebone laws was at first called "London cricket" to distinguish it from the indigenous variety. The Stonyhurst game was played upon the earthen surface of the playground the pitch being carefully rolled, whereas, of course, for the other a field was necessary. Consequently the older sport was not at once given up. Football ended with Shrovetide, and in my time Stonyhurst cricket came in very handy to fill the gap during March and April until the weather was dry and warm enough to pitch orthodox wickets on the turf.

There cannot be much doubt that in the course of the seventeenth century the English lads of good family who for the sake of religion were sent to be educated abroad at the Jesuit college of St. Omers took with them the games of football and cricket as they were accustomed to see them played at home. Cricket is likely to have become crystallized under conditions which, while allowing the essential features to be retained, inevitably introduced certain modifications. The game soon acquired definite rules, and when after a series of migrations the school, at the height of the French Revolution, was transferred in 1794 from the Netherlands to Stonyhurst, in Lancashire, the boys brought their old traditions with them. At St. Omers the English college lay within a walled city. It covered a good deal of ground, but the space for recreation must have been relatively cramped. Double-wicket cricket could not be thought of there, but by arranging a number of pitches side by side and all facing one way, as is often done at practice nets, several single-wicket games could be played simultaneously without much mutual interference. A grass surface was also out of the question, and, without turf, wickets which were destined to be continually knocked over could not be kept upright. Unfortunately we have no records concerning cricket at St. Omers, so that all this is conjectural, but we do know the conditions and rules which governed the game at Stonyhurst from 1794 down to 1873.

A wicket, of course, is a little gate or door, and anyone who studies the two uprights surmounted with a bail, as they are represented in some of the pictures of the Colman collection, will at once recognize that the term is not inappropriate. In 1744 the London rules determine the height of the uprights, still only two in number, as 22in. and the bail as 6in. in length. At Stonyhurst on a playground surface wickets could not be used, and they were replaced by stones hewn for the purpose. These had an iron ring let into the top to facilitate removal to a new position. The stones were 17in. high, 13in. wide, and 8in. thick at the bottom, though they were somewhat thinner at the upper end. This, I fancy, corresponded roughly with the objective which the bowlers in England had to aim at before the end of the seventeenth century. At Stonyhurst the batsman was out when the ball hit the stone. In the southern English game, down to 1744 and later, a bowler who sent a perfectly straight ball between the wickets without touching either them or the bail apparently gained nothing. The batsman, it seems, was not out unless the bail was disturbed; in fact the 1744 rules ordain expressly: "The Bail hanging on one Stump, though the Ball hit the Wicket, it's Not Out." It cannot have been very long, however, before the absurdity of penalizing the ball which went between the two stumps without hitting either attracted attention, and the matter was remedied by placing a third stump in the middle.

As for the bats, the Stonyhurst implement which we used in 1872 had many points of resemblance with those depicted in the earlier Colman pictures. There can be no doubt that the original weapon had no proper blade with square shoulders, though the lower end was thick and heavy. On the other hand, it was longer than those in present use and had a slight but very perceptible curve. The lower end of the Stonyhurst bat was a block of wood (alder?), roughly oval in shape, about 4½in. wide and 2in. thick, slightly curved, with the concavity on the striking side. This was spliced with strong twine to a round ash handle, the length of the whole being about 3ft. As will be readily understood, the whole driving power of the implement was near the bottom, and it was held, almost as one would hold a golf club, close to its upper end. The very make of the bat was sufficient to suggest the manner in which it was meant to be employed. All the bowling was underarm and along the ground; in fact, the bowling of sneaks was compulsory. A batsman could not be bowled out by a full pitch or even by a first bounce, unless he offered at it, and similarly a ball jerked or thrown was accounted an unfair ball. It was at the option of the striker to offer or not at any such delivery. But he was obliged to slog; he was not allowed to block or merely play the ball, and if he flagrantly offended against this rule he was out.

All these features of the Stonyhurst game seem quite in accord with the practice of the early eighteenth century, at any rate in single-wicket matches. The attitude of many of the bowlers in the pictures of that date suggests a very low ball. Moreover, the wickets were so low that not one modern length ball in 50 would hit them, however straight it might be. Meanwhile the batsman crouches watching intently to see if it will give a little hop, for then he rises to his full height and, certain of his stroke, with all the force of tense muscles sends it whizzing into the far distance. My clearest recollection of Stonyhurst cricket is of the satisfaction with which the batsman realized as the ball came hurtling along the ground that some little inequality in the surface had converted it into a long hop and that he had it for certain in his power to strike with all his force and send it where he liked.

The balls used for Stonyhurst cricket were of domestic manufacture. The inside was made by the boys themselves out of cork and worsted, wound very tightly into a sphere, and then immersed in boiling glue. For days while this was going on certain parts of the house reeked with the odour. The carcasses thus prepared, after being allowed to dry, were sent to the college shoemaker who enclosed them in two hemispheres of leather and stitched these together. This rough-and-ready method left a raised seam right round the ball, more or less like the rings of the planet Saturn. It was one of the rules of the game that the bowler should "bowl with the seam," and I think that the excrescence added a certain liveliness to the ball's movements. It travelled along the ground but not in continual contact with it, thus big hits became more possible, and that, after all, was the great interest. Speaking of cricket in the early eighteenth century Mr. Neville Cardus says with fine insight:–

> The batsman, therefore, concentrated on offence. He gave himself over entirely to a primitive appetite for honest clouting. Think of it – O ye Woodfulls and Watsons – in these pristine days of the summer game, no batsman gave much thought to defence. But this kind of cricket, happy-hearted though it probably was, can scarcely have been cricket at all. It seems to me to have mingled the crudest principles of skittles and golf. Cricket proper began with the length ball.

All this is fully in accord with the spirit which animated Stonyhurst cricket and "London cricket" respectively in the days when they were played, so to speak, side by side.

Making County Teams

BY P. G. H. FENDER

25 May 1937, *M.C.C. Number*. County cricket, in England, has always been a thing apart, by comparison with the cricket of any other country. To many players it has been the height of ambition, though a few, a very select few, have regarded it merely as a stepping-stone to the highest honour in the game, a place in England's Test side.

There is no doubt about the position of county cricket as a forcing house in the English game, for it offers to the individual player an opportunity for intensive practice of the game in competitive conditions, if he chooses so to regard his place in his county XI, and at the same time it offers him an almost day-to-day indulgence in one of the greatest pleasures possible to a cricketer, that of playing the game in good-class company to his heart's content.

County cricket is an end in itself to most players, and a most delightful one at that, and not one of those among us who have partaken of that joy in the game which it provides have failed to appreciate it on that basis, whether or not we have aspired to the greater heights.

It has been suggested that the big difference between a good club player and a good county player is nothing more than experience, and this, very probably, is as good a definition of that difference as it is possible to give. County cricket offers to those who have the time to devote to it an opportunity for playing the great game in such company, and with sufficient continuity, for it to be thought of as the "make and break" of the man as a cricketer.

A player who graduates from any other cricket into the county side meets something which he can seldom have encountered before, for even the intensity of a 'Varsity match only provides him with an opportunity of appreciating "atmosphere," while county cricket frequently, if not always, forces him to play in an atmosphere which is similar, while, in addition, he has to meet a greater degree of ability in the individual player, as well as in the matter of team work, than anything to be met in a University match.

County cricket takes the outstanding player from any other grade of the game, if he has the time to spare, and "produces" him, and he either keeps his place against other competitors for that place, or fails to do so. If he fails to do so it may be for one of two reasons, either that he has not the ability for the higher class in the game, or that he is slow to acclimatize himself to the new conditions as compared with those from which he came. If he makes good and holds his place in his county side he may either progress or merely join the main body of those who are of a certain standard of ability and can get no further, or he may be one of those who are slow to improve but well capable of holding their own. These latter seldom rise to the Test side.

For this reason county cricket is a most healthy and wholesome thing in the game, and something of great value no matter from which point of view it is regarded. It represents the high standard of the game in this country and maintains that standard, so far as it is possible to do so, by assiduous practice and the provision of opportunity for continuous practice and the gaining of experience. In England this latter is of paramount importance to the game because, in the conditions under which we play cricket, as opposed, for instance, to the Australian, the very first essential in a cricketer's make-up is versatility. The Australian makes his way along the high road of assiduous practice to perfection of stroke play on account of the constant nature of the wickets upon which he learns the rudiments of the game, whether in batting or bowling. He can always rely upon the ball doing the same thing, day in and day out, if it is delivered from the same height, and at the same speed, and pitched in the same place with the same spin. An Englishman cannot so rely, because, on account of the difference of climate and weather under which he has to study, he is likely to have to play upon several different wickets in the course of any one week.

The high road to greatness for an Australian is assiduous practice, for by that means he may achieve perfect stoke play, and after that the learning of versatility is easy by comparison with the reverse process. An Englishman has to learn versatility first, for otherwise he will not have sufficient opportunities to achieve perfection in his stroke play or in his technique. County cricket provides him with the chances to be assiduous in his practice and, providing that he can hold his place in his county side, the player can, if the ability is there, learn and progress.

There is another side, however, to county cricket, and that is what it does, through its nurseries, to improve the standard of play in the districts, and to train young men who otherwise might never be able to afford the luxury for the carrying on of the standard of cricket in the county.

Most, if not all, counties do what they can afford to train young men, especially those who are ultimately to become professionals, and it is only such organizations which provide the necessary influx of new blood into the game. The universities, in their especial categories, and the clubs in theirs, do a tremendous lot of the necessary pioneer work, but it is the counties which are the test and which, once the initial trials are justified and satisfactorily answered, take up the "higher education" of the embryo first-class cricketer.

It is true that some counties do more than others in this respect, but that is only natural, because such efforts are very largely governed by the financial position of the particular county. National cricket depends almost exclusively on the counties, while it is almost entirely through the county clubs that a club player may progress, so that the counties are really the mainspring of the game in the manner in which they provide the training ground for the advanced player on his way to the highest honours, and at the same time the facilities for cultivation of the club player.

In writing this it must not be thought that I in any way minimize the great value to the game which club cricket represents. Without club cricket there would be little, if any, cricket at all, but I do feel that without county cricket there would be a complete loss of standing among cricketing countries of the world, and that such a position would very soon lead to such a lowering of the standard of the game in this country as to be virtually the end of cricket as we know it. Some might say: "So much the better," and insinuate that the game would be the better for a return to those conditions under which the game first raised its head, but that is another point.

The game as it now is cannot get on without that which county cricket means to it – an enormous hive of intensive cultivation – the sudden withdrawal of which would mean the loss of the mainspring of the present-day game.

It is curious to note, however, that, in different parts of the country the method of preparing the material for the intensive cultivation of the counties varies quite a lot. In the South it is club cricket which provides and gives the initial training to the raw material, while in the North it is the leagues.

More often than not the clubs provide amateurs, and the league the professionals, but the very nature of the games played under the auspices of the one and the other also varies.

Club cricket, while as keen as one could wish, does not offer the same competitive opportunities to its players, and, mainly as a result, the player who comes from the league to county cricket is usually the more experienced of the two and more ready for the fiercer atmosphere of the higher grade. This is probably one of the main reasons why the North have, in the past, played such a very big part in the County Championship. The material which comes to Yorkshire and Lancashire, for example, is more "ready," and, as a result, learns more quickly and finds its new surroundings less strange.

Derbyshire, last year's champions, and Notts have a lot for which to be thankful to their local leagues, and I cannot help the feeling that the difference between the atmosphere of the clubs and the leagues is responsible for the greater consistency of the Northern sides by comparison with the Southern. Southern counties are frequently brilliant and rise to great heights, but it cannot be denied that the general form of the Northern counties is, on the whole, more consistent.

No matter how one may view the game of cricket in this country, however, one thing is certain, and that is that the game as a whole, in the eyes of the world, is viewed from the standpoint of the counties, and without the work which they do we should never be able to place a Test side in the field at all with any real hope of taking and keeping a high place in the world game.

On the Village Green

BY HUGH DE SELINCOURT

25 *May* 1937, *M.C.C. Number*. It is pleasant to notice the quickening effect of a great national occasion upon activities, however humble, throughout the country. A general rejoicing, unenforced, tips the scale naturally to the doing of what has been hitherto cautiously postponed or warily rejected.

The meeting of our cricket club in the library of the village hall bore ample witness to this spirit of derring-do. In Coronation Year – not to have a new coat of paint on the Pavilion! Absurd. Not to have water laid on – preposterous, in Coronation Year! And a small pipe extended to the square (at such trifling cost) so that in the event of a drought (we heard the perpetual rain falling outside and stamped in furious applause) – in the event of a drought (I repeat the word as the dauntless speaker repeated it) the pitch might be watered, the grass kept green, the turf in smiling, proper condition. There never was such a meeting. When enthusiasm simmered down a little from boiling point to more normal procedure the flame was turned up, relit as from fresh jets, by astute reference to his late Majesty's Playing Fields Fund, and to the 150th anniversay celebration of the great home of all cricket – "our own ground, gentlemen, being hardly less ancient; famed in story, though not named in Wisden."

There never was such a meeting. It was almost funny. It was almost frightening. The staider members were thankful that the whole meeting did not emerge *en bloc* to the ground, collecting cans of petrol on their jubilant way, apply a match to the tumbledown wooden shack that disgraced the name of pavilion, and, while they watched the glad blaze in the dark, damp Spring night, vote vociferously that a new pavilion should arise in stone glory like a Phoenix from the smouldering ashes of the old.

Much the same sort of thing, from what I hear, must surely have been happening all over the countryside. True, to our meeting came a new member, kept by years from playing cricket but whose devotion to cricket was fanned by years and made wise by years to bestir his energy for the best interests of the game. And what cards these great national celebrations put into his hand! The recalcitrant could not for once plume themselves on their policy of caution: could not fail, indeed, to appear something worse than foolish, something little better than unpatriotic. After conscientious attendance at a series of lectures in the village hall on the proper use of the gas mask – similar lectures in various languages to those being given at present all over the civilized world – it was so refreshing to be aware of our common humanity in terms that were not repulsive, that we may be excused, perhaps, for allowing enthusiasm to run high, almost to riot, in our midst. For love of country was at length being used, nor for enmity and destruction, but to spread happiness and to create.

With the glow of this meeting still warm, it seemed odd to remember how many sage heads have been sadly wagging, in bar parlours, in august club-rooms, in members' enclosures, and elsewhere, over the decline of cricket, which has been, I am told on good authority, at times even mentioned in the Press. Perhaps the fantastic changes that have overtaken all the conditions and circumstances of life in town and country – transforming the appearance of the countryside often beyond recognition, sweeping away like a high flood old barriers, old ways, old habits of mind – have induced this pessimistic outlook and forced from many a disturbed onlooker the lament that even cricket is not nowadays what it was. Last year's deplorable summer, with its cutting effect upon county finances, did not favour a rosy view. Allowance, too, must be made for the deep, concealed, yet aching sadness of men doomed by age to be lookers on merely at the game, when everything in them but their bodies – *hinc illae lacrimae*! – longs to be playing themselves.

But a man can only speak from his own experience. My own experience of village cricket ranges – with one big gap in it – over a period of 45 years, round and about the same stretch of country. I played as a boy for a village on the other side of the Downs to the village for which I have played for the last 17 seasons, and hope to play again this summer. And jolly as those early games were – driving to away matches all together in an old large two-horse brake, over crunchy roads that were roads – there can be no shadow of doubt that the whole standard of play, grounds, kit, and apparel has quite vastly im-proved. The correct public schoolboy – myself – who turned out, rather shy and stiff, possibly, became, as shy stiffness melted, the object of much witty good-humoured comment, 'im and 'is cricketin' fallals.

Bill Awker, a wiry old chap who opened the bowling for a neighbouring village, found him especially amusing. Bill scorned to be dressed up in pretties. He lurched out in huge hobnailed boots and corduroys to the wicket, took off his collar and tie, put them in the pocket of his jacket, which he removed, and handed to the umpire. Then he rolled up his sleeves, fitted his cutty behind his buckled belt, spat on his hands, took the ball from his trouser pocket, stepped two paces back, and crying out "Look out for this one, then," proceeded to deal the swiftest lob that skimmed like a frantic little wood gone crazy over the grassy pitch at a petrifying pace, a real authentic daisy-cutter, dead on the wicket. Bill gave his hands an extra rub when he observed my exquisitely accoutred approach to the wicket, and greeted my immediate discomfiture with a horrid shout of laughter. Out came his cutty, out came exuberant puffs. I could never play him then. I am sure I could not play him now. Well, old Bill has gone – rest his soul! – and many like him. I have not seen such bowling of late years (fortunately for my self-respect), and it is the man or boy not in full cricketing kit who is apt to rouse good-humoured comment now.

Gone, too, are those old stinging wooden weapons, known as bats, perfect for the slow safety of the dead bat game; we wield our lively Bradmans to some purpose, and our Surridges with Flexo handles, more anxious to test the bat's quality with drives hard and true than content to remain there, stopping ball after ball, a lifeless bit of wood in lifeless, though perhaps orthodox, hands. There is no time to wear the bowler down; he must be knocked irreverently off his length, if any game is to be won. A too slow side declared, leaving us an hour and a half in which to make the runs they had themselves taken three good hours to compile. We won comfortably with three minutes to spare. Their bowling was watched, mastered, and hit.

Grounds, like kit and apparel, have not only improved but have become more numerous. It is difficult to say what is and what is not a real village team. We are a village side, I suppose; yet I see on our fixture list for this season – not, it is true, without trepidation – matches arranged on county grounds (Hove, Horsham, and Worthing); with touring sides from London (a famous publishing house runs a team and is playing us – may we crush them!) as well as with Priory Park, Chichester, Littlehampton, and Steyning – not to mention East Preston, the village I played for as a boy. On every side, Thakeham, Ashington, Washington, Findon, Amberley, Watersfield, Pulborough, villages have their grounds and know the sides with whom they will get good games. Cricket is without any doubt whatsoever flourishing as it surely has never flourished before.

Changed conditions, with ease of transport and the growth in number and improvement of public grounds, may have adversely affected the delectable sociability of country-house cricket. There are certainly fewer private grounds; but they exist, though the games played on them may have changed their character a little. A new private ground for instance, has lately been made in this neighbourhood, where a club, known as The Triflers, composed largely of men from Cambridge, play their home games during vacation. I have unfortunately been prevented from visiting the ground, but I have played against them on other grounds, and I have never seen a keener fielding side. Really, to a man, they gave an example, a delight to watch, of how men in the field should conduct themselves, showing, indeed, an alert keenness which the usual amenities of country-house cricket, both at table and buffet, have been known to dull and damp, if not totally to extinguish.

Their keenness is not exceptional. This very April, inclement as it has mostly been, I have seen a mat placed on a lawn before a stump and bowlers doing that spade work of practice – finding their length, changing their pace with no change in delivery – for which no batsman is necessary; for which, in fact, a batsman is most definitely in the light.

The new zest for physical training which is spreading throughout the land is partly responsible for this willingness to undergo the spadework of practice. Men are beginning to learn into what good servants their bodies may be trained. Yet still the standard of bodily control among bowlers is deplorably low, as compared with the standard of bodily control common among executant musicians, though a bowler needs a twentieth part merely of the scale work to which a musician must submit.

"On his day, when he has found his length, So-and-so is without doubt a very fine bowler, whom it is a genuine pleasure to watch." Words to this effect I have seen written of a bowler in the very highest class of cricket. "On his day, when he hits the right note, there is no doubt that So-and-so is a very fine pianist, whom it is a pleasure to hear." It is merely the standard of bodily skill due to the spadework of practice among musicians and the complete lack of it among bowlers which makes the one sentence read like perfect sense and the other like arrant nonsense. A keen kid or two will come to realize the immense untapped possibilities waiting in intelligent bowling practice – the lithe conditions of body and power of control that may be developed by intelligent training – and soon will come an outcry for stumps to be lowered again.

All through April all over the countryside we have been oiling our bats, have been knocking ball on bat to hear the music, and eyeing still sodden grounds rather resentfully, trying not to think with too much envy of those lucky schoolboys already practising away at Lord's, and hoping that this Coronation year may be blessed all through the summer with Coronation weather, that our prowess with bat and ball throughout the season may be as memorable as the gallant meeting with which the season opened.

And now the season has opened: the first games have been played. Have high hopes been justified, or were they possibly set too high? The great question is being answered one way or another everywhere now; nor does the question mainly matter. What matters is that the games, win or lose, should be good games, well worth playing and having been played, well worthy of remembrance.

"How's That?"

The Umpire's Point of View

BY FRANK CHESTER

25 *May* 1937, *M.C.C. Number.* "I thought I knew all about cricket until I started umpiring," said a former England player to me once. "Then I found that I was only half an international."

The umpire sees quite a different side of the game from the player, though no man can make a good umpire unless he has had experience as a player in first-class cricket. Theory alone is not enough. Other necessary qualifications are sound health – for the physical and mental strain is greater than is commonly realized – and good eyesight and hearing. Special attention is given to these last points at the medical examination which the selected umpires have to undergo every year. They are chosen annually at a meeting of county cricket captains held in December. Reports signed by both captains at every match at which they have officiated during the past year are then brought forward and considered. Three adverse reports, provided both captains agree, involve dismissal, and there is always a waiting list of younger men ready to fill the vacant place.

About a month before the beginning of the season each of the selected umpires receives from the secretary of the M.C.C. his list of fixtures for the year, together with the M.C.C. Instructions to Umpires brought up to date. The compilation of the fixture list is an intricate business, for a man may not be appointed to umpire in a match if he was formerly qualified to play for one of the counties concerned. Distance has also to be taken into account, for no travelling expenses are allowed.

On the average we officiate in about twenty-two matches a year. In each of those matches the umpires always "lose the toss" except when it rains. They are the first to arrive on the field and the last to leave it. They get no rest except during the intervals – unlike the players, who may spend a whole day in the pavilion. They are standing, perhaps under a hot sun, and they are concentrating on cricket all the time. The strain is greatest in a Test Match. The atmosphere then is electric and the fate of the Ashes may rest on an umpire's decision.

One often hears it said that quick decision is among the qualifications of a good umpire; but I consider it unwise to make decisions too quickly, especially under the new l.-b.-w. rule. It is far better to take a second or two to think than to be rushed into a hasty decision by a smart appeal. An umpire cannot afford to make many mistakes. If a batsman makes a mistake it may be called "bad luck." When an umpire makes a mistake it is a "bad decision," and as such it is marked up against him. The most difficult decision to make, in my opinion, is on an appeal for a catch on the leg side when the ball is near the batsman's body and his bat, pads, and gloves are all tucked up together. Next to that comes a close "run out." The new l.-b.-w. rule has increased the umpire's difficulties considerably. Personally, I treat it in the same way as I did the snick rule. I give the batsman out only when he plays back. I do not consider that the new rule has improved off-side play. It has undoubtedly helped the bowler. Last summer many decisions were called for on the ground of bad light. This is always one of the most trying questions with which an umpire is faced – even worse than a wet wicket. We can do something to dry a wet wicket, but we cannot yet control the light, even to oblige the spectators.

I am sometimes asked how I count the balls in an over. I have used the same six pebbles for the purpose ever since I started umpiring sixteen years ago. I hold them in my hand and drop one into my pocket as each ball is delivered. Those pebbles have done duty now in thirty Test Matches.

I was young when I began as an umpire – so young that when I arrived at the ground for my first match at Northampton the gatekeeper asked if I was a player. When I said, "No, I am an umpire," he replied, "You've come to the wrong ground. This is a first-class match." He is still on duty there, and we enjoy a laugh over it whenever we meet again.

From the Scoring Box

BY H. STRUDWICK

25 *May* 1937, *M.C.C. Number.* Scoring in first-class matches is by no means the dull occupation that some people imagine; at times there is even plenty of excitement.

Each county has its own scorer, who goes round with the team. But although the two scorers at each county match are generally old county players the scoring box is neutral. Even a visitor to the box, if he begins to take sides, is politely told to keep quiet.

Some scorers give more details than others. There are score-books which have the spaces not only for the batting order but for times of going in and out for each batsman, and for the bowling analysis; others, besides all this, have places for the scorer to record the direction of the wind at the beginning of each day's play, the state of the weather, the chances missed, stating by which fielder and where he was fielding, and the state of the wicket. Although "weather dull" is usually a fairly safe description – at least, it was all last summer – it is not always easy to say what is the state of the wicket, and one sometimes wonders who will want to know that in 20 years' time. Again, when a player misses a very hard chance the scorer is often in doubt whether it was a possible catch or not.

The scorers see more of the game than any spectator, and should become good judges of a player, for we have to watch every ball bowled and to know every fieldsman and where he is fielding. Above all, we have to keep our eyes on the umpire, for he is dictator of every run that is recorded, and indicates how the runs shall be put down by a series of signs. . .

When the score-board goes wrong when a batsman has scored nearly 50 or 100 it always seems so much worse. If he is credited wrongly with runs and gets out before increasing his score the wrong total may be telegraphed all over England before it can be rectified. If a batsman comes in out of his turn, or a bowler is changed, and the wrong number is put up on the board even for a few seconds I get a ring from some impatient member through the office to ask if the board is right, though nearly every time I have rung up the score-board to call their attention to the mistake.

At the fall of each wicket we total up the score and the analysis to see if they balance. Then we send down the scores to the printers and answer any questions the representatives of the Press wish to ask. If it is a new man they want to know his life story. By this time the next batsman has taken his first ball.

Two examples will show the vital need for concentration. I was scoring in the Surrey trial match by myself last year. Someone opened the door behind me to ask a question. I turned round to answer him, and on looking back to the field of play I saw one of the batsmen leaving and Alan Peach pitching the ball in the air. I did not know how he was out, and though there were two men on the score-board they could not tell me. I had taken a chance and put down "caught Peach" before I received a 'phone message to say that the last man was out l.-b.-w. Again, in one of our Surrey trial games Geary was batting and Brooks keeping wicket. A ball was sent down and the wicket-keeper took it. I put down a dot in the book, and on looking up saw Geary walking away from his wicket. There had been no appeal either from the bowler or the wicket-keeper. I sent out to know what had happened. It appears that Geary had been lifting his back foot just as Brooks was returning the ball to the bowler. One of the fieldsmen had pointed this out to Brooks, so next time he did it Brooks went through the action of throwing the ball back, but did not loose the ball, and nipped off the bails. Geary was stumped, and I had missed Brooks's action by dropping my head to put down the dot.

I had an exciting time at the Oval in 1934 when Oxford University were playing Surrey. For some reason Oxford never have a scorer, and it is very difficult to score by oneself in those matches because members of the University team have so many pretty caps. A man you have noted in the morning as So-and-so, wearing such-and-such a cap, may be wearing a different one after lunch, and perhaps another after tea. I remember one scorer saying that he put down "a dirty pair of trousers" against one man; but he had changed them at lunch time.

In the Oxford v. Surrey match of 1934 Oxford declared, leaving Surrey 103 to win in less than an hour. Surrey got the runs for the loss of five wickets. They made a slow start, but the finish was very exciting. It was a severe test for the single-handed scorer, for as fast as one man was out there was another at the crease. There were four catches, and while I was trying to find out who took the catch, enter the fall of the wicket, and send it down to the printer, besides keeping the scores of the batsmen and the analysis and keeping my eye on the board, the next man was in.

The most difficult decision for the scorers to see is when a batsman plays at a ball which is very near his pads and the wicket-keeper takes the ball. It might be either l.-b.-w. or caught at the wicket. Both bowler and wicket-keeper appeal, and the appeal covers both a catch or l.-b.-w. The umpire gives the man out and leaves us to guess how he was out. When a wicket-keeper catches a man out and puts down the wicket with the batsman out of his ground both umpires may be giving the batsman out, but the catch stands. If a ball touches a batsman's leg and the wicket-keeper takes the ball and puts the wicket down and the man is out of his ground the right decision is "run out." I never agree with this decision.

Of all the good, bad, and indifferent score boxes I have worked in, I like my own at the Oval best. But the box at Lord's, I suppose, is best of all.

There the man who works the board sits at the end of the scorers' table. With a turn of a wheel rather like the steering-wheel of a motor-car he puts up the numbers almost before the run is completed. There is no worry for scorers at Lord's.

The most remarkable figures I have put down against a bowler were a hat trick and nine balls to one over to Parker, of Gloucestershire. I have recorded six 4's in one over to Peach against Warwickshire. Two successive overs off Iddon in the Rest of England v. The Champion County in 1928 were 0 6 2 4 4 6, 4 6 1 6 6 2.

The Times M.C.C. Number was a 24-page tabloid supplement to the issue of 25 May 1937, commemorating the 150th anniversary of the club. It was re-published as a book, price 1s. (5p), and subsequently reprinted because of an error in a picture caption (opposite page 48, where Storer had been incorrectly identified as Mr. G. R. Langdale in the Derbyshire championship-winning team of 1936).

Ye Batte and Balle

26 *May* 1937, *Leading Article.* By a melancholy coincidence, on the very day when *The Times* M.C.C. Number showed Broadhalfpenny Down through the genial eyes of SIR JOHN SQUIRE, news came of the threat to alter the Bat and Ball Inn, once the clubhouse of the Hambledon Club. Our Special Correspondent's account this morning may cause SIR JOHN to regret that, in shortening his quotation from JOHN NYREN, he left out one regular sixer of a phrase – "the immeasurable villainy of our vintners." In NYREN's day their offence (which he ascribes, in the Peacockian mode, to "the march of intellect") was trying to water the beer. Clearly JOHN NYREN and his amanuensis or collaborator, COWDEN CLARKE, were not afraid of the law of libel; but certain moderns are surely chafing at not being able to open their shoulders and hit out equally hard at the present successors of those im-measurably villainous ones. Every age has its tender spot. In the eighteenth century it was victuals and drink. If the twentieth century should but sip at the punch and the barleycorn gulped down by NYREN's "fine brawn-faced fellows" of Hampshire farmers it would soon be very sorry for itself and grateful for any immeasurably villainous reduction of the alcoholic content. The twentieth century's own tender spot is historical association. And that is what the proposal to alter the Bat and Ball inn has touched. The eighteenth century would have welcomed any alteration or destruction which allowed room for more people to drink more punch and barleycorn. The twentieth century drinks, by comparison, little barleycorn and less punch, and both much weaker than the Nyrenian brews; but touch the historic inn, and it is up in arms. And the protests have come not only from the "stage army," as

thwarted Vandals like to call it, the recurrent procession of National Trust, S.P.A.B., and C.P.R.E. The M.C.C. itself – no highbrow pack of aesthetes and sentimentalists – objects to the proposal; and so does the Petersfield Rural District Council.

The brewers wish to enlarge the Bat and Ball. That must mean either that they have, or that they hope to have, more custom than the inn can now conveniently satisfy. SIR JOHN SQUIRE writes of "an occasional slumbrous carter" as its only patron nowadays. But has acutest memories of Broad-halfpenny are of mid-winter; and another account, inspired at the season "when primroses are out at Hambledon," gives an impression of more activity:–

> Hither, as of old
> Come players for the game: moon follows moon,
> Still the same happy echoes fill the wold,
> Still from the down's deep wood the pigeons croon,
> About the old inn parlour village shoon
> (Ale-fragrant still the air) go clattering,
> And gardeners bowl and blacksmiths catches fling,
> And bat from ball cracks music.

If MR. ERIC PARKER is right, the brewers' need for more space may be a present need. If SIR JOHN SQUIRE is right, it may be a need that will be created by the provision of the supply. If, that is, the motorist and the cyclist and the hiker learn that at the Bat and Ball – a historic inn in a spot of singular beauty, alongside the cradle of (modern) cricket and rich in associations and relics – there is what the roadside notices ambiguously call "accommodation" (whether it includes a swimming-pool and a ballroom or only means comfortable chairs and a cocktail bar), then those pilgrims in search of natural beauty and historic interest, of the quaint, the old-world and the truly rural, will make their way thither and reward the brewers' expenditure. In either case, be the demand a fact or a prophecy, it would surely be wise to leave unaltered the parlour, the one public room, which was the Hambledon men's clubroom.

Ladies at the Oval

Lessons for Men Players

FROM OUR CRICKET CORRESPONDENT [R. B. VINCENT]

12 *July* 1937. The third and deciding Test Match between the ladies of England and Australia was begun at the Oval on Saturday, and at the close of play Australia had scored 201 runs for the loss of eight wickets.

Those who had not before been privileged to watch a cricket match between two teams of ladies of the highest class – and I admit that I had never attended such a ceremony – must have left the ground amazed at what they had seen. The normal spectator no doubt approached the ground with the impression that he would be granted no more than a curious experience of ladies attempting to achieve something beyond their physical power. What he did see was a game played with technical efficiency, liveliness, and enthusiasm, which made the thought of a county match seem humdrum. In every respect, in bowling, batting, and fielding alike, there was a lesson to be learned by men who relatively potter about at their game. Strokes were made, gallant and fluent strokes, which gathered pace as they reached the farthest end of the Oval; the bowling remained tidy until the last over of the day; and the fielding was brilliant. I had been falsely told that ladies could not throw. I hope those who had formed that idea were present on Saturday to see a lady fling the ball back from Sandham's particular corner near the gasometer, bang, full pitch into the wicket-keeper's hands.

If one may for one moment criticize what in other respects was a wonderful display it would be to say that the backing-up was a little haphazard with just too much leaping about to save overthrows. As to the placing of the field only those who thoroughly understand ladies' cricket are entitled to speak, but it did seem that at times it was a little widespread, although there was some great work done close in on both sides of the wicket, and, joy of joys, there was a lady standing at the good old-fashioned position which used to be called "point."

Australia began their innings with Miss P. Holmes and Mrs. M. Peden, both of New South Wales, to the bowling of Miss Belton and Miss Maclagan. Miss Belton, who managed to bring the ball back from the Vauxhall end, bowled at a pace sufficiently fast for the wicket-keeper, Miss Snowball, to stand back. And here a word of praise for Miss Snowball, who throughout the day took the ball cleanly and with ease, even when it had to be done with one hand on the leg-side. Miss Belton all but bowled Mrs. Peden with the first ball of the match, and Mrs. Peden having survived that discomfort went on to play an innings which consisted mainly of short-armed prods. She was clearly the Woodfull of the side. Miss Maclagan tossed the ball well up, with some variation of flight which was certainly deceiving. Miss Holmes, who has a noble stance at the wicket, with her left shoulder pointing down the pitch, played beautiful strokes from the moment that she was in. They were strokes made with a free uplift of the bat and a beautiful follow-through. She drove one ball to the off from Miss Belton which counted 3, all run, and then swept Miss Maclagan away to the square-leg boundary.

Miss Whelan came on at Miss Belton's end when 19 runs had been scored, followed by a quarter of an hour's hiatus while rain was falling. When they came out again Mrs. Davis bowled from the Pavilion end, and nothing in the day was better worth the watching. She bowls left-handed with the body arched and that free swing of the arm which reminds one of Rhodes or Blythe. High praise it may sound, but it is true, for hers is indeed a perfect action. She just had time to get Mrs. Peden out with a ball of exact length before a deluge of rain fell. In a quarter of an hour there were vast pools of water lying on the ground, and there were grave fears that never a ball would be bowled again all day.

Ladies, however, have their own ideas about the conditions in which cricket can be played. So soon as the rain stopped, and it had been falling then for two hours, the captains and umpires dragged out the groundsman and told him, no doubt quite plainly, that they wanted to get on with the match. So out they went again soon after 3 o'clock with every chance of the ladies who were fielding in the deep slipping up and being drowned.

The pitch was then playing dead easy. Mrs. Davis continued to bowl from the Pavilion end, steadily enough, but she could not make sufficient haste off the pitch to beat either Miss Holmes or Miss Pritchard. The batting of these two ladies was entirely delightful. Miss Holmes made her strokes with the left leg flung down the pitch; Miss Pritchard, who is a busy batswoman, was more inclined to jump down the pitch. Together they took the score to 84 before Miss Pritchard, who had made some grand drives to the off, was bowled by England's captain. Miss Antonio is another batswoman who looks for runs; on this occasion she was, maybe, a little greedy, for she had some narrow squeaks when nibbling at the ball just outside the off stump. In the end she fell that way.

Miss Holmes having done most of the scoring during their partnership reached her 50 with a sweep to leg which sent the ball with a crash against the boundary boarding. There followed a period of shockingly bad light, but if it had been pitch dark these ladies would have insisted on playing. Miss George clouted the ball on the off-side, while Miss Holmes both in attack and defence played with an absolutely straight bat. If a treatise on ladies' cricket is written, it well might include illustrations of the methods of Miss Holmes. The score was mounting hopefully for Australia when Miss George was out to a well-judged catch at deep-square leg and then England came in to their own, thanks to the bowling of Mrs. Davis. She bowled Miss Smith, had Miss Holmes leg-before-wicket to a twiddler, and then held a miraculous catch off her own bowling, high and wide to the left, to send back Miss McLarty.

By way of variation Miss Taylor came on to bowl round the wicket from the Vauxhall end, well enough to get Miss Walsh out. But Miss Hudson and Miss Flaherty refused to give Mrs. Davis, who in her second spell had taken four wickets very cheaply, any more encouragement. Australia certainly had shown some signs of wobbling in the middle of the innings, but theirs is a fine score which will want some passing.

AUSTRALIA 207 for 9 dec (P. Holmes 70; J. Davis 5 for 31) and 224 (H. Pritchard 66, K. Smith 45)
ENGLAND 308 for 9 dec (E. Snowball 99, M. Hide 64) and 9 for 3
Score after first day: Australia 201 for 8
Match drawn

E. A. McDonald

FROM OUR CRICKET CORRESPONDENT [R. B. VINCENT]

23 *July* 1937. The death of E. A. McDonald, who was killed in a motor accident near Bolton yesterday morning, will be mourned all the world over where cricket is played. His career was short – all too short – in first-class cricket, but during that time he had established himself as one of the greatest fast bowlers of all time. No man in so brief a period can have achieved such great things or have granted such pleasure as he did.

The great men of this, or even of a previous, generation who bowled habitually and successfully at more than a fast-medium pace are few in number, McDonald was one of them. The horrors which England suffered in the summer of 1921, when Armstrong's team conquered the best that an after-War England could offer, was attributed to a great extent to the combination of Gregory and McDonald, and of the two, with all due respect, I believe McDonald to have been the greater match-winner. Gregory was fiercely, ferociously fast; McDonald was the more restrained, the more accurate, and the more dependable. He had above all the ability, such as Lockwood had, to bowl at his full pace when the wicket was slow, and sawdust was poured into the foot-holes. He was a bowler – and a man – of moods.

It was said by the ungenerous cricketer that he bowled short to intimidate the batsman. That I am sure he would never have done. He said to me once on the Aigburth ground that if the batsman walked away from his wicket the ball had a habit of following the batsman. A fairer comment could not be made, for above all he was a fast bowler. Whatever his record may be, of his technique there can be no question.

Once there was shown in a cinematograph exhibition a slow-motion picture of McDonald which well might have been distributed to every club and every school. The slow, almost lazy, arrival from the take-off of his run, like an animal which peeps its head from rushes; the gradual acceleration of pace; and then, with the left shoulder full to the bowler's bat, an action which was perfect and joyous to watch.

McDonald was born in Tasmania in 1892, and having gone to Melbourne worked his way through various forms of cricket until he came to be recognized as a fast bowler. Before he came to England he had played in three Test Matches against J. W. H. T. Douglas's team in the winter of 1920. During that season of Test Matches he took six English wickets at a cost of 65 runs. He then came to England with Armstrong's side, and in those Test Matches took 27 wickets with an analysis of 24.

Then came his association with Lancashire in 1924. In the season of 1925 he took 205 wickets in all matches, and later relapsed to League cricket. His record, whether it be for Australia, for Lancashire, or in League cricket can never explain the bowler that he was. Those that saw him bowl will never forget.

Underhand Bowling

A Lost Art

FROM A CORRESPONDENT

28 *August* 1937. So far as I can ascertain not a single over of underhand bowling has been seen in county cricket this season. Two county captains of my acquaintance say they would willingly make use of it in an emergency – *e.g.*, when two stodgy batsmen have dug themselves in – but they have nobody in their sides with any practical knowledge of it. If an expert were available one of them admitted, the attitude of the crowd would have to be considered. His appearance as a bowler would be greeted with derisive laughter – for the average spectator thinks the "lob" is as absurd as its name, and a childish device for giving easy runs to the enemy. For this and other reasons under-hand bowling seems to be extinct in first-class cricket just as in first-class baseball the underhand pitcher has been finally extinguished, though he could jerk very nearly as his modern successors can throw and had a command of the curves.

In club cricket also the "lobster" (apt fishy facetiousness!) is despised, and some years have elapsed since I saw him plying his craft for a suburban eleven of good standing. He then took four wickets at a reasonable cost. Afterwards he told me that he had been equally successful on a Sussex green, and that his captain had privately apologized to each of his victims for subjecting him to an ordeal suspected to be unsportsmanlike. As you descend through the lower circles of cricket you find the schoolboy's aversion from "sneaks" re-appearing as a grown-up obsession.

The writer's qualifications for advocating a revival of this lost art must be briefly stated. He has studied it ever since he was at his "Prep.," and in the course of an obscure career has taken over 1,500 wickets. He never bowled in a county match, but has beguiled a number of county batsmen into getting themselves out. In his young days, he enjoyed much country-house cricket, and Alfred Lyttelton would introduce him as "a rare monster, a *left-hand* lob-bowler." And his friend in later years, Arthur Croome, Master of Games, thought he could at times produce some nasty stuff.

Despite the brilliant example of G. Simpson-Hayward, who went on first for "Fostershire" and would take his 100 wickets in county matches season after season, he is not so foolish as to believe that underhand bowling can ever again be made the main part of an attack. The batsman gets a much quicker sight of it than of the deliveries of a bowler whose "hand brushes his ear," as the saying is. The underhand bowler cannot flight the ball as could

Rhodes, who made it wander in the air like a lost soul. Though fast-medium pace can be secured (as it was by D. L. A. Jephson), only a jerk is able to make it really fast – and that is illegal, being an underhand throw. [Such bowlers have been known to profit in this matter by the forgetfulness of umpires.] But accuracy and varied spin are more easily attained than by the overhand bowler.

The higher the action, the more effective the delivery must be. Nyren says of the majestical David Harris: "He would bring the ball from under the arm by a twist, and nearly as high as his armpit, and with this action *push*, as it were, from him. How it was that the balls acquired the velocity they did by this mode of delivery I could never comprehend." The writer once saw a village bowler who had this Harrisian knack; though slow through the air, he was fast off the pitch, and had to be carefully watched.

But it is the psychological factor – *unusualness* – which would make under-hand bowling dangerous in these days. Meeting it perhaps for the first time even a first-rate batsman might become too cautious or too ready to take risks. More often than not he would expect, and be expected by the crowd, to set the figures flickering on the score-board. That is why bad lobs can be strangely effective. The classic instance is of course Alfred Lyttelton's four wickets for 19 against Australia. W. G., the English captain, said his lobs were very bad, when he ordered him back into his wicket-keeping gloves and pads, and an eye-witness told me some were "like a snail," and one bounced three times. . . . Perhaps enough has now been said to justify this plea for the revival of a venerable, if unvenerated, art of cricket.

Maurice Tate

FROM OUR CRICKET CORRESPONDENT [R. B. VINCENT]

21 *October* 1937. Cricket this last season saw the passing of two great players in Hendren and Sandham, and now comes the news that Tate will no longer be the pride of Sussex. Pride he has been, an honour richly deserved, not only on the Hove ground but also away in the North of England; greeted and recognized as one of the greatest cricketers of his generation.

The son of an illustrious father, who bowled his heart out when Sussex claimed the greatest batsmen of the time but had small answer when the other side went in, Maurice, too, had to work uncommon hard for his county, and also for his country. England in slender years sorely lacked the length bowler; Geary there was – Larwood was not allowed because he bowled too fast and too straight – and in these years since a new cricket was born after the War Tate was the model bowler, the successor to J. T. Hearne. He had not quite the fire, the versatility of Barnes, but he was on all occasions a "bowler." Some say he was inclined to bowl just a shade short of a length;

those who kept wicket to him could tell how fast the ball came into their hands. His technique was perhaps surpassed by the cheerful complexion he gave to the game. His was essentially a jolly game of cricket. He first played for Sussex in 1912, when he was only 17 years old.

The War followed, and he was not the great man we knew him until 1924, when he and his captain, A. E. R. Gilligan, bowled South Africa out at Birmingham for 30 runs – the smallest total ever recorded in a Test Match in this country. He then went to Australia to establish a record which still stands, taking 38 wickets during the series of Test Matches. From this time onward he established a record unsurpassed in this country. In eight successive seasons he made 1,000 runs and took 100 wickets, and on three occasions, in 1923-24-25, he took more than 200 wickets in a season. He has taken more wickets than ever any Sussex bowler has done before, and will be remembered wherever cricket is played long after his retirement.

The Game's the Thing

28 *May* 1938, *Leading Article.* DON BRADMAN became once more the hero of the piece – or should we say of the play? – when he established a double record yesterday by scoring a thousand runs before the end of May for the second time in his career, and scoring the thousandth on an earlier date than anybody before him. To be sure he was almost beaten in this respect by EDRICH, of Middlesex, who got to within nineteen of it some days ago; and WALTER HAMMOND has still a few days in which to equal the feat of making his May thousand for the second time in his career. The Gloucestershire batsman did it before in 1927, and the Australian captain did it on his first appearance in this country in 1930. Curiously enough, BRADMAN then completed the thousand at Southampton in the match against Hampshire, just as he did yesterday.

He is a truly great batsman, and a great captain, in spite of that pardonable lapse at the Oval the other day, about which scores of letters continue to reach this office. Hardly any of them, it must be admitted, have so far been in MR. BRADMAN's favour – except indeed our own Cricket Correspondent's, who thinks that the Oval crowd treated him scurvily. The Australian side had scored 528 (the captain's own innings, not for the first or the last time, having been the highest of the innings), and Surrey replied with a mere 271, which left them 257 behind. Now, if the Australian captain wanted to win the match, he ought obviously to have tried to get Surrey out a second time as quickly as possible. But not a bit of it. He sent in a couple of his middle-of-the-side batsmen to pile up the runs. His reason was intelligible. The team have had bad luck in the way of accidents and minor ailments – E. S. WHITE had, unfortunately, to be added to the list of casualties yesterday – and, with his eye fixed on the first Test Match about fifteen days ahead, he did not want to put a heavy strain on the best of the regular bowlers who were left to him. And he did not like the idea of doing what he could with the talent that remained. So the match dragged on without any possibility of a result; and, when DON BRADMAN eventually declared and led his men out of the pavilion to field and bowl, he had the strange experience of being booed by a section of the crowd all the way out to the middle of the ground.

It was a sad moment. But, after all, the spectators had come to see a match, not an uncompetitive exhibition of batting; and they had paid their two shillings, and they did not think it was cricket. And MR. BRADMAN himself would be the first to agree that cricket would be ruined if his example were followed. Moreover first-class cricket, when all is said and done, can only flourish on the grist which the spectators bring to its mill; so they feel entitled to have a voice in the matter – even if the Oval voice was a bit raucous, and perhaps rather hostile in its tone to a great cricketer and a great gentleman, whose whole soul is set, not on personal records, but on winning those Test Matches. Therefore he wants, as our Cricket Correspondent says, to conserve the energies of his team. The point is intelligible, but cricket will lose all its flavour if such considerations are allowed to count more than playing the game to win it.

Test Match Televised

25 *June* 1938. The televisor brought yesterday's Test Match at Lord's into the homes of thousands. The television cameras were swung smoothly about the field so that every detail of the play could be followed from the moment the ball left the bowler's hand till it reached the fielder or the boundary. The transmission was a striking example of the advance in television and the great improvement in receiving apparatus. So successful was the television of the match that a further transmission was given from 6.15 p.m. till the close of play to enable City workers to see the match in their homes. To-day the match will be televised from 11.30 to 12.30, 2.30 to 3.30, at 3.50, and again, it is hoped, for a quarter of an hour before the close of play.

27 *June* 1938. Test cricket was the delight of television viewers on Friday and Saturday, and long periods of play were visible, morning, noon, and evening. It is a happy thing to be one with the Test crowd in your own home, and to see the batsman sending the ball to the boundary and to hear the roar of the crowd. The transmissions were indeed excellent, and at times the viewer must have felt himself almost on the pitch.

Last week was the right time to televise R. C. Sherriff's delightful comedy *Badger's Green*, for it centres in a game of village cricket which changed the course of events and saved the village from the depredations of a company promoter who wanted to ruin it. It was produced by Mr. Eric Crozier, with a film of village cricket on a real village green inserted in the middle of the play to make it more actual, which was most successful.

England Declare at 903 for 7

Hutton Breaks All Records

FROM OUR CRICKET CORRESPONDENT [R. B. VINCENT]

24 *August* 1938. The Test Match at the Oval made considerable progress yesterday, for after England's innings had been declared closed with their score standing at 903 for seven wickets the Australians lost three good wickets for 117 runs. For Australia it was indeed an unlucky day, as D. Bradman when running up to the wicket to bowl fell down and sustained a fracture of the tibia, the larger of the two bones in the leg. He was carried from the field and soon after the close of play he was conveyed to his hotel. It was stated officially that he will take no further part in the match.

As there are doubts as to whether J. H. Fingleton will be able to take any further part in the match Australia are in a poor way to answer so huge a score.

As befits a time-limitless Test Match still more records were broken yesterday. In the first place Hutton by passing Bradman's score of 334 at Leeds in 1930 played the highest individual innings in the history of matches between England and Australia. It was also much the longest that has been played in these games. England's total also easily surpassed that which either country had previously amassed, the Australians having made 729 for six wickets before their innings was declared closed at Lord's in 1930. The other new record of note which was established was the partnership for the sixth wicket between Hutton and Hardstaff, which produced 215 runs, so beating the 186 by Hammond and Ames at Lord's earlier this season.

For Hutton himself the match has been a triumphant one, and when once the reason of a time-limitless match is recognized it must be said that no one could have played his part more adequately. Throughout his innings, while making it his main object to remain as long as possible at the wicket, he took every opportunity which he considered safe to score runs. Whether this is a desirable form of cricket is a matter of opinion, but the majority of a crowd of 31,000 who were at the Oval yesterday seemed thoroughly to enjoy it.

The Australians with their limited supply of bowling never wilted. W. J. O'Reilly and L. O'B. Fleetwood-Smith, both of whom were called upon to do an enormous amount of work, continued throughout to keep a remarkably good length, and keener fielding could not possibly have been demanded.

England's score when play was begun in the morning stood at 634 for five wickets. Hutton then being 300 and Hardstaff 40. O'Reilly and Fleetwood-

Smith began the bowling on a wicket which as yet was not likely to offer them much encouragement, and the large crowd sat in the sunshine waiting for the moment when Hutton assuredly must achieve his record score. Actually he had to work very hard for his runs, anxious as any man well might be in such circumstances, and those who were prepared to watch stroke play rather than revel in statistics had most to admire in the batting of Hardstaff. Fleetwood-Smith was bowling exceedingly well, and when he bowled on the leg stump to a fine short-leg and a forward short-leg, with no one in the slips, he wanted a deal of watching. Hardstaff once glided a ball away to fine-leg, but he was once drawn out to pop a ball up in the middle of the pitch before he reached his 50 with a lovely cut off O'Reilly's bowling. Bradman was again to the fore with some glorious fielding on the off side, and it was hereabouts remarked how splendid in fact the fielding of the whole Australian team had been throughout their ordeal.

Fleetwood-Smith took as many men away from the off side as he could afford when bowling to Hutton, but he had to move one back when Hardstaff was taking the strike. Hutton once was beaten by a leg-break from Fleetwood-Smith which whizzed across past the off stump, an error he covered by hitting the next ball away to deep square-leg. The score had been taken to 670, with Hardstaff taking every opportunity he could find of exhibiting his lovely off drive, when Waite and McCabe came on with the fourth new ball of the innings. That phase of attack did not last long before O'Reilly, once more starting off with a no-ball, came on again. Hutton was certainly taking his time in compiling his record-shattering runs, for he scored 21 runs only during the first hour of play, but he sent the 700 up with a late cut off Waite which flew away down to the pavilion railings. He wanted only four more runs when O'Reilly provided him with a no-ball, but he missed it, and he had to wait some considerable time before he received a ball which he considered safe to cut and to pass Bradman's 334.

This was the occasion for a great demonstration of praise, combined with relief; the entire crowd rose to its collective feet, the cheering was prolonged, and the Australian team, led by Bradman, who for some time had been lurking close to Hutton's bat, shook hands with him. The opportunity was taken for a waiter to bring out some refreshments, and thereafter the business of the time-limitless Test Match was continued. Record after record was broken, while Hardstaff, still continuing to bat elegantly and easily, approached closer to his individual century. It was noticed that McCabe was occasionally making the ball turn, but Barnes when he was given a trial provided little difficulty, and with O'Reilly given a rest in the deep field the luncheon interval arrived with the score 759.

Hardstaff reached his 100 with an off-drive off Fleetwood-Smith in the first over after luncheon. A few more runs and a miracle occurred; Hutton hit a ball from O'Reilly not only in the air but straight into the hands of cover-point, and an innings which it had seem would last so long as he was provided with a partner came to an end. He had scored his 364 runs in 13 hours and a quarter, during which time he had hit thirty-five 4's and had given an exhibition of self-control which it would be hard to surpass. Quite apart from the raids which have been made upon Test Match records Hutton's was the highest innings which has ever been played on the Oval ground, the previous highest being the 357 not out of the illustrious Bobby Abel for Surrey against Somerset in 1899.

Australia having rid themselves of an obstacle which looked likely to become permanent, there arrived the cheerful Wood to cause them more trouble. Wood, no doubt considering that the state of the game permitted some freedom, disclosed some of the strokes which he employs when York-shire have gained a reasonable lead over Lancashire. He was especially partial to the sweep to leg, caring little whether the bowler was O'Reilly, Fleetwood-Smith, or anybody else. Bradman considered the occasion to be appropriate to try out Hassett as a bowler, and he even treated himself to a short spell. Hardstaff had by then become thoroughly infected with the Test Match bacillus, and the crowd must be excused if they found his batting a little lethargic. The strokes were beautifully constructed, but their scoring value was at one time scarcely noticeable. He made a drive past cover-point off Fleetwood-Smith and another straight drive off O'Reilly which remain in the memory, but for the rest he relied mainly on deflections or pushes.

Wood when he had made 47 might have been caught at square-leg off Waite, and the partnership had produced 106 runs before Barnes held a catch off his own bowling to dismiss Wood and to allow another Yorkshire-man to have a look at the bowling. Verity had not been in long when the accident occurred to Bradman, but Hardstaff found time to make some more strokes on the off side before the tea interval arrived and with it the surprising news that England's innings had been declared closed, news which could scarcely be believed until the groundsmen appeared on the scene with their light roller and paint-pot.

Australia began their innings at 5 o'clock, and five minutes later they had lost their first wicket. K. Farnes, who started the bowling from the Pavilion end to three slips and a gully, made the ball come off the pitch at a great pace, but it was Bowes in his first over from the other end who had C. L. Badcock caught at short mid-wicket before a run had been scored. S. McCabe made three good forcing strokes to the direction of long-on off Farnes, Leyland having to toddle a long way to retrieve the ball, before he mistimed his stroke and was caught at square-leg. That was two wickets down for 19, a dismal enough start even without Bradman and Fingleton on the injured list. Hassett came to the rescue with an innings which, while it lasted, was a joy to watch. Twice in one over he turned balls from Farnes away to the leg boundary, and when Edrich came on he at once banged him away past square-leg.

Hassett was lucky to see one ball fly off his bat over the head of second slip, but in the same over he made a grand square cut. That, alas! was the end of an innings which was worthy of a proper cricket match, for in hooking a short ball from Edrich he hit the ball into the hands of long-leg. S. Barnes as soon as he was in crashed the ball square on the off side to the boundary. He was not particularly impressed when Verity came on, nor was he worried by a silly mid-off, and for all the anxiety that he and Brown showed Australia might well have been already piling up a big score. Brown made one exquisite leg glide off Verity, and if he was fortunate with one stroke which sent a ball from Edrich streaking under the hand of second slip, he was helping the runs along so well that the 100 went up when the innings was only 70 minutes old. First Farnes and then Bowes was tried again in an attempt to take one more wicket, and in one last endeavour Leyland, who bowled to three short-legs, was put on, but the day ended without any further incident.

> ENGLAND 903 for 7 dec (Hutton 364, Leyland 187, Hardstaff 169 not out, Hammond 59, Wood 53)
> AUSTRALIA 201 (W. A. Brown 69, A. L. Hassett 42, S. Barnes 41; Bowes 5 for 49) and 123 (B. A. Barnett 46; K. Farnes 4 for 63)
> Score after third day: England 903 for 7 dec; Australia 117 for 3
> *England won by an innings and 579 runs*

More Fame Comes to Pudsey

Day of Acute Tension

24 *August* 1938. Fame has come once more to Pudsey. This very plain little industrial town midway between Bradford and Leeds, with a name (pronounced Poodsa) that has been a blessing to many a comedian, like Wigan or Nether Wallop, was aglow yesterday. Round about midday the inhabitants of Pudsey were holding breath. In the homes, in the local inns, in the mills, and in the post-office the tension was acute. For once more a son of Pudsey was on the verge of a great achievement on the cricket field.

Years ago Tunnicliffe, known affectionately as Long John, had retrieved the name of Pudsey from humour. With Brown at the other wicket, he took part in many huge first-wicket partnerships for Yorkshire, and his agility in the slips has become a legend in those parts. Then came Sutcliffe, who, with Hobbs, has given the Australian bowlers gruelling hours in the heat of an Australian summer, and who, at the moment, is striving manfully to keep the Yorkshire flag flying while five of the county team are playing for England. And yesterday, one of those five, the *protégé* of Sutcliffe [*Hutton*], broke all records in Test Match cricket. He has become a fixture among the great men in *Wisden*, and the men of Pudsey are all wearing county caps.

Timeless Test Matches
Some Observations

FROM OUR CRICKET CORRESPONDENT [R. B. VINCENT]

15 *March* 1939. The welcome decision by those in authority at Durban yesterday that the exhausted players should be allowed to pack their bags and go home was an admission that there can be a limit to time-limitless Test Matches. Whether the M.C.C. team could have been transported in time to catch their boat or not, it seems to have been agreed that honours could rest easy, and that 10 days of such cricket was enough. Whatever may be said about this form of amusement, which bears as much resemblance to cricket as marathon dancing or pole squatting does to athletics, there is every respect to be paid to the players, and especially the English team.

It was a match in which no restriction was to be made as to the time taken in scoring runs, and South Africa, quite naturally, having won the toss, settled down to make the fullest use of a new wicket. It seemed after several days that they had achieved their object, and England, set the gigantic task of scoring 696 runs in order to win in the fourth innings, seemed to be in an impossible position. It appeared unlikely that the wicket, however carefully it had been manufactured, could endure for ever, but one day of rain and another day of rest on the Sunday gave England renewed hope, for when rolled the pitch became bound together, and the players were given a rest of which physically and mentally they were in greater need than their opponents.

When the game was continued on Monday it was the South African side that had to bear the strain of toiling all day and watching the match gradually slip out of their grasp. England, for their part, adapted themselves entirely to the circumstances, and the play of Edrich in particular, who has gallantly belied the unkind things that have been said of him, and of P. A. Gibb, W. R. Hammond, and Paynter as well, deserves the approval of even the most censorious Australian critic. It was without question a great feat, but one cannot help feeling that it should never have been demanded of them, and that such misapplied courage will never again be required either in this country or in South Africa, where opinion, quite clearly, is against this form of the game.

It is, and always has been, an admitted fact that time is an essential factor in a game of true cricket, and it is impossible to understand why, because the game happens to be between two countries, the time limit should be discarded. Once any regard for time is ignored, the essence of the cricket departs and the game resolves itself into a spurious run-making competition, in which little matters but the establishment of so-called "records." Those who were at the Oval last August remember the grotesque situation which culminated in tragic comedy, and this last pitiful example at Durban can only have strengthened their opinion. Certainly it is absurd to expect a team to go halfway round the world to watch rain falling, as it fell at Old Trafford last year, but there must be some middle line between no play and endless play.

The suggestion put forward by M.C.C. to the Australian Board of Control that the duration of a Test Match should be limited by the hours actually available for play and not by days, during which there might be rain, must surely be the sensible solution. Nothing can be done to make cricketers complete a match during days of rain, but something can be done to insist that they should arrive at some conclusion at the end of a specified number of playing hours. If they cannot do so then the game is drawn, and there is no harm in that, provided that each has had a fair chance of winning. But to ask lovers of cricket to accept a state of affairs which entails 10 days without providing a result is beyond reason, and one can only hope that this is, indeed, the end.

The Hon. Robert Lyttelton

9 *November* 1939. Princess Antoine Bibesco writes:–

Certain families possess defined flavours – Cecils, Churchills, Cavendishes, Lytteltons. The aroma pleases or prejudices – Bob Lyttelton belonged to his family, but even in an age of individualists he would have stood out as an individual. When you say of him "a great gentleman" it is the gentleman who benefits by the phrase.

He was a natural writer. Told that an extract from a cricket report he had written [*his account of Cobden's match-winning over in the 1870 University match, published in The Badminton Library* Cricket] was included in "Q's" anthology of English prose he could hardly believe it. Not that he was modest – he did not need to be, he was himself. His family sagas, rich with his own humour, were untainted either by admiration or censure. Figure after figure emerged intact without the misrepresentation of presentation. He had the supreme gift of the raconteur. The strong flavour of his personality never impeded the view. To those who knew him – in other words to those who loved him (it was the same thing) – his combination of dryness and warmth will remain a memory unforgettable and without possibility of counterfeit.

If cricket did not exist Bob Lyttelton would have created it. If sportsmen still exist his ghost will give them substance.

11 *November* 1939. Mr. A. A. Milne writes:–

I should like to add one story to the many which will be told of this enthusiastic lover of cricket, although, for reasons which will be seen, I feel a little diffident about telling it. I was introduced to him at a Test Match by a woman whose enthusiasms were more literary than sporting; and, to my great embarrassment, she could think of no better way of explaining me than by saying brightly, "This is Christopher Robin's father." Robert Lyttelton got the introduction back to its proper footing. Showing an interest which surprised me for a moment, he said, "Ah! Any relation to the Middlesex Robins?"

The Centenary Match at Rugby

FROM OUR SPECIAL CORRESPONDENT [U. A. TITLEY]

18 *June* 1941. There could hardly have been a more perfect day than yesterday at Rugby for the centenary celebration of Tom Brown's cricket match against M.C.C. On this occasion the school did rather worse than they did 100 years ago and were beaten by 118 runs, M.C.C. having declared at 149 for nine wickets. The school could only muster a modest 31, but considering what they were up against they might have fared even worse. J. Smith took six for eight. Luncheon, as on that other famous occasion, was taken in Old Big School, and two of those present formed a direct link with Tom Brown's team.

Both the headmaster and Sir Pelham Warner, who said that he was very happy to have lived to see this day, spoke of Mr. R. B. V. Currie and Mr. P. A. Landon. The former, a youthful 81, is a nephew of Currie Esq. major and Currie Esq. minor, while Mr. Landon, better known as vice-president of Trinity College, Oxford, is a great-great-grandson of Mr. Aislabie. Had M. M. Walford been able to accept an invitation to play, there would have been one more link. The presence of Sir Pelham Warner was extremely apt and his influence on cricket in general is too well known to need comment here. A more modern note was struck by the presence of a young gentleman who was alleged less than 12 hours earlier to have been throwing things much more dangerous than cricket balls at Germans.

The school won the toss and put M.C.C. in. This argued a certain distrust of their batting, which has been very variable on this season's wet wicket, but in the circumstances their policy was prudent, especially from the point of view of the large number of spectators – and they began well, too. R. H. Twining gave a chance at the beginning of the opening over and departed at the end of it. They had to wait some time for further success while R. I. Scorer and R. E. S. Wyatt had a long look at the bowling. Wyatt was at length out to a good catch and H. C. Munro followed before luncheon, when the score was 73 for three.

Afterwards E. R. T. Holmes got frolicsome, but Smith, to the school's regret, failed to disturb the rooks in the tops of the elms. The Boddington family had a private tussle and at 4 o'clock the M.C.C. declared. Wyatt bowled down Rugby's first two wickets before tea. The school's tale of woe continued afterwards and Smith bestirred himself to the extent of doing the hat-trick. R. E. S. Wyatt bowled very steadily and was rather too much of a handful for the boys. It was all over by a quarter to 6. Rugby may not have shone at batting, but at any rate most of their fielding was well up to scratch.

MCC 149 for 9 dec
RUGBY 31 (J. Smith 6 for 8, R. E. S. Wyatt 4 for 14)
M.C.C. won by 118 runs

A Festival Transplanted

12 *July* 1941, *Leading Article.* When the Derby is run at Newmarket there can be no complaint that the Eton and Harrow match becomes a movable feast, and to-day it will be played at Eton. In Tom Brown's match, recently celebrated, the venue seems to have been changed almost at the last moment "to the sorrow of those aspiring young cricketers who have been reckoning for the last three months on showing off at Lord's ground." Here is no such sudden disappointment, but sympathy is none the less due to those robbed by inexorable events of something of their birth-right. They are in better case than their elder brothers at the Universities who gain but makeshift blues; they will have the right caps, and these uncoupon'd, but Lord's is Lord's and there are moments that can never be recaptured. Among elder persons there will be many who find the change far from disagreeable; rejoicing not merely in green and open spaces but in the absence of tail coats and stiff collars. Nothing can ever again be so apoplectic as were such garments in a crowded carriage in the neighbourhood of Baker Street station in the dear, dead, smoky days of the old Underground. Since then, however, we have grown more in love with casual ways and demand "wentilation gossamer" almost as of right. If only the sun shines, as we are allowed to know it did in June, there will not to-day be many pleasanter spots than Agar's Plough.

With this change of battlefield comes a certain change of heart, and perhaps battlefield is no longer the right word.

> A gentleman's a-bowling
> And down the wickets go.

Their downfall will be duly acclaimed, but to a sensitive ear there may be something lacking, not merely in the volume of the shouts but in the raucous venom of them. Whatever happens, however tense the crisis, it is unlikely that elderly gentlemen will bury their faces in their hands, unable to endure the horrid spectacle, or leave the ground and wait palpitating to hear the issue outside. These amiable follies belong only to Lord's. On the face of it there has hardly ever been a more exciting match than last year's at Harrow, when, with comfortable victory in sight, the Eton wickets fell like corn before the sickle, and the last man had to go in to make, after an interval of delicious agony, the winning hit. Yet in fact the genuine agony was, by a consensus of opinion, never quite reached. Here and there a partisan may have been seen, like SIR HORACE MANN of old, "cutting about with his stick among the daisies"; but in the end both sides united in thinking that here was a good game with a capital finish, and went home neither overmuch elated nor depressed.

"There was too much levity about our game to-day," said old MR. SUTHERLAND many years ago at St. Andrews. Whether in brighter days the new spirit of vanity, almost bordering upon levity, will survive in our games no one can now tell. Doubtless we ought to hope so, but doubtless also the perfect admixture of emotion is not easy to attain. It would be a little sad to think that never again would there be that exquisite torture produced by a last over or a place-kick at goal on which the fate of empires appears, however fallaciously, to hang. As in far graver matters it is wisest not to prophesy, but simply to be glad that to-day at least we can watch a game of cricket with pleasure and without too much solemnity, likewise that we have become, if it may be so expressed, more one-day-minded. We no longer say that this is "only a one-day match." We have adjusted our point of view to the cricket that was good enough for the heroes of Hambledon; they not merely finished their match in a day but, in the words of WILLIAM BELDHAM, who lived twenty-seven miles off, "used to ride both ways the same day early and late." The players too have adapted themselves to this new order. To their cricket as to their more serious employments old NYREN might to-day transfer his famous description of the punch drunk at Broad Halfpenny and call it "good, unsophisticated, John Bull stuff."

Kenneth Farnes

24 *October* 1941. Pilot Officer Kenneth Farnes, R.A.F.V.R., whose death on active service at the age of 30 was announced in our later editions yesterday, was a fast bowler in the true sense in which the adjective is applied to Kortright, Lockwood, and Richardson, and to no other Englishman of his generation except Larwood. He was, perhaps, a bowler of moods – either destructively hostile or complacently amicable – but in his full fighting feathers he was a danger to any batsman in the world.

An easy and economical run up to the wicket was the prelude to a controlled delivery from a great height, and he had the pace to make the ball rise sharply and to excuse what in the case of others might have been regarded as a shortness of length. E. A. McDonald, that prince of modern fast bowlers, once remarked that when batsmen edged away from the wicket the ball was liable to follow them. Woe betide those, too, who ran away from Kenneth Farnes.

Son of Mr. Sidney H. Farnes and the late Mrs. Farnes, he was educated at the Royal Liberty School, Romford, and went to Pembroke College, Cambridge, in 1931 to gain his place in the University XI as a Freshman, having already had some experience of County cricket in the Essex XI. He again played in the University match in the following two years, and by then he had established himself as an outstanding bowler. In 1934 he played in two Test Matches against Australia in this country, and in 1938 was a regular member of England's team. He went out to Australia with G. O. Allen's side in the season 1936-37, and he took part in each of the Test Matches in South Africa under W. R. Hammond's captaincy in 1938-39. One of his most notable successes was in the Gentlemen and Players match of 1936, when he spread havoc among the professional batsmen. It would have required a George Gunn on that day to have tamed him. His progress on the cricket field was interrupted when he became a schoolmaster at Worksop College, but he has left a memory of a young man of a charming modesty and a gentleness of manner, who did much to lend distinction to amateur cricket at a time when talent was not easy to find.

28 *October* 1941. The Headmaster of Worksop College writes:–
The news of the death of Kenneth Farnes has come as a great shock to all who knew him at Worksop. To the majority of his countrymen the news has come of the loss of one of the greatest of fast bowlers; to masters and boys at this school it means the loss of a valued friend and counsellor. Farnes was an energetic and untiring teacher of History and Geography, and an able and much-loved Housemaster. To this latter position he was appointed at an unusually young age, and his success therein was largely due to the quite natural modesty of the man, which made him as willing to learn from boys as they were to learn from him. A giant in stature, he had that gentleness of voice and manner which so often accompanies great size and strength, and, though on the cricket-field he would rouse himself to devastating action, he never let his strength run away with him in his dealings with boys.

Sacred Turf

9 *May* 1942, *Leading Article*. Everything must give way to the winning of the war. So much being granted, many people whose patriotism is above suspicion must have been pleased to learn that, whereas parts of college gardens at Cambridge have been surrendered to vegetables, the turf of Fenner's remains untouched. That turf is primarily sacred in the eyes of cricketers as the track surrounding it is sacred in those of runners. To it belong the names of STUDDS and STEELS and LYTTELTONS, of MACAULAY and TINDALL and FITZHERBERT. Thousands of obscure mortals have drowsed pleasantly here in the sunshine or stood well wrapped up in the chilly Lent term watching the immortals at play. It has, moreover, its enduring place in literature. There

are many who do not care overmuch for blues but love their C.S.C., and, if the tap of memory be turned on, can recite on the instant :–

> I have stood serene on Fenner's
> Ground indifferent to blisters,
> While the Buttress of the period
> Bowled me his peculiar twisters.

They may not be exactly aware who Buttress was any more than Mr. Micawber was aware what gowans might be, but they are moved by the thoughts of their youth even as Mr. Micawber was when he joined fervently in Auld Lang Syne.

Some there may be who having another background to their lives believe that Fenner's has been spared its cabbages through some undue partiality, but this is not so. We are expressly told that the grass which is daily mown there has proved of exceptional value for cattle food. Fenner's like Todgers's can do it when it chooses and it is doing its bit now. It is obviously too early to assert that the cattle imbibe all unknowing some of the qualities of its great men. It would be pleasant to think that a cow would come nearer to jumping over the moon by dint of the grass on which some mighty high-jumper has lightly laid his foot. But without indulging in such fantastic speculations we know that, through Fenner's, the cow will be a more acceptable sacrifice in the cause of the nation's food.

That turf has for many of us a unique and venerable quality is beyond doubt. Each blade of grass at Lord's and the Parks, Newmarket and Epsom, Wimbledon, Twickenham and St. Andrews can give a peculiar thrill to somebody, according to his tastes and his memories. Everything changes; groundsmen and green-keepers are not the hide-bound slaves of tradition; and even the most historic of turf is relaid. The young cricketer in his first innings at Lord's is not playing on the same pitch whereon W. G. remembered having in his youth picked up a handfull of small pieces of gravel. The pilgrim holing out under critical eyes at St. Andrews is not in fact doing so on the green where ALLAN ROBERTSON holed his last putt in his famous 79 against MR. BETHUNE of Blebo. But what matter if they hold fast to their faith and think that they are? The principle is the same. On all these spots there may be heard by ears properly attuned the sounds of heroes,

> sounds
> Of undistinguishable motion, steps
> Almost as silent as the turf they trod.

If to-day, with cricket once more upon us, they are mingled with the mooings and bleatings of happily replete cattle, so much the better.

The Last Survivor

1 *August* 1943, *Leading Article*. When there dies the last survivor of some famous band of men it "leaves a gap in society." Even in these days when serious cricket seems dim enough, the death of T. W. GARRETT, the last of the Australians who played in the first Test Match, must send the mind roaming for an instant over battlefields that were once grim enough, but appear to-day wholly green and friendly. He was not the oldest of all such survivors, since there remains one illustrious player from COBDEN's year, 1870; but 1877 is sufficiently long ago and the Test Match marked the beginning of an epoch. How much the name of GARRETT means to the modern cricketer it is hard to say, but to those at least who have read their history it may still bring a sensation akin to terror, for he was an actor in two events which in their time seemed terrible indeed, the obliteration of landmarks and the opening of flood-gates. One was the defeat of the M.C.C. in a single day's play on the 27th of May, 1878; the other, on a second day of rain and puddles and ominous cloud, four years later, the first loss of the Ashes on the 28th of August. On that day GARRETT was one of the historic conference between innings at which SPOFFORTH declared that "This thing can be done" and done it was. A name always sounds the more stirring when it is indissolubly linked with others of equal fame so that they go with a swing. "Harry the King, Bedford and Exeter" are not more exciting in a cricketer's ears than those in PROWSE's often quoted line

Felix, Wenman, Hillyer, Fuller Pilch and Alfred Mynn

and GARRETT's name, though commemorated in no verse, is one of a company that haunt the memory. To 1878 belong four tremendous Australian bowlers – SPOFFORTH, BOYLE, GARRETT, and ALLAN. ALLAN, "the bowler of a century," dropped out and in 1882 come the four with an even more alarming ring – SPOFFORTH, BOYLE, PALMER, and GARRETT.

The student who murmurs to himself those four names may feel a cold thrill up the spine; he may "crawl with invidious apprehension" but, even as the small boy, pale green over a first cigar, he "likes the feeling." If it be not too close to us there is nothing like the formidable and that is surely the epithet for those early Australians, as indeed for their successors. They look formidable as we scan their photograph of 1882. Each flank is held by a black-bearded hero; on the left GARRETT himself, on the right BLACKHAM. Next to GARRETT towers the giant BONNOR with a beard of lighter hue and in the middle, bearded again, is BOYLE, with his hands casually and defiantly in his pockets. Close behind him in a rustic garden sits a stone lion, the animal destined to be so signally humiliated. In those days England itself possessed the most formidable of all men with a black beard, and perhaps beards were then less charged with meaning, but to-day they strike an awe upon the sight, and their wearers look, as MR. CARDUS wrote of SPOFFORTH, "Stark men," full of hostility and resolution. That bearded old gentleman of eighty-five who has just passed away must have had many great memories to go back and back to in his last years.

Captain H. Verity

FROM OUR CRICKET CORRESPONDENT [R. B. VINCENT]

2 *September* 1943. Captain Hedley Verity, of the Green Howards, whose death in hospital as a prisoner of war in Italy on July 31 was officially announced yesterday, had already in his 10 years of first-class cricket established his position as a worthy successor to Peel and Rhodes as Yorkshire's slow left-handed bowler, and he had played in 40 Test matches.

Always a bowler of extreme accuracy and patience, even on the truest of wickets and against the most formidable batsmen, he developed as his career advanced a greater ability to flight the ball, and on a sticky wicket he was unsurpassed. He was born at Headingley in May of 1905, and when quite young played as an amateur for Rawdon in Yorkshire Council matches, later appearing as a professional for Accrington in the Lancashire League. He played first for Yorkshire in 1930, in which season, although he did not obtain a regular place in the side, he took 52 wickets for 11 runs apiece. In 1931 he came fully into his own, making full use of many rain-damaged pitches and taking 138 wickets in the season, including all 10 in an innings against Warwickshire at Leeds for 36 runs. In the next season he took all 10 Nottinghamshire wickets for only 10 runs, and in 1933 at Leyton he took 17 wickets in a day. In 1934 when England beat Australia in an innings at Lord's he took 14 wickets for 80 runs during the course of one day, taking 15 wickets in all in the match, a feat which no one else has ever achieved in a Test Match except Rhodes at Melbourne in 1904. These were exceptional performances, but frequently Verity took seven or eight wickets in an innings at an absurdly low cost.

His career in matches on tour, during which he played in Australia, New Zealand, South Africa, the West Indies, and India, was equally remarkable, his accuracy even on the hard Australian pitches being of inestimable value to his captain, who could rely on him to keep runs down at one end. His ability to keep the batsman playing was demonstrated by the fact that even to Bradman he could place a silly point. In these tours in various parts of the world he took 224 wickets at a cost of 19 runs each, and as a batsman he at one time showed signs of following the example of Rhodes by transforming himself from a Number 11 into an opening batsman.

A keen student of the game, there never was a cricketer of a more becoming and gentle modesty than Hedley Verity, who on all grounds was regarded with the utmost respect. Before this war he had made a keen study also of soldiering, was one of the first cricketers to join the forces, and had served three years in the Middle East before he received his severe wound in Sicily.

An All-American Match

22 *September* 1943. Two teams composed of officers of the United States Army Air Force, representing Stations 103 and 112, recently met in a cricket match in this country. This is believed to be the first cricket match played by all-American teams in England, at least during this war. The batting and bowling were much above the standard expected by the English spectators.

STATION *112* 92 (Capt. Mitchell 60; Capt. Barry 7 for 56)
STATION *103* 35 (Capt. Podwajsky 5 for 13)
Station 112 won by 57 runs

Judgment against Hotel
Constantine v. Imperial London Hotels Limited

BEFORE MR. JUSTICE BIRKETT
HIGH COURT OF JUSTICE: KINGS BENCH DIVISION

29 *June* 1944. His LORDSHIP gave judgment for the plaintiff in the action in which Mr. Learie Nicholas Constantine, of Meredith Street, Nelson, Lancashire, claimed damages from Imperial London Hotels, Limited, on the ground that the defendants refused to receive and lodge him in the Imperial Hotel, Russell Square, London, in July, 1943.

The defendants denied that they refused to receive and lodge Mr. Constantine, and pleaded that, after he had been received in their hotel on July 30, 1943, he voluntarily left that evening and was provided with accommodation at their Bedford Hotel.

Sir Patrick Hastings, K.C., and Miss Rose Heilbron appeared for the plaintiff; Mr. G. O. Slade, K.C., and Mr. Aiken Watson for the defendants.

His LORDSHIP, in giving judgment, said that there was no claim for damages for breach of contract, it being conceded that Mr. Constantine had a contract with the defendants and that on breach of that contract he would be entitled to nominal damages. The plaintiff's claim was simply that the defendants were innkeepers; that the Imperial Hotel was a common inn kept by them for the accommodation of travellers; that they were under a duty receive and lodge him; that they refused to do so; and that he was compelled to go elsewhere and was put to much inconvenience.

It was conceded, for the purpose of the case, that the defendants were innkeepers; that the Imperial Hotel was an inn; that the plaintiff went there on

July 30, 1943, and requested the defendants' servants to receive and lodge him; that they had sufficient room for the purpose; and that the plaintiff was ready and willing to pay the proper charges and had paid a deposit of £2. It was further conceded that Mr. Constantine was a man of high character and attainments, a British subject from the West Indies, and that although he was a man of colour no ground existed on which the defendants were entitled to refuse to receive and lodge him.

The issue of fact was a narrow one. Did the defendants by their servants refuse to receive and lodge Mr. Constantine, or did he, as the defendants asserted, leave voluntarily after having been received into the Imperial Hotel? He (his Lordship) would first deal shortly with the question of fact. Mr. Constantine was perhaps best known as a cricketer of great renown who had won the admiration and, indeed, the affection of the cricketing public in many parts of the world. He was also employed by the Ministry of Labour as the local welfare officer on Merseyside.

There was to be an international cricket match at Lord's on August 2, 1943, and Mr. Constantine was given special leave to play in it. When rooms were booked at the defendants' hotel for Mr. Constantine and his wife and daughter, the question was asked: "Have you any objection to coloured people?" and the answer received was "No." On July 30 Mr. Constantine went to the hotel accompanied by Mr. A. R. Watson, his superior officer in the Ministry of Labour, and Mr. W. C. Leatherbarrow, the manager of the match which was to be played.

His LORDSHIP reviewed the evidence given on both sides regarding what took place at the hotel, and said that he accepted without hesitation the evidence of the plaintiff and his witnesses and rejected that given on behalf of the defendants. He was satisfied that the manageress of the hotel was grossly insulting in her references to Mr. Constantine. It was enough to say that from the outset the manageress made it clear to Mr. Leatherbarrow that Mr. Constantine could not stay in the hotel; that she used the word "nigger" and was very offensive; and that she declined to receive the party and refused to listen to reason. He (his Lordship) also accepted the evidence that Mr. Constantine removed to the Bedford Hotel, on the advice of Mr. Watson and not of his own free will, because of what the manageress and manager said.

In the witness-box Mr. Constantine bore himself with modesty and dignity, dealt with all questions with intelligence and truth, was not concerned to be vindictive or malicious, but was obviously affected by the indignity and humiliation which had been put on him and had occasioned him so much distress and inconvenience, which he most naturally resented.

He (his Lordship) found on the facts that the defendants did refuse to receive and lodge the plaintiff in their hotel without any just cause or excuse, and that Mr. Constantine did not leave voluntarily.

His LORDSHIP then proceeded to deal with the question of law raised by the defendants – namely, that the present action was an action on the case, that the gist of such an action was the damage actually suffered and proved, and that in the present case no damage was suffered and no special damage was alleged and proved. He reviewed the authorities at length, and said that there was no express authority to guide him. He held that the action was maintainable without proof of special damage, since the plaintiff's right, founded in the common law, had been violated and denied, and in those circumstances the law afforded him a remedy. He (his Lordship) had been urged to award exemplary damages because of the circumstances in which the denial of the plaintiff's right took place. He did not feel on the authorities that he could do that, having regard to the exact nature of the action, and he therefore gave judgment for Mr. Constantine for nominal damages only, which he assessed at five guineas.

A stay of execution was refused.

Solicitors. – Messrs. Isadore Goldman and Son, for Mr. Sydney W. Price, Liverpool; Messrs. Durrant Cooper and Hambling.

Ball and Beard

8 *August* 1944, *Leading Article.* There are some articles of faith which an Englishman will surrender only with his life, and of these one of the most dearly cherished is that ERNEST JONES bowled through W. G.'s beard. He would as soon discredit the story that PRINCE JOHN pulled the long beards of the Irish chieftains who came to do homage. On this sacrosanct belief doubt has lately been cast and, of all people, by SIR STANLEY JACKSON. *Et tu, Brute* will exclaim all true believers in awe-stricken chorus. This statement, akin to blasphemy, occurs in the new Wisden in a very interesting record of a talk with the greatest of all Yorkshiremen. SIR STANLEY places the incident, for he admits an incident, at Sheffield Park, not at Lord's, and here, unless indeed the thing happened twice, he will find the bulk of historians against him; but that is a small matter. In all the details but one he cannot affront the most bigoted. That W. G. came menacing down the pitch, that HARRY TROTT said "Steady, Jonah," that JONES proffered the famous apology, "Sorry, Doctor, she slipped" – on all these points he is orthodoxy itself; but then come these dreadful words, "I do not think the ball actually touched W. G.'s beard." Your true fundamentalist is impervious even to such shocks as this, but those of weaker faith will have found their spirits much refreshed by a letter from a correspondent published on August 4. He was at Lord's watching a Test Match; he was sitting square with the wicket, and on the evidence of his own eyes and those of all his neighbours, as well as on that of the Doctor's "reactions," he believed and still believes that the ball did go through the beard. England will stand behind him to the last man.

That memories of great events grow hazy, even in cricket is undeniable. Anyone who has studied in W. J. FORD's history of Cambridge cricket the accounts of COBDEN's over, given by those who played in the match, will find surprising variations. Who fielded the first ball of the over, and whether BELCHER was bowled off his legs – an insinuation which the bowler bitterly resented – are but two points in doubt. The great YARDLEY went so far under some strange hallucination as to put COBDEN bowling at the wrong end. But COBDEN's over is "another story," and as to the Doctor's beard argument is barely allowable. Once upon a time he was not the only bearded hero; the early Australian teams bristled with them: BONNOR's, BLACK-HAM's and GARRETT's beards were familiar and illustrious. To-day they have all grown dim save to those who pore reverently over faded groups. Only W. G. remains for ever *senex promissa barba*. as clear and vivid a picture to those who never saw him as to those who played with him. Even SIR STAN-LEY JACKSON admits that the Doctor came up the pitch stroking his beard. There is yet time for him to recant on the major issue. Will he not do so and so ease the hurt of many worthy souls?

> There was an old man with a beard
> Who said, "It is just as I feared,"

but he can never have imagined so fearful a heresy as this.

The evidence of the reports in The Times, *though favouring Sheffield Park, is inconclusive. On Sheffield Park (13 May 1896): Mr. Jones (very fast) and Mr. M'Kibbin were the bowlers. "W.G.", after being twice badly hit in the first over from Mr. Jones, began to force the game at a great pace, and the last two balls of the over he drove and cut to the boundary. On Lord's (23 June 1896): Jones started the bowling from the pavilion end, and from a short and fast ball Grace got a two through the slips. In the same over there was a bye and a four and a two by Stoddart through the slips.*

Mr. A. C. MacLaren

25 *November* 1944. Mr. R. H. Spooner writes:–

It was with deep sorrow that many, and particularly those in cricket circles, heard of the passing of Archie MacLaren. In my opinion he was not only the greatest captain ever, but was always a valued friend and adviser to the youthful cricketer during early appearances for his county. When captain he was always ready to give up his usual place in the batting order should he feel that that would benefit his side. He never thought of himself, and there was no one stricter in seeing that cricket was always played as it should be. Ever a delightful companion to cricketers in the British Isles, Archie Mac-Laren was a universal favourite and, rightly so, oversea, and nowhere more so than in Australia.

Australia's Good Start against England

FROM OUR CRICKET CORRESPONDENT [R. B. VINCENT]

7 *August* 1945. Lord's ground had never before held so many people as were there yesterday to see the first day of the fourth "Victory" match, during which Australia, having first use of the most perfect of wickets, had placed themselves almost invulnerable to the uncertainties of cricket by scoring 273 runs for the loss of five wickets.

The limitations of England's attack, well directed as it was by their captain and nobly supported in the field, were obvious, their medium-paced bowlers – for they had no really fast bowlers – relying over-much on the ball pitching on, but missing, the leg stump. The Australian batsmen are adepts at forcing the ball off their legs, whereas the best of them can offer a catch in the slips to the ball which goes away. W. R. Hammond for a long time was a solitary figure in the slips, while three men close in on the on-side could expect to do little else than pick up the ball or watch it pass by on the ground.

England had a most encouraging start when J. A. Workman, a useful man to be rid of, was out leg-before-wicket with only 15 runs on the board, and Australia to good fielding and accurate bowling had a severe hour's play in front of them. R. S. Whitington and S. G. Sismey maybe were unadventurous in their strokes, but it was obvious that in a side not over-strong in batting it was essential that a batsman should be well dug in to partner K. R. Miller when that potentially match-winning batsman came in later. In fact, Whitington did most of the scoring, but as events proved later it was Sismey who was the support Miller had looked for.

A short break before luncheon during a thunderstorm left Australia at the interval with 65 runs scored and only one wicket down, Whitington then having made 43. It can be truthfully said that after luncheon England's bowlers were unlucky in that D. V. P. Wright beat Sismey's bat times beyond count and Pope twice beat bat, pads, and wicket-keeper. The score had advanced slowly, but with purpose, to 70 before Whitington was caught at forward short-leg, but there well might have been another wicket if a second slip had been moved in a little sooner to Wright's bowling. Sismey when he had made 21 was all but out to a great attempt at a one-handed catch by J. D. Robertson at backward short-leg, and England had to wait until 108 before the dangerous A. L. Hassett was caught at fine-leg.

This brought forward Miller, who having survived a "yorker" to his first ball from Pope, and with a rather uncomfortable stretch, or lean, forward to Wright, settled down to take what runs were offered him, more especially from the allowance which was granted to him on the leg side. W. Roberts was tried at both ends, but he passed the bat only with those balls which could be ignored, and with Miller hastening, but never reckless, and Sismey obdurate Australia's batting policy was amply explained.

Sismey's valuable innings was interrupted when a rising ball caused him to go in for temporary treatment, and while he was away R. M. Stanford's wicket was lost, but Miller had seen to it that enough had been done by ten minutes past six, when a poor light, but nothing comparable in gloom to that in which England had at one time batted during the previous match at Lord's, ended the day's play, a curtailment which many may have thought unnecessary. More than 30,000 people paid for admission, and it is estimated that in all over 33,000 saw the game.

> AUSTRALIA 388 (K. R. Miller 118, S. G. Sismey 59, C. G. Pepper 57, R. S. Whitington 46; G. H. Pope 4 for 83, R. Pollard 4 for 145) and 140 for 4
> ENGLAND 468 for 7 dec (C. Washbrook 112, W. R. Hammond 83, W. J. Edrich 73 not out, L. B. Fishlock 69)
> Score after first day: Australia 273 for 5
> *Match drawn*

The First Day of Summer

I *May* 1946, *Leading Article*. Almanacs and dictionaries may say what they please but for thousands of people the first day of summer is that on which there first appear in modest type and as the tail end of a column the magic words "To-day's Cricket Fixtures." Therefore it is incontestable that in 1946 the 27th of April was the day. It might have come before, but where alas! are the Notts Colts of yester year? Time was when they regularly opened the ball on Easter Monday, but either they are less hardy than the Shrewsburys and Gunns and Attewells who burst on the world on that inclement date or else owing to the scarcity of paper their deeds have been buried in oblivion. Failing them there could be none so appropriate as the "unassuming" freshmen who took the field at Cambridge. There was a Surrey trial match and an Oxford one as well, but there is a bloom of youth, a coltishness about freshmen which supremely fits them for this ceremony of initiation. The earliest practice of cricketers, the first stinging of bat and of hands, is occult from observation, though there are agreeable and historic facts to tell us that they indulge in it. The pitch at The Chestnuts at Downend was always ready in March, and cricket began, subject to the immemorial rule of a quarter of an hour's innings for adult Graces and five minutes for the boys. Still earlier we know how the "Little Farmer" bowled for hours at a hurdle while tending his father's sheep and how "many a Hampshire barn resounded with bat and ball as well as threshing." But as far as our own observation goes the freshmen stepped straight on to Fenner's, straight out of spring into summer and into the glory of restricted print.

The sound of the ball on the bat is as unique and characteristic as the cuckoo's call. The one we have been hearing now for some time; for the other we may yet have to wait a little while, but at least we can read the scores, and for many people that almost suffices. Cricket is a religion on which they have been brought up and to which they adhere even though they seldom attend its celebrations. "I can remember," wrote that charming essayist The Londoner, "the varnishy smell of a new bat that I held in my hands when I was a very little boy, an innocent child that never dared doubt cricket to be part of the whole duty of man." For a while he became a heretic, but it is pleasant to know that he came back or nearly back into the fold at last, for "now that no one has schoolmasterly authority over me in the matter of cricket or the irregular Greek verbs, I can more easily sympathize with those who have kept the faith." So it is with many others; after a time of doubt they return once and for all and of their own free will to a mild but unwavering orthodoxy. On this particular first day of summer cricket had serious and superficially more important rivals, for Derby County were at length defying the gypsy's warning and winning the Cup at Wembley, while HENRY COTTON was doing some incredible number under an average of fours at Wentworth. But those were just two more matches; the freshmen at Fenner's were taking part in a solemn and a sacred rite.

Old England at the Oval

FROM OUR CRICKET CORRESPONDENT [R. B. VINCENT]

24 *May* 1946. The King was present at the Oval yesterday when the ground was *en fête*, with an immense crowd and the Union Jack flying perkily from the top of a gasometer.

The occasion was a one-day match in aid of Surrey's appeal for funds, in this the centenary year of the club, between a team styled Old England and the present Surrey side. Indeed the spectator could be excused an excess of nostalgic memories, for, with Surrey batting first, there in the fielding side was a gathering of cricketers who between them, with the two umpires, Hobbs and Strudwick, could boast of 370 Test matches.

Maurice Tate, one of England's greatest bowlers of all time, started from the Pavilion end; there was Woolley at short slip, and giants of equal eminence scattered liberally over the ground. The old men had done well enough to be rid of Fishlock with only 46 runs scored against them, but they had a toilsome time while Gregory and Squires were together. The fielding stood well up to the test, even if there was once a slight difference of opinion between two most distinguished men as to who should run away to the far distance to retrieve the ball.

Fender it was, insinuating as ever, who took Gregory's wicket and at luncheon five men were out for 190. Appropriately enough during the interval the band of the East Surrey Regiment, among other stirring airs, struck up with "Boys of the old Brigade." Another 58 runs and the innings was declared closed.

The start of Old England's innings was tragic, the great Sutcliffe, saviour of England in many a hard-fought match, being leg-before-wicket and Sandham caught high up in the slips with but two runs on the board. And so, after all these years, Woolley, greeted as ever he was all over the world, and Hendren batting together in the sunshine at the Oval. Could the heart of a cricket lover ask for more? Woolley with his elegant ease lofting the ball over the bowler's head or placing it with exquisite timing to the on; and Hendren, still nimble of foot, advancing out to tame the bowling. Together they had added 102 runs in a partnership glorious to watch before Woolley was out to a hero's death, caught in the deep. Hendren carried on the good work, and Jardine, of the immaculately straight bat, made some noble strokes, but 79 runs to be made in the last three quarters of an hour to win was a little too much to ask for even on so joyful an occasion as this.

> SURREY 248 for 6 dec (H. S. Squires 68, R. J. Gregory 62)
> OLD ENGLAND 232 for 5 (E. Hendren 94, F. E. Woolley 62, D. R. Jardine 54)
> *Match drawn*

Regency Style Cricket

Top Hats and Hard Hitting

FROM OUR SPECIAL CORRESPONDENT [PHILIP URE]

8 *August* 1946; *Brighton, 7 August.* The Regency cricket match played this afternoon on the Brunswick Lawns at Hove has been a remarkably successful event in the Regency Festival. It provided a picturesque scene and was an excellent sporting event. Indeed, the finish quite put in the shade any thoughts – friendly or otherwise – one had earlier entertained about this atmosphere. In the end, the Regency Club of Brighton beat Hambledon by nine runs.

At the beginning, the match was definitely a dress parade. The Hambledon men had it on colour, for their jackets, knee-breeches, and stockings included all those within the rainbow, and each player had an assortment of three colours all to himself. The Regency Club men were all in white, but their top hats of the Regency style varied from silver to gold, and russet and green. The one outstanding example was a black topper of exceptional width and brilliant lustre.

The bats had been made as exact copies of the famous old bat at Winchester, and so had a peculiar air of antiquity. The umpires and scorers were somewhat more elaborately dressed than the players; or was it the length of their coloured frock coats that made it seem so? Of the two scorers, one "notched" an ash stick and the other used book and pencil.

There was one other preliminary with a Regency flavour, for the captains made a formal challenge for a stake of an 18-gallon barrel of punch, which is believed in fact to have turned into beer – a solemn thought for Regency enthusiasts.

In general, the match was remarkable for the little damage it caused in proportion to the peril in which it placed modern traffic on the highway beside Brunswick Lawns. A dozen or more times a good hit sent the ball right into Brunswick Terrace, and sometimes to the beach, but not quite into the sea.

The match was played under the "new articles of the game of cricket as settled and revised at the Star and Garter, Pall Mall, February 25, 1774, by a committee of noblemen and gentlemen of Kent." That meant, among other things, that the Regency Club went in first. The bowling was all under arm, and it was obvious that neither Regency nor Hambledon have any lob-bowlers to-day. The rules allowed only four balls to the over. Another un-expected detail of Regency cricket as applied to modern times was the num-ber of players who suddenly discovered that their breeches had split in a rather vital spot, but this became so common an experience that players ceased to worry.

The Regency Club scored 183 for 10 wickets and then declared as there was apparently a time limit to the match. Hambledon made 174 all out and only just failed to win the game during its closing stages.

The Autograph Hunters

11 *October* 1946, *Leading Article.* The great mass of mankind is exempt from one of the most prostrating penalties of fame. No small boy lies in wait for them with his autograph book. They may not therefore fully appreciate the protection extended to our cricketers who have lately landed in Australia. It has been decided that neither on the ground nor in the dressing room shall there be any signing of books or score-cards or bats. This will not ensure complete immunity since the players may possibly be besieged in their hotel and will certainly be waylaid in the street, but it is a respite to be grateful for. Small boys to be sure do not constitute the only menace, for the English captain is said to have signed his name two thousand times on the voyage out, when his pursuers were presumably old enough to know better and he, poor man, short of throwing himself overboard, was entirely at their mercy. But it is the boys who are at once the most formidable and the most appealing. It must be hard to refuse that eager petition, but the celebrity who hesitates is lost. While he pauses for an instant to scrawl his signature the rest of the pack will be upon him and pull him down like so many wolves. It may well be that our cricketers will have to take their walks abroad in couples, as do

policemen in dangerous neighbourhoods, or travesty themselves by the disguise of red side-whiskers and window-glass spectacles.

It would be interesting to know when this ruthless hunting of great men first began. When Lavengro saw the bruisers of England walking on the bowling green, "the men of renown, amidst hundreds of people with no renown at all, who gaze upon them with timid wonder," no one asked TOM CRIBB for his signature and the champion might have been hard put to it to oblige. Perhaps the mania for autographs is one of the less praiseworthy results of the spread of education, but that is but one question out of many. Is there any definite table by which relative values in the market can be estimated? Do two Huttons equal one Hammond, or does it all depend on the taste of individual fans? Does the possessor of an enviable collection, being suddenly in want of something more material and less romantic, realize part of his capital and sell a second-best wicketkeeper in order to buy an ice cream? Again we should like to know the value of a test match cricketer in some alien currency, such as the names and numbers of railway engines, which are to-day, as once were alley tors and commonies, "much prized by the youth of this town." These things are hidden from such of us as do not even pass our menus round at a dinner for the signatures of our fellows, being perfectly sure first that we do not want them, and secondly that we should lose them even if we did. Without incurring too grave a suspicion of sour grapes, we can thank heaven for our own obscurity, as we pass unmolested through the wildest herd of small boys that ever tore a cricketer in pieces.

England Save the Game

FROM OUR SPECIAL CORRESPONDENT [NEVILLE CARDUS]

8 *January* 1947; *Melbourne, 7 January*. After an exciting finish England to-day just saved the third Test match, but they scarcely deserved to escape punishment for a rather unconvincing rearguard action. The innings would have been invertebrate except for Washbrook, whose first century against Australia restored among those who have known him for years faith in his stroke-play and technique generally.

Everything was a collaborator this morning to England's effort to save themselves; the wicket was easier, perhaps, than ever before for some unfathomable reason, probably geological. The ball seldom, if ever, turned and then only gently; and all the time heavy clouds overhead promised to appear as an ally for Hammond at any hour. But the army of clouds, not far distant for long, seemed to wander and vacillate and never find real contact with the main forces, like Napoleon's meandering army at Waterloo. A shower actually stopped play for a quarter of an hour after luncheon and imparted a momentary liveliness to the pitch, and it was now that Ikin got out to a hopeless stroke, caught at silly mid-on. But the mainstays of the English innings largely contributed to their own ends, apart from Washbrook and Hammond, both well and truly bowled.

For an hour after the sixth day opened Washbrook and Hutton suffered no hardship at all; Hutton was satisfied to defend, and when Hutton does not wish to score on a somnolent turf there seems to the spectator no legal means of getting him out. Washbrook played a grand innings, for though he kept a resolute watch and ward he allowed no atrophy to visit him. He was usually making strokes with ease; some of his square drives and square pulls were of the authentic Test match style and dignity. If circumstances for more then three hours compelled his bat to perform the service of a stout oak door, there was some fine carving on it.

Hutton, also a sentinel for three hours, chose at last to essay a drive from a ball of short length from Toshack, only to loft his stroke to the off near the bowler, where Bradman made an easy, but triumphant, catch, throwing up the ball as though to say, "When he's out, they're all out." Edrich, after one splendid off-drive, fumbled here and there against spin that was potential rather than actual, and succumbed leg-before to McCool, who was brought back to the attack by Bradman with only a few minutes to go before luncheon. Throughout the match Bradman has been not only a vigilant captain but quick to make deductions from evidence, psychological as well as technical.

The sad mishap or folly of the day occurred just after half past 2. Compton drove exquisitely to the off, was nearly stumped off McCool, and then he hit again with grace and speed to the offside near cover point and dashed for a run, even though the ball went quickly near to Miller, a superb fieldsman whose pick-up and return to Tallon left poor, misguided Compton swinging his heart, soul, and body round in an agonized attempt to retrieve his impetuosity. Not for worlds would the present writer chide Compton for impulsiveness in the right place and moment; to-day it was his duty to absent himself from felicity awhile. England's position here was one in which runs were a vanity, and boundaries mere baubles. Washbrook proceeded on his way, and with Hammond next as his companion there was, of course, much strength left yet in reserve for England.

Bradman asked Dooland to bowl again, and with a ball of alluring length (and Dooland had bowled much short stuff so far) he entirely broke through Washbrook's forward defensive push with possibly a googly. So a match that at 1 o'clock had seemed to have no more problems for England to solve became alive and extremely quizzical. All the time the weather was intimidatory to Australia; the sky lowered and cleared tantalizingly. After tea, to end an innings so strong and calm that it was as a classic pillar or column, Hammond was bowled by Lindwall with a ball that kept low.

The time of day was 20 minutes past four; another 10 minutes of interference by rain only stimulated the occasion, and the sight of Bedser coming out to join Yardley provoked resignation in an Englishman's breast, not unmixed with humour. Especially when Bedser put a bat to the ball of such certainty and nonchalance that it might well have been performing the great ceremony of opening an England innings with Hobbs at the other end. As Yardley, as usual, was apparently a batsman without sense of error or difficulty, 10 minutes past five arrived to find Australia after all assuming an air of impatience and frustration, while the sky glowered again as though indicating that six days of hard labour had been lavished on a cricket match.

But the combatants were back and at it again at 25 minutes past five in a gloom so encircling that only good sportsmanship prevented an appeal. Compared with this visibility, the light appealed against the other day by Barnes was as the light of the garish universe. To sustain to the end a capriciousness that has enlivened us since the New Year another cloudburst emptied the field from half-past five to 20 minutes to the close of play.

In an improved light Bedser succumbed and palpitation afflicted us in earnest; three wickets to go, opportunity for hat tricks and catches terribly missed or as terribly held. Evans faced the music with the calm and composure of Toscanini, while Yardley continued with that imperturbability which a man presumably acquires while playing in the more searching atmosphere of Lancashire and Yorkshire matches. Appropriately he was undefeated to the end.

> AUSTRALIA 365 (C. McCool 104 not out, D. G. Bradman 79, S. Barnes 45) and 536 (A. Morris 155, R. Lindwall 100, D. Tallon 92, D. G. Bradman 49, C. McCool 43)
> ENGLAND 351 (W. J. Edrich 89, C. Washbrook 62, N. W. D. Yardley 61, J. T. Ikin 48; B. Dooland 4 for 69) and 310 for 7 (C. Washbrook 112, N. W. D. Yardley 53 not out, L. Hutton 40)
> *Match drawn*

Sir Stanley Jackson

20 *March* 1947. Sir Pelham Warner writes :–
I had known Sir Stanley Jackson since 1889 when Harrow met Rugby at Althorp Park. On that evening began a friendship which grew with the years and which I prized greatly. "He was my friend, faithful and just to me," and though we all have to face the Pale Horseman there is no need to be afraid of him, and I am certain Sir Stanley faced with the same calm courage as he showed in the great matches of his day. He was a splendid all-round cricketer – one of the finest in the history of cricket – and never was he finer than in a crisis; and it was a stirring sight to see him come down the pavilion steps to set right any early failures there may have been; immaculate in his flannels and his beautifully cleaned pads and boots, with his neat trim figure every inch a cricketer. Others will deal fully with his figures, but it may be said here that

no English cricketer, not even Hobbs, Hammond, or Sutcliffe, had a finer record in England against the Australians. And then, when he gave up, he sat on the Woolsack of Cricket, as president of the M.C.C., and at the time of his death he was a trustee of Lord's, chairman of the Cricket Committee, and president of the Yorkshire C.C.C. To the end he took the greatest possible interest in M.C.C. Never a week passed, even during the winter, that he was not at Lord's, and in the summer he was the best known of all the men who delight in the charm and atmosphere of the famous ground. He was busy with every avenue and aspect of the game and his enthusiasm never flagged. That he had been seriously ill for some time was obvious, but only a few days before he died he telephoned asking me to come to see him. I found him in good spirits, saying that he felt so much better that he had good hopes of coming to Lord's for a committee meeting.

I will try to describe the sort of batsman he was. First of all he was soundness itself with all the strokes – what I call a "complete" batsman. His style was easy and natural and he inspired confidence. As a bowler, medium pace, he had a beautifully easy action, and kept a length. In 1905 he not only headed the England batting averages with an aggregate of 492 runs and an average of 70.28, but was also at the top of the bowling figures. As a fieldsman at cover point, his invariable position, he was not a Hobbs, or a Jessop, but he was a good cover point, active and quick, who missed few chances. In a gallery of great players it is impossible to have a fixed order of merit, but he was in the first class of an honours school of cricket both as a batsman and an all rounder.

When you have known and been very fond of a man for nearly 60 years it is not easy to write exactly what you feel about him, but this I will say, that he had charm of manner, was always easy and pleasant, and in the cricket world, by young and old alike, he was welcomed, appreciated and respected. He meant much to me in my cricket life and though it was in the natural order of things that he should pass on, his absence leaves a big void.

Luncheon Interval

29 *April* 1947, *Leading Article*. There are some changes in the established order which even to the least bigoted appear as the opening of floodgates and the obliteration of landmarks. Of such is an experiment which is being considered by the Leicestershire County Cricket Club. There is to be – the shocked pen almost refuses its office – no luncheon interval. Play will begin at 1 o'clock, tea will be from 4.15 to 4.45 and stumps will be drawn at 8. In itself the proposal, which only applies to the first two days, seems sensible and practical enough. Advantage will be taken of the light afforded by double summer time and spectators can do a morning's work and yet get a full day's cricket for a half-day's idleness. The players will doubtless not go hungry, and in any

case the modern rush for food has brought lunch time nearer and nearer to breakfast time. The spectators will nibble their sandwiches in their seats as of old. But no luncheon interval! It is the sheer iconoclasm of the thing that takes the breath away. Those whose memories are of a far less exalted class of cricket, perhaps in school or village matches, look back to the lunch as one of the features of the day. "Lots of beer – hogsheads; rounds of beef – bullocks; mustard – cartloads" as Mr. Jingle observed of the repast at Muggleton. And what, purely from the spectator's point of view, of lunch at Lord's, haply on a coach with the pleasant popping of corks, and the promenade afterwards on historic turf, while casting a knowing eye at the wicket? Must all these delights go?

It is the interval quite as much as the lunch, with its break in the tension and its friendly meetings, which is so essentially sacred an institution, and nothing could quite make up for it. He who occasionally goes to watch cricket, having of course a perfect excuse for a day's pleasuring after weeks of application, never ceases to be surprised at the large number of other people who are apparently in a similar situation. He wonders how the world's work is getting on without them, and supposes enviously that they are all gentlemen of independent means who can live a life of cultured ease. However that may be, there they always are, from the first ball bowled and before it. Now they will have to fill their ample leisure in some other way. Very long and blank and dreary will their mornings appear. It is impossible not to sympathize with them. And to think that this proposal should come from a proud city of which it was once written

> And Leicester beans and bacon, food of kings!

What must be must, but there are things . . . It is surely a rash and impious hand that touches the cricketer's lunch. "There was high feasting on Broad Halfpenny during the solemnity of one of our grand matches." So wrote JOHN NYREN, and he could never have been stirred to such immortal gusto by tea consumed between 4.15 and 4.45.

The Wearing of the Blue

19 *July* 1947, *Leading Article.* A famous Cambridge cricketer has lately expressed in a letter what a number of obscure persons must have been thinking. Their eyes almost popped out of their heads when they read that in the University match the opening pair of Cambridge batsmen did not wear light blue caps; one was arrayed as a Quidnunc and the other as a Crusader. This is a free country in which the tyranny of colours, like other tyrannies, is to be resisted, but to most people the wearing of the blue on this one occasion appears a usage established from time immemorial and not lightly to be disregarded. So far only one side has been heard; the other has reserved its defence, if it may so be termed. It may be that the two batsmen believed their

respective headgears to be lucky, even as VICTOR TRUMPER had a run-getting shirt which he had washed nightly till it resolved into its elements, or as one great Oxford batsman remained covered for years in his Harlequin cap. If so, the belief was justified, and the Cambridge captain may appear for ever in blue striped with yellow, in gratitude for a true captain's innings. It may be again that those detestable clothing ration books were at the bottom of it, and no one will sneer at an honest poverty in coupons. Yet, as MR. ROCKLEY WILSON says, the right caps might have been borrowed. Many a venerable blue would have been only too glad that his treasured cap should bloom again in the good cause.

There was a time, if memory serves, before Test match caps were invented, when the England eleven took the field with each man in his own club or county cap. This added a pleasant touch of colour to the scene and enabled the less instructed to know

> By post and vest, by horse and crest
> Each warlike Lucumo

though to be sure no bars of red and yellow were needed to identify the noblest Lucumo of them all. Some may regret those variegated days, but even then blues were blues and the University match a thing apart. MR. WILSON adduces a historical parallel from forty years ago, when a distinguished Cambridge batsman wore a Crusader cap, because it had a larger peak to protect his spectacles from a drizzle. That reason will never serve again, for all caps to-day have almost monstrous peaks. How much they have grown the elderly warrior will scarcely realize, unless he unearths from a drawer some coloured cap of his boyhood "with the little round button at top." He will find it hard to believe that his head has not swelled owing to subsequent if necessarily lesser distinctions. It seems indeed an absurd little garment and if he wears it at some family frolic of dressing-up, perhaps at Christmas-time, he may rely on peals of irreverent laughter. Yet the line must be drawn somewhere; blue caps are hardly a subject for merriment, and the more solemn at any rate will hope that University elevens will never again disturb their "fearful symmetry."

He Clean Bowled Grace

20 *August* 1947. Mr. H. W. Shepherd, chief rating and valuation officer for the Penge district of S.E. London, who retired yesterday, remembers when, in his early twenties, he clean bowled W. G. Grace in a match at the Crystal Palace between a Sydenham and district side and London County, which Grace captained. Grace, he said, came straight over to him, slapped him on the back and said, "My boy, if you live to be 100 you'll never send down another ball like that one."

Rolling On

5 *November* 1947, *Leading Article*. It may be that the souvenir hunter is, taken by and large, weak in intellect and feeble in memory. It should not need some monstrous vase with "A Present from ——" enscrolled among the twining roses to bring back the scent and smell of the crowded beach under the August sun and the faint, pleasant, irritant of sand between the toes, and no fragment of bomb or German helmet is necessary to recreate in the mind the horrors of air raids and war. Nevertheless every now and again it is easy to understand and sympathize with the impulse which would preserve some relic from the past, and not only the sentimental will rejoice that W. G. GRACE's old lawn-roller is not to be permitted to rust away in idleness and oblivion. It has been bought for £21 and will be handed over to a cricket club which will both use and appreciate the gift.

There is little danger of a man falling into a mania for collecting garden-rollers as others collect hats and walking-sticks which once belonged to the illustrious dead, but a roller, for all that, is not without its charm and its romantic appeal. To be sure, there is little lovable in the impersonal monsters that do duty on our Test match grounds, and the days when Dobbin, that faithful and intelligent animal, would put himself between the shafts at the fall of the ninth wicket seem remote indeed. Not all cricket grounds are first class, however, and the humbler lawn-roller, with its personal squeals and habits, has still an important part to play. Besides, did not the great Doctor learn his cricket on a lawn by a Gloucestershire orchard, an orchard not far in time or spirit from that in which Shallow and Silence nodded their heads and spoke of old Double who was dead, and perhaps the fortunate club will receive the self-same roller as that which trundled down that homely pitch and so helped the career of the man who turned the game of cricket into a many-chorded lyre destined to make its enchanting music heard the world over. The wheelbarrow and the broom are now more useful about the garden than the roller, but its day will come again, sooner than now seems possible, and once more its pleasant services will be in demand on lawns and village greens. One club at least will have reason to savour the ritual of the first rolling of the spring, and its oldest member, with the memory of a black beard and a red and yellow cap still fresh in his mind, may well murmur

> Oh! scenes in strong remembrance set!
> Scenes never, never to return!

as the veteran squeaks and rumbles its way over the lumps.

Conflict of Emotions

24 *May* 1948, *Leading Article.* The time of the first Test Match draws ever nearer and, with the first appearance of the Australians at Lord's, interest is steadily mounting. Enthusiasm for cricket takes many forms, but it has been left to the LORD MAYOR of ADELAIDE to think of a new one, at once most generous and ingenious, whereby Australians shall celebrate the feats of their players by contributing gifts of food for British war widows. The scheme appears assured of success, since already 500 country towns have agreed to take part. A tariff has been suggested of a shilling for the fall of an England wicket or for an Australian century, with proportionate amounts for boundary hits and a bonus of particular liberality "when a sixer climbs the sky." It is pleasant to picture thousands of listeners sitting up into uncharted hours of the night and, as the commentator announces a hundred by BRADMAN – or BARNES or BROWN or MILLER or MORRIS – exclaiming with tears of joy and pride "Bang goes another leg of mutton." Here indeed is a plan to be received with nothing but gratitude; and yet we may spare a moment of not too serious pity for our own enthusiasts at home. It seems that they must inevitably be torn by two conflicting emotions, one of wishing all possible good to the war widows of their own country and the other of wishing all possible ill, in a friendly way, to its formidable invaders.

Even in normal circumstances this painful alternative confronts the spectator at a Test Match. In the most unlikely event of BRADMAN being dismissed for a duck he will doubtless rend the sky with shouts of triumph, but he will also be a little disappointed since he is robbed of the sight of that terrific run-getting machine in full blast. It would not have been so in his school days, when he was a purer and a better hater, and would have hailed the opposing captain's downfall with savage glee. Now, however, he is not all partisan but has in him something of the artist, and so patriotism and selfish enjoyment of consummate art tug at his heart-strings in opposite directions. There is a story of FULLER PILCH standing umpire in a match in Kent, in which E. M. GRACE, then an infant phenomenon, was taking part. He refused an appeal, which he ought to have answered in the bowler's favour, on the ground that he "wanted to see the young gentleman bat." It is human and natural to want to see BRADMAN bat, if only he does not bat too long. Now the LORD MAYOR of ADELAIDE has intensified the struggle that must go on in many a respectable bosom. Luckily, watching cricket has much the same effect as, according to DR. JOHNSON, a man's knowledge that he is to be hanged in a fortnight; "It concentrates his mind wonderfully." Only perhaps when the day's play is over will our onlooker remember once again those kindly parcels of food.

"Greatest Cricketer That Ever Lived or Ever Will Live"

FROM A CORRESPONDENT [BERNARD DARWIN]

14 *July* 1948. On July 18, 1848, after an interlude of inconsiderable daughters, a fourth son was born to Dr. Henry Mills Grace and his wife (*née* Martha Pocock), of Downend, in Gloucestershire. It was an event destined to change the face if not of England at least of the great English game of cricket; if John Small the elder, of Hambledon, had been the "man who found out cricket," it was William Gilbert Grace who raised it to heights, alike of skill and popularity, undreamed of before his day. At the time it seemed doubtless an event of purely domestic importance and we do not know if Dr. Grace, when he came riding home from his long round, praetermitted for once his cricket practice in the evening. It is pleasant to fancy that he did not and that Mrs. Grace, who according to Richard Daft knew ten times as much about cricket as any lady he had ever met, was soothed, as she lay in bed, by the familiar sound of bat and ball amid the Downend apple trees.

Since it is primarily the birth of a hero that is being celebrated we may look back to those early years in which the small Gilbert (how impossible it is to fancy him as ever being small!) was first able to take part in the family ritual, with his father and elder brothers and perhaps a cousin or two of the clans of Rees and Gilbert. At intervals there ring out the excited barks of Don, Ponto, and Noble, that immortal trinity, as they pursue the ball into the outfield or oppose to it their dauntless breasts. Mrs. Grace is there to look on with serious, appraising eyes and the girls throw up the ball if it comes their way or perhaps bowl one in a little game of their own to the still toddling Fred. And of course there is Uncle Pocock. If anyone watches the centenary matches with exultation from Elysian wickets it should be he. He made Gilbert his peculiar care, insisting that he should not, like his brother E. M., be corrupted into the heresy of the cross bat by being given too early a bat beyond his strength; preaching to him the virtues in life that really matter, the straight bat, the left shoulder forward, defence before hitting, and, above all, patience, that endless patience that was never to desert him and caused the appetite for runs to grow only more insatiable in the making. Uncle Pocock must never be forgotten.

Comparisons between the champions of different generations are nearly always as futile as ungracious. If they are to be made at all it must be by someone with claims to which the present writer has no pretensions whatever. This is a moment when hero-worship may be given free play, and unlearned worshippers at least will accept Mr. C. E. Green's fine, defiant eulogy, "The greatest cricketer that ever lived or ever will live." But perhaps one exception to this wise self-denial is permissible. No one can ever have attained to greatness at so tender an age. The true Infant Phenomenon was not Miss Ninetta Crummles but Master Gilbert Grace. Let those who spill too fervent ink over a promising colt or a schoolboy given a trial for his county eleven, ponder over a line or two of statistics. At ten W. G. played in his first match for the West Gloucestershire Club and at 12 made 51 against Clifton. At 14 he played against the All-England Eleven and faced two famous fast bowlers, Tarrant and Jackson, whom all his life he regarded as among the very best. The bowling had to be changed and Tinley brought on with his crafty lobs before the boy was bowled – for two and thirty runs. At 15 he himself played for the All-England Eleven and not much more than a year later for the Gentlemen against the Players and for England against Surrey. The day of the Australians had not yet come and so, as far as representative honours were concerned, the boy of a little over 17 had become a youthful Alexander with no more worlds to conquer.

He had not yet reached his ultimate pinnacle, but it was not far off. In 1867, which he deemed his best bowling year, only one professional, Wootton, took more wickets than he did. We think now of a venerable bearded giant beguiling youth with slows of innocent aspect, such as old William Beldham would have called (as he did Tom Walker's) "such baby bowling." So it is worth recalling the thin, lanky boy, with an incipient black scrub on his chin, bowling fast medium round arm, straight at the stumps, with no great guile but trusting to the wicket to do the rest. And, apropos, how bad were the wickets on which W. G. was soon to gather so monstrous a harvest of runs? It is a subject on which it is for ever interesting to speculate and perhaps easy to exaggerate. We have his own word for it that in the sixties many of them, and Lord's in particular, were very rough indeed. There is further Tom Emmett's testimony to his own and George Freeman's "expresses flying about his ribs, shoulders and head." But no doubt there came an improvement and W. G., never anxious to take undue credit, told at least one distinguished batsman of a later era that many of the wickets on which he played in his prime were very good. Good or bad he soon became, according to all previous standards of scoring, thoroughly outrageous upon them, and it was in 1870, when he was still but 22, that Emmett crystallized the general feeling in a memorable sentence: "I call him a non-such; he ought to be made to play with a littler bat."

A non-such he remained from then till that far distant year of 1895 with its crowning glory of 1,000 runs in May and the hundredth 100. And all that time the vast W. G. legend was growing and growing. It is a tribute to his surpassing fame that many fine cricketers of his prime are now only known, save to the more assiduous students of Wisden, because they played with him. Emmett was a great bowler and a great character, but men remember not what he did but what he said of W. G. The first thing recalled about J. C. Shaw is that twice he got W. G. out for a duck in the first innings of a benefit match and paid dearly for such presumption in the second. Their places in the averages are long since lost; their places in the legend make their names secure.

Popular fame is not necessarily evidence of real, enduring greatness, and the immensity of the legend is not cited with any intention of making backhanded comparisons, but it does show the extraordinary position which one player of a game attained almost as a boy and never lost. As long as he lived he remained the best known man in England, at whom the inescapable finger would always point, a figure to be instantly picked out even in a Derby Day crowd, unique, not to be mistaken. To be sure this could not have been so had W. G. been merely a supreme cricketer. There were contributory causes. His huge and, as the years passed, almost lumbering frame, his mighty beard growing gradually a "sable silvered," marked him as a colossus. Furthermore he was essentially a man of character. His simplicity and his guile; his words often spoken in deadly earnest but giving delighted if concealed amusement; his boyish jollity and his occasionally boyish pettishness; his intense keenness, which sometimes led him too far but had in it nothing of rancour or malice; finally his obvious lovableness – these things were all blent in a picture which was a public possession, a picture of one who in some obscure, indefiable way was a great man.

To meet him casually, and there could be no one more friendly, was instantly to be impressed by several things – his kindliness, his true modesty which took himself for granted, his complete simplicity of demeanour and perhaps above all his great natural dignity. He was easily approachable but to take a liberty with him seemed unthinkable. If that casual acquaintance, desiring to probe further, asked questions of those who really knew W. G. and had played with him, there was but one answer. If ever he had a weakness it was an amiable one and no fault was to be hinted, no word heard against him; he was a dear old man. To be thus held in memory is surely something for which any man might be grateful on his birthday.

W. G. Grace Centenary

20 *July* 1948. SIR W. SMITHERS (Orpington, C.), on a point of order, said he had asked permission to put down a motion on the Order Paper to commemorate the centenary of W. G. Grace, but the Speaker had not allowed him to do so. He bowed to that ruling, but he could not let the centenary of the greatest cricketer of all time pass without his name being mentioned in the House. (Cheers.)

The SPEAKER. – The hon. member certainly wrote to me and asked me if he might put a motion on the Order Paper to that effect, but I declined to give my leave. It seems to me that if we put such motions on the Order Paper we might start with W. G. Grace, and we might go on to Bradman, and I do not know where we would end. (Laughter and cheers.) We put motions on the Order Paper to deal with Parliamentary matters. However much we might admire the cricket record of W. G. Grace, I do not think it would be in order to put it on the Order Paper.

SIR W. SMITHERS, pointing to the Government front bench: At least he knew how to play the game! (Laughter.)

Mr. CRAWLEY (Buckingham, Lab.). – Lest it be thought that the commemoration of W. G. Grace is a party matter, I arise to say that, had the motion been allowed, I should have been pleased to second it.

Farewell to Bradman

24 *September* 1948, *Leading Article*. If statistics were the last word in cricket, then it would be easy to prove that DONALD GEORGE BRADMAN is the greatest cricketer who has ever lived. Happily they are not and memory, warm with summer days stretching back for nearly a generation, rather than pedantry brooding over decimals, prompts the good-bye and come back if only as a visitor that speeds the Australian captain on his homeward voyage. He sailed yesterday with an unbeaten team after making a century in his last match in England as he did long ago in his first. His own summing up of all that happened between was to express a mild hope that he had made "some contribution to international cricket." A fairer way of putting it is to say that no player, since history was made in the Hambledon era on Windmill Down, has contributed more to the game.

Comparisons are odious, and when they arise in the minds of cricket lovers, who as a class take fond delight in remembering the old giants, they are apt to mislead. Who can say with real confidence what GRACE would have done against modern bowling or how BRADMAN would have adapted himself to Victorian wickets? Who, indeed, really cares? An early champion in retirement asked, as he watched a new fast bowler at Lord's, whether he himself had been faster in his youth, and on being tactfully reassured on this point went back to the country content. Lucky elders who saw GRACE and RANJITSINHJI, the middle aged who are still true to TRUMPER, and the middle ageing for whom HOBBS will always be the hero may match those great figures against the little man who has just left, but the rivalry leads nowhere except to a pleasant airing of good stories.

To have seen BRADMAN at the wicket is to have enjoyed the precision of the art of batting. LARWOOD's fierce attack and the cunning of VERITY's spin – and, in the last chapters, BEDSER's patient industry – tested his almost inhuman quickness and certainty of reaction, but only to remind spectators that he was a miracle of flesh and blood and not a little robot under a long-peaked green cap. ARTHUR SHREWSBURY used to say, when he went out to bat after lunch, "Bring me a cup of tea at half-past four." BRADMAN, but for the dusk that causes stumps to be drawn at the end of even the longest afternoon, could with equal confidence have ordered his dinner in advance to be sent out on to the field. At the top of his form there was no getting him out. Some baby now toddling after a soft ball in New South Wales may grow up to be the scourge of English Test teams in the sixties. Old stagers who then watch him piling up a century will be able, however finely he plays, to murmur: "Ah, but you should have seen Bradman."

England Win from Last Ball

FROM OUR SPECIAL CORRESPONDENT [T. D. NELSON]

21 *December* 1948; *Durban*, 20 *December*. There will never be a more stirring or breath-taking finish to a Test match than that which ended here this evening with the very last ball of the match and England winning in bad light by two wickets.

Appeals against the light, or negative tactics by the South Africans, could have closed up the game, but it was fought out to the bitter end, and the result hung in the balance throughout a long, dramatic afternoon with South Africa, who at one time had appeared to be doomed to defeat, coming within an ace of snatching a most sensational victory. The thousands of people who saw this match will never forget it, nor regret the result. It was cricket played by both teams in the highest traditions and has set the seal on the success of the M.C.C. tour. F. G. Mann must be greatly satisfied with his *début* as a Test captain, but had defeat been England's lot he would have emerged with just as much credit.

When the match was resumed this morning England were in a strong position to force a win since the South Africans, with four wickets down, still required two runs to equalize the scores. It was generally expected that unless the overnight rain had caused an improvement in the pitch South Africa would be out before lunch, leaving the road clear for a comfortable English victory. Mann relied on Wright and Bedser to take early wickets, but Wade and Begbie, batting splendidly in unfavourable conditions, gave a much better complexion to the innings than the most optimistic South African supporter could have expected.

As the morning wore on, with the batsmen beaten by the occasional lifting ball and Begbie offering a difficult chance to Simpson at deep point with his score at 13, South Africa's chances of saving the game improved. Mann, frequently consulting with Hutton, made frequent bowling changes without effect, and when he requisitioned the new ball Begbie promptly hit Bedser for a six, a most rare occurrence in Test match cricket. Bedser eventually broke this threatening match-saving partnership at 174 when he dismissed Begbie, but Wade went on to reach 63 before Jenkins bowled him round his legs. After this there was valuable time-saving batting by A. Rowan and Tuckett, but the innings closed soon after half past three.

England were set 128 runs to win and left 135 minutes to do it in. Hutton and Washbrook left no doubts about their intention of going all out for victory. Hutton cut the first ball from McCarthy fiercely down the gully where Nourse took it on the knee, causing the game to be held up for five minutes while he received medical attention. Then Washbrook should have been out in the next over. He swung at his first ball from Tuckett, giving Wynne an easy catch on the boundary, but the ball was dropped.

Then rain curtailed England's batting time by another 10 minutes. A big setback was in store for England on the resumption. Hutton had scored only five when he lifted a ball to silly mid-on. One down for 25. F. G. Mann ran out to the wicket, still intent on racing the clock, and helped Washbrook to add 24 quick runs before N. Mann got a leg before decision against Washbrook. Two down for 49.

Mann, still determined on victory and hitting out strongly, was dropped in the deep, but was almost immediately afterwards brilliantly caught in the slips by Mitchell. Three down for 52. Then, for the first time in the whole match, the South Africans came within sight of victory as McCarthy crashed through the defences of Watkins, Simpson, and Evans, and, with an hour to go, England still wanted 56 runs and South Africa wanted only four more wickets.

The match had taken a complete somersault, and now England's fate was in the hands of the imperturbable Compton and the stout-hearted Jenkins. The crowd was in a fever of excitement as they followed the tense struggle ball by ball, run by run and minute by minute. But the light was deteriorating, threatening an anti-climax to the great events of the day. With half an hour to go England required 33 runs to win. The match, however, did race to a climax, with victory in the hands of either team during the last half-hour of breathtaking cricket.

Excitement rose to a high pitch when McCarthy bowled Compton, and then, with only one run added, got Jenkins caught behind the wicket. Eight wickets were now down for 116 runs, and 12 runs wanted in the last 10 minutes, with Bedser and Gladwin left to do or die. The bad light justified an appeal, but both teams were determined to fight it out to the last. Gladwin was dropped at mid-on before he had scored, but the margin was reduced by four runs as Tuckett took the last over with eight more runs wanted. A leg bye and a four to Gladwin as he galloped up the pitch waving his bat joyously, two more leg byes as the batsmen swung desperately, and then the last ball of the match with one run wanted to win. Gladwin jumped up the pitch and swung his bat wildly as the ball went off his leg. There was a desperate scramble for the creases with a near run out, and England had won.

SOUTH AFRICA 161 (A. V. Bedser 4 for 39) and 219 (W. Wade 63, D. Begbie 48; D. V. P. Wright 4 for 72)
ENGLAND 253 (L. Hutton 83, D. Compton 72; N. Mann 6 for 59, A. Rowan 4 for 108) and 128 for 8 (C. McCarthy 6 for 43)
England won by 2 wickets

Vendetta

8 *June* 1949, *Leading Article.* It can hardly be expected that to-day's cricket match between a team of authors and a team of publishers will exhibit the normal relations between these two classes of person in any very realistic light. If they had challenged each other at (say) the Wall Game there might have been scope for their mutual antipathies to express themselves in overt or covert acts of violence, and there is little doubt that in such a case the casualties among the publishers, even if they had won the game, would have been heavier and more serious than on the other side. For no publisher could ever bring himself to kill or even to disable an author. It would not, or at least it very easily might not, pay. Even if the author's works are published by some rival house, the publisher is well acquainted with the fickleness of the species. Who knows but what the gifted creature may one day, in a tantrum, take his deathless or anyhow profitable manuscripts elsewhere? The publisher may be unable, in the heat of the struggle, to restrain himself from giving the author a little, irritable push; but he will not stamp upon his face.

No such quality of mercy resides in the author's savage breast. Incapable of gratitude, he regards every publisher as his natural enemy. Bloated middlemen, parasites who draw their over-abundant sustenance from the life-blood of his Muse, publishers arouse in him the same sort of tacit antipathy which infantry entertain for the staff. He knows, moreover, that there are plenty of them. His genius is irreplaceable; of their meagre administrative and commercial talents there is, if anything, a glut. Place one of these blood-suckers at his mercy and he will not hesitate to wreak upon him an exemplary vengeance.

In a cricket match, however – even in a cricket match between literary gentlemen – the opportunities for inflicting serious injuries on one's opponents are limited. A fast bowler might, it is true, stimulate a demand for stretcher-bearers; but authors, haled from their desks to blink like owls upon the unaccustomed turf, are not the sort of team to throw up a fast bowler, or not at any rate a fast bowler who will bowl fast for very long. Publishers, moreover, have acquired by virtue of their calling considerable evasive agility. They may not be able to return the deliveries of some insensate poet quite as smoothly and dexterously as they are accustomed to return his manuscripts; and they cannot avoid a rising ball, as they can a writer who seems unlikely to rise, by pretending to be in conference; but they are sharp-witted fellows, full of cunning, and though they may not come off scathless the authors will be lucky if the venom which inspires their attack is matched by the damage which it inflicts on their exploiters. When stumps are drawn old scores will still remain to be paid off; and whether, in the interim, any scores worth mentioning of another kind will have accrued to either side remains to be seen.

Border-line Cricket

24 *August* 1949, *Leading Article*. There are more ways of getting a man out than are known to the Laws of Cricket. A well-chosen umpire with the right ideas on local patriotism is a help and so is one who reacts easily to suggestion and can be bluffed by a loud, self-confident appeal. He is especially useful in doubtful cases of L.B.W. because nine umpires out of ten (beyond the narrow circle of professionals) are a bit hazy about the exact wording of the rule and are, in any case, seldom quick enough to see just where the ball pitched or where, if unobstructed, it would go. The wicket-keeper (who used to be called the "Aunt Sally" and has to put up with all the knocks) is sometimes accused of crouching, with outspread gloves and protruding pads, over the stumps, intent on flipping off a bail, morally dislodged by a ball that beat the batsman. Jocular remarks between overs may serve (but not with Australians) to induce a momentary care-free mood that is good for a dolly catch. Queer stories in this *genre* are told of W. G. himself.

Such artful aids to a bowling analysis are strengthened by freaks within the law. Hitherto, the record in this class has, perhaps, been held by the entry, still surviving, in an old County score-book, "C. G. Taylor, hat knocked on wicket, b. Hillyer, 89." That white beaver, skittled down from the head of its wearer by a fast, rising ball, must have gone long since to the moths and, now, its claim to fame is surpassed. It cannot compete with "Townsend, j R.A.F. Pilots, c. Eagar, b. Carty." This unlucky Warwickshire batsman, who fell to an attack consisting of two Hampshire men and three diving aircraft, may console himself with the thought that he has been "jetted" into cricket history. At the cost of no more than the loss of his wicket, he joins the sparrow which shares with the ball it fatally obstructed a glass case in the pavilion at Lord's. Destruction from the air is evidently a two-way traffic and it remains for some Jessop to land one in the cockpit, thus starting a new variant of the schoolboy question about what happens in a match – without boundaries – if the ball is hit into a passing train. The proviso of no boundaries seems unnecessary with a stroke into an aircraft, for, however high it went, it could hardly be ruled to have crossed the line. A long-winded pair of batsmen might run it out until the ball was returned from the airfield; but, if they did so, they might find themselves cut down to a beggarly six. They might be tripped up by the rule about a ball that "cannot be recovered" or even – although this seems a far-fetched definition of jet-propelled flight – by the one about being "finally settled."

Projection of the hazards of cricket into another dimension will be poorly viewed by players for whom the turf and the fauna upon and around it already get too effectively in the way of their centuries. Spectators prowling behind the bowler's arm, flies and wasps dancing above the pitch, and sun-light catching on glass have all taken wickets – or at least batsmen, as they took off their pads, have been heard to say so. Providence kindly tempers the wind of these misfortunes for the weaker brethren. The worse a batsman is the more stoutly he often triumphs over distraction. Let the sight-screen be wrongly placed and the light fade and the band blare away at the neighbouring flower show and he is just as likely as not to get runs – or to get out. He rises above the pettiness of fate just as he scorns the bowler's skill. Googlies are wasted on him, for he could not, if his life depended on it, tell by the delivery which way the thing was coming at him and, if he could, how would the foreknowledge help him? Against such a man – and he is the salt of cricket – dive-bombing is a farce. All he needs is a straight ball; he is not particular about its length.

Oh, What a Beautiful Season!

10 *May* 1950, *Leading Article*. Once more the court of King Willow resounds with the gladsome music of bat meeting ball. . . . Perhaps nobody writes quite like that in these days; but it is one of the standing duties of occasional literature to salute the opening of the cricket season, and this duty is now being faithfully discharged on all sides. Though their language may be rather less lyrical than of yore, though it is comparatively rare to find a closing paragraph which begins "But ere long the lengthening shadows will caress the verdant green-sward," the writers still contrive to strike that note of seemly jubilation which has always been *de rigueur* on this occasion. What they are saying is, in effect, that it is now once more possible for Englishmen to play cricket; and, though they cannot exactly be accused of mafficking, they say it in accents vibrant with a deep and holy joy.

It cannot be said that, this year, they have quite succeeded in capturing the atmosphere in which many of us played the first game of the season. Not insensible though we were of the privilege of being allowed to play cricket again, it was the idea of desisting from this sacred pastime and getting into a nice hot bath that was uppermost in our minds during the actual game itself. Far above our heads the rooks clung precariously to the thrashing elms or, becoming air-borne, were whirled instantly into the next parish. The tins on the telegraph rattled like a Bren-gun carrier. Underfoot the ground was sodden, and in (among other things) its colour and consistency the bowler's pile of sawdust resembled sausage meat. The ball which occasionally, and so far as the batsman was concerned unintentionally, came our way was a raw, pink, slightly swollen object; it did not skim along the turf, but progressed in a series of long, low, venomous, squelching bounds until after punishing our frozen finger-tips it struck us upon the knee-cap with fearful force. The sleet which fell from time to time was never quite enough to stop play.

Upon the football field there would have been violent exercise, at the point-to-point there would have been cherry brandy; but at the court of King Willow there was only cricket, an odd enough game at the best of times; in the rough winds of this May a rigorous ordeal. Shivering, grumbling, dropping catches, falling over and getting run out, we played the summer game in winter weather. And, so strange is the British character, so oddly formed by this and similar pursuits, that when the match was over and we trooped off the desolate field in our damp, discoloured flannels, some of us had actually enjoyed it and the rest of us believed that we had.

Lord's Calypso

30 *June* 1950, *Leading Article.* Playing on their own sunny ground West Indian cricketers have beaten English teams before. Once, at Sydney nineteen years ago, they beat Australia, with BRADMAN playing. But yesterday was their finest hour. They have handsomely laid an All England XI low at Lord's. JOHN GODDARD and his men have made a new mark in cricket history. To win by 326 runs at the headquarters of cricket, in spite of the brave English recovery led by WASHBROOK on Wednesday, puts these West Indians for good among the great ones. There have been giants before in West Indian cricket – GEORGE CHALLENOR, LEARIE CONSTANTINE and GEORGE HEADLEY, each of them among Wisden's best through the ages. This is the first West Indian team to bring the promise of so many fine cricketers to full fruition.

These West Indians play cricket – as their fellow countrymen watch it – in their own gay way. Even if this game had gone against GODDARD's team these men would have stayed in the memory: RAE's solid hundred dotted with hard hits to the ring, STOLLMEYER's elegance, the flowing eagerness of WORRELL, the forceful skill of WEEKES, the happy mastery of WALCOTT behind the stumps and his massive batting – above all the spinning duet of RAMADHIN and left-arm VALENTINE, striplings both with more experience gained in this one match than in all their brief career before. The proper Test cricketer mixes the right alloy of patience, precision in technique and attacking spirit. Only patience and the dourer experience of more sober cricketers have been lacking before. This time the West Indians mixed the elements right. Under GODDARD's long-headed leadership West Indian cricket has come of age. There will no doubt be a calypso about it all. Perhaps it has been already composed by the knot of gleeful islanders on the stand behind the sight-screen, with their cries and calls, their songs and music sounding pleasantly strange in the Lord's hush. It will be sung as a battle-honour wherever West Indians bat and bowl.

Australia Well Beaten

FROM OUR SPECIAL CORRESPONDENT [R. C. ROBERTSON-GLASGOW]

1 *March* 1951; *Melbourne*, 28 *February*. Shortly before 5 o'clock this afternoon Hutton turned a ball from Hassett to leg for a single and England had won the fifth Test match againt Australia by eight wickets. So victory came after 13 years. It was a resounding victory won against chivalrous, but tough, opponents by a team of cricketers who, if late in the series, answered both the leadership of a true captain and their own latent powers.

Luck did not unduly help either side. The pitch remained good to the end. To the end, too, if we allow for the pleasing comedy of the last six balls from Hassett, the Australians strained spirit and sinew in defence of their invincibility. Their fielding was superb and when Washbrook was out at the total of 32 and only 65 runs were needed still, we were half ready to believe that Iverson would suddenly reveal some further freak of spin, or that Lindwall and Miller would rise to demoniac strength and unearthly brilliance and snatch victory from England at the last. But whatever fantasies may have clouded or illumined the minds of the spectators, there was one man out in the middle, Hutton, who stood no nonsense from sceptic or bowler.

As is the way of greatness, he controlled and commanded without fuss. Early in the innings he hit Lindwall for a sizzling 4 past cover. Then, when Iverson came on, he knew and showed himself to be the master. Praise, too, to Simpson. Late, but not quite too late, he found his own high artistry of stroke-play, put away the pedestrian accuracy of the mere workman, and turned a position of doubt to one of lively hope.

So much for the batting. In the bowling Bedser once more showed that he is the best of his kind in the world to-day. Throughout the match, indeed throughout the series, no Australian batsman wholly mastered his late swerve either way, his accuracy of direction, and his stinging pace from the pitch. His was a double task to quell runs and to take wickets, and he achieved it. Wright also, that variable genius, had his share in the victory. He ended both Harvey and Hassett when each was set and happy. As an old Yorkshire player once remarked: "Any fool can bowl batsman when he's made nowt."

In the morning when Hassett and Hole continued from a total of 129 for 4, Brown was faced with a tactical problem, mild perhaps in retrospect, but real enough when every Australian run was a drag on hope. Should he or Bedser bowl during seven overs before the new ball was due? Bedser has no dislike of work or of a ball of moderate age, but this part-rended ball had apparently grown senile early. So Brown took it and in the first two overs by him and Wright singles came with an ease that was alarming or reassuring according to party.

Hole did once glide Wright in the air not far from Bailey's outstretched hand, and Hassett did have some trouble with Wright's googly. But the googly on the middle-and-leg is ever the spinner's second best, and it was a beautifully pitched leg-break which, at 142, beat Hassett's back-stroke and hit his middle and off stumps. Wright, a man of quiet temper, jumped in triumph. That was the second ball of an over. The seventh Johnson ballooned to very deep mid-on, and Brown never looked as if he would not catch it.

So Lindwall joined Hole and Bedser came on at the Richmond end for Brown. He harassed Lindwall, who was almost caught by Sheppard diving to the right at short-leg. Suddenly Wright lost accuracy, and Hole, who now carried the Australian innings and hopes with debonair courage, cracked him thrice in one over to the boundary – two hooks, then a late cut off the faster ball. Forty minutes before luncheon Bedser took the new ball and Bailey succeeded Wright. Drinks, irrelevant to most, were brought out. Then Bedser had a duel with Hole. Evans missed a chance of stumping on the leg side, and Hole made an uppish stroke wide of the slips, then a beautiful drive for 4 past mid-off. Soon after Hole reached his 50. Lindwall, never so convincing in his more sedentary mood, edged Bedser for 4 between the slips, who rearranged themselves with postdated care.

At the pavilion end Bailey lapsed into eccentricity with two overhead full tosses, then he cooled himself down to a more methodical attack at the leg-stump with three close leg fielders. Hole was quietened and when he did try a drive Bailey almost caught and bowled him with a goalkeeper's fling to the right. Then Bedser, as if tired of other people's oddities and luck, bowled Lindwall, who was framing vaguely for a cut. That was 192 for seven and Tallon walked in very slowly with head cocked a little to the side as one who hears the deadly approach of the tumbril. He scored one run to leg. And so to lunch – 193 for seven and Australia only 90 ahead. Hole had then scored 61.

After lunch the air was heavily humid and a slight mist as of autumn come too soon hung over the scene. Bailey tried no more ballistic experiments and bowled Hole with a fast and well-pitched-up ball. Hole will surely be seen with the next Australian team in England. He batted for two hours and 40 minutes. And now Bedser who had taken the first two wickets, took the last two also. He pierced Johnston's airy defence and caused an outswinger to whizz from the edge of Iverson's antique bat into Compton's hands at second slip. No nonsense about it. He had taken 30 wickets in the five Tests.

After use of the light roller Hutton and Washbrook went out to face Lindwall (pavilion end) and Miller just before a quarter to three. Lindwall went through more unlimbering exercises than usual and some prophesied an attack of much height as well as speed. But it was speed only, and in the very first over Hutton drove a 4 off Lindwall like the crack of a pistol. Miller once passed Hutton with a beauty, but Hutton did not mean to play any game with time and 17 runs were on the board, 16 to Hutton, when after two overs each, Lindwall and Miller were succeeded by Iverson and Johnston, the latter using his slower method. Washbrook, never happy to Iverson, swatted away in a whole over without effecting anything except complicated fusion of himself with Tallon, who kept wicket in quite his old style. Hutton, by contrast, interpreted Iverson as flowingly as a scholar translates a once puzzling passage. At the other end Washbrook hit Johnston square to the off boundary. Then he cocked up the easiest of catches to short-leg. Sixty-three to win when Simpson came in and rain now threatening.

Simpson began with a few deflections, then attacked, hooking Johnston violently for 4 past short-leg's head. Twenty minutes before tea Johnson bowled an over of convenience to let Iverson and Johnston change ends. Harvey's fielding at cover-point was a sight to see. Still Hutton batted with a free certainty, and the issue must now be sure. But at 62 Simpson drove Iverson to Harvey's right and ran. Harvey, who had once already thrown down the bowler's wicket, did so again and Simpson was far run out. Now the spectators began to cheer nearly everything, and Compton came in. He turned Iverson to leg for 1, and so to tea with 31 needed for victory. Hutton had scored 40 out of 64.

Afterwards some thought that Hassett might bring on Lindwall and Miller again for a last fling. But he kept on Iverson and Johnston. A light rain now fell. In 2's and singles the runs came and Hutton reached his 50 – 16 to win. When 8 were needed Hole came on for Iverson; with 4 to win Hassett took the ball from Johnston. With humorous care he called long-leg in closer. A run to Compton, a run to Hutton, another to Compton. Then Hutton, with ironical precision, pushed a single to leg and all was over. And soon the two captains, Hassett and Brown, were making speeches on demand to the cheering throng.

AUSTRALIA 217 (A. L. Hassett 92, A. R. Morris 50; Bedser 5 for 46, F. R. Brown 5 for 49) and 197 (G. Hole 63, R. N. Harvey 52, A. L. Hassett 48; Bedser 5 for 59)
ENGLAND 320 (R. T. Simpson 156 not out, Hutton 79; K. R. Miller 4 for 76) and 95 for 2 (Hutton 60 not out)
England won by 8 wickets

Only Four Bats

24 *March* 1951, *Leading Article*. "Washbrook broke his bat." What a tragedy might have lain behind that bald statement of our Special Correspondent in New Zealand if the player had not gone on to make a creditable fifty-eight in the Christchurch Test and if the rest of the team had not raised the score to the nowadays un-English total of more than 500. Every sportsman or player of games knows how a particular bat, club, gun or fishing rod can bring to its wielder just that touch of added confidence which may make the difference between success and failure. In this instance the accident might have had even graver results. Our Correspondent adds that "owing to restric-

tions on luggage carried by air, M.C.C. have only five bats in New Zealand between them. These are now reduced to four, so M.C.C. are now no better equipped than Much Grabham on tour." This is indeed reducing cricket to a game, and brings visions of the Much Grabham team on its way to Snatchem Parva in a horse-drawn brake, which lurches through flower-scented lanes. Some of the side wear bowler hats and high collars, and the bars are as gnarled, mahogany-faced and wrinkled as any veterans should be. In fact, our apparent lack of cricket impedimenta in New Zealand seems to have narrowed the gap between our Test team and those real enthusiasts who pass the one bat to friend or foe indiscriminately, and whose wicket is a pile of boys' caps or a chalk mark on a wall.

No doubt, if a real crisis arises during to-day's Test at Wellington, New Zealand will come to the rescue with some loans. If so, M.C.C. will be able to congratulate themselves that they are not engaged in a golfing encounter. Though the golfer has the seemingly generous limit of fourteen clubs in which to carry out his task, the Royal and Ancient demand that "the addition or replacement of a club or clubs must not be made by borrowing from a partner, opponent, or fellow-competitor." But it is the well-worn favourite that counts, and it is to be hoped for the sake of M.C.C. to-day that the weather (in spite of all forebodings) is such as our Correspondent described in the Otago match at Dunedin, when "it was cool like an English October morning," and a hit to long-leg "scattered the parliament of seagulls." We cannot afford a risk of heat of the West Indian intensity which blistered Jingle's bat in his memorable encounter with Sir Thomas Blazo and Quanko Samba. Without reflection on England's tail, which has often wagged so effectively, it may be wished that the four remaining bats belong to the four best performers. Some particular virtue attaches itself to the bat of the great. Even the stamped signature on a blade may deceive the indifferent club player or schoolboy into thinking that one day he will be a Compton or a Hobbs. How much greater confidence can be gained by handling the master's very own. If before flying to New Zealand the team had been reduced to such scarcity, and HUTTON could have been prevailed upon to lend his bat, or, when he carried it through the innings, even his second favourite, to some of his colleagues, there is no knowing what might have happened, even in Australia.

The Occasional Cricketer

30 *July* 1951, *Leading Article*. The occasional cricketer is in some ways a rather pathetic figure. He is not to be confused with the man who has not touched a bat for fifteen years, who has a different outlook and different coloured trousers and very often makes fifty. Roped in to fill a gap at the last moment, this carefree fellow starts with all the advantages of the licensed

jester. He may not actually wear braces, but as he advances to the wicket his costume makes it clear that this was not the way in which he had planned to spend the afternoon. As the ironic applause and the facetious exhortations die down the fieldsmen close in like a wolf-pack waiting for the kill. Laughter greets the batsman's ungainly flourish at his first ball, the convulsive undulation with which he avoids the impact of the second; but at the third there is a sudden, mellow crack and the cheers take on a different timbre as mid-on jogs back to retrieve the ball from the winter oats beyond the boundary. After that all is plain though often hazardous sailing, and in no time at all the buffoon has become a hero with a strong claim to local immortality.

To the occasional cricketer this sort of thing never happens, even during his day dreams at long leg. For one thing, he would be miscast in this particular role. He cannot claim not to have touched a bat for fifteen years. The whole point about him – if there is any point about him at all – is that three or four times in every season he does touch a bat, though it seldom amounts to very much more than that. By a diminishing number of people he is still thought of, if not exactly as a cricketer, at least as a cricket-playing person. There is in practice almost no limit to the number of feats which he will never accomplish upon the cricket field; but to make an unorthodox invasion of the game from outside it is the only triumph of which he has not – in imagination – been the protagonist.

Since he cannot bowl, or anyhow is not asked to, and since his innings, even if the time spent in walking to and from the wicket be included in it, is never a very long one, the occasional cricketer has plenty of opportunity for exercising his imagination. As he stands out there on the greensward he does not look a very formidable figure; his white trousers are too short and the moth pastures show like snowdrifts upon the summit of his faded cap. He himself realizes, now, that it is not much good dreaming, as he used to years ago, of centuries, and no good at all – unless two or three of his fellow-players sprain an ankle – even thinking about the hat-trick; but he still sees himself achieving some minor, unexpected distinction – a faultless late cut to the boundary, an almost impossible catch taken and held with the left hand, low down. The truth is that he needs these dreams. Were it not for them he might read the writing on the wall in the unhesitating regularity with which the batsmen cry "Come one!" every time they hit the ball in his direction. Were it not for them he might divine too easily the thoughts of his opponents when – batting rather earlier than usual, owing to somebody's car having broken down – he comes in at No. 8. A slogger? They soon see he is not that. A spin-bowler? Before the match is over they realize that he was not being played for his bowling. He is only – as the more astute of them will have divined from the moment he took guard – an occasional cricketer; the bowler's friend when he is at the wicket, the batsman's accomplice when he is in the field. Every summer his trousers, and his breath, get shorter; every summer it gets harder to decide why he is asked to play. But he is a likeable chap, he lives near at hand, and in another year or two no doubt he will do the Big Thing. "No, I won't play," he will say, "but I'll come and umpire if you like." And as he stands out there, year after year, in his white coat the players will no longer be faintly puzzled by his presence.

Cricket on the Screen

22 *August* 1951. For all those lovers of cricket who devoured the daily dispatches of the M.C.C. tour in Australia last winter and later completed their education, in a detached way, by reading of the tour again in concentrated book form, there has now come a film on the same subject, one hour in length. It is called *Elusive Victory*, photographed and assembled by Mr. John Woodcock, with Mr. E. W. Swanton as the chief narrator, and supporting commentaries by Mr. R. C. Robertson-Glasgow, Mr. Rex Alston, and Mr. S. C. Griffith.

As a tranposition of the printed word into terms of vision and sound it has an unquestioned educative and entertainment value. More than a mere pictorial impression – the first of its kind on this subject – it brings one closer to the heart of an undertaking across the breadth of a continent. Here one can see and feel the game in Australia; the huge crowds, vast enclosures, and sense of urgency surrounding the Test matches. One can sense, too, the strain of such a tour with its exhausting travel, and its heat, brought into relief when the players are caught in their moments of relaxation.

Clearly the film faced certain problems and limitations. Every ball bowled, for instance, could not be recorded. Yet in spite of that the camera has effectively caught many vital moments of the struggle. It shows, above all, the full implications of an Australian "sticky" wicket at Brisbane, where batsmen fell like ninepins.

Application for hire of the film, in either 16mm. or 35mm size, by clubs, firms, and other organizations should be made to Mr. John Woodcock, Bodley House, Vigo Street, London, W.1. Schools – the enthusiasm of the young cricketer is perhaps the main target – should apply to Mr. John Green at the same address. The film is an hour well spent of a winter's evening.

Averages and Asterisks

12 *September* 1951, *Leading Article*. To-day the final table of averages announces all too clearly that cricket and summer are done. Already the appearance one by one of the county averages had warned us of the impending doom, but still, on its very brink, many of the players continued to indulge in the feverish gaiety of festivals. It was but a putting off and now the neat patterns with their columns spotted with the little asterisks that signify

"not out" make the temporary epitaphs of those who have cheered us during the past months. They are tucked up in their dark wintry beds till "spring shall blow her clarion" to waken them once more, when we shall have un-gratefully forgotten the less illustrious of their names.

The list as a whole makes necessarily sad reading, but it is in the details of the county averages that individual pathos is to be found. Look, for instance, at the names of those who find no place in the tables, but figure only in the postscript as "Also batted." Here is one whose entire contribution to his county's score was o not out. For all we know he never made contact with a single ball, since as soon as he had taken his place at the wicket his colleague incontinently allowed himself to be bowled. What sad stories we can invent for ourselves about him. With what joy he received the invitation to play, believing his fortune made. What a send-off he received from his village; how he lay awake half the night wondering and hoping, and all for o not out. He may not have had it in him to make a hundred, but double figures – those he might have achieved and they with an asterisk would have been at least a cheering memory, but he never had a chance. Yet he will always be able to muse on what he might have done, a pleasure scarcely to be enjoyed by the man who in four completed innings achieved an average of 1.75.

Apart from such palpably heart-rending cases fate seems strangely capricious in this matter of asterisks. As we know they are of great value in swelling an average, since the total of runs is increased, but not the number of innings by which it must ultimately be divided. He who goes in last is likely with ordinary luck to accumulate a little treasure of asterisks, but the tables show that among the eminent persons who go in high on the list some are much more richly dowered than others. In one county are two batsmen who have each gone to the wicket five and forty times; each has a highly respected average and to neither has fate awarded a single one of her mathe-matical favours. Another and possibly rather more distinguished batsman on the same side has a positively miserly store of seven. There seems here some malignity of fortune at work. Again some tables are entirely honest and produce precisely the expected results. Here is Yorkshire with HUTTON easily head in the batting and that new and romantic figure, APPLEYARD, in the bowling. The proper gods are in their respective heavens and all's right with the world. Now and again, however, we find one who has toiled and sweated and carried his county on his back relegated to second place by some little over-asterisked being of whom we have barely heard. Then our only comfort must be that figures can prove anything.

Nawab of Patuadi

4 *January* 1952. The Nawab of Pataudi, who died at New Delhi suddenly on Saturday, from a heart attack while playing in a polo match, will be long

remembered for the pleasure he gave to countless spectators in various parts of the British Commonwealth by his cricketing prowess.

Nawab Muhammad Iftikar Ali Khan Bahadur was born in March, 1910, and at the age of 19 succeeded to the rulership of Pataudi, a small State in the Gurgoan district of what is now East Punjab. He came to this country in 1926 to go up to Oxford. He was coached by Frank Woolley, the Kent and England batsman, who forecast a brilliant cricket future for him and gained his Blue in 1929 scoring 106 and 84 against Cambridge. Two years later he established a new record by making the highest individual score in these University matches in remarkable circumstances. In the Cambridge first innings A. Ratcliffe scored 201, so breaking the record which had been held for 27 years. Ratcliffe's honour lasted only a few hours, however, because Pataudi obtained 238 not out for Oxford. It is said that before going in to bat Pataudi declared his intention of trying to pass Ratcliffe's score.

Pataudi went to Australia as a member of D. R. Jardine's team in the 1932-33 tour. He scored a century in his first Test but, after one more game for England, was left out of the side. He reappeared for England when Australia came here in 1934, by which time he was playing for Worcestershire, but his next Test appearances came in 1946, when he led the Indian Test team to England and played in all three Tests. On that tour Pataudi did not enjoy the best of health and he disappeared from first-class cricket after his return home, but last autumn he returned to England for a visit after finding a school in Switzerland for his 11-year-old son. When he was in England Pataudi made contact with his former county and Worcestershire successfully applied to the Advisory County Cricket Committee for him to be regarded as still qualified to play for them. He hoped to turn out for them occasionally next season when visiting his son at school.

After a long engagement arising from tardy consent by her father, the Nawab of Bhopal, one of the most important Muslim-ruled States in India, he married the second daughter of that prince in 1936, and he leaves a son and three daughters.

C. B. Fry

25 *April* 1952, *Leading Article.* If MR. CHARLES BURGESS FRY had never been born, as, fortunately, he was, eighty years ago to-day and in Surrey of all Home Counties, it would have been necessary to invent him. The authors of serial stories in a boy's own paper – say in *C. B. Fry's Magazine* – had to learn that life is not a bed of roses. They, feebly letting truth set the pace for fiction, had for long allowed their heroes a blue or two, a goal here, a try there, a decent show in school sports, and just enough book-learning to avoid rustication. More than that, they feared, was over the odds of probability, and then a Reptonian was elected Senior Scholar of Wadham, with

the future Lord Birkenhead coming in fourth. After that, fiction gave up the race and sat gasping in amazement while truth sprinted off down the straight. The facts about MR. FRY's record as an undergraduate are so famous and so familiar that any writer must blush to recite them in detail. Captain of Oxford against Cambridge at cricket and at Association football was not enough – a century had to be made at Lord's (not out, of course), and a blue for Rugby football only missed through a last-minute accident. A perform-ance for the O.U.D.S. as the Prince of Morocco in *The Merchant of Venice* crowded a second night house to enjoy an athletic rendering of the line "Oh, Hell, what have we here?" A meeting with MR. MAX BEERBOHM of Merton led to the coining of the phrase "Golf is glorified croquet." A taste for taking exercise against Cambridge, without the distractions of a ball, caused the setting up of a world's record for the long jump.

Those were salad days triumphs. The best was yet to come. Among the many good reasons for having been alive and taking notice in the earliest years of this century must have been that K. S. RANJITSINHJI and C. B. FRY were Sussex batsmen together. This partnership, it has been said, turned MR. FRY from a good to a great player. He needed little turning. Upright at the wicket, with bat lifted back over the middle stump, he made the Hove ground seem too small to contain a cricket-ball. His straight drives and his on strokes were a delight and, when deluded fielders suspected him of being weaker to the off, he taught them better. Statistics embalm the thousands of runs in a season and the row upon row of centuries. They cannot recapture the grace of the artist at the wicket.

Sport, even at this high Olympian level, had to take its place in the queue of MR. FRY's accomplishments. He has written well in prose and verse. He has stood as a Liberal for Parliament. His long service in the Mercury rightly earned him at the age of seventy-four the honorary rank of Captain, R.N.R. A horseman and an angler, a marksman and a motorist, he has preserved through all his strenuous versatility as an out-of-doors man an unquenchable zest for good talk. Those who have been privileged to hear him agree that there is no subject, from Greek music to the gold standard, in which he will drop a catch. The great sportsman is a good companion and his memories are rich. He recalls MEREDITH asking him if the whip stroke was better than the long swing, and BARRIE – that ardent amateur of cricket – "not minding a bit" when his Scottish terrier nipped her fellow-countryman in the Achilles tendon. With so much gaiety and such well-earned fame behind him, MR. FRY should go forward confidently to complete his century.

A Caravan of Bats

12 *May* 1952, *Leading Article*. Neither the Foreign Office nor the M.C.C. has seen fit to comment on a report from Kalimpong that a large consignment

of cricket bats, transported on the backs of mules, is on its way to Lhasa at the behest of the education authorities in Tibet. Accustomed as we are to being baffled by International affairs, it is difficult to recall any recent development in that sphere of which the significance was harder to evaluate. There is, of course, nothing odd in the Tibetans wanting to play cricket; the natural and salutary aspiration does them credit. The mountain torrents of their native land and her frequently frozen lakes severely limit the opportunities open to wet-bobs, and it was perhaps inevitable that a passion for our national sport, repressed for centuries, should break out sooner or later.

It is, all the same, a little surprising that King Willow should come into his own at a time when Tibet is under Communist control. It may, of course, be that the new régime in Lhasa sees in cricket an opiate or anodyne which will confer upon the people partial oblivion of their sufferings; and it is certainly true that the history of the game is unsullied by any connexions with counter-revolutionary activity. But there are, after all, other sports less closely associated with the Imperialist tradition; and, however much one reveres cricket and however little one knows about Tibet, it is difficult to believe that this incomparable game is ideally suited to the conditions obtaining on the Roof of the World.

There may – indeed there must – be more in this business than meets the eye. It looks like some sort of a move in the Cold War. Readers with romantic minds will toy with the idea that the whole thing has been organized for subversive purposes, by the British Secret Service – that at the head of the caravan (humming the Eton boating song to put people off the scent) strides, heavily disguised, some agent of the calibre of Colonel Egham or Big White Carstairs. Alas, it is more likely to be the other way round. World Communism, though it has many conquests to its credit, has as yet made little impression on cricket; but its outward indifference to the sport (the Russians have not even bothered to claim that they invented it) may well mask a respect for its civilizing influence and a determination to adapt it to conform with the exigencies of Marxist doctrine. It is true that Tibet does not seem a particularly sensible place in which to initiate this project; but it is remote and secluded, and the inhabitants have no preconceived bourgeois ideas on the subject which need to be eradicated. It seems all too probable that the report from Kalimpong may foreshadow the launching of a vast conspiracy throughout the New Democracies to undermine the influence of cricket by evolving a similar but ideologically sounder game. How fast or how far this threat to one of our dearest institutions may develop it is impossible to say. It depends to a certain extent on whether the people in Lhasa remembered to order any balls.

Hutton Captains England

Break with Tradition

26 *May* 1952. L. Hutton, the Yorkshire professional opening batsman and first choice for England for many seasons, is to captain England in the first Test match against India at Leeds on June 5. N. W. D. Yardley, Hutton's county captain, who is chairman of the England selectors, announced this after a meeting at Nottingham yesterday. He added that the side for the first Test would be selected next Thursday.

All four selectors were at the meeting. Besides Yardley, they are F. R. Brown, who had stated that he would like to give up the England captaincy for a younger man, R. E. S. Wyatt, and L. E. G. Ames, who was the first professional to be appointed a member of the selection committee.

Our Cricket Correspondent [Geoffrey Green] writes:–

For the first time a professional player has been chosen to captain England. Though there are many who will look back with anxious eyes and with sorrow at the passing of an age, there are yet those who will welcome the ending of an anachronism. The amateur, in the older meaning of the word, no longer truly exists. He has largely been destroyed by the economic circumstance of mid-twentieth century. Further, to find such a man, both with the character to lead and also the quality indisputably to hold a place in an England team, has progressively become more difficult. When F. R. Brown was called on by the selectors two years ago the writing was on the wall. Brown's unqualified success, heartening though it was, solved nothing. It merely postponed the hour that has now come.

The selectors, who for some time have been struggling to balance the requirements of tradition with the needs of the moment, are to be congratulated on the action they have taken. They have shown a boldness that one had not expected of them yet. But sooner or later this last step seemed to be due. It was presaged by the reinstatements of W. R. Hammond, who led England after the war against Australia, and W. J. Edrich, joint-captain of Middlesex; by the responsible parts played in the counties by Compton, Dollery, and John Langridge.

In this age of so-called equal opportunity for all the professional player has at last attained his fullest stature, and it is now up to Hutton to prove not only himself but also his colleagues worthy of the new principle which has been established. Certainly tradition has died hard and to Hutton now goes the new honour.

Actually there have been instances in the past of England being led on the cricket field by a professional in the absence through illness or injury of the amateur captain. Hobbs, of Surrey, once captained the side against Australia in the fourth Test match at Manchester in 1926 after A. W. Carr had been struck down by tonsillitis; Compton took over from F. R. Brown in the fourth Test match in Australia during the 1950-51 tour after Brown had been hurt in a car accident; Hutton himself was at the helm for an hour or two at the Oval last season against South Africa while Brown was having a strained leg attended to.

Whether this new title will become a burden that will affect Hutton's full efficiency as a great batsman remains to be seen, but the eyes of the country will be upon him as he accepts the accolade before his own Yorkshire people at Headingley.

Art for Sport's Sake?

20 *October* 1952, *Leading Article.* There are many signs that the great gulf which once separated the Hearty from the Highbrow is gradually being narrowed. The contemptuous hostility with which each used to regard the other has been modified to a quizzical tolerance, and a sort of demilitarized zone has been created where both are apt to find themselves on common ground in their liking for detective fiction, village cricket, and the drawings of MR. OSBERT LANCASTER. One symptom of this *rapprochement* is the tendency for people who write about sport to write about it in a prose liberally incrusted with cultural allusions. The dexterity of a late cut is compared with the virtuosity of an epigram by OSCAR WILDE, the names of leading ballerinas are invoked to convey to the reader the peculiar prowess of a stand-off half, and a rally on the Centre Court is described in terms of contrapuntal orchestration. Nobody quite knows whether the Hearty actually likes this sort of thing; but it undoubtedly makes it easier for the Highbrow to follow his activities.

It has been very noticeable, however, that in the partial reconciliation between these two factions the concessions have all been made by one side. Accounts of cricket and golf, of football and steeplechasing, have – often at the cost of baffling the sportsmen themselves – steadily increased their potential appeal to persons of culture and refinement; but from the other side, from the Highbrow camp, has come no gesture of response. One does not know for certain whether or not MR. ALEC BEDSER has ever been compared, in print, to MR. T. S. ELIOT, but one would not be particularly surprised if he had. One does on the other hand, know – absolutely for certain – that MR. T. S. ELIOT has never been compared to MR. ALEC BEDSER. This unforthcoming attitude on the part of the Highbrows may be due to arrogance, to a sort of constitutional inability to mix a few acorns with the pearls they cast before the swine; or it may be simply that they do not know where to go for acorns.

Whatever the cause, it is reassuring to be able to report an indication, even if it is only an isolated one, that they are prepared to repay the Hearties in their own coin. A review recently published in a Bloomsbury periodical of an exhibition of abstract paintings (just the sort of homework a Hearty most needs help with) concluded as follows:–

> His most successful paintings, such as the large yellow canvas with the black bicycle-framed grid and the lopsided blue carboard planet, are only successful within their own absurdly limited terms; terms which make it impossible for the spectator to be involved in their success. One is reminded of a good shot only shooting duck which he himself has released.

The intention here is excellent. Partially successful abstract painting, if it has got to be interpreted, must be interpreted in terms of something; and to select for the purpose a Philistine pursuit like wildfowling shows a laudable desire to reach out to a wider and more oafish audience. It would be hyper-critical to suggest that a one-man *tir aux canards* is not a spectacle of which many of us can claim to be reminded, even by a lop-sided blue cardboard planet. The main thing is that the ice has been broken, and if all goes merrily forward in the right direction, we may soon hope to hear KAFKA being discussed in terms of beagling, and to be told that M. ANOUILH is the P. B. H. MAY of the Paris theatre.

Giants in those Days

13 *December* 1952, *Leading Article.* "Ah! but you should have seen Kort-right." Those words, heard so often as LARWOOD or LINDWALL or FARNES was bowling, echo to-day in the December half light from the news that, ripe in years, the fastest bowler of all time has died. Great sportsmen share with great actors a fate from which authors and other artists in lasting media escape. They depend for their fame on action and once they quit field or stage they become ghosts, doomed to flit to and fro in the memory of a dwindling few. But here and there a GARRICK or a GRAY projects so vivid a shadow into the future that he stirs curiosity in younger generations as to what exactly he was like in his prime. KORTRIGHT stands out in this way among those he himself called "the old-times men of pace."

There is a thrill about fast bowling especially when it is watched from the safety of the stands. KOTZE, GREGORY, MCDONALD, KNOX, FIELDER, CONSTANTINE – the roll-call could go on to make a full eleven – return easily to the mind's eye of anyone who saw them and bring back vanished days of hot summer sunshine to dispel mid-winter gloom. Purists may say that the subtle beauty of the game does not lie in speed, and nobody will contradict them. But the thrill remains. KORTRIGHT once recalled how one of his yorkers rebounded from the bottom of the stumps and went back past him almost to the boundary. Some of us would rather have seen that than have sat through a whole scientific century by A. N. Other. A batsman for whom fast bowling has no terrors is deservedly a hero. That was one side of the splendour of GRACE, who reached three figures against KORTRIGHT when his partners were making no secret of their discomfort.

Recollection, aroused by thoughts of KORTRIGHT, turns to an even farther away giant whose prowess earned ever greater praise. If the tales are true SPOFFORTH was the demon king of bowlers. Speed served him but it is his legendary cunning that looms larger in retrospect. He would lie awake at night turning over the best ways of attacking the mighty opponents who were to face him in the morning. When he was at his most deadly he brought London swarming up to Lord's for an afternoon in which he mowed down the flower of English cricket. That was an occasion as famous as an Irving first night. But SPOFFORTH never, as KORTRIGHT did, bowled a ball which rose almost straight and went out of the small ground without a second bounce, thus giving away a unique six in byes. Such was this Victorian out of Essex and he found a wicketkeeper in MACGREGOR to stand up to him in spite of his "muzzle velocity" which SIR PELHAM WARNER has reckoned probably to have been a hundred miles an hour down the pitch. Giants there indeed were in those days.

Jack Hobbs at 70 not out

Birthday Memories of Great Games and Players

BY OUR SPECIAL CORRESPONDENT [JOHN HARTLEY]

16 *December* 1952. John Berry Hobbs is 70 to-day. This astonishing fact has come as a surprise to many lovers of cricket for whom the memory of this legendary figure is still as green as the Oval table in the days, not so long ago, when he stood slim and erect in the middle and the runs flowed in an effortless stream from his bat.

To Hobbs himself the achievement of threescore years and 10 has come as no less of a surprise. But for the publicity it has aroused and the requests for interviews – such as the one he gave to your Correspondent – the date might have passed unnoticed. For at 70 he is still slim, still alert and nimble; there is scarcely a line of his face and his hair is not, as he claims, "picked up eleven-a-side."

As a batsman Jack Hobbs was always a delight to watch. He attacked the bowling, scored freely and fast, except when occasion demanded he should just stay there, and he delighted in short runs. He had a zest and passionate enjoyment for cricket as a game which was transmitted to the crowd. He has always been modest, but, having decided to delve into the past as a form of birthday celebration, he has brought up memories and comments all reflecting a love of the game.

From his early days he was a natural batsman. His father was groundsman at Jesus College, Cambridge, and in Jesus Close he used to practise hitting the ball. He would set up a stump as a wicket, and with a stump as a bat would get a friend to bowl to him with a tennis ball – "and stumps were thin in those days, too."

His trial and acceptance for Surrey came on Tom Hayward's recommendation after an unofficial trial on Parker's Piece, where a wicket was set up and Hayward and Reeves (of Essex) bowled to him. In his first game for Surrey, against the Gentlemen, Hobbs came up against Dr. W. G. Grace. "I had never seen him before, except at a distance. It was a very proud moment for me when I faced up to him. He bowled those donkey drops of his. I cannot say I found him difficult; but I did not take any liberties with him, I must admit."

In his next match – against Essex – he made a century. "I thought I knew it all then. Later I found I did not. Opening with Tom Hayward, I learned what balls to leave alone and what to go for. I learned the scoring strokes to improve and those to drop." Later he came to prefer other partners. "Poor old Tom, he did not like the short run, he was too heavy. It was lovely with Wilfred Rhodes when we started the short run business. Sutcliffe and Sandham liked cheeky runs, too. I think a lot of short runs are missed these days."

Jack Hobbs looks on the period 1910-14 as his most brilliant. He could attack the bowling with zest when he felt like it. "You could play cheeky shots and make 50 or 60 and feel life was worth living. Then came the exasperation when they started counting your hundreds, publishing averages, and it was all figures. They think too much of figures these days." This from the man who made more runs than anyone else has ever done – 61,221 – and whose 197 first-class centuries is also a record. [*61,221 was the figure given in the 1952* Wisden. *The following year it was amended to 61,237, which is now generally, though not universally, accepted.*]

Batsmen to-day have all Hobbs's sympathy. Bowling has become defensive and wickets are slower. In-swingers across the wicket from outside the leg-stump do not give batsmen a chance. "If you try to glide them now you get caught, and all the beautiful shots on the off-side that one used to see have been shut up. An off-drive by Hutton or Compton is something to admire, but you no longer get much wristy cutting. It is much easier to stay in now, but not so easy to score runs. Players like Hayward would have adapted themselves to it, but Hayward would have been a bit better than most to-day. I think I might have adapted myself. I do not see why I should not also have scored runs."

There was fast bowling in the old days. "A fast bowler to-day is an event. They tell you the wicket is too easy paced, but a fast bowler is a necessity; he is always likely to get a wicket at the beginning of an innings. Pace bowlers are still the same type, but they have lost a bit of their devil. If Trueman keeps free from injury he should 'make the grade.'"

The game is more commercialized now, he says. There must be good gates and lively cricket is necessary. Surrey played lively cricket last summer and had some handsome gates. He did not want to compare the team of last year with that in which he played when Surrey last won the county championship in 1914. "I do not think we were inferior, but they played magnificently last summer and gave me a thrill or two. There is such a good spirit in the side."

The difference between players then and now is not so much of quality as of quantity. "There were more stars then; many good amateurs are lost now because of high costs and taxes." But English teams have been improving since the war. "With young Len Hutton as skipper we have the best chance of beating the Australians next summer that we have had for years. The Australians seem to be in the doldrums now; with an even break in the luck, we should win. They do not seem to have as many good players as in the Bradman era.

"Bradman was a team in himself. I think Don was too good; he spoilt the game. He got too many runs. The pot calling the kettle black? No, I was human; he got hundreds every time he went in. I did cheer the hearts of the bowlers even in my most palmy days. He was mechanical; he was the greatest run-getting machine of all time. I do not think we want to see another one quite like him. I do not think we ever shall."

Hobbs spoke of his favourite strokes. "We always liked to hook a good ball. Then I liked a good square cut, you could get a lot of power into it, it was a beautiful shot to make. I liked a cover drive, but . . ." he paused and gave a slow smile, "you like them all when you can hit them hard."

Of all the bowling he faced he preferred the googlies above all. "They put you on your mettle and there is always a loose one – and then you crack it." Sydney Barnes was perhaps the best bowler of all and would have been even better on present wickets.

Hobbs qualified two comments that have been made on his game – his improved fielding, and a tendency to be l.-b.-w. It was said that he developed suddenly from a comparatively poor fielder into the most brilliant cover-point of his generation. He denies he was ever poor. "I had a minor injury – I had thrown my arm out – and nobody knew about it at the time." The way he used often to be out he explains on the ground that to play a straight bat he had to stand behind the flight of the ball. Sometimes he missed it. "If you miss a straight ball, you get out. Some people get bowled, I was l.-b.-w."

He really enjoyed the Tests, but it is not always the big occasions that are fixed in his memory. His most enjoyable innings was in a private match in 1921 when he played for Lionel Robinson's XI against a side captained by MacLaren which included Australians. Everything went right and he felt he could not get out. After making 87 he retired hurt, having pulled a muscle going for a desperate run.

Hobbs remembers every innings he played on a bad wicket. There was the terrible "sticky" at Melbourne on the 1928-29 tour when he and Sutcliffe put on over 100 for the first wicket after people had prophesied that England would be out for under 70. England won by four wickets. He considers his most valuable innings was that at the Oval in 1926 when he and Sutcliffe each made centuries on a bad wicket and England won the rubber against Australia for the first time for 14 years.

He will never forget the game against Kent at the Oval in 1919 when he and Jack Crawford, batting against the clock, made 90-odd in 35 minutes and the crowd went mad. He remembers the excitement when he needed a hundred to equal Grace's record of 126 centuries. It was a long time coming; then he scored 91 one day at Taunton and had to make nine the next morning. "We started a quarter of an hour late while they let the crowd in. I remember feeling a bit jittery waiting." He recalls his highest score, 316 not out at Lord's in 1926 at the age of 43. "I did not get tired. I never got tired batting, though cricket is a game of intense concentration."

When Jack Hobbs retired in 1934 after making 197 centuries, regret was expressed universally; but he was certain then, as now, that he was right. "I gave up before my 200th century because I thought I had outstayed my usefulness with the Surrey side. You cannot go on for ever keeping people out of the side. Also I did not want to be an object of sympathy. Some people said I was playing as well as ever, but I knew how I felt, what I could and could not do. Looking back, though, it is a pity I did not get the 200; I should like to have been the first."

Jack Hobbs was a cricket idol then. To-day he is a sporting legend.

The Fight for the Ashes

Australian Hopes for Coming Test Series

BY SIR DONALD BRADMAN

21 *February* 1953. In 1926 an Australian team went to England to do battle for "The Ashes." Since then it has been my good fortune to be a member of every Australian team which has followed in their footsteps until now, when it is my turn to be on the side-lines. That period of history covers 27 years, and so I confess to a slight feeling of nostalgia at staying behind, for I love England and her people.

When a touring team is chosen critics usually find several good reasons why the selection committee should be sacked. This year is no exception. However, for once I was not on the committee and could afford to smile. After the team had been announced and I was returning to my hotel I accosted three strangers and out of pure devilment said to them: "What do you think of the team?" The first simply said, "Horrible"; the second, "Too old"; and the third, "We'll lose the Ashes with that selection." These opinions rather shocked me, so I sat down and made a quiet analysis to myself of my miniature private Gallup poll. If the team is "horrible" it must be conceded that it contains the best 11 cricketers in Australia, even though we may argue about some of the remainder. If it is "too old" at least it includes the youngest player ever to be selected for Australia. Whether we lose or not still remains to be answered.

The South African team which has just toured Australia won two, lost two, and drew one Test in the series. This is being used as an argument to discredit Australia, for at the beginning of their tour the visitors were not conceded any chance of winning. But let me say at once that these South Africans moulded into a combination of formidable strength. They were young, full of enthusiasm, and remarkably fit. I never once saw a man sit down on the field when a wicket fell, even towards the close of the hardest day. No greater fielding team has ever been seen in Australia, according to even the oldest spectator. Their batting improved until finally, without having a shining star around whom to build, they had an even quality down to number ten which merited comparison with true international standard. Only in bowling did I feel they were below it. The lack of real speed was evident at once and was sadly missed in spite of lionhearted efforts by the medium pacers. A vicious leg spinner would have been invaluable on many occasions. Marvellous fielding, including some of the most incredible catching, helped to hide these deficiencies, but to the discerning eye the attack was very limited.

Here, then, to my way of thinking, we come to probably the most important question about Australia's potential weakness. Our batsmen (in the selectors' eyes the best we have), under conditions more suitable for run-making than they are likely to find in England, did not collectively make enough runs against South Africa. The same players will need to improve if they are to make higher scores against Bedser, Trueman and Co. Our touring team has only two regular openers. The older and more experienced of the two is Arthur Morris, and a great deal will depend on whether he can recapture his 1948 form.

If the openers fail to provide a good start heavy responsibility will fall on Hassett (should he elect to bat first wicket down) or Harvey. The latter was positively brilliant against South Africa. His powerful hitting, aggressive attitude, and at times unorthodox methods made him stand out above his colleagues. He is at the peak of his form and should play many grand innings on the tour, but it will be flirting with providence to have him at the crease while the ball is new and the bowlers fresh. Possibly Hassett will prefer to trust his own greater experience and more sedate methods to try to lay the foundations for the attackers. Come what may, Hassett is no longer cast in the role of the aggressor but Harvey is, and in that category is best likely to serve his team even though in defence he is now tighter and sounder than ever before.

Of the other batsmen, it will be interesting to see who develops most quickly. In Hole, Craig, and de Courcy we have a trio who are very different in method but all very talented. Perhaps attention will first be focused on Craig because of his youth. In a country where youth is rewarded sometimes more than experience it was thought remarkable that a boy of 17 could be good enough to play for Australia. The selectors believed he was, and his batting in the fifth Test against South Africa probably surpassed even their high expectations. Surely here is a great player in the making.

Australians think highly of Graeme Hole, whose offside play possesses a fluency and grace of the classical variety. He also bids fair on recent form to remedy a weakness in our slip fielding. The West Indians were surprised that de Courcy was not chosen in the Tests against them. He is a versatile, quick-footed batsman who should benefit from continuous play and the knowledge that he is in the team. These things have been denied him in the past. Englishmen know the debonair, unpredictable Keith Miller. He will thrill them again when the mood strikes him, but recurrent back trouble has caused grave fears as to how much longer he can be a star fast bowler without being unfair to himself. Anxious eyes will be on him those first weeks.

In young Benaud will be found a cricketer who could easily be mistaken for Miller as he moves lithely after a ball. Their movements, build, and mannerisms are similar. Benaud is a lovely field and a batsman who can hit with tremendous power, but strangely enough in bowling he reverts to slow leg spinners. He may easily be called upon to do a lot of work and if so will obviously enjoy it. There are two other leg spinners. Of these, Ring is well known to Englishmen and is regarded as our number one. The second is Jack Hill – the surprise choice of the 17. He bowls faster than the orthodox leg spinner but on our pitches does not turn to any extent. His length is usually impeccable and without any doubt his inclusion is an insurance against the failure of our other leg spinners, coupled with the thought that he may force his claims to a place in the eleven on his own prowess.

In Bill Johnston Englishmen will find a stout-hearted bowler who from the pavilion appears just the same as the 1948 vintage. He laughs even more, and his infectious joviality on the field even makes fun of a bumper which might from anyone else cause resentment. His understudy is Davidson – a glorious fieldsman, a more than useful hard-hitting batsman, and a left-hand bowler of the Johnston type. If the opportunity presents itself Davidson could easily join the top flight.

Of Lindwall one can say that his bowling against South Africa had not quite the fire of earlier years, except when he deemed it necessary to put forward a special effort. Nevertheless it was at all times intelligently directed and his absence from the attack in the fifth Test was sorely felt. Here again, unfortunately, there is the lurking fear of a leg injury, and Hassett will certainly take all precautions to keep Lindwall fit for the important occasions. He, too, has an understudy in young Ron Archer – a lad of 19 summers. Perhaps Archer would admit he was a lucky boy, on his limited experience of first-class cricket, to catch the selectors' vote, but they have shown courage in trying to develop a young virile athlete who shows distinct promise in all departments of the game. As yet he can scarcely be termed fast, and this tour should decide whether he can find the extra pace to lift him beyond the realms of fast medium.

Of wicket keepers it is enough to say we have two reliable stalwarts, both tested and proved in the crucible of international cricket. Tallon is still a great artist, and even if Langley has not the polish, do not be misled. Wait until someone touches a swinger. Our bowlers are confident that no safer pair of hands exists to-day. As for courage, he is a real bulldog. There, in a brief review, is Australia's team.

I am not going to forecast the result of the series. All signs point to a very even struggle. However, I think England may very reasonably contend she has at least an equal chance, on the grounds that Australia's batting appears to be weaker than in 1948, and her bowling and fielding no stronger. On the other hand, England's claims that her own bowling, fielding, and batting have improved seem to be well founded. These variations in strength can, of course, be quickly altered by the luck of the toss, a sudden storm, or even an umpire's decision.

Irrespective of the result, I may perhaps make a plea in the interests of cricket and on behalf of the general public. It is just simply that the teams endeavour to play a bright, attacking game, and not shut out by defensive strategy those glories of stroke play which are exclusive to our national game. Cricket in Australia was stimulated by the South Africans. Their whole attitude to the game was delightful, and their departure is regretted on all sides. I, for one, hope our players and those of the Mother Country will in the forthcoming series do still more to popularise a sport which is unquestionably an invisible asset in the Empire balance-sheet.

THE AUSTRALIAN TEAM

*A. L. Hassett, aged 39, Victoria (capt.)	*A. R. Morris, 31, N.S.W. (vice-capt.)
R. Archer, 19, Queensland	R. Benaud, 22, N.S.W.
I. Craig, 17, N.S.W.	A. Davidson, 23, N.S.W.
J. de Courcy, 25, N.S.W.	*R. N. Harvey, 24, Victoria
J. Hill, 29, Victoria	G. Hole, 21, South Australia
*W. A. Johnston, 31, Victoria	G. Langley, 33, South Australia
*R. R. Lindwall, 31, N.S.W.	C. McDonald, 24, Victoria
*K. R. Miller, 33, N.S.W.	*D. Ring, 34, Victoria
*D. Tallon, 37, Queensland	

* Member of 1948 touring team.

The party will sail from Perth, Western Australia, in the Orcades on March 22, and is due at Tilbury on April 13.

Lights Up at Lord's

12 *March* 1953, *Leading Article*. With everybody tumbling over themselves to be thought up-to-date and progressive, last ditches to-day are unoccupied areas, but surely a few stalwarts will man them and make their protest against the alterations which have now been made to the scoreboards at Lord's. The numbers one to eleven have been added, with the letter S for substitute, and then the ball is caught or fielded the scorer will press a button and a light above the player's score-card number will shine out on the board. Lord's, indeed, will be more like Piccadilly Circus than a respectable cricket ground, and gone will be the favourite occupation of the expert onlooker, that of gently but firmly correcting the erroneous notions of his neighbour. When the man in the row in front has loudly applauded a piece of fielding and con-fided to his impressed companion that Dash is the best cover-point in the country, no longer will he be able to remark, with an air of mild yet un-mistakable superiority, "That, sir, was not Dash, the ex-Cantab., but Blank, the old Oxonian."

Besides, to carry through such a reckless revolution at this particular moment is to surrender a point in the psychological warfare which is now the recognized prelude and accompaniment to all respectable games. Even when the Australians were rolling us in the dust, there was always comfort in the thought that at least we did things in our own and, therefore, the superior way. If Sydney and Melbourne chose so to conduct their business that the crowd could turn its back on the game and watch its progress on boards huge in size and correspondingly lavish with information, that was their own affair and we had no intention of following suit. In the good old days of not so very long ago it was part of the fun to bamboozle the paying spectator and keep him in a stage of comic ignorance as to what was going on. If it rained and then stopped, he was seldom told when play was likely to begin again, and, on some grounds, score-cards before luncheon were a treat. He, stout fellow, stood it all with the utmost good humour but now all is changed. The man is positively pampered, a decent anonymity is no more, and cricketers, to all intents and purposes, are as the poor footballers who carry numbers as though they were horses or articles at an auction sale. Still, last ditches are uncomfortable places to linger in, the Oval and Trent Bridge have already gone part of the way with Sydney and Melbourne and the hope is that this summer the lights of Lord's may shine out as brightly as the sun itself.

Butterfingers

6 *April* 1953, *Leading Article*. The comparative shortness of the present school holidays before the long vistas of the summer term does not excuse those parental duties which the young expect to be performed. He who has cricketing offspring is fortunate indeed if he has been sufficiently old-fashioned to have a quiverful, for he may then delegate some of the burden of "hardening up" for the season. There were famous cricketing families in the good old days in which father, mother, sisters, and even well-trained fielding dogs were enlisted to give practice to the son or sons of the house. But in these modern times smaller families are more usual, so that an unwarranted strain is likely to fall upon father – mother is too busy in the home; sister despises cricket and is playing lawn-tennis; dog is, maybe, a dachshund of a serious turn of mind, and, in spite of springing from a stock once famous for badger-hunting, is now more interested in a five-year plan for the storage of bones rather than in any form of sport.

If the cricketing offspring has reached double figures in years he has probably also outgrown the home ground on the lawn, and, for fear of the neighbours, father is forced to agree to practice on the nearest public open space, perhaps a corner of the village green or local pitch, still uncut and unrolled, and from which the ball is likely to rise at any angle. Woe to the parent who has given his son a new ball as a part Christmas present. There was a time when that same parent probably prayed to be asked to go on to bowl when the shine was still on the ball, but now the vicious-looking unworn seam is apparently only there to lacerate the palms. Having contracted that the son shall retrieve everything within moderate range – in other words, father must not hit too hard during his own innings – the parent cannot resist making his one scoring stroke, a chancy slash through the covers from which the ball indubitably ends up in the pond. Its pristine loveliness muddied, there follows a torrent of protests from its young owner.

As the single wicket match progresses through one of the bleaker April afternoons, father goes on to bowl, and has to stop some stinging returns. It is little comfort to him that soon those tougher types, the Australians, will be experiencing an English spring on the field of Worcester. Father tries to remember some of the more pleasant interludes of his cricketing past – the smell of hay from the paddock by the leg-boundary, the pavilion flag just stirring in the lightest of breezes, and the whole white and green rhythm of a cricket match on a perfect summer's day. Suddenly he realizes that the ball is descending upon him from a height; one of those deceptive, spinning catches that usually seem to go to mid-on from a mishit. As in the days of long ago the ball falls feebly to the ground, and, borne on the east wind, father hears a reedy, scornful, but still unpleasantly familiar cry of "butterfingers."

"The Final Test"

Mr. Rattigan's Film about Cricket

[BY DUDLEY CAREW]

13 *April* 1953. The ultimate feeling left by *The Final Test* (London Pavilion) is one of deep admiration for the consummate cleverness of Mr. Terence Rattigan as a playwright – *The Final Test* is a film, but the word is apposite and must stand.

Cricket is a game for the contemplative, and, as its literature shows, for the poetic. It reveals character, certainly, but through the medium of action on the field; it is blessed with both emotion and humour, yet, here again, these qualities belong to the actual pitch and are not easily transferable to stage or screen. And yet Mr. Rattigan, who is a good cricketer himself [*opening batsman for Harrow 1929-30*], has so contrived that in the 90 minutes the film takes to run, character, emotion, humour, and the essence of the game itself shall all have their innings, and in this he has been greatly helped by the director, Mr. Anthony Asquith.

His story is cunningly thought out and the film gets off the mark in the first scene. Mr. Rattigan has decreed that Sam Palmer – a batsman of Sutcliffe-Leyland calibre – shall be playing his last match for England against Australia at the Oval. Sam has a son, Reggie (Mr. Ray Jackson), who has, however, no intention of following in father's footsteps. Reggie writes poetry and hero-worships not Hutton – who, incidentally, has a not so very small part in the film and acts it admirably – but an advanced poet, Alexander Whitehead. Reggie, on the morning he should be watching his father play his last innings for England, goes instead to visit Whitehead only to find. . . . Only to find, of course, that Whitehead has no thoughts for anything but the Test match and, on hearing that Reggie has a spare ticket, rushes him to the Oval. Add to this neat contrivance the fact that Sam is in love with Cora (Miss Brenda Bruce) who is a barmaid and who, through her calling, can introduce on to the screen the solemn Englishness of a public-house crowd listening to a Test match on the wireless, and it will be realized just how clever Mr. Rattigan has been.

The scenes at the Oval, both on the field and in the dressing-room, have the stamp of authenticity and realism, and if, with Whitehead, Mr. Rattigan allows himself a degree of farcical exaggeration, it is, perhaps, because Mr. Robert Morley is so very willing to play. He makes the poet a most endearing eccentric, and the scenes he shares with Mr. Jack Warner's solid, likeable Sam, who, in spite of his lack of accent, must have played for Yorkshire, are the most delightful in a delightful film. Miss Adrianne Allen runs up a not inconsiderable score as Sam's sister, and Miss Bruce makes Cora a pearl among barmaids.

Eightieth Birthday Tribute
to S. F. Barnes

BY OUR SPECIAL CORRESPONDENT [JOHN HARTLEY]

14 *April* 1953. Sydney Barnes, the former England Test cricketer, will be 80 on April 19, and to celebrate his birthday he will bowl at the beginning of a match in his honour at Stafford on April 26. As the tall, erect figure runs slowly up to the wicket and delivers the ball from the outside edge of the crease, cricket lovers will be seeing one of the greatest cricketers of all time.

It is many years since Australian mothers frightened naughty children with the name of Sydney Barnes. It is years since Australian and South African crowds sat stunned into horrified silence as Barnes shattered the might of their batsmen on their own perfect wickets.

But Barnes's reputation has lived on. It tells of devastating bowling; of an attack that came like summer lightning, impersonally destroying wherever it struck.

In 1901, when Barnes was 28, A. C. MacLaren dropped a bombshell into the cricket world when he announced that S. F. Barnes would go on the next Australian tour.

Yet after two Tests the Australians were hailing him as the finest hard wicket bowler ever sent from England. Six years later, after another tour, M. A. Noble was describing him as the finest bowler in the world, and P. F. Warner said that Barnes was the best bowler he had played against.

But Barnes did not reach his peak for another six years – during tours of Australia and South Africa in which his performances have moved into legend. He was then widely acclaimed as the finest bowler the world had ever seen.

At 80 Barnes is neither frail nor infirm. Anyone seeing him striding easily and quickly each day up the long flight of steps to his office in the Shire Hall, Stafford, must be impressed by his vigour.

His manner is courteous and gentle. It is only when an incautious word is uttered that one realizes that the internal fires are not completely banked down, that age will never entirely mellow this rock of a man. The fateful, kindling word is "batsmen." At its sound a frosty look overtakes the bright blue eyes, and a hard edge comes into the Staffordshire accent. Mention of the ancient enemy takes Barnes back in his memory through the stages by which his attack was built up.

He began as a fast bowler, playing occasionally, but without much success, for Warwickshire. He was taught the off-break, but decided that the ball moving away from the batsman was more difficult to play. He developed a leg-break which was spun with the third finger so that it could be whipped down from the same height as the off-break. "It is speed off the pitch that counts." The "Barnes ball" was a leg-break that pitched on the leg stump and came off very fast to hit the top of the off stump. The action was very similar to that of the off-break, and Barnes never bowled googlies – "I did not need to."

He learnt much about swing in his first Test tour, and on a later tour Charles Macartney, in his first innings for Australia, saw Barnes bowl Victor Trumper. The ball was fast on the leg stump, but just before it pitched it swung suddenly to the off. Then it pitched, broke back, and took Trumper's leg stump. Macartney said afterwards: "It was the sort of ball a man might see if he was dreaming or drunk."

Barnes could make the ball swing one way and break the other and he could do it for both off- and leg-breaks. What is more, through variation of pace and flight alone, he could change both the spot at which the swing would become effective and the amount of the break. Finally he decided to bowl from the outside edge of the crease to make the line of flight of the ball more deceptive.

He was accurate and kept a perfect length. His bowling was directed against the weaknesses of batsmen. "I never bowled at the wickets: I bowled at the stroke. I intended the batsman to make a stroke, then I tried to beat it. I tried to make the batsman move. The time a batsman makes mistakes is when he has to move his feet."

Barnes's field was meticulously set. He would stand impassively, sometimes being barracked for delay, with long forefinger flicking every fielder to the exact spot. After a few balls he might move a man just a yard and a half – where he would take the catch straight to him.

The bowling to-day makes him impatient. "The l.-b.-w. rule is mainly responsible. It has shut out the lovely off-side strokes; there is too much defensive bowling outside the leg stump and too much playing off the back foot. If you are going to get wickets you must attack the batsman."

Barnes thinks we have one good bowler – Bedser – and a very promising bowler – Trueman – and that we can beat the Australians. "We should have beaten them years ago if we had attacked them." He would like to have bowled at Bradman. "He did not like one going away."

Barnes could bat, and once, with a 38 not out, including the winning hit, saved a Test for England. But he often threw his wicket away. "Why don't you try to make runs?" asked C. B. Fry. "If I make a century and took no wickets, would the selectors pick me for my batting?" was the reply. He once undertook to make 50 if allowed to go in first. He opened against Tasmania, but made only 47.

Barnes is not prepared to say who he thinks was the best batsman of his day – "there were so many really good men then." He would sometimes "just plug them down at Jack Hobbs and hope he would have a fit or something." Clem Hill was probably the most difficult to get out.

Although he had an immensely long playing career – from 1893 to 1936 –

Barnes played little first-class cricket. After his Test *début* he played two seasons for Lancashire – 1902 and 1903 – and thereafter played no first-class cricket except representative matches. In 22 seasons for Staffordshire he took 1,432 wickets for an average of 8.03 runs, and in 38 seasons of League cricket he took 3,741 wickets for an average of 6.68 runs.

The battles with the Australians provide his most treasured memories. Of these the most vivid is the classic occasion at Melbourne in 1911 – one of the finest feats of bowling in Test history. Australia with a powerful, triumphant side had won the toss and went in first on a perfect wicket. The crowd settled back happily in expectation of a huge score. F. R. Foster bowled the first over, then Barnes, who had been ill all week and was scarcely recovered, took the ball.

His first ball swung in to Bardsley, hit him on the toe and went on to the wicket. "He would have been l.-b.-w. if it had not." Shortly afterwards Kelleway stepped in front of the wicket and did not attempt to play a ball going past his legs. "It dipped into him and he was l.-b.-w." Clem Hill, the left-hander, was next. "I gave him one that was an off-break to him and then an in-swinger. Then I sent him one going away and he let it go. The last ball of the over pitched on his leg stump and hit the off. Clem said afterwards he had never had such an over."

The crowd was thunderstruck. But worse was to follow. Trumper and Armstrong, grim and determined, seemed to be making a stand. "Then a leg break to Armstrong went across nicely and very quick off the pitch. He played back, snicked it, and was caught at the wicket. I turned to Douglas, who was captain. Everything was going round. I said: 'I'll have to chuck it. I can hardly see the other end.'" He came off, having bowled nine overs with six maidens and taken four wickets for three runs. He did not bowl again until after lunch.

Then, in his first over, three runs were scored. In the next Minnett played forward to a leg-break, did not get it in the middle, and was caught by Jack Hobbs at cover-point. Barnes had taken five wickets for six runs.

In spite of his successes Barnes was not a popular idol. He was then too stern, too reserved, and he played too little first-class cricket. There was never any national tribute paid him, and though the game on Sunday comes for his eightieth birthday it is gratifying that Barnes is now as able as at any time in a distinguished career to appreciate the feelings of regard that cricket lovers everywhere will feel for a very great player.

Cricketers' War Memorial

28 *April* 1953. The Duke of Edinburgh yesterday opened the Imperial Cricket Memorial, constructed at Lord's to commemorate cricketers who died in two world wars. The ceremony was attended by High Commissioners

of Commonwealth countries and representatives of many cricketing organizations, among them members of the visiting Australian team.

The DUKE of EDINBURGH spoke of the almost universal delight in cricket throughout the British Commonwealth, and said that as a result it attracted a wide and devoted following, bound together by ties of affection for a wonderful game. They formed a great brotherhood of kindred spirits from every corner of the world.

It was appropriate that the memorial should have been provided at Lord's to cricketers from many different walks of life. Many would have been commemorated by their regiments, services, or in their home towns. Their friends would rather remember them as cricketers.

The DUKE of BEAUFORT, president of Marylebone Cricket Club, said that an emergency committee recommended in 1945 that the disused rackets court at Lord's be adapted for use as a cricketers' war memorial composed of a picture gallery and library. Mr. J. H. Markham was commissioned to prepare plans to provide gallery space on two floors.

Responsibility for the cost of the building was borne by the M.C.C.; no appeal for funds was made to the general public, but one was sent to M.C.C. members, and copies were addressed to county clubs and other cricket organizations that might wish to be associated with the scheme.

In response, about £4,200 was subscribed. The fund was still open, and donations were being made in a fairly steady volume.

The Duke of Beaufort referred to presentations of pictures by Sir Jeremiah Colman and cricket bodies overseas. Those from overseas were displayed on the ground floor in a small gallery that housed the commemorative tablet.

A notable exhibit, on view for the first time since the war, was the original urn that contained the ashes presented to Ivo Bligh during the successful tour of an English team in Australia in 1882-83.

The memorial was dedicated by the Bishop of London.

With the Gloves Off

5 *June* 1953, *Leading Article.* The rules of cricket were simply defined by Brigadier Gerard when he was a prisoner of war in this country. It is, he reported home to France, a brave pastime, a game for soldiers. Each tries to strike the other with the ball, and it is but a small stick with which you may ward it off. Three sticks behind show the spot beyond which you may not retreat. "I can tell you," the Brigadier exclaimed, "it is no game for children, and I will confess that, in spite of my nine campaigns, I felt myself turn pale when first the ball flashed past me." But he had reason to look back with complacency on his introduction to this stern sport. His aim was so true that he struck the batsman, a brave man who fell upon the wooden pegs behind him and, even in that moment of anguish, was sporting enough to confess

that there had been no accident in the victory. Again and again he cried aloud, "He did it a-purpose, he did it a-purpose!"

No such balm of righteous self-indignation soothed poor MR. REVILL, the Derbyshire batsman who was given out "hit wicket" after being struck on the hand so that he shook off his glove in pain and it removed a bail. That grand and genial sportsman MR. A. V. BEDSER must have been the sorriest man at the Oval when he took the wicket by this freakish and unprecedented chance. Nothing so odd has happened at the Oval for more than eighty years. A certain J. SOUTHERTON, playing for Surrey against the M.C.C. in 1870, skied a ball and, being evidently of a pessimistic turn of mind, unusual in batsmen, hurried off to the pavilion without waiting to watch what seemed to him a certain catch. The fielder dropped it, but MR. SOUTHERTON did not return, and so he is recorded as having "retired, thinking he was caught." MR. WARD, in a Lancashire against Derbyshire match at Old Trafford, half a century ago, was given out "hit wicket," when a ball knocked a shoulder off his bat on to one of the stumps.

More fortunate, and well within living memory, was MR. PEARCE, whose experience has its memorial in the Long Room at Lord's. A ball bowled to him by MR. JAHANGIR KHAN killed a sparrow in flight which, the batsman having played his stroke, fell dead against the wicket, but without removing the bails. Presumably, even had the wretched bird taken a bail off the verdict would have been "Not Out." The rule confines itself to the hitting down of the wicket with bat or any part of the person and the sparrow was not, and had no wish to be, in any way connected with MR. PEARCE. The law may have been fulfilled at the Oval, but the spirit of the game was certainly flouted. Would a batsman struck in the stomach by a viciously rising ball and caused to sit down, winded, on the stumps, be given out? Tough old gentlemen in the pavilion, their playing days safely behind them, may, here and there, mutter that the bat is provided to hit the ball with and that to miss with it lays you open to all the consequences. But most cricketers will join in a chorus of "Bad luck, Revill."

England Have Last Word

Three Yeomen foil Australia

FROM OUR CRICKET CORRESPONDENT [GEOFFREY GREEN]

1 *July* 1953. Out of darkness, through fire into light. Thus did England yesterday rise like some Phoenix from the ashes of apparent defeat to save the second Test match at Lord's and so gain a remarkable draw against Australia with a final score of 282 for seven wickets, just 61 runs behind their original aim for victory.

The age of miracles it proved was not yet past, nor could all the ranks of

Tuscany scarce forebear to cheer this most dramatic and most honourable ending to a match already full of the oddest twists. But within the climax there came the longest and most agonizing last half-hour of a match it is possible to imagine, for in that last span Australia stood to snatch back with leg-spin bowling all that three yeomen of England had denied them for nearly the whole of this last gruelling day.

The yeomen, the heroes, stood apart. They were Watson, Bailey, and Compton, and the greatest of them was Watson. The left-handed Yorkshireman, in the centre of the batting order, was the soul and the pulse of England's rearguard action, and he now became the twentieth man in history to score a century on his first appearance in an England v. Australia Test match. From six o'clock on Monday evening, when the desperate peril of England was shown in her 12 runs for three wickets, he held the crease until 10 minutes to 6 last evening. A moment before he finally left, mentally and physically exhausted after a personal battle of five hours and three-quarters against all the odds, England stood at 236 for four. Therein lay the measure of his triumph, though mere figures alone can never disclose the heart of his achievement.

But he was not alone. First at his side there stood Compton. Theirs has been a happy association in the past. Three times against South Africa in the summer of 1951 they fashioned century partnerships. But none could now compare with the 61 vital runs that were born of an hour and three-quarters struggle that first turned back the Australian assault. Compton for the second time in this perplexing exciting match batted finely and for the second time it took a really good ball to claim him. It was at 20 minutes to one yesterday that the bounding, left-handed Johnston, loose and long of limb, suddenly had him l.-b.-w. with a ball, a yard quicker through the air, which kept low.

England then were 73 for four and a long, long way yet from any harbour of safety. But already Compton and his partner, footballers both, had achieved something. They had lit a tiny flame of hope. More practically Compton, with three crashing off-drives to the boundary in a single over, seemed to destroy all Benaud's confidence in his own length and leg-spin that lasted far into the day. That was of considerable importance.

So with four hours and 50 minutes left Bailey walked down the pavilion steps. Each stride to the crease took him nearer his part in what was to prove an epic achievement of courage, concentration and will power, not to mention skill. For all but three-quarters of an hour of that wide ocean of time did he and Watson stand firm in the face of all that Hassett and his Australians could hurl at them. Together they fanned that first tiny flame of hope until it spurted up into a sturdy fire. Their fourth-wicket partnership of 163 runs was the greatest of all this great match. And it has been a great match, worth every penny of its world record receipts of over £57,716, a match that day by day took one by the hand down new and unexpected paths.

There were four crises on this last desperate day. The first came at the beginning as Watson and Compton faced Lindwall and Johnston. This crisis at last was passed as Hassett turned to the leg-spin of Ring and Benaud. It was now that Compton set Benaud back with an attack that saw 52 runs arrive in the first hour, three overs costing Benaud 22.

The second critical moment came with Compton's dismissal. This, together with a third anxiety – the arrival of a new ball in the hands of Lindwall and Miller at 3 o'clock with the score 149 for four – was neutralized by the glowing courage and concentration of Watson and Bailey as the bowlers tore at them with pace and lift. Twice indeed at this last point in mid-afternoon Bailey suffered the sharpest of blows on his knuckles from Lindwall that searched out the tendrils of his spirit.

For 40 minutes they met the barrage, scraped together 10 runs and won through. So tea came with England almost miraculously 183, still for four wickets, with Watson 84, Bailey 39 and a 100 partnership already under their pads. The runs had ticked up at a declining rate of 52, 44, 35, and 29 through succeeding hours which showed the intensity of the struggle and the fact that Hassett by now was clearly a worried man. Things had slipped through his fingers slowly, largely because the spin of Ring and Benaud had failed him when most he needed it.

Through all this long span Watson had been passed on the forward stroke once each by Lindwall and Miller and once had snicked Davidson just short of the slips. But mostly he had been firm in his stroke play, turning the ball beautifully off his legs to the on side, whence most of his runs came. Bailey, also beaten once by Miller, again, as he had done before, got his head down well and his bat along the strict line of the ball to present a teasing barrier, sweeping every now and then any loose ball that was offered and, on one occasion particularly, cutting Johnston beautifully for 4.

The Australian bowling, when faced by this growing problem, seemed strangely out of gear. Its sharp edge of earlier was now surprisingly blunted, though Ring, who occasionally worried Watson, Johnston, and Miller, tried everything from both sides of the wicket to various combinations of close fielders outside the leg and off stump.

It was all to no avail until Ring, in a long, last spell after tea, finally began to get some work on the ball down the hill from the Nursery end. But by half-past 5 Watson was past his great hundred, nearly out incidentally at long leg, as he swept Ring for 4 to a mighty cheer; Bailey, too, was beyond his 50. Together they had all but piloted England to safety.

But at 10 minutes to 6 things suddenly began to happen. Watson, almost on his last legs, snicked Ring's googly to slip, to receive a wonderful ovation on his return home; 236—5—109. Then, just short of 6 o'clock, Bailey loosely tried to drive Ring's away spin, pitched well outside the off-stump, and holed out at cover-point; 246—6—71. He, too, another footballer, received the applause of a hero.

Now came the last fearful half-hour as Australia, suddenly revitalized and on tiptoe, strained every nerve for a dramatic breakthrough. How Brown and Evans at times survived the spin of Ring and Benaud none could truly tell. But Brown at least showed himself a man for this last crisis. With no little sense of discrimination, and some thumping drives, he hit the spin away for four telling boundaries that helped to preserve all that had been built up so patiently through the long hours.

Every ball played was now met by nervous applause as the assembly sensed the tingle of the fading battle. Though Brown, with five minutes left, finally fell to Benaud in the slips, the battle at last was over. The enemy had been deprived of his prey.

> AUSTRALIA 346 (A. L. Hassett 104, A. K. Davidson 76, R. N. Harvey 59; Bedser 5 for 105, Wardle 4 for 77) and 368 (K. R. Miller 109, A. R. Morris 89, R. R. Lindwall 50, G. B. Hole 47; F. R. Brown 4 for 82)
> ENGLAND 372 (Hutton 145, Graveney 78, Compton 57; R. R. Lindwall 5 for 66) and 282 for 7 (Watson 109, T. E. Bailey 71)
> *Match drawn*

Test Cricket Triumphant

20 *August* 1953, *Leading Article.* Some of the players in yesterday's Test Match were unborn when England last won the Ashes at home, and the oldest of them was no more than a small schoolboy. It is natural, after so long and at times so bleak an interval, for lovers of English cricket to rejoice. But looking back over the exciting – and even the nerve-wracking – ups and downs of this season, victory once again at the Oval is seen to be only one reason why hearts should be light to-day. Test cricket, like other traditional institutions, reflects social change. A game that has its roots in a more leisurely age than the present has been thought by some loyal supporters of past glory to be in danger. The bloom of freshness, it has been said – more often privately than in public – must wilt in the hothouse atmosphere of daily and, indeed, hourly publicity.

So fierce a concentration of limelight was, according to this pessimistic view, bound to lead to demand for "brighter" play, to disputes about selection, and to new and worse outbreaks of ill-feeling between the countries. The tireless pens of the critics and the ceaseless voices of the commentators could be taken, with the ominous, slow hand-clapping of the crowds, as "noises off," sounding the death knell of cricket as the special summer's pleasure of those who understand it. A wider, casual public was being brought in to transform a glorious game into a branch of high pressure and highly professional sport.

The genius – it might almost be called the imp – of cricket has now stepped in to confound these prophets. Australia sent over a side less formidable, or at least less fortified with terrible names, than she has sometimes done before, and England was no better placed. The robot quality of skill that, in other seasons, has made a finish a foregone conclusion, temporarily vanished. Scores were low. Neither side reached four hundred in any innings and there were only six centuries – two of them from HASSETT and one from HUTTON – in the series. Each of the struggling and changing elevens was lucky to escape decisive defeat. The fortunes of the players rose and fell so unpredictably that honours were spread, and no single man towered to HOBBS or BRADMAN height.

This, had the melancholy thesis proved sound, would have led to a season of discontent and frustration. Instead, it has been a bumper season and everyone, including the players, has enjoyed almost every moment of it. HASSETT and his men will go home knowing that, though they leave the Ashes behind them, they leave, too, as happy memories with their hosts as did any of the sides that came before them. They and our own men have triumphantly survived ordeal by stop-press, loudspeaker, and television camera. No cricket season in history has seen a series of Test matches between England and Australia played more closely in the spirit of the clubs and villages from north of the Trent to south of Sydney on which the health – and the fun – of the game depends. Is there an Englishman who, putting his hand on his heart, can swear that, when he went to bed on Tuesday night, he knew for certain that all was over bar the cheering round the pavilion? Eleventh hour upsetting of probability is the salt of cricket and 1953 has brought it in full measure.

Lord's Turns to Lacrosse

BY OUR SPECIAL CORRESPONDENT

7 *October* 1953. There is a place for Lord's Cricket Ground in the hearts of all lacrosse players, for besides its congenial surroundings and excellent turf, it has a long historical connexion with the sport. Indeed, a history of lacrosse at Lord's covering the last 70 years would make fascinating reading.

Although the appearance of the players of to-day and the form of their equipment have changed since the Canadian pioneers of 1833 played at Lord's, the skill, teamwork, and character have been maintained. This Saturday Kenton and Old Thorntonians, meeting there in a championship match, begin a new chapter in this history. Other games will follow every Saturday until November 14.

In First Ball

10 *April* 1954, *Leading Article.* Breathes there a man with past so dead that not even an ember in it is made to glow by the window display, currently on

view, of a "Junior Cricket Set," complete for fifteen and fourpence? Completeness consists of one bat, one ball, four stumps, stuck into a stand, and a string "carry bag." That, shockingly though the prices of sports gear have risen, is bumper value for money to-day. Seeing the complete set, shiny and immaculate, in the window is to be reminded that the seasons come stealthily on city dwellers with always a surprise in store. Let the countryman keep his familiar nests and flowers bravely trying to avoid the staleness of annual repetition; it is only the townsman who gets such a novel reminder as this that the time for cricket is round the corner.

How diverse will be the fates of those complete sets when they go out into the world. All will lose their present look of being as neat and clean as choir boys on Sunday mornings. Many will quickly be divorced from their stand. It will be useful, indeed essential, on asphalt but, wherever there is turf to be punctured, the three stumps will go in at one end and the singleton at the other. Bat and ball may be the first of their kinds ever to be handled by their new owner. They cannot guess, until they leave the shop, in whose fumbling fingers they will be made, dramatically speaking, to serve the masters of the game. Hutton will hit a six (and wreak havoc in the process among out-of-bounds flowers) with the bat. The Bedsers will take turns with the ball and, between overs, it will be thrown at the smallest fielder to remind him not to lose interest in the proceedings because he has just been given out leg-before-wicket.

The first taste of cricket is, for many men, the sweetest. Played on recreation grounds, on the sands and in back gardens, it is free from umpires and other spoil-sport conventions. All players can and do loudly refuse to admit that they are out or that they have been bowling for too long. Competitive instinct and little or no nonsense about the old school tie reign supreme. We are all little Graces when we first play cricket. White flannels, net and fielding practice and all the mature glories of the game come later and are not, by every one, loved as much. The holidays enjoy for embryo cricketers what the lawyers call privilege. Then, and only then, can the Hutton and the Rabbit of to-morrow join in an uninhibited shout of "Got your off stump! Give Bill the bat." If, as is highly unlikely, Bill is given the bat there and then, what matter that it may take some time before his dog can, by chasing and persuasion, be induced to disgorge the ball?

Jet Cricket

17 *April* 1954, *Leading Article.* The full results have not yet been made public of an experiment, fraught with interest for the British race and indeed for most of the British Commonwealth, which was carried out the other day. A jet aircraft engine was used to dry out a cricket-pitch and naturally did the job much quicker than Dame Nature, even at her most cooperative, could

have done it. The unreliability, often verging on malice, of our climate constantly menaces the best interests of our national game, disappointing crowds, playing havoc with averages, and perverting the ends of justice by saving the other side from defeat (occasionally, of course, it is the other way round and we remind ourselves complacently that there is no game quite like cricket). Nothing will do more to reduce frustration and delay and to lessen wear and tear on the gramophone records which enable the B.B.C., when rain stops play, to substitute for the commentator's voice a medley of intensely unpopular tunes, than a device which will dry out a pitch many times quicker than the brightest of bright intervals.

Reactionary voices will no doubt be heard complaining that the balance of Nature is being upset, and wet-bobs will take pleasure in concocting, only in order to rebut them, rumours that oil is going to be sprayed over the course at Henley in the event of rough weather during Regatta week. But most people will welcome anything that will make it possible for more actual cricket to be played during cricket matches. One pleasing feature of the new device is that it is absolutely useless to foreigners. All too often in the past British pioneering in the field of sport has been requited in the long run by national humiliation. Other races have learnt our rules, borrowed our equipment and some of our vocabulary and come back to trounce us. There is no danger of this boomerang process happening this time, and it is comforting (though possibly a shade mean) to reflect that – within, so to speak, the family – a means of drying the pitch quickly is not nearly such an important requirement in Australia as it is here.

It will take a little time to get the hang of the new device, and the M.C.C. will have to draw up very carefully the rules governing its use. Will captains, between innings, have the choice between the light jet and the heavy jet? Problems of finance will obtrude themselves, for grounds equipped with this new gimmick will, like cinemas equipped with 3D, offer spectators something of which they have never before had the advantage, and no enterprising club will be able to dispense with one. Who will operate them? What should they be called? If the final results of the recent experiment turn out satisfactorily, the coming cricket season may be full of surprises – unless of course there is just one surprise, the biggest of the lot, in the shape of a really fine summer.

George Hirst

11 *May* 1954, *Leading Article.* Posterity's memory being the wayward and parsimonious thing it is, it can easily be said that cricket has already too many "immortals" for so comparatively young a game. But it can be said with equal certainty that the newest comer to the Elysian fields will last with the longest. GEORGE HIRST was more than a great cricketer. He was a great character. Already in his lifetime he had begun to be a legend. Not that the

deeds of the cricketer should be forgotten. They are remarkable enough for any man. The *Wisden* of 1922, marking his fiftieth birthday and also his impending retirement from the game, records a page of astonishing figures. In thirty-one years of first-class matches HIRST batted in 1,211 innings, scored 36,196 runs, with an average of 34.14 an innings. In those same years he bowled 122,592 balls, and took 2,723 wickets at an average of 18.75 runs a wicket. But what no figures can give was the wonder and the beauty of his fielding at mid-off. Whatever credit he deserved for the swerve, it was one of the lesser parts of the fame of this very all-round player.

There are many men – and indeed women, for HIRST was the idol of all Yorkshire – now advancing in years, who can remember the joy of seeing HIRST in his prime. It was not merely the joy of achievement – he could on occasion fail as humbly as any other man – but he brought to everything he did a courage, an integrity, a vigour and a tenacity that meant that no game in which he took part was decided until the last ball had been bowled and the last stroke made. One of the few remaining links with W. G. GRACE, he belonged to cricket's Homeric age. At least, so those who ever saw him in the field must now think. No doubt the Homeric days of cricket are always with us, and there are probably small boys at this time building pedestals for their own idols of the future. Fortunate indeed will any generation of them be that can count upon seeing the peer of HIRST.

18 *May* 1954. Sir Francis Meynell writes:–

In 1904 when George Hirst took his Benefit I sent him from my preparatory school a hard-saved half a crown; and I asked him how to make the ball swerve. His reply – in his own round and careful hand, for Benefits had no first, second, and third secretaries in those days – was as follows:

"Dear Sir [and this alone was worth the money to a schoolboy] thank you for the 2s. 6d. I cannot tell you how to make the ball swerve, hold the ball with the seam between the first two fingers. Yours faithfully, George Hirst." But that was not the end. There was a gap of an inch and then, generously, another "George Hirst" – detachable, as a "swop."

Complacent Masters Beaten by Their Pupils

FROM OUR CRICKET CORRESPONDENT [JOHN WOODCOCK]

18 *August* 1954. The young cricketers from Pakistan had their finest hour, and England one of their less glorious, at the Oval yesterday when the fourth and final Test match was won and lost there by 24 runs. Pakistan gained a victory which carried with it a sharing of the rubber and England

suffered a defeat which came as a rather unwelcome awakening within a month of sailing for Australia.

Some may say that the full strength of England was not in the field, some that the losers had the worst of the wicket, but first and foremost all should acknowledge a performance of great merit by Pakistan, and one upon which they are to be congratulated most warmly. By seizing their chance with both hands and winning this Test match on English soil on their first tour they have achieved in less than four months what it took Australia two years, South Africa 28 years, and West Indies 22 years to achieve, and what to this day has eluded New Zealand and India.

Pakistan's particular hero was Fazal, who brought his tally of wickets in the match to 12, and who throughout the series has established himself as a bowler of medium pace fit to rank near our own Bedser. Next to Fazal one would put Wazir and Zulfiqar, whose ninth wicket partnership of 58, when all seemed lost, gave birth to the recovery from which victory sprang. Kardar, when suddenly he saw the heel of Achilles exposed, captained his side in every respect as astutely as he has done all summer, and there was an alert response from those under him.

Much of England's play, from the moment that Wazir and Zulfiqar came together on Monday morning, was almost too bad to be true. The bowling of Loader and Tyson became lifeless and inaccurate; the fielding became casual; and the inadequacy of the batting on a good wicket is reflected in the score-book. May and Simpson played well, but they got themselves out, and Compton's 29 would have been nearly 50 had he made the most of the loose balls he received. Graveney failed in the crisis, as he had in the first innings, and the tail proved to be no shorter than one had feared. Nor, should Bailey by some mischance be out of action, and if five bowlers are played as they surely must be, will it be any shorter in Australia.

The odds, when play started yesterday with England's last four wickets needing 43 runs, seemed to be slightly in Pakistan's favour, and one simply hoped that England would put up a fight. Their main chance rested with Wardle, who has made a good many runs against Pakistan this year. Given the opportunity he could have won the match off his own bat in 10 minutes, but Kardar sensibly chose Mahmud to bowl with Fazal, and speed does not suit Wardle's book so well as spin. The result was that Wardle was prevented from using the long handle and never flourished.

There was an impartial cheer for anything of note from the small crowd, and the sense of strain in the middle was soon shown in an injudicious single. Then at 129 Wardle was dropped at second slip off Mahmud, a none too difficult catch as slip catches go, and presently the same batsman survived two leg-before appeals from Fazal. After 25 minutes only six had been scored, but by then Tyson seemed to be finding his feet, and Pakistan badly needed a wicket. It came just on noon, when Tyson felt speculatively for an out-swinger from Fazal and gave Imtiaz his seventh catch of the match. Loader now came in ninth instead of his usual eleventh, and at once forced a 4 to long-on, followed by a quick single which took the score to 138.

With 30 needed from three wickets it was anyone's game, and yet within a quarter of an hour the end had come. At 138 Wardle was caught round the corner turning Fazal off his legs, and Loader, hitting out desperately, immediately sent a steepling catch to cover-point, where Waqar, after an agony of suspense, held it and threw it aloft. There remained only some missing and snicking, a run out escape, and then a fatal call by McConnon, who underestimated Hanif's quickness and accuracy of throw from cover-point to the bowler's end. Hanif hit the stumps, umpire Davies adjudicated, and Pakistan, who had come to learn, had come and conquered.

> PAKISTAN 133 (Tyson 4 for 35) and 164 (Wazir Mohammad 42 not out; Wardle 7 for 56)
> ENGLAND 130 (Compton 53; Fazal Mahmud 6 for 53, Mahmud Husain 4 for 58) and 143 (P. B. H. May 53; Fazal Mahmud 6 for 46)
> *Pakistan won by 24 runs*

COURT OF APPEAL
Professional Cricketer's Tax

D. E. Moorhouse (Inspector of Taxes) v. Dooland

BEFORE THE MASTER OF THE ROLLS, LORD JUSTICE JENKINS, AND LORD JUSTICE BIRKETT

20, 22, 23 *November* 1954. The COURT reserved judgment in this appeal by the Crown from a decision of Mr. Justice Harman on May 27, 1954, confirming a decision of the Commissioners for the district of Blackburn, Lancashire, that benefits received by Mr. Bruce Dooland, professional cricketer, were not liable to income tax.

Mr. R. E. Borneman, Q.C., and Sir Reginald Hills appeared for the Crown; Mr. F. N. Bucher for the cricketer.

The respondent was the cricket professional to the East Lancashire Club, a member of the Lancashire Cricket League. In August, 1949, he entered into a written agreement with the club to act as their professional for the seasons 1951 and 1952, at a salary of £800 a year.

A clause in the agreement provided that "collections shall be made for any meritorious performance by the professonal with bat or ball."

In 1951 the respondent became entitled on 11 occasions to have a collection made on his behalf, and £48 15s. was so collected. The question in the case was whether the money so received was a taxable profit within the wording of schedule E as being "salaries fees wages perquisites or profits whatsoever" from the exercise of an office or employment of profit for the year of assessment.

MR. BORNEMAN, in opening, submitted that the money received by the respondent was not a mere token of esteem but was payment for services rendered. A professional footballer's benefit was taxable; and if a cricketer's was not there was an anomaly which the Crown considered should be removed.

The MASTER OF THE ROLLS said that he was quite unmoved by the assertion that there was an anomaly; whether there was or was not was immaterial. Cricketers had had many things to put up with, including summers like that of 1954. Cricket was the only game which distinguished us from all others.

Counsel argued that while the tax anomaly remained footballers, parsons, who had to pay on Easter offerings, and taxi drivers, who were taxed on tips, might feel that they were being dealt with harshly.

LORD JUSTICE BIRKETT. – You could remove the anomaly by saying that they should not be taxed. The tax in this case would be something trivial.

LORD JUSTICE JENKINS. – I hope this is being done at the Crown's expense.

Counsel replied that, if successful, the Crown would not ask for costs. He could imagine nothing more generous than that.

LORD JUSTICE BIRKETT. – I can.

Counsel said that Mr. Justice Harman took the view that as only some £20 was involved the matter might well have been left alone. The Crown felt, however, that it had to administer the law. There was no question of sympathy for anybody.

The MASTER OF THE ROLLS. – If you bring this sort of case you expose yourself to this sort of bowling.

LORD JUSTICE JENKINS. – Do they never have a collection for an umpire?

The MASTER OF THE ROLLS. – For rejecting five or more appeals?

The MASTER OF THE ROLLS, later referring to the tax on clergymen's Easter offerings, said: "I regard it as the gravest case of misplaced fiscal enthusiasm. When one thinks of the expenses the unfortunate clergy have to bear I cannot understand it." On the taking of tips, he said that the inspectors taxed every person suspected of getting them. "How on earth is the amount of the tip ever discovered?" he asked. "Presumably only the honest pay."

LORD JUSTICE BIRKETT said that the law became rather absurd if it could not be observed in a uniform way.

During further argument the MASTER OF THE ROLLS said that if the Crown indulged in its "passion for uniformity" Christmas boxes ought to be taxed.

MR. BORNEMAN, continuing his argument, submitted that the words in the schedule could not be wider: all "profits whatsoever" included money received from any persons, not only from persons with whom the recipient had a contract. The remuneration of the respondent was to be partly in the form of collections, and was liable to tax. It might be said that the law was too harsh, but that was a matter for the Legislature to consider. Whether a payment was made in pursuance of the terms of a contract or was a gift independent of contract must depend on the particular facts of each case, and on the facts of this case he submitted that the finding of the Commissioners could not be supported. The only cases where such payments were not liable to tax were cases where the payment was on some exceptional occasion, such as the end of a career, which could not recur, and was not in respect of the performance of the duties of an employment.

SIR REGINALD HILLS, following, said that the money was received by the respondent because he had played well in a match in which he was employed to play. It was plainly a profit from his employment.

The MASTER OF THE ROLLS asked what the position would be of a young man employed by the club whose father gave him a shilling for every run he made. Would that gift from his father be liable to tax?

SIR REGINALD HILLS submitted that the right to have collections was part of the respondent's contract.

The MASTER OF THE ROLLS told counsel in the next case (Prescott v. Birmingham Corporation) they could go away since Sir Reginald was not out yet and the other side had to go in.

MR. BUCHER, for the cricketer, submitted that for money to be taxable it must be a payment made in return for services rendered by the payee to the payer. Where there was no service relationship the payment was spontaneous, and was not within the scope of "emoluments." There was no certainty about the amount to be raised by a cricket collection, and the cricketer could not claim any sum at all as a right. Easter offerings were taxable because they were not a personal gift to the incumbent for the time being but were a tribute to the office. The real question here was whether the money came to the respondent as the club professional, or as Mr. Dooland. It did not come to him as the professional for the time being, but it came to him in his personal capacity. Whether a particular case fell on one side or other of the line was a question of fact for the Commissioners; and their finding here should not be disturbed, unless it could be held to be such a conclusion as rational men could not have reached. The yield from the collections was so small that the Commissioners, as local men, could hold that the right to such collections was not an inducement to Mr. Dooland to serve his club. They were a spontaneous sign of appreciation from the spectators.

Solicitors. – Solicitor of Inland Revenue; Messrs. Gibson and Weldon for Messrs. Crockford and Anderson, Nottingham.

The appeal of the tax inspector was allowed, in the judgment delivered the following month, on the grounds that the collections constituted part of the earnings of Dooland's profession under the terms of his contract.

Commentary before Breakfast

26 *November* 1954, *Leading Article.* The thoughts we entertain in the early morning remain for the most part unrevealed, for as a nation we are notoriously uncommunicative until the breakfast things have been cleared away. Whatever may go on behind those inexpressive features as they greet the new day it is certain that to-day the thoughts of many will have been with our Test players in Australia. Before daylight has asserted itself the hand of the cricket enthusiast emerges from the bedclothes to grope for the switch on his wireless set and to satisfy a powerful curiosity. For weeks he has followed the triumphs and failures of our players. The last time they were in Australia he was plagued by news of injuries. If it was not COMPTON's knee it was WRIGHT's neck or BAILEY's shoulder. This year the casualty list has been shorter and the achievement already substantial, but he has been kept on tenterhooks by the in-and-out form of the English batsmen. Now the rehearsals are finished. The captains, the teams, and the umpires have been picked; the pitch has been appraised for the last time, the coin has been tossed, and in the cold light of breakfast time speculation gives way to fact.

The news may not always be to the audience's liking – in 1946 BRADMAN was already on his way to a double century after the first day's play – but the score is not everything. The hard figures of the day's play may be heard in later bulletins, but nothing can quite destroy the fascination of listening to the ebb and flow of the commentator's voice as he describes, from the other side of the world, LINDWALL running in to bowl or a sweep to leg by COMPTON. So absorbing can this become that the whole routine of a household may temporarily be set at naught. The listener wanders about distractedly, carrying cups of tea and listening for the quickening of the commentator's voice as it tells of a boundary or the muffled roar that greets a fallen wicket. Sustenance is taken not necessarily at the breakfast table but wherever the loudspeaker stands. Children are hushed into silence. Sooner or later the passage of time forces the listener back into the rhythm of another working day, but before he slips on his overcoat he will have relished the sound of cheers from an Australian crowd on whom – or so he imagines – the sun is beating pitilessly down.

A Cricket Lover's Bequest

Local Ground the Pride of Darley Dale

FROM OUR SPECIAL CORRESPONDENT [PHILIP URE]

20 *December* 1954; *Darley Dale*, 19 *December.* A village cricket club that in these stringent times is bequeathed the sum of £5,000 must be accounted

fortunate indeed. But Mr. Alfred Smith of Darley Oak was a lover of cricket, and the club and ground of this his native village near Matlock gave him all the pleasures of the game that he ever desired. He died last summer at the age of 82 and under his will, which has just been published, Darley Dale Cricket Club comes into £5,000.

Alfred Smith first played for Darley Dale in 1887 at a time when he had to borrow the club subscription of half a crown from his mother. He continued to play for 50 years and in his prime was acknowledged the club's best bowler. He became a wealthy man – his estate is valued at more than £200,000 – and during his lifetime spent much money in making the cricket ground of Darley Dale one of the finest in all the Midlands.

His most intimate surviving friend says of Alfred Smith: "He had two drawing rooms – the cricket pavilion in summer and the billiards room in winter." He is said to have been an exceptionally shy man, and it is pleasant to think of the cricket field and the cricket club as the places where such a man felt most at ease with his neighbours.

Outside his devotion to the cricket club he was frugal in the spending of money, in spite of his substantial fortune. But no one in Darley Dale thinks of Alfred Smith as ever having been mean; it was just that he had been brought up strictly. This showed itself in a lifelong opposition to Sunday play, and in his will he expresses a wish that there shall continue to be no Sunday play at Darley Dale. But his wish was not written as a cast-iron stipulation, for he recognized how feeling on this question was changing with the march of time.

Now that he is gone, the field that was his great pride will remain the pride of Darley Dale and, through his beneficence, can be kept in the first-class condition that he would wish.

Tyson Levels Test Series for England

FROM OUR CRICKET CORRESPONDENT [JOHN WOODCOCK]

23 *December* 1954; *Sydney*, 22 *December*. At Brisbane, tragedy; at Sydney, triumph. Here this afternoon England won a memorable victory by 38 runs after one of the most exciting Test matches for many years. At 10 minutes past three Tyson and Statham, heroes at the head of England's team, were cheered from sight through one pavilion gate, and through the other went little Harvey, undefeated after a masterly effort to steer Australia home.

There have been many Test matches in which the technical standard has been higher, and, for that matter, several in which the margin of victory has been smaller. But few can have followed a more winding course or reached so great a climax as did this one. And in few can there have been so courageous and sustained a piece of fast bowling as Tyson's to-day. For four days England's cricket alternated between the pit of depression and, very occasionally, the heights of expectation, until this morning it seemed that Australia would most likely win.

Indeed it had seemed that way since England were bowled out for 154 in their first innings. But Tyson, with a bump on the back of his head the size of an egg, swung the balance after 15 minutes to-day with two shattering yorkers in an over. Thereafter England fought like lions, paralysing all Australia's batsmen except Harvey. Statham supported Tyson with great heart and determination, Appleyard got a valuable wicket, and Evans took a staggering catch. Nor must one forget the batting of May and Cowdrey or England's last-wicket partners. Yet the match should be remembered more than anything for Tyson's fast bowling to-day on an easy wicket.

Only last week at Melbourne he changed to a shorter, more controlled, run. Now he has also learnt the value of a full length by watching Lindwall, and 10 wickets in a Test match is the result. He is strong, and it is difficult to see how a man can bowl much faster than he did at times to-day. Within a fortnight he has acquired for himself a considerable ascendancy over Australia's leading batsmen through being genuinely too good for them.

M.C.C. can thank him for being able to spend Christmas with happy hearts, and England are in the elevating psychological position in which Australia found themselves after Brisbane. Had this match gone the other way, however, as it came within an ace of doing, much of the interest might have gone from the series.

Now it is ablaze with possibilities, with Hutton's side restored to confidence and their doubters faithful again. Hutton captained calmly and with judgment to-day. It was not easy for him with runs so precious and with Tyson and Statham to be conserved and yet released.

Nor is Harvey an easy man to keep down. This innings of his was altogether better than his century at Brisbane, and it would have gone down to posterity had he somehow won the match for Australia, as there was a chance he was going to during a, to English eyes, torturing last-wicket partnership of 39 with Johnston. For the first time on this tour Harvey looked a great player. Never before has one seen him so scrupulously behind the line of the ball, and never has one seen his bat have fewer edges. Almost always before when playing against England he has looked brilliant but unsound; to-day he played hardly a false stroke.

When Harvey and Burke made their way to the wicket in cool and sunny weather this morning it needed only an over apiece from Statham and Tyson to reveal that the pitch was dead and remarkable things would have to happen if England were to win. Remarkable things did happen in Tyson's second over, for off the third ball the obdurate Burke was yorked, and off the seventh Hole met a similar fate.

Benaud was struggling, Harvey was hemmed in, the bowlers' length was checking many drives, and for almost an hour the battle went slowly yet tensely on with 29 runs being secored. Hutton soon had Bailey on from the

M. A. Noble stand end, with Tyson and Statham in short bursts from the other, but it was Appleyard who made the next vital contribution to England's day when he replaced Bailey. Appleyard is forever likely to beat in the air someone to whom he has not bowled before with the ball he holds back, and sure enough in his second over he caused Benaud to sweep too soon and send a high swirling catch to Tyson off the top edge of the bat. Tyson was at backward square leg half-way to the boundary, and he caught the ball so far from his body that for an awful moment one feared the catch might go to ground.

Australia's innings, if not now open as England's would have been, was at least ajar and Archer survived until luncheon, when Harvey had passed his 50 in 165 minutes. During the interval nobody could make up his mind who was going to win. Some said two to one against England, some said even money, few yet favoured England, but the first half-hour of the afternoon virtually settled the issue. Tyson and Statham began the bowling and the former bowled Archer in his second over. The ball fairly whipped back off the pitch and Australia, with four wickets to go, still needed 101 to win. One had lurking fears of Davidson and Lindwall, both of whom are highly inflammable drivers, and yet before Harvey could get at the bowling to shield and prepare them they had gone. Davidson was the victim of Evans's resilience, for he flicked at an out-swinger and there was Evans throwing himself to the ball in front of first slip.

The crowd savoured the meeting of Tyson and Lindwall after Tuesday's accident and at 136 Tyson got ample revenge with his one stroke of luck to-day. He pitched one well up outside the off-stump and Lindwall, trying to chop it, dragged it on. Four times had Tyson hit the wickets and he deserved all the praise his colleagues gave him. But the game was by no means over yet, for it was now that Harvey began to rule it while he had the chance. He pulled Statham for four and hooked Tyson for three before losing Langley, bowled by Statham in trying to keep a half-volley out of his stumps with a shot of his own.

Surely all was as good as over and, one felt, Hutton thought so too when he called for drinks to let victory linger on the palate. Nor did Johnston do anything to destroy the feeling of exultation when he missed his first three balls and escaped an l.-b.-w. appeal off his fourth. These were the last four balls of Statham's over and 78 were needed with one last wicket to fall. But for 40 minutes Harvey and Johnston tortured all Englishmen present. Women in the crowd began to get hysterical and the spectator in front of your Correspondent mistook his dark glasses for his pipe. In seven overs Johnston had only nine balls to face. He ran where there was no run and got away with it. He hooked over Bailey's head at long leg when Bailey would have had a catch had he been where he should have been, on the fence. He drove and he glanced and all the time Tyson and Statham were wearing themselves out.

There were terrible visions of anticlimax as the lead dwindled and the fielding became ragged. Finally Bailey had to replace Statham, who had been playing an important part by bowling most gallantly into the wind for 85 minutes, and Harvey hit Bailey for two fours. Tyson, too, after 90 minutes' bowling since luncheon, was almost on his knees when at last he had Johnston before him on the first ball of an over. Johnston maddeningly hit a four one-handed to fine leg off the fourth ball but off the fifth he glanced a catch down the leg side to Evans and the umpire's finger was up.

ENGLAND 154 and 296 (P. B. H. May 104, M. C. Cowdrey 54)
AUSTRALIA 228 (R. Archer 49, J. Burke 44; Tyson 4 for 45, T. E. Bailey
4 for 59) and 184 (R. N. Harvey 92 not out; Tyson 6 for 85)
England won by 38 runs

Wit and Wisden

Centenary of a Versatile Writer on Sport and Stage

FROM A CORRESPONDENT [ALAN PITT ROBBINS]

23 *September* 1955. Tribute is paid on the front page of *The Times* this morning to the memory of Sydney H. Pardon, who was born a hundred years ago to-day. Although it is a few months short of thirty years ago since he died his name is remembered with affection and gratitude wherever cricket is played, and wherever *Wisden's Cricketers Almanack* is studied by lovers of the game who look upon it with awe as one of the most complete reference books ever placed upon the market.

"S. H. P.," who combined for some years the positions of Editor of "Wisden's," Cricket Correspondent of *The Times*, and a partner in the Cricket Reporting Agency, established a unique individual position in cricket. As far as his closest friends knew, he had never played the game in his life. But he became the recognized authority on the game whom county captains and even the M.C.C. were glad to consult. His descriptive writing was admirable and he had an uncanny knack of picking out the promising young player. To be selected as one of the five hopefuls of the season in "Wisden's" was an honour greatly prized. On the first occasion that Pardon saw Victor Trumper his innings consisted of six balls only, but at the end of it Pardon was convinced that he had seen the greatest bat that Australia had ever produced. When Sir Jack Hobbs made his first appearance for Surrey Pardon wrote in "Wisden's" that there was a new player "from whom a great deal can be expected and who can be regarded as the best batsman brought forward for years."

In those days writers on cricket had not to face the competition of com-mentators on the air. Pardon would not have made a success at broadcasting. His voice was too gentle and his sight was so poor that he could not follow cricket without the most powerful glasses. He would probably have been impatient with those who were compelled to take snap decisions on a meritorious batting, bowling, or fielding performance. He preferred to form more leisurely judgments, and events rarely proved him to be wrong, as any who care to read the Editor's notes in successive issues of "Wisden's" will discover. It is a coincidence that John Wisden first opened his "cricket and cigar depôt" in London in the year of Pardon's birth. He launched his Almanack in 1864. Pardon took over the editorship in 1891 and held it until his death in 1925. One of his greatest friends, happily still with us, was Sir Pelham Warner, who wrote after his death that on all questions which agitated the cricket world his views were always balanced and judicious and that he never wrote an unkind word about a cricketer because, although criticism was sometimes imperative, the charitable touch was never wanting. Nor was his sense of humour. His quiet but piercing wit always entertained, and he had a wonderful memory for the lighter incidents of the game.

But, although cricket was both his business and his hobby, it was always Pardon's proudest boast that he had written special articles for *The Times* on four widely different subjects – cricket, the drama, opera, and horse racing.

Touring Cricketers

29 *February* 1956, *Leading Article*. No sportsmen have earned, over the years and on and off the field of play, a better reputation than have English cricketers. When they go oversea they have been counted upon not only to give a good account of themselves in the game but also to win the friendship of their hosts. Unfortunately the hooliganism – no ligher word fits – of some members of the M.C.C. team in Pakistan has blotted this record. It would be comforting to be able to say that their breach of decent manners was without precedent. But it is common knowledge that a recent touring side left a bad impression behind them in the West Indies. This, it may be hoped, will be corrected by MR. SWANTON's eleven, which will shortly begin a West Indian tour. Meanwhile, the Peshawar affair cannot be dismissed with the apologies that have been given and accepted.

This is an affair in which the M.C.C. must, and, no doubt, will, intervene as soon as a full report has been received and considered at Lord's. Rough horseplay, of which an umpire is a victim [*as a prank Idris Begh had been doused with cold water*], would be quite beyond the bounds if all concerned were here at home, Englishmen among themselves, at Old Trafford or the Oval. But our men are guests in an Eastern country, and they should have known better than to forget themselves as they evidently did. Old stagers will certainly say that such a thing would not have happened in the palmy days of captains who, while remaining on the friendliest terms with their men, kept discipline and stood no nonsense during games or in the intervals between them.

But the control of a touring cricket side, as of other bodies that need authority set over them, can no longer be exercised in the traditional way. The greater freedom now given to the individual imposes on him a stronger obligation to be self-disciplined. Every man involved in this sorry business must be aware that, in the fullest sense of the phrase, he has let England's side down. When our men are booed by a crowd oversea, as has just happened, and we at home have to admit to one another that they had brought it on themselves, matters have come to an ugly pass. The air will not be cleared until the M.C.C. has spoken, and spoken in no uncertain voice.

The President of M.C.C., Lord Alexander of Tunis, offered to cancel the rest of the tour, but it was completed. On the team's return M.C.C. laid responsibility for the incident on the captain, D. B. Carr, who had been present.

Hutton's Refusal

2 *May* 1956. Mr. L. Hutton, former England Test captain, has declined an offer by East Bradford Conservatives to be their prospective Parliamentary candidate.

Memories of Watching Cricket since 1878

BY SIR HOME GORDON

10 *May* 1956. It would seem reasonable to believe that I am the last surviving spectator of the game between Gentlemen of England and the Australians played at Prince's (now Cadogan Square) in June, 1878. The feature of a low-scoring struggle, in which no batsman made 30, was that the crowd surged into the playing space. I, a startled child in his seventh year, was removed. It was an odd commencement to my prolonged career of an unwearying onlooker.

Probable also is the presumption that I alone among those still alive watched the first Test match ever played in England at the Oval in 1880. Some may be surprised to learn that there was an open-air skating rink at the Vauxhall corner. It was a fine gesture of Lord Harris to accept the captaincy, because, during the preceding winter, he had been the victim of a violent mob attack at Sydney, burly George Ulyett defending him with a stump.

Though Spofforth was not playing, the contest was tremendous. W. G. Grace amassed a magnificent 152. The Australian captain, W. L. Murdoch, bet him a sovereign he would surpass this and actually compiled 153 not out. Subsequently, wearing it on his watch chain, he showed it to me when captain of Sussex. Those he led at the Oval were crude bats so far as style was concerned, but they revolutionized cricket in the placing of the field. Blackham came here as second string wicketkeeper to Murdoch, but was at once recognized as supreme. It was not he but diminutive Henry Phillips, of Sussex, who led to the dispensation of long-stop.

One feature of this historic match was a phenomenal catch. Bonnor, who stood 6ft. 6in. in his socks, hit such a terrific skier that two were run before the ball was beautifully judged by G. F. Grace. There has been controversy as to where the fielder took it. I am certain he ran at top speed to grasp the ball in front of the second gasometer. A month later he was dead, due to sleeping in a damp bed at Chichester. At the final fixture of the tour at the Crystal Palace, the Australians wore black bands on their left sleeves.

In the Test match of 1882 W. G. Grace, when bowling, put down the wicket beside him because the batsman, S. P. Jones, was backing up too eagerly. In 1924 so much was said about this by Australians to A. E. R. Gilligan, leader of our side out there, that he cabled me to know the facts.

England's cricket sank to its lowest in that game, which we lost by seven runs in trying to get 85. C. T. Studd – later a missionary in China – that year had made more than a thousand runs. Yet he was put in tenth by A. N. Hornby and never received a ball because Peate was bowled in attempting a reckless smite. Horan, who always batted in brown pads, has related that in the desperate tension one spectator dropped dead and another gnawed pieces from the handle of his umbrella.

Often I am asked what Spofforth was like. Long, lean, with flying arms and running at great speed, he came like a whirlwind towards the batsman, using cleverly varied pace and direction. Subsequently, when he was manager of a tea company, I knew him well. He was pleasant but very conceited, persisting that he was the fastest bowler ever.

This was sheer nonsense, for he never acquired the pace of E. Jones – who bowled through Grace's beard – nor of N. A. Knox, Kortright, or the South African Kotze. In the later nineties many Australians regarded C. T. B. Turner as a better bowler.

The first Test match at Lord's was in 1884. I have seen all played there since, as well as others at Old Trafford, Headingley, Edgbaston, Trent Bridge, and Kennington. A. G. Steel amassed a superlative 148, the sort of effort Neville Cardus would ascribe to a d'Artagnan of the game. Alfred Lyttelton afforded invaluable support. He was the only man I ever saw keep wicket wearing a hard straw hat. This was for Middlesex against Gloucestershire at Clifton in 1880.

The rubber was instituted in 1886. Shrewsbury was at the wicket at Lord's for seven hours for 164. Both Sir Aubrey Smith and W. Newham told me that, when touring with them in Australia in 1887, he wore a wig which did not fit and insisted upon eating all his meals with a hat on his head. Lohmann declared him to be the most difficult bat to bowl at he ever opposed.

Turner and Ferris showed us how to disregard the state of the wicket when bowling. Between them they claimed 514 wickets for 6,195 runs in one season. After the first war J. M. Gregory and McDonald transformed cricket by starting any match under any conditions with fast bowling at both ends. The last-named had the most beautiful rhythmic delivery I have ever seen.

The partnership of "the pair of midgets," as S. E. Gregory and Graham were called, completely demoralized England at Lord's, arousing wild enthusiasm by their smart running between the wickets. How different from the stolidity of Iredale and Darling, which provoked onlookers on the Mound to whistle the Dead March in Saul, quite harmoniously.

It was because Sir F. S. Jackson and some Yorkshire professionals preferred to play for their county rather than for England that selectors were appointed. At Leeds "the governor-general" Macartney scored a dazzling century before luncheon. During that interval Mrs. Sutcliffe, with a baby in her arms, explained that she had brought her son so that when he grew up he would be able to say he had seen his father's first Test in Yorkshire. To-day that infant is captain of Yorkshire and I had the pleasure of proposing him for M.C.C.

Frequently it is put to me: what has been the greatest innings I have watched. Perhaps it was that of J. T. Tyldesley at Birmingham in 1902 on a rain-soaked wicket unfit to play on. Or was it that supreme demonstration of "pulling it off" by Gilbert Jessop – 104 out of 139 in 75 minutes? He assured me that the more accurate the bowling the easier he found it to hit in every direction.

Or could there be more glamorous batting than that of Victor Trumper – "perfecting the dexterity of MacLaren"? Most modest of men, it may be that he foresaw his early death, for it was curious, as Doctor Rowley Pope pointed out, that he never made plans but existed from week to week.

Was batting ever more controlled than that of K. S. Ranjitsinhji? He told me repeatedly that he himself had only begun where W. G. Grace left off and that his own success could be ascribed to exceptional concentration as well as numberless nets. In the field he always wore his shirtsleeves buttoned round his wrists. Hammond occasionally did so. As my host in India for the Durbar, the Jam Sahib was superlative. But he would not praise the perfection of his nephew Duleepsinhji for fear of turning his head – which was absurd.

I remember an Indian prince – the beloved Duleep – when twelfth man in a Test match at Trent Bridge, taking out a sweater to an English professional, Maurice Tate. Both those great judges, Ranjitsinhji and P. A. Perrin, said they regarded Maurice as an inferior bowler to his father, Fred.

Superfluous to dilate on the wonder of the batting of Bradman, Hobbs, or Hammond, academic to discuss whether Clem Hill or Frank Woolley was the greater left-handed bat. Bardsley lacked the grace of either, though so difficult to oust. Of the many masters behind the stumps Oldfield comes first. All honour to him for the unselfish way in which for so long he was second string to Carter.

No more pleasant pastime can be cited than picking representative teams.

It entails temerity because the inquiry is provoked: "How can you leave out So and So?" My answer is that there are only 11 places to be filled. Whom would you omit? Anyhow, here are my selected sides, past and present, for others to consider. Australia – Bradman, McDonnell, Trumper, Macartney, Clem Hill, Keith Miller, Turner, Noble, Oldfield, Mailey, Spofforth or Lindwall. England – W. G. Grace, Hobbs, Ranjitsinhji, Hutton, Rhodes, Lohmann, Larwood, Ames or Evans, Maurice Tate, Sydney Barnes. How invidious to choose so few out of so many that have afforded delight. How keenly do I anticipate watching the Test at Lord's next month.

Sir Home supplied the name of his eleventh English player – Woolley – in a letter to the Editor published four days later.

All Ten Australians Wickets
and 19 in the Match

FROM OUR CRICKET CORRESPONDENT [JOHN WOODCOCK]

1 *August* 1956. England won the fourth Test match against Australia at Old Trafford yesterday by an innings and 170 runs, so retaining the Ashes, and Laker made the achievement possible by taking all 10 wickets in Australia's second innings. Either feat is notable enough; but when one leads to the other a mockery is made of all laws of probability. Last Friday Laker captured nine wickets in Australia's first innings and his remarkable tally of 19 wickets for 90 runs must always make this one of the most memorable games of cricket ever played. Indeed, it is unlikely that Laker's performance will ever be equalled. Cobden's match and Fowler's match and many others have their own place in history. This one will always be remembered as Laker's match for the way in which his off breaks paralysed Australia.

There are many tedious records which have singularly little meaning, but those which the 34-year-old Laker surpassed yesterday were all of consider-able significance. In the first place he became the first bowler ever to take 19 wickets in any first-class match, let alone a Test match. In Test matches S. F. Barnes headed the list with 17 for 159 against South Africa in 1913. Against Australia, H. Verity and W. Rhodes both took 15 in a match, and for Australia F. R. Spofforth took 14 in 1882. But Laker's crop leaves all these far behind and now with 39 wickets in the series, he has equalled the number established by A. V. Bedser as a record against Australia in 1953. At the Oval, Laker will almost certainly exceed Bedser's total and the whole affair, which is already stranger than fiction, is made even more incredible by the fact that Laker also bowled out the Australians on his own for Surrey in May.

Now he has enabled England to hold the Ashes on three successive occasions for the first time since five matches in a series became the rule in 1897. It is also the first time since 1905 that England won two matches at home in one summer against Australia. And to make Laker's achievement all the more extraordinary is the fact that Lock, who is generally so irresistible when the ball is turning, plugged away for 69 overs in the match for one wicket. That to some extent is a comment on the state of the pitch. Lock did not bowl particularly well, nor did things go his way, and Laker bowled magnificently. But the pitch was very far from being a travesty.

This match will always be talked about as much as any of the 171 played between England and Australia before, not only because of Laker's analysis but also because there arose on the second day a widespread controversy over the condition of the pitch. Then the ball spun from dry turf. Yesterday it did so after persistent rain and the batsmen's task grew progressively harder. Yet for a long while it seemed that the grass would not dry sufficiently or quickly enough for England to win and as nothing was foregone the play was full of tension. One knew that the turn would not have to be ridiculously awkward for England's purpose and during the long partnership between Craig and McDonald the batting was so good that the art was made to seem perfectly feasible. As soon as Craig was out, it was made at times to look impossible. In reality it was somewhere between the two when the game finally hurried to its conclusion.

McDonald's innings was a triumph for his fighting spirit. He is no great technician, but once he is entrenched he is as stubborn as they come. To score runs he waited for a chance to cut. For the rest of the time he played forward or back in a way too open to please the purists, but he was wonderfully watchful and there could have been no better example of unyielding concentration. Craig, who was his partner for so long, played an innings of almost equal value. He could hardly have had a fiercer baptism in Test matches against England, but the experience of it will always stand him in good stead.

Craig is still only 21, yet he had a long time in the wilderness awaiting a chance to show his skill. Now his patience and perseverance in the face of all manner of disappointments have been rewarded and there are many series ahead for England to appreciate his beautiful method. Two hall-marks of class are stamped on his play. In the first place he has plenty of time in which to make his strokes, in the second his judgment of length is extremely sound, and not until Laker dislodged him yesterday did England start striding towards victory.

Play was begun only 10 minutes late, although it had rained heavily through the night until 5 o'clock, and before luncheon the pitch was too saturated to be of any use to anyone. May explored every move. He began with Bailey, who was inclined to bowl too short, and later he gave Oakman a turn. Statham, too, tried with the new ball to hammer some life from the pitch. But of course the attack was based primarily on Laker and Lock, and what they wanted most of all was some sunshine to dry the turf. There was a stiff wind, which sent the many lowering clouds scudding over the ground, but that was not enough, and towards the end of the morning some blue sky began to appear. And with it the pitch perked up and the ball showed signs of misbehaving.

At luncheon McDonald and Craig were still together. They had then added only 59, but the important thing was that they had each been batting for more than four hours. Ahead of them stretched another four and only 15 minutes of these had ticked away when Laker struck his first blow. Craig, still showing a full sense of duty after 259 minutes, played back where he might have been better advised to go forward, and was leg-before. Several other Australians were to do the same and the departure of Craig revealed a hollow middle to Australia's innings. Mackay splashed about in deep water until he sank pushing forward at Laker and being caught off the edge of the bat at second slip. Miller undermined himself, by choosing to take everything he could on the pads. One has never seen him so completely dispossessed and he was out at 130 lunging myopically at a ball he might have made into a full pitch. Archer at once was caught by the middle of three backward short legs playing back to Laker and the day was not yet half run. The sun, too, was now blessing the scene, the threat of showers was fading and as Laker's spin quickened it seemed that there might be a collapse of the kind that had been witnessed on Friday.

Perhaps if Benaud had fallen at once there would have been, for Mackay, Miller, and Archer had not scored a run between them and between 25 past two and five to three four wickets had gone for 16 runs. But McDonald stood immensely determined amid this crumbling world, and now Benaud stayed with him until tea. That was for 80 minutes, and it began to seem again as though England might be thwarted. Benaud carried gamesmanship almost to an extreme by asking for guard in every over, and slowly and deliberately taking a botanical interest in the pitch after every ball. It is fair enough to repair each divot mark which the ball makes, but Benaud's way of doing it irritated the crowd, just as his admirable powers of resistance must have worried England.

When the final two hours of the evening started, whichever side was to win still had a long way to go. Someone was going to be denied and the likelihood that it would be Australia increased when McDonald's monumental vigil of 337 minutes was ended by the second ball after tea. He pushed forward at an off-break and Oakman at backward short leg took his fifth catch of the match. The next two balls from Laker must have settled any doubts that had been sown in English minds. Both of them turned viciously and now it was only a matter of time and a question of whether Laker could take the last three wickets himself.

This was suddenly a fabulous possibility, and three-quarters of an hour later it was an accomplished deed. First Benaud was forced back on to his stumps and bowled by a generously flighted off-break, then Lindwall was snapped up in the leg trap, and finally Maddocks was trapped leg-before. Australia were beaten, the crowd flooded the ground, there were smiles and handshakes, and the hero jogged off as though nothing very much had happened. Close behind him was May, who could feel justly proud at having led England to the Ashes at his first attempt. His splendid efforts must not be overlooked, but this now was Laker's hour, and here to end with and for all time are his figures. In Australia's second innings he took 10 for 53, in the match 19 for 90 in 68 overs, and yesterday eight for 26 in 36 faultless overs. Surely there may never again be anything like it.

> ENGLAND 459 (Rev. D. S. Sheppard 113, P. E. Richardson 104, M. C. Cowdrey 80, Evans 47, P. B. H. May 43; I. W. Johnson 4 for 151)
> AUSTRALIA 84 (Laker 9 for 37) and 205 (C. C. McDonald 89; Laker 10 for 53)
> *England won by an innings and 170 runs*

Memories of Old Wicket-Keeper

FROM OUR SPECIAL CORRESPONDENT [A. P. RYAN]

3 *May* 1958. Mr. Herbert Strudwick is beginning his sixtieth and – so he says – last season in the service of Surrey cricket. But you would not think it as you watched him darting across his little score box by the side of the Oval pavilion to show you how a ball, low on the leg side, should be taken behind the wicket. His hands would be diagnosed at a glance, even by Dr. Watson, as those of an old wicket-keeper. Every finger bears honourable proofs of what happened when gloves were thin ghosts of their present plump and well-protected selves. His memories, keen and racily put, go back to his native Mitcham in the eighties, when he and the other village boys would hurry to the station to watch the Australians arrive in a special saloon coach for practice on the famous common.

You cannot pin him down to the past. For he rushes off from it in conversation as quickly as he used to leave the wicket and career towards the boundary. ("You had to; we didn't have all those men on the on side – often only one. That's why I always used the smallest pads I could get hold of. Ernie or I had to chase all the balls played to square leg. Not much above the knee. With them you were light on your feet.") First-class cricketers, he says, are as good and – allowing for changes in the wicket and laws – as fast scoring as ever they were. The crowd, he thinks, know less of the game than they once did. ("Almost everybody who watched played a bit. There were more to choose from at the top. We could have the county, the second eleven and two club and ground teams playing on the same day. Spectators didn't expect every batsman to be a Jessop or a Woolley. If he were they'd soon get tired of seeing boundary after boundary. You chaps on the Press are partly to blame. What I'd like to see (and here Mr. Strudwick plays with his fingers on the buttons he presses to light up the numbers of the fielders on the score board) is more reports of who did a good piece of ground fielding. If all the members in a team to-day got their fair share of praise it would encourage them no end. They are putting up as good a show, by and large, as any men have done in my time. There have always been slow scoring patches in any well fought game. They are part of the excitement.")

Back to wicket-keeping and Mr. Strudwick, leaving the buttons and his chair, crouches to make his points. ("Hands matter more than pads. Once, when I was a youngster at Dorking, all the chaps started chucking balls at me as fast as I could take them, before the start of a match. I did not realize that I had no pads on until I was taking the first ball of the match. The chaps had been trying to hit me on my shins. But my eye was in and they hadn't. Stand nice and comfy, drop the hands with the fingers pointing down. Watch the ball from the bowler's hands and then off the ground. If you don't you can't tell what it's going to do next. Above all don't stiffen as the ball leaves the ground. If one part of the body is stiff, it'll all be stiff.")

Did he, as has often been said, put raw meat inside his gloves? ("Never. Most of them did. But I thought it too messy. So I was glad when the gloves and the inners got better. At first I had only brown leather round the fingers and inners with nothing much to them. For my first two years I hadn't a box protector. When it did come in it was like cardboard. It didn't save you but it gave you confidence. I never had a long-stop. Hardly any of them did except Harry Butt and he only for Vine. Albert Trott used to turn round and try to hit the ball past the wicket-keeper's head when the ball was outside the leg stump. He used a very heavy bat and it was not a nice feeling when you felt this bat somewhere near your face. I remember Trott hitting Butt a nasty blow from a ball pitched outside the leg stump. You didn't dare to drop out even if you had a groggy finger. There were two or three waiting to take my place. Once the middle finger of my right hand was so swollen that I wanted to rest. I reported to the doctor. He said 'Let's see your tongue.' I told him it wasn't my tongue that was sore. He said again 'Let's see your tongue.' I did. He glanced at it and told me 'You're quite fit. Out you go on to the field.'")

What is the most awkward bowling to take? ("A slow bowler is trickier than a fast one. Razor Smith was about the worst. He could turn the ball so sharply from the off. Kirk, our Surrey left-arm swinger, delivered the ball with his feet at all angles across the popping crease. Tarrant of Middlesex once came out to play here, padded as high as he could get them, and with towels wrapped round his body. He told me there wasn't a chance of being given out l.b.w. So he meant to stand in front of his wicket. I said 'What about me? I can't see round you.' I had a word once with Kirk for having made an l.b.w. appeal he shouldn't have done. His answer was 'Well I get 'em out like that in club cricket.'

("Simpson-Hayward was another tricky one with his underhanders. He was the only bowler I ever kept to who could twist the ball in his hand as though it were a billiard ball. When we were in South Africa one of their batsmen, Zulch, put a bit of white paper to mark where Simpson-Hayward's good length ball would pitch outside the off stump. His idea was to play any ball from further out with his legs. But I wasn't having that. The paper would have put me off and so I picked it up.")

Mr. Strudwick admits that all fast bowlers were not easy. ("N. A. Knox was the hardest of the lot. You never knew what he was going to do next. He did not know himself. As the ball whizzed past the batsman's head our captain would say 'Well bowled Neville.' Richardson was faster but safe to take. He was one of our heroes when I was a kid. I used to see him on Saturday morning down at Mitcham after I'd helped my mother and then gone for a day's watching. We used to shout 'Hullo, Curly' at Richardson, and he always gave us a smile. I got into a bit of trouble in those days through sitting right by the sight screen so as to be as near behind the wicket-keeper as I could get. When I came to keep to Richardson there was one ball of his that *was* difficult. He could make them go past the off-stump in such a curve that I had to take them far away to leg. I believe Richardson would be pretty well unplayable with the bigger stumps of to-day and with this new l.b.w. rule.")

"Batsmen," says Mr. Strudwick, "can make a lot of difference to a wicket-keeper. I noticed Jack Gunn when standing back to the bowler always fell flat down if the ball was pitched very short, and out of his ground. So I asked Mr. Crawford to 'Send him down a short one as fast as you can bowl it.' He did. Jack Gunn went miles out to it and fell flat. And I stumped him. As he was going back I said, 'Jack, I've been trying to stump you for years.' He was very cross with me. W. G. Grace was a tricky one. He never stopped talking or muttering. I've heard him at point keep on saying 'Get him in a minute, get him in a minute.'" Four visits to Australia and two to South Africa have left him with pleasant memories of playing on matted wickets. ("They give you a better chance. They're faster and truer. Turf wickets are much slower than they used to be. Balls got up above stump high much more than on these modern wickets – and much faster – I used to think after the first ball, I will never be able to stop them to-day. But during the last years of my playing I was taking the ball below my knees.")

The last has, it seems, not been heard of Strudwicks behind the stumps. There is a grandson, beginning his first term at Brighton and his grandfather, who has coached him in the garden, says he shapes well as a wicket-keeper.

Cricket has not been Mr. Strudwick's only game. He broke his nose at football, he was a keen hockey player. ("They wanted me to keep goal. But I wasn't having that. No thank you.") He took up golf in his early days and at 78 still plays it. He and Sir John Hobbs have a round at West Hove regularly once a week. The conversation then must, surely, be the best cricket talk to be heard in the world to-day.

Mr. D. R. Jardine

24 *June* 1958. L. E. J. [Sir Lawrence Jones] writes:–

It is always a little disconcerting to the friends of great players of games to read obituary notices which confine themselves to the field of play. Jardine himself always regarded cricket as "only a game." He never wanted to talk about it. His main preoccupation, in the years when I knew him both in a City office and in my own home, was Hindu philosophy. He had a speculative mind, intent on ethical and religious problems. Kindly and high-minded, he had in those years an antipathy to Christianity, to which he always referred as "Rewards and Fairies," equal to Gibbon's. Nor, in his manner and bearing, was there the faintest trace of the stern, aloof, decisive cricket captain. He was gentle and diffident in all his ways; slow and hesitant in speech, and, as it seemed to us, in thought; he chewed things over and came to cautious and tentative conclusions, except when attacking "Rewards and Fairies." Then he could be trenchant, and we realized how this mild-mannered philosopher could have been the instigator of "body-line" bowling.

It must be seldom that a great cricketer can have played the game so seriously and yet, on retirement from it, have put cricket so firmly in its proper place.

Former Test Cricketer Fined

19 *September* 1958. Herbert Sutcliffe, the former Yorkshire and England cricketer, of Tubham Rise, Ilkley, Yorkshire, was fined 20s. at Bow Street Court yesterday for passing a traffic signal at red in the Strand. In a letter to the court, he wrote: "I have no wish to doubt the accusation made by the police, but I should like to state that my eyesight and concentration are almost as good now as when I had the honour of playing for England along with my old partner Sir J. B. Hobbs. I must confess I find it difficult to think I have proceeded through traffic lights at red."

Quite Like Old Times
Lindwall Scourge of M.C.C.

FROM OUR CRICKET CORRESPONDENT [JOHN WOODCOCK]

1 *December* 1958; *Brisbane*, 30 *November*. M.C.C. got a thoroughly bad day out of their system here yesterday when they were dismissed by Queensland for the miserable total of 151. Up to a point it was quite like old times, for Lindwall took five wickets for 57 runs and it was his bowling alone that

distinguished the day. The old warrior's arm is lower than it was – the surprising thing would be if, at the age of 37, it were not – but of all the bowlers in Australia he is still the finest craftsman and England's batsmen must be relieved that he will not be playing against them on Friday.

The great natural cricketers of this world can go on for years if they remain as fit as Lindwall, and in his case guile compensates for any loss of speed. Moreover he is as keen as he has ever been, so that his ambitions even now comprehend a return to the Australian side, and, from what we have seen in the past few weeks, he remains a better bowler than either Davidson or Meckiff, who have been chosen for the first Test match.

Australian selectors are always reluctant to fall back on a favourite once he has been discarded. Lindwall's last Test appearance was two years ago. Since then he has been overlooked for a South African tour, even when a replacement had to be sent for, and, until yesterday, he has not seemed a candidate for this series. But now he found a useful wicket to bowl on, with sufficient grass to help the seam and enough humidity in the air to encourage swing. Certainly it was the best seam bowler's wicket we have come across on this tour, and, even when he returned after tea to finish off the innings, Lindwall was still moving the ball about.

Four years ago this corresponding match started in the same way, with Lindwall sending back Cowdrey and Bailey in a fine opening spell before Compton and Simpson retrieved the situation with a century apiece. Now Lindwall had Watson caught at the wicket after half an hour and Milton at forward short leg 10 minutes later. May was taken low down at slip off Mackay's first ball, and after that M.C.C.'s innings was a tedious and, at times, humiliating struggle.

It has been so for some time that when May fails runs are scarce. Things are made worse at the moment by Cowdrey's inhibitions. Cowdrey is such a fine player that he is sure to come good, as they say, in the Test matches again, but since Perth he has become increasingly diffident and subdued. He pens himself in, allowing the bowlers to take the initiative, and is reluctant, it seems, to go through with his strokes. It is sad to see a player with such an outstanding talent becoming the butt of the barrackers.

Bailey, of course, is entirely different. He is in such a defensive groove that if he can possibly lie doggo he will do so. Yesterday he saved an ugly situation when M.C.C. were 39 for four, having just lost Milton, Watson, May, and Cowdrey for 17 runs in 35 minutes, and by the time Subba Row was bowled the score had reached 112. Bailey then was well set and, on Subba Row's departure, he should have made some effort to get the bowling away. Instead he contributed precisely three runs in 70 minutes before tea and not for the first time on the tour a good Saturday afternoon crowd were baffled by his refusal to play what appeared the right game for his side.

The remaining batsmen inevitably suffered from watching Bailey make the bowling look so difficult, and it was a mercy when the innings was over at a quarter past four, having lasted for four hours and a half. Lindwall revived old memories again when he found an immediate yorker for Laker, and Bailey was denied the not out which he seemed so intent on achieving when Lindwall made a ball lift to have him caught in the gully.

The Australian spectators, delighted as they were at Queensland's excellent showing, must have been mystified that this was the strength of England, for, apart from Milton, who is in encouraging form, and Subba Row, whose determination is beginning to find some reward, there was nothing to cheer. No doubt M.C.C. would have been seen in a more favourable light had they been bowling rather than batting, for Statham, Bailey, and Tyson would have been a nasty proposition during the morning when traces of moisture were to be found. By half past four the pitch was more placid than the man who tends it.

He had been in evidence at the tea interval but half an hour later, when the wicket was being rolled between innings, he had resigned over the employment of one of his assistants. His resignation was accepted and a former Woolloon-gabba groundsman, now nearing 80 and watching the play as a spectator, was called in and entrusted with the preparation of the Test wicket. That was until the groundsman put an end to the pantomime by withdrawing his resignation. Whether or not his wicket will be so temperamental on Friday no one knows. At present it is heavily grassed and everything may depend on how closely it is shaved, a matter which, as a writer of detective fiction, the groundsman is keeping a closely guarded secret.

MCC 151 (R. Subba Row 51; R. R. Lindwall 5 for 57) and 71 for 4
QUEENSLAND 210 (R. G. Archer 83; Laker 4 for 27)
Score after first day: M.C.C. 151, Queensland 30 for 1
Match drawn

The Decay of Initials

17 *February* 1959, *Leading Article.* Various reasons have been given for the present rather dull and depressed state of English cricket. Some are technical and others fanciful and nostalgic. Among the latter is the lack of players having three initials. Where are the great three-deckers of yesteryear? The most illustrious player in England at this moment is properly dowered but his initials do not run trippingly off the tongue as they would once have done. No one talks of P. B. H. MAY. It might be said of him as of the Bishop of Rum-Ti-Foo in the *Bab Ballads*

> They called him Peter, people say,
> Because it was his name.

He is rapidly become Petermay in a single word in the manner of Peterloo.

It is hard to lay a finger on the cause of this deplorable phenomenon. It is probably this odious familiarity of Christian names which has overflowed the world in a great vulgar tide.

One who laments it has written down without the book some five and thirty examples of the trebly endowed and they make a rich feast. Here are just a few of them: S.M.J. and L.C.H., H.D.G. and B.J.T., A.J.L. and D.L.A., F.G.J., P.G.H., A.P.F., and, should something, as Sherlock Holmes would say, a little more recondite be wanted, what will the reader make of P.J.T. and S.A.P.? And this is but a small selection; our memory man has plenty more up his sleeve. He finds modern times miserably poor by comparison. Being a Sussex man he remembers first G.H.G. and then from Warwickshire – just to pass the reader a hint – M.J.K.

It may be simply that parents have gradually grown more niggardly at the font, although they have on the whole fewer children to christen. Again it may be that to-day far fewer amateurs can afford to play cricket and it was they that used to have the larger number of initials. Once upon a time indeed professionals had no initials, at any rate on the programme. If by some fortunate accident he learnt their Christian names the adoring small boy could hug to himself knowledge of Luke or Ephraim, Saul or Mordecai; but such things were to be thought, not uttered. It is all a little sad but there is some strange comfort in compensation. If some columnist of to-day had flourished in the days of W. G. he would never have been satisfied with those initials to simply and severely great. He would have called him GILBERT or, even, gracious powers! have shortened him to GILLIE.

Walking by Himself

20 *June* 1959, *Leading Article.* A fair minded man might well assert that the most composed of all those who have taken the field at Lord's during the past two days was the resident cat – the cat which, in the middle stages of India's first innings and in fine full view of the spectators and the television camera, fielded for a short period at square leg, changed comfortably to mid-off at the end of the over and then stalked majestically off the field. Though he was unable to improve on his pause before the last ten yards by taking off a cap or waving a bat, many a player must have envied him the easy grace and the absence of self-consciousness with which he made the long walk between the wicket and the pavilion. That walk, whether it is at the school fathers' match or at one of the more skilful if less exacting contests that take place at Lord's or the Oval, tries even the strongest nerves. The difficult thing, on a lone public occasion, is to have nothing to do except just walk. The occasional century-maker has, it is true, various gestures of acknowledgment as well as his inner joy to sustain him. Even the duck-maker can indulge in some comic by-play – provided his ducks are rare enough. The poor wretch who has

made about five, and usually does, has no saving grave.

But the real test is the walk to the beginning of a performance, whether at a wicket or, say, a rostrum. Slow speed, like that of the Lord's cat, is certainly the essence of the technique – confident slowness, conveying the impression of knowledge that the crowd is expectant and that the walker has something so good to bestow that he can well keep them waiting. Mr. Pickwick would never have kept such a grip on the Club if he had not "slowly mounted into the Windsor chair." Of nobody less than a Beatrix Esmond can it be said that their "motion, whether rapid or slow," is "always perfect grace." It is useful to keep to a practised standard gait and mien; though this is little help to the hardest tested of all solitary walkers – the young athlete who is called up successively at the school sports prize-giving to receive the trophies of, say, the 100 yards, 220, 440, long jump, high jump, hurdles, and Victor Ludorum. In all these things cats have it over human beings. They are used to walking slowly and by themselves, and they are creatures of habit. A long, solitary walk suits them, and they share with all animals the lack of self-consciousness which creates public dignity. They gain by the facility for doing a bit of what comes naturally. At which point truth compels us to admit that the Lord's cat directed his stately walk from the wicket not to the Pavilion but to the Bar.

Pain in the Neck

29 *June* 1959, *Leading Article*. We have so long been accustomed to irreverence in biography that such works of piety as FORSTER's *Life of Dickens* or MORLEY's *Gladstone* seem farther back in time than actually they are. Even so we are, where venerable figures are concerned, still capable of being shocked. LORD CHANDOS certainly administered a blow the other day when he revealed that when, as a child, he asked an uncle what it was like to play with W. G. GRACE, he received the crisp reply "The dirtiest neck I ever kept wicket behind."

The words are as vivid as they are unexpected, and on the instant the bearded formidable figure who bestrode the cricket field, and, if it comes to that, the later Victorian era, like a Colossus is reduced to the stature of a small and grubby boy. A man is not a hero to his valet, but a great batsman has the right to expect a measure of admiration and respect from an opposing wicket-keeper, and was it not the REV. A. P. WICKHAM, one of Somerset's clerical wearers of the gloves, as the old sporting journalese had it, who, after "keeping" to W.G. during an innings of mammoth proportions, recorded that not a single ball had passed the bat? No pat on the back for technique, however, can make up for the comment that soap and water had neglected to work backwards from the face, and if W.G. were alive to-day there is no doubt that he would regard the whole race of wicket-keepers with the gravest suspicion.

On the other hand he would, if possible, be even a greater hero to the juvenile members of the population who, when the state of their ears and the back of their necks came in for public criticism, could cite the great man in defence and, what is more, point out that he was a doctor as well as a cricketer. The medical attitude towards what is sometimes breezily called a little healthy dirt was, in truth, more liberal then than it is now, and the masculine neck, when all is said and done, is nothing to make a fuss about. Female necks, on the other hand, were highly thought of at the time the DOCTOR was breaking the hearts of bowlers, and to own one which could, with no more than a moderate degree of poetic licence, be described as "swan-like" was as good as possessing a pair of eyes like twin stars. CALIGULA amiably wished that his subjects had one collective neck so that he could dispose of them with a minimum of inconvenience, and small boys – and, as it seems, W.G. – are inclined to forget that they have them at all. To be reminded that they do and that they are in need of attention is a pain in the neck indeed.

Keep Your Shirts On, Please

17 *August* 1959. About 30 men sitting shirtless in the sun watching the Middlesex-Yorkshire cricket match at Lord's on Saturday were asked by an M.C.C. attendant to replace their shirts. The attendant said this move was a result of complaints from women spectators during the recent hot spell. "After all, Lord's is Lord's," he added.

Later, a Lord's official said there was no ground rule enforcing the wearing of shirts, "but we do have regular complaints from ladies who object to seeing men with bare chests. We do our best to comply with their views and to persuade men to wear shirts."

Unforgettable Words

26 *October* 1959, *Leading Article*. MR. GEORGE LYTTELTON's letter about HIRST's immortal words to RHODES, "We'll get them in singles," sheds at first sight a gentle melancholy upon the soul. HIRST seems to have denied all knowledge of them. It is true that he only said he had no recollection of using them and that is some comfort. So is MR. LYTTELTON's suggestion that if he had but said not "singles" but "wuns" (which appears to be the Yorkshire idiom) memory might have come flooding back. Still, it is saddening and makes us wonder what we can believe. Did TOM EMMETT never say of W. G. that he ought to be made to play with a littler bat? That is a dreadful thought. Did WILLIAM PALMER not say, "It was the riding that did it," nor JACK MYTTON, after setting light to his nightshirt, "The hiccup has

gone, by God"? Most tragic of all, what of "Up Guards, and at 'em"? CROKER asked the DUKE in a letter whether he had used those words, and the DUKE, in his reply, did his best for posterity. He wrote: "What I must have said or possibly did say was 'Stand up, Guards' and then given the commanding officers the order to attack." We must be content with what we can get.

Yet perhaps it does not really matter so very much, save for the sake of pedantic accuracy, whether HIRST said it or not. To the younger men coming in at so tremendous a crisis he would have addressed some reassuring words, and what could be better than those long since enshrined in our faith – if he did not say it he ought to have. After a time it is surely more important that history should be romantic than that it should be precisely true. There ought to be a statute of limitations about great words whereby, after a certain period, they should be unquestionably accepted, and we may feel sure that, at the bottom of his heart, MR. LYTTELTON would agree. For all we know, CAESAR's memory about "*Veni, Vidi, Vici*" may have become a little shaky, but he did his duty in remembering it. We should abolish from all our admirable dictionaries the sceptical letters "attr." Let there be no attributions! At any rate, we may thank Heaven that HIRST did not say in the words of a most uncricketing poem, far too often quoted: "Play up, play up, and play the game." He would have known better than that.

Prince Duleepsinhji

7 *December* 1959. Prince Duleepsinhji, the former Sussex and England cricketer, died at Bombay on Saturday at the age of 54. His cricketing career was cut short by illness, but it lasted long enough to establish him as one of the great batsmen of his generation.

Kumar Shri Duleepsinhji was born on June 13, 1905. He was a nephew of Ranjitsinhji, with whose style his wristy elegance and attacking spirit had some affinity. When he came to England to be educated, he made his mark on the cricket-field almost at once. He was in the Cheltenham XI in 1921 when he was only just 16, and in his last season at the college he was probably the best school batsman of the year. For the Lord's schools against the Rest, he scored 108 and took five wickets for 41 runs.

He went up to Cambridge in 1924, and was awarded his Blue the following summer, making 932 runs during the university season, with two centuries. In 1926 he became qualified for Sussex, and showed himself as great a run-getter in county as in all other classes of cricket. It was in 1927 that the first interruption took place, for early in the season he was pronounced to be seriously ill, and after May he played no more. A winter spent in Switzerland set him up, and he came back to England with restored health. Then began an even more notable run of success. His highest score for Sussex, which he captained with tact and ability, was 333 against Northamptonshire at Hove. He scored two separate hundreds in a match three times, and a hundred and two hundred once in a match against Kent in 1929. He made four hundreds in successive innings in 1931. Outside the county championship he was particularly effective in Gentlemen and Players, making three centuries. And finally, in the first of his 12 Test matches, against Australia at Lord's in 1930, he distinguished himself with a splendid innings of 173. In his three golden years of 1929–31 he scored over 2,500 runs each season.

The curtain fell all too soon. In 1932 his health again gave way. This time his visit to Switzerland did not have the desired effect, and the pulmonary disease from which he suffered grew worse. In 1933 he retired from the Sussex captaincy, and towards the end of the summer he knew definitely he would not play first-class cricket again.

He joined the Indian foreign service in 1949 and was appointed High Commissioner for India in Australia and New Zealand. After his return to India in 1953 he became chairman of the public service commission in the state of Saurashtra of which his brother was Rajpramukh. He married in 1936 Shrimati Jayaraj Kumari, who survives him.

"The Greatest Test Match of All Time"

FROM OUR SPECIAL CORESPONDENT [MICHAEL DAVIE]

15 *December* 1960; *Brisbane* 14 *December*. The first Test match between Australia and the West Indies ended here at four minutes past six tonight with the first tie and the most sensational finish in the history of Test cricket.

After the game, with sweat pouring off his brow, the Australian captain, Benaud, said that this had been "the greatest cricket match I have ever played in and the finish could only be described as fantastic". The West Indies captain, Worrell, took the same view: "I have never played in a game like it before." And to Sir Donald Bradman it was "the greatest Test match of all time".

Overnight the West Indies had been 207 runs ahead with one wicket standing, and this morning and afternoon there was much palpitating cricket as they finished their innings and Australia set out after a total of 233. But it was at the tea interval that the tension really began to mount.

At tea the game could scarcely have been more evenly balanced. Australia, 109 for six, needed 124 to win in exactly two hours. The wicket was the colour of pale straw, scarred with black patches around the crease: though anything but easy, there were still runs in it.

The Australians, plainly and characteristically, decided to go for the runs. Valentine bowled to Benaud and Benaud hit him high over mid-on's head for four. Hall, who had wrecked the start of Australia's innings with a fine, sustained spell of fast bowling (his figures were 12–3–38–4) came back for his second spell and Davidson clipped him easily into the covers. Ramadhin replaced Valentine and with his first ball baffled Davidson completely. But the Australians kept on the attack, driving firmly and running quick singles.

At five o'clock, with an hour to go, Australia needed 61 with the new ball between them and victory. Davidson picked Ramadhin off his stumps and hit him a colossal blow in the air to the mid-wicket bounday to put up his 50. If he were not the best new ball bowler in the game, Davidson would be in the Australian side for his batting. When Worrell now took himself off and put on Sobers to bowl his left arm tweakers over the wicket, it seemed to be the critical moment to the entire match. Benaud seemed to think so too, for he watched Sobers on to the bat with deepest concentration before he swung him out to midwicket for four off the last ball. The Australians were keeping in exact step with the clock.

Davidson drove Ramadhin straight for four and swung him round to the fine leg boundary to bring up the 100 partnership in 95 minutes. Forty-three minutes to play and 40 wanted. The West Indies fielding hereabouts was magnificent and so was the Australian running of safe, quick singles. Benaud hit Ramadhin straight for one run and Australia had reached 200. With half an hour to go, with Hall taking the new ball and the crowd alight with excitement, Australia needed 27, still with four wickets intact.

Benaud hit Hall in the air not far short of Hunte at square leg, and Davidson hooked him first bounce to the midwicket boundary. With 20 minutes left and 19 runs to get Worrell brought back Sobers at the other end bowling his faster ones, but Benaud, looking now more sallow than ever, drove him to mid-on for four. Benaud had his 50 in just over two hours. With 15 minutes left Australia needed 10, and then nine in 10 minutes after Hall had bowled a long over for one run.

At last, with seven minutes left, Benaud pushed Sobers to mid-wicket for one quick single too many. Solomon hit the stumps and Davidson who had made 80, was run out. Six minutes left, seven runs to win and three wickets remain. Grout was hit on the leg and the whole crowd seemed to appeal. But he was not out and he then took a single to mid-on. So, as the last over of the match started, Australia needed six to win and Grout faced Hall. Grout was hit in the stomach and Benaud dashed through for a run when the ball dropped at Grout's feet. Benaud swung at the next ball with all the power at his command, got a touch, and Alexander caught it: the crowd went through the roof. Six balls to go, five runs to get and two wickets to fall.

Meckiff kept Hall out on his first ball and gave a nervous smile. The next one went through to the wicketkeeper, who threw it to Hall, and if Hall had hit the wicket when they took another quick single, Meckiff would have been out. Four balls to go and four to get. Grout struck the next ball high and straight up in the air; everyone rushed forward and Hall, knocking Kanhai out of the way, got under it and, to roars of ecstasy, dropped it while the batsmen went through. Three balls left for the three runs wanted.

Meckiff got hold of the next ball and it soared out towards the midwicket fence looking like six and the end of the match. But Hunte cut it off on the bounce as the batsmen, running like men possessed, went through for a third run and now Grout was run out by a foot. The sides were level with two balls to go.

In came Kline, looking pale and drawn. He took guard and not a bird moved. He lashed out like a man in a nightmare fighting off phantoms: the ball flew to midwicket, there was a flurry of desperate fieldsmen, Solomon flung at the wicket and to an incredulous shout of joy and anguish, scattered the stumps. The umpire's finger shot up and Meckiff was out. It was a tie. Four wickets had fallen in 13 balls, three of them run out, and three of them in seven balls.

The day had started with an hilarious stand between Hall and Valentine who kept out Davidson and Benaud in full cry for nearly 40 minutes to add another 25 runs to the West Indies overnight score of 259 for nine. The time they took was as important as the runs they made, for they left Australia 233 to win in 312 minutes, or a rate of 45 an hour. Even so, it had seemed well within Australia's power to get them with time to spare.

But the Australians got off to a bad start. Simpson, who showed little sign of liking Hall in the first innings and was even less comfortable in the second, when Hall was bowling up to his reputation, tried to pull the sixth ball of the fast bowler's second over and was caught by the forward of three short legs. Harvey took a four off his first ball and then played back, got an outside edge and Sobers dived unbelievably to pick up the ball an inch from the ground in his right hand. He dislocated a finger doing so and left the field grimacing with pain to have it strapped.

At luncheon Australia were 28 for two. Then, a quarter of an hour after the interval, O'Neill was caught at the wicket off Hall and Australia seemed on the run. They were 49 for three. Favell was nearly out to the next one, and from the next ball of the new over McDonald played forward to what seemed a straightforward ball from Worrell and was clean bowled. The West Indies were then right on top. When a quarter of an hour later Favell turned Hall straight into Solomon's hands at short leg and Australia were 57 for five it seemed all over.

The next wicket went to Ramadhin. He came on at three o'clock, just about the time Australia needed 150 in even time with Mackay getting dug in. His first ball to Mackay was a googly. Mackay, wholly baffled, followed it to give a catch to slip which, agonizingly, was dropped. But this affected Mackay's temperament and it was not surprising shortly afterwards when Ramadhin got one to turn a little more sharply to hit the leg stump.

That brought together Benaud with Davidson for a stand of a lifetime. But it nearly never began, for the second ball Benaud got from Ramadhin he never saw and he could scarcely believe his luck when he found it had somehow missed the stumps. Then both batsmen began to settle down and Benaud off-drove Valentine just before the tea interval to bring up the Australian 100 in 175 minutes.

Until that interval, and its extraordinary sequel, it had scarcely seemed possible that Australia could win the match. Subsequently it seemed impossible they should lose. There seems every likelihood, indeed, that historians of the game will decide that this was not only the first tie in Test cricket but one in which, of all Tests, the expectation of victory most frequently oscillated between two teams. The second Test match of the series, which starts in Melbourne on December 30, should fill that airless and mammoth stadium.

> WEST INDIES 453 (G. Sobers 132, F. M. Worrell 65, J. S. Solomon 65, F. C. M. Alexander 60, W. Hall 50; A. K. Davidson 5 for 135) and 284 (F. M. Worrell 65, R. Kanhai 54, J. S. Solomon 47; A. K. Davidson 6 for 87)
> AUSTRALIA 505 (N. O'Neill 181, R. B. Simpson 92, C. C. McDonald 57, L. Favell 45, A. K. Davidson 44; W. Hall 4 for 140) and 232 (A. K. Davidson 80, R. Benaud 52; W. Hall 5 for 63)
> *Match tied*

Lord's Will Have Music

3 *June* 1961. For the first time in memory there will be music played at Lord's during a county cricket match. The Middlesex Regiment's band, in this country during a summer for the first time since the last war, offered its services and the Middlesex club accepted. So musical selections will be played during the lunch and tea intervals at the Middlesex and Warwickshire match today. Bands do play at Lord's during the season, but only when Services teams are taking part.

Seven Runs Decide Exciting Knock-out Match

[BY GORDON ROSS]

3 *May* 1962. In a finish which would have gripped the most unemotional and carping critic Leicestershire beat Derbyshire by seven runs in the one-day Midlands knock-out competition at Leicester, and thus qualify to meet Northamptonshire at Leicester next Wednesday.

This absorbing day's cricket – which clearly stamps the experiment with considerable success, a happy augury for the future – produced 493 runs in a little under seven hours, yet at no time did the proceedings give the impression of prostituting the basic skills of the game.

There was no suggestion of a carnival. In fact only three sixes were struck.

It was just a question of bowlers bowling a liberal ration of overs in the time and batsmen getting on with it by playing strokes and using their pads only for protection.

This enterprising experiment arises from a desire expressed by all the counties to acquire a practical knowledge, before 1963, of just how one-day cricket can operate successfully, and how different is its image from the accepted format for county cricket. The Leicestershire secretary, turning this over in his mind, discovered that Leicestershire, Derbyshire, Nottinghamshire, and Northamptonshire had these available dates and took swift action.

The geographical position of these four means that no hotel accommodation is involved and, as it turned out, the fees received from the Independent Television Authority defrayed all the expenses of the competition, including the purchase of a cup – the Midlands Counties Knock-out Cup – to be competed for annually.

Laws framed for this match limit each innings to 65 overs, prevent any one bowler from bowling more than 15 overs, restrict the off side field to six players, and authorize the umpires to be the sole judges as to whether or not extra time shall be played in order to finish the match. The technique of this sort of cricket has yet to be evolved. Carr made one obvious point when, on winning the toss, he put Leicestershire in. The side fielding first have more manoeuvrability, since they know exactly what they must do in the batting time allotted to them.

Kirby and Hallam, for instance, opening for Leicestershire, feeling the pulse of something foreign to them, took 10 minutes to score their first run before a crowd which barely constituted a quorum on a bitter morning. The rash discarding of early wickets would be folly; some heavy artillery must be kept in hand for an all-out assault when the end of the 65 overs is in sight.

After 20 runs in 10 overs the pace of the morning soon quickened and in due course showed a brisk acceleration upon the old formula. After two hours' cricket and 41 overs Leicestershire had made 148 for one, so that practically all their resources were still available to mount a blistering attack from a position of strength, with Hallam 85 not out and batting beautifully.

Plans, however, went awry at this point when Hallam was run out and Wharton was stumped. Carr, having worked out this process with his customary shrewdness, had kept half a dozen overs apiece from Jackson and Rhodes up his sleeve. This, as it transpired, produced the remarkable sight of Jackson being hit by Jayasinghe for three fours in one over, not quite as Carr had intended, but in the main it did stop any undue high jinks. Leicestershire finished with 250 for five in three hours and 20 minutes off the prescribed 65 overs.

Derbyshire began like a house on fire. Carr (who apparently has always had a sneaking feeling for opening the innings) and Lee put up 50 in the twelfth over and 100 in the twentieth, Carr hoisting the hundred with a six.

He also hit seven fours.

Barratt enjoyed a spell of seven overs, four maidens, five runs and one wicket, yet many a captain has shown consistent reluctance to put a spinner on when wickets are wanted, for fear of his being hit. Barratt, who is 19, was an economic proposition. The real excitement came at the end when Derbyshire seemed to be sailing home with a score of 229 for 6, but they failed to get there.

> LEICESTERSHIRE 250 for 5 (65 overs) (Hallam 86, Wharton 50,
> Jayasinghe 49 not out)
> DERBYSHIRE 243 (61.4 overs) (D. B. Carr 62, Lee 50, Oates 46)
> *Leicestershire won by 7 runs*

Day of Memories at Lord's
Old England Win Lightheartedly

FROM A STAFF REPORTER [BRIAN MOORE]

18 *June* 1962. "Go on, Keith, bowl him a bumper", came the cry as Compton took guard with the shadows beginning to inch their way across Lord's on Saturday evening. Miller, ever the man for such a moment, tossed that fiery mane of his, an action still capable of chilling English blood, and duly parted Compton's hair with what can only be called a fizzer. Howls of laughter from all sides.

In that moment there was crystallized the whole purpose of this day's sparkling cricket between an Old England XI and the Lord's Taverners. For, corseted within an agreeable wrapping of good humour and pure farce, the not-so-old heroes (some of them it is sad and surprising to find, already greying) evoked memories for all.

There was something for everyone, in fact, even the captive tea lady who said she had managed to abandon her urn long enough to watch "that smashing bit of nonsense between Norman Wisdom and Roy Castle", the Taverners hilarious ninth wicket pair. And wasn't that Roy Castle a good bowler, too, she gravely opined, getting that chap out like that. That chap being no less a batsman than Robertson, stumped far from home for 51, and not worrying over much about it either.

But for the most part it was the Comptons, Edriches, Browns, and Wrights in the cast who made the more genuine and lasting impact. And about the only concessions that they made to the growing number of Wisdens that stand between 1962 and their own great deeds were perhaps a certain reluctance to bend and chase in the field and to bowl off a shortened approach.

Wright, for example, no longer runs up as though hotly pursued by a swarm of angry bees, all flailing arms and kangaroo hops, although he still turns over a most respectable leg break at some pace off four or five yards;

Gover shuffles fussily over the same distance, with enough nip still to quicken the stroke (54 years old? Impossible); Brown's right arm looks a good deal lower than once it was; and little Edrich, for a time after the war an impoverished England's fastest bowler for half-a-dozen overs, now trundles down some improbable, looping off breaks.

There were more authentic touches, too: Bedser's clockwork toy run up, for example, with its efficiency unimpaired, and still he finds Evans's red palms, eager and impeccable as of old, with a resounding thud; Washbrook, too, brooding in the covers waiting to swoop.

And, of course, there was the dynamic Miller. He came in when the Taverners ("a cheerful collection of cricketers, cricketing actors and acting-cricketers", the programme said) were 28 for three. A situation ripe for such a showman. In a twinkling he had hit Compton for four sixes, one of them, a massive blow, scattering the unsuspecting as well as the "Read Compton on Cricket" signs in St. John's Wood Road. He smacked 53 in half-an-hour.

Subba Row (too young for Old England?) aroused painful reminders that he has retired too soon with a well struck 82, Barnett made a prim 92, and the Taverners, after scoring 257 for six *by luncheon*, declared with 319 for nine at three o'clock.

Washbrook and Robertson soon made inroads into this score with 100 in 45 minutes, having seen off Miller and the new ball, a point that would have had a much more satisfying ring about it some 10 years ago. Even so it was a dazzling start, with Washbrook matching Miller's six into the road in his pugnacious 73.

Robertson, Edrich, Ikin, and Compton then played their full part – although what a pity we were denied the last tantalizing glimpse of Edrich and Compton at the wicket togehter – so that Old England, to everyone's delight, overhauled their truly cheerful opponents with two wickets standing. Lord's had been revisited to be sure, worthily and with splendour.

LORD'S TAVERNERS 319 for 9 dec (B. A. Barnett 92, R. Subba Row 82, K. R. Miller 53)
OLD ENGLAND 321 for 8 (C. Washbrook 73, J. T. Ikin 63, J. D. Robertson 51)
Old England won by 2 wickets

A Chance to Win in 1963

BY SIR LEARIE CONSTANTINE M.B.E.,
HIGH COMMISSIONER FOR TRINIDAD AND TOBAGO

31 *August* 1962, *Supplement on Trinidad and Tobago*. The Summer of 1963 will find the stage all set for one of the most interesting struggles in the history of test matches between England and the West Indies.

Many have wondered at the effect the breaking up of the West Indies

Federation would have on West Indies cricket, sad as this must be for all of us. West Indies cricket existed long before anything was done to create Federation, and its eventual dissolution can only mean that cricket is one of the essentials of common services.

I am by now noted for sticking my neck out, and I begin with the prediction that the West Indies will defeat England in this series [*They won 3-1*]. It is important to go into a few details to confirm this first impression, and I begin with the West Indies tour of Australia two winters ago.

Worrell as captain threw out a challenge to Benaud the Australian skipper; Benaud accepted it and cricket the world over benefited by this enterprise. I stated without hesitation that if Worrell could only improve the West Indies fielding from what hitherto had been its most backward department, we could defeat Australia. The fielding did improve, in fact it reached a high standard, and considering the farewell that Australia gave to Worrell and his men, the lawyer could be forgiven for noting, so far as results were concerned, the disparity between the *de jure* and the *de facto*.

England has of late been developing along the proper lines and the counties have been trying to revive the old tradition of bright play. It takes a Robins as chairman of the English Selection Committee to encourage a player of the calibre and outlook of Dexter as captain as against a more cautious and exact scientist. He would do a good job in Australia; he will create a brightness hitherto absent from the English batting. This would be good for the English players, but I do not believe that it could be developed sufficiently to thwart the efforts and stratagems of the West Indies players. On the other hand, the England bowling is and will remain suspect, and although the West Indies batting will be "tops", it is their bowling that should pave the way for their eventual victory. To talk of Hall as being the fastest bowler in the world today is to talk in terms of real speed, and there are other fast bowlers too who could be included in the side to keep Hall a terror right up to the end of the series. The job of the West Indies selectors, therefore, is to pick such a bowling combination that Hall could be spared the ordinary chores of county matches.

In that connexion, I would like to feel that whatever were Ramadhin's failures in Australia, he would be considered for the tour of England as I believe that he is and will always remain a mystery to the uninitiated.

Sobers is one of the finest bowlers in the world, a left-hander bowling the wrong-un and the top spinner with such facility that the captain would have a difficult job to determine whether his bowling or his batting should predominate. West Indies batting should be strong with McMorris, a disciplined opening batsman, Kanhai, Solomon, Sobers, Worrell, Hunte and a few others who should give the England bowlers some long, tiring days in the sun.

Worrell has been selected as captain. I am usually accused of bringing up the subject of colour in my deliberations on this great game. I do not need to make any excuses for so doing because the fact that it is the first time that a black man has been selected to captain the West Indies side in England leaves the field wide open for other people to make the excuses. Worrell is a student of the game. He knows it inside out. He has had a lot of experience, including a close study of present-day players, and I would wager that he makes a contribution in tactical manoeuvring equal to some of the greatest masters of the game. He will, I imagine, outwit Dexter; and if he does not, then like the Yorkshireman I say "it would be a glorious draw".

One aspect that must not be omitted in considering the relative merits of the side is that most of the West Indies are achieving independence. To us this means self respect and an opportunity to make, among other things, our characteristic contribution to this great game. It will have a psychological effect on the West Indies side and it is bound to reflect itself in their play. The motto of the newly independent Trinidad and Tobago – "Together we aspire, together we achieve" – is apt in the circumstances. Do not underrate it. I am happy that I shall be present to watch this great battle between my country and my almost adopted country.

Cricket Breaks with the Past

End of the Distinction between Amateur and Professional

27 *November* 1962. The 17 first-class cricket counties decided at Lord's yesterday by a clear majority to do away with the amateur status. In future, all players will be known as cricketers. Approval is necessary from M.C.C. before this can come into force, but it is expected that this will be forthcoming when the M.C.C. committee hold their next meeting at the end of January.

Lawn tennis has for three years been deliberating upon whether or not to make their Wimbledon championships an open meeting. Cricket, along with table tennis, will now be the only sport without recognized amateurs, although cricketers can continue to play without accepting payment if they wish.

This means the end of the Gentlemen v. Players match, which dates back to 1806. It is expected that M.C.C. will substitute another representative match in its place at Lord's next summer, possibly the former North v. South game, and there will have to be an alteration in the Scarborough Festival games which also include a Gentlemen v. Players match. . .

The committee have accepted a block grant of £6,500 by the Gillette Razor Company, who will sponsor the new KNOCKOUT CUP COMPETITION which starts next season. Apart from the grants, a trophy will be presented to the team winning the final at Lord's. It will be known as the Gillette Cup or Trophy, and there will also be awards in respect of each of the 16 ties on the basis of meritorious individual performances. The Gillette awards will be made to the "man (or men) of the match". There will be two rounds, a semi-final round and a final, together with a bye round to be arranged between the two counties occupying the bottom places in the county championship. The draw for the knock-out competition will be made today.

England and West Indies have accepted an offer by Wisden to provide a perpetual trophy for the winners of the Test series between the two countries. This is in celebration of the Wisden Cricketers' Almanack centenary edition in 1963, when the West Indies tour England. It is hoped that the WISDEN TROPHY will play a similar role in the matches between England and the West Indies as the Ashes do between England and Australia.

Our Cricket Correspondent [John Woodcock] cables from Brisbane:–

The abolition of the distinction between the amateur and the professional in cricket is a realistic decision. For some time the borderline between the two has been spurious and E. R. Dexter's admission in Melbourne recently that he made a good deal more from cricket than business emphasized the anomalous situation.

In principle the amateur outlook is a fine thing. It charms away routine. Yet the day of the genuine amateur who cultivated the game purely as a pastime has gone. The attitude now among the leading amateurs is becoming increasingly mercenary. Without making money from cricket they could not afford to play, so that they advertise and write and receive liberal expenses, which amounts in some cases to considerably more than a professional's salary. The distinction is therfore largely theoretical. To remove it is at once a break with a tradition which has, in its day, been a great strength to cricket and an acceptance of changing times.

Yet I see no reason why a cricketer, if he chooses, should not remain unpaid and thereby retain his independence. The change might attract new blood to the game. It might draw in a part-time player who has the potential of a top-class cricketer but lacks the time or the inclination or the resources to devote a full summer to the game. The "amateur spirit" would still be there. Many young men can introduce this by their natural way of playing. It is in their character or the upbringing and it always will be, whether they are called Gentlemen or Players or just cricketers.

Wisden's Century

17 *April* 1963, *Leading Article*. The little top-hatted figure of JOHN WISDEN, a Brighton builders' son, is familiar to all lovers of old cricket prints, and in his day he was a terror to batsmen. Although he stood 5ft. 4in. and weighed seven stone his prowess as a fast bowler, who, among other feats, once took six wickets in six balls, has become legendary. But his lasting claim to fame rests on his almanac – that hardy annual which this season reaches its century.

JOHN WISDEN, like THOMAS LORD, was a man of many interests outside cricket. He kept a tobacconist's and sports shop in Leicester Square and had a shrewd eye for advertisement. What would this businesslike sportsman make of the current issue of the almanac and of the state of play of the game it so faithfully records?

As one who had played overseas – though in Canada and the United States – he would be pleased to find an article, rich in good stories, by SIR ROBERT MENZIES, the Prime Minister of Australia. Inevitably he would be out of it when he came across MR. NEVILLE CARDUS choosing as the six giants of the Wisden century, GRACE, HOBBS, BRADMAN, RICHARD-SON, BARNES, and TRUMPER. But remembering the rivalries and arguments of his own day he might sympathize with MR. CARDUS for nervously and promptly following that list with: "I can already hear in my imagination a thousand protesting voices (including my own)." What might well give him most satisfaction would be to learn that the sale of the almanac is now steady, averaging 21,000.

How far does this reflect healthiness in cricket? Certainly it is proof of keenness in a large minority of followers. Loyalty shown to the Cricket Society points the same way. But the quick eye of WISDEN would, we may be sure, light on MR. JOHN SOLAN'S look "Through the Crystal Ball", in which it is noted that the attendance paying at the entrance at county matches last year was 933,000, compared with nearly two million just after the Second World War. Six-day cricket, MR. SOLAN reminds us, has no future. "It is one of county cricket's most melancholy anomalies that the dullest day's play is almost invariably reserved for Saturdays." The future pattern, he argues, must have at its centre a "virile and satisfying spectacle on that im-portant day". It is a measure of *Wisden*'s contemporary vitality that such plain truths appear in its centenary number. If this interest in the personalities and statistics of cricket is to be kept up at past level, imaginative reform cannot much longer be delayed.

Talking of Cricket

13 *June* 1963, *Leading Article*. It must have interested elder listeners when they recently heard one of the B.B.C.'s fluent commentators on Test match cricket call the wickets the timbers. There was a time when the sports re-porters on papers of widest appeal took a professional pride in avoiding the obvious word. Simile and synonym were unremittingly pursued. In Rugby football no try could be simply converted; the oval had to be propelled through the uprights and players were not tackled but grassed. In descriptions of cricket there was an even greater practice of this habit. The ball that kept low had to be a daisy-cutter although a first-class cricket pitch has surely been sufficiently mown to lose all likeness to a flowery meadow. The timbers,

recently restored to favour, were constantly appearing. A series of pulls which ended with a catch at the wicket would appear in this form: "After several cow-shots into the Great Beyond, Basher was neatly pouched by the timber-watcher." The wicketkeeper was also the custodian of the woodpile. Fielding was leather-hunting and the bat was always the willow. The weather had its own lingo, in which traces of a classical education, though possibly limited, were on view. It was Old Sol and not the sun that shone. If rain stopped play it was Jupiter Pluvius who intervened.

The custom dwindled, partly because it grew tiresome and partly because reporting of games was taken up by authors of repute, critics of the arts, and other servants of the Muses. A remarkable salute to culture was made in a paper of large circulation which headed its accounts of cricket-matches with "Poet and Novelist" after the writer's name. Now plain speaking is the general rule. But the jargon of games retains some curios. Much has been written of the origin and naming of the googly, which has its Oriental cousin, the Chinaman, attached to a similar form of deceptive spin. The commentator who was restoring the timbers to use mentioned this twister; he implored viewers not to drench him with letters of inquiry about the word. It was a natural precaution, but at least he could assume that mention of the timbers would get by without attracting massive correspondence. He might have included the willow in his arboreal references. This makes one wonder whether any of the aforetime Latinists ever called a bat a salicaceous implement. They might have done. Those were the days.

Close, Cricket's Enigma, Now a Hero

Unforgettable End to Lord's Test Match

FROM OUR CRICKET CORRESPONDENT [JOHN WOODCOCK]

26 *June* 1963. The second Test match between England and West Indies had, as it deserved, a finish of unforgettable, unbearable excitement. When Cowdrey came to the wicket with two balls to go, his left arm encased in plaster, any of four results was technically possible. England needed six to win, West Indies had one wicket to take, the light was fading fast, the crowd could scarcely cast their eyes upon the scene. That Allen settled for a draw was understandable and took nothing from the drama.

No sooner had he done so than hundreds of West Indians poured across the ground. They besieged the pavilion and called for Worrell as though it was election night. It was the epilogue to one of the greatest Test matches Lord's has ever seen. England, requiring 234 to win, were 228 for nine when time was called. From 2.20, when play began, until six minutes past six, fortunes had swayed this way and that, and while Close was playing his finest innings England looked the likelier winners. As the result of it all, the series is established. By the interest that it will engender the next instalment at Edgbaston is a success in advance.

West Indies sought victory with the battering ram. For three hours 20 minutes Hall bowled from the pavilion end without relief. His energy was astonishing, his stamina inexhaustible, his speed awesome, from the first ball to the last. Forgetting the fact that he took an unconscionable time about his overs, it was a stupendous piece of bowling. His partner for all but five overs was Griffith, likewise a man of the fiercest strength. Standing against them until 20 minutes from the end was Close, the enigma of English cricket.

Barrington stayed for a while; so, too, did Parks and Titmus. And without Allen, who braved the flames of the last three-quarters of an hour, England would probably have lost. But England's hero of the day was Close. There were those, when he was out, who blamed him for losing his head. It was more gracious to acclaim him for having kept it through a struggle as tense and unrelenting as any he will know.

Through the afternoon Close played with a sense of responsibility with which few have credited him. After tea he was obliged to take a risk to keep England abreast of the clock. He chose to do so by running out to the fast bowlers before they had delivered. This is a recognized way of distracting a bowler and upsetting his rhythm. That it was Close's downfall in the end was a venial sin, reckless though it may have appeared.

At the start of play Close was seven not out and England were 116 for three. When he was caught by Murray, heaving mightily at Griffith, they were 219 for eight. Perhaps if Close had been prepared quietly to glean the remaining runs, England would have won. It is a reasonable line of argument. Had he done so the misdemeanours of his career, if you can call them that, would have vanished in the evening air. As it was they mostly had, for without him there would not have been the climax that there was.

Fifteen runs were wanted when Close departed and Shackleton joined Allen. With only Cowdrey to come they kept the winning chance in mind without daring to attempt too much. Thus, when the last over started. England were still eight runs short. From the balcony came instructions for a death or glory bid, and Shackleton threw his bat at the first ball without making contact. He and Allen took a short single off the second, with Hall in his follow-through making a spectacular attempt to run Allen out. The third ball was glanced by Allen for one, leaving six to make in the remainder of the over.

At the fourth ball Shackleton lunged in vain; it went through to Murray, and Allen ran for a single without Shackleton's knowledge. By the time Shackleton was aware of what was happening Murray had thrown the ball to Worrell at forward short leg, and Worrell, remaining inscrutably calm, raced for the bowler's end and took off the bails before Shackleton made his ground.

It was now that Cowdrey emerged, cheered for his bravery. He had a long consultation with Allen, deciding in the course of it that six runs off two balls from Hall with the fielders scattered far and wide was not a proposition. No one could blame them for reaching this conclusion. The run-out had left Cowdrey at the bowler's end, which was merciful, and Allen lay doggo for the last two balls. Both were straight and fast, and Allen moved resolutely into line.

In spite of morning rain there had been thoughts of resuming play as early as 12 o'clock. The covers were removed and there was to have been a start at 12.15 had there been no further rain. In the event the rain hung about until half past one. An early luncheon was taken, and at 1.50 the umpires announced the pitch as fit but not the light. Soon after two o'clock the sky cleared, and at 2.20 the match was on. The pitch was unaffected, having been protected all night, and the field was surprisingly dry. There was no need of a towel for the bowlers, and the piles of sawdust remained unused.

Barrington, who had played so well on Monday, never picked up steam. In 55 minutes he managed only two scoring strokes. The first, after three-quarters of an hour, flew to fine leg off the shoulder of the bat, the shot being a protective one against a short-pitched ball. The other was a boundary to square leg. Barrington was persuaded ultimately to spar at a short off-side ball from Griffith, which led to his being caught at the wicket.

Most of the scoring during these opening exchanges was done by Close, and there was not much of it. Parks was freer with his strokes after surviving, off his first ball from Griffith, a concerted appeal for leg-before. He lived for long enough to add 28 with Close and to display two ravishing cover drives off Griffith. Close, by now, looked as much at ease as could be expected in the circumstances. He was being hit about the body a good deal by Hall, but already we were revising opinions about his temperament for the big occasion.

Parks was beginning to look positively happy when he was leg-before to a short ball from Griffith which bounced less than most. Parks was trying to push it away past the short legs. At tea, 20 minutes later, England were 171 for five. In one hour 55 minutes West Indies had bowled 28.1 overs. Apart from the last over at the Nursery end these had been bowled exclusively by Hall and Griffith. Of the 55 runs England had added Close was responsible for 28.

So long as Titmus stayed with Close England had their noses in front, and he did so until only 33 were wanted. The first four overs after tea took 20 minutes to bowl, which was an unconscionably long time. Close now was looking for runs more eagerly than before. Care turned to urgency. He began to swing at balls down the leg side which earlier he had allowed to pass. He gathered a four to fine leg off Hall and would have had another but for a brilliant save by Butcher. At 182 for five, with 65 minutes left, Gibbs replaced Griffith.

With an hour remaining and four effective wickets standing England needed 48 to win. A few minutes later word came through that Cowdrey was changed. The England dressing room must have been a place of shattered nerves. Titmus was clinging on like a burr and running well between wickets, and at 196 he joined the applause for Close's 50, reached with a hook to fine leg for four off Hall. The pavilion was filling up as businessmen arrived in bowler hats from the city.

This, then, was the position when Titmus pushed Hall firmly to the middle of three short legs where McMorris held an excellent catch. Next ball Trueman was taken at the wicket and England in a trice had their backs to the wall. It was Close or no one now and he continued to edge England forward. Two more hooks brought two more fours, with Allen hanging on for his life.

Once, perhaps twice, an over Close was charging down the wicket. The first time he did so Hall pulled up before delivering the ball, clutching his back as though in pain. A gentle word from Worrell wrought a miracle of healing. Griffith returned in place of Gibbs. Twenty minutes later Close was out and as he made his way in the pavilion rose to receive him. We had endured already an agony of suspense, and there was still more to come.

> WEST INDIES 301 (R. Kanhai 73, J. Solomon 56, C. Hunte 44, G. Sobers 42; F. S. Trueman 6 for 100) and 229 (B. Butcher 133; F. S. Trueman 5 for 52, D. Shackleton 4 for 72)
> ENGLAND 297 (K. F. Barrington 80, E. R. Dexter 70, F. J. Titmus 52 not out; C. Griffith 5 for 91) and 228 for 9 (D. B. Close 70, K. F. Barrington 60; W. Hall 4 for 93)
> *Match drawn*

Tricky Wicket for Mr. Dexter

Caution on Politics

FROM OUR SOUTH WALES CORRESPONDENT

2 *August* 1963; *Cardiff*, 1 *August*. Mr. E. R. Dexter deserves more net practice before he faces the demon bowler of Cardiff South-East, Mr. James Callaghan.

This morning England's cricket captain held a press conference after his selection by the divisional Conservative Association as prospective candidate to fight the seat now held by Labour's shadow Chancellor.

Mr. Dexter agreed that he had never before spoken for the party from a political platform or been a "physical member" of the Conservative Party or a Young Conservative. Much of his life had been spent out of the country, he explained, and it was now that he was settling down with a growing family that he had the opportunity of helping the Conservative Party. By conviction he had always been Conservative.

Mr. Dexter was reminded by a questioner that he had put down one of his interests as economics and that Mr. Callaghan might also have something to say on this subject. What did Mr. Dexter think about the problems of international liquidity?

He wisely took his bat away. "I would rather not tangle with Mr. Callaghan on that one", he said. Those were specialized things with which he had not had time to get seriously acquainted. As from October (after the end of the cricket season) his time was going to be his own. He would then get better acquainted with Cardiff and with such specialized fields.

As a captain Mr. Dexter was able to answer with some fellow feeling a question about his views on the Conservative succession. "I would align myself behind Mr. Macmillan", he said. "If he thought we should have a successor then I would align myself behind him."

When asked what he did have strong views about (coloured immigration, perhaps) Mr. Dexter stonewalled. He did not really want to be tied down to such matters of policy, he said. He obviously had personal feelings about these things, but did not want to make comments on them at this juncture.

Would not the electors of Cardiff South-East expect him to? When he was knocking on doors in October, he said, he would give them his own considered views.

A reporter wondered what Mr. Dexter would specialize in. That, he replied, would emerge in his visits to Cardiff, but he thought he would specialize in the particular problems of Cardiff South-East. "I do not pretend to know those in detail at the moment." But he hoped to put that right in the future.

Mr. Dexter was drawn into saying he would be against renationalization of steel and that the Government was remarkable in what it had achieved in education, thus deserving a further term of office.

In an introductory statement Mr. G. V. Wynne-Jones, chairman of the local association, said those people who had met and known Ted Dexter would realize it was Dexter the man and not Dexter the cricketer who had been chosen.

Sussex Achieve Success through Attrition

FROM OUR CRICKET CORRESPONDENT [JOHN WOODCOCK]

9 *September* 1963; *Lord's*. Manifest in the final of the one-day knock-out competition were several of the best features of this type of cricket and a number of the worst. Sussex, the first winners of the Gillette Cup, achieved their success through attrition rather than attack, which is, of course, contrary to the aims of the competition.

Because of the loyalties involved and the great gathering of supporters who had travelled from Sussex and Worcestershire, the atmosphere was full of excitement. It was like Yorkshire and Lancashire with the lid off. There was some of the ribaldry of Eton and Harrow before the war; and at times devotees from Dudley and *aficionados* from Angmering found themselves reacting to a boundary hit more like West Indians than Englishmen of traditional reserve. From this point of view it was only a pity that the ground was far from full, in spite of all the tickets having been sold and all the private boxes taken.

In the matter of weather the organizers were remarkably fortunate, as they have been all along. The groundsman had excelled himself in producing a table dry enough for play, and although the last hour of Worcestershire's innings took place in Stygian gloom and occasional rain there were no interruptions. If Worcestershire had appealed against the conditions the umpires could hardly have turned them down; instead, they struggled on against Dexter's protective fields, and thanks in the end to Booth they made an exciting finish of it. The anticlimax of leaving a few overs to be bowled this morning was mercifully avoided.

There is not much doubt, I think, that those who began the day with an open mind mostly turned sooner or later to supporting Worcestershire. In the first place Worcestershire bowled 34 overs of spin, which was a welcome break from the season's motto theme. It was their clear intention to get Sussex out. Sussex, on the other hand, went into the field after making 168 with the main purpose of containing Worcestershire. Where Kenyon had, for the opening overs, placed two slips, a gully and a short leg, Dexter had only one close fielder, a slip, for Thomson and Buss. This made for a hard match and a slow rate of scoring.

For Sussex, only Parks played with the dash and distinction of other rounds. Oakman and Langridge provided a good beginning, with Langridge the more forceful. Their opening stand of 62 had a big influence on the match. After Gifford had dismissed them both in the same over wickets fell with regularity. Dexter was caught at slip off bat and pad, the umpire being more sure than the batsman that ball had made contact with bat. Suttle was out before luncheon and Lenham soon afterwards, both to Gifford, whose four wickets for 33 runs in 15 overs earned him the special prize for the best individual performance of the day.

Sussex scored their runs at 2.8 an over as against 4.7 in their three earlier matches. The pitch was inevitably slow; the ball would turn, and only Parks's handsome driving gave impetus to the innings. Worcestershire in the field were shrewdly directed by Kenyon. With the bat the initiative eluded them.

Although the pitch had dried out a little by the time Worcestershire went in, it still frustrated all but the finest drivers. Sussex's tactics were unashamedly defensive and insidiously effective. Once Kenyon was leg-before to a break back and Horton had been brilliantly caught and bowled it was up to Headley and Graveney to mount the challenge.

This was a crucial phase in the match, and it was by their successful suppression of Headley for two hours and a quarter that Sussex settled the issue. Headley played any number of good strokes for nought, the ball hit hard and straight to a fielder. It seemed not to occur to him to try to upset Sussex with the short single on the off side. Eventually Graveney got himself out in the effort to accelerate and at 103, Headley skied Bates to mid-on. Thereafter it was a race against the light, the rain and, for Worcestershire, against time.

After a few lusty hits by Broadbent, Snow took three quick wickets which reduced Worcestershire to 133 for nine. With eight overs left and the last pair together, Worcestershire still needed 36. That they got 21 of them was due largely to Booth. In every era there are a number of worthy cricketers who do yeoman service for their counties without ever quite achieving fame. Booth is one of these. He batted now with unexpected ease and quickness of foot and not until Carter, his partner, was run out a few minutes before seven o'clock were Sussex assured of victory. Had Carter beaten Suttle's throw as he went for a second run, Worcestershire would have required 14 to win off 10 balls. The end, in fact, was close enough for anyone, even if the means on the way had, at times, been a perversion of positive cricket.

No doubt the one-day knock-out match, contested by first class cricketers, has come to stay. A knock-out draw, with all reasonable entries accepted, provides, to my mind, enough yet not too much of this type of cricket. Perhaps next year Saturdays will be put aside for the competition: the final, too, may be played earlier in the season when the days are longer and less of a premium would be put on winning the toss.

This inceptive tournament, generously sponsored, has come through unscathed by the weather, and that is miraculous. It has provided, with its brilliant fielding and interesting tactics and fast running, a happy diversion from three-day matches. It was won, however, by a side which bowled, in four rounds, only 23 overs of spin and deployed their fielders with unremitting caution. That, in itself, exposes an undoubted weakness of this kind of cricket in our kind of climate.

SUSSEX 168 (60.2 overs) (J. M. Parks 57; N. Gifford 4 for 33)
WORCESTERSHIRE 154 (63.2 overs)
Sussex won by 14 runs

Sir Jack Hobbs

30 *December* 1963. Mr. J. W. Chance writes:–
Some years ago I bought a cricket bat at Sir Jack Hobbs's shop in Fleet Street. This was required for a raffle as part of a programme to raise funds for repairs to a church in Buckinghamshire. Having completed the purchase I asked Sir Jack Hobbs whether he would do me the honour of autographing the bat. On learning the charitable nature of the request he immediately

agreed to do so, and then asked whether I would care to collect as well the signatures of the Surrey XI, at that time in the middle of their reign as champion county. I said that I would be only too grateful, but how should I set about it. He then produced his own Oval pass and told me to use it to introduce myself to Mr. Surridge, the captain. I did so one afternoon when Surrey was playing Cambridge University at home. Within a short time I had all the team's signatures on that bat, including the twelfth man and the umpires. But that was not all. A day or two later I received £1 from Sir Jack for tickets in our raffle. I have subsequently heard from another Surrey cricketer that anything to do with the church always evoked his sympathy and support.

Apology to Cricket Captain

Wheatley v. Beaverbrook Newspapers Limited and Others

BEFORE MR. JUSTICE SACHS
HIGH COURT OF JUSTICE: QUEEN'S BENCH DIVISION

1 *August* 1964. The settlement was announced of this libel action by Mr. Oswald Stephen Wheatley, the well-known cricketer and captain of the Glamorgan County Cricket Club, against Beaverbrook Newspapers Ltd. and the Daily Sketch and Daily Graphic Ltd., in respect of reports in the *Daily Express* and *Daily Sketch* of July 18, 1963, of an incident at Colchester on Wednesday, July 17, 1963, when Glamorgan were playing Essex.

Mr. Brian Neill appeared for the plaintiff; Mr. Douglas Lowe, Q.C., and Mr. David Hirst for the defendants.

MR. NEILL, for the plaintiff, said that on Tuesday, July 16, the plaintiff had been playing at Dover for Glamorgan against Kent. He was due to attend the annual dinner of the Hawks Club in London that evening, but he realized that it would be impossible for him, if he left Dover at the close of play, to reach the restaurant where the dinner was to be held in time if he were to change into his dinner jacket in London. For this reason he made the change in Dover. All the plaintiff's clothes were sent with the club bags direct from Dover to Colchester.

The plaintiff left the dinner about midnight, went to bed shortly thereafter and left next morning dressed in his dinner jacket. He arrived at Colchester in time for the toss, which took place well before the start of play, with only a few people at the ground and with the plaintiff still in his dinner jacket.

The *Daily Express* and *Daily Sketch* on Thursday, July 18, reported this incident. The plaintiff would have had no objection whatsoever to their doing so had they confined themselves to the facts, but the articles in both newspapers were so worded as to suggest that the plaintiff, instead of going to bed, had attended an all-night party. The plaintiff regarded that quite unfounded suggestion as most damaging to his reputation as a professional cricket captain, and had felt it necessary to bring these proceedings. The defendants had agreed to express their apologies to the plaintiff in open court and to pay him a sum of money appropriate to the injury to his reputation, and also his costs.

MR. LOWE, for the defendants, said that the defendants fully accepted what had been said by counsel for the plaintiff, and sincerely regretted that the articles were worded so as to convey the imputations suggested, which they fully accepted were untrue.

The record was, by leave, withdrawn.

Solicitors. – Messrs. Norton, Rose, Botterell & Roche, for Messrs. Bickley, Wheatley & Co., Birmingham; Messrs. Oswald Hickson, Collier & Co.; Messrs. Swepstone Walsh & Son.

Graveney 15th to Achieve Century of Centuries

FROM OUR CRICKET CORRESPONDENT [JOHN WOODCOCK]

6 *August* 1964; *Worcester*. This is an encomium, or an acclamation, of a famous player rather than a commentary upon a successful side. Worcestershire's total of 309 for eight declared was a fine one, on a dry pitch emitting puffs of dust. But yesterday belonged not to Worcestershire but to Graveney, who became the fifteenth cricketer to score a century of centuries.

Here is the constellation which Graveney joins, with the number of hundreds they have made. – J. B. Hobbs (197), E. Hendren (170), W. R. Hammond (167), C. P. Mead (153), H. Sutcliffe (149), F. E. Woolley (145), L. Hutton (129), W. G. Grace (126), D. C. S. Compton (122), D. G. Bradman (117), A. Sandham (107), T. Hayward (104), L. E. G. Ames (102), and E. Tyldesley (102). Graveney became one of them just after half past five, towards the end of a scorching day.

He had played, characteristically, an innings of distinction and grace. Most of his 19 boundaries were drives, beautifully made with a flowing swing of the bat. We shall remember him for the high stance, the tanned face, the long peak to his cap, and the shoulders slightly rounded, the right rather lower than the left. When we are old we shall recall, nostalgically, the charm and rhythm of Graveney's stroke play. "Ah," we shall say, "you should have seen Graveney: there was elegance for you."

Yes, Graveney expresses as well as anyone the beauty in batting. Whether he is leaning on his bat between overs or playing a feathered glance or a delicate cut, he *looks* a cricketer. All the strokes are there, they have given pleasure in all the cricketing countries of the world. And now, at 37, Graveney is as good a player as he ever was.

That should be an example to those who think of giving up too soon. And let it be an encouragement to them that Hobbs scored more than 100 hundreds after he was 40. Graveney has many more to come, I hope. It is only a pity that someone of such infinite gifts should not have given more to England. As a Test match cricketer the best has seldom been got out of him, and now, it seems, the selectors have set him to one side.

Another large crowd watched yesterday's cricket. The game has the whole county by the ears at present, and by the middle of the afternoon there was scarcely a seat unfilled. For a long time the play was predictably slow. With the pitch likely to worsen, and the ball already turning, Worcestershire set cautiously about their business. In the two hours and a quarter of the morning they made 76 for two. Kenyon lost his off stump to Watts and Headley forced Scott to mid-on. Andrew soon had his spinners on, both of them slow left-arm over the wicket. After luncheon P. D. Watts had three overs of rather extravagant leg breaks.

Steele, who is a cousin of Crump, had much the longest stint of his career, without proposing himself as a strong spinner of the ball. He bowled an accurate line, on and outside the off stump, and well deserved his wickets. Scott stands fifth in the bowling averages with 81 wickets. He has a nice high build for a bowler of his type, though the action itself is square. Of the four orthodox left-arm spinners in the match, I imagine Gifford turns the ball the most. Today it will be interesting to see what he and Slade achieve.

Apart from Graveney, the best of Worcestershire's batting came from Horton, Richardson and Booth. Horton is a good, four-square player in his own right. Batting for so long in Kenyon's presence has brought him on. S. M. Brown learnt a lot from watching Robertson at close quarters, as Lowson did from watching Hutton, and Sandham must have done from watching Hobbs. Horton now made 54 solid runs before Milburn at silly mid-off, caught him off Steele, anticipating the stroke and diving to his right. Somewhere, I am sure, a seismograph must have recorded Milburn's fall. Horton and Graveney had added 75 and laid the basis of the innings.

By luncheon Graveney was installed. From the start his defensive technique was proof against the turning ball. Gradually the strokes began to flow, liquid as a mountain stream. He was never missed; he was seldom beaten; he was never hurried. During the afternoon he made 52 with an ease and a style that concealed the problems of the pitch. For half an hour Ormrod used his feet as Graveney's partner. And then Booth came to see him pass this great milestone in his career, and stayed on to share the celebrations. A sixth wicket partnership of 108 ensured a powerful position for Worcestershire in, to them, a vital game.

Graveney went to three figures with a succession of hooks off Larter. Everyone congratulated him, as is customary on these occasions. Graveney acknowledged the cheers to the manner born. I was at Canterbury when Ames reached his hundredth hundred. Here was another glorious natural batsman. Hutton was the last to do so, in 1951. May could be the next if he chose, his tally being 85. Cowdrey, with 69, probably will be. In any day and age, to achieve such a feat is a sign of abundant ability and the outcome of many years delightfully spent.

> WORCESTERSHIRE 309 for 8 dec (T. W. Graveney 132, M. J. Horton 54, R. Booth 51; D. S. Steele 4 for 65) and 112 (J. D. F. Larter 5 for 44, B. Crump 4 for 39)
> NORTHAMPTONSHIRE 212 (P. D. Watts 91, B. L. Reynolds 50; M. J. Horton 4 for 59) and 142 for 5 (P. D. Watts 48)
> Score after first day: Worcestershire 309 for 8 dec, Northamptonshire 0 for 1
> *Match drawn*

Cricket for Russians

15 *August* 1964, *Leading Article.* A gallant effort is made by *Anglia*, the official British magazine in Russian that circulates in the Soviet Union, to add to NIKITA SERGEYEVICH'S well-known store of proverbs and popular sayings. Quite rightly *Anglia* draws its offerings from Britain's national game *kriket*, otherwise cricket. First it gives a scholarly explanation of the game itself, telling all about the *betsmeny*, *boylery*, *fildery* and the two commands of eleven men apiece. Having set the field, the talented author then goes on to give what all Marxists would call a valuable generalization based on experience and with a just application to the tasks for today. He points out that cricket has enriched the English language with many very popular phrases, each with a moral. Pride of place he properly gives to "That is not cricket", *Eto nye kriket*, and explains it means "That's not fair", *nye po-sportsmensky*.

The good work is taken up in yet another article in the magazine, this time in English. If, as one may confidently expect, MR. KHRUSHCHEV is given a translation he will find it hard to resist the cricketing metaphors which it lists. He may not go so far as to complain to MAO TSE-TUNG that the Chinese are always trying to get him "on a sticky wicket". But there are the British. The Russians frequently assure us that they wish relations to be excellent – or, next on the list of *Anglia*'s examples, "on a good wicket".

There would be no better way of warming and softening SIR ALEC DOUGLAS-HOME's cricketing heart than by Moscow's assuring him in a friendly letter that, though NIKITA SERGEYEVICH may occasionally "send down a fast one" in negotiations, he recognizes that (relying on *Anglia* again) it is SIR ALEC's job to try to "hit it for six" – "a phrase commonly used to describe the complete frustration of an opponent in almost any context". On the other hand MR. KHRUSHCHEV, having read on, may feel it no less right to point out that if an opponent has "no fit reply to an apparently unanswerable question" he may be said to be "clean bowled" or "stumped". There are many new opportunities for enlivening diplomatic correspondence along such lines. *Anglia* is certainly on a good wicket.

Personal Column

24 *November* 1964. A first class County Cricket Club [Lancashire] invites applications from persons with first-class cricket experience for the position of Captain of the County XI. The position will carry a salary in accordance with experience and an allowance to cover expenses. – Write Box J.961. The Times, E.C.4.

Mr. Wilson Plays Himself In

15 *December* 1964. Mr. Wilson yesterday forced a draw – or should it be tie? – between himself and Sir Alec Douglas-Home. The Prime Minister whipped off his own green tie at Lord's and replaced it with a Lord's Taverners' tie.

He was accepting honorary membership of the Lord's Taverners, an exclusive charitable cricket club established at the famous tavern. Earlier this year Sir Alec, who has played in first-class cricket, brought roars of approval when he slipped off his own tie in favour of the club's. As Mr. Wilson did likewise yesterday, a wag among the cheering members called out: "Pull it tight."

Mr. Wilson said: "The first time I was here was one of the grimmest evenings in British cricket. We had lost three for 14 before nightfall, including Hutton, in the second Test of 1953. But all was saved next day by Willie Watson.

"I was a very bad cricketer, but I did get into my house team for Huddersfield – I was last man in", Mr. Wilson said. He recalled a match when the opposition were all out for 15. "We were 15 for nine. I went in; there were three balls, bumpers, and blinding light."

His partner came half-way down the pitch and said in "Yorkshire language" that he should not try to score but keep his end up. "I swiped at the first one and missed, and the same thing happened to the next two balls. Then my partner got the bowling and was clean bowled. He was Willie Watson."

Lord Reith was also made an honorary member of the club.

Mr. Raymond Robertson-Glasgow

6 *March* 1965. Mr. Raymond Robertson-Glasgow, who died on Thursday at the age of 63, was a man of many parts, scholar, athlete, wit, and first-class conversationalist. All these talents were focused on his favourite subject in life, cricket, and made him a notable and in many ways a unique figure among the brotherhood of cricketers.

His career as a performer started at his preparatory school, developed at

Charterhouse and came to full power on going up to Oxford. He played for Oxford in four University matches but, having bowled Hubert Ashton in the first, failed to take a wicket in his following three appearances. This was one of many unusual and original performances for which he had a most endearing flair. It was the more remarkable for he was a fine bowler of fastish pace who made the new ball leave the bat. His bowling career with Somerset and Oxford from 1920 to 1935 brought him almost 500 wickets, and many of these were defended by the greatest professional batsmen of a prolific age.

He was no mean batsman himself when called upon to exert himself to the full but his normal attitude, as a member of the lesser half of the order, was one of immense if ephemeral enjoyment. The most serious engagement of this extremely unserious but wholly devoted cricketer was one appearance for the Gentlemen (at Lord's) in 1924.

His time with Somerset was spent among some gay and colourful companions, such as Sam Woods, John Daniell and "Farmer" White, whose friendship filled him with great joy, and whose feats and foibles gave him a wealth of reminiscence which he retailed by spoken word or pen with a touch and gusto unexcelled in sporting talk or writing.

For 10 years from 1923 Robertson-Glasgow taught at St. Edmund's School, Hindhead. He entered journalism as golf and then cricket correspondent for the *Morning Post* in 1933, later working for the *Daily Telegraph*, *The Observer*, and *The Sunday Times*. He also contributed to *Punch* and other magazines.

His autobiography, *46 Not Out*, was published in 1948. Among his other books were *Cricket Prints* (1943), *More Cricket Prints* (1948), and *The Brighter Side of Cricket* (1951).

His writings were a departure in cricket journalism. His practical knowledge made him a dependable and informative observer, but the immense fascination of his work sprang from a warm and kindly wit which lay close beneath the surface of every sentence he spoke or wrote.

To those who knew him it came as no surprise that the open scholar of Corpus Christi College, Oxford, should later have written a wartime book *I Was Himmler's Aunt*.

Much of his writing was achieved against a background of ill-health, and there can be little doubt that but for this his talents would have been more widely known. He was the unrelenting enemy of all humbug and solemnity in sport; to him the brighter side of the game, whatever it might be, was all-important. This made him the perfect chronicler of cricket matches far below his own standard of play, and of such golfing pleasures as the meetings of the Oxford and Cambridge Golfing Society and the Halford Hewitt.

He married, in 1943, Elizabeth Edward, widow of P. Y. Hutton.

9 *March*. Our Cricket Correspondent [John Woodcock] writes:–
Raymond Robertson-Glasgow, known to his countless friends (with great

affection) as "Crusoe", possessed a warm and wonderful way of delighting his companions. He had, for one thing, a laugh which was as infectious and uninhibited in its enjoyment of the jokes of other people as of those he made himself. He had the background of a classical scholar, combined with a riotous imagination and a sense of humour which lit bonfires of good will. You had only to cross the threshold of a pavilion to hear and to know whether "Crusoe" was there.

In 1950, on the M.C.C. tour to Australia, I drove through the country with "Crusoe", and with his wife, Elizabeth, and watched them while they made a trail of friends. He reported the tour for *The Times*. Subsequently, his appearances dwindled. Ill health had much to do with that, for he would suffer long periods of depression when, to all but those who knew him best, he seemed in cracking form.

From 1953, when he retired from regular cricket writing, "Crusoe's" influence on the cricketing scene and his generous nature were badly missed. To him, cricket at every level was a game to be enjoyed. In his reporting of it there was an understanding of the difficulties involved, and a knowledge of the finer points which commanded everyone's respect. Solemnity was scorned. It is no coincidence that first class cricket has tended to become a more serious business and a less amusing one since "Crusoe" no longer inhabited, as a chronicler, and a sportsman, a humorist, and a wit, the grounds where it is played.

10 *March. From our correspondent, Reading, 9 March.* A widow said at an inquest here today that her husband, who had been suffering from melancholic depression, became depressed at the sight of the snow last Thursday and took an overdose of drugs.

Mrs. Elizabeth Robertson-Glasgow, of Lime Tree Cottage, Buckhold, Berkshire, said that usually her husband, Mr. R. C. Robertson-Glasgow, aged 63, author and former Somerset cricketer, was first downstairs to make the morning tea. On this day she was first down. She had swept the snow away from the kitchen door when she saw her husband. He told her: "Please telephone the doctor. It's urgent, darling. I am sorry for what I have done."

He said he had taken about 20 tablets.

A verdict of Suicide while the balance of the mind was disturbed was recorded on Mr. Robertson-Glasgow, who died in hospital at Reading. Dr. Frank Hampson, a pathologist, said that an analyst's report showed that he died from barbiturate poisoning.

M.C.C. Plan for Tavern Bar at Lord's

6 *May* 1965. Beer-drinking spectators of cricket outside the Tavern at Lord's this summer will need to order an extra pint to drown their nostalgia. For at

their backs, as they drink, time's winged chariot will be drawing near in the form of a redevelopment plan which will obliterate their century-old haven behind cover point, or mid-wicket, depending on which end is bowling.

M.C.C. yesterday published the details of the comprehensive £1m. redevelopment plan for the south-west corner of cricket's headquarters. In the plan the Tavern will be demolished and rebuilt with an added restaurant next to the Grace Gates and out of sight of the wicket.

A new stand, seating about 2,000 spectators, will be built on the site of the existing Tavern, members' dining room, and clock tower. In the background a 12-storey block of flats will be erected, partially overlooking the ground, and presumably in great demand as a vantage point during Test matches.

But thirsty spectators can sip their pints in security all this summer and next, while they watch the run-stealers flicker to and fro; demolition of the existing Tavern will not start until September, 1966, when the new Tavern will be ready for them.

M.C.C. have also realized that there is a need for some therapeutic haven with a view of the cricket in which their customers can find liquid inoculation against bitter weather and tedious stone-wallers. So on the site of the present Tavern they will build a smaller Tavern bar. And from here in the future, as in the past, hearty cries of comment and advice will be hurled at any batsman who tries to put the shutters up in the last few overs before luncheon.

McKenzie and Hawke Rout West Indies

FROM OUR SPECIAL CORRESPONDENT [C. L. R. JAMES]

18 *May* 1965; *Port of Spain*, 17 *May*. Australia gained an astonishing victory here today in the fifth Test match against West Indies and with it they lessened the disappointment of having already lost the series. They won by 10 wickets with three full days to spare, having dismissed West Indies in their second innings for 131. Simpson and Lawry scored without difficulty the 61 runs which Australia needed for victory, thereby underlining the memory of a beautiful day, a large crowd, and some notable bowling.

Of the 11 wickets to fall today the fast bowlers claimed ten, Griffith setting the fashion by getting rid of his opposite number McKenzie, with the last ball of his only over this morning. Australia's first innings thus ended without addition to the starting score of 294 for nine. When West Indies batted, Sincock, with his unorthodox medley of left arm chinamen and googlies, played an important part. Although he bowled many bad balls – there was not a single maiden among his 18 overs – Simpson never took him off, once he was on, for he unsettled all the batsmen except Hunte.

But it was McKenzie, with five for 33, and Hawke, with three for 31, who set Australia on the way to their remarkable victory. Only Hunte, who carried his bat for 60, saved West Indies, with their great batting strength, from total rout in their second innings. Butcher, who helped Hunte to add 41 for the third wicket, was the only other West Indian batsman to reach double figures.

At the start of the day the groundlings had been out for a good time, their setbacks unforeseen. They applauded Hunte straight driving McKenzie for three and doubled the applause when Booth returned that ball over the bowler's head straight into Grout's hands. Davis showed his strength by a perfect off drive from Hawke and was then leg-before to one that squatted.

Kanhai at once made vintage strokes and played Hawke watchfully forward. Hawke was moving the ball into the batsman in the air. Apparently one did not move in the air and Kanhai's stumps were spreadeagled. The ball did nothing awkward off the pitch. At 27 Sincock bowled some dreadful long hops and presumably strategic full pitches. Butcher hit one of each for four, but seemed over-anxious to hit Sincock about and achieved a number of would-be potent but ineffective hits. Not so Hunte, who was very much the anchor with 16 to Butcher's 20 at luncheon when West Indies were 53 for two.

Butcher hit a high full pitch from Sincock straight into the hands of mid-wicket. Nurse was leg-before to Hawke, and four wickets were down with West Indies still four runs short of the deficit of 70.

Sobers seemed comfortable but was not. He missed quite a few leg hits at Sincock. Then, trying to force McKenzie off the back foot, he was convincingly beaten and bowled. McKenzie was going all out and the crowd hummed awesomely at the pace he was making off the pitch. The Australian fielding, always of a high order, was giving nothing away. The 100 came with Hunte 39. Allan scored only seven; but he showed a readiness to resist and the crowd made much of him.

Sincock is not only master of the deadly full pitch. His long hops, pitched half way, possess the faculty of evading the most carefully aimed cuts. What prevents an unvarnished statement of how bad the West Indian batting was is that it would diminish the merit of the Australian bowling and fielding.

Hunte's 50 came out of 121 and he celebrated by digging out two creepers in an over from McKenzie. McKenzie bowled Hall and Griffith. Gibbs gained applause by stopping the hat trick but was bowled next ball.

WEST INDIES 224 (R. B. Kanhai 121) and 131 (C. C. Hunte 60 not out; G. D. McKenzie 5 for 33)
AUSTRALIA 294 (R. B. Simpson 72, R. M. Cowper 69; C. C. Griffith 6 for 46) and 63 for 0
Australia won by 10 wickets

Festival Cricket

27 *August* 1965, *Leading Article.* All too soon now festival cricket will be taking over from the Test and championship variety, a familiar sign that the season is at its last gasp. The word "festival" in connexion with the technical intricacies of the contest between bat and ball may seem a little out of place. It suggests clowns and false noses, whereas cricket, if it is to have any meaning or attraction, must be played seriously – which does not mean solemnly.

Festival cricket has interpreted this basic truth genially, with Scarborough, which has over the generations established itself as the leader in this particular field, setting the example. Much excellent and exciting cricket, the real, as against the spurious, kind, has been seen on that friendliest of all the Yorkshire grounds with Trafalgar Square at one end to attract the attentions of such hitters as C. I. THORNTON, whose name is so intimately linked with the place. The gentlemen v. players match is no longer played and it is now under the name of T. N. PEARCE and not H. D. G. LEVESON-GOWER that teams go out to do battle. But the knack of combining light-hearted enjoyment with earnest endeavour has been preserved.

Other places have had – and still have – their cricket festivals, but not always with Scarborough's success. At Blackpool, understandably enough, the accent was too much on the holiday spirit. At a match there in the twenties the umpires announced that they had been instructed to be "very generous about l.-b.-w. decisions". The characteristic comment of GEORGE GUNN on this, was, according to R. C. ROBERTSON-GLASGOW, "And I suppose if anyone's bowled (rhyming with 'scowled') it's just a nusty accident?" Folkestone has seen some good games, although the wide open spaces there, in the absence of large crowds, have sometimes seemed a little intimidating. Hastings, now back in favour, is compact enough with the castle guarding the ramparts overlooking the sea, and always has, as it were, a festival atmosphere. Festival cricket all the season is a horrid thought. So is the idea of a summer without any at all.

Marylebone Cricket Club

18 *October* 1965, *Personal Column.* Full members should attend special general meeting 5.30 p.m., Wednesday, October 20, 1965, to oppose proposals to provide funds for grandiose building programme. Proposals include increasing members' subscriptions by 50 per cent, pledging property, selling investments and building site lease. Members have received no explanations. Financial justification very large expenditure seems very slender. – Inserted by a member of the Club.

The Seamy Side of Cricket

8 *March* 1966, *Leading Article*. If SIR ALAN HERBERT – that dauntless stormer of seemingly impregnable strongholds and doughty tilter at windmills – were given to saying, "I told you so", he has now good reason for saying it again. What is more, he would be justified in doing so to the wise men of Lord's. Nestling modestly and to a large extent undetected among their latest layings down of the rules of cricket is a paragraph headed, "Polishing ball". This strikes with revolutionary thoroughness at bowlers who polish their missiles or rub the shine off them. They must in future find other ways of taking a wicket, and even wiping and cleaning will be allowed only under the supervision of the umpire.

At first sight this may not appear as earth-shaking news. Those unhappy people for whom cricket is no more than a game may greet it in the Johnsonian spirit of – In a world bursting with sin and misery, you come prating to me of string. But opening a parcel by cutting instead of untying the knot is surely an offence far more trivial than that of tampering with a ball before bowling it. Like so many insidious lapses from virtue, the habit grew up slowly.

It is part of the *mystique* of the "seamer" of whom so much is heard in cricket reporting. He has brought his verbs in with him. He "seams" and is "seaming". The once fashionable "swing" bowler has been made to take a relatively back seat in the idiom of the sports commentators, and, as for "fast", it has almost become a dirty word. If the new rule leads to more spin bowling and to wicketkeepers less often standing half-way back to the boundary, it will cheer those who are tired of some recent trends. It will certainly gladden the heart of SIR ALAN. He has had to wait for his triumph. As long ago as 1959, he denounced in these columns the rubbing of the ball as "inelegant and laughable" and called for an amendment of the law. Were his letters, one wonders, read aloud lately to this august sub-committee of the M.C.C.?

Successful Sunday for Essex and Somerset

FROM OUR CRICKET CORRESPONDENT [JOHN WOODCOCK]

16 *May* 1966. If the first objective of first-class cricket on Sundays is to make it more accessible to the public, the experiment got away to a notable start at Ilford yesterday. For the second day of their match with Somerset, Essex had one of their largest home crowds for years. The cricket itself was less auspicious.

On Saturday 21 wickets fell for only 259 runs on a pitch which allowed the ball to move readily off the seam. Yesterday there was no such movement and

Somerset, who were 54 runs behind on the first innings, spent the four hours and a half of play easing their way back into the game. Clayton, the night watchman, gave them a good start by making 42 and Virgin played nicely for 51. After tea G. Atkinson and Kitchen made sure that Somerset's recovery became well established.

It was a pleasant family scene, mother being there with the best of them to see whether it was all worth while. The ground, set in a park, was a congenial place for the outing, and the afternoon was warm and sunny.

East, recruited straight from village cricket (he joined the Essex staff from East Bergholt), showed promise as a left-arm orthodox spinner, and Hobbs had the luxury of a long spell. Bailey, on the field as player and off it as secretary, was happy to take a part in the launching of a new scheme.

Not many years ago people were saying that Sunday cricket would "never come in our lifetime". Now it is here – to stay, if there are many more days as congenial as this.

SOMERSET 102 (B. R. Knight 6 for 36) and 343 for 6 dec (M. Kitchen 76, G. Atkinson 76, R. Virgin 51, G. Clayton 42)
ESSEX 156 (B. R. Knight 56; B. Langford 4 for 10) and 286 for 7 (B. Taylor 77, K. Fletcher 73)
Score after second day: Somerset 102 and 239 for 3, Essex 156
Match drawn

Definitely Not Cricket

2 *January* 1967, *Leading Article*. Indian cricket fans will have been disappointed by yesterday's newspaper placards about the second Test match against the West Indies in Calcutta. "Riots stopped play" was the news from that sprawling, uncontrollable city.

By now the world has become used to rioting students, intransigent Sikhs, no less determined defenders of the cow, and crowds that turn to violence at almost any railway station for almost any reason. This troubled Test match might seem only another proof of India's growing taste for violence. Others might take a different view. Was it not Britain that gave the game to India? And was it not an enthusiastic crowd, cramming the ground to a capacity of 80,000, with more trying to force their way in, that started the rioting?

But what of the scene at the holy of holies – the pitch? There a small tragedy was enacted. Some cricket-lovers tried to save it, but these brave fellows were overcome by angrier sportsmen who set about the most fiendish desecration of the pitch.

Come to think of it, the Calcutta police might find a cause of the rioting in a wily anti-imperialist of the Sukarno type. "Was not cricket an imposition of the British imperialists?", he would demand. And here, he would go on, in this Test match between the West Indies and India was a most subtly corrupting trick of neo-colonialism.

Happily the game has its built-in defence. If Britain is saved from the destruction of yet another of its missions overseas it will be because Indians would find it not cricket thus to turn on the importers of the game. All credit to the ordinary, workaday Indians that their anti-colonialism does no more than occasionally chip the nose from the statue of some long-departed viceroy.

Sir Frank Worrell

14 *March* 1967. Sir Frank Worrell, the great West Indian cricketer, died yesterday in Kingston, Jamaica, at the age of 42. His death will come as a profound shock to cricket lovers around the world for it is little more than three years since he ended his first class career as captain of the triumphant West Indian touring team in England. He was one of the finest all-rounders in the history of the game, but he will be remembered as much for his leadership as his play. It was he who moulded the West Indian Test team from a group of talented, entertaining but erratic individuals into what it has now become – probably the finest side in the world. In doing this he not only won personal fame but raised the status and dignity of the West Indian coloured cricketer.

Frank Mortimer Maglinne Worrell was born at Bridgetown on August 1, 1924. As nearly a natural cricketer as may be – for he was never coached and rarely practised – he was a leading figure in the remarkable upsurge of Barbadian cricket in the 1940s. He was an outstanding player from boyhood; at Combermere School he was primarily an orthodox slow left-arm bowler and as such – and a number eleven batsman – was first chosen for Barbados – when he was 17. A year later while still at school, sent in as "night watchman" he went on next morning to make 64 and to establish himself as a batsman. In the same West Indian season he scored 188, the first of his 40 centuries against Trinidad. In 1943-44 at 19, he made 308 not out in an unfinished partnership of 502 with John Goddard, a record for the fourth wicket which he and Walcott broke two years later with an unbroken 574, also against Trinidad. When world cricket recommenced after the Second World War, he and his fellow Barbadian batsmen, Walcott and Weekes, were the legendary "three Ws".

Worrell was the most orthodox of the three; his self-taught technique was so correct that he seemed incapable of a crooked stroke. Lithely built and superbly balanced, he was a stylist with an elegantly unhurried air, although his wide range of strokes, off front or back foot, was based on rapid movement into correct position. His cutting was delicate, his driving, for all its easy execution, powerful; he was strong on both sides of the wicket; and he combined ability to relax when not actually playing with the unremitting concentration of those who build long innings.

The demands of League cricket changed his bowling method from slow to fast-medium left arm; he exploited English conditions in sharp movement off the seam and his pace from the pitch was so hostile as at times to be little short of genuinely fast. Latterly his speed declined but to the end of his Test career his experience and control enabled him to seal up an end. He was a safe fieldsman and a clean catcher anywhere and latterly his fielding at silly mid-on was a considerable tactical asset for his bowlers.

As a young man he was markedly sensitive to criticism and some schoolday bitternesses rankled so deeply that, in 1947, he made his home in Jamaica. So it was as a Jamaican player that he established his Test place in the series of 1947-48 against England.

His performances brought him the offer which few West Indian cricketers have found it financially possible to resist and in 1948 he joined the Central Lancashire League club, Radcliffe. There, and subsequently with Norton and Church, he spent some dozen happy and successful years as a league professional. Meanwhile, he read first Optics and then Economics at Manchester University. He contrived, however, to take part in all the West Indies' Tests of that period except those of 1958-59 in India which coincided with the final terms before he took a B.A.(Admin.) degree. He made three tours of India with Commonwealth sides.

For the team of 1950, which was the first from the West Indies to win a Test, and a rubber, in England, he was top of the batting averages with 539 runs at 89.93 and made an important contribution to team-balance by his fast-medium bowling. At Trent Bridge after taking three important English wickets he scored 261, then the highest innings by a West Indian in a Test in England.

In the West Indian side which was beaten in Australia in 1951-52 he emerged as a genuine all rounder of Test standard. Apart from his technical ability, the quality of his temperament was strikingly apparent in Goddard's defeated and dispirited team of 1957 in England, when he made good the lack of an opening batsman and opened the bowling. He took seven English wickets in the innings at Headingley and finished second in the batting and first in the bowling averages for Tests.

It was now apparent that only internal politics could prevent him from captaining the West Indies. He himself wisely took little part in the occasionally acrimonious controversy which ended when he was asked to take the 1960-61 team to Australia; the first time a coloured West Indian had been appointed to the captaincy of a touring side.

On that tour, which included the famous tied Test at Brisbane, cricket in Australia was raised to such heights of public esteem as it had not reached since the days of Bradman. Australian opinion was reflected in the institution of the "Worrell Trophy" for all future series between the two countries.

When he captained the touring side of 1963 to England, he was almost 39, a veteran by West Indian standards; indeed, all his famous contemporaries of the 1940s had retired from Test cricket. He himself was no longer the player he had been but, as batsman, bowler and fielder, he was still useful and he was one of the few men whose captaincy was so outstanding as to make a major contribution to a side's strength. He declared his purpose as not merely to win the Test series, but also to make such an impression as to bring West Indies to England again appreciably before the 1971 season of the Conference schedule. He achieved both his aims. The West Indies won the rubber three-one.

Worrell's captaincy was outstanding. Sharp in tactical perception, astute in attack and defence, quietly spoken, yet firm to the brink of ruthlessness, he outwitted his opponents and sustained his colleagues. As lately as 1957 a West Indian team had crumpled psychologically in face of defeat. Now, at one crisis after another, Worrell, with what sometimes seemed exaggerated calm, held them steady. His achievement may best be described as instilling in his players a professional attitude and stability which has endured. As in Australia, his side's cricket roused such immense public interest as achieved his second design. In the following winter the tour programme was revised, bringing another West Indian team to England in 1966.

By the time that decision was taken, Worrell had returned home to a magnificent public reception, the Post of Warden in the University of the West Indies at Kingston and a seat in the Jamaican Senate; a knighthood followed in the New Year Honours of 1964. In 1966 he was appointed Dean of Students for the branch of the University of the West Indies in Trinidad.

He was a non-smoker who kept enviably fit with a minimum of training. Convivial and conversational, he would talk gaily far into the night in his pleasant, slightly husky voice; he was quick and flexible in debate, fond of England and his many English friends, courteous in manner and he only rarely revealed the depth of his feeling on racial matters.

In 51 Test Matches he scored 3,860 runs at an average of 49.48 and took 69 wickets at 38.37.

He married Velda Brewster of Barbados in 1948; they had one daughter.

Magic of Lord's – Even Without the Tavern

BY JOHN WOODCOCK

17 *June* 1967. It is no use arranging to meet a friend on the Tavern forecourt, as it used to be called, or under the Clock Tower boxes during next week's Test match against India at Lord's. If you do, you will find yourself hidden by boarding from a view of the play and in the way of men working on the new stand, which it is hoped will be finished by the start of the 1968 cricket season.

The Tavern today means the new pub which has just been opened to the

west of the Grace Gates, complete with banqueting facilities. For old times'
sake, the M.C.C. were keen to erect a temporary bar in front of where the
original tavern stood; but the contractors resisted lest it should delay their
progress. As things are going, it will be possible to watch next year's Test
match against Australia from where the workmen's sparks now fly.

That, of course, is a great occasion. England against Australia at Lord's,
like the Royal meeting at Ascot, has nothing quite to match it. Yet for any
touring side this particular Test match is the showpiece of their tour. It will
be the same for the Nawab of Pataudi's side next Thursday, in spite of the
steel girders and the building operations, and happily the Indians have found
the form which should enable them to enjoy themselves.

May is now a bad and costly memory – for the majority of counties as
much as the Indians themselves. I shall always remember, though never
willingly, the lugubrious expressions of Mr. T. Tarapore, who is their
manager, and his treasurer, Mr. Chinnaswamy, who was always huddled at
his side, in those melancholy weeks. Only at Headingley at the beginning of
this week did they allow themselves a smile as India, against all the odds,
made their highest total against England.

Each touring side brings to Lord's its own distinctive cricketing character.
And in some felicitous way they generally manage, when they come there, to
be at their best, at least for a time. The Australians are still the toughest of
them all and their feathers the most prized. Only a pair of Australians would
spend the day on their feet, barracking from the stand reserved for Members'
friends. And only Keith Miller, two of whose many friends they were, would
have put them there in the first place.

Only an Australian, too, would pay off a taxi at the Grace Gates a quarter
of an hour before the start of play on a Monday morning when he was the
"Not out" batsman. Richie Benaud, having been caught in the traffic on the
way, did so in 1956, and in the next two hours he increased his score from
three to 97. Yet the Australians are the first to say that no other ground in the
world has the same quelling atmosphere as Lord's, that great "cathedral of
cricket" as Sir Robert Menzies has called it.

The New Zealanders offer more homespun methods, and a modesty that
is inhibiting except when they have a Donnelly or a Sutcliffe in their side. Of
all the fine innings played at Lord's since the war, Martin Donnelly's double
century in the second Test of 1949 is among the very best. Donnelly had the
irresistible qualities, when they are allied to one another, of greatness and
humility. You will find him now, unchanged except that his hair is grey,
fishing the mountain streams of Australia or boating with a large family in
Sydney harbour.

South Africans have a special affection for Lord's as being the scene of
their first Test victory in England. In 1935, when leather jackets lived in the
wicket, Xenophon Balaskas, a Greek chemist from Johannesburg, destroyed
England with his leg breaks. Sir Pelham Warner described Lord's that season

as looking like "the sand on the sea shore".

It was at Lord's, too, that the West Indies beat England for the first time over here. That was in 1950, when the calypso writers set Ramadhin and Valentine to music, and gaiety and passion broke loose. It was the start of the West Indies' rise to power. On their next tour, in 1957, Everton Weekes played so magnificently on a flying wicket that Mr. Ronnie Aird, secretary of the M.C.C., wrote on the club's behalf to congratulate him.

In 1963 came the epic match which ended in a draw, with England three runs short and West Indies needing only the wicket of Cowdrey, whose arm was encased in plaster. Several West Indians who got drunk that night were excused the next day by a magistrate. "I don't blame you", he said. "It was worth it."

Now it is India and Pakistan whom people will go to Lord's to watch; and many of the pleasures will be the same as if the Australians were there. Planters from Assam will arrange to meet sheep farmers from Victoria in the Long Room Bar, as they did when last they were at home. Whoever the visitors, it is always a full and beautiful time of year, with the hay being mown, strawberries in the Memorial Garden, and the buttonholes matching the members' complexions.

Next week the Indians may feel with a sense of relief that they have already proved themselves after their great recovery at Leeds. Their bowling is critically weak, and at any time, as Trueman had a way of proving, a genuine spell of fast bowling tends to find them out. Probably they have too many weaknesses to win.

But if all goes well they will show with the bat those gifts peculiar to themselves – of quickness of foot and eye, and flexibility of wrist – that can make them so attractive at the crease. If Pataudi, Chandra Borde, Hanumant Singh and Farrokh Engineer feel the sun on their backs and a firm and true wicket at their feet, the grazier and his friend will soon leave the bar.

Surrey's Great Effort Fails

FROM JOHN SILCHESTER [JOHN ARLOTT]

1 *July* 1967; *The Oval.* In an hour of sharp, well-organized out cricket, Kent came from prospective defeat to beat Surrey and move to second in the championship table.

A little before five o'clock Edrich and Stewart, batting better than anyone else in the match, were in command, and Surrey needed 111 to win with nine wickets and 95 minutes in hand.

In the next half-hour Underwood and Graham broke through. Cowdrey caught Smith at slip in a fashion to recall Hammond, and only Edrich remained to dispute the issue.

But it was resolved by Underwood. He achieved little turn, occasionally he spun enough to straighten, but largely by steady line and slight variations on his slow-medium theme, he took five wickets for 28 in his last nine overs. After the best innings of his life in the morning, his day was happily complete.

The Kent innings was a curious, uneasy affair of fits and starts, as one batsman after another tried to create the position for a declaration. Prodger fretted in rigid orthodoxy: his eight runs took, altogether, 80 minutes. Meanwhile, in strong contrast at the opposite end, Underwood, sent in on Thursday as night watchman, sensibly, and without any apparent difficulty, made the highest score of his career.

Cowdrey's 27, at a run a minute, was like a Turner watercolour sketch, tiny perfection in its own right, but only the outline of a major work from such a hand. He obviously considered the life of an orthodox batsman precarious on this pitch, an opinion he emphasized by declaring at lunch-time, and asking Surrey a scoring rate of less than 63 runs an hour.

As if this were their cue, both batsmen began to make aggressive strokes. It was a triumph of mind over marl: the pitch which hitherto had inhibited all who batted on it suddenly seemed full of runs. Had it dried a little?

Suddenly it still had no real pace but Edrich's bat made a rich noise when he drove, Stewart hooked the faster bowlers jauntily: the field retreated farther, and, by tea, Surrey were 120 for one, nearly halfway home, as nearly as made no matter up with the clock, and holding advantage for the first time in the match.

The pair were gathering momentum again after tea and their partnership had made 133 when Stewart, changing his stroke to a ball from Underwood which straightened, sent an awkward catch to cover where Shepherd, a lithe, prehensile fieldsman, held it. The remainder of the day belonged to Kent, and then still had half-an-hour of it to spare at the end.

KENT 220 (B. W. Luckhurst 96; S. J. Storey 5 for 47) and 161 for 8 dec (D. L. Underwood 47)
SURREY 132 (J. H. Edrich 55) and 177 (J. H. Edrich 92, M. J. Stewart 61; D. L. Underwood 5 for 59)
Kent won by 72 runs

'Hello! Is There a QC on the Ground?'

BY DENZIL BATCHELOR

23 *August* 1967. Olympus broods over the case of Brian Close after his acquisition of what *The Times* described as "two dishonourable points" in last week's match against Warwickshire. No doubt, had he not resorted to the more questionable tricks of the trade, he would by now have been appointed England's captain for the West Indian tour.

His case would be *sub judice* were the M.C.C. Committee a court of law. Public opinion observes, not for the first time, that morality can be a matter of geography: just as, if you have several wives in a man-depleted tropical island you are the best of citizens, though you would hardly be rated so highly in a London police court.

In this case, the Yorkshire columnist of a Sunday paper believes "Close's tactics to be entirely justifiable" though one, possibly without the advantages of his background, openly wished that Mike Smith, rather than Close, had been chosen to captain England in this season's last Test.

Even Richie Benaud, outstanding as a broadcaster and critic as he was as a player, took sides against him, saying that such tactics would kill cricket within a year. And Benaud fully realizes the flexibility of cricket's morality. When he came to England as Australia's captain in 1961 he announced that he had given orders to his team to "walk" when they knew they were out, without waiting for the umpire's decision. [*In a letter published two days later Benaud said that, as a result of a team meeting, it was their general policy to walk but that the matter was left entirely to the individual.*]

On the same day his book *Way of Cricket* was published, in which he told how in the Lord's Test of 1956 he had been caught at the wicket when three, had been given not out, and, according to the Australian custom at that time, had stayed on to score 97, which many of us thought had a great deal to do with Australia's victory in the match.

Time-wasting tactics are, I think, a modern invention. W. G. Grace, accused of most forms of sharp practice, never attempted them: he believed, like Mrs. Battle, in the rigour of the game – or perhaps he never thought of them. They are an off-shoot of one of the greatest evils cricket is heir to, the fact that at the highest level games of cricket are not played – only rubbers. In this case, of course, it was participation in a league table rather than a match against Warwickshire that was to blame. C. B. Fry told me that when England won the famous Oval victory in 1902 nobody grieved that the rubber and the Ashes were already lost: all rejoiced in victory in a match against Australia. In those days people knew no better than to suppose that a game was a game.

But the fact remains (though Mr. S. C. Griffith points out that M.C.C. has previously dealt with two cases of alleged time-wasting this season) this trick of the trade has come to be a recognized tactic today. You might say that it is all part of gamesmanship – to potter and not quite cheat.

My feeling is that we have only touched the fringe of the art. What have spectators to complain of: a bowler's practice run, walking back to bowl slower than ever, changing over languidly and repeated consultations due, according to Mr. Close, to the noise the crowd was making, rendering him inaudible?

Pretty primitive stuff surely. What about gaining time with a slip fields-man's broken shoelace? Or a bowler sending to the pavilion for his lucky cap (to be given to the umpire as soon as it arrives)? Or a cover-point who pleads that the crowd's noise has made him deaf and has to wait while the captain writes out instructions for him, possibly in triplicate, to provide the county committees with a copy apiece?

Then – telegrams. They used to be part and parcel of cricket, but seem to have gone out of fashion. What is to stop an imaginative captain from sending two or three to players – it always takes a valuable couple of minutes to open, read, and say there's no answer? A really thoughtful captain could send fielding orders to members of his team by telegram, if the crowd was really booing.

Then there is the wicketkeeper. Is the captain satisfied with his performance? Why not change wicketkeepers, especially if the bowler is of the pace of Hobbs, who, of course, would take a 20-yard run to the wicket to send down the slowest ball of the season?

You can try anything once, and at least puzzle the umpires. I can hear the announcer asking: "Is there a Q.C. on the ground?"

Wilfred Rhodes Reaches 90

BY A. A. THOMSON

28 *October* 1967. Mr. Wilfred Rhodes, who celebrates his ninetieth birthday tomorrow, is one of the surviving great figures of cricket's golden age. He has lived long, travelled widely, and has always been a shrewd observer of the human scene, but it is fair to say that cricket has been his life.

He and his lifelong friend, the late George Herbert Hirst, came from the same tiny hillside village in the West Riding and when, in their heyday, the question arose, "Who is England's greatest all-rounder?", the local worthies would nod sagely, murmuring enigmatically: "He bats right and bowls left; and he comes from Kirkheaton". No two men, in character and outlook, could have been more different – Hirst, dashing, exuberant; Rhodes, cool, relentless, technically a perfectionist – but, together, for Yorkshire and England, they were the consummate pair.

Rhodes's career reads like that of the industrious apprentice, blessed with a fairy godmother. In 1898 he came into the first class game as heir to Yorkshire's line of slow lefthanders, Peate and Peel; he retired 32 years later, after taking his regular 100 wickets up to the age of 50 and, more astonishingly, after enjoying a middle period as England's No. 2 batsman, opening with Hobbs, England's greatest No. 1. In the historic tour to Australia in 1911-12 these two set up a first-wicket Test record, only surpassed by Hutton and Washbrook 37 years later.

The old Yorkshire cricketers called W. G. Grace a "nonesuch" and, by any standard, Rhodes has been a nonesuch, too. In cricket there has hardly been a prize that he has not won, an objective he has not attained; 16 doubles, over 4,000 wickets, nearly 40,000 runs. His first Test match in 1899 was W.G.'s last. In his year of retirement he bowled against Bradman, who, he thinks, was the finest of all batsmen.

His career has touched the high peaks of cricket history. In the first match of the epic rubber of 1902 he and Hirst crushed the Australians for 36, and in the last – Jessop's match – he joined his fellow-Yorkshireman when 15 runs were needed. Whether they "got them in singles" or not, get them they did in an electrifying finish which brought triumph to England by one wicket.

His exploits in Warner's Australian tour of 1903-04 ranged even higher. In the second Test he exploited a Melbourne "glue-pot" to take fifteen wickets, while in the first, at Sydney, he had shared what is still a record last-wicket stand with R. E. Foster and bowled all day on a billiard-table pitch at the brilliant Victor Trumper, who hit 185 not out, but not many of them off Rhodes. Before the day's last over Trumper begged, with a rueful smile: "Now, Wilf, give us a bit of mercy."

Whereupon Rhodes bowled him the most diabolical maiden over of the day, which no one but Trumper could have survived.

Heads were shaken when in county cricket Rhodes started to score runs. "Now, Wilfred", said Lord Hawke, "no more than 20". But his scores multiplied; soon he was opening for Yorkshire and then for England. That perfect understanding between partners which we associate with Hobbs and Sutcliff sprang to life with Hobbs and Rhodes. Asked to explain the secret of this remarkable harmony, Rhodes replied with his own gruff humour: "Here's the secret: if I'm coming I say Yes; if I'm not, I say No."

In the 1914-18 War he worked on munitions, playing League cricket at the weekend. When county cricket restarted he was over 40 and the Leagues tried hard to entice him away. ("They sat on my doorstep with their contracts," he told me.)

But Yorkshire retained his allegiance, and, season after season, in devastating fashion, he headed the first class bowling averages until in 1926, another Australian year, he was dramatically recalled.

"Can you", he was anxiously asked, "still pitch them there?"

"There", he replied, "or thereabouts".

He was two and a half months away from his forty-ninth birthday and three members of the England side, including his captain, had not, at the time of Rhodes's first Test, been born. Yet it is history that in the last Test at the Oval England won the rubber and regained the Ashes. It is also history that in Australia's second innings Rhodes clinched the issue by taking four for 44.

Thirty years later he told me: "The pitch was improving. They should have put me on sooner."

That was the last of his 58 Tests, but he went on four seasons longer, taking 100 wickets in both 1928 and 1929. After his retirement in 1930 he played a season with a Scottish county and here the shadow of tragedy fell.

"I got bowled by a slow full toss", he said, "and I knew something was wrong with my eyes".

Twenty years passed before total blindness overtook him. Its onset was a double blow, for his keen, clear eyesight was the envy of all cricketers.

"Is it true", he was asked, "that when you batted with Jack Hobbs you could see the seam on the ball?"

"Ah", said he, "you should have played with Ranji. He could see the stitches."

In the years following the Second World War his sight grew worse but he faced the enemy indomitably. Seeing the ball as a small white blur, he played a remarkable game of golf. ("I've no trouble keeping my head down. I don't have to watch the ball.")

In the 1950s I watched him tending his garden. "It's no trouble", he said, "I can work between those two big white stones".

For many Septembers his friends have greeted him at the Scarborough Festival, and apart from the war years I do not think that, as player or patron, he has missed a trip to Scarborough between 1898 and 1966. He sits on the bench outside the Yorkshire dressing-room, "watching" the play by ear, criticizing the sound of an edgy stroke, holding court among old admirers.

In his blend of inflexibly firm character and splendid skills, he has been the complete cricketer. No bowler before or since has matched his classic art, his rhythmic action, his supreme command of length and flight. To the impatient batsman he was the subtlest tempter since the Serpent of Eden. His batting lacked the sheer beauty of his bowling. ("The cut was never a business stroke.") It was utilitarian, but massive, and you cannot score 39,797 runs without gifts of the highest order.

In old age and blindness there is pathos, but in Wilfred Rhodes at 90 there is no pathos, but something far, far from it. He has attained the highest reaches of his profession, which happens to be an English way of life; he retains his dry humour, his acute intelligence, his delightfully youthful complexion and, above all, the unaffected dignity of a life well lived. No pathos, indeed, but a kind of human grandeur.

Cockney with Melody in his Name and Poetry in his Action

BY ALAN GIBSON

8 *November* 1967. It is 50 years this month since Colin Blythe was killed in action, in one of those pointless attacks at the end of Passchendaele. His name was a melody in itself, his bowling action by every account was a poem; he played the violin; people who saw Rhodes, Peel, Peate, Briggs, Parker and

Verity averred that Blythe was the best slow left-arm bowler cricket has ever known.

This is probably still true. The only modern contender, I suppose, would be Lock – a great bowler, without doubt, but so different in style from Blythe as to invalidate close comparisons.

Nevertheless, Rhodes – and, later, Woolley – usually kept Blythe out of the English team. In a career lasting 15 years he played in only 19 Test matches. This was not just because Rhodes and Woolley were better batsmen. It was held that Blythe's temperament too often let him down upon the big occasion.

The figures do not bear this out. In 19 Tests he took exactly 100 wickets. This is a higher ratio of wickets to matches than any English bowler (who has reached 100) except Barnes. It is true that 59 of Blythe's wickets were taken against South Africa, but they were a strong side in that period. His 41 wickets against Australia, in nine Tests, were taken at an average of 21. His average for all Tests was under 19.

His greatest triumph was against the formidable South African side of 1907. On a turning wicket at Headingley only his bowling, and Fry's batting, won England the decisive match of the rubber. Blythe took 15 for 99 in the match, and England had 53 runs to spare after being out in the first innings for 76. According to Fry, in this match Blythe never bowled a bad length ball. But he was a sick man for days afterwards. He was one of those in whom nervous strain produces severe physical reactions.

He was perfectly happy bowling for Kent, and in all first-class matches took 2,506 wickets at an average of 16.81. Of the 11 bowlers who have taken more wickets, only Rhodes has a better average – by .10 per cent.

This aversion to Tests was rather a strange thing, since in those days county matches were usually considered almost as important. In 1893, for instance, F. S. Jackson declined to play for England against Australia, preferring to play in an important match for Yorkshire. But it was undoubtedly so, and after the first Test in 1909 Blythe was left out of the England team on the advice of a nerve specialist. He had taken 11 wickets in that Test, his best performance against Australia. He came back for the fourth, taking seven more wickets, but was unfit again for the fifth. His absence may well have cost England the rubber.

Blythe was born in Deptford in far from luxurious circumstances, and Sir Neville Cardus has recorded his astonishment at discovering that this man of the poetic run-up and musical tastes talked with a broad Cockney accent. He first played for Kent in 1899. He had gone to watch Kent play Somerset at Blackheath.

"I don't think", he said, "there were many more spectators than players. Walter Wright came out to practice and asked me to 'bowl him a few'. Captain McCanlis happened to be present and took my name and address." The following year he headed the bowling averages for the county.

From then until the outbreak of war, in spite of some fine performances from Fielder and the advent of Woolley (who modelled himself upon his forerunner), Blythe was Kent's principal attacking weapon. His most remarkable single achievement was against Northamptonshire in 1907 when he took 17 wickets in a day, for 48; all 10 for 30 in the first innings.

He was deadly on a turning wicket, but contemporaries praised as highly his ability to keep runs down when the wicket was plumb. Flight, rather than spin, was his principal ally.

He took a lot of wickets with the ball that moved on with the arm, and could make the new ball swerve (he often opened the bowling). He varied his pace subtly, kept his arm high, and often surprised batsmen out with the ball delivered from a yard or two behind the crease.

Blythe seemed an improbable soldier. Sir Home Gordon commented: "How he ever passed the medical examination must be dubious." But he became a sergeant in the Kent Fortress Engineers. At the time of his death he was attached to The King's Own Yorkshire Light Infantry, in which one may see a pleasant irony, since it was against Yorkshire that he had obtained some of his greatest successes – always a test of a cricketer. In 1903, for instance, when they were not far from their peak, he took 13 for 61 against them at Canterbury. The same season he took 11 for 97 against Lancashire at Old Trafford. I wonder if anyone else has achieved such a double as that?

He was 38 when he was killed. His powers had shown little sign of decline, and it seems probable that he would have played for England again after the First World War, since slow left arm bowlers do not usually wear out easily. It was a loss comparable to that of Verity in the Second World War. It seems singularly bitter that the fates, in succeeding generations, should have struck down so savagely two thoughtful, gracious practitioners of so delicate an art.

Rain Stops Film

28 *May* 1968, *Diary*. The film debut of Gary Sobers yesterday wasn't. Sobers was to have been performing at Vincent Square, Westminster School's pleasant tree-lined ground near Victoria, for a film called *Two Gentlemen Sharing*, but – thanks to Saturday's rain – was engaged instead in the Gillette Cup at Worcester.

Cricket may be, as they say, too leisurely for this bustling age, but – without Sobers anyway – film-making couldn't survive one summer as a spectator sport. Infinitely slowly, a camera backed before Robin Phillips and Esther Anderson, two of the stars, as they walked by slumbering extras in front of the pavilion, and Phillips fumbled with two deck chairs. Again and again. Film executives – major and minor – buzzed about.

Sobers – who should now be making his debut today – will in fact be merely an expensive "double" for Hal Frederick, an American negro actor, who plays a cricketing West Indian law student in *Two Gentlemen Sharing*.

Frederick is not a cricketer. But, said Mr. Ted Kotcheff, the genial Canadian director, he does have a coach. "Alf . . .". He turned to a knot of executives: "What's his name?" . . . "Glover" . . . "Grove" . . . "Alf Grover" . . . "Alf GOVER", one read from a list. "The Surrey" . . . "English" . . . "Test" . . . "bowler, I think" . . . "COACH".

In Sobers's absence, Frederick did face up to a couple of deliveries from John Snow, the England fast bowler, "We hired him because he can land the ball on a sixpence", said an executive. Snow landed the ball on Frederick's bat, and then thigh. "It's an Indian ball. It swings about like a pebble", Snow explained. Bad light stopped filming.

The Woman Behind the Hailstones

24 *June* 1968, *Diary*. Cricket and the occult make strange companions. But last Thursday a woman telephoned Lord's when the ground was covered in hailstones, and said: "I'm responsible for this storm. And there will be more such storms until the Australians pay their debts." Mr. Donald Carr, assistant secretary of Lord's, told a colleague of the incident at the dinner which the M.C.C. gave on Saturday night to commemorate the 200th Test match between England and Australia.

The Lord's switchgirl, he said, asked the caller for a little more information about herself. "I have occult powers so far as the weather is concerned", said the voice. "Several years ago I used these powers to break the drought in Australia. The Australians have not yet paid me for my services. My spell over their matches will continue." The Australian fast bowler, Graham McKenzie, received a similar call during the rainy second match at Leicester, evidently from the same person. Again the drought debt was her main theme.

"This woman said she wasn't fooling", continued Mr. Carr, "and she proceeded to put a spell upon our Jean over the telephone. At the end of a few seconds, Jean felt so dizzy that she cut the caller off."

In fact, using my own highly developed occult powers, I can tell Mr. Carr precisely who the sinister caller was: Mrs. Doris Munday, of Applegarth Road, W.14.

"I've been doing this for a long time", she confessed, clearly not in the least rattled at being discovered. "It was three years ago when the Australians asked me to break up their seven year drought and when I did it, they gave all the credit to the aborigines.

"They also promised to take up a collection for me, and didn't; not that I wanted the money, but I was annoyed. So I started off by smashing the Brisbane Test in 1966. I've been bashing them ever since."

Mrs. Munday, who is 49, broke into the psychic business a long time ago as a hypnotist; then about four years ago she was told by a hypnotist friend that she was a "weather manipulator".

"I was so shocked I told him to leave at once. But then I took a few tests in psychic phenomena, and sure enough I found I could do it", she recalls. Since then she claims to have broken droughts in India, China and the United States, brought freak storms throughout Britain and given countless friends sunny holidays.

Cowdrey 100 Not Out

BY JOHN WOODCOCK

10 *July* 1968. At Edgbaston tomorrow, Colin Cowdrey plays in his one hundredth Test match. It is a landmark reached by no other cricketer and one which Cowdrey will pass without thinking for one moment that a bottle of champagne is called for. He is too unassuming and abstemious for that.

Such a vast collection of "caps" is possible only in these days of regular touring. W. R. Hammond, whose Test career spanned 20 years, compared with Cowdrey's 14, made 85 appearances for England. Godfrey Evans, who is next in line to Cowdrey, made 91. Len Hutton made 79 and Denis Compton 78, with the war years intervening.

Neil Harvey, with 79, is the leading Australian; John Waite, with 50, the leading South African, Gary Sobers, with 65 the leading West Indian; John Reid with 58, the leading New Zealander, and P. R. Umrigar, with 59, the leading Indian. Of Pakistan's 53 Test matches Hanif has played in 51.

In 19 years "W.G." played in only 22 Test matches. S. F. Barnes took his 189 Test wickets in just 27 matches. Fred Trueman's 307 wickets came in 67 Tests, Don Bradman's 6,996 runs in 52.

Cowdrey so far has held 112 catches and made 6,940 runs. No one has taken more catches; only Hammond, Bradman and Hutton have made more runs. As things are going Cowdrey will soon have left them all behind with only Barrington and Sobers on his heels.

Cowdrey's baptism was in Brisbane in 1954, as the youngest member of Hutton's side. England lost that match by an innings and 154 runs, though Cowdrey's own batting was more auspicious. He made 40 in the first innings there, and 23 and 54 in the next Test at Sydney. His 102 at Melbourne, immediately after that, is, to this day, as fine an innings as he has played.

I can see him now, driving England out of trouble in the classical manner, on a green wicket with Keith Miller's mane escaping in all directions as he made to destroy England. Cowdrey was then 22: an undergraduate at Oxford on an extended vacation.

In the years that have followed, he has filled us at times with sheer delight and at times with utter despair. At his best he is such a superb batsman that one wonders why he should ever become, as he sometimes does, so deeply introspective. The answer lies somewhere in his makeup.

His modesty is a drawback to his batting. If he had ever realized just how good he really is he would have been, to an even greater extent, the despair of his opponents.

Of Cowdrey's 99 Test matches, I have seen all but a few in New Zealand. This has meant sharing the pleasure of success, the disappointment of failure, and the anxiety of the big occasion. To play in an important Test match is not the fun that many people may imagine it to be, especially for a batsman carrying the chief burden.

In Melbourne at the beginning of 1963, when England had just won a Test match, I congratulated Cowdrey on his considerable part in the victory. It was some hours after the match had finished and he had made 113 and 58 not out. I said how relieved he must be that it was all over. To which he replied: "Yes, but now there's the next one to worry about."

The strain of Test cricket, in these days of mass publicity and exaggerated criticism, is great, especially for the captains and the kings.

It is one of Cowdrey's worthiest achievements that he has stuck it for so long. While others have retired before their time, and when England could ill afford to lose them, Cowdrey has battled on, through triumph and setback, because of his love for the game and the life that goes with it.

His players admire him for this, and it is a fine reward for his perseverance and keenness that his stock stands higher now than ever before.

If he retains his form there is no reason why his remaining years for England should not be his most influential. What he would like to do, I think, is lead M.C.C. to South Africa next winter and to Australia in 1970-71 before retiring from Test cricket.

After that he should still be fit enough, and young enough in spirit, to play another three or four years for Kent, leading, one would like to think, a crusade for bold, unselfish play.

Cowdrey has four children, three of them boys who are encouraged but never forced to find fun in games. From a large house set in a beautiful garden on the borders of Kent and Surrey, he leads a busy life. His appointments book is invariably full, even when he has a match off.

Last Friday, for instance, he followed a few holes of golf with Brian Huggett in the early morning with his daily correspondence. He lunched at his old prep school, where in the afternoon he played against the boys in a match organized to raise funds for a new playing field. Having made 50 and a short speech there, he moved on to the Sports Day at his daughter's school.

I am often amazed by the things he finds time to do and the number of letters that he writes and lessons that he reads. He loves the simple life, has a quick sense of humour, a wonderful eye for ball games, a lot of friends, a stubborn streak, a rare gift for organization, and a hundred "caps" as well as a healthy desire to see the Ashes regained.

Test Selectors Win an Apology

Insole and Others v. Parkinson and Another

BEFORE MR. JUSTICE NIELD
HIGH COURT OF JUSTICE: QUEEN'S BENCH DIVISION

26 *July* 1968. Apologies were offered to Mr. Douglas Insole and his fellow Test selectors over suggestions, in an article in *The Sunday Times* of June 25 last year critical of the dropping of Geoffrey Boycott from the Test team, that in choosing it they had been actuated by "unworthy and discreditable motives".

Mr. Insole, Mr. A. V. Bedser, Mr. Donald Kenyon, Mr. Peter May and Mr. Brian Close had brought an action for libel against Times Newspapers Ltd., publishers of *The Sunday Times*, and Mr. Michael Parkinson, the writer of the article.

Mr. Michael Kempster for the plaintiffs; Mr. Brian Neill, Q.C., for the defendants.

Announcing a settlement of the action, Mr. Kempster said that Mr. Parkinson had written a long and highly critical article concerning the plaintiffs' decision to drop Mr. Boycott from the Test team notwithstanding the fact that in the previous match he had scored 246 not out. Mr. Parkinson considered that the selectors had done Mr. Boycott a very considerable injustice.

Had the matter ended there the plaintiffs would have had no wish to complain since they fully accepted that their decisions as selectors had to be open to full discussion and criticism in the press. Unfortunately certain passages in the article went considerably farther and were such as to suggest that in choosing the team the selectors had been actuated by unworthy and discreditable motives.

After the matter had been drawn to their attention the defendants had published in *The Sunday Times* an express disclaimer to the effect that it was not their contention that the selectors were actuated by any such motives, although they did not accept that the article complained of conveyed those imputations.

On further consideration, however, the defendants had realized that the article was capable of such construction. They therefore attended by counsel to withdraw the suggestions.

As the plaintiffs' object in bringing the action was to clear their names, they were content to let the matter rest. The defendants had agreed to pay their legal costs.

Mr. Neill, on behalf of the defendants, said that he associated himself with all that had been said. Without withdrawing or departing from their criticisms of the selectors' decision to drop Mr. Boycott, they were happy to make it clear that they accepted that, in reaching that decision, the selectors had not been actuated by any improper or unworthy motive and were seeking to further the best interests of the game.

The Sunday Times and Mr. Parkinson apologized to the plaintiffs for the distress which the passages in question had caused them.

Solicitors. – Halsey, Lightly & Hemsley; Theodore Goddard & Co.

Test Bowled Two Maidens Over

BY RITA MARSHALL

27 *July* 1968. In a room with three cricket photographs on the wall, and a view of St. Pancras station, sit some of the most telephoned girls in London.

They are the G.P.O.'s "Test team", and thousands of people ring them every day – dialling UMP – to hear the latest Test match score. During the present series with Australia more than six million calls have been made.

Four girls provide the voices on a continuous commentary, Miss Margaret Woodin, Mrs. Ellen Moelly, Miss Pamela Hawes and Miss Yvonne Biddulph, who comes from Guyana. Miss Biddulph said: "It got exciting when the West Indians played here. But we didn't exactly come to blows."

The girls work in teams of three. An editor is in direct link with the ground on which the Test match is being played, and two telephonists take it in turns to record the score or to check the telephone commentary against the information from the ground. The average time between getting a new score from the ground and putting it on record is 25 seconds.

Most of the girls are cricket enthusiasts, and two who were "not all that interested" are now fascinated by the game. Miss Hawes and Miss Woodin have never seen a Test Match, but said: "We are going to try and get to the Oval for the last match if we can get some tickets".

The two editors, Miss Pat Weighall and Miss Sheila Keogh, both Post Office telecommunications traffic officers, are self confessed cricket addicts. "We've offered to take our equipment to the ground", Miss Keogh said. "We have even said we would not mind the overseas tours, but we are still here".

Although they have no favourite cricketer, all the girls speak affectionately of "Uncle" Tom Graveney. Mrs. Moelly, who supports Sussex, thinks Ted Dexter is "lovely".

The Post Office Test team "reserve" is Mrs. Thelma Cumberbatch, a mother of two, who comes from Barbados and is something of a cricket expert because "I used to play it back home". She is learning the job, but said: "I haven't done very much yet. Every time it is my turn rain seems to stop play."

Bards Rejoice

Eisteddfod in the Wings

BY DAVID PARRY-JONES

6 *August* 1968. Yesterday was the first day of the 1968 national Eisteddfod in Barry, but even the bards carried transistor radios tucked under their robes as they strove to keep up with the fall of wickets 30 miles along the coast. The sheer elation when the final news came through was such that all 11 Glamorgan men must stand a chance of election to the Gorsedd.

Of course, this is the second time running that the Australians have fallen to Glamorgan, and if there were any Ashes at stake between Wales and Australia, they would now be firmly enshrined in the Guildhall at Swansea 100 yards or so from St. Helens. Sooner or later some nationalist wag is sure to say that Australia should now drop the weaker cricketing countries, such as England, from their Test engagements in order to concentrate properly on a series with Wales.

Not that Glamorgan are quite the Welshmen that they were six or eight seasons ago. Like many other counties, they are starting to resemble a Commonwealth side. Though I would be inclined to say that only Cordle, a West Indian, is a real odd man out; the other West Indian, Bryan Davis, has a name that is as Welsh as the Mumbles; while the exciting No. 4 batsman, Majid Jahangir comes from Pakistan but boasts an accent identified as mid-Rhondda.

The foundation of this victory though – and Glamorgan achieved it without their captain, Tony Lewis, who has a throat infection – was laid on the first morning with a fine 99 by Alan Jones, the left-handed opening batsman, who is a real local boy.

Now entering his 30s, Jones has served his county well, and it both puzzles and saddens us in Wales that he has never represented England (which sounds paradoxical, but you know what I mean) or toured with M.C.C. His average is at present over 40, in a low scoring season, and surely he deserves a place on the winter tour of South Africa.

Don Shepherd, the veteran off-spin bowler who acted as Glamorgan's captain, said that yesterday was one of the greatest days of his life. That is roughly what Keith Catchpole said two years ago when he led Australia to a surprise Rugby victory over Wales at Cardiff Arms Park. Revenge is very sweet.

League at Cost of Cavaliers

BY JOHN WOODCOCK, CRICKET CORRESPONDENT

21 *August* 1968. The International Cavaliers, who have given so much pleasure to cricket watchers, both around the country and on B.B.C.2, may have to go out of business next season because of the ruling, made by the counties and announced from the Lord's yesterday, that the only Sunday cricket to be televised live in 1969 will be the new one-day league. This is bad luck on the Cavaliers, who, after appropriating the name by which they are known, themselves pioneered this popular form of Sunday cricket.

A sponsor has been found, though not yet named, for the Sunday League, and both B.B.C. and I.T.A. have been invited to tender for the television rights. It is hoped that between them the new sponsors (who are not, in fact, dependent on television) and one or other of the television channels will contribute about £80,000 compared with £40,000 which the Cavaliers, in conjunction with B.B.C., had agreed to pay. This would make the Sunday League the game's richest source of income.

Of the money available, a large share will be used for making direct payments to the players who take part. It will amount, for them, to a fairly substantial pay rise.

Each county will meet the remaining 16 once in the new competition, and there will be no Sunday play in three-day championship matches.

The regulations for the Sunday League will be made known in October. It will involve an uncomfortable amount of extra travelling, though to offset this the county championship will be reduced from 28 to 24 three-day matches.

The Sunday League will be conducted on the lines of the present Cavaliers' matches – with a limited number of overs for each side, a limitation of the bowler's run-up, and special rules for days when rain takes a part. It should, in fact, be just as much fun to watch on television as the Cavaliers' matches have been, with a greater competitiveness between the sides compensating for a reduction in the all-star quality of the cast.

Sponsored by Rothmans, the cigarette company, the Cavaliers have presented the world's leading players to the English cricketing public. The large sums paid for the right to televise their matches have been ploughed back into the game; the gate money has been given either to charity or to cricketers whose benefit year it has been. Last Sunday, for instance, Don Bates, of Sussex, received a cheque for £1,200 from the match between Sussex and the Cavaliers at Hove.

To encourage the Cavaliers to continue their good work. I had thought they might be admitted into the Sunday League as the eighteenth side, so that their matches could still be televised. They were prepared to import three or four overseas players to replace those who will in future be regularly engaged with their counties. But that is not to be.

The Cavaliers have not yet committed themselves as to whether or not, in the absence of television they will fulfil their provisional programme for 1969. But a joint statement with Rothmans last night said that: "There must now be considerable doubt whether these matches can take place as envisaged."

Free Lunch for Cricket Watcher

30 *August* 1968. Loudspeakers at the Hampshire and Nottinghamshire county cricket match at Portsmouth yesterday warned a schoolboy on the ground: "Don't eat the sausage sandwiches – the sausages are off." It was from his father. The boy, Paul Brown, of Clay Hill Drive, Gosport, was then invited by loudspeaker to lunch in the members' room at Hampshire Cricket Club's expense. Afterwards he confessed: "I was so hungry that I had three of the sandwiches before I heard the warning. But I feel all right."

Mr. Vorster v. M.C.C.

19 *September* 1968, *Leading Article*. To the outside world Mr. Vorster's speech about Mr. D'Oliveira was one more indication of the mental weakness of apartheid, which is a fetish rather than a policy. To hear it said that Mr. D'Oliveira had been chosen by the anti-apartheid league sounded like the murky justifications of Pravda or Izvestia. No one ever thought that Mr. Vorster or his Government wanted a South African born man of colour to show his equality in a touring side. Nevertheless, faintly permissive noises had been made about him at the time when South Africa still hoped that its mixed team would be accepted at the Olympic Games. If the Olympic decision had not been reversed, Mr. D'Oliveira's inclusion in the M.C.C. side would have been swallowed. And even after the Olympic rejection. Mr. Vorster could not easily have objected to his initial selection on merit, without exposing himself to the charge of political interference in sport which he levelled at the Olympic committee and now levels at the M.C.C.

The offer of a contract for Mr. D'Oliveira to go to South Africa as a sports writer, and the unfortunate havering over his inclusion in the side when a vacancy occurred, gave Mr. Vorster his chance to justify exclusion to his own people. Sensible South African cricketers will not accept his absurd allegations, but they will be accepted by the mass of Afrikaner opinion which is sore about Mexico but not so keen on cricket. There may be trouble over the All-Blacks Rugby tour, which touches the Afrikaners more closely. The M.C.C. is the perfect Aunt Sally.

Mr. Vorster is thus able to give a sop to the right-wing malcontents in his party, the "Verkramptes". They denounced the racial concessions made to the Olympic committee, and exploited the ensuing humiliation. They would have opposed the relaxation of the rules of "petty apartheid" at social occasions for Mr. D'Oliveira, just as they do relaxations in favour of the black diplomats whom Mr. Vorster's "forward policy" will supposedly bring to Pretoria.

These extremists are not dominant, but Mr. Vorster has shown he is willing enough at times to appease them. The fact that they have won another point should caution those who think political principle has been vindicated now that the M.C.C. is virtually precluded from touring South Africa. Among Afrikaners the way this issue has emerged is a political defeat, not victory, for liberal ideas.

Sport is possibly not a "bridge" into South Africa that can bear much ideological traffic. It did carry some. It was worth preserving because contacts with South Africa cannot be ended, but they will be less beneficial when they are confined to diplomacy and business. More and more cut off from reality and the world, South African society will increasingly accept the paranoid decisions and dogmas of the ruling party and that party's inner clique. A hunger for respect and recognition by the world nevertheless remains – as was shown by South African pride in Dr. Barnard's achievements. So long as South Africa retains any sensitivity to outside opinion, so long as its conscience can be kept alive by any means, the loss of contacts must be regretted.

Freddie Trueman Retires

BY JOHN WOODCOCK, CRICKET CORRESPONDENT

11 *November* 1968. Frederick Sewards Trueman, now in his thirty-eighth year, has announced his retirement from first-class cricket. "Time marches on", he said. It takes with it a character who has enriched the game and a fast bowler of monumental achievement.

Trueman holds the record bag of Test wickets. Between 1952 and 1965 he took 307 in 67 appearances for England. These are figures which tell well enough of a wonderful natural talent.

He was born with a rhythm for bowling and a strong physique which assured him of cricketing success. But what marked him out from other cricketers, apart from his ability, was his temperament, which was forthright, and his sense of humour, which was basic.

His best years were from 1958 until 1964, though right from the start he was attended by success. His first series for England was in 1952, when he took 29 wickets in 119.4 overs and put the Indians to flight.

In 1953 he had a part in England's at last regaining the Ashes, and in 1955 he established a partnership with Brian Statham which became as famous and as fecund as that between Larwood and Voce or Lindwall and Miller. Both Trueman and Statham were superb fielders, and the years of their prime coincided with a period of English ascendancy.

But it was Trueman's personality as much as his prowess that made him star quality. Wherever he appeared – from Bradford to Brisbane, via Bridgetown and Bombay – he was cheered on sight.

Of England's fast bowlers since the war, Tyson, for a short time, was the fastest, Statham the most accurate, and Trueman the most volatile. He emerged from the coal face, as it were, of a mining village – rough hewn and with a strong disinclination to compromise his character. Because of this he blotted his copybook in the West Indies in 1953-54 and was left out of M.C.C. teams to Australia in 1954-55 and South Africa in 1956-57.

I am reluctant to believe that characters are many fewer now than they were; but it may be a long time before another comes along of Trueman's calibre. Last year he took only 66 wickets, so that he is wise to give up before his powers fail and to accept a lucrative offer from the International Cavaliers.

Undoubtedly, Trueman goes down as one of the greatest of all fast bowlers. Sometimes with spectacular success he wielded a bat like a pickaxe, and had he put his mind to it he could have made many more runs than he did.

Because of who and what he is, many of the best cricket stories are attributed now to Fred. That is a compliment initself. But here, as an example, is an authentic specimen.

During the M.C.C. tour to Australia in 1962-63, at a civic reception in Perth, a bishop mounted the platform. Trueman to David Sheppard, wearing a dog collar for the occasion: "Is that your senior pro?" This, for once, is an unexpurgated version.

Wilson's Hitting Fails to Save Yorkshire

BY JOHN WOODCOCK, CRICKET CORRESPONDENT

28 *April* 1969. Considering the weather, which was cold but dry, and the fact that the sides were short of confidence and practice, the Player's Sunday League got away to a most encouraging start at Lord's yesterday. Middlesex beat Yorkshire by 43 runs, in one of the lower scoring matches of the day, and I am sure the 5,000 spectators who watched them do so will look forward to coming again.

Yorkshire were without Trueman and Illingworth. But for a swashbuckling effort by Don Wilson, who made all but half their score, they would have been humbled rather than merely beaten. None of their bowlers was anywhere near as accurate and lively as Price, and their five main batsmen managed only 21 runs between them. Where Yorkshire excelled was in their fielding, which was splendid. But so, too, was the Middlesex fielding.

For Yorkshire there were some brilliant saves by Wilson, and Balderstone threw Hooker out from mid-off in just about a perfect piece of work. Sharpe, too, made his usual blinding catch at slip. For Middlesex, Parfitt started the Yorkshire rot by a fine diving catch at second slip in Connolly's first over in his new colours, and Price, whether bowling or fielding, was in irresistible form.

Price found it about as easy squeezing that long and stuttering approach into 15 yards as he might do trying to fit himself into a baby's cot. But once he had done it he worked up a good pace, and following through to his own bowling he ran out Boycott, who had been called for a sharp single by Padgett.

For most of the time the wicketkeeper stood back. For much of it the field was far flung. Yet the overall impression was one of urgency. There is really no time for much else in a match beginnng at 2 o'clock and scheduled to end by 6.30. Yesterday's game was over by 6.10, by when Wilson had earned himself three shares of £1,000 – the sum to be distributed among all those who hit a six in the competition.

Middlesex were indebted to Parfitt and Radley for pulling their own innings round after a rather wanton start in which Smith and Russell cast away their wickets. Parfitt got things going with some brisk running and a succession of spirited strokes. Radley picked up the idea, and later on Keith Jones, an all rounder from Shepherds Bush, played uncommonly well.

Yorkshire's chance of winning was virtually gone within a dozen overs. Price saw to that. There was Parfitt's catch and Price's run out, and then Padgett and Hampshire were both out to balls that lifted. There followed a partnership between Wilson and Binks which added 48 and was ended by Hooker just as it was getting dangerous for Middlesex.

MIDDLESEX 137 for 8 (40 overs)
YORKSHIRE 94 (32.2 overs) (D. Wilson 46)
Middlesex won by 43 runs

Milburn May not Play again in Tests

BY JOHN WOODCOCK

26 *May* 1969. With his spirit unimpaired, Colin Milburn was receiving visitors and messages and gifts at the General Hospital, Northampton, yesterday. He has already got fruit enough to open a stall, though when I saw him on my way to Leicester he was wanting a newspaper so that he might catch up with Saturday's scores. Not surprisingly, none was delivered with his morning tea.

Having spent 24 hours feeling quite sick at the news of Milburn's accident, I left him encouraged, as everyone will be, by his cheerfulness. He was never unconscious following the crash, and when the ward sister told him after the operation of the loss of his eye, he was not surprised. A shattered windscreen did the damage, and he does not believe that a seat belt would have saved him. He has several nasty cuts about the forehead and face, and there are seven stitches in his right knee; but on his right eye there is only one slight scratch.

It is hard to believe, even with such unquenchable spirit, that Milburn will ever play Test cricket again. He, bless him, has no doubt that he will. "Buster" Nupen played for South Africa with one eye, but he was a bowler; and more recently, the Nawab of Pataudi has batted wonderfully well after having an eye badly cut, also in a motor accident.

But in Pataudi's case it was the right eye that was injured, and, as he has written himself, the light which the bad eye let in was a great help to the good one. He tried unsuccessfully to bat with a pirate's patch. These are worn sometimes in the shooting field to counter a master eye, but they create their own problems of judgment and timing. It is necessary only to put a hand over one's right or one's left eye to realize this.

Again, to a right-handed batsman, which Milburn is, the left eye, even when it is not the master eye, is still the less dispensable of the two. To play with his right eye only would necessitate an unnaturally open stance. A specialist at the hospital thought that Milburn's master eye was almost certainly the right one, which would, of course, be a help. It generally is, apparently, in the case of good right-handed games players. In the specialist's view, the extent of a man's adjustment to such a handicap depends first of all on the individual; and if anyone can overcome it and still be a first-class batsman, I am sure Milburn will.

That the accident should have happened to him of all people, at a time when the game is short of characters, is particularly cruel. He is looked upon with genuine affection by friend no less than foe and by everyone who meets him. In the last two or three years he has played a number of innings of incredible devastation, and he is still only 27. Only last winter he scored 181 between luncheon and tea playing for Western Australia against Queensland, and in his only championship match this season he made 158 against Leicestershire.

Before his accident he was English cricket's greatest asset and its most lovable personality. If surgery permitted it, I am sure thousands of cricketers would gladly present him with an eye, and in an effort to disperse the gloom it would be nice if his first-class colleagues were all to have a Milburn day – when they played the game for fun and not for figures. He hopes to leave hospital within a fortnight's time and to have a false eye fitted within a month or two of that.

Glamorgan Have a One-sided Victory

BY ALAN GIBSON

18 *June* 1969; *Bournemouth*. "When the umpire shall call 'play,' the party refusing to play shall lose the match." This, referring both to the state of play, and to intervals (including the fall of a wicket) was set down in the Laws of Cricket as revised by the Marylebone Club in 1830. It has always been, and remains, the basic assumption of any match at cricket.

I suppose the result of this match should be recorded as: "Glamorgan won because Hampshire refused to play." Not that they refused in any deliberate sense. They had simply gone away under the impression that the match was over.

To set the scene: at the beginning of the day Glamorgan faced with Hampshire's declared total of 337, had scored 256 for seven. A. R. Lewis, the Glamorgan captain, slightly surprisingly, decided to bat on. He was presumably hoping for a few more quick boundaries from E. Jones, who indeed got a couple of lusty ones. But when Jones was caught and bowled, after 20 minutes, Glamorgan declared, which was sad for Williams, who was just beginning to get his eye in.

The Hampshire second innings had not really begun to take shape when the rain started. It was slow, persistent, dismal rain. Lunch was taken early. The rain drizzled on. We longed for a storm to end the futility of hanging around. Duty, not hope, kept us miserably waiting.

The public, such as them as were present, was given no indication of what decisions might be taken about the future of play, and gradually drifted away. At four o'clock, sitting in the little pavilion and contemplating a cold, flat beer, I saw the Hampshire team leave, changed and off to the next engagement. I concluded that all was over, and ordered a taxi.

Perhaps five minutes later the Glamorgan team came out of their dressing room, also changed, packed, and ready to depart. A. R. Lewis spoke, casually but sensibly enough, to the senior umpire, Wight. Lewis said: "I suppose it is all off?" Wight replied to this effect: "There are more than two hours to go, the rain is not heavy, the wicket will be playable almost as soon as it stops. It is far too early to abandon the match." Someone said: "Does Marshall know?" Wight replied: "I have not been asked."

In this decision Wight was, in my view, unquestionably right, and his fellow umpire, Budd – a former Hampshire player – was strong in agreement with him.

So Glamorgan stayed on the ground. Efforts were unsuccessfully made to contact the scattered Hampshire team. At 5 o'clock the rain had almost stopped. The umpires made an inspection and ordered mopping up operations. Satisfied with these, they decreed a resumption of play at 5.30.

Glamorgan, unnecessarily, changed back into flannels (or thereabouts Walker was partly revealing a fetching pink undergarment) and took their places on the field. Budd, the bowling umpire, called "Play". It was all quite properly done. There was no unseemly hurry, Cordle marked out his run.

And then, at 5.31 – believe me I do not exaggerate – the flimsy drizzle developed into serious rain. A batsman might have been justified in walking off, but there were no batsmen. Glamorgan stoically stuck it out in the field (Walker had taken up an aggressive position within the return crease), Wight looked at his watch, measuring every agonizing second, and after the necessary two minutes turned back towards the pavilion.

Glamorgan had taken 10 points for a win, because the other party had refused to play. This gave them 12 points to Hampshire's seven, though I suppose it is arguable, and will be argued, whether a side failing to come up to the scratch is entitled to any points at all.

No criticism can be made of the umpires. The weather was good enough at 5.30 to resume play, and though it rained shortly thereafter both sides had played through heavier rain in the morning. The question why Marshall, the Hampshire captain, was so confident that the game was over, is more difficult. I was assured by the umpires that they had said nothing whatsoever to give him such an impression. My own guess is that it started from one of those well meaning busybodies who are sometimes found at cricket grounds. A glance at the foreboding sky, a wave of the hand, and "all off!" they knowingly say. And the rest of us, also liking to be busy and knowing, pass it on to our neighbours – "All off! All off!" – and it percolates to the dressing room. Still, it is a captain's job to make sure.

HAMPSHIRE 337 for 5 dec (R. M. C. Gilliat 114, B. A. Richards 80, P. J. Sainsbury 66) and 28 for 1
GLAMORGAN 270 for 9 dec (E. Jones 85, Majid Jehangir 74; D. W. White 6 for 58)
Glamorgan won by default

The decision was later overturned and the matched declared a draw.

A Great Day for the Irish

BY RICHARD STREETON

3 *July* 1969. Even the Duke of Wellington – the Iron Duke of Napoleonic fame, that is – who played cricket for Ireland in his youth, never quite achieved a comparable victory. A hard man to please, he would have been proud of his successors yesterday. For the mighty West Indian cricketers, straight from the Lord's Test match with England, were routed for 25 runs in their one-day game against Ireland.

This piece of cricket history will scarcely be credited in the sugar cane fields of Barbados or the rum shops of Kingston. But they know differently in Sion Mills, a village some 15 miles outside Londonderry, where it all happened. The little people were in good humour yesterday morning and the rest was inevitable.

Now, of course, Sion Mills will appear for ever in Wisden. But the staid prose of the cricketers' Bible will hardly tell the whole story. There is little scope between the covers for mention of the part played by the leprechauns in Ireland's triumph. Wisden will mention how reaction after the stress of a Test match affected the West Indians. Wisden will also speak of a tiring journey from London and the difficulties of batting on a wicket both green and wet from overnight rain.

The West Indians actually lost their first six wickets for eight runs, and they heard the howling of Irish wolves. Clyde Walcott, the team's manager, making a rare appearance, then called on all his experience to thwart his opponents – both seen and unseen – to the extent of making six runs. Grayson Shillingford, from Dominica, where it is too hot for leprechauns, did even better and made the top score of nine. The West Indians at least reached double figures as the fairies relented a little.

When Ireland batted they established a lead of 100 runs and then declared with two wickets in hand – an imperious gesture but an opportunity not to be missed. It had the added advantage of letting the crowd see the touring team bat again.

The official result under the laws of cricket goes down to posterity as a win for Ireland by nine wickets on first innings. The details will be pasted in many a scrapbook in Sion Mills, described by a helpful assistant in the local library as having one street, 1,569 souls at the 1966 census and with linen mills providing the main source of employment. In the Caribbean the same details will be regarded with awe for a long time.

Emmott Robinson

19 *November* 1969. Mr. Emmott Robinson, the Yorkshire all-rounder, died on Monday.

Emmott Robinson was 35 before he first played for Yorkshire. Between 1919 and 1931 he scored nearly 10,000 runs and took just over 900 wickets, helping to form, with Rhodes, Waddington, Macaulay, Kilner and E. R. Wilson, one of the two strongest county attacks in cricket history. In such a powerful side his chances of shining were limited, yet year after year he would bat creditably and take his 60 or 70 wickets, never quite achieving the double, but coming near to it several times, notably in 1928, with 926 runs and 113 wickets. In 1926 he shared with Leyland Yorkshire's record sixth-wicket partnership of 276 and for a dozen seasons he fielded with prehensile audacity in the close positions.

Though not a cricketer of princely rank, like Hirst or Rhodes, Sutcliffe or Hutton, he was as true a Yorkshireman as any; indeed, the Yorkshire terrier might have been his symbol: tenacious, belligerent and slightly shaggy. For him the smoking chimneys of Bramall Lane were as happy a background as were the green trees and bright bannerets of Canterbury for Frank Woolley. To him Yorkshire cricket was everything; victory for Yorkshire was a law of life; defeat an outrage. He tried with heart and soul to capture a wicket with every ball he bowled and from his fine grey head to his turned-in toes, he was Yorkshire incarnate.

North-country crowds knew him well and savoured his image with a kind of wry affection: his concertina trousers, the Christopher Robin hoppity-hop in the middle of his run-up, the wicked outswinger that took the batsman's breath (and bails) away. They chuckled over his uncanny judgment of a wicket's texture, which enabled him to advise his captain on matters of declaration in terms of minutes rather than hours ("No, Mr. Wilson, not twenty-five past – twenty past.")

He held high place in Yorkshire's long line of rich comedy characters, which stretches from Tom Emmett to Freddie Trueman. Anecdotes of his pugnacity are innumerable and, even when apocryphal, highly characteristic. Fielding at suicidally silly mid-off, he was warned by a dashing but humane batsman to step back out of mortal danger. "Thee get on with thi lakin', Mr. Foster", said Emmott austerely, "and I'll get on with mine".

A Cambridge batsman, after a few flashing hits, was bowled by a superlative ball which pitched on the leg-stump and whipped away his off-bail. "By jove", he murmured, as he passed on his way out of history, "that was a beauty."

"It was an' all", said Emmott. "It were wasted on thee."

In his later playing years he nobly served the game by the encouragement and cunning coaching he gave to the youthful Bowes and Verity. Not for them the cinema in the evening; in their hotel bedrooms, with the aid of shaving sticks and tooth-brushes, Emmott would demonstrate just how badly they had bowled that day. To refrain from obloquy was his only praise. And they loved him for it.

Race Vindication for Yorkshire

21 *November* 1969. Yorkshire cricket club's policy of allowing only Yorkshire-born players to represent the county is not a breach of the Race Relations Act, our Race Relations correspondent writes.

This was stated yesterday by the Race Relations Board, who said that the 76 M.P.s who have signed a Commons motion on the subject appeared to have misunderstood the Act completely. The motion urges that the Act be amended to allow the club to continue its policy.

The board said: "To be born a Yorkshireman is undoubtedly a distinction. But merely being born in Yorkshire does not in any way distinguish a man by colour, race or ethnic or national origin – and that is what the Act is all about."

Rhodesia Snubs Asian Boy

15 *December* 1969; *Salisbury*, 14 *December*. A 17-year-old Asian schoolboy cricketer, Haroom Ismail, who won the prize for the best batting performance at the national school trials last week, has not been selected for the Rhodesian team which is to play in South Africa. He was not allowed to eat in the same room as his white team mates.

Mr. A. I. Kassim, chairman of the boy's league club, said: "If we had known he was going to be subjected to all this humiliation, we would have asked him not to go. Rhodesian sportsmen have always boasted that politics does not enter sport."

Six Killed in Stampede at Test

FROM OUR CORRESPONDENT

17 *December* 1969; *Calcutta*, 16 *December*. Six people were killed and at least 30 seriously injured in a stampede outside the Eden Gardens stadium in Calcutta this morning, three hours before play began on the fourth day of the fourth Test between India and Australia.

A large crowd had been waiting for tickets at the stadium since last night and an hour before the counters opened this morning, many people broke away from the queues and tried to force their way through the gates. Police used tear gas and batons to disperse them and they retaliated by throwing stones.

Seized by panic, the whole crowd started running and a stampede resulted.

The situation was soon brought under control and play began on time. Australia won the match with all its wickets intact.

It was inside this stadium three years ago that a day's play in a Test between India and the West Indies was disrupted by rioting because more people had been sold tickets than could be accommodated.

The trouble today occurred because the demand for tickets exceeded the available accommodation.

Hobbs's Home Goes

28 *January* 1970. The terraced house in River Place, Sleaford Street, Cambridge, where Sir Jack Hobbs grew up and learnt to play cricket is to be pulled down under a slum clearance order.

Graeme Pollock without Peer

FROM JOHN WOODCOCK

31 *January* 1970; *Cape Town*, 30 *January*. Graeme Pollock, South Africa's greatest batsman and regarded by many as the best in the world, has no army of supporters or aircraft of his own, no fetish for fitness or yearning for retirement. He is just a mild, straightforward, easy-going fellow with a gift for batting, which it pleases him to use.

He enjoys living in Port Elizabeth, where he was brought up, because it's "away from the rat race". He is very much a home town boy. His father was editor of the *Port Elizabeth Herald* until he died last year; his wife is a Port Elizabeth girl and his young son is being nourished on Port Elizabeth air. When Graeme has some spare time from his new job as sales manager of a large group of clothing companies, he likes to round up two or three friends for a few frames of snooker at the club. It's a game with a tempo that suits him. Anything for the quiet life. In the field he likes to stand at slip. This involves a minimum of running and there is always someone close by with whom to discuss the less important matters of the day.

On the afternoon before a Test match when the teams are at practice you will see Eddie Barlow or Graeme's brother, Peter, or Trevor Goddard with their shirts clinging to their backs. Graeme will scarcely break out of a canter if he can help it. When last summer he was in England playing for the International Cavaliers, he and his wife rented a flat within a long iron shot of Lord's but it would never have occurred to him to go there for a net. He played for me in a village match in Hampshire and produced the perfect innings. In the evening he drank beer with the village side without the least embarrassment either to himself or them.

Graeme's grandfather was a Scottish Presbyterian minister. His own father had a year or two at Heriot's before the family came to South Africa to settle. The ability to play games is inherited though not until the present generation has it been so marked. Graeme and his elder brother, Peter, who is still South Africa's opening bowler, are the sons of a father who kept wicket for Orange Free State and a mother who played tennis for Natal.

Graeme could walk when he was eight months old and he was making centuries by the time he was nine years old. Just before he was 17 he became the youngest South African cricketer to score a first class 100 and just after he was 19 he scored a double 100 at an earlier age than any other South African. "For a long time," says his brother, "I thought he was sure to be found out. He was always so much better than the rest of us and we were all quite a bit older." But it has yet to happen. Graeme is still, at the age of 25, in a class of his own. But he is old enough now to worry about it. The more that is expected of him the more nervous he becomes. This is never evident but he assures me it is so.

He was at Grey High School in Port Elizabeth from the age of six to 16. The coach there at the time was George Cox, of Sussex, himself a true son of nature. Realizing that he had a rare talent in his hands Cox left well alone. I wish Graeme could have seen George on one of those days at Hove when his cap grew more faded in the sun and the shots he played were too brilliant to have come from any text book. A year after leaving school Graeme visited England with his parents and, at Cox's suggestion, he played half a dozen matches for Sussex second eleven.

By the time he was 18 he had decided to concentrate on cricket. It was not as rough a game as rugger, at which he excelled as a stand-off half, and it was less strenuous than tennis. Like Cliff Drysdale, with whom he played a lot of tennis, he had a two-handed backhand and at one time there was nothing to choose between them. By 1962 the New Zealanders were returning home from a tour to South Africa and saying that they had seen in Port Elizabeth the player of the future. And when the late Ron Roberts took a side to South Africa at the end of that year he came back with reports of a prodigy who had made 209 not out for Eastern Province.

A year later Graeme began his Test career. It was in Australia on a tour which started with his making nought and one against Western Australia in the first match. In the following week, after he had scored a century in 88 minutes against a combined eleven, Don Bradman said to him: 'If you ever play an innings like that again I hope I'm there to see it." Well, he has been doing so ever since – the last of them was against the Australians at Port Elizabeth recently when he made 105 in 102 minutes. On that tour of Australia he treated Bradman to an innings of 175 at Adelaide (he and Barlow added 341 for South Africa's third wicket) and another of 122 at Sydney. On his only tour to England his 125 at Trent Bridge ranks among the finest innings of post-war cricket.

But if Bradman applauded Pollock's style of batting I am not sure that he can have approved of his view of records. In the Don's heyday there used to be a general exodus from shops and offices to watch him bat. If he was not out at lunch it was a safe bet that he would be there well into the afternoon if not the evening. When he made 309 in a single day against England at Leeds he described it as "a nice bit of practice for tomorrow". With Graeme Pollock it is different. Once past his 100 he is happy enough for someone else to take a turn.

As a captain he receives only moderately good notices. It may be that he is too phlegmatic for the job or not sufficiently dedicated, or perhaps because he has never really had to work at the game himself, he finds it difficult to comprehend the problems which lesser batsmen have to contend with. The most successful captains are not always the most talented and popular cricketers.

From his colleagues in the South African side come, quite independently, much the same observations . . . "Just a nice uncomplicated guy. . . ." "If he were twice as ambitious they'd never get him out. . . ." "Tricky to run with because he's always after the strike. . . ." Bill Lawry, the Australian captain, is less enthusiastic – "A good bad ball player – but he's always giving the bowler a chance." Richie Benaud on the other hand puts Graeme on a pedestal partly because of the caning he got from him in Australia. Bobby Simpson does the same and so I fancy does Gary Sobers.

When Sobers joined Nottinghamshire he was asked whether there was anyone else he'd particularly like the county to try to sign. The name Sobers gave was Pollock, who was approached and for a while thought seriously about it. What the struggling bowlers of other counties would have said I am not sure. I doubt whether the seam bowlers would have liked it, for they are Graeme's favourite dish. "Good fast bowlers and good spinners are a challenge. The easiest to attack are the medium pacers."

But Sobers and Pollock will never play for Nottinghamshire together. After one more visit to Australia in 1971, Graeme intends, though he will be only 28, to confine his cricket to South Africa. If so, South Africa's forth-coming tour to England may provide English cricket lovers with a last look at a splendid batsman. He is not the most elegant player of the day, as with his considerable height he might be, and he is certainly not the fittest. But with less fuss and effort than the rest he inflicts the greatest damage on a bowler's pride.

Champion County Face Giant Bolster too

BY ALAN GIBSON

25 *April* 1970. Cornwall today at Truro make their first appearance in the Gillette Cup. They will be the fifteenth of the 19 Minor Counties to play in the competition, and they have every intention of becoming the first to beat a first-class county, and the champions [*Glamorgan*] at that. Certainly they can expect a large and enthusiastic crowd to watch them try.

Cornish cricket has never made much of a stir in the world; nothing comparable with Cornish rugby. They earned their place in the cup by finishing third last season, and only narrowly missed being able to challenge Bucking-hamshire for the championship. But that is the highest position they have ever held. Yet there is considerable enthusiasm for the game in the county, and much care in its organization.

For many years league cricket has been popular among Cornish clubs, and the approach has been strongly competitive; more so than, for instance, in the gentler if more polished atmosphere of club cricket in Devon. I have spent many afternoons watching Cornish league matches which were not only pleasant (for some of the grounds are lovely) but compelling.

I remember particularly a perfect day at Mullion, and a fine innings, which just failed to win the match, by the professional Billy Strauss (who won wider fame as a footballer with Aberdeen and Plymouth Argyle). There was much excitement at the climax. Crowds used to be quite large at these matches, the holiday visitors swelling them in season, though I gather that – as with other forms of cricket – there has been a decline in recent years. Still, this familiarity with competition ought to help a minor county to make a respectable showing in the Gillette.

One attractive feature of the game in Cornwall is that quite small places, little more than villages, are able to compete effectively against the sides of the larger towns. Mullion always used to have a good side. Troon has pro-duced some fine cricketers, and Gorran, and St. Just-in-Penwith, as well as the more obvious places such as Falmouth and Camborne and Penzance. Cornwall's captain last season, G. R. Harvey, came from St. Columb. A former captain of Blundell's, he averaged 58, which put him at the top of the Minor Counties' averages.

From St. Columb, too, came Jack Crapp, who is, I suppose, the best cricketer Cornwall has produced, at least in modern times (though R. T. Weeks was in the Warwickshire championship side of 1951). He joined the Gloucestershire staff in the mid-thirties, and when in 1938 he scored 1,700 runs, it was clear there was a good one on the way. Wisden commented that year that he "would have improved further by the more general use of his natural aptitude to force the game", which reads oddly to those of us only familiar with him in his latter years, when he used frequently to get out through genial attempts to hoick the spinners over long on. Crapp was a left-hander, who played with credit against the terrible Australians of 1948 and again for England in South Africa the following winter. In his career he scored 23,500 runs at an average of 35, with 38 centuries. His warm and tranquil personality was, and remains today in the umpire's white coat, a splendid advertisement for Cornish character and Cornish sport.

Harvey's predecessor as captain was R. W. Hosen, a capable all-rounder, and one of the many rugby players who have also represented Cornwall at the summer game. R. A. W. Sharp, a wicket-keeper who was in the running for a blue at Oxford, is another.

I am sure that the improvement in Cornish standards of play must owe a good deal to the end-of-season tours undertaken in recent years by the Crusaders XI, organized by Mr. Ross Salmon, and containing many of the best cricketers in the country. These matches have not only enhanced the popularity of the game, but given Cornish cricketers experience against top-class players. Lack of such experience has always been a handicap: they play only eight matches in the championship, all in the south-west. They used to venture further – Cornish sides have played at the Oval – but the difficulties of geography and finance have become too severe. Thanks to the Crusaders, the mountain has come to Mahomet, or, more appropriately one might say, to the Giant Bolster, who once reigned over west Cornwall.

I think it was Edmund Blunden who put forward the theory that the first known cricket match was played between the Giant Cuchullain and a hundred Colts of Ulster (score: Colts, b. Cuchullain, o; Cuchullain, not out, 1). Now Cuchullain and Bolster were not only contemporaries but in all probability relations.

What more natural than that the Irish giant should have passed on a few tips to his Cornish cousin? Let Cornwall therefore take the field this morning confident in the knowledge of an illustrious and venerable history. Surely old Bolster will be there, six miles high, one foot on Carn Brea and one on St. Agnes Beacon, peering down over the Truro ground to urge them on.

Why Not to Cancel

2 *May* 1970, *Leading Article*. The Times has expressed the opinion that the M.C.C. should have called off this year's tour by South African cricketers immediately after the refusal of the South African Government to admit Mr. D'Oliveira as a member of the M.C.C. party to tour that country in the winter of 1968-69. The reason for doing so was not the objection that is taken here to the South African manner of selecting their players, for that would have been to offer South Africa the very discourtesy that was complained of in their case, namely interference in the other people's prerogative to select whom they want to. The 1970 tour should have been cancelled in order to make it absolutely plain to the South Africans that we will brook no inter-ference of that kind. That was a sufficient reason in itself. There was a further reason for withdrawing at that stage in that Mr. Vorster's action made it inevitable that the 1970 tour would not pass without a great deal of bitterness.

The M.C.C. took a different view. Primarily in the interests of cricket, also in the belief that the maintenance of links with South African cricketers is more likely than their severance to promote the cause of multiracial sport in South Africa, the M.C.C. decided to proceed with the tour. Though in our opinion wrong, the decision was reasonable on both counts, and it was one which the M.C.C. was fully entitled to make. It is of the essence of a free and plural society that persons and organizations may make decisions and act lawfully upon them, however vehemently other persons and organizations may hold those decisions to be wrong. That is toleration, a principle with difficulty established and precariously preserved during the long course of British civil history.

In the meantime explicit and credible threats have been made to bring about the unlawful disruption of the matches by physical means. These threats make it more difficult for the Cricket Council (to which responsibility has been transferred from the M.C.C.) to reverse the decision. They also make it imperative that it should not. For there is now at stake something of more importance than the disputable question whether playing with the South Africans does more than not playing with them to dent apartheid. We are now posed within our own society with the proposition that one section of people may, in what seems a good cause, forcibly impose their view on another section of people by unlawful means. That is to substitute mob rule for the rule of law.

The disorders that may be expected to occur could be ridden out, and would be worth riding out in order to indicate the principle of civil toleration. But there is another dimension to the affair which causes some who would otherwise concur with that to withdraw and demand that the tour be now cancelled. They are deeply and justly anxious about the effect of disorder surrounding these matches on race relations.

It is possible to share these anxieties to the full without concluding that it would be expedient to cancel the tour. In the first place its enforced cancellation at this stage and in these circumstances would be deeply resented by some non-demonstrating sections of the community, and the resentment would be directed if not against coloured people at least against the fervent propagandists of racial integration. Secondly, it needs to be asked precisely how racial disharmony is likely to be provoked by the tour. It will not come primarily and directly from resentment on the part of the coloured communities at the presence here of white South African cricketers. The main impetus of the campaign to stop the tour has not come from them; their organizations have entered the lists at a fairly late stage in the agitation. The damage will be done by mass demonstrations, menacing or violent at the fringes, by battles with the police, by disorders in or around the grounds on which the games are played – all having at their root a conflict of ideas about racial policy. They will not be race riots (if riots they become) but they will be riots concerning race, which are almost as poisoning and polarizing in their effect.

It is said that the whole blame for this prospect rests with the Cricket Council for its "provocation" in persevering with the tour. It is almost as if to demonstrate or go in for disruption in the face of this provocation were an incontrollable impulse. It is not. It is a calculated act. And if it is a reasonable calculation that mass demonstrations will provide cover for disorders, and that disorder will lead to a deterioration of race relations in our cities, then those whose primary concern in the matter is not to seek release for their moral indignation but to prevent the hardening of racial antagonism may be asked to draw the conclusion that they had better not turn out on the streets and had better use their influence to persuade others not to do so. Of all the advice which has been so freely given by important people to those among whom they have influence, that of Mr. Victor Feather is the most sensible: if you disapprove of these matches, have nothing to do with them.

Plan to Disrupt Cricket Tour with Locusts

11 *May* 1970. A London University student said yesterday that a plan had been devised to wreck the South African cricket tour with an army of locusts. By the time the tourists arrived 500,000 would be ready for release on cricket pitches so that they would eat the grass, he said.

Mr. David Wilton-Godberford, a biology student aged 20, already has 50,000 of the insects at his home at Colwyn Bay. He said that friends were also breeding them in secret in other parts of North Wales.

The breeds he intends to use are the desert locust and African migratory locust. They will be up to $1\frac{1}{2}$in. long, harmless to human beings, and unable to fly.

In a brick building behind his home rows of small glass-fronted cages contain thousands of locusts, kept warm by the heat from electric bulbs. There are also scores of bottles containing eggs.

Mr. Wilton-Godberford, who said he was against violence, explained: "I abhor apartheid and this is to be my personal protest. Anything up to 100,000 locusts will be let loose at a particular ground and I think the plan is foolproof. They will ravage every blade of grass and green foliage. The greatest care will be taken to ensure they are in the correct physiological stage. So that their insatiable appetites will not be impaired they will not be fed for 24 hours before the moment of truth.

"It takes 70,000 hoppers 12 minutes to consume one cwt. of grass. The crack of a solid army of locusts feeding on the grass will sound like flames. The South Africans are going to dread this trip; they will see more locusts than they have ever done back home."

He said the insects would probably die within a month because of the climate and certainly before their wings developed.

The tour was called off on 22 May following a request from the Home Secretary.

Sobers Gets Ovation in Rhodesia

FROM IAN SMITH

14 *September* 1970; *Salisbury*, 13 *September*. Gary Sobers, the West Indian cricketer, left Salisbury tonight after a two-and-a-half day visit to Rhodesia, during which he won the hearts of Rhodesian cricket fans.

After he had made a short, farewell speech today at the end of play on the police ground, 7,000 fans gave him a standing ovation and three cheers and then sang "For he's a jolly good fellow".

Throughout his visit, Sobers played the diplomat, avoiding comment on the political issues which have bedevilled Rhodesia's sport with the outside world since the Unilateral Declaration of Independence (U.D.I.) nearly five years ago.

He told the crowd today that his visit had given him "something to think about", adding, "I enjoyed it very much indeed". His partner in a $1,000 single-wicket competition, Ali Bacher, the Springbok captain, said he would like to see Sobers play again – further south.

Sobers said in an interview that he would like to see the Rest of the World XI play in Rhodesia and South Africa.

Gary Sobers is the first world-class non-white cricketer to visit Rhodesia since U.D.I. When he arrived on Friday he was cheered by a large crowd on the balcony at Salisbury airport and members of the Indian community put a garland of flowers around his neck.

This morning he met Mr. Ian Smith, the Rhodesian Prime Minister, and his wife. He sat beside Mr. Smith watching the competition, won by Mike Procter, of Rhodesia, and Lee Irvine, of South Africa, who gained full points from their three games. Each of the other pairs won one of their games.

India's Three Exciting Hours to Fame

BY JOHN WOODCOCK, CRICKET CORRESPONDENT

25 *August* 1971; *The Oval*. India's victory, received amid scenes of great enthusiasm, stands as one of the finest achieved by a visiting side to this country. It is something they have been striving for since they first played Test cricket 39 years ago, and it came from an apparently hopeless position.

Just think of it. They had been saved from defeat at Lord's and Old Trafford by rain, and last Friday evening no one gave them the slightest chance of winning. With a first innings total of 355 England, it seemed, were secure from defeat. With Australia, West Indies, New Zealand and Pakistan already under their belt, they were moving to another cold and calculated victory. Or so we thought. But, Chandrasekhar fooled us all, and yesterday India kept their nerve where Pakistan and Australia have recently lost theirs.

England fought, as they have been guaranteed to fight. Never was a match more reluctantly conceded, and this was all to England's credit. It was a desperately slow pitch, so slow that Illingworth gave Price not a single over and Snow bowled only six. He relied upon himself and Underwood to win the match, and for once there were too few runs to play with. Hardly a ball turned, and Snow might as well have bowled a poached egg as a bouncer.

Yet when Wadekar was run out without a run added to the overnight score of 76 for two, it looked as though England might ·get away with it again. D'Oliveira, from cover point, took advantage of a moment's hesitation to beat Wadekar's dash for safety after Sardesai had called him for a single. For some time after that Underwood, Illingworth and D'Oliveira probed away, hopefully, thoughtfully, patiently, persistently. And with the luck they needed through the slips Viswanath and Sardesai survived.

For the most part Illingworth gave Underwood the pavilion end, from which the ball was more likely to turn, and Underwood, for all his accuracy, lacked the flight or spin to win the day. Laker and Lock would have fancied their chances no doubt, but Locks and Lakers are few and far between. Illingworth ringed the bat, to try to delude the batsmen, and his fielders gave him all they had. But Sardesai and Viswanath, and then Engineer, were too good for them.

When Underwood got a ball to turn at Sardesai and Knott took a good catch, there was still a chance for England. So there was when Underwood stuck out his left hand to take a spectacular return catch from Solkar. That was 134 for five and, as Illingworth said afterwards, he believed then that England could win if they made short work of Engineer, which they failed to do.

Sardesai defended stubbornly for two hours, 40 minutes, and with great skill Viswanath kept England at bay for almost three hours. Without these two India would not have won. And without Engineer they would have won less comfortably. He came in with 39 still needed, and of these he made 28 himself.

Having got out going for the winning runs, Viswanath was not there to be garlanded as Engineer was. He was caught by Knott off Luckhurst, brought on by Illingworth as a last desperate throw. It had taken India three hours to make the 97 they needed when the day began; three tense, exciting hours which culminated with an invasion of the field by the Indians of London.

So, at last, the tightrope snapped. England have walked it several times this year. During the winter they did so at Sydney and then at Auckland; and again this summer at Edgbaston, Headingley and Lord's. They are not a good side, as England sides go, and their performances this summer have reflected, quite starkly, the hapless state of Australian cricket. But their way of playing makes them devilishly difficult to beat.

Both India and Pakistan have appeared to enjoy their cricket more than England. They have contributed more liberally to our summer's pleasures. In Illingworth's time as captain, England have now won eight Test matches, drawn 12 and lost only one. Before that, under Cowdrey, they played seven more without defeat. But an unbeaten record has its complications. Now that England have lost they should think in terms of building a side which plays the game with more of a smile and less of a frown.

This, of course, was a wonderful result for Indian cricket. Always they have bred fine, natural players, whose temperament has been suspect. Yesterday was their festival of Ganesh, which is one of the great Hindu festivals. Ganesh, a god with an elephant's face, comes to the succor of the distressed.

Well, it was England who were in need of his help. And if, as they should, they proclaim their readiness to tour India this winter, they may need it again. For in a short time Ajit Wadekar has made this Indian side into a match for anyone. Within six months they have beaten West Indies and England away from home – and climbed the highest peaks in the cricketing world.

ENGLAND 335 (A. P. E. Knott 90, J. A. Jameson 82, R. A. Hutton 81,
J. H. Edrich 41) and 101 (B. S. Chandrasekhar 6 for 38)
INDIA 284 (F. M. Engineer 59, D. N. Sardesai 54, A. L. Wadekar 48,
E. D. Solkar 44; R. Illingworth 5 for 70) and 174 for 6 (A. L. Wadekar 45,
D. N. Sardesai 40)
India won by 4 wickets

Wilder Notes than
Sweet Music of Ball on Bat

BY PHILIP HOWARD

15 *September* 1971. No gaudy celebration or victorious pennant fluttered over the ancient sporting arena in south London yesterday. One of the gas-holders was at half-mast. Surrey, the champion county for the first time since 1958, were still finishing their last match of the season at Southampton.

Old scorecards blew around the gutters, urban autumnal leaves that show that summer is over in Kennington. Groundsmen were refreshing the famous turf, which is battered, brown and hard after a season of attribion for bonus points. And workmen were carrying huge chessmen into the ground for Saturday's pop concert.

At the Vauxhall end a stage was being hammered together from which new echoes will startle the ghosts of the Oval, and provoke more vigorous approval than the customary sleepy ripple of applause from the members' stand.

The Oval is full of shades and echoes of golden summers long ago:

Richardson flashing down balls so fast that even before they became ghostly they beat the eye; Hobbs stroking the ball past cover; Hayward and Abel, Lohmann and Lockwood; Strudwick and Sandham; May, Bedser and other names that are incantations.

But a larger crowd than watched any day's cricket there this summer will take the Underground and the No. 3 buses to the Oval on Saturday to sit on the grass and listen to The Who, the Atomic Rooster and non-cricketers so withered and so wild in their attire that look not like the inhabitants of the Oval and yet are about to make history by being on it.

The staff were up till midnight last night dealing with requests for tickets. They have already sold more than 5,000 and are prepared for a crowd worthy of Bradman on Saturday. The square will be covered by coconut matting; and not many of the crowd are likely to be wearing shoes that tear the turf as roughly as cricket's spikes.

Cricket has always been a leisurely, backward-looking obsession, glorying in ancient paladins and Old Wisden. The great days of cricket, when summers were golden, it never rained and Hayward was permanently at the wicket, always have been 50 years ago – even 50 years ago.

In the golden days at the Oval, before 1939, club membership was never as high as it has become since the war. It was always relatively few people who went to the Oval even when Hobbs was batting.

In the golden days the managerial and professional classes who belonged to the club left the office for the Oval at four, and at close of play caught steam trains to Camberwell and Croydon, where they employed two servants and lived in respectable style on £500 a year.

Vast oil paintings and yellowing photographs in the pavilion show them posing in silk hats, mutton-chop whiskers and sporty expressions all over the playing area, with a formidable 11 of dukes and earls at their head.

Anyway tradition is always changing. Hobbs would have been as startled by the absence of trams rattling past the wall and by the need to provide parking space for motor cars as he would have been by the pop concert.

In the nineteenth century the FA Cup Final and England-Scotland soccer internationals were played on the Oval; in those days 20 groundsmen were employed all the year instead of four today, Mr. Geoffrey Howard, secretary of Surrey County Cricket Club, says: "We have to adapt to the demand of the times, just as the old cricketers would have adapted to the demands of modern cricket.

"It is better that people should use the Oval than that it should be empty. We badly want to go on providing cricket here, because we love it. We cannot force the new generation to love cricket. But if we can make a little money by promoting what people enjoy, it must be a good thing for cricket."

In his office in Curzon Street, full of hubbub and beautiful people moaning from behind dark glasses about having been up late last night, Mr. Rikki Farr, the producer of Saturday's show, said that he aims to provide a form of circus relevant to 1971. "If rock and roll can help to salvage the financial situation of the Oval, then cricket should be in awe of rock and roll and not the other way round.

"The astonishing thing about Saturday is that thousands of the generation that is the whipping donkey of the establishment will be paying £1.25 each, knowing that the profits from the concert will go to the relief of refugees from East Bengal.

"What cricket needs is some new rules to hype [derived from high-power] it up as a change from all this boring old nonsense with batsmen prodding about. I should love to do a concert in the true bastion of the old days, Lord's."

Commentators and Credibility

BY JOHN HENNESSY

6 *January* 1972. If there is anything more depressing than a cricket field guarded by covers against the summer rain it is the spurious attempt to create Test matches out of a computer. This is the brainchild of the BBC, who now regularly tell us how Boycott, who can hardly even have seen Bradman play, is setting about outwitting the old master. The bats really do seem to have gravitated from the bag to the belfry.

Foreigners (which for this purpose include the Scots) have always regarded cricket as an English disease. They must now see it as a form of madness, when a sham excitement is breathed into a run-out that never was or a wicket that never stood let alone fell.

There seem to be two ways of looking at this form of sporting charade. Either the BBC know their business, which does not say much for those on the other end of the transmissions. Are they in such a pathetic state of deprivation, in spite of the proliferation of Test matches nowadays, that they must dream impossible dreams in their dotage to keep body and soul together during the long winter months?

Or is it the BBC who have taken leave of their senses? No doubt a "spokesman" will leap forward with a set of statistics to prove that the transmissions are a roaring success, that people turn off their electric razors or television sets, according to the time of day, by the millions to hear Bradman bowled for a duck by Bedser. But who is to say that the statistics themselves have not been regurgitated by a computer programmed by a madman in quartered cap and multi-coloured blazer?

These words, I should add, are not the ravings of a cricket hater. Certainly a disenchantment has set in with the antics of the governing body (under whatever name) in recent years and the drift towards thud-and-blunder cricket, but I still demand the blood of the Australians as vociferously as the next man and will do so through the coming summer. What blood, though, can anyone extract from a computer, with a transistor where the heart should be?

The series does, however, raise one important issue – the credibility of the commentator. It may be recalled that John Arlott declined to comment on matches involving the South Africans on the ground that broadcasting was a matter of mutual enjoyment and there could be none on his side. I could not quite understand his position then, but I think I can now.

Brian Johnston does such a remarkable job in simulating the real thing that it is hard to tell that the bails are not flying before his very eyes. But what happens when he takes his place at Lord's or Leeds with 13 men of flesh and blood paraded before him? How shall we know that the excitement he is displaying is genuine and not vamped up at the behest of some voiceless producer talking through an instrument thrust in his ear?

Some commentators switch from one mood to another so quickly that it is impossible to believe that the transformation is genuine, arising solely from deeds of derring-do being performed before them. Mr. Johnston is of a different breed, or has been until now. However irritating his digressions into matters of laundry or bird-life may be, he has generally seemed to be a man honestly trying to convey to the listeners what he feels and thinks. It will be hard to take him on trust in the future.

It is surprising to find Arlott himself and Sir Neville Cardus associated with this tomfoolery. But whether either has so lowered his professional standards as to offer a commentary I could not say. If so, it has been my good fortune to be otherwise engaged at the time.

To be fair, the BBC is not alone in its midwinter madness. One paper, not particularly distinguished for its cricket coverage, not only gives the full ghostly scoreboard but also a fairly lengthy report. There we learn that Bradman was bowled by a "late inswinger pitching middle-and-leg and cutting away to bowl Bradman off his pads". It must be suffering from a touch of the sun.

Duncan Fearnley

Cricketer and Bat Maker Who Works Hard at his Pleasure

BY ARTHUR OSMAN

17 *January* 1972. The river Severn is running fast and high, five miles away the Malvern Hills are lost in rain clouds, and the view from the cricket ground to the cathedral has a veil of rain across it. It is hardly a day for daydreaming about cricket prospects. But the thoughts of one man, who works a couple of six hits from the county ground, are occupied with little else.

Duncan Fearnley admits to devoting his working life and leisure to cricket. He works hard at his pleasure. At the age of 31 he has tasted success as a county professional and is now emerging as one of the world's few individual makers of high quality cricket bats.

He can claim to be the only cricketer playing today who makes for himself, and for a growing number of world batsmen, the most valuable tool of their trade. All are fashioned from selected clefts of Suffolk and Essex willow which have been seasoned and dried for up to 14 months.

The affinity between a cricketer and his bat has a certain mystical quality. Mr. Fearnley knows this well and insists that no bat leaves his workshop which has not been case-hardened, spliced and balanced by himself.

Players at professional and club level treat a bat with the sort of respect that a weekend motorist gives to the family car.

Mr. Fearnley's life has revolved around cricket since he was a child, which is not surprising, since he was born at Pudsey, Yorkshire, played for England as a schoolboy and hoped to follow illustrious fellow townsmen such as Sutcliffe and Hutton into the Yorkshire team.

As events turned out this was not to be, and in 1961 he moved to Worcestershire, where he soon established himself as a notable opening bat. In 1968 the county engaged Turner, the New Zealander, and Mr. Fearnley moved on to Lincolnshire to play in the Minor Counties. This season he will captain Worcestershire second eleven.

When he left school he had learnt the batmaker's craft at a one-man shop in Bradford, and later he always kept equipment at home.

His family had a tradition of working in wood, his grandfather having partnered Ray Illingworth's in a cabinetmaking business and his father being a woodwork teacher at a local school.

The turning point for Mr. Fearnley came at a party at Ilkley for the England and Rest of the World teams in 1970. He had in his pocket several rough drawings of a suitable marque to put on his bats, and after some hilarious suggestions it was decided that only one would do – a perspective view of a set of bails and wickets.

The sign has become known as the Black Wicket, and from a distance it looks like a large black triangle on the back of the blade. It has intrigued many armchair viewers of the game, has kept Mr. Fearnley's wife, Mary, busy this winter cutting out 4,000 of them, and all in all has proved a potent asset.

John Snow took three of the first 12 bats produced to Australia, and another, which was a spare in the bag of a player, produced five centuries. It is now the centrepiece of what Mr. Fearnley hopes will be a distinguished collection.

Its impact was sufficient to produce an order for 3,000 bats from Australia during the 1970-71 tour, and another order for 1,000 received in the past few days will be shipped out this summer. New Zealand is another developing market, as is the West Indies.

He says: "My involvement as a player has been an invaluable asset, because

I know what batsmen are looking for. I have been through it all myself. When I watch cricket on television I feel like a split personality, for I am watching the performance of my bat just as much as that of the player." When Mr. Fearnley lifts a bat, his highest praise for it is "Aye, it's not a bad stick". When he adds "It taps up nicely" one feels that nothing short of a crisp 100 on its first outing will do.

Greek Translator Required

20 *March* 1972, *Diary*. The Cricket Society is looking for a Greek scholar to translate the laws of cricket into Greek. The society's chairman, Christopher Box-Grainger, is offering a cash prize for its completion. The translation is required by the members (and, more particularly, by the umpires) of the two local cricket teams in Corfu – Gymnastikos and Byron – both of which can claim seniority over The Cricket Society. (Corfiot cricket was begun, it is thought, by Lord Byron.)

This year at least three English teams are going to Corfu to take part in a cricket festival in September – Lord Orr-Ewing's XI, H. P. F. Forster's "Cricketer" XI and The Cricket Society's XI. The society has prepared a handbook which has a glossary of local cricketing terms such as *bombarda* (full toss), *pintz* (Yorker) and *apo psila* (caught).

An Eastern Potentate Who Became Prince of the English Game

BY ALAN GIBSON

6 *May* 1972. We are now so accustomed to the fact that many of the world's best cricketers are of other than English stock, that it is hard to realize what a surprise it was when Ranjitsinhji, born a hundred years ago, appeared on the sporting scene in the early eighteen-nineties. In 1892 he was clearly one of the best batsmen at Cambridge, but was not given his Blue. The captain was F. S. Jackson, who later readily admitted his mistake, but who had by his own account made very little attempt to find out how good a cricketer this Indian prince was. Jackson was captain of Cambridge again in 1893. In the winter he had been on a cricket tour of India, and this broadened his horizons. That summer Ranjitsinhji was given his Blue.

There were many who felt that an Indian, however high-ranking, had no business in a cricket match between Oxford and Cambridge. Sir Home Gordon, who was very far from being a wild radical, recalled in later years that he had been abused by a committee-member of M.C.C. for having "the disgusting degeneracy to praise a dirty black". The outcry did not last long, partly because it was soon apparent that Ranji (the abbreviation rapidly became popular) was an astonishingly good cricketer. The further question remained: should he be picked for England?

In 1896, the Australians were here. At the time the England side was chosen by the authorities of the ground on which the match was played. Ranji was not chosen at Lord's, it was said, because of the disapproval of Lord Harris. The Lancashire committee asked him to play at Old Trafford, and he said he would be delighted, if the Australian captain had no objection. Harry Trott cheerfully agreed.

This was one of the best matches ever played between England and Australia. Ranji scored 62 and 154 not out. His second innings, when his side was in a losing position, against Ernest Jones on a fiery wicket, was considered by many the best he ever played. That season he was at the head of the first-class averages, and scored 2,780 runs. It was the highest aggregate ever recorded, beating W. G. Grace's 2,739 (in 1871).

But his greatest years were 1899-1901. In 1899 he broke his own aggregate record, scoring 3,159. In 1900 he scored 3,065. At this point, therefore, the three highest aggregates ever made stood in his name. No wonder men called him a marvel. Most of these runs were made for Sussex, with C. B. Fry at the other end. In 1901 Fry reached the 3,000 mark, and so did Tyldesley. Ranji was not so successful, with 2,468 runs. But he only batted 40 times (to Tyldesley's 60) and his average was 70.51.

His other occupations, and in later years his duties of state, often limited his appearances. In some seasons he was out of the country altogether. When he made an occasional return he did not always easily find his touch. In his last appearances, after the First World War, he had only one eye. In spite of these handicaps, during his career he scored 24,567 runs at an average of 45, with 72 centuries.

In the seasons 1899-1901 he scored 8,692 of those runs (Fry 7,838 in the same three seasons). Against Australia, he also averaged nearly 45, despite the astounding events of 1902, when his Test match average was 3.75 (which was nevertheless a notable triumph over Fry, who averaged 1.25 for the same number of innings).

I have given this statistical outline of his career because to a later generation he became a legend as much for what he was as what he did, and we need to remember that in those early dramatic years he surpassed, even in terms of figures, what any batsman had ever achieved. But, of course, it was the way he made the runs that also caught the public's imagination, and set the press-men scratching their heads ("magic of the east", and "Oriental conjuror" are only good phrases once). Nobody, not even W. G. Grace or Bradman in their heydays, ever filled the grounds as Ranji did. He developed new strokes and new variations of old ones.

There have been many technical analyses of his batting, none entirely satisfactory, even that by Fry. The action photographs of him were taken too

late to show him at his best. He put on weight early. We have to content ourselves with tantalizing glimpses. For instance, once when he was playing a
fast bowler to leg, that stroke something between a hook and a leg glance, he
missed, and the ball broke the skin of the lobe of his ear: his left ear.

He explained that when playing short balls to leg, it was necessary to get
an entire sight of the ball (with both eyes). No doubt he had marvellous eyesight. Indeed, he was responsible for the belief, widespread among cricketers
for many years, that all Indian cricketers had marvellous eyesight. I played
some cricket in university days with M. J. Kalyasunderam, a distinguished
scholar with a rich talent for a song in the evening, but not – he will forgive
me for saying – a formidable cricketer. As soon as Kalyasunderam went in
the field would spread, and when his first off-drive went to long-leg (his most
productive stroke) be sure an elderly spectator would say: "Wonderful eye
these chaps have."

Ranjitsinhji was a prince and potentate, and only subordinately a cricketer.
The monarchs of the Raj lived in a peculiar tension, between the lures of the
western world, and their own long habits and glories. This is why they sometimes seem to us, unimperial Englishmen of 1972, so odd.

None can have suffered this strain more acutely than Ranji. He became,
in one aspect, so much the English gentleman, that there is an occasional note
of pained surprise in the comments of his English friends. Sir Home Gordon,
for instance, who knew him well, and received many favours from him,
wrote: "When we all met him, the Jam Saheb was thoroughly western, apart
from due assumption of his dignity as an Indian prince when occasion arose.
But I have been told that out there he had phases of going entirely native, not
speaking English for weeks and subsisting then solely on rice with some condi-
ments in the curries." Imagine it! A Cambridge Blue, an England cricketer,
not speaking English for weeks and subsisting on curries!

In 1912, Ranjitsinhji was of much value to the King-Emperor at the Delhi
Durbar, and was rewarded with an increase in the number of his guns, which
gave him much delight. He attended the Durbar in a silver coach, which he
wished to present to the King-Emperor. The offer was declined.

His income at the time was £75,000, and his entertainment for the fortnight
of the Durbar cost him £36,000, even though his palace was not then built,
and he had to put up his guests in huts. Afterwards, the special train in which
he was taking his party back to Nawanagar was held up for five hours, because
he had no money to pay for it, and the railway company insisted on cash in
advance. He had not expected to succeed to the throne of Nawanagar, which
goes by nomination of the ruler (though within the family), and this must
have been an additional strain for him. He is often referred to in English
accounts as a model prince, but there does not seem much evidence for this,
apart from what he told his friends. However, he was made Chancellor of the
Princes, and was an Indian representative at the League of Nations, and
there is no doubting the quickness of his intelligence, any more than of his

eye. There is a remarkable book waiting to be written about him by someone better versed in Indian affairs and the politics of the 1920s than I.

He was always, in England, the English gentleman, no more eccentric than an English gentleman of the period might legitimately be (a good deal less eccentric, for instance, than MacLaren). He much enjoyed the part, and entertained lavishly at his home at Staines, though possibly it took the Staines tradesmen some years to recover from the shock.

He died in 1933. His death was sudden, but cannot to him have been unexpected, for the night before he had given to his British political officer, urgently summoned, a special copy of his nomination for the succession. An autopsy found no traces of foul play, or apparently of any other cause of death. His mother and sister observed strict purdah.

How Cricket Came to Argentina

FROM RICHARD WIGG

8 *June* 1972; *Buenos Aires*, 7 *June*. A typical Buenos Aires Taxi driver asked "Cree-ket? You mean that English sport?" as he took me, one hot summer afternoon in January, to watch the North versus the South game, the principal fixture of Argentina's cricket season.

The familiar smack of bat hitting ball and the appeals to the umpire were sufficient to make any Englishman homesick.

Everyone that afternoon was speaking English as a mother tongue, but it was accent-less and a fine ear noticed that the vocabulary was occasionally old-fashioned. These are all the distinguishing marks of a remarkable breed of men, the Anglo-Argentines.

This month the Argentine Cricket Association is sending the first fully Argentine side to play in England and Wales, concluding with a match against the MCC at Lord's.

Last century, when the British gave this South American country the biggest sustained economic development it has ever enjoyed, they threw in as a bonus the introduction of football, rugby, tennis, golf, rowing, boxing, and polo. All these games have since become native sports, several of them developed by Argentines to world standards, as in the case of football and boxing.

Cricket has proved a sport idiosyncratic enough to fascinate only the already highly idiosyncratic Anglo-Argentines.

The team is captained by Mr. Frank Forrester, a 28-year-old broker in a Buenos Aires insurance business; several members have the Anglo-Saxon surnames of Anglo-Argentine families. One of the players was born in Brazil of British parents and one of the best bowlers, who works for a local British bank, was born in England. Of the rest of the team, some are farmers, engineers, accountants, business executives or students.

Englishmen and Anglo-Argentines, were playing cricket more than one hundred years ago. Sometimes under unusual conditions. In 1859 when General Justo Urquiza was besieging Buenos Aires during one of the frequent civil wars the cricketers insisted on their game going ahead and obtained from the fiery general permission to cross the lines to get to their pitch. They played their game – in spite of a dead horse on the pitch.

The North versus South matches date back to the 1880s when British staff ran the Argentine railways and much of the country's meat producing industry.

In 1926, when British prestige reached its zenith, the Argentine President (accompanied by the Army general who was to succeed him in a coup) thought it proper to attend a first "Test match" at the Hurlingham Club (the Anglo-Argentines' holy of holies) against a visiting MCC side.

But then came Perónism and difficult times for Britons, Anglo-Argentines and, of course, for cricket.

In 1948 "Evita", wife of the former dictator, allegedly disgusted at her cool reception in Britain, caused "difficulties" to be made for the Buenos Aires Cricket Club and for its famous cricket ground in the high class suburb of Palermo.

The British Ambassador managed to stave off a showdown with General Perón. But the final blow came when one night Perónists burnt down the club house, removed the fences, and drove bulldozers all over the pitch.

Cricket is played regularly at weekends from November to February by enthusiastic Anglo-Argentines and younger members of the surviving British community (the "Ancient Britons" in diplomatic circles).

The coming British tour is important to Argentine cricket. It should raise the sport's prestige sufficiently to encourage efforts to "graft" cricket into the Argentine school curriculum, and so make cricket a fully national sport.

Clash over Cricket Money Back Offer

BY A STAFF REPORTER

13 *June* 1972. Wilfred Wooller, secretary of Glamorgan County Cricket Club, took an unusual step to register a protest at the way Somerset were conducting their innings at Swansea yesterday. He announced over the public address system that if any spectator felt he was not getting value for money an application for a refund would be sympathetically considered.

At that point Somerset, standing at 245 for four at luncheon on the second day, elected to continue their innings into the afternoon. Welsh resentment, already stirred by Somerset's slow play on Saturday, welled over.

Brian Close, the Somerset captain, met the situation in the most effective way possible. Having scored a century himself, he set his bowlers to scatter the Glamorgan batsmen and before close of play Glamorgan were batting again, having followed on 169 runs behind Somerset's 314 for seven wickets declared.

Wooller said: "The spectators are the people who matter in this. They pay the players' wages, and Somerset's tactics in batting on after lunch seemed to be quite unreasonable. It is a very pleasant afternoon but I doubt if we have collected £20."

Close's immediate comment was "bloody ridiculous". He promised another forthright statement by close of play, but in the event he confined himself to saying that Somerset had given their answer on the field of play. "I am not", he said, "going to get as cheap as he [Wooller] was."

Three Question Marks over England Team

BY JOHN WOODCOCK, CRICKET CORRESPONDENT

26 *June* 1972. Those who left Lord's on Saturday evening despondent at having seen a Test match lost – and there were a lot of them – could, with advantage, have looked at things from a different angle. For they had seen a summer made. If Australia win today, as they surely will, the series will be level, and the last three Tests (at Trent Bridge, Headingley and the Oval) should be worth going a long way to watch.

I confess to having had a dread of seeing England sitting on a lead of two matches before decreasing crowds. But if Australia win this one there need be no fear of that. In three days they have discovered a gifted bowler and established some faith in themselves. It is the England selectors who have the worries now, and fairly substantial ones they are. Illingworth has been reappointed as captain for the last three Test matches, but Price, Gifford and Luckhurst all have question marks above their names.

How has it all happened? How, on a pitch that is basically firm and sound and of a good pace, did England come to lose nine wickets for 86 runs in 48 overs? Especially after Australia's last five wickets had added 107 runs, with Marsh, their wicketkeeper, making an entertaining 50 in an hour and a quarter against an England attack armed with a new ball. It amounted to a day's cricket which many must have been at a loss to understand.

While great credit is due to Greg Chappell for a wonderful innings of 131, to Edwards for his part in steadying Australia's innings on Friday, to Lillee for making the first breaches into England's innings, and to Colley for lending valuable support, the man who has put Australia into an apparently invincible position is Massie. So far he has taken 15 wickets for 122 runs in 56.5 overs. He is the first Australian to have taken 15 wickets in a Test match, and only Jim Laker (19 for 90 against Australia at Old Trafford in 1956) and S. F. Barnes (17 for 159 for England against South Africa at Johannesburg in 1913) have taken more. That is in over 700 Test matches, at all times and in all places.

But who *is* Bob Massie? And where has he been hiding his light? He is 25, a bank clerk from Perth in Western Australia, and what the Australians call a "Bonzer bloke". He had three seasons (1969, 1970 and 1971) in Scottish cricket, playing for Kilmarnock, the arrangements for that being made by Tony Lock, who was then captain of Western Australia.

In his first match for Kilmarnock, in the Western Union competition, Massie took all 10 wickets against Polock, who had Sadiq Mohammad, now with Gloucestershire, playing for them. In his time up there Massie married a Kilmarnock girl.

Last December, while having varying success for Western Australia in the Sheffield Shield, he worked the scoreboard in the Test match against the Rest of the World at Perth before playing in the last two Test matches of that series. By taking the first six wickets (Gavaskar, Ackerman, Zaheer Abbas, Graeme Pollock, Sobers and Asif Masood) for 27 runs in the match at Sydney, he earned his place for the present tour.

Those who played both at Sydney and on Saturday say that he moved the ball rather more at Sydney than at Lord's. He has also been known to swing it quite prodigiously into the breeze that blows off the Swan river in Perth.

At Worcester in April he showed signs of doing it, with six for 31 in Worcestershire's second innings, and he was looking like it again at Lord's in May against MCC when he strained a muscle in his side. This kept him out of the first Test at Old Trafford, where he could have been well nigh unplayable, and when he returned to play against the Combined Universities on June 14 he had trouble with his control. It was partly this which has led to his bowling round the wicket at Lord's with such astonishing success.

It was decided that he should do so at a team meeting before the match, Neil Hawke, who came to England in 1964 and 1968, being cited as a bowler making the switch to good effect, unlike most bowlers who go round the wicket as a variation to their normal style. Massie has no trouble in avoiding the pitch in his followthrough. Neither Constant nor Fagg, the umpires at Lord's, have needed to warn him about this.

With eight for 84 in England's first innings, Massie was suddenly a name to be reckoned with, and on Saturday he held the whole ground in thrall. England began their second innings half an hour after luncheon, 36 runs behind Australia, with Massie bowling from the nursery end and Lillee working up a genuine pace at the pavilion end.

At 6.30 Massie was still at it, having had a break only for tea and taken seven for 38 in 24 overs. At 6.15, when feeling sick from the effort of it all, he sent for a tablet, and had the rest of the Australian side chaired him off the field it would have been no surprise. It was as though he had worked a miracle for them. The clouds had lifted from the hill and the long, cold night was over.

In having a humid, overcast day to bowl on, Massie was fortunate. It helped to accentuate his swing. The ball moved at times as though radio-controlled, and the fact that seven catches were taken at the wicket or in the slips shows how much he made it leave the bat. His pace is a brisk medium, his action economical, and for the rest of the tour he must expect to find himself treated with the care of a crown jewel.

As for England's batsmen, they were up against a superb piece of bowling, which they never looked remotely like containing, although between them they have scored 36 Test hundreds. Boycott was out unluckily, when the ball dropped off his body on to the stumps, with just enough impetus to remove the off bail.

Luckhurst never looked up to it (his scores in four Test innings this season are 14, 0, 1 and 4) and Edrich failed for once to stick it out. With no rescuing act from D'Oliveira or Knott, the score was 52 for six soon after 5 o'clock. Standing among the ruins, needing all his resolution to survive, was Smith, and when Illingworth, after holding on for 45 minutes, left him, it was 74 for seven. With Smith's own departure soon afterwards went England's last chance of leaving Australia a total to test them today.

What we all wondered, would Hammond have made of the bowling, or Compton, or Hutton, or Hobbs and Sutcliffe? It is difficult, indeed impossible, to say. But from some there would have been an attempt to hook and cut when Lillee pitched short. And these great players of the past were more accustomed than those of today to playing the ball that leaves the bat. The bowler saw more of the English left shoulder than he does now, and felt more of the cover drive. For sheer determination Smith's was a fine effort. But it was not enough to steal the thunder from a bank clerk from Perth.

ENGLAND 272 (A. W. Greig 54, A. P. E. Knott 43; R. A. Massie 8 for 84) and 116 (R. A. Massie 8 for 53)
AUSTRALIA 308 (G. S. Chappell 131, I. M. Chappell 56, R. W. Marsh 50; J. A. Snow 5 for 57) and 81 for 2 (K. R. Stackpole 57 not out)
Score after third day: England 272 and 86 for 9; Australia 308
Australia won by 8 wickets

Cricketers Told to Get their Hair Cut

11 *July* 1972; *Singapore, 10 July.* Zealous immigration officers told two Oxford University cricketers here today to get their hair cut or face deportation.

They confiscated the passports of Mr. Simon Corlett, aged 22, and of Mr. Bryan Hamblin, aged 20, and gave them three days to comply with the order.

Mr. Corlett, one of 15 members of an Oxford-Cambridge team which arrived here today for a tour, said they had no choice but to visit the barber tomorrow.

Tourists Keep Steam in the Dressing Room

BY JACK FINGLETON

19 *August* 1972. It was a happy part the Australian cricketers had in the Oval dressingroom last Wednesday, Ian Chappell, the most casual of all Australian captains, wore a yellow and blue track suit and a gay tam-o'-shanter from Scotland. Most, with draped towels, were in their birthday suits and champagne corks popped with musical rapidity. Malcolm Chappell, whose third son, Trevor, could also one day play with Ian and Greg in the same Test side, quietly and proudly packed the Chappell gear.

I much appreciated being invited to join in the conviviality. As an old cricketer, I am a bit of a fogey when it comes to the privacy of dressingrooms, which belong exclusively to players, and I have purposely not stayed at the same hotels as the Australians. If players on a tour as long as this want to let their hair down occasionally, they are entitled to do so in privacy and it would be more than odd if fit-to-busting young athletes did not want to go on the rampage occasionally with a few drinks and songs.

This Australian team has had some severe, but most isolated, criticism of its behaviour on tour. Incidents happen on any sporting tour when tensions are released and this Test series has known plenty of tensions. Dressing-room incidents can be written of any team. Bats are flung, feelings are got out of the system.

Possibly a reason why one or two critics have turned to "team behaviour" this tour could be because, forecasting that the Australians were a poor side and would not win a Test, they have gone off at a tangent. Cricketers of any country are not parlour saints. The Australians did not emerge with flying colours from Scotland and Northampton. They were careless in their approach to both games and at Northants apparently offended the shop steward of the waitresses by helping themselves to cheese and biscuits.

Manager Ray Steele, a splendid manager with discipline but no stuffiness, dressed them down in no uncertain terms over their playing approach. He did not mention the cheese and biscuits.

In an interview he gave me in his Adelaide club before he left Australia, Ian Chappell said he would not tolerate any suggestion by any of his players of disagreement with an umpire's decision. Nor has there been an instance of this. I wish I could repeat what Chappell said to Mallett at the Oval the other day when umpire Rhodes gave Mallett his final warning over running down the pitch after delivery. There have been other occasions, when a bowler has been warned for intimidation or pitch trespass, when a skipper has argued the point for his bowler with the umpire.

Not so this time. Umpires Rhodes and Spencer have said that this was the easiest touring team they have had to handle. That's nice, for Australians, to know. It could not have come from a more informative source.

The dominant feature of this Australian team, apart from its friendliness, has been its youth, yet it could well be that not many of them will come again because the Australians, due to some odd itinerary quirk which happened many years ago, are not due to come to England again until 1977. Many of them will have given their bats away by then. There is talk of some World Cup series in England in 1975 but, as the huge gate takings have shown – and that despite the disadvantages of weather – no game appeals like an honest-to-goodness Test match between England and Australia. Officials of both countries should sort this one out. I would think England will want us again in the four years usual time. We certainly would like it that way.

Now comes the hardest part of the Australian tour. There is inevitable reaction after a Test series and these one-day games, with all their rushing and scurrying, are not only comparatively new to the Australians but are the very deuce for the players. Fitness does not go off on a long tour. It is the mental attitude that gets blunted.

I do hope my fellow Australians see it through. Coming as a young, untried side, I think they have done magnificently, although I could be biased. My hackles rise when I think they are criticized unfairly and it often strikes me as odd how the bare one or two, who were possibly no plaster saints on the field themselves, are so eager to dip their pens in vitriol against Australians. You would think we are not of the same stock; that hundreds of thousands of Britishers have not, in recent times, made Australia their home.

Of course, a healthy young Australian has fire in his belly and red blood in his veins. Field Marshal Montgomery did not find anything wrong with the Australian Ninth division in the Middle East. (The team before this one was rocked to its haunches when the Field Marshal walked into the Australian dressingroom at Southampton and asked: "Were any of you chaps with me in the Desert?")

Once again, I say I am proud of these young Australians, even if they do not ask for the biscuits and cheese to be passed. I hope the sun will shine on them for the rest of their tour and especially when they sing the chorus of their song: "And the rain, rain, rain comes pouring down; on the Aussie cricket tour." The word, by the way, is not pouring!

One fashion – or domestic note – to end. Those evil looking, drooping Chinese moustaches that Messrs Sheahan and Edwards wore for most of the tour disappeared overnight when Mesdames Sheahan and Edwards arrived in England. Which proves that the word is mightier than the pen.

Social Joys of an Off-duty Cricketer

BY JOHN WOODCOCK

30 *December* 1972; *Delhi,* 29 *December.* I am often asked which of the cricket tours that one undertakes is the most enjoyable. Is it to Australia, West Indies, South Africa or India and Pakistan?

The answer I think is that they are all enjoyable and yet all different.

From a purely cricketing point of view there is nothing to equal a visit to Australia. To sail from Tilbury as we used to do and three weeks later to see Fremantle through one's port-hole, having watched the team become a team on the voyage, was wonderful fun. Even now, when the journey is made by air, there is something very special about arriving in Australia to fight for the Ashes. And except for Lord's the players will say that the best Test ground in the world is Sydney.

Round the crescent from Perth to Brisbane the entertainment seldom ceases: from the first of the civic receptions and the first of a thousand speeches. Where else can a cricket team in its off moments sign for a dozen oysters or be given the courtesy of so many beautiful golf courses or enter so many welcoming homes or by their identity stir so many memories? Nor on the field of play can there be anything quite to compare with routing an Australian side.

In the days when we went to South Africa, to sail into Table Bay and to watch cricket at Newlands was the introduction to a tour when the hospitality was every bit as lavish, yet the glare of publicity less fierce. At the time of the last MCC tour there in 1964-65 South Africa were not quite the cricketing force they would be now, but they were not far from it.

There, as in Australia, the players were never left to fend for themselves.

It is the same in the West Indies. A steel band is there to serenade them when they arrive, and life thereafter is as exotic as they choose to make it. On the field this is a hard tour, with lighter interludes in lovely places like St. Lucia or Nevis or St. Vincent or St. Kitts. Where we are now, in India, the enthusiasm for the game is even greater than in the West Indies, and the matches are even harder to win.

In Bombay every open space it seems is given over to cricket. Sometimes on the pavements one has to wait for an over to end before passing on. In Hyderabad 100,000 people watched a three-day match. In Indore a monument in the shape of a bat 145 feet high and bearing a replica of the signatures of Ajit Wadekar's side has been erected to mark their victory over England in 1971. In Delhi where a Test match has just been played every day was a sell-out.

Yet nowhere else is a touring side so dependent upon its ingenuity for its recreation, or so acutely uncomfortable when it is uncomfortable, or for that matter more comfortable when it is comfortable. If less than it was, India is still a country of extremes: of poverty at the palace gates, of finery and filth.

In Indore where this present team were assigned to rooms like prison cells, they sang like an army on the march to sustain their spirits. In Delhi they spent 10 days in a tower of luxury. Instead of singing themselves they listened in smoochy restaurants to Indian singers "dreaming of a white Christmas".

On the Tuesday following their Test victory, the team made the pilgrimage to Agra to see the Taj Mahal. The week before they went to the Golden Temple in Amritsar. To visit such places is one of the delights of an Indian tour. There is golf too for the declining number of cricketers who play it. In Delhi there was a fine course – well kept and with caddies to get one out of trouble if they could. With their toes they perform prodigies of manipulation in the way they provide a lie for a wooden club, even in the densest country.

Besides a lack of opportunity, what holds the Indians back from making a mark at golf is the cost and shortage of equipment.

I played recently with a merchant of great wealth who can lay his hands on only one new ball a month due to import restrictions.

This week it is Calcutta, next week Bangalore, the week after that Madras. And so it goes on. For one reason and another there has developed on this tour the best spirit I have known and it was this not least which led to England winning in Delhi. Through there being fewer diversions the team are usually together and therefore working out their cricket. There is more of this here than in Australia, South Africa or West Indies.

A day for the players goes something like this. A coach to the ground at nine o'clock with a net for those not playing in the match. Play starts at 10 a.m. or 10.15 a.m. and lasts until 4.50 p.m. or 5.05 p.m. More often than not there will be a warm bath at the hotel after play followed by a beer in the manager's room (thanks to a British brewery whose supply of cans makes for a great saving, with local beer at the equivalent of 50p a bottle). The evenings are passed either at a reception in a gaily lit garden, the curry taken standing up, or more often in the hotel. There are few British homes to go to any more except in Delhi where the High Commission is based.

A massage being a good way to pass the time, the physiotherapist is seldom idle. It is he who insists upon the team doing their teeth in soda water, and allowing no water to pass their lips unless it is known to have been purified. The team's bill for soda water on this tour will come to something in the region of £250.

On the last tour they were said by one of the Indian authorities to have eaten over £150 worth of bananas, mostly in lieu of a cooked lunch on the grounds. There is as you will see less sophistication than on most tours, more making do. But going into the New Year with a victory behind them, Tony Lewis and his side are happy at the moment to settle for that.

Ward Sent Home and Coloured Bats Are Out

BY RICHARD STREETON

19 *June* 1973. The image of cricket as a tranquil sport, free from acrimony and purely routine away from the field, was a little dented yesterday by a series of incidents and announcements in a variety of places. Easily the most momentous event was the sending home of Alan Ward, the Derbyshire and England fast bowler, for seemingly disciplinary reasons before play ended. Next, perhaps, for rapidity of action and drama came the banning by the authorities at Lord's until the full implications are studied of coloured bats. An enterprising manufacturer had introduced them only on Sunday as a sales gimmick.

Cricket is unused to people being sent off and nobody at Chesterfield was saying very much after Ward left the ground with the game against Yorkshire still in progress. Brian Bolus, the former Yorkshire and Nottinghamshire player now captaining Derbyshire in his first season with them, can hardly have dreamt when play started that by the close he would have joined Lord Hawke (Yorkshire) and Lord Tennyson (Hampshire) as the only English captains previously to have deprived their side deliberately of the services of a player before a match was completed. Peel and Newman respectively – both bowlers – were the men "sent off" in the past.

All Bolus would say afterwards was: "You saw what happened. It is up to you to put your own interpretation on what you saw. I have nothing further to say on the matter. This is the concern of the Derbyshire County Cricket Club."

Onlookers had seen Ward savagely punished by the Yorkshire batsmen early on, being hit for 19 in one over by Hampshire and after one further over in the afternoon, finishing with figures of one for 56 in nine overs.

Later, as Yorkshire's total continued to grow, Bolus approached Ward and then left the field. He returned and approached Ward again only to turn to the pavilion and beckon the 12th man to take the field, at the same time waving Ward off.

Major Douglas Carr, the Derbyshire secretary, would not confirm that Ward had been sent off but he did say: "I can confirm that he has been told to go home and that I will be seeing him formally in the morning. He is not injured as far as I am aware." He confirmed that Bolus had sent a message from the field asking to see him but he declined to say what was discussed and what had gone on between Ward and his captain. Ward also declined to comment on the matter before leaving the Chesterfield ground.

Meanwhile, the last comparable uproar over cricket bats before yesterday's issue of coloured bats was in 1771 when one Thomas "Shock" White of Reigate "arrived with a bat which completely covered the width of the stumps". The quotation is from the minute book of the Hambledon Club, who at the time governed the game, and almost overnight they instituted the first regulations governing the size of the bat.

In the 200 years since nobody has found it necessary to think much about the bat's size, or anything else and certainly not its colour until on Sunday Richards used an orange bat for Hampshire and Roope a blue one for Surrey in John Player League games. Roope was quoted as saying that he would use his blue bat in the Lord's Test match this Thursday. The complications which might arise from, say, the use of a bat coloured the same red as the ball or the distastefulness of manufacturers and their contracted players from trying to outdo each other in public are obvious.

One of those lengthy solemn statements that give the impression of having been drawn up by a bevy of judges and Queen's Counsels at Lord's was immediately forthcoming and most people's sympathies are with the officials. One does hope, however, that the appropriate committee meets and acts quickly – as their forebears at Hambledon did. Just occasionally cricket committees tend to defer problems too long.

The text of yesterday's broadside read: "Coloured bats shall not be used in matches under the control of the Test and County Cricket Board. This includes the Test match against New Zealand at Lord's on Thursday. While in general principle the board has never sought to restrict the type of equipment used by players, it is considered only right that the board have the chance to consider the implications of using equipment to which the opposition might justifiably object, or which could conceivably make the task of the umpires more difficult." All fair enough, perfectly reasonable and no doubt a compromise will be reached in the usual way of English cricket.

The Skill is Undiminished

BY JOHN WOODCOCK, CRICKET CORRESPONDENT

21 *June* 1973; *Cricket – A Special Report*. It has been said before that cricket never was what it used to be. Pick out, at random, any one of the 110 *Wisdens* contained in a full set, and somewhere the game or those who play it will be under fire.

This is worth remembering when taking a look at the contemporary scene. The young shavers sitting on the boundary's edge at Trent Bridge during the recent Test match there, will be saying in 30 years' time how no one compares with Amiss, Greig and Congdon. They will hold their children spellbound with the story of New Zealand's great recovery.

In English cricket there can seldom have been a greater wealth of skill, but only a small part of it is English skill. In the golden age of batsmanship, so incomparably described by Sir Neville Cardus, I doubt whether there were so very many finer batsmen playing in the county championship than there are now, but they were all English then.

To Sir Neville, Barry Richards, Gary Sobers, Mike Procter, Clive Lloyd, Rohan Kanhai, Majid Khan, Geoff Boycott, Asif Iqbal, Mushtaq Moham-mad and the rest are not to be compared with "Ranji" and Charles Fry and Gilbert Jessop, and Tom Hayward and Archie MacLaren and Stanley Jackson. Whether or not when stood side by side they are as good, I believe they are playing a more difficult game not a better game, but a more difficult one.

Just as in football, more emphasis is being placed on saving goals than scoring them, so, in cricket, captains and bowlers think increasingly in terms of containment rather than attack. To some extent this is the outcome of limited-over cricket; but it is a development which was taking shape before the one-day game was introduced on anything like its present scale. There is no way in which it can be for the best, and no way, so far as I can see, in which the trend can be reversed.

To get an idea of how much the game has changed it is worth wondering what would have come of "Tich" Freeman, the second leading wicket-taker in the history of cricket, had he been starting today. Between 1914 and 1936 he took 3,776 wickets, 1,122 of them in four seasons between 1928 and 1931, with leg breaks and googlies.

In 1973 it is most unlikely that he would have found a county to give him a start. He gives too much away, they would say. Wickets are not bought any more, as Freeman used to buy them. From Test cricket down to the village green the game is dominated by bowlers all of much the same pace. For this reason much of the technical variety has left it, to be replaced by variety of a different kind.

Whereas a dozen years ago the championship was the only domestic competition in which first-class cricketers took part, there are now three others, all of them sponsored and designed to appeal to a public which no longer has much time or the inclination to watch the three-day county game.

There is not a single spectator sport that has not been faced in the last decade by falling gates. Rugby and soccer, racing, boxing, tennis and golf have all had the same worries as cricket. Only the great traditional fixtures can still be sure to draw the crowds: the Open Championship, the FA Cup, the Derby, a fight for the heavyweight title of the world, or the battle for the Ashes. This is a fact of life to which different sports have reacted in different ways and at different speeds. Cricket has not, on the whole, been dilatory.

First as a gimmick, then as a lifeline, the one-day game has been developed. The players accept it as a necessary expediency; it makes their life more hectic but financially more rewarding. Television accepts it as a sellable product, and that is vital. There is between television and sport a love-hate relation-ship. To cricket the liaison is worth £150,000 a year; yet in the course of a season there is no knowing how many would-be spectators it keeps at home.

A good many more, no doubt, than it encourages to come.

Sponsorship extracts less of a price for its patronage, and it is doubtful whether without it all 17 first-class counties would still be in existence. Last year more than £400,000 was invested in the game by almost everyone from cigarette manufacturers to the makers of toys and prams. It is not least because of them that the best overseas cricketers migrate each year to England, to play their game and make their living. It is a migration which has been insufficiently curbed, but which, overall, has been of undoubted benefit to the English game.

Take Lancashire, for instance. In 1968 they were joined by Clive Lloyd, the West Indian left-hander. At once he brought a revival in their fortunes. His fielding and batting and zest for cricket were as much of an example to the side as an attraction to the public. Yet the fact that Lloyd went to Old Trafford, to be followed almost immediately by Farookh Engineer, the Indian wicketkeeper, has kept Frank Hayes, one of England's bright young men, waiting longer than he would otherwise have done for a regular place in the Lancashire side.

All round the country, except in Yorkshire, there are examples of this. It is no use anyone who is not a Yorkshireman applying to play for Yorkshire. Other counties must soon insist on a tighter control of imported players, as well as on no further increase in one-day cricket at the expense of the championship programme.

I think cricket holds as high a place as ever in an Englishman's affections, in spite of all its ups and downs. When England played Australia last year the Post Office dealt with 15 million telephone calls from people asking for the Test score. Opinion polls have shown that, next to football, cricket has by far the largest readership of any game in the newspapers.

At the grass roots the game is healthy enough, except that it mirrors the imperfections at the highest level. Driving through the countryside on a Saturday or Sunday evening you will see as many games as you ever did, many of them with a new competitive element. If fewer boys now play cricket at school those who are lost to other sports are mostly those that would simply have been making up the number.

To some extent the enthusiasm for taking a bat and a ball to the park, rather than the infernal football, varies with the success which England's footballers or cricketers are having at the time. When England beats Australia cricket does well for recruits, and for those who choose it as their summer pastime it continues to provide as happy a way as there is of making the friends and memories of a lifetime.

The Art of Captaincy

BY MICHAEL BREARLEY

21 *June* 1973; *Cricket – A Special Report*. The effects of the changes in the structure of county cricket have been and are being discussed *ad nauseam*; but it is perhaps worth mentioning the differences these changes have made to the captain's job.

It is widely believed, I think, that the arts of captaincy are among those numerous skills which disappear as soon as limited-overs cricket starts. Tactics are thought to be unnecessary and absent.

In all types of cricket there have been captains, no doubt a majority, who work to rule, following whichever book happens to be fashionable at the time. They merely set things in motion and await results. And it is especially tempting to think of the job along these lines in limited-overs cricket. As usual, if he has a good side under him, the captain who follows a rigid pattern will usually achieve adequate results; but this approach is a pale shadow of proper captaincy.

It is of course essential to have some sort of plan or outline of policy. But situations vary enormously; no simple formula can fit all contingencies. The perfect captain will have a feeling for the moment when a batsman has taken the measure of one of his bowlers. He will know which of his bowlers is least likely to be heaved to the short boundary on the leg-side.

He will gauge accurately the time to stop worrying too much about saving singles and to concentrate on saving fours. In the midst of impending chaos he remains calm, juggles his bowlers sensibly, and keeps weak fielders out of the way.

From the batting point of view, the tempo of the side's approach requires constant reappraisal. In 40-over matches one must, I am sure, go for one's strokes from the start of the innings. At the same time the batting should almost never be reckless. Every batsman has to play himself in a little; the special skill lies in doing so without destroying the momentum of the innings.

Team selection and batting order call for clear-headedness. Many of the most successful Sunday league players have been young enough not to have founded their whole game on three-day cricket. Yet one-day cricket can easily induce bad habits among the less experienced. It is often hard to weigh the contribution of a steady batsman against that of a chancy all-rounder. What, one must ask, is the average value of X's fine fielding or Y's ability to bowl a few overs in a pinch?

I personally like one-day cricket and enjoy captaining Middlesex in their games. I find myself totally absorbed in what is going on. I have always found the tactical aspects of the game as intriguing and fulfilling as batting. This absorption is, for me, the main attraction of the job.

A danger, for me, is the tendency to a sense of omnipotence which tempts a captain to exaggerate his own responsibility both for success and failure. Others rarely help, for one receives, as captain, as little sensible praise as sensible blame. There are, of course, the trials and rewards of positions of responsibility in many areas. But it is rare that the overall assessment appears to be so easily calculable or so publicly available.

Different captains are temperamentally suited to different forms of cricket. For this reason, and to dilute the pressures which many captains fell, it would be feasible for a county to appoint different players as captains for three-day and one-day competitions. There was a certain irony in the choice last year of Brian Close to captain England in the one-day internationals. For in one-day cricket the guiding principle is to restrict the opposition, whereas Close is by nature an attacking captain, who, I suspect, took some time to come to terms with the challenge of limited-overs cricket.

One last point on this subject. Twelve years ago there was only one inter-county competition, the championship. Now there are four. One entirely happy result is that most counties have something to play for during at least some stages of the season. Middlesex, so far, have done little in the championship or in the Benson and Hedges Cup. But we are, touch wood, doing well in the John Player League. Last year we had a chance in the last two; the year before, in the championship. The increased range of potential success keeps up the morale of players and members alike.

Changes in social structure, though less tangible, have had no less an influence on the role of the captain. The aristocratic tyrant has to some extent given way to the collaborating foreman. Some older players yearn for the old-style discipline. Cricket still provides a locus for both snobbery and inverted snobbery.

At the same time the administrators of the game have brought into the committees of the Test and County Cricket Board several current players, mostly county captains. The captain can find himself betwixt and between. He is often the only representative of the players on the county committee, yet he is also a member of that committee.

The biennial captains' meetings at Lord's, under the persuasive chairmanship of Doug Insole, have been represented as the voice of the cricketers. This picture may with justification be resented by the players, as happened this year over the issue of fines for county sides who fail to average 18.5 overs an hour. The rise of the Cricketers' Association may in retrospect appear to have been as important a development of the 1960s and 1970s as the introduction of one-day cricket.

Prince Ranjitsinhji wrote beautifully about the duties of a captain in *The Jubilee Book of Cricket*. Much of his sensible and sensitive account of this complex job in personal relations, administration, tactical sense and leadership still applies. Shall we see, in the next few years, a dividing-up of these functions?

Will there arrive in county cricket managers and trainers, the apparatus of soccer and, for that matter, of American sport, to plan and dictate policy, and to lay down rules and procedures for training and discipline? Tentative steps in this direction have been made. I am doubtful about how far they can profitably go. I do feel, however, that there is room for greater professionalism, in the best sense of that tarnished word, in cricket.

This professionalism will have to extend to the running of clubs. I will end with one illustration of the success this can produce. Two of the most improved sides of the past five years, Leicestershire and Northamptonshire, owe their improvement largely to the powerful and incisive influence of their secretaries, Mike Turner and Ken Turner. It will, I think, increasingly become clear that success will require secretaries (call them managers if you will) among whose tasks will be the finding and signing-on of players.

Adventure in Each Ball Bowled

BY BEN TRAVERS

21 *June* 1973; *Cricket – A Special Report.* Mystique, my dictionary avers, is a "secret known to its inspired practitioners"; a definition to be treasured by anybody confronted with the challenge: "Why on earth do you give up all that time and thought to cricket?"

"Ah", he can reply, "that is my mystique." The trouble is that the true reason for his obsession remains a secret even from the inspired practitioner himself.

Thousands of his lifetime's precious hours he spends with his eyes glued on other men playing cricket or on the rain which has stopped them doing so. Why? Is the love of the game born in him, lurking in his system from the outset among the lesser but delectable natural appetites? Or is it, as the dictionary seems to think, an inspiration stimulated by early hero-worship and maturing into the insistent bigotry of the mystique?

In my case, I honestly suspect it was inbred. Although, as a boy, I sat enthralled watching W.G. and Ranji making a hundred apiece in partnership and, a few years later, Jessop's classic century at the Oval, the love of cricket was deeply implanted in me long before it embraced such glorious revels.

But the game's survival and prosperity depend not upon the fanatic but upon the normal discriminating supporter. His first reason for going to see cricket played is to see the players who play it. His interest lies in the performance or promise of individual players, to be appreciated, criticized, argued about.

And in every generation along come hundreds of cricketers of swingeing ability and entertainment value with, here and there, some star performer whose outstanding abilities are enhanced by a personality which makes him a compelling attraction for the regular worshipper and tickles the curiosity of the sceptic – Grace, Ranji, Jessop, Hobbs, Hammond, Bradman, Compton, Dexter, Trueman and who you will beside.

Suddenly, not so long ago, the cricket-lover, like everybody else, found himself caught up in the whirl of the speed age. Life is now one perpetual rush-hour. The long-drawn-out three-day county match soon felt the strain. Somebody had to do something pretty drastic. Somebody did. He was in-spired to institute and sponsor the one-day, result-guaranteed contest. It caught on.

The Test match still thrives with a glamour and box office value of its own; meanwhile the authorities struggle to recapture the interest of the preoccu-pied public in the three-day county game. But their well-intentioned system of bonus points appeals only to the faithful county partisan; the hardened old bigot ignores it as beyond his comprehension or concern.

Yet, so long as cricket endures, he and his progeny will likewise endure; still creating upheaval and protest in the crowded railway carriage in an effort to glimpse just one ball being bowled in the club match alongside; dawdling on the seafront promenade to study the form of the little boy on the sands wielding a spade one handed as a bat and with the outsize bucket for stumps.

The basic question remains – why do I love cricket? First, I think it is the allurement of keen continuous anticipation which makes every ball bowled a fresh, isolated adventure. I love, too, the whole setting and atmosphere, the traditional dignified amplitude. For me, the moment of the umpires' emer-gence from the pavilion at the opening of a Test match (preferably against Australia) is one of unparalleled bliss. I relish it in silence, merely turning my head to exchange a wink with another old inspired practitioner in the row behind me.

This Special Report *on Cricket was an eight-page supplement to* The Times *of 21 June 1973.*

Close of Play at the Lane

BY BRIAN CASHINELLA

4 *August* 1973. The last county cricket match ever to be played on the historic turf of Bramall Lane, Sheffield, starts this morning. Fittingly, the ground's professional career ends with (what else?) a Roses battle between Lancashire and Yorkshire.

More than ever before, if that is possible, Yorkshire will want to win this one and offer the victory to the memory of the surroundings which have witnessed some of their finest successes.

Messrs Boycott and Lloyd, the captains, will be aware that, whatever happens, their names will forever be linked with one of the most famous cricket grounds in the world and lodged firmly in the knowledgeable memory banks of the local cricket fraternity.

The demise of Bramall Lane is the cricket equivalent of a state funeral and who is to say that the ghosts of the famous – Rhodes, Makepeace, Duckworth, Verity, Lord Hawke, Leyland, Jackson, Tyldesley and many others – will not patrol the boundary rope and watch the latest chapter in the deadly serious clash between the great rivals.

It was alleged to be in the old "grinders' stand" there that a man was complaining about the slow scoring rate in an earlier confrontation between the red and white roses. "Is thee from Yorkshire?" he was asked roughly. "No", he replied. "Well, is thee from Lancashire, then?" Again "No." . . . "Well, what th' 'ell's it got to do wi' thee?"

While Yorkshire and Lancashire have had their fair share of cricketing punch-ups at the Lane, few of the players down the ages were likely to remember their reception with any regret. On the other hand, Surrey's memories are somewhat different.

For just over a century ago, one of their teams was almost lynched by the irate Sheffield crowd after a thunderstorm had apparently put an end to a tightly-balanced game with Yorkshire. The Surrey skipper was William Caffyn who accepted the umpires' decision that further play was impossible and began preparing his team for the return to London.

No such luck. The Sheffield crowd had decided the game must go on and the Surrey players, already on their way to the railway station, were confronted by an angry section of the spectators and threatened with a fate worse than death if they did not resume immediately.

It was an offer they could not refuse. The unfortunate Surrey players literally paddled their way back on the pitch and slopped the ball down until Yorkshire clouted enough runs to win by two wickets.

Douglas Jardine, the Bodyline tour captain, much criticized by some sections of the cricket community, was loved at Sheffield, and so was "Big Bill" Bowes, another fast bowler. Both players and the crowd had one thing in common: they played to win.

For it is the crowd, rather than the ground itself, that players remember. F. G. Mann, the Middlesex captain, will always recall the Lane as the place where he put Yorkshire in to bat on what proved to be a good wicket. The home batsmen proved difficult to move and a wag in the crowd bawled at the fielding skipper: "Tha put us in, nah get us aht!"

Herbert Sutcliffe scored his 100th century for Yorkshire there and, as Cyril Washbrook describes in his autobiography: "The whole vast crowd stood up, and it was the finest reception given to an English cricketer I have heard anywhere in the world."

But, you can take any match you like, load it with as many exciting boundaries as your mind can muster, fill it with bowling like you have never seen before, and it will not compare with a "Roses" duel – no matter how dull.

These games are not about scoring runs, getting wickets, snatching bonus points. They are matters of honour, pride and prestige, twice-yearly encounters where scores are settled.

Nobody outside these two Northern counties will ever understand what is at stake. Makepeace, the old Lancashire skipper, made a firm rule: "No fours before lunch against Yorkshire." And he meant it.

Sir Neville Cardus, the doyen of cricket writers, perhaps grasped the essence of the battle best with a story he told some years ago. Lancashire were 499 for nine wickets and their captain, Leonard Green, was at the wicket. He decided that, even if it killed him, he would score the 500th run.

Wilfred Rhodes bowled, Green pushed the ball gently on the off side and ran like a hare. There was a rapid throw to the bowler's crease. Green was safely home but the ball hit Rhodes on the arm. As the Lancashire captain was thanking his lucky stars he heard Rhodes muttering to himself: "There's somebody runnin' up and down this wicket. Ah don't know who it is, but there's somebody running up and down this wicket." As Cardus pointed out, the classic operative phrase was: "Ah don't know who it is."

So what more could Bramall Lane want as a farewell? It has seen a Test match, tourists by the score and county games that are listed as among the finest ever played. But Roses games have something special and today's is the last it will see.

Let us hope it is a fitting epitaph to a famous ground that will now see only football.

S. Africa Accept Non-Whites on Cricket Tour

27 *September* 1973; *Cape Town,* 26 *September.* The Government has approved the inclusion of two non-whites, John Shepherd, of the West Indies, and Younis Ahmed, of Pakistan, in Derrick Robins's cricket team which is to tour South Africa from October 20 to December 11. This announcement was made by the Sports Minister, Dr. Piet Koornhof, at The Cape Town University "Sportsman of the Year" dinner.

Cricketers Charged

15 *October* 1973. Cricketers who took part in a multiracial match in Pietermaritzburg yesterday are to be charged with contravening new Government proclamations, according to an official of the Group Areas Board.

Officials and detectives took the names of players and spectators at a private club during a match between a multiracial team and a white university side. The match was later continued.

British Author Knocked out at Test Match

FROM OUR CORRESPONDENT

7 *January* 1974; *Sydney, 6 January*. Laurie Lee, the British poet and author, was knocked unconscious today by a flying beer bottle on Sydney Cricket Ground's notorious "Hill". He was taken to hospital and had four stitches in his head. He was hit during the last 10 minutes of play after the Australian batting had collapsed to the New Zealand pace attack.

Mr. Lee, who is 59, said afterwards at his brother's home in Paddington, a Sydney suburb: "I enjoyed it, but if I go back again I will wear a tin hat." He is returning to England next Friday.

Jamaican High Court Judge Knows the Score

23 *February* 1974; *Kingston, 22 February*. There was a hush in Kingston High Court. The judge spoke in sombre tones. "I have to tell you, gentlemen, that Boyce is dismissed," he said.

"But m'lud", offered the defence counsel, "my client's name is Bryce." "Ah, quite so," said his lordship, "but I thought you would like to know the latest Test score from Sabina Park."

The bank robbery trial was halted and everyone in court, including the accused, sat and listened as the judge read out details of the West Indies–England cricket match.

Occupational Complaint Strikes at Greig's Spinning Finger

FROM JOHN WOODCOCK, CRICKET CORRESPONDENT

29 *March* 1974; *Port of Spain, 28 March*. A spin bowler you can tell by his fingers, a wicketkeeper by his hands. Ask any old wicketkeeper to show you his hands and he will take you round them, bumps and all, saying where this bone was broken or how that one was cracked. I never had a better morning listening to a cricketer talk than when I asked George Duckworth to go round his hands.

It was on a boat to Australia and they were like one of those relief models of a golf course or a mountain range, all humps and crags and hollows. "That was Gubby at Perth", and there would follow a colourful account of how a knuckle had got knocked out of place, or whatever it was. In those days I doubt whether a wicketkeeper's gloves gave quite the protection they do now. Knott's hands have hardly a scar on them, which is a tribute to his skill as well, of course.

Today, on the flight from Georgetown to Port of Spain, the most interesting exhibit was Greig's spinning finger – the forefinger, that is, of the right hand. As a result of changing his bowling style, from medium pace seam to off cutters and off breaks, he is suffering from the spin bowlers' occupational complaint of a finger on which the skin has been broken, as a result of spinning the ball.

Laker's spinning finger is swollen and arthritic after years of service. Pocock's is generally quite raw during a season: Gibbs's too. In the Test match in Bridgetown Pocock had to leave the field to get his spinning finger treated, and now Greig is trying to grow the skin again on his before the last Test match starts here on Saturday.

Greig's new-found skill has answered the question that was worrying him before the tour began of how, at his usual medium pace, he could do much good. After failing in the first Test match to take a wicket he decided to slow down his pace and change his method. He bowls now more as Appleyard did with such success in Australia in 1954-55, or as Shepherd did for so many years for Glamorgan, using the crease for variation and changing his pace between slow and slow-medium.

His height is a virtue, occasionally giving him a bounce which others fail to get. As a direct result, in the last three Test matches he has been the most successful bowler on either side. England have taken 21 wickets in that time, Greig 11 of them.

This is bad news for Pocock, whose job Greig has taken over. Six weeks ago, had one written down a likely MCC side to go to Australia in October, Pocock would have been in it. Now Greig gets pencilled in as the "off spinner". With the new restrictions allowing only five fielders on the leg side applying in Australia by then and making things a lot harder for the off spin bowler, only one of their kind may go, and Pocock is not at the moment the first choice – or the second, for that matter. In Georgetown, Birkenshaw was preferred, as he probably will be again on Saturday if the balance of the attack stays the same.

It may not be until just before the match that England decide whether or not to bring back a third fast bowler. Meanwhile, Greig will be dipping his spinning finger into some sort of potion to try to toughen it and wondering whether or not to continue in England next season to bowl more slowly. Probably he will be one thing one day, and one another, according to the conditions, but it is in his slower vein that he is having such an impact on this series.

A Batting Machine they Called 'The Croucher'

BY ALAN GIBSON

"At one end stocky Jessop frowns,
The human catapult
Who wrecks the roofs of distant towns
When set in his assault".

18 *May* 1974. So wrote an American rhymester in 1897, when G. L. Jessop, a young man scarcely over the threshold of his career, was playing in Phila-delphia. "The human catapult" was a fine hyperbole. The way Jessop sprang at the ball, the moment the bowler had realeased it, is what those who saw him most vividly remember.

English cricket has had bigger hitters than Jessop (he did not try for specially long hits; the boundary was good enough). English cricket has had batsmen who scored more runs with a higher average. But there has never been an English batsman who hit so hard, and scored so fast, and yet still scored runs so consistently. In his career, which lasted from 1894 to 1914, Jessop scored 26,698 runs, at an average of 32.63, and if one believes all one hears – those in Gloucestershire who remember him never tire of talking about him – hardly played a defensive stroke.

Shortly before Roy Webber died, he was talking to me about some statis-tical investigations he had been making to Jessop's career. Jessop scored 53 centuries in first-class cricket, with a highest score of 286, and so far as Roy had been able to discover, he had never batted for more than three hours. I don't know if Roy had time to confirm this, but it is an astonishing thought*. Take into account your different social climate, your changed over rate, your negative bowling tactics; take into account anything you like, but to score all those runs and all those centuries, and not to bat for more than three hours. . . .

In his early days Jessop was a successful fast bowler, twice taking 100 wickets in a season; and throughout his career he had a reputation for being one of the world's best cover fieldsmen. A. C. MacLaren, recalled to the England captaincy in 1909, demanded before the series began that Jessop should be picked for every Test, "because he will run Victor Trumper out for me". This plan did not work – rather the contrary, for Jessop strained his back while fielding in the third Test, and never played for England again – but it is a remarkable example of the value placed upon his fielding.

I felt I glimpsed a little of G. L. Jessop once, when I saw his son, the Rev.

---

* Gerald Brodribb's biography of Jessop, published a few months later and reviewed in *The Times* by Alan Gibson, revealed that Jessop took 200 minutes over his 240 for Gloucestershire against Sussex at Bristol in 1907.

G. L. O. Jessop, score a fast 80 or so for Dorset against Cornwall at Camborne. G. L. O. Jessop was then middle-aged himself, but a beautiful striker of the ball. He used the sweep a lot, as his father is said to have done, sometimes in the most daring circumstances, but he also had a splendid straight drive back over the bowler's head.

C. B. Fry always insisted that Jessop was not "a slogger", which used to be a pejorative term, but a true batsman who took risks, who stretched his technique to the limit, sometimes attempting more than he could achieve; but was nevertheless basically a sound player. That innings by G. L. O. Jessop, though he has never sought to compare his merits with those of his father, gave me a fairly clear idea of what Fry meant.

In Test cricket, it must be said, Jessop's record was disappointing. Although he was usually picked when he was available, over a period of ten years, he scored only 569 runs in 18 matches, at an average of 21.88.

Nevertheless, Jessop did win a Test, the famous one against Australia in 1902, when he redeemed a forlorn English cause in the last innings, scoring 104, his only Test century, in 75 minutes. The philosophy behind picking him must always have been, "Ah! But whatever his average, he's the kind of man who can swing a match", and that was an occasion when he did.

The number of times he did it for other sides, and particularly Gloucestershire, it would be a labour to count. He came to the Gloucestershire captaincy soon after the departure of W. G. Grace. Grace had left amid a large and loud rumpus, and Jessop's task was not an easy one. But although he was unable to lead the side to the championship, which was hardly surprising with the resources at his disposal, he kept up the gates and the spirit of Gloucestershire as much by his own marvellous example as anything else, and today his name is spoken of in the county in the same breath as those of Grace and of Hammond.

He was nicknamed "The Croucher". He bent low at the wicket, and sometimes would stoop down so far that his cap was on the level of the bails. He said that this helped him to judge the length of a ball early. It must have added considerably to the psychological and dramatic effects of his sudden spring, his pounce, his leap at the ball. But in later life, at least, he disliked the name.

About 1948, when I was a junior producer on the staff of the BBC, I was sent a capital script about Jessop, by Harold Gardiner, called "The Croucher". We put the programme into production, and billed it in the *Radio Times*. As a matter of courtesy, we sent a script to Jessop, though, as it was an almost entirely laudatory script, we hardly thought he would complain. But he did. He complained most sharply, particularly about the title: indeed, it took all the tact of Frank Gillard to calm him down, and the programme was postponed, to be broadcast at a later date under the less inflammatory title of "G. L. Jessop".

Well, most old men have cantankerous moments, but this incident has always baffled me. Did he resent the nickname because it was put upon him by the press? He did a good deal of journalism himself at one time and another. Did he resent it because the Gloucestershire public relished it? Amateurs in those days were inclined to disregard public esteem, but he must have been proud of the affection in which Gloucestershire held him (he was born and brought up at Cheltenham), and it is as "The Croucher" – the great cat about to jump – that he is still happily and proudly remembered.

Boycott Back in Swing

BY JOHN WOODCOCK

18 *June* 1974. Better after his bout of 'flu and keen to get back to the wicket, Geoffrey Boycott found a game in Bath yesterday – for the Lansdown Club against Selwyn College, Cambridge. He made 108 before retiring, with the same satisfaction, I imagine, as a crack shot killing low pheasants.

He was lucky to find a wonderfully good pitch. It was here that Vivian Richards, now playing for Somerset, re-wrote the local record book last season. The ground is beautifully kept and fast scoring, and had the sight of Selwyn's left arm opening bowler, operating from over the wicket in the style adopted so successfully by Solkar, unnerved the Yorkshire captain, there was a hospital behind the bowler's arm.

But all was well. In one of the early overs Boycott hit the second, third, fourth and fifth balls for four and took a single off the last. Soon afterwards he had the ball changed, not because it was out of shape or swinging too much but because of the red marks it was leaving on the blade of his bat.

Little can Selwyn have thought, as they left for their West Country tour, that they would be called upon as cannon fodder for England's most prolific batsman. As improbable, you might say, as a side of clerics finding that their opponents in the Diocesan Cup have a certain Prebendary Trueman opening their attack.

Two-match Suspension for Arnold

BY JOHN WOODCOCK, CRICKET CORRESPONDENT

8 *August* 1974. To Geoffrey Arnold, of Surrey, has fallen the unenviable distinction of becoming the first cricketer in modern times to be suspended from playing for his county for his behaviour on the field. Although available to play for England in the second Test match against Pakistan at Lord's today and also in the third Test in a fortnight's time, he will miss Surrey's championship match against Middlesex, starting on August 17, as well as their John Player League match against Northamptonshire on the following day.

While bowling for Surrey against Warwickshire in a Sunday match last month, Arnold bridled when Peter Wight, the umpire, signalled a wide. Mr. Wight and Arnold gave evidence at Lord's yesterday before the disciplinary subcommittee of the Test and County Cricket Board, as did David Evans, who was the other umpire, and John Edrich and Arthur McIntyre, Surrey's captain and coach respectively.

In the chair was David Clark, manager of MCC on their last tour to Australia when there was enough of this sort of thing on the field for the Cricket Council to issue a strong warning that they and the TCCB, through their disciplinary committee, would not hesitate "to use their wide powers, including the termination of the registration of a player" to put a stop to "incidents involving dissent from umpire's decisions whether by word or deed".

Arnold is a superb bowler in this country. Colin Cowdrey told me the other day that he considered him one of the best he had ever played. He might have added that on the field he was also one of the grumpiest. It will therefore come as no surprise to cricketers in West Indies, India and Pakistan, as well as in England, that Arnold has at last found an umpire who complained.

In South Africa and Australia, as well as in England, swearing on the field has recently caused concern. Swearing for the sake of it in everyday life is accepted as it never used to be in a less permissive, more gracious age. Swearing at an umpire is still, mercifully, a good enough reason for a cricketer to be censured, as it is even in football, which tolerates most of the more excessive forms of conduct but still cautions a player for firing four-letter words at a referee.

Llewellyn Suspended

9 *August* 1974. Glamorgan have suspended Michael Llewellyn, an all-rounder, who was sent off by the umpires during a second XI match at Pontypridd this week for allegedly refusing his captain's request to field at short leg.

Sobers Gives Notice of Retirement

BY JOHN WOODCOCK, CRICKET CORRESPONDENT

17 *August* 1974. Only for another three weeks will it be possible to watch Gary Sobers, arguably the greatest cricketer of all time, playing the game which has brought him such fame and which he has played so gracefully for over 20 years. He gave notice yesterday of his intention to retire at the end of the present season.

Nottinghamshire have eight matches left, three of them on Sundays, in which to take a last look at Sobers, and I advise those who can to do so. I say that for two reasons: first, because he will be really trying and secondly, because we shall seldom see his like again. Already this month he has made the fastest championship 100 of the year, in 83 minutes, for Nottinghamshire against Derbyshire.

Sobers is 38. He played his first first-class match, for Barbados against the Indians, in 1953. Chosen as a slow bowler, he sent down 89 overs in the match, at the age of 16. His first Test match was against England the next year, since when his all round record in Test cricket has surpassed anything ever achieved before. He has scored 8,032 runs in Test matches, including 26 hundreds, and taken 235 Test wickets and 110 Test catches. He played an innings of 254 at Melbourne which Don Bradman described as the best ever seen in Australia and one of the most perfect ever played. He could equally well have bowled an opening spell with the new ball to strike terror into the hearts of the best batsmen in the game.

It is this incredible versatility that has made Sobers pre-eminent in the game. I have heard famous and greatly gifted cricketers saying of him that it was simply not fair for one man to be so impossibly good at so many things. He has been as likely to win a Test match with a breathtaking catch in the leg trap as with a brilliant throw from cover point; as likely to turn another with a spell of orthodox, left arm spin, as he did only last February in Port of Spain, as with a dozen overs of chinamen and googlies or a couple of fast inswingers; as capable of a long defensive innings as an attacking tour de force.

As a captain, in Test and other cricket, he was never prepared sufficiently to involve himself with the whole running of a side, both on and off the field, to be particularly successful.

He saw his job, I think, as starting at 11.30, or whenever he led his side on to the field, and finishing when the day's play was done. Dedication was not in him. I suppose it never needed to be. Without trying, or without appearing to try, he was better than anyone else, and he has always considered that life is for the living. I have not often passed more than a few moments with Sobers without him laughing about something. He had the rare gift to go with his wonderful talent of being able to see that cricket is a game for the playing and not a war for the fighting.

At the end of MCC's tour to West Indies in 1967-68, Colin Cowdrey, who had led England through a hectic series to a narrow victory, said that if he had at that moment to choose one word to apply to Sobers it would not be his agility or his temperament or his eyesight or his footwork, or even his virtuosity, but his sportsmanship. In victory and defeat he was the same person, born in a humble Barbadian home, the son of a seaman, but with a remarkable way of getting the game in perspective. While others around were working themselves into a frenzy, Sobers was sharing a joke with the opposition, fortified by the thought that, win or lose, it was not going to be the end of the world.

There were times when his own players felt that he batted too low at No. 6, always his favourite place in the order. Often the effort was made to persuade him to go in higher, but even in his prime he rarely did. This suited England, of course. Deflating as it was, after taking the fourth wicket of an innings, to see Sobers walking out to bat, he would undoubtedly have made even more runs than he did had he batted higher up. Then, though, he would have had less time to study the racing form and that would never have done.

Away from cricket, Sobers has always been happiest either at the races or on the golf course. There was never a rest day last winter, during the Test series against West Indies, when he was not looking for 36 holes of golf. Out of the clubhouse window of the new Barbados Golf and Country Club, on the rest day at Bridgetown, I saw a file of golfers and caddies in the distance walking down a path from the 15th green to the 16th tee. Leading them was Sobers, with his unmistakable walk – sparing one leg because of the knee which has given him so much trouble but still extraordinarily feline and keen to get to the next hole, although it was his second round of the day.

He had played in the morning with David Marsh, a former British Walker Cup captain, who said of Sobers that he was a lovely hitter of the ball, long off the tee and with a good touch. In his retirement he will play a lot of golf and have a chance, he hopes, to put something back into cricket. Not that after such generous a career he is in its debt.

Life Jail for Man who Killed Cricketer

FROM OUR CORRESPONDENT

4 *October* 1974, *Bristol.* A promising young county cricketer was murdered by a man who had been planning a killing for two years and said he wanted to do it again, it was stated at Bristol Crown Court yesterday.

Simon Kerr, aged 20, a Rhodesian, who had paid his fare to England to join Gloucestershire County Cricket Club, died after being stabbed 10 times at a party.

Mr. John Hall, Q.C., for the prosecution, said that Desmond Carroll, aged 24, an engineer, who admitted murdering Mr. Kerr, had described the killing as "sheer ecstasy". Mr. Carroll, of North Road, St. Andrews, Bristol, was jailed for life.

Sir Neville Cardus

1 *March* 1975. Sir Neville Cardus, C.B.E., who died in a London hospital yesterday at the age of 85, began as a sickly child in a Manchester slum, and ended an octogenarian who had richly fulfilled his two-fold ambition, to make a name as a music critic and a writer on cricket. He had no formal training in either field. The start of cricket for him was bowling for hours at a bucket, shielded by a broad piece of wood. Music came to him naturally and gave him his first chance of getting into print. As a sporting writer, he ranks with the old masters of the art from Hazlitt to Bernard Darwin; his cricket books became classics in his lifetime.

A versatile all-round journalist, Cardus delighted in commenting on the contrasts he had known in the social scene over the years. He could talk as well as he wrote and he was as welcome in exalted music circles as among cricketers in a pub. No compliment pleased him more than that he had made many people wish they had actually been at a cricket match or actually attended a concert. He wrote on cricket as a cricketer; on music as a listener.

Born on April 2, 1899, Cardus was brought up in the home of his grandfather, a retired policeman. He never knew his father and the most he ever heard of him was that he had been one of the first violins in an orchestra.

In his *Autobiography* (1947) he wrote that his Aunt Beatrice, "a great and original girl", frankly, and his mother, more discreetly, joined "the oldest of professions".

A brief Board school education was interrupted by an illness which kept him in bed for nearly a year. Earning his first money as a pavement artist, he went on to scrape a living from a miscellany of odd jobs, selling papers in the street, delivering the washing for his mother and aunts, pushing a handcart for a builder, and serving as a junior clerk.

Learning to spin an off-break that whipped up viciously, he played as an occasional pro in club cricket, and answered an advertisement for an assistant to William Attewell, the old Nottinghamshire player and head coach at Shrewsbury School. He was taken on, and stayed for five seasons from 1912 to 1916. One day the headmaster, Alington (later headmaster of Eton and Dean of Durham), found him on the field reading Gilbert Murray's translation of the *Medea* of Euripides. This happy chance led to Alington making him his private secretary. Cardus always acknowledged his debt to Alington, who gave him the run of the library. But the clerical headmaster never shook his young assistant's faith in free thinking.

Having volunteered in August, 1914, for military service and been rejected, "Not to my surprise or dismay", owing to extreme short sight, he was placed in an awkward dilemma when Alington went to Eton. He became a casual labourer and sold policies covering funeral expenses among the poor for a burial society. Escape from this dreary task came when he wrote to C. P.

Scott asking for employment in the counting house of the *Manchester Guardian* and enclosing cuttings of what little he had written. Scott was impressed and took him on briefly as secretary, and, later, invited him to join his staff as a reporter at 30s a week, with 10s for expenses. This was in 1917, and for the next two years he did all sorts of work for the paper.

He became its cricket correspondent by chance. In March, 1919, he suffered a breakdown and, after he returned to the paper, the news editor, later editor, W. P. Crozier, suggested that he might convalesce by spending a few days at Old Trafford. His first cricket report appeared in June, 1919. Next year he began writing on cricket every day, covering the most important matches up and down the country and his salary was raised to £5 a week. Between 1920 and 1939 he wrote roughly eight thousand words a week on cricket every summer from mid-May to August, nearly 2,000,000 words in 20 years. He brought to this task an unusual combination of qualities. First, he was a player in his own right who knew from first-hand experience how professionals reacted, and, secondly, he had absorbed the passion for writing good prose which was the tradition of Scott's young men. He put everything that was in him into his reports, catching the atmosphere of a ground, the personalities of the men in the field, the excitement and the tedium of the day's play – all distilled through his literary and musical enthusiasms. For him, Macartney was the Figaro of cricket, MacLaren the Don Quixote with his stonewalling partner, Makepeace, as Sancho Panza, and J. W. Hearne the Dickensian Turveydrop of the crease. This often bewildered the players he was writing about, but they respected him for his technical knowledge of the game. He put his experiences as "Cricketer" into a number of books, including *A Cricketer's Book*; *Days in the Sun*; *The Summer Game*; *Cricket*; *Good Days*; *Cricket all the Year Round* and *Close of Play*.

Delighting in cricket, he never wavered in his regard for music as his first string. He had first got into print in 1910 with an article in *Musical Opinion* on "Bantock and style in music", which tempted him to throw up his job as a clerk and devote himself to freelance journalism. But a postal order for only 7s 6d in payment for this article made him prudent, and he stuck to his job. He wrote musical articles in his early days in the *Manchester Guardian*, acting as assistant to its great critic, Samuel Langford, who taught him much, and with whom he always maintained a disciple to master relationship. He succeeded Langford in 1927, and held the post up to 1940 when he went to Australia. After his return to England, he had a spell on the staff of *The Sunday Times* in 1948-49, and rejoined the *MG* as its London music critic in 1951. From 1941-47 he was with the *Sydney Morning Herald*, and, later, he again visited Australia to broadcast on music for one hour weekly.

Reflecting on the two themes which engaged him, he once confessed "I could say that the Hammerclavier Sonata was the last thing that Beethoven wrote, and I'd get a couple of dozen letters, perhaps, 75 per cent from foreigners. But, if I said that Hutton made 363 at the Oval in 1938, I'd get thousands from Yorkshire alone." He admitted, though, that "Cricket opened my door of escape; cricket brought me enough economic independence whereby to educate myself". His books on music, some of which were translated into German and Swedish, included *Ten Composers*; *Musical Criticisms of Samuel Langford*; *Kathleen Ferrier Memorial Book*; *Talking of Music*; *Sir Thomas Beecham, A Portrait*; *Gustav Mahler: His Mind and His Music* Vol I; and *The Delights of Music*.

He married in 1921, Edith Honorine King, who died in 1968. There were no children. He was made C.B.E. in 1964 and knighted in 1967.

7 March 1975. Mr. Yehudi Menuhin writes:

What made Neville Cardus unique and uniquely British was his love and loyalty to both music and cricket. As a small boy, when I was still alien to these shores, it came as a wonderful shock when after only a few bars Sir Edward Elgar left the responsibility of playing his Violin Concerto in my immature hands, to go to the races.

I was equally surprised to learn that the great critic, Neville Cardus, knew as much about a cricket bat as about a violin bow. These two memorable experiences convinced me ever since that sport and fresh air were in no way inimical to a profound knowledge of music.

Neville Cardus was indeed unique. No critic has interpreted music and performance to the public with greater insight and sensitivity. He always searched for and recognized the intention and the message of the performer as well as the character of the occasion. He was as alive to the public response, to the pulse of the audience, as he was to the specific performance and its ambience. His vision and integrity were such that he could preserve a balance between the diverse facets of his writing.

Above all he knew that music exists in time as an organism, not only as theory or law, above and independent of time. He lived the music and the occasion. He wrote not as a one-man dictionary, but with the combined reaction of heart and mind.

Danger Should be Crucial Word in the Laws

BY JOHN WOODCOCK

1 March 1975. No matter where one goes, or who one talks to, the conversation comes round to short-pitched bowling. So far as the Auckland incident is concerned, in which Ewan Chatfield so nearly lost his life, opinions vary widely: from that of the *Guardian*'s man at the match who wrote that "no one I have met in Auckland has held Lever in any way to blame for what happened", to my own that Lever's was a calculated act to take unreasonable advantage of a bowler's inability to bat.

In their efforts to keep such bowling within bounds, the authorities are thinking for the moment more in terms of persuasion than legislation. Any proposal for a change in the law would, in any case, have to await the next meeting of the International Cricket Conference, which is not to be held until the end of June. Pakistan have cabled Lord's asking for this meeting to be brought forward so that what is an urgent matter can be discussed before, rather than after, the World Cup.

The law as it stands ("The persistent bowling of fast short-pitched balls is unfair if in the opinion of the umpire at the bowler's end it constitutes a systematic attempt at intimidation") lends itself to too casual an interpretation. When, for example, does an "attempt at intimidation" become systematic? And when does "persistent" become persistent? For the sake of an easier definition, would it not be better to say simply, that "the bowling of fast short-pitched balls is unfair if in the opinion of either umpire it constitutes dangerous play"?

Specifying the number of bouncers to be bowled at each batsman according to his position and the order is altogether too cold-blooded. Neither, as we saw in Australia, is it practicable. How many, if you like, do you assign Walker, who, although he batted at number eight for Australia, and is primarily a bowler, averaged nearly 50 in the Test matches?

As for a line drawn across the pitch, who is going to watch it, unless (heaven forbid!) a kind of service-court judge is brought into the action? It would be asking too much of the bowler's umpire, with all he already has to do, to decide which side of the line each ball pitched. In the case of the square leg umpire, he is at too wide an angle and too far away to make a hairline judgment.

Baseball went a part of the way towards solving a related problem by making the wearing of helmets compulsory for the striker. It is also accepted as being morally wrong for a pitcher to aim at the striker. Although at baseball the ball is hurled at a faster speed than at cricket, and over a shorter distance, only one striker has ever been killed. Helmets, no doubt, have had something to do with this, though if they were to be worn for playing cricket, they would probably lead to more reckless bowling than there already is.

In seeking to make the game less hazardous, it is crucially important not to drive fast bowlers out of it. Some of the most thrilling innings ever played have been against bowlers bowling both fast and short. There are batsmen (but not bowlers) playing today who, with their eye in, would give a guinea a time for Lever's bouncers; just as there are thousands of people in England who are counting the days to the time when they can go and see for themselves just how fearsome Thomson and Lillee are. If, in the meantime, they were to hear that the bouncer had been banned, they might change their minds about going. "Have you got another Larwood, Bill?" asked the secretary of the Australian Board of Control of Bill Bowes, when he landed in Australia just after the war, "because if you have the grounds won't be large enough". This winter, on one or two occasions, they hardly were, because of Thomson and Lillee.

Should it be thought that we are getting soft in our old age, Mr. Bowes makes some relevant comparisons between the bodyline tour, on which he went as a player, and last winter's tour, snatches of which he watched on television. Although not liking to see the lack of mettle shown by some of England's present batsmen, he believes they had more to contend with than the Australians did in 1932-33 from Larwood, Voce and Allen. For one thing, the lbw law, as it applied then, made batting easier than it does now. You could only be out when the ball pitched between wicket and wicket, which meant that you needed to play nothing that was wide of the stumps. Today you can be leg before to a ball pitching outside the off stump.

More contentiously Mr. Bowes insists that Larwood never aimed to hit the Australian batsmen, which Lillee ("I bowl bouncers for one reason, and that is to hit the batsman and thus intimidate him") and Thomson both do, and which Lever ("I wanted to get him caught off the glove") did to someone whose highest first-class score was eight. This is what Mr. Bowes finds so horrifying: that there should be at large bowlers whose aim it is to hit the batsman. Some Australians, not surprisingly, would say that Larwood did. It was because of him, after all, that the word "intimidation" appeared in the laws. Now, because of Chatfield, the game's conscience is being troubled again – the conscience not least of the captains and the managers, for if the umpires are undecided what is fair, you can be sure the players are not.

Why Chinese Will Not Play Politics with Cricket

FROM RICHARD HUGHES

2 *April* 1975; *Hongkong, 1 April.* Harold Larwood, D. R. Jardine's incomparable bodyline Test bowler, will be specially invited to bowl a nostalgic over at the historic match which will finally draw stumps at the century-old Hongkong Cricket Club this year. Larwood, now an Australian businessman, who lives in Sydney but prefers to watch Tests from "the Hill" rather than the Sydney Cricket Club members' stand, has accepted an invitation to attend the requiem ceremonies at the colony's original cricket club.

Officially, he will be included in the "non-playing" guest-list, together with notable Australian Test veterans: Bert Oldfield, Lindsay Hassett, Bill O'Reilly and Bill Brown. But it is predicted that not only Larwood but also Oldfield, Hassett and O'Reilly will be asked to appear for a symbolic one-over appearance in their old roles as wicket-keeper, batsman and slow bowler.

The invited guests of the "playing" contingent of former Australian Test players will include: Neil Harvey, Bobby Simpson, Ian Craig, Alan Davidson, Jim Burke, Ron Archer, Ray Lindwall, Rod Marsh, Les Favell, Keith Stackpole, Ian Meckiff and Ian Johnson.

After this memorable final match, the old club will be moved from its honourable site in the congested heart of the colony to a cleared wasteland halfway up the Peak. On present plans, the old site will become a public park, topping one of the central underground stations on Hongkong's projected mass transit system. Sceptics are already suggesting however, that the land areas is too valuable to be preserved indefinitely as a park and that the site will inevitably become another skyscraper office complex, overshadowing both the adjacent Hongkong Club and the Communist People's Bank of China.

The ancient ground will certainly be crowded to standing accommodation to see the immortal Test veterans in action once more. There are unofficial hopes that one of the invited Australian batsmen may finally achieve the unique distinction of breaking a window of the towering People's Bank across the road with a six and thereby win the legendary but still unclaimed prize of a case of champagne.

One of the several urbane officials of the Communist bank who occasionally stroll into the cricket club to watch the curious foreign-devil game of cricket has said privately that no party protest would be made if a six did break a window of the bank. "Our ping pong balls have occasionally struck friendly foreigners watching our players in action abroad", he pointed out. "We well understand the rules and traditions of good sportsmanship,which have nothing to do with differing views on politics or ideology."

Pavilion Sale

3 *June* 1975. Lowdham Cricket Club, near Nottingham, has had to sell its pavilion because of a £36 rates demand. The building, which cost £225 seven years ago and had no services, fetched £25.

Sri Lanka Prospects Please until Thomson Injures Two Batsmen

BY ALAN GIBSON

12 *June* 1975. I was having a drink with this beautiful girl from Ceylon. It was rather a lot of years ago, perhaps it would be unchivalrous to say how many. She is now a famous broadcaster in her country. I had just begun as a cricket commentator. "One day", she said, "you will broadcast upon England against Ceylon at Lord's." We had another beer on the prospect. It was an evening when every prospect pleased, and the spicy breezes blew soft o'er

Ceylon's isle. "But", she went on to say, her golden eyes hardening, "when you do, you are to be kind to Ceylon."

Well, I have not yet seen Ceylon play England at Lord's, but I saw Sri Lanka – as they are now called – play Australia at the Oval yesterday, something which would have seemed even more improbable those years ago. As to being kind, there is no difficulty. They played extremely well, they batted better than they bowled, and their fielding varied between brilliance and wildness. Nevertheless, at one stage they had the mighty Australians worried, almost fumbling. Consider, Australia were 178 for no wicket in 34 overs at lunch, and went on to make 328 for five. All we expected of Sri Lanka was that they would do their best to bat it out and gain experience. But in the 32nd over they had scored 150, and lost only two wickets. Mendis and Wettimuny were going so well that anything seemed possible.

At this point Thomson laid Mendis out. It was not strictly a bouncer, but a short ball, aimed at the body. Thomson hit the batsman on several other occasions with similar balls. He was booed by the crowd, alike by those from the Indian subcontinent and those forthright souls from the Elephant and Castle. It will not, I am afraid, be a pleasant occasion when Australia meet West Indies.

Mendis was carried off, and in Thomson's next over so was Wettimuny, who had had several bangs on the legs and midriff. He limped most of the way, but had to be picked up before he reached the Pavilion. They were both taken to hospital for treatment. With two new batsmen needing to play themselves in, Sri Lanka could not keep up the scoring rate. Thus vanished their hopes, but not their bravery. They did not duck or dodge the fast bowling. They kept playing strokes: glances and cuts are what they do best. They will beat Australia one day.

Perhaps they were wrong to put Australia in, on a fast and true pitch. I suppose after their last experience they were afraid of an attack of early nerves, a sudden, irretrievable breakdown. They certainly played better as the day went on. They were not helped in the morning by an invasion of the field by some young supporters who were, I understand, protesting against the selection of their side.

Sri Lanka's 276 for four was the highest score made in the second innings of a Prudential Cup match: not that that breaks any long-standing records, but it was done against Australia and their dreaded attack. Although Australia dropped some catches, they were not fooling about. The man of the match, Laurie Fishlock decided, was Turner, whose innings we had almost forgotten in the flux of events. Not that he did not deserve it. The woman of the match was a golden-eyed girl from Ceylon who prophesied long ago.

AUSTRALIA 328 for 5 (60 overs) (A. Turner 101, K. D. Walters 59, G. S. Chappell 50)
SRI LANKA 276 for 4 (60 overs) (S. Wettimuny 63 ret hurt, M. H. Tissera 52, A. Tenekoon 48)
Australia won by 52 runs

The Great Day when London was Lloyd's

BY JOHN WOODCOCK, CRICKET CORRESPONDENT

23 *June* 1975. By the time the curtain calls had ended at Lord's on Saturday it was 9 o'clock. By the time the last of the speeches had been made, and the last of the lights put out, it was past midnight. As much as a cricket match, the final of the World Cup for the Prudential trophy, won by West Indies by 17 runs, had been a piece of theatre; of drama, tragedy, carnival and farce all rolled into one.

Already a great enterprise, the tournament ended as a great success. We shall know later this week where and when it is to be staged next. It went so well this time that it could even be in England again. As the most compact and cosmopolitan of the cricketing countries it makes in many ways the ideal setting, especially when the weather is as it has been for the past fortnight. Saturday was as beautiful a day as any there had been, and as eventful.

Worthy and colourful champions as the West Indians are, Australia will be kicking themselves for the blunders they made. Of these, perhaps the most expensive was the missing of Clive Lloyd when he was 26. Had Edwards, at short midwicket, held the low catch which Lloyd offered, as he would have done more often than not, West Indies would have been 83 for four with little chance of making as many as they did. There is no better Australian fielder than Edwards, either. Then, when Australia batted, needing 292 to win, they made a succession of irredeemable mistakes between the wickets. If either side was to be let down by errors of excitement I had thought it would be West Indies, not Australia.

Although Australia will be criticized for putting West Indies in I am not sure that that is fair. If at any time in the match the pitch held something for the bowlers it was during the morning, while there was still a little damp about; and the risk that Australia were taking of batting themselves in fading light was lessened by a cloudless forecast. In the event, as Thomson and Lillee showed in a last wicket partnership of 41, the ball could be picked up perfectly well, even at the end of the day.

But this is far enough to have gone without mentioning an innings of 102 by Clive Lloyd, which will always be talked about by those who watched it. To dwarf so many of the world's leading batsmen, as Lloyd did, was of itself the mark of greatness. Physically, and in terms of cricketing authority, he towered above the rest. He was larger than life. To have such gifts of height and power and timing is one thing; to use them at a time like this is another. Lloyd made the pitch and the stumps and the bowlers and the ground all seem much smaller than they were.

It was possible, because of the game that Lloyd played, for Kanhai to go from the twenty-third over of the West Indian innings to the thirty-fourth without scoring a run and yet do a service for his side. Kanhai cut loose eventually, when the crisis of 50 for three was safely passed. Boyce, turning three somersaults when he tripped over where one would have done, made a whirlwind 34, Julien a useful 26; and in the penultimate over even Murray hooked Lillee for six.

Yet Australia would have won, I think, had they not kept running themselves out. It was a supremely easy pitch by now, and a fast outfield, and when they reached 80 for one after 20 overs they had made just the start they needed. If the target was still far distant the ease with which Turner and his captain were batting, and with which others batted after them, showed what might have been, but for three fatal hesitations and the deadly aim of Vivian Richards. Turner and the Chappell brothers were all run out by Richards; each time when the single would have been safe, albeit narrowly, had the batsmen not wavered.

At 167 for three, with Ian Chappell and Walters together and 21 overs left and the West Indians worried, it remained an open match. At 233 for nine, after 53 overs, only Thomson and Lillee thought Australia still had a chance. With no pretence at style these two made us wonder whether the last twist of an enthralling game was to be the most dramatic. For 40 minutes the thousands of West Indians ringed the boundary, rocking, rolling, shouting, clanging, as they waited their victory to proclaim.

Standing on their balcony the Australians felt their hopes returning. Once, when Fredericks caught Lillee, off a no-ball, the floodgates burst, the crowd pouring across the grass as Fredericks's throw at the bowler's stumps, an attempt to run out Thomson, disappeared among them. By the time the field was cleared and the ball recovered, and the umpires had decided how many runs had been run there were three overs left and 21 were needed. When, at last, Murray ran out Thomson, bowling the ball at the stumps as Thomson, the striker, made a despairing dive for safety after being sent back by Lillee, we had had all that we could stand. Players, stewards, barmen and watchers had reached the end of their tether. So, too, had Thomson, when he emerged from an encircling horde of West Indians, without gloves and bat and sweater, perhaps, for all I know, without his box. As a seasoned surfer this was the worst dumping he can have had.

There it was then: West Indies were the champions, Australia the gallant losers, cricket the deserving winner. Whether, as the match went on, Prince Philip rang his home to ask for his supper to be put in the oven I wouldn't know, but it was not a match to leave. The cup and the award as Man of the Match he presented to Clive Lloyd, the hero of he day, the toast of every West Indian island from Camberwell to the Caribbean.

In 119 overs there had not been one of spin, which was more than sad; in all the excitement there had been several dropped catches. Of fast bowling which took the breath away there had been surprisingly little. Yet as a production to remember it was, as the sponsors themselves might put it, an "assured" success.

WEST INDIES 291 for 8 (60 overs) (C. H. Lloyd 102, R. B. Kanhai 55;
G. J. Gilmour 5 for 48)
AUSTRALIA 274 (58.4 overs) (I. M. Chappell 62, A. Turner 40; K. D.
Boyce 4 for 50)
West Indies won by 17 runs

Naked Runner is Fined £20

6 *August* 1975. Michael Angelow, who ran naked across Lord's cricket
ground on Monday, was fined £20 when he appeared at Marylebone Magis-
trates' Court, yesterday.

Mr. Angelow, aged 24, a merchant seaman, of St. Albans, Hertfordshire,
admitted insulting behaviour. When told that the escapade was for a £20
bet, Lieutenant-Colonel William Haswell, chairman of the bench, said: "The
court will have that £20; please moderate your behaviour in future."

England Women Dispel Flippancy
and the Australian Challenge

BY ALAN GIBSON

5 *August* 1976. The notices were still there on the pavilion doors: "The
attention of all members of MCC, and Middlesex, their guests and visitors,
is drawn to the conditions contained in regulation 3 (v) of the regulations
of MCC which require them to wear a necktie and jacket whilst in the
pavilion."

Regulation 3 (v) has never taken such a battering as it did yesterday. The
doorkeepers turned their eyes away as the skirts whisked up to the dressing
rooms. For this, as you will already know – it is not Rachael Flint's fault if you
do not – was the first time the women had taken over Lord's. The editor of
The Cricketer told me he had raced to the ground to be sure of seeing the
first ball bowled. Not many others had. Only a few hundred were there at the
start, and when Australia lost a wicket to the second ball, the noise was
rather less than it will be if the same thing happens in the men's match next
year. But, as a sunny afternoon drew on, more and more people came along
until there was a larger crowd than Middlesex often get.

They saw Australia all out, for 161. When nine wickets were down for 127,
it looked as if they would score less, but a last wicket stand gave them something to bowl at, and prolonged the innings to the sixtieth, and in any case
last, over. Marie Lutschini batted very well in this stand, as Sharon Tredrea
had done earlier. It cannot have been often that players of Italian and

Cornish extraction (as I presume these two to be) have made so big a contribution to an innings at Lord's.

I have never thought cricket a particularly suitable game for girls to play – I mean, I shall not grieve if my daughter Felicity does not take it up – but if they wish to, they should be encouraged by fellow-cricketers, not patronized or snubbed. I am glad Lord's has opened its door to them, in the jubilee year of the Women's Cricket Association.

In my student days, I played often against and with women's teams. Some of these matches were quite serious. Westfield College, for instance, were not a side you could take chances with. The batting of the women then was much better than their bowling. They could catch, and field smartly on the ground, but their throwing was poor, and I do not mean just through lack of physique.

Watching the cream of the game yesterday (I use the metaphor advisedly: they were playing for the St. Ivel Cream Jug) I thought that they still batted better than they bowled. They would score runs against a county, but it would take them a long time to get one out. The throwing, however, especially the Australian throwing, has improved vastly.

I dislike some of the W.C.A. publicity, those giggly bits about leg-glances, etc. I was disappointed at some of the antics at the fall of a wicket, like so many huge, hairy footballers (Australia were less emotional than England). They do not do themselves justice by these things. But I see their difficulties. They feel they must not spurn any chance of publicity.

Women's cricket, for all its well-established international pattern (England first toured Australia in 1934, and Australia returned the visit three years later) rests on a small numerical base. In 1970, Rowland Bowen estimated that one woman cricketer in a hundred plays for England, whereas the figure for men would be nearer one in a hundred thousand. Things have improved since then, but not by much.

Flippancy dropped away from the crowd, though, as England set out to get the runs. They were given a good start by two famous players, Enid Bakewell and Lynne Thomas. Thomas was caught at mid-on in the 38th over, Bakewell run out in the 41st. The score was then 93 for 2, with two new batswomen to play themselves in.

Chris Watmough, a Lancastrian, who now plays for Kent, and her captain, the pride of Wolverhampton, saw them through, amid genuine enthusiasm, with three overs to spare. Australia, however, took the St. Ivel Jug, because they had won at Canterbury on Sunday, and had a faster scoring rate over the two matches combined. So everyone had something to celebrate.

AUSTRALIA 161 (59.4 overs) (S. A. Tredrea 54)
ENGLAND 162 for 2 (56.2 overs) (C. Watmough 50 not out)
England won by 8 wickets

A Dish to Set before the Queen

FROM COLIN COWDREY

18 *March* 1977; *Melbourne*, 17 *March*. As the light began to fade after five gloriously sunny days of enthralling cricket, Knott was dismissed by Lillee, his fifth wicket and eleventh in the match, and Australia had won the centenary Test match by 45 runs.

By some coincidence, on March 17, 1877, a hundred years to the day, England were set a target of 154 and also lost by 45 runs. Today it was a stiffer task. In scoring 417, England achieved the highest total in the fourth innings of an Anglo-Australian Test match and in doing so have won all hearts.

The last day began with England left to score just 272 to win – 90 in each session, a task by no means beyond them on the slow, easy paced pitch. Provided that the early overs were negotiated safely only the clock might have presented a problem. As the ball becomes softer and the outfield is slow here a batting side can so easily get bogged down. So it was important that they did not lag behind and at lunchtime they were well in contention.

The first hour was fascinating, for Chappell had a problem. With Gilmour injured, Lillee was the trump card. He had to be thrown in to the fray to make the early break, if possible, but the new ball was available in 12 overs. O'Keeffe bowled tidily and took two vital wickets later on. Walker, faced with the prospect of some marathon spells later in the day, was discarded temporarily.

Needing just 13 for his first Test hundred, Randall was confronted with a burst from Lillee. If he was nervous he showed no trace of it. Brearley had provided the helpful word early in his innings and now he was fortunate to have the steadying influence of Amiss at the other end. In the event he played quite superbly, a deft sweep, a glorious late cut and he was soon on 99, facing Lillee. Next ball he tucked him away to fine leg for his first Test hundred and became the fourteenth batsman to score a hundred in his first Test match against Australia. The Yorkshireman, Willie Watson, was the last to do so in 1953.

I was delighted for him after his rigours in India where his previous best in a Test match had been 37, but he had made a huge contribution to the team's success by his enthusiasm. It would have been understandable if he had shown the odd lapse of concentration in the excitement of his achievement but he just played better and better as he went along. He is something of an irrepressible Jack-in-the-box both in batting and fielding but today he assumed a responsibility to fit the occasion. His timing never left him; only fatigue slowed him down and, in part, contributed to his downfall.

All the while Amiss looked a class player with plenty of time. He seems to have the broadest bat in English cricket today and Lillee did not unruffle him as much as I expected. His sudden dismissal by a ball that kept rather low was the turning point of the day. True, that while Greig and Randall were together we could still have won but somehow I had the feeling that we were beginning to live too dangerously.

When Randall made 161 he edged Greg Chappell low and wide where Marsh appeared to have scooped his glove under the catch. As he rolled over and over the umpire upheld the appeal and Randall departed a disconsolate figure. Without delay Marsh leapt to his feet and rushed down the wicket to tell his captain that the ball had bounced. The umpires conferred and Randall was recalled. It was indeed a chivalrous gesture at such a critical moment of the match.

Just before tea England were slowed down by some good bowling from Chappell himself and he elected to gamble with O'Keeffe. In his first over, Cosier dived full length to take a magnificent catch off bat and pad and Randall's historic innings had closed on 174. The whole ground rose to him.

Through the tears of joy he went out through the wrong gate, finding himself at the end of the path leading to the special box where the Queen and the Duke of Edinburgh were sitting. Within a few yards of them he discovered his mistake and stopped in his tracks and, much to the amusement of all, bowed before beating a hasty retreat across the public seats. It was a happy touch for the day had belonged to him.

It might be arguable that Lillee's great bowling could have earned him the prize of Man of the Match, but without doubt Randall was the man who had made the match complete. There were not four gladder hearts in Melbourne today than Larwood, Voce, Hardstaff and Simpson, giant names from Trent Bridge.

If the game tilted fairly sharply towards Australia after tea Knott made it clear that they were not going to have it all their own way. He played a series of astonishing shots, treating Lillee with utter contempt. He is a genius of improvisation.

But the day finished with Lillee summoning up energy and fire from I do not know where. He was bowling faster at the end than he was at the beginning and deservedly he was carried aloft, first by players and then by some of his ecstatic countrymen, while a dozen or more policemen surrounded him to keep him intact.

But alas, his medical advisers have determined that he is not quite intact although you could never have guessed it today. Sadly for the English pubic but to the relief of the English batsmen, he has withdrawn from the forthcoming tour of England.

We have had a remarkable week and life will be rather flat until we have had time to absorb it all. I do not know when I have enjoyed the last day of a Test match more than this one. It had everything, both captains playing their part in the challenge, both wicketkeepers making their mark, some wonderful fast bowling, good sustained spells of leg spin bowling, some fine fielding, a generous gesture and a large crowd. The result was open until near the end. When Randall and Greig were raking the embers just before tea there was still the prospect of an English victory. What a dish it was to set before the Queen.

AUSTRALIA 138 (G. S. Chappell 40) and 419 for 9 dec (R. W. Marsh 110 not out, I. C. Davis 68; C. M. Old 4 for 104)
ENGLAND 95 (D. K. Lillee 6 for 26, M. H. N. Walker 4 for 54) and 417 (D. W. Randall 174, D. L. Amiss 64, A. P. E. Knott 42, A. W. Greig 41; D. K. Lillee 5 for 139)
Australia won by 45 runs

11 *May* 1977, *Personal Column.* In affectionate remembrance of International Cricket which died at Hove, 9th May, 1977. Deeply lamented by a large circle of friends, and acquaintances. R.I.P.   N.B. The body will be cremated and The Ashes taken to Australia and scattered around the studio of TCN9 Sydney. NTJCBM.

Tony Greig Dismissed as England Captain

BY JOHN WOODCOCK, CRICKET CORRESPONDENT

14 *May* 1977. Tony Greig has been deprived of the England Test captaincy. Meeting at Lord's yesterday, the emergency committee of the Cricket Council announced that they would be instructing Alec Bedser, the chairman of the selectors that "Tony Greig is not to be considered for the position [captaincy of England] for the forthcoming series against Australia".

The committee said that, in reaching this decision, they had taken into consideration "the current England captain's clearly admitted involvement, unknown to the authorities, in recruitment of the players for an organization which has been set up in conflict with a scheduled series of Test matches. His action has inevitably impaired the trust which existed between the cricket authorities and the captain of the England side." The committee were referring to a projected series between Australia and a world eleven in Australia next winter, under a contract with Mr. Kerry Packer, a television proprietor.

Freddie Brown, chairman of the Cricket Council, added: "The captaincy of the England team involves liaison with the selectors in the management, selection and development of England players for the future, and clearly Tony Greig is unlikely to be able to do this as his stated intention is to be contracted elsewhere during the next three winters."

Yesterday's decision, besides being a great personal disappointment to Greig, is bound, to some extent, to be a setback to the recovery which the

England team launched with some success in India last winter. Disloyalty, though, such as that shown by Greig in involving himself and two more of England's leading players, Knott and Underwood, in a scheme which drastically reduces their availability for England, deserves what punishment it gets.

However plausibly Greig may claim that what he is doing is for the good of English cricket, however unselfish an act he may say it is, however truculently he may express the hope that the authorities at Lord's will be "sensible" in how they react to the Packer circus, no one is likely to be convinced that he has acted less than miserably as the reigning captain.

Like Knott and Underwood, Greig can play for England in the coming series – unless the International Cricket Conference, who may be convened within the next fortnight (their annual meeting is not due until July 26), should rule that any one who has already signed for Packer has, by doing so, excluded himself from official Test cricket. As the Packer party include most of the Australian team currently touring England and the Australian manager has said that no sanctions will be imposed on any of them for the duration of their tour, what action the ICC decide on is unlikely to take effect until the Australian tour is over.

There have been various occasions since he became an England cricketer when Greig has overplayed his hand. The most famous, or infamous, was at Port of Spain in 1975, when he ran out Kallicharran as he was making off to the pavilion after the last ball of a day's play. There was always this danger that, for some reason or other, his impulsiveness, or his commercialism, or the strangely insensitive streak which exists within a normally charming and considerate person might be his undoing.

What has to be remembered, of course, is that he is an Englishman not by birth or upbringing, but only by adoption. It is not the same thing as being English through and through. At the same time, I do believe that making the England team into a winning one has meant a great deal to him. There was a lot of truth in what he had to say after the Melbourne Test match about the strength of his team's team spirit.

For this reason, whoever is appointed to succeed Greig will have a difficult job. Within moments of being informed of the Cricket Council's decision, the England selectors met at the other end of the Lord's pavilion to decide where to go from here. The favourite for the captaincy must be Michael Brearley, of Middlesex, who was Greig's understudy in India. Like everyone else, he was rather dwarfed by Greig out there. But he is liked and respected by the players and he will almost certainly get into the England side on merit. Tactically, too, he is Greig's superior, which is not to say that he will make a better captain. Greig's aggressiveness and his fearless example on the field will be hard to replace.

There is no intention at present of asking Mr. Packer to come to England, or of requesting Mr. Bob Parish, chairman of the Australian Cricket Board, to see Mr. Packer before he himself flies over. One of the ironies of the whole affair is that it is with Mr. Packer's company that the Test and County Cricket Board signed a contract for £150,000 for the Australian television rights of this summer's fight for the Ashes. Mr. Packer's offer was preferred to the Australian Broadcasting Commission's which is the establishment of Australian broadcasting.

If, when they meet, the member countries of the ICC decide that no one shall be considered for his country while giving priority to the cause of Mr. Packer, Australia, West Indies and Pakistan, as well as England, are all going to have a lot of rebuilding to do. I hope yet that some compromise may be reached. It should be possible. It might even have happened already, and saved Greig his job, had his own part in a month of negotiations not smacked of concealment.

Referring to the payment which the England players will receive for playing in a Test match this summer, against Australia (£210), Mr. Peter Lush, speaking after yesterday's meeting, said that it was realized how inadequate it was. When the present pay restraints are lifted it will improve. As it is, the two sides this summer will be playing for prize money of approximately £20,000 – less than Mr. Packer would put at stake, but a great deal more than any one has ever before had the opportunity to win.

A Victory to Celebrate Jubilee Year

16 *August* 1977, *Leading Article.* Our new national obsession with the antics of the antipodean television tycoon can for a while, be laid aside for happier thoughts. England has won a mightily convincing and historic victory. What more fitting Jubilee event can there be than the recovery of the Ashes in this country for only the third time this century – the feat last being performed in 1953, the year of her Majesty's coronation, and before that in 1926? It was even longer ago, in 1886, that England last won three consecutive Test matches against the traditional foe in a home series, although they have done it several times in Australia.

It was little more than two years ago that the English side returned from their Australian tour, thoroughly beaten, dispirited and demoralized. A decade of Australian supremacy was predicted. That the tables have been so completely turned lies largely to the credit of Greig. He took over a side being compared with the very worst in England's cricketing history, made its members believe in their individual and collective abilities, and by his own flamboyant, perhaps over-aggressive example instilled confidence into a team that had become accustomed to losing. In particular, his insistence on the importance of good fielding has paid handsome dividends. The superb athleticism and sticky fingers of the English side contributed in large measure to its success.

It is not disparaging to the virtually flawless captaincy of Brearley to say that he inherited a side already filled with the enthusiasm and motivation to perform splendid feats. He took over, nevertheless, at an unsettled time in less than happy circumstances, and, with great tactical perception, went on to lead England's team to comprehensive victories in three matches. That makes him a very good captain indeed.

The dominant memory of the Test series will undoubtedly be of Boycott, returned like some banished prince to assume his birthright, bestriding the narrow crease like a Hutton, suspending belief in the possibility that his wicket, too, could fall like that of mere cricketers. But Boycott is already of a certain age. In the longer term, the youth of all but a few members of the team and the sudden embarrassment of talent among even younger players promise well for the future of English cricket.

There are those of little faith who say that the Australian team was the weakest ever sent to these shores, and that they were worried by the un-mentionable commercial activities that have formed a backdrop to the season (why then did Greig, Knott and Underwood not suffer?). Why entertain such quibbles? England have achieved a magnificent victory. The Ashes are back. It is a time for every Englishman to feel proud.

America Wins its First Cricket Match

5 *September* 1977; *New York, 4 September.* The Americans beat the West Indians yesterday on what the stadium announcer, with characteristic hyperbole, called the playing field of history. Yet you could not gainsay him, for according to the promoters it was the first professional cricket match ever staged in the United States.

It was played in a vast bowl-like arena, on artificial turf, under floodlights for the last 90 minutes and with an electronic scoreboard which provided instant replays and at the dramatic highlights of the game, would flash out phrases like: "Ouch!" "Did you see that", "Give 'em a hand, fans".

In spite of such blatant differences from Kennington Oval, it remained recognizably cricket. When Sir Gary Sobers was bouncing his cover drives off the bright blue boundary fence, it was cricket of a vintage kind.

The game attracted a crowd of 6,674, rather above the average for a week-end one-day county game in Britain. Nearly all were West Indians, and they had paid between $6 (£3.50) and $10 for their tickets. If you tell the organizers that this is a modest start for a sport they hope will sweep the country, they wag their fingers and say, "Yes, but what about soccer?"

The success of soccer is the big sports story in the United States just now. The New York Cosmos, champions of the season which has just finished (as, with a team that includes Pele and Beckenbauer, they should be), drew a capacity crowd of 76,500 for their last home game.

The local equivalent of the F.A. Cup was televised nationally. Soccer is being played at more and more schools and colleges. Yet only a few years ago it was hard to persuade anyone but a few homesick Europeans to watch. "Who would have thought," asked one of the backers of yesterday's cricket, "that 77,000 people would turn out to see guys in short pants bounce a ball off their heads."

The cricket match was played at the Cosmos home stadium, part of the new Meadowlands sports complex in New Jersey, just four miles from Manhattan. It is also the home of the New York Giants, who play American football.

The wicket was marked out amid the numbered lines used in American football to calculate yardage gained. Because stumps cannot be poked into artificial turf, they were fixed to a wooden platform which was made fast to the surface.

I could tell it was going to be a Caribbean crowd as soon as I stepped on to the bus at the Eighth Avenue terminal. My family and I were the only white people on it, apart from the driver. As we arrived at the stadium women were parading round the arena bearing placards with the names of the countries from which the players hailed. Each player was introduced individually to the spectators, waving as his name was announced.

The American side batted first, and the first ball bowled for money in America was a sensational one. Wes Hall, the formerly redoubtable but now balding fast bowler, delivered it to Peter Merritt, an Englishman who opens the batting for Staten Island, and of whom the programme note said that he "represented the United States in Bermuda with fair success".

I thought this a rather uncertain recommendation and so it proved. Hall's first ball sent the bails flying and the electronic scoreboard went beserk. "Did you see that?" it asked. (In Merritt's case the answer was clearly "No". "Give that man a hand"; and there appeared an animated picture of two hands clapping.

Yet the American side (itself composed mainly of West Indians) improved after that blow. Charlie Griffith, Hall's old partner, was ineffective, and Lance Gibbs was the only bowler who had consistently to be treated with respect. The ball bounced high on the artificial surface, but at no great pace.

As the innings progressed the Americans took advantage of the tiring and aging attack and at the end of their allotted 40 overs had scored 194 for eight.

The tea interval was unduly prolonged because the steel band due to perform in it took more than half an hour to set up their equipment. After an interval of an hour and a quarter the players and umpires had to take the field to persuade Lord Observer, the improvisation king of calypso, to leave it.

The Americans, a much younger side than the West Indians, bowled and fielded with enthusiasm and had soon sent back to the pavilion (or rather to the dugout below the stands) such eminent players from the past as Roy Fredericks, Lawrence Rowe and Seymour Nurse. They spent an embarrassingly short time "at bat", in the baseball parlance which the scoreboard was using to describe the action.

The scoreboard, and the commentator who was giving a ball-by-ball account of the game over the loudspeaker system for those unfamiliar with its mysteries, reserved their greatest enthusiasm for Sobers. "Sir Gary" was the message passed in electronic letters. "Fantastic" and "Attack" were flashed out as he stroked his fours and sixes.

It would have been a terrible anti-climax had he been out cheaply, but he was the highest scorer with 57, although limping badly. Apart from David Holford nobody else did much, and the West Indians were out for 170.

It was all very different from the county ground at Weston-super-Mare on a damp Tuesday.

On the debit side, there was nothing of cricket's bucolic tradition, unless you count the vaguely unpleasant smell drifting in from a sewage plant nearby.

The man behind the event was Bert Smith, a West Indian photographer, who managed to get the sponsorship of an airline, using the argument that if it had happened to soccer, why not to cricket?

But there were precious few genuine Americans there yesterday and whether it will catch on like soccer has I would not be so bold as to predict. It is, as they say in these parts, a whole new ball game.

Echoes of a Month-long Hearing in the High Court

9 *November* 1977.

The alacrity with which they [the players] joined was frightening – *Kerry Packer*

They want the penny and the bun – *Geoffrey Boycott*

I've heard the only way to get out of a Packer contract is by becoming pregnant – *Raymond Steele* (Australia)

Bob Taylor is one of the best wicket-keepers the world has ever seen – *Alan Knott*

Alan Knott is the best wicketkeeper in the world – *Boycott*

Cricketers [at the Cricketers' Association meeting] thought that if we got rid of a few more [overseas players] it would be nice – *Tony Greig*

We're not a philanthropic organization – *Packer*

The ban is a disservice to cricket – *Asif Iqbal*

The presence of Greig, Knott and Underwood would have been a great help to bring the crowds along – *Walter Hadlee* (New Zealand), referring to this winter's England tour

Mr. Packer waved a big stick – *Steele*

I don't think John Arlott is very knowledgeable on the game of cricket – *Jack Bailey*, ICC secretary

I'm always open to offers – *Boycott*

We were very anxious, indeed still are anxious, to avoid an horrific situation – *Douglas Insole*, TCCB chairman

The moment that one of my players is banned is the moment you have me for an enemy – *Packer*

There's a little bit of a whore in all of us – *Packer*

It's England first, last and all the time so far as I'm concerned – *Greig*, confirming an earlier newspaper interview.

The press get it right, the press get it wrong – *Greig*

It's degrading to have to virtually beg for benefits – *Michael Procter*

No one has to have a benefit – *Boycott*

We are the poor relations of world sport – *Greig*

". . . makes the language boggle" – *Robert Alexander, QC*

I'm a press man's dream – *Greig*

Gloucestershire want me to go on playing – *Procter*

I'm not a legal expert – *Derek Underwood*

I'm sure you [Underwood] are far better off being a cricketer – *Andrew Morritt, QC*

They thought they could have the best of both worlds – *Steele*

Pandora's chest – *Bailey*

A more severe ban is justified – *Boycott*

Tests are not built in a day – *Mutthian Chidambaram* (India)

We were prepared to fly our players home from Pakistan and fly them out to New Zealand six weeks later – *Insole*, discussing a possible compromise

I admire umpires – *Greig*

I've had nightmares about it – *John Snow*, on the prospect of becoming an umpire

I suggest they [the TCCB] are being dishonest – *Packer*

Unfortunately the Cricketers' Association is looked on as something of a joke – *Snow*

I would say the Cricketers' Association exists full stop – *Procter*, invited to say what the Cricketers' Association existed for

It [Test match revenue] goes to the counties, where it's to a large part wasted – *Snow*

I suppose I was a bit young and naive at the time and I let them [*Sunday Mirror* journalists] in – *Knott*

Australian players tend to pop out of holes in the ground when the opportunity's there – *Ross Edwards*, Australian cricketer

They [Australian cricketers] seem to come out in their thousands when they're knocking hell out of the Poms – *Boycott*

Thank heavens I don't have that prospect – *Edwards*, asked what happened if a batsman faced Dennis Lillee and got injured.

The next game could be your last. If you're playing against Lillee and he smashes your elbow you'll never play again – *Knott*

I didn't trust the Australian Cricket Board, and I don't trust them – *Packer*

They [the authorities] have undersold the game – *Greig*

I said there'd be a strike or something like this [the Packer series] – *Snow*

The tour [England to Pakistan this winter] is very doubtful because of the political situation – *Asif Iqbal*

World Series Cricket is essentially parasitic in its nature – *Michael Kempster, QC*

Test matches are vital to our survival financially – *Hadlee*

They [the TCCB] were trying to white-ant us – *Packer*, using an Australian expression derived from an insect that bores into wood and leaves the shell intact

Someone's white-anted my copy – *Mr Justice Slade*, examining a document in evidence

The establishment could benefit from a jolly good shake-up – *Greig*

The TCCB are not as dishonourable as the Australian Cricket Board – *Packer*

It's very depressing to go into a ground with 400 spectators – *Greig*, referring to county championship cricket

I'm not sure the British public would want four-day matches – *Boycott*

You have to play enough cricket to satisfy 13,000 members at 12 guineas – *Boycott*, arguing that the county championship should not be reduced to 16 matches a county

I would deny that absolutely – *Insole*, asked if the Australian Cricket Board were opposed to any compromise with Mr Packer

Ghulam Ahmed said "Soon there'd be 10 Mr Packers on the scene" – *Chidambaram*

Procter is one of the casualties of the battle – *Peter Short* (West Indies)

Being available to go to cocktail parties – *Greig*, explaining the work involved in earning the free use of a car

They [the Australian Cricket Board] were telling me untruths – *Packer*

"You're men of honour" – *Steele*, quoting Mr. Packer's reference to the ACB television negotiating sub-committee.

Give them the opportunity to draw back from the brink – *Insole*

I wish I'd never said "Draw back from the brink"; there are so many problems – *Insole*

Draw back from the drink, sorry, the brink – *Kempster*

Wars are not won by appeasement – *W. H. Webster*, ICC chairman

Chamberlain's Churchill – *Mr. Justice Slade*

We [the West Indies] had grave reservations as to the morality of a retroactive ban – *Short*

There was a deliberate attempt by the ICC to break down the negotiations – *Packer*

After that we had our toes insured – *Greig*, referring to an injury suffered by Fred Titmus in a swimming accident

They can play at Brighton in the water if they want – *Packer*, confirming his players' availability in the English summer

When we went into this we knew exactly what we were doing and it would probably get us banned from county cricket – *Snow*, confirming an earlier interview

When the donkey kicks you know which way it kicks – *Snow*

I did not expect they would blackball us altogether – *Greig*

You didn't have to be an Einstein to foresee the ban – *Packer*

Gloucestershire want me to go on playing – *Procter*

It's everyone for himself now and let

the devil take the hindmost – *Packer*

Nineteenth century lockout – *Alexander*

The changes in rules are no more stringent than are required to protect the conventional game – *Kempster*

Derek Randall [a big attraction] at Trent Bridge? I thought they were Yorkshiremen who'd come to watch me – *Boycott*

One should go to another county – *Knott*, referring to the competition between him and Paul Downton in the Kent team

Television of Mr Packer's series would have a very serious effect on official Tests. The public could sit at home and watch the circus match – *Steele*

The press, on behalf of the authorities have always tried to lampoon our games – *Packer*

We were in the gloaming if not in the dark – *Bailey*

We believed they [the players] were going to do irreparable damage – *Steele*

The players should be treated as outcasts – *Steele*

Mr Packer wanted exclusive television rights there and then – *Bailey*

The offer would have had to be quite a big one if I was to be banned from Yorkshire – *Boycott*

The word "grovel" followed me around – *Greig*

They [his cricketers] must be like Caesar's wife – *Packer*

David Brown [chairman of the Cricketers' Association] and I couldn't have changed anything in a million years – *Greig*

I considered the Cricketers' Association vote [in favour of the ban] unfair and biased – *Underwood*

I would not have got a gun and shot Mr. Packer – *Steele*

We're not perfect – *Bailey*

He [Tony Greig] said "How the hell did you get involved in this" – *Boycott*

There is no fat at all – *Insole*, questioned about county clubs' finances

Our players had let us down because on their behalf we had negotiated a $350,000 team sponsorship and we'd taken on agreements to which they'd agreed – *Steele*

If there are no good guarantees, tours may have to be cancelled – *Short*

If overseas players are absent from a Sunday League match between Hampshire and Gloucestershire, the cricket ratings will go down and those of High Chaparral will go up – *Alexander*

Any believability in my word would be destroyed – *Packer*, if his series were cancelled

If Tests wane the game as a whole will languish – *Kempster*

The Australian Cricket Board would do anything, even to eating crow or humble pie, to prevent a holocaust – *Bailey*

. . . body and soul contract, more on his side than my side – *Boycott*

The series will be considerably better than first-class in the eyes of the public – *Packer*

I kissed them goodbye – *Steele*, referring to players who had already signed contracts

I was riveted – *Bailey*, by Mr Packer's appearance on David Frost's television programme

Kerry Packer picked my brains – *Boycott*

"Fabrication" is your word, not mine – *Boycott*, to Alexander

They found a very good living – *Insole*, referring to engagements in league cricket of Sobers, Lindwall, Ian Chappell and others

They'll fight . . . like Kilkenny cats – *Packer*, of the Australian Cricket Board

Since May 9 [the date of public knowledge of the Packer series] I think that's correct – *Steele*, asked if modern cricketers had become too commercial

They [the ICC] didn't want to compromise in any way, shape or form – *Packer*

We still hoped to prevent a hijacking situation – *Bailey*

We're all getting underpaid, except a few overseas stars who're getting all the money – *Boycott*

The county championship is the lynchpin of English cricket – *Insole*

The effect on the first-class game if the Test match profits diminish would be serious, very serious, or catastrophic – *Bailey*

The world cricket authorities are carrying the can for Australia – *Packer*

I don't know about that [Michael Brearley's double first] but he's certainly very brainy – *Boycott*

When a Yorkshireman shakes your hand that's all you need – *Boycott*

No, you should be expected to play as your form warrants – *Boycott*, asked if he thought Test cricketers should have more security

One can take only so much – *Greig*

Cricket Boards Face Huge Costs after Packer Victory

BY JOHN HENNESSY AND RICHARD STREETON

26 *November* 1977. Mr Kerry Packer and his group of cricketers gained a crushing victory in the High Court yesterday. In deciding between them on the one hand and the International Cricket Conference (ICC) and the Test and County Cricket Board (TCCB) on the other, Mr Justice Slade came down heavily on the Packer side.

He was giving reserved judgment after a hearing that had lasted 31 days. The judgment ran to more than 60,000 words and took five and a half hours to deliver.

The judge found, in particular, that the bans proposed by the TCCB and imposed by the ICC on Test and county cricketers were an "unreasonable restraint of trade" and thus void.

The Packer players are now free to reclaim their places in Test and county teams, should they be wanted. The judge also found for the Packer group in the lesser aspect of inducement to breach of contract.

The costs, amounting perhaps to £250,000, fall virtually on the cricket authorities in their entirety. The TCCB, which meets next Tuesday, will discuss the result of the case and decide whether to appeal.

The members of the ICC, who are spread around the world, will be consulted by telephone. The TCCB had withheld £10,000 from each county's share of this summer's profits in case of an unfavourable end to the case.

Mr Jack Bailey, the ICC's secretary, said of the judgment: "Of course we are disappointed. It is a blow; as the judge himself said, we acted in good faith and in the best interests of cricket but in law it was not enough." He thought that conventional Test cricket would still survive.

Mr Douglas Insole, the TCCB chairman, said the judgment would not make cricket administration any easier in the short term. "There is going to be no great joy in it either way for people who love the game."

He was asked if with hindsight he felt the authoritities had acted too hastily. "On the basis of this judgment we were obviously wrong, but I would not say we were necessarily hasty at the time." He added: "The purpose of the ban was to try to draw a clear line. That was its only purpose."

In Australia Mr Packer said he believed the court's decision was a vindication of the players, according to Reuter. "I can say with some assurance that we are incredibly delighted at the decision."

Mr Packer forecast that the lifting of the bans improved the climate for a compromise with cricket authorities. "We can at last all get down to just playing cricket," he said.

"Now that the players are available for their country and counties the authorities have less to lose and maybe we can look at the good of the game rather than the interests of individual groups."

Mr Richard Rossiter, treasurer of the Gloucestershire county club, said that cricket's authorities should now sit down with Mr Packer and work towards a settlement, "something which should have been done four months ago."

The judge said yesterday that he had seen a number of people giving evidence on behalf of the authorities who were among the top administrators of cricket in one or other of the Test-playing countries. Without exception he had been "impressed by their obvious disinterested dedication and concern for the game.

"If they can be regarded as fairly representative of it, I am not surprised that cricket has traditionally been regarded by many as embodying some of the highest professional standards in sport.

"These witnesses all clearly regarded the official Test match structure as something which should represent the pinnacle of any cricketer's ambition.

"They thus find it difficult to understand how any cricketer could, even for good commercial reasons, bring himself to do anything which could be thought likely, directly or indirectly, to damage the structure of international cricket, of which Test matches at present form the all-important part."

The importance of Test cricket, however, was far from being based solely on sentimental or emotional grounds. They were extremely profitable.

"The Test matches played by the Australian touring team in England during the summer of 1977", the judge said, "are together likely to produce a net profit for United Kingdom cricket of not far short of £1m."

The very size of the profits that could be made from cricket matches involving star players must, for many years, have carried the risk that a private promoter would appear on the scene and seek to make money by promoting cricket.

"The risk might perhaps have been more limited", Mr Justice Slade said, "if the structure of official cricket in the Test-playing countries had been such as to offer the most talented a secure and remunerative career structure."

The decision for the court was whether the steps which the ICC and TCCB had taken to deal with the situation were justifiable in law. On July 26 the ICC passed a resolution changing its rules, the effect of which was that any player who, after October 1, should remain with Mr Packer would be disqualified from Test cricket.

Mr Justice Slade said he was not surprised that many of the plaintiffs' witnesses had expressed the view that their remuneration in county cricket was inadequate, or that similar views had been expressed about the level of Test match payments, "at least until the season immediately past".

The judge "totally rejected" suggestions that the authorities were careless of the difficulties and needs of people who played cricket for a living. But some of the officials who gave evidence for the defence gave the impression that, though dedicated lovers of the game, they found it hard fully to understand the feelings and aspirations of those who sought to make their living out of it.

The judge did not share the view that all the English players who had joined Mr Packer were in breach of any moral commitment.

He could see some criticism could be applied against Tony Greig, who had recruited others for Mr Packer when he was still generally regarded as the England captain. But it had to be borne in mind that neither the ICC nor the TCCB had entered into any commitment, legal or otherwise, ever to offer employment to Mr Greig or the other players.

It was straining the "concept of loyalty too far for authorities to expect players to enter into a self-denying ordinance not to play for a private promoter during the winter months."

There was no sufficient reason why the players, with the possible exception of Mr Greig, could justifiably be criticized on moral grounds for maintaining strict secrecy. "The subsequent actions of the defendants have made it abundantly clear that, had they been informed in advance of the World Series project, they would have done their utmost to prevent it from taking root."

Addressing himself to the nine questions he had earlier identified as requiring decision, the judge first dismissed the defence argument that the contracts were void. On the second question he ruled that there had been direct interference by the ICC with the contracts of World Series Cricket (a Packer organization).

The ban "contained a threat" and its publication in a press statement "was applying direct pressure, by means of an implicit threat, to the minds of all contracted cricketers". The TCCB ban, too, applied pressure or persuasion to the minds of the cricketers.

Holding that the proposed TCCB and ICC ban was "void as being an unreasonable restraint of trade", the judge said that to deprive, by a form of retrospective legislation, a professional cricketer of the opportunity of making his living in a very important field was both a serious and unjust step to take.

The last four questions related to the amended defence appeal under the Trade Union and Labour Relations Act, 1974. Mr Justice Slade gave judgment for the plaintiffs on all counts.

The judge accepted Mr Packer's evidence that, "contrary perhaps to some popular belief, he liked cricket". Discussing the collapse of a compromise meeting at Lord's in July, he thought Mr Packer had good reason for not thinking he would be fairly treated by the Australian Cricket Board of Control.

The Judge said the World Series venture had offered promise of greater rewards for star cricketers and regular remunerative employment during the English winter. It had stimulated new sponsors for traditional cricket. It had brought back to the game in Australia several talented players.

It had initiated a useful coaching scheme for young players in New South Wales. Finally, it had increased public interest in the game.

Mr. Herbert Sutcliffe

23 *January* 1978. Mr. Herbert Sutcliffe, one of the famous cricketers of his time, has died at the age of 83.

From Hirst, Rhodes and Jackson to Leyland and Hutton, Yorkshire has always provided England with cricketing backbone and at no time was the old saying, "When Yorkshire is strong, England is strong", so true as when Herbert Sutcliffe stood, in the words of his autobiography, ". . . For England and Yorkshire". His playing career spanned almost exactly the period between the two world wars and by any standard his figures were massive. In all, he scored over 50,000 runs, including 149 centuries. His England caps were 54, though he was seldom seen to wear one, and, of his 16 Test hundreds, half were taken off Australian bowling. In each of 21 home seasons and on three tours he made his thousand runs, a dozen times 2,000 and three times 3,000. Four times he scored two hundreds in a match and twice four successive hundreds. His records flowed opulently like the bequests of a generous millionaire.

He was born on November 24, 1894, in Pudsey, the West Riding hometown of his predecessor John Tunnicliffe, and his eminent successor, Sir Leonard Hutton. In his teens he caught the eye of the Yorkshire authorities and had already made an appearance or two for the county's second eleven when the First World War broke out. He enlisted in The Sherwood Foresters and later was commissioned. In the first post-war season Yorkshire called on him at once and after an attractive innings in the first game against M.C.C. at Lord's, he found himself in possession of his county's No. 1 batting position. By the end of the summer he had established himself so firmly that he was named as one of Wisden's Cricketers of the Year.

Each season saw him steadily advancing and his first 2,000 runs came in 1922. Two years later his selection for England against South Africa marked the beginning of his long association with Sir Jack Hobbs, the most impressive and prolific partnership that English batting has known. Their first stand produced 136 runs, the second 268 and the third 72, and this initial success brought Sutcliffe an invitation to tour Australia where, though the rubber was lost, his personal performance was magnificent, producing four successive hundreds and a Test average of over 80.

With that gayest of good companions, Percy Holmes, he broke virtually every Yorkshire batting record. Their century partnerships numbered 69 for Yorkshire (74 in all) and their highest was the record-breaking 555, scored at Leyton in 1932 at a rate of 74 runs an hour. This was Sutcliffe's richest season, bringing him 3,336 runs and keeping him at the head of the first class averages, a place he had held in 1928 and 1931. His three-figure partnerships with Hobbs totalled 26, of which 15 were against Australia. The understanding which inspired their almost uncanny running between wickets – daring, but safe – was foreshadowed in the days when Rhodes was Hobbs's prewar partner and was brought to perfection with Sutcliffe's intelligent cooperation. Of their combined exploits two at least are outstanding. In the fifth Test of 1926, with the rubber still undecided, England began their second innings 22 runs behind. In poor evening light Hobbs and Sutcliffe scored 19, but a thunderstorm in the night made the morning's pitch at first dead-slow and then as the sun came out, vilely treacherous. If either Hobbs or Sutcliffe had succumbed, England could have been out for a hundred. As it was, the pair batted valorously, adding 112 by lunchtime and after Hobbs had been bowled for exactly 100, Sutcliffe stayed till the last over of the day. His share was 161 and sharply rising deliveries had bruised him all over. Connoisseurs of his batting speak with even greater awe of his innings for Chapman's side of 1928–29 on a Melbourne "sticky dog". In hideous conditions the two Englishmen fought their way to a total of 105, when Hobbs was out, and afterwards Sutcliffe went serenely on to take his individual score to 135, bringing England within sight of victory.

Sutcliffe's success sprang from his personal character, based on tenacious courage and unshakable concentration. In an age when bat dominated ball, he was among the giants; Hobbs, Hammond, Bradman and Woodfull at one end and Hutton, his own disciple, at the other. Though he fell short of the consummate artistry of Hobbs or the sheer brilliance of Hammond, he was a handsome batsman with an armoury of powerful on-side strokes and a defence that was a bowler's despair. He could score steadily or swiftly, as he judged the situation, and once, with Leyland, hit 102 off six overs against Essex.

As a mark of respect to his famous England first-wicket partner, Sutcliffe named his son, who was later to captain Yorkshire himself, William Herbert Hobbs. Sutcliffe's wife, Emily, died in 1974.

His appearance at the crease, from elegant buckskin boots to perfectly smoothed black hair, was as immaculate as his defence. His quiet voice masked a tremendous combativeness. Congratulated on his superb innings at the Oval in 1926, he replied softly: "Ah, Mr. Warner, I love a dog fight". And after his equally valiant effort at Melbourne Sir Jack Hobbs observed: "There was Herbert, black and blue, and not a hair out of place". Under the harshest of stresses, he was unruffled and unrufflable.

It was once said of Yorkshire's opening batsmen that, while Holmes looked as if he was off to the races, Sutcliffe had the air of an alderman about to lay a foundation stone. There was truth in the jest, for a characteristic innings by Sutcliffe formed the foundation of many a Yorkshire and England victory. Though he looked young all his playing life, he was England's "Old Imperturbable".

May Elegant not only in Style but in Manner

BY ALAN GIBSON

2 *January* 1980. Fifty years ago, on New Year's Eve, Peter May was born. Early in his life it became clear that he was going to be good at cricket. He was captain of Charterhouse in 1947, scored hundreds against both Eton and Harrow, and for the Public Schools against the Combined Services. He went on to Cambridge, after his national service (he made his first first-class appearance for Combined Services – and had played for Berkshire – he was born at Reading – in 1946).

For Cambridge he scored nearly 3,000 runs in three seasons, at an average of more than 60. In 1950 he played for Surrey, winning his county cap, and in a Test trial. In 1951 he played for England, against South Africa, and scored a century in his first Test innings. He played in all four Tests against India in 1952, and did well. There was something exceptional in the making.

In 1953 there was a mild setback. He played against Australia only in the first Test and the last. He failed in the first, in which he batted at No 6. He was always happier, even when young, with the responsibility of batting No 3 or 4. When he came back for the last Test, the decisive one, at No 3, he scored 39 and 37, both innings of much consequence in the context.

Thereafter, except for injury or illness (of which he had rather more than his share) he was always an England player. Before his early retirement in 1963, he had played in 66 Tests, in 41 of which he was captain. The number of captaincies is a record, although we should not make too much of it, because so many more Tests were being played. He averaged 47 in Tests, and 51 in first-class cricket – 27,500 runs, 85 centuries.

I put the figures in because they deserve it, but you may be thinking, especially those of you who did not see him, or only saw him when you were very young, "Yes, we know all that, we know he was one of the great English batsmen, but how would you describe his play?"

The word that occurs to me is *elegance*. "Elegant but not ostentatious", as Johnson said of Addison's prose. May, even if he was beaten, never looked uncouth. People who were there tell me that this was true even on the 1958–59 tour of Australia, when English batsmen were constantly reduced to inelegant attitudes by the "dubious actions" of the bowlers – rather as Australians had been, a quarter of a century earlier, on the "bodyline" tour.

May's style was the kind we call classical. The upright stance, the back-lift, the immediate judgment of length and adjustment of feet, the pounce to the overpitched spinner, the quick step back, almost to the stumps, for the cut: these were the things we had always associated with the Edwardians, the amateur batsmen of the golden age. May of Charterhouse made a fit companion for MacLaren and Jackson of Harrow, Fry of Repton, Foster of Malvern. At least he would have done, had he not been a couple of genera-tions late.

You might say that, although not the least of the apostles, he was one born out of due time (you could say much the same of Cowdrey of Tonbridge, who came along a little later). Yet in another sense he was very much a man of his time. Only rarely, in Test cricket, did he display all his stroke-making gifts. Yet he had a mastery of concentration which none of the Edwardians had, except Jackson. He had greater patience than any of them but then he could afford it, since he did not have to face the challenge of three-day Tests.

He was often seen at his best for Surrey, when Surridge was captain. Surridge was a man who hated draws. As an England captain, and an Eng-land batsman, May crammed himself into the mould of his predecessor, Hutton, who was an even more beautiful batsman and an equally wise captain, but became increasingly cautious in both aspects. I have always thought that May was appointed to the England captaincy too soon. Another couple of years without the responsibility might have given him the confi-dence to be a little more adventurous. Also, we might not have lost him as early as we did.

May was elegant not only in style but in manner, not only in his cricket but his character. He came to the front at a time when pressures on top class cricketers were intensifying, although they were not so terrifying as those of today (of course the rewards were correspondingly less). A captain's lot was a particularly difficult one, with the press almost dictatorial in demands for constant attempts to pry into private life.

The more brash among them sometimes thought May remote, although he was always polite and tactful. When the 1958–9 side returned from Australia, he was immediately asked for his views on throwing. He replied that Englishmen should look forward to seeing Norman O'Neill, one of the best throwers (from the deep) that he had ever seen. His field manners were what we expected (rightly or wrongly) from the old-style amateur. There was one unfortunate mix-up about the use of a runner in the West Indies, when May was in the wrong, but it was no more than a misunderstanding, and May, although it was not generally known until he returned, prematurely, to England soon afterwards, was unwell.

Of his many great innings, the one that comes most readily to my mind was in the first Test against the West Indies in 1957. It was, in its earlier part, a defensive innings, but the circumstances demanded that. The West Indies bowled England out for 186, and scored 474. England had conferences and interviews, and lost three for 113 in the second innings, when May and Cowdrey came together. The next wicket, Cowdrey's fell at 524. He had made 154. May went on to 285 not out, until he declared at 583 for 4, E. W. Swanton wrote that "the concentration, the restraint, the technical excellence of these two innings could not be overpraised. Never have two young cricketers built such a monument to patience and determination". I did not see the match, but I would bet that they were, both of them, *elegant* innings.

May came in for some criticisms because he did not declare earlier, and certainly the weary West Indies' score at the end, 72 for seven, suggested that he might have done. But it was not unreasonable to feel that he had saved a match that looked hopelessly lost, and that would do for now. The West Indies were never the same side again that season.

I am afraid our sage and beloved Cricket Correspondent is not enjoying himself too much at present in Australia. I dare say, as he wilts beneath the barrage of ballyhoo (how inadequate a word that has become) he reflects on better days and better manners, and that his tours with May are often in his thoughts. And I dare say that May, from his ripe and rounded middle age (although remember that Woolley, Hobbs, and Rhodes, to take three, all played first-class cricket when they were older) feels relief to be well away from it, despite the monetary attractions. Of all leading English cricketers, at least since the first war, he would have looked the most incongruous in this setting. So perhaps he was not, after all, a man born out of due time.

French are Stumped by Lord's Taverners

FROM IAN MURRAY

23 *June* 1980; *Meudon*, 22 *June*. The French language and French credulity were strained this afternoon when a team of Lord's Taverners made merry with bat, ball and champagne on their first match in France.

Their opponents were the Standard Athletic Club, which boasts the only cricket pitch in regular use in France. For the occasion the club's gates in this Paris suburb were opened to as many of the local population as might be tempted to learn about the game of cricket.

The onlookers were not all that numerous. One of the girls, who had put together the publicity hand-out, frankly confessed: "The French are not that crazy, you see." The only celebrity on the Taverners' side who meant anything here was John Taylor, who not so long ago was a familiar scourge of the French rugby fifteen when he donned the red shirt of Wales. Names like Nicholas Parsons and Colin Milburn meant nothing.

And then the game itself was so strange. During the tea break, while a recorded brass band played "Abide with Me", small knots of puzzled men gathered round the *guichet* and stared in silence at the footmarks made by the *lanceur* as he hurled the ball at *batman*. They inquired of any English present which of the players was the "maiden".

The predominantly British crowd did their best to help explain what was going on.

For the benefit of a perplexed television crew, Mr. Willie Rushton tried to explain, in an accent that would even encourage Mr. Edward Heath to speak more French, the importance to the game of a cup of tea. A fellow Taverner wearing a donkey's head mask nuzzled his shoulder, "*Poussez-off Euroâne*", roared Mr. Rushton as the producer snatched back his microphone. "*Poussez-off*, or it's French cricket at Lourdes for you next week."

Despite their overall incomprehension the French onlookers came away, perhaps, with a better idea of why Britain is so difficult to beat at EEC negotiations and why the word "fair play" is untranslatable in French.

The afternoon produced a profit for French and British charities.

Language of the Terraces Comes to Lord's

BY RICHARD FORD

1 *September* 1980. Has civilization as we know it ended with the disgraceful scenes in the Members Enclosure at Lord's before the start of the third day of play in the Cornhill Centenary Test?

Even the august and dignified members of the world famous MCC would appear to have among their number an element who are not averse to using a rather coarser sort of language than one expects on the cricket field.

The abusive language and jostling that took place as the two captains and umpires returned to the Long Room is the kind of behaviour we have come to expect on the football terraces but not from the gentlemen of the Pavilion at Lord's.

It just is not cricket and today the MCC will start an inquiry into this most unsporting behaviour.

Many might prefer a dignified veil of silence to be drawn across the unseemly incidents on Saturday in which Ian Botham, the England captain, was hit on the head and David Constant, an umpire, grabbed by the tie and jostled. But they have received so much publicity that an investigation will begin with Botham and Greg Chappell, the Australian captain, being seen by Mr. Jack Bailey, secretary of the MCC.

He had heard a complaint from Chappell that intimidatory and abusive language was being used and that one of the umpires had been jostled as they returned from making a fourth inspection of the pitch, where 22,000 spectators were waiting for play to start. Mr. Bailey investigated this and spoke to two members pointed out by Chappell but said he thought, from what they had told him, that they had not been behaving unreasonably.

Mr. Bailey said: "I spoke to the men and felt they were innocent, but of course it could have been a case of mistaken identity. There is no question about it, the members were not pleased at having to wait and made their feelings known, but I thought they were doing it in the reasonable English way and that it would not go beyond this."

From the hotel where he is staying in London, Botham described the incidents as "the behaviour one expects from football hooligans." He added, "I was walking out to make the final inspection with Chappell and the two umpires when I was hit on the back of the head by a hand.

"I did nothing about it but as we were all walking in a man in his twenties grabbed the umpire David Constant by the tie and shoved and jostled him. Greg Chappell and I moved in to break it up."

He said the man thought he was being clever and added that the abusive language being shouted in the Pavilion had disgusted him. "It was a disgrace especially as it involved the captain of an opposing team. I feel very sorry and embarrassed about people who to my mind are a disgrace to the game."

So the language and behaviour of the football hooligan has at last invaded the home of English cricket. W. G. Grace would turn in his grave at the thought.

The Voice of Cricket Declares

BY ALAN GIBSON

3 *September* 1980. When the centenary Test match came to its end yesterday, there also came to an end, at least as far as Test matches were concerned, the most famous of cricketing voices.

Broadcast cricket commentary began soon after broadcasting itself, but for a long time it was rather amateurishly done. The usual practice was to find some distinguished old cricketer, such as Pelham Warner, prop a microphone in front of him, and leave him to get on with it.

In the 1930s, Howard Marshall appeared, and after him E. W. Swanton (and we must not forget Arthur Wrigley, who founded the technique of modern scoring).

But it was only after the war that we heard the voice of them all, John Arlott.

He came from Basingstoke, and his Hampshire accent was in those days sharp. The Hampshire accent is not naturally a mellow one, such as that of Dorset, which helped to make Ralph Wightman such a broadcasting success.

It took a year or two for the public, brought up on Marshall and Swanton, to grow accustomed to Arlott. He did not sound like a member of MCC. But by 1948 he was established, and ever since has remained, for every Test in England, a necessary part of the scene.

He did that because he was a cricketer and a poet. He was never, I think, expected to be an outstanding cricketer, though he had a passion for the game, and when he abandoned his first-class ambitions he was determined to stay in touch with it somehow.

He became very knowledgeable, partly because he pestered cricketers for information: not the dressing-room gossip, but technical stuff. "What does he *do*? What's his dangerous ball?" he would demand if a new bowler appeared.

"We all loved and admired John in the Hampshire dressing-room", said his old friend, Desmond Eagar, then the Hampshire captain, "but we did sometimes wish he would stop asking questions".

The greatest honour that he feels he has been paid is to have been invited to be chairman of the Cricketers' Association, a post he will retain in retirement. Not that he really retired: he is going to live in his beloved Alderney, but he will speak and write as long as he lives. He has immense industry, a constant urge to work, more than any man I have known.

But he would not have become so famous had he not been a poet. He was considered one of the most promising post-war poets. He gave that up too ("The words don't come any more"), but his adventures in poetry gave him a command of words, a gift of phrase such as no other cricket commentator has possessed.

He also had an unforced sense of humour. When he used phrases such as "the fieldsmen are scattered in the wilderness like missionaries", people used to think he had thought them up beforehand. Sometimes, I suppose, he may have done, but he never needed too.

I remember one Test morning at Trent Bridge when I was in the commentary box with him and Trevor Bailey. Trevor began, as usual, with his introduction about the state of the game, finishing with "and now come the umpires in their new-style short coats, looking like dentists. Over to John Arlott".

John immediately said: "It occurs to me, Trevor, that it is rather suitable for the umpires to look like dentists, since one of their duties is to draw stumps".

Everything but the Real Thing at Bristol

BY ALAN GIBSON

18 *September* 1980. England played the Rest of the World at a game purporting to be cricket last night, on the Bristol City ground at Ashton Gate. I had been warned that I would find it a repellant spectacle, but the half had not been told me. I felt bitterly towards our cricket correspondent who had been unavoidably prevented from attending by a previous sporting engagement (boating on the Thames with Brian Johnston). Not since I played for Yorkshire against the Rest of the World on a rough common outside Smolyensk have I seen a more gross caricature of the game, but the competitors at Smolyensk were a coach party of tourists, and at Ashton Gate they were some of the best cricketers in the world. In this was the tragedy.

No doubt floodlit cricket has a future, for this is the age of the sporting stunt, and it is only fuddy-duddies who remember that it was once the meadow game with the beautiful name. I did meet one or two regular cricket followers among the crowd – about 9,000 it was estimated – and they muttered shamefacedly things like "a bit of fun" and "does no harm".

I suppose the harm has already been irredeemably done. But how any cricketer with any feeling for the game at all can regard the sight of the best players in the world bashing monotonously into the stands on a narrow football field as fun passes my comprehension. Never mind. In 10 year's time, mark my words, we shall have the pylons up at Lord's and the riots to go with them. They have had a promising trial run for rioting already.

The emetic-yellow pads, the umpires dressed in red nightgowns like Chinese mandarins, the white ball, the black sight screens, the indiscriminately yelling crowd (I imagine the things they like most about soccer are sudden death penalties) the artificial pitch, combined to make it all a hideous nightmare.

England were sent in to bat, and lost four wickets for 31, but Boycott and

Botham put a stop to these brief hopes of an early finish. It was just the game for Botham, able to mis-hit as much as he liked, and still score sixes. Boycott, whose inner soul must have shrunk from what was going on around him, could not resist the temptation to play a proper cricketing stroke now and then. Doshi showed that even in such conditions bowling a length could bring a reward. The fielding was of high quality, even in the difficult period when daylight gave way to floodlight. These are the only polite things I can think of to say.

The English innings ended for 214 in the 38th over. The Rest of the World scored 220 for two. The players, and Bristol City both made some money, and Bristol City, at any rate, need it. But the end does not always justify the means, and I would have thought it much better to see Bristol City in the third division than survive by such tales told by an idiot, full of sound and fury, signifying nothing.

> ENGLAND 214 (I. T. Botham 84, G. Boycott 68; D. R. Doshi 6 for 48)
> REST OF THE WORLD 220 for 2 (S. M. Gavaskar 67, Sadiq Mohammad 64)
> *Rest of the World won by eight wickets*

It Was an Exceptional Summer for Batting

BY ALAN GIBSON

26 *November* 1980. Most county cricket championships have been won by bowling. The one great exception was the victory of Middlesex in 1947. It was a summer of sunshine, the golden season of Compton and Edrich; Compton scored 3,816 runs, Edrich 3,539, still the two highest aggregates, and unlikely ever to be bettered, certainly not while the present pattern of an English season lasts (the next highest are Hayward in 1906, Hutton in 1949, and Woolley in 1928, the year he was dropped for the Australian tour). But that was not all for Middlesex in 1947; Robertson and Brown, the openers, scored more than 2,000 each. These four scored their runs at such a pace, something like 80 runs to the hour, that they gave Middlesex the time to bowl the other sides out.

And they did need plenty of time, for they were short of bowlers. Jack Young, a slow-medium left-arm spinner, had made a big advance since the war. He was 35, but, with an economical action, could still bowl a long and accurate spell; he was chosen for England once that season and seven times more in the next couple of years, though he performed without much success (17 wickets at 44). He was a sound county bowler, rarely more. Jim Sims, a tall and genial leg-spinner, who had played for England four times before the war (11 wickets at 43) was nine years older than Young; he was a cunning old warrior, of whom Robertson-Glasgow had written only a few years earlier that he could "unbuckle about the most difficult googly in the game today" (I presume he was not including Australians).

So the Middlesex spin bowling was at least adequate, but there was not much in the way of pace. Gray, who was 32, had lost his best years to the war, a more severe imposition in the case of a fast bowler than a spinner. The edge of his speed had gone. Edrich could bowl fast for a few overs – some said he was then the fastest in England, not a large claim to make. He had some bowling successes, and so did Compton, who was beginning to develop his back-of-the-hand left-arm spin. Robins, the captain, had been a leg-spinner of high class before the war, but he was 41 and did not bowl much. With three other spinners turning the ball from the leg, he could not give himself many opportunities. It was an uneven attack, not at all that of a champion side, yet it proved sufficient because of the flood of runs.

Middlesex played 26 matches that season, won 19, lost 5, and drew 2. The last figure was the most significant. Robins was a captain in the style of Sam Woods, half a century earlier, who believed that draws were only any use for bathing in. Two instances illustrate the Middlesex approach. At the Oval they scored 537 for two on the first day (the only occasion in the season when Robins allowed his side to bat through after he had won the toss). Brown scored 98, Robertson 127, Edrich and Compton (both not out) 157 and 137. So Middlesex had two days to bowl out Surrey twice – and managed it.

The other match was at Leicester. Middlesex had difficulty in getting Leicestershire out in the third innings and it seemed as if the match was saved when the last wicket fell: Middlesex had to score 66 in 20 minutes. Robins was not playing that day and Edrich was captain. As Middlesex walked from the field, he came alongside Compton, and said: "We'll go in first, Denis, and get these runs." So they did, with a minute to spare. I remember someone in Common Room saying next morning, "Aren't Middlesex marvellous?" and there was not a dissenting voice, though we were, mostly, a North Country college.

I remember feeling that nothing was going to stop them. Yorkshire, to whom Middlesex had been second in 1937, 1938, 1939 and 1946, were out of it halfway down the table (hardly believable to a Yorkshireman in those days); but Middlesex did have a challenge, from Gloucestershire, whom they played at Cheltenham in August. The Cheltenham pitch was then known as Tom's Delight, because Tom Goddard, though 47 years old, had had many triumphs there and was still about the best off-spinner in the country (Laker was some years from his peak). It was a very good idea, at Cheltenham, to win the toss; Gloucestershire lost it, and the match. Tom did his stuff with 15 wickets, but Middlesex won by 68 runs. They were without Compton and Robertson, both playing in the Test against South Africa; however, they did have Edrich, who would also have been playing for England but for a strain. He had told the selectors that he could manage to bat, but not bowl or throw. Middlesex chose him simply as a batsman and he made 50 in the first innings, the highest score of the match.

When it began, Middlesex were four points ahead of Gloucestershire, each side having played 21 matches. Gloucestershire fielded three seamers, which seemed silly when Goddard and Cook had Cranfield, another useful spinner in reserve. The Gloucestershire seamers wasted some overs, especially during Edrich's innings. Middlesex brought in Harry Sharp, a middle order batsman and off-spinner, nearly 30 years old (what a match it was for the not-so-young!) who had learnt his trade on the ground staff before the war without winning a place. It was only his second championship match, but he made the Middlesex attack more balanced and suitable for the occasion. In the last innings he took the wickets of Neale, Emmett and Wilson, after scoring 46 going in as nightwatchman. Young took nine wickets and Sims eight, but you could say that Sharp did as much to win that match as anybody. He took those three wickets in seven balls after Gloucestershire, 67 for two in their second innings, were still in with a good chance.

This shows the strength that Middlesex had in reserve; so did the performances of some of their amateurs, the two Manns (J. P. and F. G.). Fairbairn and Bedford. It also shows the shrewdness of their captain. Robins resigned at the end of the season, and though he returned as nominal captain in 1950, he did not play much more. He was a remarkable and, so most found, an agreeable man, and nothing in his cricketing life can have given him so much pleasure as to lead Middlesex, in the evening of his career, to their first championship (and the first championship of any southern county) in 26 years.

It was a victory compatible with Warner's in 1921, in several ways; but it was the batting that did it: the first four batsmen all having the season of their lives at the same time. Brown never played for England; Robertson did, 11 times (average 46) but only twice at home, and never against Australia. But when you remember that nine times in 1947 they put on more than 100 for the first wicket, you can see how much they helped to polish the golden path. Imagine the feelings of a bowler on a hot day: second wicket just fallen, 150 or so, momentary relief, long time to tea. And now who had he got? Compton and Edrich, thank you, both gently settling in. The only thing to do was to bowl for run-outs, in which Compton would sometimes cooperate.

I must add that in those days the match, Champion County v. Rest of England, was played over four days, and taken seriously (I am sorry it was ever abandoned; the shivering spring match, M.C.C. v. the previous champions, is no sort of substitute). Only Yorkshire had ever beaten the Rest of England before; Middlesex now did so, against a strong side which was trying hard, by nine wickets. Bedser had Brown and Robertson quickly caught at the wicket when Middlesex batted first. Edrich and Compton then made 426 between them. Compton hit Goddard for four to mid-wicket while falling flat on his face; it was that sort of season for him.

But there was a worrying sign. His knee was in bandages, and for all he thereafter did, it was never to be quite that sort of season again; nor, indeed, for Edrich, nor, for a long time, for Middlesex. They shared the championship with Yorkshire in 1949, but they have returned to the lead only in the past few years. By then it had become a different game in a different world – though Brearley has some things in common with Robins.

When Dark Blues Radiated a Certain Light

BY DAVID GREEN

20 *January* 1981. Many reasons can be advanced for the current low standard of Oxford and Cambridge University cricket. Two particularly valid ones are the increased emphasis placed by examiners on academic ability, and the ending of National Service which effectively lowered the average age of sides by two years from 1960 onwards. It is interesting to reflect that, even when unemcumbered by such handicaps, the universities had their problems.

In the five seasons from 1954 to 1958, of 85 matches played by Cambridge only 13 were won against 35 losses: of the wins, only seven were against counties, and this during a period when they included players of the quality of C. S. Smith, Barber, Dexter, McLachlan, Pretlove, Wheatley and Goonesena. Oxford's record over the same period is even more dismal: they lost 42 of their 76 games, and could manage only three wins against county sides, though they could call on players like Cowdrey, Mike Smith, Chris Walton, J. A. Bailey and Esmond Kentish.

Against this grim background the achievements of the Oxford sides of 1959 and 1960 glow with a certain radiance. In those two seasons 10 out of 31 first class matches were won, and only eight lost: against counties, of 24 matches played seven were won and 10 drawn. Much of the credit for this change of fortune must go to A. C. Smith who was captain and wicketkeeper in both years. It could be argued that he inherited seven Blues from the previous year, but I have it on good authority that the morale of the 1958 side was so low that it spent much of its time with its collective eye on the roof of Keble College, for when clouds came from that quarter, play for the day was normally washed out.

Sinister cloud banks were referred to as "good weather coming up" and were seen as the only means of avoiding defeat. A.C.'s inspiration was mainly responsible for a complete change in attitude. He told us that if we got our minds right we would certainly field better than our opponents, and that we should not assume that counties would necessarily bat or bowl better than us.

Though 1959 was a glorious summer, April was wet, and I remember finding batting in the nets extremely difficult. I looked around to see if anyone appeared to be a worse player than me. I was relieved to see a small Indian trying to get a big bat on the ball, with notable lack of success. He was alleged to have played first class cricket for Hyderabad, which was manifest fantasy, and I wrote him off as competition for a batting place. It is adequate commentary on my judgment of a player to state that this was Abbas Baig, who was to score 1,149 runs for Oxford that year at an average of 46, make a century for India at Old Trafford in his first Test, and in all play 10 times for his country.

Abbas was Oxford's leading batsman in 1959, and he got reasonably solid support, but their greatest strength was in their bowling. The spearhead was David Sayer who, in an era when England were not short of fast bowling (e.g., Trueman, Statham, Harold Rhodes, Flavell, Jackson, Loader, "Butch" White), was considered to be among the more hostile performers. He was tall and very strongly built, with a rhythmic and powerful approach followed by a very full body turn before delivery. He possessed a spiteful bouncer, with which he was fairly liberal, and very occasionally, when the body-turn got slightly mistimed, let fly a truly terrifying beamer; he was known as "The Slayer".

Andrew Corran, his partner with the new ball, was tall and angular, possessed of boundless stamina, and moved the ball around in the air and off the wicket at fast medium pace. He had firm opinions on a wide variety of subjects: the freedom and frequency with which he expressed them caused him to be known as "Oracle".

The off spinner was the slim, red-haired Dan Piachaud, from Ceylon. Though he bowled fairly quickly, he had a peculiar looping flight and a skilful change of pace, so that he was effective on flat wickets, as well as when the ball turned. In three seasons Sayer took 146 wickets at 21 each, Piachaud 138 at 23, and Corran 108 at 19. John Raybould, a chunky Yorkshireman, bowled leg spin which on good days could trouble the best.

Abbas's chief support came from Javed Burki, a strong, stocky man, who captained Pakistan in 1962 and scored a century at Lord's. Alan Smith and I usually opened the innings, and the batting line-up was completed by Charles Fry, Mike Eagar and Richard Jowett. Fry had to operate under the considerable handicap of being "grandson of the great C.B.". He made himself into a useful performer, and was a most brilliant fielder at cover. Eagar, a fine hockey player, was also a high-class fielder and a good batsman, though prone to excessive theorising. At one stage he worked out that the only safe attacking shot was the sweep, or "lap", as he called it. This obsession, which was the cause of some strange-looking innings, was fortunately dominant only for a few weeks.

In 1960, Alan Duff replaced Raybould as the leg-spinner; Colin Drybrough, an all-rounder later to captain Middlesex, replaced Jowett and the Nawab of Pataudi came in instead of Eagar. I am not alone in believing that, but for the loss of an eye, Pataudi would have been numbered among the greatest. Though small, he could drive powerfully and was strong off his legs, but his chief glories were his cutting and his hooking.

He was normally addressed as "Noob", which apparently had been the practice at Winchester, but this seemed an unsatisfactory arrangement to one young man, who insisted that A. C. Smith told him what the Nawab's Christian name was. A.C., wondering how a Muslim could have such a thing anyway, regarded his interlocutor in perplexed silence. The question was repeated and, after some deliberation, A.C. replied "Sidney". This amused the Nawab greatly, and thereafter he was more often than not addressed as "Sid" by his team colleagues.

The object of any Oxford side is to defeat Cambridge. This was achieved in 1959 by 80 runs: Oxford batted disappointingly, but "Slayer" and "Oracle" bore all before them, taking 15 wickets between them in the match. The 1960 match would almost certainly have been won but for the loss of two and a half hours on the last morning. Cambridge finished 90 ahead in their second innings with one wicket standing, the Nawab, in his first University Match, having made a beautiful 131. Cambridge's second innings resistance depended entirely on an elegant and resolute 95 from Tony Lewis. In this game "Oracle", in 76 overs, took 12 for 118.

The side was happy, played some excellent cricket, and had an enormous amount of fun. I do not suppose that Alan Smith would wish for any other summary of his teams' achievements.

Chappell: Skipper whose Ship Died of Shame

FROM DILIP RAO

3 *February* 1981; *Sydney*, 2 *February*. There could not be a lonelier man in the cricket world today than Greg Chappell, Australia's captain, who yesterday took the unorthodox and unethical measure of having his younger brother, Trevor Chappell, deliver underarm the final ball of the third match in the best-of-five final against New Zealand in the Benson and Hedges World Series Cup one-day competition at the Melbourne Cricket Ground. He has been assailed by angry words from all directions, Ian Chappell, another brother, not excluded.

The tactic, which Chappell now regrets having employed, was designed to prevent Brian McKechnie, of New Zealand, hitting a six and levelling the scores. It succeeded and Australia advanced to a 2–1 lead in the series. The remaining legs will be played at the Sydney Cricket Ground tomorrow and on Wednesday, although an additional match may be played on Thursday if either is washed out or tied.

As is their practice in an emergency, the Australian Cricket Board "met" today by telephone hook-up and decided that if New Zealand agreed, the playing conditions of the competition would be amended "to prohibit the use of underarm bowling in the remaining matches". But they also decided that as no existing rule had been infringed, the Melbourne result must stand.

But Philip Ridings, chairman of the board, said after the meeting: "The board deplores Greg Chappell's action and has advised him of the board's strong feelings on this matter and of his responsibility as Australia's captain to uphold the spirit of the game at all times. "We acknowledge that his action was within the laws of the game, but that it was totally contrary to the spirit in which cricket has been, and should be, played".

Chappell, after being rebuked by the board, said: "While I took a decision which was within the rules, I recognize in the cool light of day that it conflicted with its spirit. I made my decision in the heat of the moment, when I was under pressure. But I regret it now. It is something I would not do again".

The board's censure would have hurt Chappell less than the outburst in *The Sun* this afternoon from Ian Chappell, never known to be a great upholder of cricketing traditions. Several former Australian captains waxed eloquently on the issue and not one of them with any sympathy or support for Greg.

Ian, forthright as ever, wrote: "Fair dinkum, Greg, how much pride do you sacrifice to win $35,000?" Another rebel of his time, Keith Miller, said: "Yesterday one-day cricket died and Greg Chappell should be buried with it."

This plea from Miller did not fall on deaf ears for, it is widely said here, some of the members who "attended' the telephonic board meeting wanted Chappell relieved of captaincy but were dissuaded by the prospects of a bitter feud over his succession.

Premiers react: The Prime Ministers of Australia, and New Zealand Malcolm Fraser and Robert Muldoon, respectively, joined the fierce controversy over Greg Chappell's action. In Wellington, Mr. Muldoon said the underarm delivery was an act of cowardice" and it was appropriate that the Australian team were wearing yellow.

In Canberra, Mr. Fraser said that he would not respond to Mr. Muldoon's comment, but he said that Greg Chappell had made a serious mistake, ontrary to the traditions of the game.

Chappell's action has engendered such hostility that the good cricketing relationship between Australia and New Zealand has probably been irreparably damaged and Chappell's own international reputation as a sportsman severely impaired.

A Sydney radio station said that several callers had urged that Australia's ambassador be recalled as an expression of national shame.

AUSTRALIA 233 for 4 (50 overs) (G. S. Chappell 90, G. M. Wood 72)
NEW ZEALAND 229 for 8 (50 overs) (B. A. Edgar 102 not out, J. G. Wright 42)
Australia won by 4 runs

It Is for the Selectors to Select

27 *February* 1981, *Leading Article*. The failure of the Guyana authorities to respect the right of the English selectors to include Robin Jackman in the side for the Test to be played there, and their insulting demand that he be removed from the territory, left the Cricket Council with no choice but to cancel the fixture and take the players elsewhere.

The council will now have to ascertain whether the same attitude prevails where the remaining Tests are to be played. If it does (and Jamaica indeed seems to have done something to urge upon Guyana the need to make an example of Mr. Jackman on account of his South African connexions) that is the end of the tour. Guyana's decision is a serious blow to the future of Test cricket and may mar Commonwealth harmony.

The British position has been stated before and it was right for Mr. Hector Monro to restate it yesterday, for it needs to be understood by West Indians and Africans who oppose it from feelings which must be respected. The Commonwealth Gleneagles agreement on sport and apartheid does not abridge the freedom of the selectors who choose any team of sportsmen to represent Britain in international events: of this basic principle cricket is only a particular case. At Gleneagles in 1977 the governments committed themselves to discourage their nationals and sporting bodies from playing South African teams as long as apartheid in sport is practised there. But it was recognized that such commitments would be differently interpreted under different systems of law. Countries with all-powerful governments can (and do) make it illegal for their sportsmen to have contacts with South Africa. This is not possible for countries where individual liberty is prized as the first article of democracy: neither British public opinion nor Parliament would tolerate a Bill making it illegal for British citizens to participate in sport in South Africa, Russia or any other country. That is a fact – more easily understood in the West Indies indeed than in Africa.

The British government has repeatedly sought to discourage British sports bodies from playing in South Africa, and not without success at times. But what eventually brought about the cessation of Test cricket with South Africa was the rejection of Basil d'Oliveira as a member of the English side by Mr. Vorster in 1969. The (then) MCC wobbled, but eventually set the rule that it would not be interfered with. Those events have a direct bearing now, and they should, if read correctly, enable President Burnham to reject, not emulate, the Vorster line.

Many British sportsmen, after consulting their consciences, do decide that it is licit for them to participate in South African games. Several of the England side now in Guyana have exercised their rights as British citizens to ignore their government's advice and play in South Africa. Guyana accepted them. It is for the West Indian authorities to explain how one degree of contact with South African sport is more or less heinous than another. They need to remember that Britain is a very heterogenous country nowadays: it is multiracial, but also every part and strand of the "old empire" is represented in the composition of its nationals, South Africa included. We are not ready to have anyone discriminated against – anyone.

If British principles cannot be reconciled with West Indian priorities on this issue then, on occasion, international cricket will not be possible. Everyone will have to accept such casualties as the product of politics becoming so entangled with sport. On the issue of personal liberty Britain cannot give way, even if cricket suffers.

The Players who Came in from the Icy Cold

BY RICHARD STREETON

25 *April* 1981. What was believed to be the unique occurrence of a first class cricket match being halted because of the cold took place at Fenner's yesterday. The umpires took the players off the field to give them some relief from the wintry weather. A biting, gusty south-easterly wind made the near-freezing temperature almost unbearable. The bowlers were unable to grip the ball properly and Pringle, the Cambridge batsman, who wears contact lenses, was troubled by his eyes streaming and could not see.

At first the scorers assumed the match had been stopped for bad light, but the umpires sent them a message to say that "extreme conditions" should be recorded as the reason. Don Oslear, the senior umpire standing in the game, said that after seeking the captains' agreement, the umpires had invoked the law which – under the new 1980 code – allowed them to suspend play when conditions were so bad that it would be unreasonable or dangerous to continue.

Both factors applied, Mr. Oslear said. (It is not inappropriate at this point to note that Mr. Oslear, a former footballer with Grimsby, Hull and Oldham, is also the only championship umpire who used to play professional ice hockey.) It was a little after noon when the umpires stopped the match after what had been a miserable 70 minutes for everyone. An early lunch was taken and a further 35 minutes lost before play resumed.

The match was finally abandoned an hour later when it rained.

The reference books closest to hand show no instance of the cold stopping a first class game before, though it will probably have influenced bad light decisions on occasion. Before overseas cricketers claims about the English weather finally being acknowledged even by the English as being too cold for cricket, it should be noted that England also provides the only known case of a match being halted because it was too hot. This happened between

Surrey and Lancashire at The Oval in July, 1868 when the heat brought an hour's postponement after lunch.

Gerald Brodribb's *Next Man In* (Putnam & Co.) is always the main source of this sort of information. Mr. Brodribb also lists instances where cricket had been interrupted by an earthquake at Lahore in 1937-38; by a deranged monkey (Poona 1951-52); and a runaway horse (Scarborough 1892). Perhaps we were fortunate at Cambridge merely to flirt with pneumonia.

Cambridge, resuming at 82 for 4, soon lost Goldie, the night watchman, but both Pringle and Russom played some good strokes as they added exactly 100 runs in the same number of minutes against bowlers and fieldsmen who showed stoic perseverance. Lever, who missed the morning's play because of a funeral, and Foster had just taken the new ball and Pringle had edged a slip catch, when the rain brought a welcome end for everyone.

One other piece of history must also be recorded. Cambridge's three-day match against Hampshire starting today includes Sunday play for the first time at Fenner's against a county. The University officials have secured the agreement of Hampshire, and that of the TCCB that play should start at 11.30 tomorrow. Cambridge do not charge admission at Fenner's so the statutory 1.30 Sunday start can be waived.

> CAMBRIDGE UNIVERSITY 146 (S. Turner 4 for 20) and 204 for 6 (D. R. Pringle 66, N. Russom 47 not out, J. P. C. Mills 43)
> ESSEX 244 (M. S. A. McEvoy 54, K. W. R. Fletcher 46; D. R. Pringle 4 for 56)
> *Match drawn*

Model Cricketers Make a Bishop Very Happy

BY GERALDINE NORMAN, SALE ROOM CORRESPONDENT

18 *July* 1981. Cricket brought good fortune to the Assistant Bishop of Hereford, the Right Rev. W. A. Partridge, at an Andrew Grant sale in Droitwich on Thursday. He had consigned for sale 15 biscuitware models of Victorian cricketers of a type sold as cake decoration for a few pence in the late nineteenth century. They comprised two umpires, two batsmen and 11 fielders, rather a large team, and he had been told to expect about £5 a figure.

In the event the collection was sold for £210, almost three times that estimate. They were bought by Mr. A. Berg, a Warwickshire dealer, on behalf of a friend who is a cricketing enthusiast. Mr. Berg told the auctioneers afterwards that his friend had been prepared to bid up to £800.

England Awake to a New Jerusalem

John Woodcock Reports on a Famous Victory

22 *July* 1981. England's victory in the third Test match, sponsored by Cornhill, at Headingley yesterday was greeted by the kind of scenes reserved for great sporting occasions. After Australia, needing only 130 to win, had been bowled out for 111, the crowd massed in front of the pavilion, cheering their heroes and waving the Union Jacks they were saving for the Royal wedding.

While at one end of the balcony Brearley and his victorious team were being serenaded, at the other Allan Border, who had not long before been out for nought, was to be seen with his head buried in his hands. It was a moment of disaster as well as triumph.

Kim Hughes, even so, was gracious in defeat, giving credit where it was due and saying that, whereas from tea-time on Monday the luck had gone mostly England's way, before that the Australians had had the greater share of it.

If Botham's unforgettable innings made the recovery possible, it was Willis who crowned it with a marvellous piece of bowling after Australia had got to within only 74 runs of their target with nine wickets standing. When play started yesterday morning the chances seemed to be that Willis was playing in his last Test match. He had bowled below his best in England's first innings and it was not until his second spell now, after he had changed ends, that he caught the wind.

That was where Brearley came in. His return to the England side has not only released Botham to play his game unhampered by the burden of captaincy; it meant that England, with so few runs to play with, were under the command of a supreme tactician. To everyone on the ground, except those who wanted Australia to win, it was a great reassurance to see Brearley handling the situation with calm and understanding.

After England's last wicket had added only another five runs at the start of the day, Brearley opened the bowling with Botham and Dilley, England's third different new ball partnership of the match. His reason for this was partly psychological: Botham and Dilley having shared such a decisive partnership with the bat, it was worth seeing whether they could repeat it with the ball.

In the event Dilley, though he was to hold a great catch later in the innings, was taken off after two unimpressive overs. Although in his second over Botham had Wood caught at the wicket he looked hardly in the mood to move another mountain.

That Willis was the man to do this, at the age of 32, and with knees that have often had to be supported by sticks, was a mark of rare courage. He had started with five rather laboured overs from the Football Stand End. At

48 for one, half an hour before lunch, Brearley gave him the breeze, the decision which launched him on his devastating spell.

It was noticeable even in his first over from the Kirkstall Lane End that Willis was bowling faster than in his earlier spell; not only that, he was making the ball lift as well. At 56, he got one to rear almost geometrically at Chappell, who cocked it up for Taylor, running forward, to take the catch. At 58, in the last over before lunch, Hughes and Yallop both went without scoring, Hughes beautifully caught at second slip by Botham, diving to his left, and Yallop also out to a very good catch. Gatting, standing his ground at short leg and reacting quickly to Yallop's desperate attempt to keep down another kicking delivery, threw himself forward for the ball.

Whereas at the start of the day the skies were clear, by now the clouds were rolling in, causing the ball to move about rather more, even to bounce more steeply. To keep his hands warm for the slip catch that could have gone his way, Brearley was constantly blowing into them.

With Yallop's departure, off the fifth ball of an over, lunch was taken. I harboured a fear that during the interval Willis might stiffen up; but not a bit of it. Brearley had him on again straight away afterwards, bowling as furiously and well as I have ever seen him. When in making a superhuman effort he was occasionally no-balled, Brearley told him not to bother: bowl your fastest, he said, and keep digging it in.

After Old had knocked out Border's leg stump, a vital contribution, Willis did the rest. At 68 he had Dyson caught at the wicket, hooking, as important a wicket as any in view of the skill and resolution with which Dyson had played.

At 74 Marsh, a dangerous customer, hooked Willis to long leg where Dilley, only a yard in front of the crowd, judged to perfection a high and horrible catch. At 75 Lawson gave Taylor his 1,271st first class catch, a new wicket-keeping record, though in all the excitement few knew it.

There followed a partnership between Bright and Lillee which rekindled Australia's fading hopes. Taking their lives in their hands, they added 35 in four overs before another fine catch, this time by Gatting, accounted for Lillee. Running in from mid-on, Gatting dived forward for a mis-timed hook. The ball was a long time in the air and Gatting had a lot of ground to cover.

With only 20 needed and Lillee and Bright going as well as they were, Lillee's wicket was a vast relief. There was only Alderman to be dealt with now and to finish things off Brearley brought back Botham in place of Old. Botham would have done it, too, had Old, at third slip, not dropped Alderman twice in the over. As it was, in the next over Willis yorked Bright and the match was won.

It was not a good Test pitch. Nor it was at Trent Bridge for the first Test of the series. At Edgbaston next week it should be different. In trying to produce something fast and true, the groundsman at Headingley made one that was unpredictable and patchy. But at least he tried.

England's choice of four fast bowlers proved, after all, the right one. Had Australia followed suit Lillee, Alderman and Lawson would not have been as tired as they were on Monday evening when Botham played his marvellous innings.

But what does that matter? They shared in a match that was a victory for cricket. To hear them singing Jerusalem down below you would think that it had revived a nation, too.

"Ian Botham, they call him Jessop in the paper today. It was the most remarkable innings I've ever seen". That was Brearley on his young lion. Botham's 149 not out, as Hughes has said, must be one of the finest innings of all time. Very few could have played it, not only among contemporary cricketers, partly because of his enormous strength. He weighs 16 stone, all of which went into the marvellous drives that made up the majority of his 28 boundaries.

> AUSTRALIA 401 for 9 dec (J. Dyson 102, K. J. Hughes 89, G. N. Yallop 58; I. T. Botham 6 for 95) and 111 (R. G. D. Willis 8 for 43)
> ENGLAND 174 (I. T. Botham 50; D. K. Lillee 4 for 49) and 356 (I. T. Botham 149 not out, G. R. Dilley 56, G. Boycott 46; T. M. Alderman 6 for 135)
> *England won by 18 runs*

Where Cricket is 20-a-side and Rich in Laughter

BY GEOFFREY WATKINS

28 *July* 1981. Samoan cricket has to be seen to be believed. It is rich in laughter, has elements of farce, echoes of tribal warfare, a touch of the Glee Club, gives a nod or two in the direction of MCC laws and is played in noisy enthusiasm against exotic backgrounds of blue lagoons, waving palms, rubber trees and the beautiful feathery tamalingi with its red flowers.

It is a game that is played with pleasure by men and women equally. In Apia, the capital of Western Samoa, it is played on an area of land recovered from the sea called the Eleelefou. The concrete wicket is slightly longer than ours and four feet wide. It is raised about three inches off the ground so this makes no-balling virtually impossible. The bats are three-sided and 44 inches long, tapering to a rounded handle bound in coconut cord. Individual marks in bright colours are painted on the base part.

Some people are reminded of baseball when they first see the bats, but I see tham as tribal clubs, smashing the hard rubber ball which the players make themselves from strips of raw rubber off the trees, as they used to crack the skulls of their Tongan or Fijian enemies. There are no bails as the strong sea breezes would keep shipping them off.

The teams are 20-a-side and it is a picturesque sight when they take the field in their colourful lavalavas (cotton wraparound skirts worn by both sexes), wearing T shirts and bare-footed. Each side brings its own umpire. In the harbour tall-masted yachts gently swayed at anchor, and overlooking the town and the pitch is the thickly wooded Mount Vaea where Robert Louis Stevenson lies in his simple tomb on the summit in the paradise he made his own.

The batting side does not repair to the pavilion when the game begins as there is no such place. Instead the other 18 players sit in a semicircle in the position of the slips. Most of the fielders being on the leg-side as the game proceeds – runs are called points – the seated batting side will break into song: sad traditional melodies or war chants accompanied by handclapping. Leading the musical entertainment is "the teacher", a chorus master-cum-cheer leader of charisma, and whatever he does the rest of the team dutifully follows. He also has a whistle which he blows from time to time and he will go into rhythmical gyrations as if on a dance floor, followed by his team.

Now it might be thought that this was done to encourage the batsmen at the wicket or to put the bowlers out of their stride. Not a bit. It was just done out of Polynesian *joie de vivre*. But the fielding side had their secret weapon also.

The "teacher" would blow his whistle, leap in the air with whoops, twisting and turning in impromptu dance and grimacing like a gargoyle. He would end by jumping up and clapping his hands above his head with his team emulating him. This, too, was an expression of unhibited joy and had nothing to do with intimidation.

When a wicket fell, however, the performance was intensified with leaping and shouting and laughter and with the more athletic doing cartwheels and somersaults. It made me think that Derek Randall might have visited this pearl of the Pacific; he would be in his element in this game.

The batsmen have two stances. Some will rest the bat over their shoulder as if waiting to brain some creature emerging from the swamps, while others point it to the ground like a golfer lining up for a prodigious drive; and both men and women, perhaps a little inelegantly, thrust the folds of their lavalavas between their muscular thighs before taking guard.

All the bowlers are fast and they only take three or four paces before hurling the ball down. Women bowl underarm. The ball is always well pitched up, usually middle and leg, and rises sharply. Sometimes the batsmen were hit in the tenderest of places. As they scorn such sissy aids as helmets, boxes, gloves and pads, I winced for them. But they seemed unaffected and just laughed when they were hit.

In fact, whatever the players did they laughed in doing it: dropping a catch, being out first ball, missing a run-out or whatever were causes for loud laughter, and they laughed just as loudly when making a mighty hit into the sun or into the long grass in the outfield where fielders were up to their waist in couch grass.

The ball is bowled from whichever end it lands – there are no overs – and the bowlers are also the wicketkeepers. Although most of the batting reminded me of the village blacksmith having a bash after a skinful of scrumpy, the other aspects of the game were more skilful. Men and women throw straight and hard – learned from their childhood when they threw stones at tins and other objects – and they all seemed to have a flair for wicket-keeping, going through the motions of whipping off the imaginary bails like a Rodney Marsh.

Batsmen always go for the big hit as it is too tiring to run for singles in the heat. When it was time for a break – the lunch or tea interval – both teams sat on the grass drinking soft drinks and eating biscuits and chatting.

One of the happy sights in Apia between 4 p.m. and 6.15 p.m. is to see a few hundred women of all ages and shapes and in a variety of costumes, playing cricket on the Eleelefou. The scene is a happy blend of colour, noise and enthusiasm and when it comes to the histrionics of the game the men pale beside the women.

The woman "teacher" will grimace grotesquely, thrusting her arms to her side and waggling her fingers. Then she will bend her knees, roll her buttocks, kick out in puppet-like movements, straighten up and jump up and down as if demented, all the time blowing her whistle. Then she will kick her left leg as if getting rid of a persistent admirer and leap into the air with both arms extended. She was followed in all her actions by the rest of the team.

On occasions the performance would end with the women facing the men and lifting up their lavalavas for what could have been a full frontal if they had not been wearing a kind of cut-down cotton long johns. It must have frightened the living daylights out of their enemies in the old days.

The men's cricket season has now ended and I saw the last game between the town area and the village of Ifilele Aasa. The town team had 15 Mormon bishops playing for it and one of the umpires was Bishop Afamasaga Laulu, who is also the tribal chief of Fasitootai. He was a splendidly dignified figure in his creamy jacket, ecclesiastical purple lavalava and his clipboard.

As each side had won a game they played a decider – but only 15 players each this time to shorten the proceedings – and the game was won by the visitors.

Last Saturday saw the start of the women's cricket season with a game between Vineula ladies, of Apia, and Miliemo. The home team scored 60 points, the visitors 24. So it was a comfortable win of 36 points for the locals, ranging from slimlegged, doe-eyed schoolgirls to muscular, big-busted and broad-beamed ladies.

Although Samoan cricket is fun from beginning to end it once had a tragic sequel. In a match not far from Apia a visiting batsman was given out when the ball was caught by a young spectator. The batsman protested, but the home umpire, proud of his young brother who had made the catch, stuck to his decision. The batsman killed him with one savage swipe of his bat.

But things like that do not happen today. Samoan cricket seems to make many of its rules as it goes along. But who cares? It has a logic of its own, and so long as it is an occasion for so much laughter and pleasure long may these Polynesian "flannelled fools" in their cotton lavalavas make a spectacle of themselves and make an entertainment for us.

Was Botham's Innings the Greatest Ever?

BY JOHN WOODCOCK, CRICKET CORRESPONDENT

17 *August* 1981 (*front page*). Ian Botham's innings of the fifth Test Match at Old Trafford on Saturday was, of its kind, perhaps the greatest ever played. It began just before half past two, when England, in their second innings, were 104 for five after starting the day at 70 for one. With a relentless display of tight fielding and accurate bowling, Australia had recovered from an apparently hopeless position to one from which they could well win.

In 34 overs, Boycott, Gower, Gatting and Brearley had fallen to Alderman and Lillee, while a mere 34 runs were being scored. Although still in, and batting with the utmost resolution, Tavaré, England's No. 3, had made only nine in the two hours of the morning, and another two in the first 20 minutes of the afternoon. The light was grey, the pitch not unhelpful to the faster bowlers.

When Botham walked out to bat he left an England dressing room in which few could bring themselves to watch the play. There is nothing worse than to see a hard won advantage against Australia being gradually whittled away. Contrasting with England's abject surrender was Australia's unconcealed joy.

The cheers which greeted Botham were of desperate encouragement, the position being scarcely less fraught than at Headingley where he made his historic 149 not out. His 118 on Saturday was an even finer innings. It was more calculated for one thing, and less chancy.

At Headingley, he played a wonderful, unforgettable slog, but it was also a lucky one. On Saturday, with a full sense of responsibility, he played himself in. If Brearley said anything to him as they passed on the pavilion steps, other than the customary "Good luck", it might simply have been: "Now, take your time" – and to the Australians it must have been increasingly worrying the way he did so.

Off his first 32 balls Botham scored five runs. With a new ball available in only 17 overs from the time he took guard, Bright was bowling at one end and Whitney at the other. When Alderman did take the new ball, immediately it was due, Botham had made 28 from 53 balls. At the other end,

Tavaré was taking good care of himself, not scoring much but relieving Botham of the anxiety of seeing a partner in distress. Of the 149 they added together, Tavaré's share was 28.

Botham had been in for 65 minutes when the new ball was taken. At 150 for five, one or two of the England side were to be seen watching the cricket again. Tavaré, wrapped in his cocoon, had completed the slowest half century ever made in a Test match in England. Then, suddenly, the floodgates opened.

Rather than finishing off the England innings, as they were expected to do, Lillee and Alderman took a dreadful hammering. Lillee had already bowled 14 overs in the day and Alderman 16. If they had lost their edge, it would not have mattered had it not been for Botham.

When, 13 overs later, Botham was caught at the wicket, he had made another 90 runs in 49 balls. Off Alderman's first over with the new ball he took seven; off Lillee's, 19. In the remaining nine overs in which he received a ball he made six and 10 off Alderman, five, six and 13 off Lillee, eight and seven off Bright and one and eight off Whitney. I refuse to believe that a cricket ball has ever been hit with greater power and splendour.

Where England's earlier batsmen, apart from Tavaré, had found survival impossible, Botham made the boundaries seem far too short and the wicket far too good. When Lillee bowled bouncers to him he hooked them off his eyebrows for six. When Alderman tried one it was pulled to mid-wicket for six. The crowd became a mass of dancing people and waving flags. Never before in Anglo-Australian Tests has anyone hit six sixes in an innings. Having reached his hundred with one, a sweep off Bright, Botham drove Bright over the sightscreen for another. He also hit 13 fours.

The fastest hundred in Test cricket, in terms of balls received, was by the West Indian, Roy Fredericks, at Perth in 1975. It took him 71 balls. In 1902 the mighty Jessop scored 102 against Australia at the Oval in 75 balls. On Saturday, with the Ashes in the balance, Botham's hundred took 86 balls (one fewer than at Headingley), though he went from five to 118 in 70 balls.

It was an innings that could have been played in the first place only by a man of astonishing power. Botham's attack on the new ball was a mixture of crude strength and classical orthodoxy.

At Trent Bridge in 1938, while Stan McCabe was scoring 232, Bradman called from the balcony to those in the dressing room: "Come out here, you may never see the like of this again."

So it was on Saturday. Botham, as McCabe occasionally did, is able to scale heights beyond the reach of ordinary men.

Till Cricket Us Do Part

26 *August* 1981. Mrs. Mildred Rowley, a nursing sister, of Helming Drive, Wolverhampton, was granted a decree nisi yesterday on the grounds of her husband's unreasonable behaviour. She had complained that he was "cricket mad".

After the hearing at Wolverhampton Divorce Court, Mrs. Rowley said: "Cricket was not just a hobby – it was a total obsession. I had just had enough of it." Her husband, Mr. Michael Rowley, was not in court because he is on tour in the West Country with Stourbridge Cricket Club.

He was in Torquay yesterday with his team playing under their touring name of the Worcestershire Marauders battling it out against Torquay Cricket Club.

When asked to comment on his divorce he said: "Really there is nothing more that I can say. I cannot stop . . we have got to get on with the game."

An Open Letter to the Yorkshire Chairman

17 *September* 1981. *At a series of emergency meetings at Headingley today, attempts will be made to resolve the latest crisis within the Yorkshire club arising from last week's suspension of Geoffrey Boycott by the Yorkshire manager and former England captain, Ray Illingworth. Remarks made by Boycott on radio and television, in which he said he was not being given a fair deal by the county, brought the trouble to a head.*

Here we publish an open letter from our cricket correspondent, JOHN WOODCOCK, *to the chairman of the Yorkshire club, Mr. M. G. Crawford, whose day begins at 10.30 this morning when he meets members of the York-shire Reform Group, who are calling for Illingworth's dismissal. At 2 p.m. the cricket committee will meet to discuss the position and consider what proposals to present to the full committee convened for 5.30.*

Dear Michael,

Poor you, having to give up a golfing holiday in Scotland to knock two such illustrious heads together! If it is any comfort to you, you have a fine reputation within the Yorkshire club for fair dealing. "No one better than Michael", they say, "to sort things out."

As soon as Ray's appointment as your manager was announced there were those who saw as inevitable a clash between him and Geoff. It seems that they have come to resent one another in a way that was never evident in Australia when Ray was regaining the Ashes. There, they both wanted their own way and got it. Geoff was allowed to do as he pleased because Ray needed his runs. When Geoff threw his bat on the ground at Adelaide, in disgust at being given out, it suited Ray to have as small a part as possible in censuring him.

Now that you have discovered what happens when an implacable nature meets an iron will, we are all agog to see what you do about it. I suppose you will feel beholden to Ray because of the free rein you have given him. It is too late now to realize that it never does to reengage someone you have sacked, let alone to make him foreman.

It seems to me that the role of team manager in cricket, certainly when you have a captain who is worth his salt, can be so difficult to define as to be hardly worth the bother. The idea of a supremo running English cricket alarms me almost as much as a Reform Group running Yorkshire's.

What troubles you do have up there! Bill Bowes says it never used to be so, but I am not so sure about that. I always think there is nothing to compare, for pure vitriol, with one Yorkshireman talking about another if he doesn't care for him, or for rabid loyalty, when the same two people may be moved to defend each other.

Those of us looking in from outside are getting a good deal more amusement from Benn v. Healey than from Boycott v. Illingworth. When Yorkshire tear themselves apart it is bad news for English cricket.

It is true to say, I think, that Yorkshire have more support among the cricketing public now than they have ever had before. This, of course, is because of your admirable resolve to make do with your own kith and kin. I hope the present dispute won't change that. What we are hoping to see is a rapprochement between the two protagonists, but to achieve it you will need to be at your most cogently persuasive.

Both, clearly, are very angry. Neither, as you well know, likes to be run out. Both have an eye for the main chance. Both have their futures to consider. Both have powerful support, though some of those who, up to now, have thought that Boycott could do no wrong, must be beginning to wonder about that when he falls out with Illingworth. Not all of them can be aware of how difficult both can be – as David* found out in Australia.

I suppose England can more afford to lose Boycott today than they could Johnny Wardle when Yorkshire suspended him in 1958 and he was withdrawn from our side to Australia. Johnny was a bad loss to the first-class game. But I hope it won't come to that this time.

My sympathies are inclined to be with Geoff, my money on Ray, and my hopes are for seeing the two of them forgetting their differences and doing what is best for Yorkshire cricket – which they profess to have so much at heart.

With best wishes for a quick end to the turmoil and a happy return to the links.

Yours, John.

*David Clark was manager of the M.C.C. side to Australia in 1970-71, captained by Ray Illingworth.

Moreover . . . Miles Kington

24 *September* 1981. DITHERING HEIGHTS – a rip-roaring novel of passion and searing emotion.

"There's trouble up at t'crease!" The dread cry went up and was taken round the little Yorkshire town of Hutton-on-t'-Moor. A beautiful little town it was, although the grimy and dreary moorland was only 10 minutes' walk away, and its one industry was cricket. Generations of Hutton men had gone to work on the county ground, patiently hewing runs out of the resistant pitch. It was man's work in which women took no part, yet when a disaster was reported it was the womenfolk who crowded round the pavilion doors, weeping and waiting for the worst.

This was one of those days. The flag had gone up over the pavilion, meaning that men were trapped inside in a sudden and violent committee meeting. They could be there for days, and nobody knew who would come out alive. The crowd was silent.

"They do say as 'ow big Geoff Boycott has bought it", said an old man whose crouching stance showed him to be an ex-middle of the order batsman.

"But there have always been Boycotts at the ground!" exclaimed a woman.

"It only seems that way, lass", said the old man. "It's always been Geoff, the greatest cricketer Yorkshire ever produced."

"Any news of Ray Illingworth?" someone asked. Ray Illingworth! The greatest player Yorkshire had ever produced. The man who had gone down south to seek his fortune and had come back again to Hutton-on-t'-Moor as they all did with the possible exception of Mighty Brian Close, the greatest cricketer ever to come from those parts.

Suddenly the crowd pressed forward as the doors opened, then fell back slightly as two stretchers were carried out. The women gasped and the men went pale as the two recumbent forms proved to be those of Boycott and Illingworth.

"Are they dead?" asked the old man. No one answered him. In true gritty, direct Yorkshire style he went up to Boycott and bent over him. "Art tha dead, lad?"

There was no reply. The women moaned. Then a microphone was thrust in his face and a soft voice said: "BBC here, Mr. Boycott. Have you any comment to make in the light of today's disaster?"

The words had a magical effect. The eyelids fluttered, the lips opened and with a great effort the wounded man said: "I am fighting fit and raring to play for Yorkshire every day of my life and I demand to see my solicitor". The roar that went up from the crowd awoke the other man, and Ray Illingworth suddenly sat up from his coma.

"I am the manager!" he cried. "What I say goes! I think, therefore I am! Consider the spinners of the field! Tha shalt have no other manager!"

Exhausted, both men fell back and were carried off. Before the crowd could look grief-stricken again, the doors opened once more and out strode a spruce figure carrying a suitcase. It was the greatest cricketer Yorkshire had ever produced – John Hampshire.

"'Appen you'll not see me round 'tton again, lads!" he cried. "I'm off to bonny Derbyshire. If you need a new manager or captain, give me a ring!"

"I always doubted he were a true Yorkshire lad", growled the old man. "There's got to be summat wrong wi' a man who names hisself after a southern county."

As Hampshire pushed his way through the crowd, a young man came the other way with all his worldly goods in a small bag. "I have come to play for Yorkshire, good folk", he said loudly. "Tell me to whom I should apply."

They looked at him. They noticed that he was jet black. They smiled. Even the women laughed. "Th'art a gradely lad", said the old man to him, "but no one not Yorkshire born can ever dig for runs on 'utton pitch."

"Know then, old man", said the black youth, "that I was born and bred in Bradford and proud of it." There was a short, stunned silence. "Lord be praised!" shouted the old man. "We've got our own West Indian at last!"

And that is how Heathcliff, the greatest cricketer Yorkshire ever gave birth to, came to play at Hutton-on-t'-Moor.

No Ball

2 *March* 1982, *Leading Article.* "I think it will be treated as one of total deception", said the Minister for Sport, Mr. Neil Macfarlane, yesterday, referring to the action of a dozen English cricketers in touring South Africa. He was right: what is at issue is not a question of judgment but a matter of trust. There are certainly two points of view about the merits of resuming sporting contacts with South Africa at this time. It can be argued that there is no longer a case for continuing to ban South Africa from international competition in those sports where outside pressure has led to people of different races playing with and against each other, that to maintain a boycott in such circumstances is not to protest against apartheid in sport but to use sport as a political instrument against the wider evil of apartheid in society. It may also be argued, less controversially, that it would be an infringement of personal rights for any government or sporting authority to forbid anyone, as an individual, to play wherever he wishes.

But neither of these arguments can be deployed to justify this tour. These cricketers are not going as a bunch of carefree, if irresponsible, individuals in search of some enjoyable play in a pleasing climate. They are being paid large sums of money to compete against a representative South African team, who will receive international caps for their endeavours. That is in direct contravention of the policy of the Test and County Cricket Board, which wrote to every first-class player in England towards the end of last summer warning them that if they played in any international or representative match in South Africa they would jeopardize their chances of being selected for England.

If that policy is mistaken it should be changed: if it is changed it should be done so openly. The worst way for it to be challenged is for players to slip out of England secretively, "playing it very close to their chests", as the TCCB spokesman put it with sour restraint.

The impression of deception is all the greater because of the assurances that were given before this winter's tour of India was allowed to proceed. The Indian Government was wrong in the first instance to raise objections to Geoffrey Boycott and Geoffrey Cook as members of the English team because they had played or coached in South Africa. But to allay Indian suspicions the TCCB emphasized its disapproval of representative tours of South Africa and the two players publicly expressed their opposition to "the principle and system of apartheid".

Boycott's words have now been made to appear as no more than a gesture of convenience; and there will inevitably be doubts over the sincerity of the TCCB's assurance, even though the board has in fact acted impeccably throughout. This is the most serious aspect because the thoughtless or selfish attitude of this touring party will put in jeopardy the future structure of Test cricket. There could all too easily be a division between the white and non-white cricketing nations, which would be tragic for the development of the game and a denial of its spirit.

The correct course now would be for the TCCB to live up to the spirit of its earlier warning and ban these players from selection for England. However, to go further, as some would like, and bar them from county cricket would be wrong. But to do less would almost certainly lead to the cancellation of this summer's tours by India and Pakistan, and quite possibly to the end of Test cricket as we have known it.

The players were banned from Test cricket for three years.

A Restrained Innings against Pace Attack

FRANK JOHNSON IN THE COMMONS

3 *March* 1982. "Maggie Fury at South Africa Cricket Tour" said a headline in *The Sun*. Other morning newspapers had variously described the Prime Minister as dismayed, and concerned and angry.

Some of us went into Prime Minister's question time, then, with foreboding, being dismayed and concerned at her anger. For that is not what we regard her as being for. We like her fury to be directed at the great liberal causes.

But it turned out that all was well. Throughout the exchanges she bore the rebellious cricketers' action with marked composure. She preferred to dwell on the importance of allowing citizens of a free country to travel where they liked. This, for a minority of us, is the true issue. So the Maggie Fury at the South Africa tour was presumably that day's page three girl, a descendant perhaps of the pop artiste of old, Billy Fury. ("Maggie's ambition is to travel. She will be in South Africa for the cricket tour".)

It was an historic question time. Mrs. Thatcher presumably entered *Wisden* by becoming the first Prime Minister to bat steadily through an entire Commons uproar without once supporting the Government.

The pedantic may object that she is the Government. Well, not always. All the evidence suggests that she regards the Government as a vast force with a life of its own. It is entirely made up of such uncontrollable phenomena as Sports Ministers who have no alternative but to denounce cricket tours of South Africa, and various spokesmen who have to put it about that she is "concerned" about such visits to forbidden lands.

For these purposes, she tends to include the official Opposition, much of the press, and the BBC, as part of the Government; certainly the SDP is included, indeed she probably sees it as the permanent government.

But, like Mao Tse Tung, every now and then she generates cultural revolution against the regime over which she nominally presides. Such an occasion was yesterday. The right winger Mr. Nicholas Winterton (Macclesfield, Con) rose. He is a co-author of a Commons motion congratulating the errant cricketers. He has a loud voice, as befits a man who bullies for England. He demanded that Mrs. Thatcher defend the principle that "any law-abiding citizen of this country has the right to travel where he wants to".

Some of us more delicate souls might have preferred that our cause be championed by a more *verlichte* figure than Mr. Winterton, but one cannot always choose one's allies. Matters were not helped by the fact that Mr. Winterton is burly, blond, and has a military background.

Mrs. Thatcher replied that all citizens were free to travel and no restrictions would be placed upon them. With that she sat down. There was no condemnation of the tour. It was in this not entirely subtle way that she revealed her lack of fury. One assailed oneself for ever having doubted her.

The Labour benches were enraged. Actually, they were delighted. What one means is that they made out they were enraged. Mr. Foot rose. He denounced Mr. Winterton's motion as "deeply humiliating to the House of Commons". He urged her to condemn it. She rose again and repeated that citizens were free to travel. If they were restricted, we would no longer be a free country".

Mr. Foot got up again and condemned the Tory motion. Mrs. Thatcher returned to her theme about freedom. Some Labour Members shouted at her to condemn the tour. "Say it, say it", said others, taking up the cry. She did not. Mr. Foot and Mrs. Thatcher continued their exchange on the same lines as before. Two Tory wets, Mr. Hector Munro, the former Minister for Sport, and Mr. Peter Bottomley, did condemn the tour. This intensified the Prime Minister's lack of fury.

The other *Wisden*-type fact to be recorded is who was the first Labour Backbencher to shout "racialist!" and after how long into the question time. (Mr. Martin Flannery: five minutes.)

The Unmasking of a Dashing Oriental Star

BY ALAN GIBSON

19 *May* 1982. Fifty years ago I saw the Indians play at Leyton. I can tell you the date: it was May 28, my ninth birthday – no, I tell a lie, because there was no play on the Saturday, but I had a chance of watching them on the Monday and Tuesday.

Our house overlooked the Leyton ground and on the Saturday, as a birthday treat, I had been allowed to go in, paying sixpence, to watch from closer quarters. It was a disappointment that there was no play, after numerous consultations, but I can remember several things about the rest of the match, though by then I was only surveying it from the balcony at home.

I had bought a scorecard (twopence, a stiff price we thought) and conned it eagerly. No. 1 in the Indian side was described as H. H. Porbandar, with an asterisk to show he was captain. When India went in, after bowling Essex out for 169, their No. 1 played some handsome strokes.

We had some romantic ideas about Indian cricket at that time, because of Duleepsinhji, and the Nawab of Pataudi, and vague folk memories of Duleep's uncle, Ranji. So, although neither Duleep nor the Nawab were available for the Indian party, we expected magic. When the Indian No. 1 was so dashing, I thought that this Porbandar was going to be another oriental star.

"Cor, old Porbs looked good", I said to my friends. I wondered what the H.H. stood for. 'Arry? my friends suggested, or 'Erbert? I cannot swear to this, but I do believe I suggested 'Orace, because I knew he was something foreign.

Alas! I discovered later that though Porbandar had played in that match, he had not batted, and that the No. 1 who had played the strokes was Naoomal Jeeoomal – or words to that effect (even *Wisden* was uncertain in its transliteration of Indian names in those days). Naoomal played three times against England and averaged 27, so he cannot have been too bad. He made 1,300 runs in that 1932 season, 1,500 in all matches. So I had seen a pretty good innings; but it was a disappointment that he had not been Porbandar.

H.H., I also discovered, stood for "His Highness', and the full title was "The Maharajah of Porbandar". *Wisden* of 1933 described his appointment as captain of the Indian side (there had been touring sides from India before, but this was the first to be granted a Test match) in these terms:

"Some little difficulty was experienced with regard to the captaincy, and after one or two disappointments the choice fell upon the Maharajah of Porbandar . . . For reasons apart from cricket, the necessity existed of having a person of distinction and importance in India at the head of affairs, and it was almost entirely because of this that Porbandar led the team."

(Did anyone murmur anything about sport and politics?).

Wisden continues: "No injustice is being done to him, therefore, by saying that admirably fitted as he was in many respects for the task, his abilities as a cricketer were not commensurate with the position he occupied."

I checked Porbandar's figures for the tour:

At Pelsham, v. Mr. T. Gilbert Scott's XI (not first-class): b R. S. G. Scott o; b Owen-Smith 2.
At Hove, v. Sussex: b Tate o.
At Maidenhead, v. Mr. H. M. Martineau's XI (not first-class): b Lowndes 2.
At Cardiff, v. Glamorgan: b Jones 2.
At Cambridge, v. the University: c Titley, b Rought-Rought o.

He did not play again after the Cambridge match in the second week of June: at least, I can find no trace of it in *Wisden*, which nevertheless attributes 8 runs to him in all matches (average 1.14). Where are the missing runs? I can agree with their verdict on first-class matches (2 runs, average 0.66), but there is a problem here which I feel the Society of Cricket Statisticians should immediately investigate. There is no record of his bowling or taking a catch.

That is not all there is to say about the Maharajah. The tour was difficult, experimental, and it passed off happily. India ("All-India" as the team was then called) did well and though they lost the only Test match, it was not before they had given England a shock or two. E. W. Swanton wrote that Porbandar "made a creditable success of keeping his men a happy and united party". It was also graceful, if inevitable, for him to step out of the side.

That it was not so easy to captain an Indian side in England was shown on the next tour, in 1936, when the amiable Vizianagram ("call me Vizzy", he used to say in the commentary box) struck trouble, and Amarnath, the best all-rounder, was sent home. In a later book Swanton refers, rather unkindly, to Porbandar's "fleet of white Rolls-Royces", but also states that he had made only two runs on the tour – "from a leg-glance at Cardiff, I seem to recall".

Fifty years later, with cricket between England and India still going on, I think we owe a salute to him. Porbandar – the state – produces limestone, which, according to the *Encyclopaedia Britannica*, "is used for buildings in Porbandar without mortar, and is said to coalesce into a solid block under the influence of moisture". Well, the limestone still holds, and he applied his touches of moisture in those early days.

8 *June* 1982. It was a pleasure at Edgbaston to meet Robert Brooke, the editor of *The Cricket Statistician*, who has solved the Porbandar mystery, of which I wrote in these columns some weeks ago, and which has perplexed a number of correspondents. Brooke has confounded *Wisden* and demonstrated that the Maharajah did make two more runs, equalling his highest score, in a match, twelve a side, against Blackheath in 1932. This confirms his tour average, for all matches at 1.14. He still holds the record for a touring captain.

Turner: Man of Principle and a Perfectionist

BY JOHN WOODCOCK

2 *June* 1982. Of the 19 cricketers to have scored 100 first class hundreds none can have been more of a perfectionist than Glenn Turner, or have reached the landmark in a more spectacular way than when he scored 311 not out in one day against Warwickshire last Saturday.

He has no time for the slovenly, whether in his own game or anyone else's. As a young man he dedicated himself to developing a technique based on the teachings of the text book, realizing that was the surest way of achieving consistency. A career average of 50, as near as makes no matter, shows how successful he has been.

To be such a very good player and yet find it necessary to score 239 not out against a weak Oxford University attack, as he did in his first innings this season, tells, as well as anything could, of Turner's single-mindedness. Some of Worcestershire's later batsmen were hoping for an early-season knock. Yet by doing things his way Turner wins more matches for them in a season than even Vivian Richards does for Somerset. That this is so is an indication of how over the years he has widened the scope of his game.

In his time he has twice carried his bat through a Test innings, with infinite patience and in vastly different conditions, and yet so dominated an attack in a county championship match (Worcestershire v. Glamorgan at Swansea in 1977) as to score 141 not out out of a total of 169, a record in percentage terms. In most recent seasons he has made a habit of scoring at least one hundred before lunch.

Only Walter Hammond has ever scored a hundred in each innings of a match more often than Turner. Hammond did it seven times to Turner's six. Turner's 10 hundreds in a season (1970) for Worcestershire constitute a record for the county.

In 1973 he became the seventh and last batsman and the only one since the last war to score 1,000 runs before the end of May. In the West Indies in 1971-72, playing for New Zealand, he scored 672 runs in the Test series at an average of 96. In successive innings in Georgetown, against Guyana and then in the fourth Test match, he scored 259, and batted altogether for nearly 22 hours. So one could go on.

Turner was born in Dunedin, in the South Island of New Zealand, in 1947. He was 35 on May 26, and now that he has put his 100th hundred in the bag he will probably retire at the end of the season. Once Billy Ibadulla, then coaching in New Zealand, had persuaded him to try his luck in England soon after leaving school, Turner's course was set. Besides being fastidiously correct, for a long time he was tediously slow. Yet today, of all the batsmen playing first class cricket, he makes as good a model as any for youngsters to study.

If he has not been a great success as a captain it may be because of the permissiveness of the age: he sets higher standards both on and off the field than many today find acceptable. He made no secret of his distaste for the way some of the Australians played the game in New Zealand when they were there in 1974, or for the antics of the West Indians, also in New Zealand, in 1980.

It was unlike him when, to show the West Indians what he had thought of them then, he refused to bat properly while playing for Worcestershire against them soon afterwards. It would have been in character had he kept them in the field for a couple of days with an immaculate display of manners and batting method.

In New Zealand there are those who feel, not altogether surprisingly, that he should have made himself available to play for them more often. His last Test match was in 1976 when he was only 29. He has preferred in recent years to spend his time out there in the commentary box rather than at the wicket, watching far less good players trying to cope. Because of this he has never proved himself at the highest level against the fiercest pace. Some say he never could, though I disagree with that.

His record entitles him to be ranked as the foremost right-handed batsman New Zealand has produced (Martin Donnelly and Bert Sutcliffe, both great players, stood the other way round) and with such character, determination and technique he could, I am sure, have made a hundred against Holding at one end and Roberts at the other. The last batsmen to reach 100 hundreds were Geoff Boycott and John Edrich in 1977; the next will almost certainly by Zaheer Abbas who needs only nine more.

Match that Needs a New Home

BY ALAN GIBSON

28 *June* 1982. On Saturday Oxford won the toss, batted and six overs were bowled, enough to see several handsome strokes from their captain, Ellis. But nobody was deeply interested, for obviously the rain would soon blot

things out, which it did so comprehensively that play was abandoned for the day at half past two.

This was sad, sadder than usual when a day's cricket is washed away, because we had some hopes of this match, hopes that it might do something to restore the quality of the occasion. Both sides had played presentably against the counties, Cambridge actually beating Lancashire.

They have plenty of good batsmen, though, as usual with university sides, the bowling has been weak or at least inexperienced. They should have done better in the Benson and Hedges Cup, though they did well enough against the Indians. I felt the bowling lacked an aged, prayerful character like Wingfield-Digby, but I suppose even theologians have to end their courses sometime or another.

What we expected, given the weather, was a high scoring match, with admirable batting, a cautious declaration by whoever was batting on the third morning, and a draw. You could expect a draw anyway. Since 1960, of the 21 matches played, 17 have been drawn. In the first 100 years of the fixture, which began in 1827 (though irregular in the early years) nine were drawn.

The object then was to win at all costs. The object now is to avoid defeat at all costs. This is why this historic game has lost public interest: even if it had been fine on Saturday, few more people would have been there to watch.

The only man who might have stirred some interest, because he was the only bowler with the talent to get the other side out, and had an air of class about him, was Pringle, who preferred to play for England, although he was the Cambridge captain. A previous Cambridge captain, Majid, chose his university before Pakistan, although he had played for Pakistan twice that season. It clashed, he felt, with the duties he had accepted when he accepted the captaincy.

Pringle's decision, and I see the force of the argument that a young man needs money and must not risk his place in the England side, reduced the status of the university match to a second class fixture. That his colleagues should be reported as being "delighted" with his decision reduced it even more.

I wrote some years ago that the match would be better played at Bletchley, or possibly Scarborough, or Torquay. I was confirmed in my view by a letter from the Bletchley Cricket Club, an old established club enjoying a boom since it is adjacent to Milton Keynes, saying they would be delighted to house it and could guarantee a good gate. All the authority, grit and dignity of the occasion at Lord's has been lost. And I do not say this just because of Saturday's rain. The sooner the fixture is moved, the better.

OXFORD 249 for 5 dec (R. G. P. Ellis 86) and 136 for 6 dec (R. J. Boyd-Moss 4 for 42)
CAMBRIDGE 114 for 2 dec (R. J. Boyd-Moss 41 not out) and 272 for 3 (R. J. Boyd-Moss 100, S. P. Henderson 50, N. E. J. Barrington 48 not out)
Score after first day: Oxford 23 for 0
Cambridge won by 7 wickets

Window on the World of Lord's

Gubby Allen at 80

BY JOHN WOODCOCK

31 *July* 1982. Eighty today, G. O. Allen has become as intrinsically a part of Lord's as Father Time or the Grace Gates. Whatever the match in progress, he is to be seen framed in the window of the Committee Room, dispensing the wisdom of his long experience.

The years have not so much wearied as mellowed him. Although it is still sometimes said that this or that decision is "one for Gubby's Lawn", the term is used by way of definition, not of resentment. He is more a father figure now than a high priest, more the Emeritus Fellow than the Secretary of State.

Lord's, almost literally, is his own back garden. Only the pavilion prevents him from seeing "the green circle" as he lies in bed. On August 9 he is being honoured with a dinner in the Long Room. The only other dinner to have been held there was for Sir Pelham Warner in 1953, also to mark his 80th birthday. It is a little like giving a dance on the Centre Court at Wimbledon.

As one of three Trustees of MCC, Gubby Allen is still the holder of an important office at Lord's. At some time or other he has been both president and treasurer of the club, captain of England, chairman of the Test selectors, a constant guardian of the welfare of the game and a tireless worker for youth. For most of this century no important decisions have been taken at Lord's without first having been through the hands of Plum Warner or Gubby Allen.

When at his best as a cricketer, Mr. Allen was busy enough in the City never to be able to play anything like a full season for Middlesex. Twice, though, he went to Australia – as one of Douglas Jardine's formidable array of fast bowlers in 1932-33 (Allen never bowled bodyline himself) and again as captain in 1936-37, when he suffered the agonies of losing the last three Test matches after having won the first two.

After the war, at the age of 45, he took MCC away again, this time to West Indies. On his 50th birthday Mr. Allen made a hundred, playing for the Arabs against Sir William Worsley's XI at Hovingham Hall in Yorkshire. At 80, with a notable collection of hip operations to be incorporated in his swing, he still plays golf, a game with whose theory, like that of cricket, he has had a long and romantic attachment.

In Adelaide earlier this year, Sir Donald Bradman, his erstwhile adversary, commenting on a piece of Mr. Allen's in the 1981 *Wisden* entitled "Fifty Years On", said: "To have been more critical would have been much easier but much less helpful." There was in the article a strong note of understanding, the contentment of twilight.

Peerless Percy George

BY RICHARD STREETON

21 *August* 1982. The world's senior Test match cricketer, P. G. H. Fender, is 90 tomorrow, the last famous survivor from the golden age of English cricket before 1914 when his early contemporaries were such legendary figures as Ranjitsinhji, Sydney Barnes and Jessop.

The First World War delayed Fender's Test debut until the 1920-21 MCC tour to Australia, J. C. W. MacBryan (Somerset) is a month older than Fender, but he did not win his solitary England cap until 1924. "Stork" Hendry, Australia's longest surviving senior, played his first Test a few months after Fender and is a mere 87.

Fender's last games for Surrey were in 1935. Senior citizens down Kennington way can still be found who claim that nobody at the Oval since "Percy George" has been such fun to watch; whether as a ferocious hitter, guileful spinner or controversial captain. Fender in his elongated sweater – immortalized in Tom Webster cartoons – has remained a vivid memory for them.

These days Fender is recalled most often as the scorer of first-class cricket's fastest 100 in history and also for the failure by England to choose him as captain.

It was at Northampton in 1920 that Fender reached three figures in 35 minutes, having faced between 40 and 46 balls. The precise number cannot be deduced from the only surviving scorebook.

It remains uncertain why Fender never led England. He was regarded as the shrewdest cricketing brain in the country and he worked near miracles in the early 1920s with Surrey's limited bowling attack on unhelpful Oval wickets. In his thinking and behaviour, though, Fender was frequently ahead of his time. Several minor skirmishes with authorities probably did little for his cause.

Fender, now blind, celebrates tomorrow with a family luncheon party in Horsham, Sussex, where he lives with his son. He still deals with telephone inquiries on behalf of the family firm, the London Wine Exchange, but the 1980 Lord's centenary Test was his last major outing. He cannot see the screen and follows cricket by listening to the television. In a typically succinct Fender remark, made without malice, he says: "Can't get on with those radio chaps, but Benaud is worth listening to."

Plans to make a film about the bodyline series have aroused his interest. "I shall write and protest if anyone blackens Jardine's name. I still maintain he was blameless."

Dissent by players and other bad behaviour appals him. He was delighted when Peter May – an occasional visitor – became chairman of the selectors this summer. As Fender recently said: "You know, Streeton, I was always considered a bit of a rogue but I would never have done, or allowed to be done, half of what goes on these days . . . I do hope those in charge of the game can get it back on the right rails."

Twist Again

Qadir Brings Back the Leg Spin

BY DONALD WOODS

26 *August* 1982. Many old gentlemen of England will have a smile in their hearts today because of the revival of an art they had thought lost forever.

For years they had lamented the passing of leg spin bowling. Where were the successors to Bosanquet, Mailey, Grimmett, Tich Freeman, Peebles, Faulkner – or even that young feller Benaud? Gone and forgotten, it seemed, was the wristy, back-of-the-hand delivery so hard to control that it was too expensive in this era of limited-over cricket.

Now the lament is no longer necessary, thanks to Abdul Qadir, of Pakistan, who proves with the essence of the risky art of leg spin that he can weave spells around England's best batsmen without squandering runs to buy victims. But never mind the figures. It is the way in which he does his devious work that makes Qadir the embodiment of all the composite characteristics of classical leg spin.

It is, after all, the most subtle and sinister of all the cricketing arts, and it is not for your open-hearted extrovert. To go to the unnatural trouble of screwing the ball out of the back of the hand over a cocked wrist requires a nature both complicated and contrary, as well as a readiness to wrench the shoulder, elbow and other parts of the body into unconventional positions.

Action pictures of the great leg spinners give some idea of the sheer inconvenience of this method of delivery. Douglas Wright's action was once described as a cross between the barn dance and the swallow-dive. Roly Jenkins, by all accounts, did a sort of hornpipe. "Tiger" O'Reilly grimaced as if in agony, and perhaps he was.

But it gets to you. Dabble in the dark arts of leg spin and your whole approach to life is affected. I knew a schoolmaster so addicted that he seemed unable to walk an ordinary pavement very far without going compulsively into the tangential foot-shufflings and shoulder-shruggings apparently inseparable from preparation to bowl a leg-break.

Yet the real leg spinners are the true princes of cricket, and if they have to do a sort of Mephistophelean deal to reach the top orders of the mystical rite they certainly pay the price.

It seems that Qadir could not be other than a leg spinner. He even walks like one between deliveries, with his feet apparently magnetized to the turf for preparatory purchase (remember Colin McCool?) and he has the right face, too, one of calculation and conspiracy.

The eyes narrow ominously and the fringe of dark beard hints at brigandage and plunder, not at all like the straightforward yeoman growth of Gatting.

You could imagine that face emerging from the mystic gloom of a Karachi bazaar to whisper dread tidings of deceit in high places and intrigue in the back streets, and the name Abdul is somehow appropriate, hinting at the mystery and magic that is about to be worked on some poor plodding Englishman at the crease.

As is fully to be expected, Qadir goes into a most complicated set of movements to begin his bowling action. He holds his left hand high as if in final salute to the doomed batsman, while his right hand twirls the ball urgently to appraise it of future rotational requirements, then squirts the ball into the upraised left hand while his feet begin a ritual dance on the spot.

The left hand brandishes the ball momentarily, then transfers it back into the right, which is already beginning a series of small circular sweeps as he bounds and gambols into his curving (of course) approach run.

In all this activity his entire body is the mere servant of the cocked right wrist as it sweeps over out of a flurry of wheeling arms to float the buzzing ball at his victim, and so complete is all bodily involvement that even after releasing the ball Qadir twirls after it up the pitch as if urging it on to work its own wickedness, and his bowling arm repeats an echo motion of the delivery to quench itself of every last vestige of spinfulness.

What the ball then does is variously astonishing. Taking on a life of its own it loops and dips, pitching to spin vastly to left or right or to spear straight on with topspin, and if it raps the batsman's pads Qadir has a range of appeals for lbw – one supplicatory, one accusatory, one challenging and one slyly inquisitive, then the major one, the total and ultimate appeal.

With this one he dances an angry tattoo upon the turf, jumping up and down and uttering fierce cries of the sort that surely terrified whole generations of marauders clear out of the Khyber Pass. At such times Qadir makes John McEnroe seem like a calm exponent of reasoned remonstration.

But ultimately it is his superb art that one remembers, and it is a fitting irony that the torments of the googly which he now inflicts on innocent Anglo-Saxon lads had their origin not in the mystical regions of the East but on the playing fields of England.

Bosanquet knew not what he was visiting upon later generations of his countrymen, but Abdul Qadir certainly does, and as a worthy custodian of the rescued art of legspin he will surely continue to delight millions with his magic.

A Master of the Mind Game Steps Down for a Back-bench Role

BY JOHN WOODCOCK, CRICKET CORRESPONDENT

14 *September* 1982. Garlanded with honours, the latest of them the county championship of 1982, Mike Brearley retires today from first-class cricket. His next career will be as a psycho-analyst; his first was as a university lecturer. Such is his knowledge of the game and those who play it, as well as the goodwill which attaches to him, that his recent election to the cricket committee of the Test and County Cricket Board is much to be welcomed.

It is 21 years ago that a Cambridge undergraduate, a little under medium height and a scholar to St. John's from the City of London School, began to be talked about as a batsman of unusual promise. When the 1961 Australians came to Fenner's, three weeks after Brearley had played his first first-class match there, he made 73 and 89, batting at No. 8 in the first innings and going in first in the second. Jack Fingleton commented that he had seen a great batsman in the making.

In the event that was something Brearley never became. His record during his four years at Cambridge was so outstandingly good, and he has scored so consistently for Middlesex in the years that he has played regularly for them, that it has to be one of the disappointments of his career to have no better a batting average in Test matches than 22.88 and in 66 innings for England never to have made a hundred.

Despite that, he was a winner of Test matches, more so than many a great batsman, and a veritable thorn in Australia's side, because of his qualities as a captain.

Some captains are Olympian, some genial, some bluff, some autocratic, some are confused, some fussy, some anonymous. Brearley was brilliantly analytical. He has worked out the modern game better than anyone else except perhaps for Ray Illingworth. Few have had more to do with the most recent stages of cricket's evolution on the field or more strongly influenced trends off it.

He looked more objectively than most at the Packer intrusion, his aim, right from the start, being that some good should come out of it. He has been ruthless in his pursuit of success for Middlesex, whether that has meant going against the wishes of many of the county's members by importing fast bowlers from South Africa, West Indies and Australia, or preferring, as he did last week, a young Oxford Blue, Richard Ellis, to such a trusty servant as Clive Radley.

Owing, though, to Brearley's reputation for clear thinking, his decisions, although they may not always have brought agreement, have inevitably been respected. Rodney Hogg, the Australian fast bowler, once said of him that whatever other degrees he may have, he certainly has one in "people". When it has come to getting the best out of his players he has had few failures.

Having, some years ago, been a sort of cricketing Wedgwood Benn, he retires from active service more as a Joe Gormley, prepared, as it were, to take a seat in the House of Lords so long as that did not mean having to wear a tie. If he were, in fact, the next cricketing knight, it would be no surprise.

His fellow players will miss his counsel, the game his prestige, the reading public his fascinating books on the Ashes. He has scored 44 first-class hundreds and over 25,000 first-class runs. He led England to 11 victories over Australia (as against four defeats), the most gratifying of them coming last year when he returned and pulled together, so dramatically, a dejected and disjointed team.

Under Brearley's captaincy, Middlesex have won four county championships and two Gillette Cups, and if, at some time in the future, they find themselves in desperate straits, and he has no patients for a day or two and has been playing a little, he would help them out. As someone who likes to be fully stretched he probably will.

Causing a Stir

20 *September* 1982, *Diary*. The metal bat with which Dennis Lillee gained headlines almost three years ago has proved a failure as a soup stirrer. Six of the aluminium bats were tested by the West Australian Department of Mental Health, which hoped they would prove more durable than big wooden spatulas used to stir huge vats of soup being prepared for patients. The bats have been declared out by the catering staff, who find them hard to clean.

Lillee, who hurled his bat towards the dressing room when told he could not continue using it in the Perth Test of December 1979, said: "It should have been an ideal soup stirrer – bacteria free and virtually indestructible." He and his partner, Graeme Monaghan, are still seeking alternative uses for the redundant hit-wear.

Kortright – the Quick and the Dread

BY ALAN GIBSON

11 *December* 1982. While in chase of some quite different information recently, I noticed that C. J. Kortright died on December 12, 1952, only 30 years ago. I say "only" because we think of him as one of the great fast bowlers of the 1890s. He died, however, just short of his 82nd birthday.

Arguments about the relative speeds of fast bowlers of different generations are often entertaining but inevitably fruitless, although I suppose in future the electronic eye may give us some rough guide. Up to 1914 it was commonly accepted among English cricketers that Kortright was the fastest. Australians were inclined to prefer the claim of their own Ernest Jones. Englishmen agreed that Jones was fast, although suspecting he was a chucker. It was Jones who was said to have bowled a ball through W. G. Grace's beard (there are various versions of the story, all improbable).

As late as 1942, E. H. D. Sewell described Kortright as "the fastest bowler, right or left, ever". Sewell's judgment was marred because he could never bring himself to believe that much good cricket was played after the First World War; but he had played and reported cricket for more than half a century when he wrote those words, and fielded in the gully for Essex when Kortright was bowling. So he had some experience on which to base his assertion.

He quotes, in partial support, J. T. Hearne, who said that the fastest bowlers were Kotze (South Africa), Knox (Surrey), and Kortright. Sewell adds that Hearne "did not specify the fast ones in that order, but if he places them in the order in which he wrote them, I am surprised. I have held catches in the slips off Kotze and Kortright and managed to get a hundred with Knox doing his full share of the bowling, and, on those experiences, I put Kotze third and Kortright always head, shoulders, arms, legs and brain, easily first."

Well, we might minimize the importance of Sewell's tribute, but it was not unsupported. Altham wrote that in 1895 Kortright "was probably as fast as anyone who has ever lived"; and confirms it in a different part of his *History* (written in 1926) by saying that Kortright was "by fairly common consent the fastest of all bowlers within living memory". H. D. G. Leveson-Gower, writing in 1953, says that "the fastest of them all was C. J. Kortright."

P. F. Warner, in 1911, wrote that "I think Kortright at his best was just a shade faster than anyone else. Tall, loosely built, and very strong in the back, Kortright, with his long, springy run up to the wicket, was at times almost terrifying. One had to shut one's teeth very tight, and to remember that for honour's sake one could not run away, to face him on a rough wicket. Some of the professionals, in particular, feared him with a mortal fear!" In a footnote to a later edition of the book in 1943, Warner adds that "Larwood is probably as fast as anyone in the history of the game".

There is, however, substantial evidence from these comments that Kortright was PDQ. But he never played for England. He probably would have done in 1899, but for an injury. He played often for the Gentlemen. He began at Brentwood, then Tonbridge in 1887, played for Essex, not regularly, from 1889 to 1907 (captain in 1903), and took 489 first-class wickets at an average of 21. He also had a batting average of nearly 18, with a couple of centuries. A lot of his time he spent playing country house cricket. He was very much the amateur and used to boast that he had never done a day's work in his life.

I must pinch John Arlott's account of a conversation, from his introduction to David Frith's *The Fast Men*. Kortright was asked: "What did you *do*, Charles?"

"What do you mean, *do*?"

"Well, you know, for a living?"

"Didn't have to earn a living, father left enough for me and my sister."

"Well, what did you do except bowl fast?"

"Bowled leg-breaks and played golf."

In the 1948 *Wisden* Kortright said he had always wanted to "project things further and faster than anyone else". He recalled the time he once bowled six byes in a club match at Wallingford. He was a temperamental character, and had a famous row with W.G., amicably settled when they shared a last-wicket partnership in a tight finish against the Players.

It is sad, as Frith says, that we have no action photographs of Kortright; it is sad, too, that a man who could take seven for 73 against the Players was never pitted against Australia. Sad for us, that is. I doubt if it ever occurred to him to care tuppence about such details.

Pavilioned in Splendour

BY RUPERT MORRIS

27 *April* 1983. Today's cricket match at Lord's between MCC and Middle-sex, the county champions, is not only the traditional opening fixture of the season, when Test match hopefuls aim to impress the selectors. It is also the cricket follower's annual opportunity to cast off the leaden cares of winter and imbibe the sight, sounds and smells that are an irreplaceable part of an English summer. More than that, it enables him to escape into a time-warp.

The ground, which opened in 1814 as the home of MCC, is universally regarded as the Mecca of cricket. Despite many structural changes to the international game it remains the administrative headquarters; the President and Secretary of MCC still automatically occupy the same positions within the International Cricket Conference, cricket's supreme body, and MCC still makes the laws of the game.

Hardly surprising, perhaps, that Lord's today should remain cocooned in traditions that comfort those who belong there and warn strangers to mind their manners.

Unless you have a match ticket, a membership card or a specific appointment you will have trouble passing through the huge wrought-iron Grace Gate. Middlesex players arriving for practice in a car they have used all the previous season have been known to find difficulty getting in.

Bill Leonard, at 81 the most venerable of those who mind the gate, arrived at Lord's in 1922. He became a gateman in 1965; six years ago, when his wife died, he was told he could stay in the job as long as he liked. The club's generosity is the reward for his instinctive loyalty, and epitomizes the benevolent feudalism fundamental to Lord's and the Marylebone Cricket Club – a well-defined hierarchy which perpetuates, in subtle ways, the old cricketing distinction between "gentlemen" (amateurs) and "players" (professionals).

The home of the gentlemen of Lord's is, of course, the members' pavilion, a magnificent late Victorian three-tier stone building, a bastion of male privilege, where women and children are admitted only at specially ordained times.

Downstairs, the members take their ease, strolling among the cricketing memorabilia in the famous Long Room, or in the reading room and bars, while on the first floor Jack Bailey, the Secretary, and his three assistant secretaries run the show.

Mr. Bailey cut short a holiday in Majorca last week to return for another in a seemingly endless round of committee meetings. At the back of his mind is the special meeting later this summer when the members will decide whether or not to send an MCC team to South Africa, an issue that threatens to throw the cricketing world into a turmoil with repercussions as far-reaching as those of the D'Oliveira Affair. This morning, however, his main concern will be the weather.

That, too, will be the chief preoccupation of Lieutenant-Colonel John Stephenson, assistant secretary in charge of cricket, who will have bicycled in from Swiss Cottage shortly before 9 a.m., and will soon be on the telephone to RAF Northolt for the latest forecast.

Known to everyone as "Colonel" ("It's not quite pally-pally, but it's not too formal", he says), his is the unmistakably military figure that strides out to the wicket during weather-induced stoppages in matches to talk to the umpires and discuss the prospects for resumption of play with Jim Fairbrother, the groundsman. His arrival – as impressive in its way as the famous walk to the wicket of "Lord Ted" Dexter, or that of the arm-swinging superman Ian Botham – invariably prompts a cheer.

In his office, with its fine view of the pitch, the Colonel was explaining last week how the MCC organizes its 260 annual away fixtures and its foreign tours.

The average MCC club side is rather stronger these days than it used to be. Probationary playing members, of whom there are between two and three hundred, are given five matches in which to prove their worth under the eye of the match manager, before their applications are considered in August. Half are rejected.

Match managers' reports and records of every player's performances are kept in the Cricket Office, at the corner of the pavilion, where they are constantly updated by the manager, Steven Lynch, assisted by a clerk and a typist. In the files lie such fascinating details as the performance of I. T. Botham in his first MCC match in 1972 against the Universities Athletic Union. He made nought and took no wicket for 23 runs.

Botham was once an MCC Young Cricketer, a group of 20 school leavers taken on by Lord's for up to three seasons. It is their chance to learn the game (28 of them have gone on to be current county players), with the benefit of daily coaching, but they have to earn their keep by doing odd jobs, bowling at members, and occasionally being drafted into MCC sides at short notice.

They arrived fresh faced on Monday to be given a pep talk by the Colonel. Today they will sell scorecards, man the scoreboards and be ready to help Jim Fairbrother with the covers.

The chief coach is Don Wilson, a genial 45-year-old Yorkshireman who played for England just before the sudden explosion in cricketers' pay in the 1970s, and who keeps a fatherly eye on the Young Cricketers, the schoolboys who come to Easter coaching classes, and even some seasoned professionals.

Few games encourage such eccentricity and give so much time for contemplation as cricket; it is no coincidence, for example, that many cricketers love music.

One day recently the indoor school was brought to a halt by a sudden burst of beautiful choral singing. Those familiar with Don Wilson's eccentricities may have carried on playing, but others dropped their bats and listened. He had been coaching the boys of the Westminster Abbey choir school, and at the end of their net, he asked them to sing. He always does.

Another music-lover is Christopher "Gus" Farley, a small, rotund, Pickwickian figure who is the ground superintendent, responsible for policing, general upkeep, and hiring winos. Winos? Surely they'd never get through the gate?

"Without them this place wouldn't be open", he replies. "They know there's casual work here, so they come from the arches at Charing Cross to paint the seats and clean. We give them a meal and pay them in cash.

"Mind you", he adds, "you have to look closely at their eyes before you take them on. And if there's one propped up between two others, you have to make sure he can stand up."

Two of the regular winos are, curiously enough, trained opera singers. Sometimes, after dark, when the cleaning is done, their fine voices echo across the deserted square.

In lyrical mood Mr. Farley describes the peculiar atmosphere of Lord's: how it livens up on the Monday when the Young Cricketers arrive, how on the morning of a match the ground "opens out like a flower", and how the life drains out of it at the end of the day as the last spectators leave.

Elsewhere in the pavilion Roy Harrington, the 62-year-old dressing-room attendant, prepares to bring the players their 10 a.m. tea, attend to any repairs to equipment, then bring lunch, towels, tea, and clean up the showers and baths afterwards.

This summer there will be no Geoffrey Boycott, always grabbing one of the two dressing-tables with a looking-glass. And Roy regrets the departure of characters like Denis Compton, who would often arrive late and rush out to smite centuries with a borrowed bat.

Behind the scenes, undoubtedly the most important figure is Jim Fairbrother, the groundsman. Foreign visitors, anxious to learn from the man who, as curator of the Lord's pitch, is the most distinguished practitioner of his art in the world, assume that he earns at least £20,000 a year, and drives a Mercedes. He does not.

To the cricket watcher, the square over which he presides is just a flattish patch of grass, albeit carefully trimmed. To Jim Fairbrother, it is 18 numbered pitches. The Test match pitch is No. 10, bang in the middle; no one else will play on it all year. He and the Colonel will have decided yesterday whether pitch No. 12, on the Tavern side of the centre, has dried out sufficiently to be used for today's game, or whether to switch to Pitch No. 3, higher up on the square. (There is a notorious "hill" at Lord's which runs down towards the Tavern.)

By the end of a season, the earth on the whole square has tightened as hard as a pavement. It has to be softened up by sprinkling over two days; then it must be raked with a scarifier, brushed with a besom, hollow-tined by machine, treated with a sorrel at the batting ends, grass seed inserted to a special formula, holes filled in with a top-dressing of soil with a high clay content, then covered with more soil and levelled with a lute. Jim illustrates this highly sophisticated procedure with an artist's hand gestures.

He had been thinking of taking a holiday last week, but the weather put paid to that. With rain about, it is all a matter of hairline decisions: which roller to use, how low to cut the grass, when to allow the Middlesex players to have nets or use the practice ground.

Under the Grand Stand work the Lord's printers, a team of three long-serving men, updating scorecards during matches, printing annual reports, invitations and notices for the club's 18,000 members.

"It's not like working in a factory", says 62-year-old Charles Reason. "They are not unreasonable people here. Also you've got the atmosphere of the match, with people coming in and out wanting scorecards. You get caught up in it. I used to belong to a union, but you don't need it here."

A similar attitude prevails elsewhere round the ground. The Clerk of Works, Ted Collins, has an office next to the Grand Stand. His deputy, Dave Norman, is also the Lord's electrician – happy to work round the clock if necessary to get the place ready for a big game. Like many others, he often works seven days during peak cricketing periods.

The staff canteen, a homely place with cricket pictures on the walls, is run by Sharon Clarke, the 22-year-old manageress, and her mother, Anne. They provide special lunches at Christmas and at the end of the season when the nursery ground comes into its own for the use of the Cross Arrows, the club for permanent members of MCC staff. Finally there is the annual staff fixture between two fairly ramshackle teams, one captained by Colonel

Stephenson, the other by Wing Commander Lawrence, the chief accountant. The result doesn't matter, of course. The game's the thing.

Art of Cricket

BY JOHN RUSSELL TAYLOR

3 *August* 1983, *Galleries*. The British Museum's current *Sporting Life* exhibition seems to open up an infinitude of possibilities. Why range so widely – would there not be more than enough material in just one sport? Why be so narrow – how about including paintings and sculptures as well as prints? As though in answer to both these questions, John Player has sponsored a sizable exhibition, and a substantial book to go with it, devoted exclusively to that most English of games, cricket. *Art of Cricket*, at the Fine Art Society until August 13, begins at the beginning, in the approved manner, and goes on, if not until the end (for who would dare to predict that?), at least up to Ruskin Spear's lively Pop-Arty portrait of Fred Trueman.

Inevitably in such a show, the balance between art-interest and subject-interest is at times a little precarious. Funnily enough, this is not much of a problem with the earliest works, perhaps because for any artwork to survive for more than two centuries it is likely to have some sort of artistic quality, while any scrap of evidence about the origins of the game is bound to have its own historical significance. The cricket enthusiast can observe the gradually changing forms of the bat in the long series of cricketing portraits (almost a genre of its own in portraits of boys and young men during the second half of the eighteenth century), while those whose interest is mainly artistic will appreciate rather the variety of character painters like Francis Hayman or Joseph Wright of Derby were able to get into what might be strictly stereotyped works.

Cricket even managed to get into family groups and conversation pieces like Thomas Hudson's *Mrs. Matthew Michell and her Children* or Thomas Beach's *The Tindall Family*. It crops up in Victorian times in the occasional rustic genre piece, such as the Tate's charming *A Country Cricket Match, Sussex* by John Robertson Reid (now when, I wonder, did the Tate itself last find wallspace for that?), and we have probably forgotten that before he made himself into a Victorian sage Watts earned an honest penny in 1837 by making five lithographs to illustrate the finer points of batsmanship. We may also forget that Camille Pissarro was sufficiently charmed by the atmosphere, if not the technicalities, of the game to paint it a couple of times on his visits to England. Its impact seems to have been less on twentieth-century painters – you have to look quite hard to determine why Carel Weight's *The First Cricket Match of Spring* is actually so called. But there is still plenty of material left undisturbed: Sir Gerald Kelly, for example, painted some of his most evocative small panels at the Oval facing towards the gasworks during cricket matches, but none of them is included. So the way is open for further explorations – not to mention *Art of Football* and all the rest of the sports in turn.

West Indies' Finest Batsman Bore his Burdens Lithely

BY ALAN GIBSON

14 *December* 1983. I once took part in a television programme with Lord Constantine and Harold Pinter. We were asked to play the old game of choosing an all-time cricket XI. An odd selection committee, you will agree, but we enjoyed ourselves, whatever the viewers thought. We settled on Hobbs and Trumper for the opening pair, and then considered batsmen to follow.

"Headley", said Learie, at once. "Bradman?" suggested someone. "Yes," agreed Learie, "we will have Bradman as well, because after all, he was the white Headley." This was a reference to the constant description of Headley by English and Australian journalists as "the black Bradman", a description which did not altogether please Headley or his fellow West Indians.

George Headley, whose recent death we mourn, was not perhaps quite so good as Bradman, but had to bear heavier burdens. He was probably the best West Indian batsman there had ever been, despite the magnificence of Worrell, Weekes, Walcott, Sobers and Richards. None of the others was so unsupported as Headley.

When he began, shortly after West Indies Test cricket began, it was usually a case of "Headley out, all out". He had no comparatively easy Tests to boost his figures: his opponents were England and Australia. Nevertheless, he scored 10 centuries in 40 innings in 22 Tests. His Test average was 60.83: in all first-class matches, from 1927 to 1954, it was 69.86.

He played his first Test in 1930, when he was 20. England sent a side to the West Indies. It was not a full Test side (another "England" team was playing in New Zealand at the same time), but a strong one, including Hendren, Ames, Wyatt, Sandham, Voce, Gunn (aged 49) and Rhodes (aged 52). Rhodes took Headley's wicket in the second innings of the first Test, but only when he had scored 176, one of four centuries in the four-match series. Rhodes played his first Test in 1899, Headley his last in 1954; it must have been an interesting confrontation.

In 1930-31 West Indies made their first tour of Australia. Headley was then almost entirely an off-side player and the Australians tied him down for a while, as they did Hammond, by attacking his leg stump. He realized an extra dimension was needed, with the result that Grimmett, who had been causing him problems, later said that he was the greatest master of on-side play whom he had met.

Headley toured England twice and was particularly effective on wet pitches. His record in such conditions was, as C. L. R. James points out in his remarkable book, *Beyond a Boundary*, much better than Bradman's. He had a successful series at home in 1934-35, ending with 270 not out in a Test which West Indies won by an innings. After the war he was not quite the same force again. He mostly lived in England. He was the first black man to captain West Indies, when England toured in 1947-48, but had to retire after the first Test because of a back injury. In 1953 the Jamaican public subscribed to bring him home for the next England series, but he played only in the first Test and Lock got him twice, for 16 and 1.

I saw Headley bat before the war. I have quite a clear recollection of his innings at the Oval in 1939. He scored 65 and a century seemed sure, when he was run out. The culprit was Victor Stollmeyer, and it must have been a horrifying moment for him in his first and, as it proved, only Test, although he made amends with a brave 96. What impressed me about Headley was his lightness of foot, his litheness. You would have to say that he was primarily a back-foot player, as Bradman was, but he always seemed to be dancing.

I saw him again after the war, indeed I saw what I think must have been his last first class match, in 1954, when he played in the Torquay Festival, batted beautifully for an hour or so for 64, and capered happily around the field. He seemed as nimble, as lithe, as ever. The circumstances were not, of course, testing, but I remember I was sitting next to Jack Walsh, one of the best Australian leg spinners of the day, and Jack said: "I'd love to be bowling to that blighter, just for the pleasure of watching him carve me about."

Dismissal of Franks Sets off a Collapse

BY ALAN GIBSON

24 *April* 1984. Our sports editor, generous man, in sending me a note about plans for the season, said: "I will do all in my power to keep you away from Didcot." He then sent me to Oxford, and it is very difficult to get to Oxford from the south except via Didcot. However, I examined the timetable, and found that by leaving Bath at 1.26 a.m., and changing at Bristol, Cheltenham, and Worcester, with peaceful halts at Moreton-in-Marsh and Ascott-under-Wychwood, I could arrive at Oxford at 1.02 p.m., If I cheated a bit and left early, catching the 7.03, I would arrive back at Bath at 6.40 a.m.

Still, we respect our sports editors: but unfortunately I had not noticed that the initial 1.26 from Bath was marked MX-Monday excepted. So it had to be Didcot after all, and though there were some trifling difficulties, I reached the Parks well before lunch.

The Oxford innings fell into three phases: a collapse, a brave recovery, and another collapse. The fifth wicket fell at 47. Then there was a stout stand of 76 between Carr and Franks. Carr we already know to be a good one. Franks, a St. Edmund Hall man, was new to me but looked just the kind of solid character a university needs in the middle of the order. . .

16 *August* 1984, *Announcements.*

IN MEMORIAM
ENGLISH CRICKET
which finally passed away at The
Oval, 14th August 1984, will be
sadly missed.
R.S.V.P.
T.I.S.

England has just been beaten 5-0 by West Indies.

Gower's Side Fight for their Pride

BY JOHN WOODCOCK, CRICKET CORRESPONDENT

27 *August* 1984. England's cricketers are being paid £1,500 each for playing in the current Test match against Sri Lanka, sponsored by Cornhill, and by Saturday evening I was feeling that most of them deserve to have the money withheld. Their batting, following an exhibition of supreme mediocrity in the field, was of unprecedented indifference. In reply to Sri Lanka's 491 for seven declared, they made 139 for two in four hours 20 minutes, the last 107 of them in 56 overs.

If, from lunchtime onwards on Saturday, they had set out to be seen in a worse light, they could hardly have managed it. No self-respecting club side would have been content with the way England batted. In two hours and a quarter Tavaré made 14, four of those off the edge. The longer Broad lasted, the less convincing he became. He was dropped twice while on his way to 69 not out. As for Gower, he even slunk off at the end, having scored 16 in 70 minutes before the clock showed six.

There must be hundreds of batsmen in England – yes, hundreds – who could have played better than Tavaré, Gower and Broad did now against the bowling as it was. That England had bowled so poorly on Thursday and Friday was partly because Sri Lanka had batted so unexpectedy well; but for England's batsmen there was no such excuse. By playing as they did they not only let themselves down but the whole body of English cricket.

Instead of making 500, as they easily could have, Sri Lanka decided to give England 20 minutes' batting before lunch on Saturday. This was a nice, positive move. Yet one felt that if England were to play anything like properly, they could run the Sri Lankan bowlers off their feet and still win the game. I doubt whether Sri Lanka, when they took the field, had banished from their minds all thoughts of defeat. Three hundred by close of play, a not unreasonable target for England, would have opened up the game.

Lamb, it is true, was unfit to bat, having done something highly improbable like pulling a muscle while drawing his bedroom curtain, but it was the sort of day and pitch on which Botham could have made 150 in an hour and a half, with the Sri Lankan bowlers, several of them carrying injuries, powerless to stop him. Instead, Tavaré played like a frightened rabbit, Broad like a man terrified of not making a hundred and Gower like a captain who had lost all urge to lead.

Countless sides would have been disappointed not to score at five runs an over on Saturday evening. Instead, de Silva, though handicapped by a badly sprained ankle, was allowed to bowl 10 overs of gentle leg-breaks for 18 runs, and play ended with Broad treating Madugalle's even gentler off-breaks with laughable respect. The Sri Lankans must have suspected some unfamiliar, unfathomable joke.

Why, then, do I think that good will come to England from the match? For several reasons. It has shown that Agnew is hardly ready yet for an overseas tour and that to take Tavaré to India (a week ago he was the odds-on favourite to be Gower's vice-captain) would be to settle in advance for stalemate. Broad's limitations are better known than they were at the end of the West Indian series, and the need for a constructive influence behind Gower, to prevent the winter expedition from getting bogged down, is clearer than it was.

Perhaps, too, the team will come to realize how much they need help. Cricketers tend these days to spurn the advice even of the old masters. Yet to bat at No. 3 for England as Tavaré did on Saturday, in the footsteps of some of the greatest batsmen of all time, seems heretical to me. It was because Fletcher condoned such cricket, as well as a truly shocking over-rate, that he lost the England captaincy. It smacked then, and still does, of funk.

So today England really are on trial. If on a public holiday not many turn up to watch them, that will be not least because of the way they batted on Saturday. Unless they set out to erase the memory of that, this will be remembered as the England side who had no pride, and they surely cannot want that.

One last stricture. On Saturday morning, when he persuaded Mendis to slog him to deep mid-wicket, where Fowler held a good boundary catch, Pocock leapt and danced and raced across the field like a child on his way to the Christmas tree. Come on England, be your age and play the game.

SRI LANKA 491 for 7 dec (S. Wettimuny 190, L. R. D. Mendis 111,
A. Ranatunga 84) and 294 for 7 dec (S. A. R. Silva 102 not out, L. R. D.
Mendis 94; I. T. Botham 6 for 90)
ENGLAND 370 (A. J. Lamb 107, B. C. Broad 86, D. I. Gower 55, R. M.
Ellison 41; V. B. John 4 for 98, A. L. F. de Mel 4 for 110)
Score after third day: Sri Lanka 491 for 7 dec, England 139 for 2
Match drawn

Record Breakers still not Home

FROM JOHN WOODCOCK, CRICKET CORRESPONDENT

16 *January* 1985, *Madras.* There seemed not to be many batting records left
by the close of play in the fourth Test match here yesterday, and who should
have spent the day breaking them but England's much maligned batsmen?
In reply to India's first innings total of 272 they have so far made 611 for five.
Fowler scored 201 and Gatting 207.

England made 318 runs yesterday against mainly protective fields, fielding
that was an appreciable improvement on Monday's and bowling that was
never unarguably ragged. It is, I need hardly say, a mercilessly easy pitch.
There is little pace left in it, and the ball is hardly turning. It is this that may
yet prevent England from winning. They can be expected to declare some
time tomorrow morning (today is the rest day) and if India get anything of a
start they could take a lot of bowling out, even in a day and three-quarters.

On Monday Fowler batted through the day, yesterday Gatting almost did.
Never before, in over 600 Test matches, have two Englishmen scored double
hundreds in the same Test innings. Bradman, first with Ponsford and then
with Barnes, did it for Australia, as did Simpson and Lawry. Mudassar and
Miandad have done it for Pakistan, and Hunte and Sobers for West Indies.
But not even Compton and Edrich in 1947, did it for England. England's
total is not yet their highest against India – that still stands at 633, made at
Edgbaston in 1979. But they have never before had such a total on the board
(563) at the fall of their third wicket.

Until Gatting beat it, Fowler's was the highest score by an Englishman in a
Test match in India. So far as I saw, Gatting gave only one chance, a low and
barely catchable one to Siva off his own bowling. More than once, on Monday and again yesterday, he must half have expected to be given out leg-
before; but this was a triumph after many disappointments.

One of the first to congratulate Gatting was Peter May, chairman of the
England selectors, who at one stage in England last summer had grave
doubts as to whether it was worth persevering with him. The best analogy
could yet be Bobby Simpson, who, once he had scored his first Test hundred
in his 52nd innings for Australia, never looked back. Yesterday's was
Gatting's 58th innings for England, his first Test hundred, at Bombay,

having come in his 54th. His dynamic game is just what England need. He is as strong as an ox, has a good feeling for cricket and his best years lie ahead.

Monday's play had ended with Pocock padded up for the second evening running, to act as nightwatchman should it have been necessary. Yesterday a refreshed Fowler and a much more confident Gatting made 39 in the first hour and 36 in the second. Gatting was the first to find his form. Right from the start he played very well. For half an hour or so Fowler, by comparison, looked insecure. To make it harder for the batsmen to assume total command, Gavaskar slowed the tempo of the game right down.

Watching him do so, it was easy enough to see how, at times, India bowled only 10 overs an hour when England were here last. Under the quite excellent regulation which requires a minimum number of overs to be bowled in a day, India were obliged now to tot up 80 – and there was no chance that the light would go yesterday before they had done so. There is a good hour's more daylight in Madras than in Calcutta. Even so, they took over six hours about it, this despite the spinners bowling a majority of them.

India, in fact, bowled consistently better than they had on Monday. Kapil Dev began with an admirable spell, with a ball that was still fairly new, and Siva was never to be treated lightly. The batsmen, therefore, had to work for their runs. The crowd, numbering some 25,000, were wonderfully generous, welcoming each landmark almost as though it was India who had passed it. The first of these came when Fowler reached 180. Until then Amiss's 179 at Delhi in 1976-77 had been the highest individual score by an Englishman in India. Before lunch the nearest thing to a chance was when Fowler, then 160, edged a ball from Siva past Kirmani's chest.

Early in the afternoon Fowler pulled and then on drove Yadav for two towering sixes in the same over. Next, Gatting went to his hundred; and soon their partnership had broken the record for England's second wicket against India, held previously by Amiss and Edrich with 221 in the Lord's Test of 1974.

Until a breeze blew up off the sea the day was very hot. But India, to their credit, showed few signs of wilting, and 55 minutes after lunch they had the consolation of the wicket of Fowler, caught behind off a ball from Kapil Dev which left him off the pitch. Fowler had batted for nine hours 25 minutes (an hour longer than Amiss for his 179), faced 411 balls and hit three sixes, 21 fours and one five. He and Gatting had added 241 in 72.3 overs.

By now India were under the command of Amarnath, Gavaskar being off the field from lunchtime onwards with an allergy which was soon being known as "Fowlergy". As Gatting had been on Monday, Lamb was some time getting off the mark. By the time he was bowled, though, taking a great heave at Amarnath, he had scored 62 of a third-wicket partnership of 144. Ten over were left and it was disappointing that Gower thought it right to send in first Edmonds, when Lamb was out, and then Foster, when eventually Gatting was out, even if their intention was to attack. In the end, when

Foster was out, Gower appeared himself.

It was nice for India that they took a late trick or two. They deserved to. Having just reached his double hundred and passed Fowler's score with the same stroke, Gatting was caught on the long-on boundary. He had gone from 192 to 198 with two of those awful reverse sweeps. His innings had lasted for 506 minutes and included 20 fours and three sixes. He faced 308 balls and was cheered in all the way, wet through but very happy. So was I.

INDIA 272 (M. Amarnath 78, Kapil Dev 53, M. Azharuddin 48; N. A. Foster 6 for 104) and 412 (M. Azharuddin 105, M. Amarnath 95, S. M. H. Kirmani 75, Kapil Dev 49; N. A. Foster 5 for 59)
ENGLAND 652 for 7 dec (M. W. Gatting 207, G. Fowler 201, R. T. Robinson 74, A. J. Lamb 62) and 35 for 1
England won by 9 wickets

INDEX